Beginning Web Programming with HTML, XHTML, and CSS

Beginning Web Programming with HTML, XHTML, and CSS

Jon Duckett

WILEY

Wiley Publishing, Inc.

Beginning Web Programming with HTML, XHTML, and CSS

About the Author

Jon Duckett published his first Web site in 1996 while studying for a BSc (Hons) in Psychology at Brunel University, London. Since then he has helped create a wide variety of Web sites and has co-written more than ten programming-related books on topics from ASP to XML (via many other letters of the alphabet) covering diverse aspects of Web programming including design, architecture, and coding.

After graduation, Jon worked for Wrox Press first in its Birmingham (UK) offices for three years and then in Sydney, Australia, for another year. He is now a freelance developer and consultant based in a leafy suburb of London, working for a range of clients spread across three continents.

When not stuck in front of a computer screen, Jon enjoys listening to music and writing.

Credits

Senior Acquisitions Editor
Jim Minatel

Development Editor
James H. Russell

Production Editor
Eric Newman

Copy Editor
Nancy Rapoport

Editorial Manager
Mary Beth Wakefield

Vice President & Executive Group Publisher
Richard Swadley

Vice President and Executive Publisher
Bob Ipsen

Vice President and Publisher
Joseph B. Wikert

Contents

Contents

Contents

Contents

Contents

Contents

Contents

Contents

Contents

Contents

Introduction

There are a lot of books about designing and building Web pages, so thank you for picking up this one. Why do I think it is different? Well, the Web has been around for quite a few years now, and during its life several technologies have been introduced to help you create Web pages, some of which have lasted, others of which have disappeared. Indeed, even enduring technologies such as HTML have had features added and removed over the years. Many books that teach you to write Web pages are revisions of earlier versions of the same book and therefore still take the same approach as the previous edition did. This book, however, is completely new, written from scratch, and its purpose is to teach you how to create Web pages for the Web as it is today and will be for the next few years. Once you have worked through this book, it should continue to serve as a helpful reference text you can keep nearby and dip into when you need to.

About the Book

At the time of this writing, Internet Explorer version 6 and Netscape version 7 are the main Web browsers, and each of the previous versions of these browsers had added new features as the Web developed (and sometimes old features were removed). As all this change might suggest, there is more than one way to build a Web site. For example, if you want to have a heading for a page displayed in a bold, black, Arial typeface, you can achieve this in several ways. However, you can also consider this a very good time to come to the Web, as many of the technologies used to create Web pages are maturing, and favored methods for creating Web sites, or "best practices," are emerging.

Writing Web pages today thus requires a balance. On the one hand you want to use the latest and best methods, while on the other hand you have to remember that not everyone who visits your Web site has the latest browser software. So you need to be able to write pages that take advantage of the features of the latest browsers while at the same time ensuring your sites can be viewed in older browsers. (Indeed, if you want to make a living from working on Web pages, you will *need* to be aware of some of the older ways of doing things.) In this book, I teach you the best practices that you *should* be learning, and, where necessary, I expose the older techniques that help you achieve the results you want.

Over the past few years there have also been innovations and changes in the way people access the Internet. The Web is no longer just viewed on desktop computers; Web sites are becoming available on devices with small screens, such as mobile phones and PDAs (personal digital assistants), and some devices such as televisions have lower resolutions than computer monitors. There are even stories in the newspapers about how we will all soon have refrigerators and other appliances that will allow us to browse the Web. So, while most of the examples in this book are written for a computer, I will teach you to code your Web pages so that you can make them available to other devices without rewriting your whole site. Learning to code for the emerging generation of applications will make your Web sites and your skills last much longer.

Another area where the Web has changed from a few years back is the increased emphasis on usability and accessibility. *Usability* refers to making the site easy for users to get around (or navigate) and achieve what they came to your site for, whereas *accessibility* addresses making a site available to as many users as possible, in particular people with disabilities (who may have impaired vision or difficulty using a mouse). Many governments around the world will not issue a contract to build Web sites for them unless the site will meet strict accessibility standards. A little careful thought before you build your Web site means that people with vision impairments can either view your site with larger text or have it read to them by a screen reader. There are books dedicated to the topics of usability and accessibility that are aimed at Web developers who need to learn how to make their code more accessible and usable, but my aim is to teach you to code with these principles in mind from the start.

By the end of this book, you will be writing Web pages that not only use the latest technologies, but also are still viewable by older browsers. Pages that look great can still be accessed by those with visual and physical impairments—pages that not only address the needs of today's audiences but can also work on emerging technologies—and the skills you learn should be relevant for longer.

Who This Book Is For

This book is written for anyone who wants to learn how to create Web pages, and for people who might have dabbled in writing Web pages (perhaps using some kind of Web page authoring tool) but want to really understand the languages of the Web to create better pages.

More experienced Web developers can also benefit from this book because it teaches some of the latest technologies, such as XHTML, and encourages you to embrace Web standards that not only meet the needs of the new devices that access the Web, but also help make your sites available to more visitors.

You do not need any previous programming experience to work with this book—even though these big red Wrox books are published under the trademark Programmer to Programmer (because the books are written by programmers for programmers). This is one of the first steps on the programming ladder. Whether you are just a hobbyist or want to make a career of Web programming, this book will teach you the basics of programming for the Web. Sure, the term "programmer" might be associated with geeks, but as you will see by the end of the book, even if you would prefer to be known as a Web designer, you need to know how to code to write great Web sites.

What This Book Covers

By the end of this book, you will be able to create professional looking, and well-coded Web pages.

Not only will you learn the code that makes up markup languages such as HTML, but you will also see how to apply this code so you can create sophisticated layouts for your pages, positioning text and images where you want and getting the colors and fonts you want. Along the way, you will see how to make your pages easy to use and available to the biggest audience possible. You will also learn practical techniques such as how to put your Web site available on the Internet and how to get search engines to recognize your site.

The main technologies covered in this book are HTML, XHTML, and CSS. XHTML is not actually a completely different language than HTML; it is more like the latest version of it. What would have been HTML 5 was named XHTML, rather like how Microsoft called what would have been Windows 2001 Windows XP. XHTML stands for eXtensible Hypertext Markup Language; it describes the structure of Web pages such as the headings, paragraphs of text, tables, bulleted lists, and so on. CSS is then used to apply styles the documents, to change things such as colors, typefaces, sizes of text, and so on. Once you have learned the basics of these languages you will learn some more practical aspects of applying them. You will also learn the basics of JavaScript, enough to work on some examples that add interactivity to you pages and allow you to work with basic scripts. Along the way I introduce and point you to other technologies you might want to learn in the future.

The code I will encourage you to write is based on what are known as Web standards; HTML, XHTML, and CSS are all created and maintained by the World Wide Web Consortium, or W3C (`http://www.w3.org/`), an organization dedicated to creating specifications for the Web. You will also learn about some features that are not standards, but it is helpful to know some of these in case you come across such markup and need to know what it does (where these are introduced I make it clear that they are not part of the standard).

What You Need to Use This Book

All you need to work through this book is a computer with a Web browser (preferably Netscape 6 or higher, or Internet Explorer 6 or higher), and a simple text editor such as Notepad on Windows or SimpleText on Mac.

If you have a Web page editor program, such as Macromedia Dreamweaver or Microsoft FrontPage, you are welcome to use it, but I will not be teaching you how to use these programs. Each program is different and entire books could be and have been written on the individual programs. Even if you were to use one of these tools, you can write much better sites when you really understand the code such programs generate. Like many of the other books on the shelves, these programs were created years ago and do not address the best way to write pages today. They get jobs done, but not necessarily in the best way possible, so you will often want to edit the code they create.

How This Book Is Organized

The first chapter of this book gives you the big picture of creating pages for the Web. It explains how all the technologies you will be learning in this book fit together. In this very first chapter you will also create your first Web page and learn how the main task in creating a Web site is *marking up* the text you want to appear on your site using things called *elements* and *attributes*.

The next six chapters of the book describe the different elements and attributes that make up HTML and XHTML and how you can use them to write Web pages. The chapters are organized into task-related areas, such as structuring a document into headings and paragraphs, creating links between pages, adding color and images, displaying tables, and so on. With each task or topic that is introduced you will see an example first to give you an idea of what is possible; then you can look at the elements and attributes used in detail.

These task-focused chapters are followed by one on *deprecated markup*, which is markup that is no longer part of XHTML, and browser-specific markup, which was introduced by the main browser vendors but not used in the W3C HTML and XHTML recommendations. While you should not rely on this markup for writing your pages, you are likely to come across it when working with older Web pages.

At the end of each are exercises that are designed to get you working with some of the concepts you learned about in each chapter. Don't worry if you have to go back and review the content of the chapter in order to complete the exercises; this book has been created with the intention that it should be a helpful reference for years to come, so don't feel you need to learn everything by heart. Along the way you see which browsers support each element, and you learn plenty of handy tips, tricks, and techniques for creating professional Web pages.

Once you have seen how to create and structure a document using HTML and XHTML, you then learn how to make your pages look more attractive using cascading style sheets (CSS). You'll learn how to change the typefaces and size of fonts used, color of text, backgrounds and borders around items, and alignment of objects to the center, left, or right of the page.

Having worked through these chapters, and using the examples in the book, you should be able to write quite complex Web pages. These chapters will serve as a helpful reference you can keep coming back to and the examples will act as a toolkit for building your own sites.

The next chapters look at important Web page design issues. You see some examples of popular page layouts and how to construct them; you learn how to create a good navigation bar to allow users to find the pages they want on your site; you find out what makes a form effective; and you learn how to make your Web sites available to as many people as possible. These chapters really build upon the theory you learned in the first half of the book and help you create professional looking pages that really attract users and make your site easy to use.

The final chapters then take you through some more advanced issues. There is a chapter on Modularized XHTML, which is the future of XHTML, and which will allow you to create pages for devices other than desktop computers. Indeed, you will see an example of a site that uses XHTML to send pages to a mobile phone. Then two chapters introduce you to JavaScript, a programming language known as a *scripting language* that you use in Web pages. While the entire JavaScript language is too large to teach you in two chapters, you should get a feel for how it works and see how to integrate scripts into your pages. The last chapter prepares you to put your site on the Internet and covers Web hosting, FTP, and validating your code. Finally, I give you some ideas of where you can go now that you've worked through this book; there are a lot of other things you might want to add to your site or learn to advance your Web skills, and this chapter gives you an idea of what else is possible and what you need to learn to do that.

Conventions

To help you get the most from the text and keep track of what's happening, this book uses a number of typographical conventions.

> **Boxes like this one hold important, not-to-be forgotten information that is directly relevant to the surrounding text.**

Tips, hints, tricks, and asides to the current discussion are set off and placed in italics like this.

As for styles in the text:

❑   Important words are *italicized* when first introduced.

❑   Keyboard strokes appear like this: Ctrl+A.

❑   Filenames, URLs, and code within the text appear in monospace, like so: `version="10"`.

❑   Code appears two different ways:

```
In code examples, new and important code appears with a gray background.
```

```
The gray highlighting is not used for code that's less important in the
present context or has been shown before.
```

Source Code

As you work through the examples in this book, you may choose either to type in all the code manually or to use the source code files that accompany the book. All of the source code used in this book is available for download at www.wrox.com. Once at the site, simply locate the book's title (either by using the Search box or by using one of the title lists) and click the Download Code link on the book's detail page to obtain all the source code for the book.

Because many books have similar titles, you may find it easiest to search by ISBN; this book's ISBN is 0-7645-7078-1.

Once you download the code, just decompress it with your favorite compression tool. Alternately, you can go to the main Wrox code download page at www.wrox.com/dynamic/books/download.aspx to see the code available for this book and all other Wrox books.

Errata

I've made every effort to ensure that there are no errors in the text or in the code. However, no one is perfect, and mistakes do occur. If you find an error in this book, such as a spelling mistake or faulty piece of code, I would be very grateful for your feedback. By sending in errata you may save another reader hours of frustration and at the same time you will be helping to provide even higher quality information.

To find the errata page for this book, go to www.wrox.com and locate the title using the Search box or one of the title lists. Then, on the book details page, click the Book Errata link. On this page you can view all errata that has been submitted for this book and posted by Wrox editors. A complete book list including links to each book's errata is also available at www.wrox.com/misc-pages/booklist.shtml.

If you don't spot "your" error on the Book Errata page, go to www.wrox.com/contact/techsupport .shtml and complete the form there to send us the error you discovered. We'll check the information and, if appropriate, post a message to the book's errata page and fix the problem in subsequent editions of the book.

p2p.wrox.com

For author and peer discussion, join the P2P forums at p2p.wrox.com. The forums are a Web-based system for you to post messages related to Wrox books and related technologies and interact with other readers and technology users. The forums offer a subscription feature to e-mail you about topics of your choosing when new posts are made to the forums. Wrox authors, editors, other industry experts, and your fellow readers are present on these forums.

At http://p2p.wrox.com you will find a number of different forums that will help you not only as you read this book, but also as you develop your own applications. To join the forums, just follow these steps:

1. Go to p2p.wrox.com and click the Register link.
2. Read the terms of use and click Agree.
3. Complete the required information to join as well as any optional information you wish to provide and click Submit.
4. You will receive an e-mail with information describing how to verify your account and complete the registration process.

> *You can read messages in the forums without joining P2P, but in order to post your own messages, you must join.*

Once you join, you can post new messages and respond to messages other users post. You can read messages at any time on the Web. If you would like to have new messages from a particular forum e-mailed to you, click the Subscribe to this Forum icon by the forum name in the forum listing.

For more information about how to use the Wrox P2P, be sure to read the P2P FAQs for answers to questions about how the forum software works as well as many common questions specific to P2P and Wrox books. To read the FAQs, click the FAQ link on any P2P page.

Beginning Web Programming with HTML, XHTML, and CSS

Untangling the Web

At one time, you had to learn only one language to write Web pages: HTML. As the Web has advanced, however, so have the technologies you need to learn in order to create effective and attractive Web pages. As the title of this book suggests, you will be learning a few different languages: HTML, XHTML, CSS, and a bit of JavaScript. But before you start learning each of these languages individually, it helps if you understand what each of these languages does and how they fit together.

This is not just a theory and history lesson, however; you will be writing your first Web page sooner than you might think, and along the way you will also learn some of the essential background information, such as what a markup language actually is, the difference between a tag and an element, and how a Web page is structured.

As you are about to see, a Web page is made up of not only the text or images you see when you visit a site, but also information about the structure of the document, such as what text is a heading and where each paragraph starts and finishes. Each Web page can also contain general information such as a title for the page, a description that can help search engines such as Google index your Web site, and links to things called style sheets that change the appearance of fonts, colors, and so on.

In this chapter, then, you will:

❑   Meet HTML, XHTML, CSS, and JavaScript and learn what each does

❑   Learn the difference between tags, elements, and attributes

❑   See how a Web page is structured

❑   Learn why rules that say how a document looks are best kept separate from the content of the Web page

❑   Cover the differences between writing HTML and XHTML

❑   Meet some of the tools you can use to help you write Web pages

❑   Learn the basics of how a Web page gets to you when you request it

By the end of the chapter you will have a good idea of how Web pages are created, and you will have built your own first Web page.

A Web of Structured Documents

To start off, you need to consider the concept of the Web as a sea of *documents*. In its relatively short life, the Web has grown to feature millions of sites and billions of pages. For the moment, think of each of these pages as a document. Many documents on the Web bear a strong similarity to the documents you meet in everyday life, and all documents have a structure, so think for a moment about the structure of some of the documents you see in everyday life.

Every morning I used to read a newspaper. A newspaper is made up of several stories or articles (and probably a fair smattering of advertisements, too). Each story has a headline and then some paragraphs, perhaps a subheading and then some more paragraphs; it may also include a picture or two.

I don't buy a daily paper anymore as I tend to look at news online, but the structure of articles on news Web sites is very similar to the structure of articles in newspapers. Each article is made up of headings, paragraphs of text, the odd picture (and, yes, maybe some ads, too). The parallel is quite clear. The only real difference is that each story gets its own page on a Web site, which is usually accessible from a headline and a brief summary either on the home page or the title pages for one of the subsections (such as the politics, sports, or entertainment sections).

Consider another example: Say I'm catching a train to see a friend, so I check the schedule to see what time the trains go that way. The main part of the schedule is a table telling me what times trains arrive at and when they depart from different stations. Like paragraphs and headings, a lot of documents use tables. From the stocks and shares pages in the financial supplement of my paper to the TV listings at the back, you come across tables of information every day—and these are often recreated on the Web.

A different kind of document you often come across is a form. For example, I have a form sitting on my desk (which I really must mail) from an insurance company. This form contains fields for me to write my name, address, and the amount of coverage I want, and boxes I have to check off to indicate the number of rooms in the house and what type of lock I have on my front door. Indeed, there are lots of forms on the Web, from a simple search box that asks what you are looking for to the registration forms you are required go through before you can place an online order for books or CDs.

As you can see, there are many parallels between the structure of printed documents you come across every day and pages you see on the Web. So you will hardly be surprised to learn that when it comes to writing Web pages, your code tells the Web browser the structure of the information you want to display—what text to put in a heading, or in a paragraph, or in a table, and so on—so that the browser can present it properly to the user.

The languages you need to learn in order to tell a Web browser the structure of a document—how to make a heading, a paragraph, a table, and so on—are HTML and XHTML.

How the Web Works

Before you learn how to write a very basic Web page, you should understand a little about how the Web works, such as what happens when you type a Web address such as `http://www.wrox.com/` or `http://www.google.com/` into the browser and a page gets returned.

Every computer that is connected to the Internet is given a unique address made up of a series of four numbers between 0 and 256 separated by periods—for example, 192.168.0.123 or 197.122.135.127. These numbers are known as *IP addresses*. IP (or Internet Protocol) is the standard for how data is passed between machines on the Internet.

When you connect to the Internet using an ISP you will be allocated an IP address, and you will often be allocated a new IP address each time you connect.

Every Web site, meanwhile, sits on a computer known as a *Web server* (often you will see this shortened to *server*). When you register a Web address, also known as a *domain name*, such as wrox.com you have to specify the IP address of the computer that will *host* the site.

When you visit a Web site, you are actually requesting pages from a machine at an IP address, but rather than having to learn that computer's 12-digit IP address, you use the site's domain name, such as google.com or wrox.com. When you enter something like http://www.google.com, the request goes to one of many special computers on the Internet known as *domain name servers* (or name servers, for short). These servers keep tables of machine names and their IP addresses, so when you type in http://www.google.com, it gets translated into a number, which identifies the computers that serve the Google Web site to you.

When you want to view any page on the Web, you must initiate the activity by requesting a page using your browser (if you do not specify a specific page, the Web server will usually send a default Web page). The browser asks a domain name server to translate the domain name you requested into an IP address. The browser then sends a request to that server for the page you want, using a standard called *Hypertext Transfer Protocol* or *HTTP* (hence the http:// you see at the start of many Web addresses).

The server should constantly be connected to the Internet—ready to serve pages to visitors. When it receives a request, it looks for the requested document and returns it. When a request is made, the server usually logs the client's IP address, the document requested, and the date and time it was requested.

An average Web page actually requires the Web browser to request more than one file from the Web server—not just the XHTML page, but also any images, style sheets, and other resources in the page. Each of these files, including the main page, needs a *URL* (a *uniform resource locator*) to identify it. A URL is a unique address on the Web where that page, picture, or other resource can be found and is made up of the domain name (for example, wrox.com), the name of the folder or folders on the Web server that the file lives in (also known as directories on a server), and the name of the file itself. For example, the Wrox logo on the home page of the Wrox Web site has the unique address wrox.com/images/mainLogo.gif and the main page is wrox.com/default.html. After the browser acquires the files it then inserts the images and other resources in the appropriate place to display the page.

The final chapter of the book covers putting your site on a Web server, but first you must learn how to build your site.

> *You may have noticed on the Web that Web pages do not always end in* .html. *There are lots of other suffixes, such as* .asp *and* .php. *You are introduced to the languages ASP and PHP in the final chapter; they usually run extra code on the server to generate a page especially for you. Meanwhile,* .htm *files are just HTML files like those you have already started creating—because you can save HTML files with either the suffix* .htm *or* .html.

For an example of how all of this works, see Figure 1-1 and the explanation that follows it.

Figure 1-1

Here's what's going on in the figure:

1. A user enters a URL into a browser (for example, `http://www.wrox.com`). This request is passed to a domain name server.

2. The domain name server returns an IP address for the server that hosts the Web site (for example, 212.64.250.250).

3. The browser requests the page from the Web server using the IP address specified by the domain name server.

4. The Web server returns the page to the IP address specified by the browser requesting the page. (The page may also contain links to other files on the same server, such as images, which the browser will also request.)

Introducing Web Technologies

Now that you are thinking of the Web as a huge collection of documents, not dissimilar to the documents you come across in everyday life, and you know how a Web page gets to you when you type a URL into your browser, it is time to look at the technologies used to write Web pages.

In this section you meet HTML, CSS, XHTML, and JavaScript. You will get an idea what each language is used for and start to see the basics of how each works. With a basic understanding of each of these technologies you will find it easier to see the big picture of creating pages for the Web.

Introducing HTML

HTML, or Hypertext Markup Language, is the most widely used language on Web. As its name suggests, HTML is a *markup language*, which may sound complicated, although really you come across markup every day. Markup is just something you add to a document to give it special meaning; for example, when you use a highlighter pen you are marking up a document. When you are marking up a document for the Web, the special meaning you are adding indicates the *structure* of the document, and the markup indicates which part of the document is a heading, which parts are paragraphs, what belongs in a table, and so on. This markup in turn allows a Web browser to display your document appropriately.

When creating a document in a word processor, you can distinguish headings using a heading style (usually with a larger font) to indicate which part of the text is a heading. You can use the Enter (or Return) key to start a new paragraph. You can insert tables into your document, create bulleted lists, and so on. When marking documents up for the Web you are performing a very similar process.

HTML and XHTML are the languages you use to tell a Web browser where the heading is for a Web page, what is a paragraph, what is part of a table and so on, so it can structure your document and render it properly. But what is the difference between HTML and XHTML? Well, first you should know that there are several versions of both HTML and XHTML, but don't let that bother you—it all sounds a lot more complicated than it really is. Whereas there are several versions of HTML, each version just adds functionality on top of its predecessor (like a new version of some software might add some features or a new version of a dictionary might add a few extra words), or offers better ways of doing things that were already in earlier versions. So, you do not need to learn each version of HTML and XHTML, nor do you need to focus on one variation. This book teaches you all you need to know to write Web pages using HTML and XHTML. Indeed, as I mentioned in the Introduction, XHTML is just like the latest version of HTML, as you will see shortly (although to be accurate, while it is almost identical to the last version of HTML, it is technically HTML's successor).

Let's have a look at a simple page in HTML. (Remember that you can download this example along with all the code for this book from the Wrox Web site at www.wrox.com; the example is in the Chapter 1 folder and is called ch01_eg01.htm.)

```
<html>

  <head>
    <title>Acme Toy Company: About Us</title>
  </head>

  <body>
    <h1>About Acme Toys Inc.</h1>
    <p>Acme Toys has been making toys for popular cartoon characters for
    over 50 years. One of our most popular customers was Wile E. Coyote, who
    regularly purchased items to help him catch Road Runner.</p>
  </body>

</html>
```

This may look a bit confusing at first, but it will all make sense soon. As you can see, there are several sets of angle brackets with words or letters between them such as <html>, <head>, </title> and </body>. These words in the angle brackets are known as *markup*. Figure 1-2 illustrates what this page would look like in a Web browser.

Figure 1-2

As you can see, this document contains the heading "About ACME Toys Inc." and a paragraph of text to introduce the fictional company. Note also that it says "Acme Toy Company: About Us" right at the top of the window in the middle; this is known as the *title* of the page.

To understand the markup in this first example, you need to look at what is written between the angle brackets and compare that with what you see in the figure, which is what you will do next.

Tags and Elements

If you look at the first and last lines of the code for the last example, you will see pairs of angle brackets containing the letters <html>. The two brackets and all of the characters between them are known as a *tag*, and there are lots of tags in the example. All of the tags in this example come in pairs; there are *opening tags* and *closing tags*. The closing tag is always slightly different than the opening tag in that it has a forward slash character before the characters </html>.

A pair of tags and the content it includes is known as an *element*. In Figure 1-3 you can see the heading for the page of the last example.

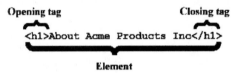

Figure 1-3

Again, the tags in Figure 1-3 come in pairs. I mentioned earlier in the chapter that markup adds meaning to a document, and in HTML it is the tags that are the markup. The special meaning these tags give is a description of the structure of the document. The opening tag says "This is the beginning of a heading" and the closing tag says "This is the end of a heading." Without the markup, the words in the middle would just be another bit of text; it would not be clear that they formed the heading.

Now look at the paragraph of text about the company; it is held between an opening <p> tag and a closing </p> tag. And, you guessed it, the p stands for paragraph.

> Because this basic concept is so important to understand, I think it bears repeating: *tags* are the letters and numbers between the angle brackets, whereas *elements* are tags and anything between the opening and closing tags.

As you can see, the markup in this example actually describes what you will find between the tags, and the added meaning the tags give is describing the structure of the document. For example, between the opening <p> and closing </p> tags are paragraphs and between the <h1> and </h1> tags is a heading. Indeed, the whole HTML document is contained between opening <html> and closing </html> tags.

If you were wondering why there is a number 1 after the h , it is because in HTML and XHTML there are six levels of headings. A level 1 heading is sometimes used as the main heading for a document (such as a chapter title), which can then contain subheadings, with level 6 being the smallest. This allows you to structure your document appropriately with subheadings under the main heading. (You look at this in detail in the next chapter.)

You will often find that terms from a family tree are used to describe the relationships between elements. For example, an element that contains another element is known as the *parent*, while the element that is between the parent element's opening and closing tags is called a *child* of that element. So, the <title> element is a child of the <head> element, the <head> element is the parent of the <title> element, and so on. Furthermore, the <title> element can be thought of as a grandchild of the <html> element.

Separating Heads from Bodies

Whenever you write a Web page in HTML, the whole of the page is contained between the opening <html> and closing </html> tags, just as it was in the last example. Inside the <html> element, there are two main parts to the page:

❏ **The <head> element:** Often referred to as the head of the page, this contains information *about* the page (this is not the main content of the page). It is information such as a title and a description of the page, or keywords that search engines can use to index the page. It consists of the opening <head> tag, the closing </head> tag, and everything in between.

❏ **The <body> element:** Often referred to as the body of the page, this contains the information you actually see in the main browser window. It consists of the opening <body> tag, closing </body> tag, and everything in between.

Inside the <head> element of the first example page you can see a <title> element:

```
<head>
   <title>Acme Toy Company: About Us</title>
</head>
```

Between the opening and closing title tags are the words Acme Toy Company: About Us, which is the title of this Web page. If you remember Figure 1-2, which showed the screenshot of this page, I brought your attention to the words right at the top of the browser in the center. This is where Internet Explorer (IE) displays the title of a document; it is also the name IE uses when you save a page in your favorites.

The real content of your page is held in the <body> element, which is what you want users to read, and is shown in the main browser window.

> The **head** element contains information about the document, which is not displayed within the main page itself. The **body** element holds the actual content of the page that is viewed in your browser.

Adding Style

The first example page isn't going to win any awards for design. Indeed, when the Web started it was a rather gray place filled with drab pages like this one. While the Web was originally conceived to transmit scientific research documents (so that existing research could reach wider audiences), it did not take long for people to find other uses for it. No one can question that the speed with which the Web has grown is phenomenal, and it did not take long for people to start creating Web pages for all different kinds of purposes—from individuals setting up homepages about their family or hobbies to big corporations setting up vast sites that highlighted their products and services.

As the Web grew, people who were building these pages wanted more control over how their pages appeared. In order for this to happen, the W3C (which stands for World Wide Web Consortium, the body responsible for creating the HTML specifications), and the people writing the Web browsers (in particular Netscape and Microsoft) introduced new markup. Soon there was markup allowing you to specify different fonts, colors, backgrounds, and so on. It was in catering to these new requirements of the Web that new versions of HTML were spawned.

Consider the possibilities: You could take the first brief Web page from earlier in the chapter, specify the typeface (or font) you want the page to use, change the color of the text in the main paragraph to red, and indicate that some of the text should be in a bold or italic font. The whole of the page could also have a very light gray background, in which case it would look something like Figure 1-4.

Figure 1-4

This page is still not going to be a hot contender for any design awards, but it shows that you do have control over how the page looks. The typeface has been specified, the paragraph is in red text (which you can't see from the black and white figure), and it also features bold and italic text.

Here is the code for this example (eg01_eg02.htm):

```html
<html>

  <head>
    <title>Acme Toy Company: About Us</title>
  </head>

  <body bgcolor="#EFEFEF">
    <font face="arial">
      <h1>About Acme Toys Inc.</h1>
    </font>
    <font face="arial" color="#CC0000">
      <p><b>Acme Toys</b> has been making toys for popular cartoon
      characters for over 50 years. One of our most popular customers
      was <i>Wile E. Coyote</i>, who regularly purchased our items to help
      him catch Road Runner.</p>
    </font>
  </body>

</html>
```

First you should note how parts of the text in the paragraph are in bold and italic typefaces. The `<b>` element is used to indicate the parts of the text that should be in a bold typeface, and an `<i>` element is used to indicate which parts should be in italics.

The most obvious changes to this page, however, are the `<font>` elements, which specify that the page should be displayed in an Arial typeface. If the book were in color you would also notice that the paragraph text is in red. (This is just one way of indicating which typeface to use, and you will meet a preferred way in Chapter 9.)

Attributes Tell Us About Elements

In order to specify which font you want to use, the `<font>` element must carry an attribute called `face`. It is important to take a moment now to look at attributes, as they are used a lot in HTML.

You can use *attributes* to say something about an element. They appear on the opening tag of the element that carries them. All attributes are made up of two parts: a *name* and a *value*:

❑   The *name* is the property you want to set. For example, the `<font>` element in the example carries an attribute whose name is `face`, which you can use to indicate which typeface you want the text to appear in.

❑   The *value* is what you want the value of the property to be. The first example was supposed to use the Arial typeface, so the value of the `face` attribute is `Arial`.

The value of the attribute should be put in double quotation marks, and is separated from the name by the equals sign. You can see that a color for the text has been specified as well as the typeface in this `<font>` element:

```
<font face="arial" color="#CC0000">
```

This illustrates that elements can carry several attributes, although an element should never have two attributes of the same name.

You might have noticed that the value of the `color` attribute is #CC0000, which might seem a strange way to describe a red, but there are many shades of red and this notation allows us to describe lots of different reds. Don't worry about it for now; you learn all about color in Chapter 4. As you will see in that chapter, colors on the Web can be described using six-digit codes preceded by the pound (or hash) sign # and the characters after it represent the amount of red, green, and blue used to make up the color. The same notation is used for the `bgcolor` attribute on the `<body>` element, which indicates that we want the background of our page to be a very light gray. (Appendix D also lists over 100 color names and their corresponding numbers.)

> **All attributes are made up of two parts, the attribute's name and its value, separated by an equal sign. Values should be held within double quotation marks.**

Keeping Style Separate from Structure and Semantics

By the time the W3C had released version 3 of HTML, it contained all kinds of markup that indicated how a document should look. Markup that indicates how the document should look, rather than describing the structure or content of the document, is known as *stylistic markup*. The <font>, <b>, and <i> elements, and the color and bgcolor attributes are examples of stylistic markup.

You can contrast stylistic markup with the markup from the first example. The first example contained only *structural markup* indicating the structure of a document (the paragraphs and headings), and *semantic markup* telling us something about the content of the data, like the <title> element. But that first example also looked plain and gray, which is why the stylistic markup was introduced.

Stylistic markup made Web pages look more interesting, but the result was that even the very basic Web pages became longer and more complicated. Furthermore, the markup no longer just described the structure and contents of the document. Whereas in the first example the markup added information about the document's structure and its content only, the second example used markup to describe how the document should look.

You see, a heading is a heading whether it is printed in black and white or shown on a Web browser in bold, red, Arial typeface. Similarly, a title is the title of a document, no matter whether it is on the front page of a document or at the top of each individual page. But when you use markup to indicate what should be in an Arial typeface, 12 pt in size, red in color, and bold, you are saying how the document should look rather than just saying "this is a paragraph" or "this is a heading."

Introducing CSS

By the time the W3C released version 4 of HTML, it had decided to move away from including stylistic markup in HTML and instead created a separate language with which to style documents called *cascading style sheets* or CSS. CSS uses *rules* to say how a document should appear (rather than elements and attributes). These rules *usually* live in a separate document rather than in the page with the content, thus keeping the presentation rules separate from the structural and semantic markup.

Each CSS rule is made up of two parts:

❑ A *selector* to indicate which elements a rule applies to.

❑ *Declarations* indicating the properties of an element you want to change, such as its typeface or color, and the value you want this to be, such as Arial or red. Declarations are very similar to attribute names and their values.

Figure 1-5 shows an example of a CSS rule that would apply to the <body> element of a document. Because it is used on the <body> element, it also applies to all of the elements between the opening

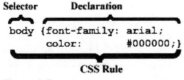

Figure 1-5

<body> tag and the closing </body> tag. It says the text inside a <body> element should be shown in a black, Arial typeface.

CSS is covered in detail in Chapters 9 and 10, but it might help to look at an example of CSS so you can see how it fits in when writing Web pages. So, let's go back to the first example in this chapter and create a style sheet for it so that it looks more like the second example (with the Arial typeface and red text in the paragraph), but keeping the extra stylistic markup out of the HTML document.

Some people add their CSS rules inside the <head>element of the HTML document, but if you are writing more than one page for your site, you might as well use the same style sheet for all of the pages rather than repeating the rules in each page, which is the approach taken here.

To make an HTML page use a separate CSS style sheet you need only to add the <link> element into the <head> element (this example is ch01_eg03.css):

```
<head>
  <title>Acme Toy Company: About Us</title>
  <link rel="stylesheet" type="text/css" href="style_01.css" />
</head>
```

This will be covered in detail in Chapter 9, but for now you know that it creates a link to the following style sheet called style_01.css. You can see the selectors on the left and the declarations on the right in the curly brackets:

```
body     {font-family:arial;
          color:#000000;
          background-color:#EFEFEF;}

p        {color:#CC0000;}
```

Here, the first rule selects all markup inside the <body> element and says that the typeface (font-family) used for all text inside this element should be Arial, the color should be black, and the background color (background-color) should be light gray. The second rule selects the paragraph elements and says the color of anything within that element should be red.

You can now see why CSS has the word "cascading" in its title. The directions applied to the <body> element indicated that everything inside the <body> should use the Arial typeface, and this rule has cascaded to other elements contained inside the <body> element, such as the <p> element.

Now, imagine you had a Web site with 20 pages. If you had included the rules for how the Web site should look in every page (using stylistic markup such as the <font> element and color attributes you saw in the second example), and you wanted to change the color or typeface of the text in all paragraphs, you would have to alter 20 pages. With the presentation rules in a style sheet, however, you can change the appearance of 20 pages simply by changing the style sheet. Thus, you do not have to add all of those extra stylistic elements and attributes to each page, which means your Web pages are smaller and simpler.

You learn more about styling your documents and using CSS in Chapters 9 and 10, where you will also meet some more of its advantages.

Introducing XHTML

When the W3C released HTML 4.1, almost all of the markup that had been used to style documents had been marked as *deprecated*, meaning that it would be removed from future versions of HTML and therefore Web page authors should stop using it. This was the W3C's way of encouraging people to use only structural and semantic markup when writing HTML documents and to use CSS for styling documents; the result is a separation of style from content.

> *You will still meet a lot of deprecated markup in this book, and where you do it is clearly noted. Some of it is included because occasionally you have to use deprecated markup when creating pages so that they work in older browsers, and other times you should just be aware of it because you are likely to come across it when you look at older pages.*

Having released HTML 4.1, the W3C did not release an HTML 5.0; it may sound confusing, but the W3C decided that its successor should be called XHTML—rather like when Microsoft released Windows XP instead of calling it Windows 2001.

The X at the front of the name came from a new language called XML (eXtensible Markup Language), which has gained huge popularity in all aspects of programming. XML is a language you can use to create your own markup languages, and therefore it was decided that the new version of HTML (Hypertext Markup Language) should be written in XML. In practice, this means that authors writing XHTML have to be more careful about how they write their pages (as XHTML uses a stricter syntax than HTML did). One benefit of this stricter language, however, is that browsers can be a lot smaller in size (and will therefore fit better on smaller devices such as phones). Another benefit is that a lot of tools are written for use with XML, and you can use any of these with XHTML.

The good news for you is that you do not have to learn HTML *and* XHTML because when XHTML was created it was designed to be backwards compatible with browsers that display only HTML pages (unless specifically noted).

> **I should reiterate here that most of the elements and attributes you use in XHTML are exactly the same as those that were available in HTML 4.1; you just have to be precise about the way in which you use them and obey a few new rules.**

To help Web developers make the transition from HTML to XHTML, three versions or flavors of XHTML were released:

❑ Transitional XHTML 1.0, which still allowed developers to use the deprecated markup from HTML 4.1 but required the author to use the new stricter syntax.

❑ Strict XHTML 1.0, which was to signal the path forward for XHTML, without the deprecated stylistic markup and obeying the new stricter syntax.

❑ Frameset XHTML 1.0, which is used to create Web pages that use a technology called *frames* (you meet frames in Chapter 7).

If by now you are feeling a little overwhelmed by all the different versions of HTML and XHTML, don't be! Throughout this book, you will be primarily learning Transitional XHTML 1.0. In the process, you will learn which elements and attributes have been marked as deprecated and what the alternatives for using these are. If you avoid the deprecated elements and attributes, you will automatically be writing Strict XHTML 1.0.

Having learned Transitional XHTML 1.0, you should be very able to understand older versions of HTML and be safe in the knowledge that (unless specifically warned), your XHTML code will work in the majority of browsers used on the Web today.

Before you take a look at JavaScript, it is helpful to note the differences between writing HTML and XHTML as discussed in the next section.

Differences Between Writing XHTML and Writing HTML

As mentioned previously, XHTML uses a stricter syntax than HTML. This section looks at the difference between writing HTML and XHTML. If you have written any HTML before, this section will give you a good idea of the stricter syntax you need to learn in order to write XHTML. If you are a beginner, this section will help you work with code that may be written using earlier versions of HTML.

Include XML Declaration

Because XHTML is written in XML, an XHTML document is also technically an XML document. Therefore it can start with the optional XML declaration that all XML documents can start with:

```
<?xml version="1.0" encoding="UTF-8" ?>
```

If you include the XML declaration it must be right at the beginning of the document; there must be nothing before it, not even a space. The encoding attribute indicates the encoding used in the document.

An encoding (short for character encoding) represents how a program or operating system stores characters that you might want to display. Because different languages have different characters, and indeed because some programs support more characters than others, there are several different encodings.

While it is advised that you use the XML declaration, Netscape Navigator 3.04 and earlier or Internet Explorer 3.0 and earlier will either ignore or display this declaration, so you may choose to leave it out of your pages if visitors to your site are likely to use one of these browsers. You look at browser versions and support in Chapter 8.

Include a DOCTYPE Declaration

A DOCTYPE declaration indicates the version of HTML or XHTML you are writing. It goes before the opening <html> tag in a document, and the contents are different for each different version you write. If you are writing Transitional XHTML 1.0 (and include stylistic markup in your document) then your DOCTYPE declaration should look like this:

```
<!DOCTYPE html PUBLIC "-//W3C//DTD XHTML 1.0 Transitional//EN"
    "http://www.w3.org/TR/xhtml1/DTD/xhtml1-transitional.dtd">
```

If you are writing Strict XHTML 1.0 your DOCTYPE declaration will look like this:

```
<!DOCTYPE html PUBLIC "-//W3C//DTD XHTML 1.0 Strict//EN"
    "http://www.w3.org/TR/xhtml1/DTD/xhtml1-strict.dtd">
```

For frameset documents (discussed in Chapter 7), your DOCTYPE declaration would look like this:

```
<!DOCTYPE html PUBLIC "-//W3C//DTD XHTML 1.0 Frameset//EN"
  "http://www.w3.org/TR/xhtml1/DTD/xhtml1-frameset.dtd">
```

> A Strict XHTML document *must* contain the DOCTYPE declaration before the root element; however, you are not required to include the DOCTYPE declaration if you are creating a transitional or frameset document.

Elements and Attributes Use Lowercase Names

Whereas HTML allowed you to use uppercase characters, lowercase characters, or a mix of both, XHTML requires that all element and attributes names be written in lowercase.

```
<body onclick="someFunction();">
```

Of course, the element content (between opening and closing tags) and value of an attribute are not case-sensitive; you can write what you like between the opening and closing tags of an element (except angle brackets) and within the quotes of an attribute (except quotation marks, which would close the attribute).

The decision to make XML case-sensitive was largely driven by internationalization efforts. While you can easily convert English characters from uppercase to lowercase, some languages do not have such a direct mapping—in some cases there is no equivalent in a different case; there can even be regional variations. So that the specification could use different languages, it was therefore decided to make XML case-sensitive.

Close All Tags Correctly

In XHTML, every opening tag must have a corresponding closing tag. The only exception is an empty element. In HTML you could write paragraphs like so:

```
<p>Here is some text in the first paragraph without a closing tag.
<p>Here is a second paragraph without a closing tag.
<p>Here is a third paragraph, which again misses a closing tag.
```

Each time an HTML browser runs across a new <p> tag it assumes that the previous paragraph has finished. But all elements in XHTML must be closed, so this should read:

```
<p>Here is some text in the first paragraph with a closing tag.</p>
<p>Here is a second paragraph with a closing tag.</p>
<p>Here is a third paragraph, which again has a closing tag.</p>
```

Some elements, however, do not have any content between an opening and closing tag. These are known as *empty elements*. Examples of empty elements are the <img> element for including images (which you meet in Chapter 4), and the line break element. In HTML the line break element looks like this:

```
<br>
```

This one tag on its own is all that is required to add a line break in HTML. In XHTML, empty elements must include a forward slash character to represent the empty element correctly. For example:

```
<br />
```

Note that there is a space before the trailing slash character. If you did not include this space, older browsers would not understand the tag and would ignore it.

Attribute Values

You need to be aware of three points when writing XHTML attributes:

- ❑ All attribute values must be enclosed in double quotation marks.
- ❑ A value must be given for each attribute.
- ❑ Whitespace (see the definition at the end of this section) is collapsed, and trailing spaces are removed.

In some versions of HTML, you could write attributes without giving the value in quotes. For example, the following would make a heading element appear in the center of the page:

```
<h1 align=center>
```

In XHTML, however, all attribute values must be put inside double quotation characters like so:

```
<h1 align="center">
```

Furthermore, HTML also allows some attributes to be written without a value. It is known as *attribute minimization,* and where a value is not given, a default is used. This is not allowed in XHTML—all attributes must be given a value in quotes.

Finally, you should note that any trailing spaces—known as *whitespace*—at the end of an attribute value will be stripped out of the XHTML documents, and any line breaks or multiple spaces between words are collapsed into one space, rather like most processors treat spaces in HTML.

The HTML Element Must Be the Root Element

The opening tag of any XHTML document must be:

```
<html>
```

and the last tag in the XHTML document must be:

```
</html>
```

The only things that may come before the opening <html> tag are the XML declaration and DOCTYPE declaration because all XML documents must have one unique root element, which contains the rest of the document. In the case of XHTML documents, it is the <html> element.

Tags Must Nest Properly

When you read that tags must nest properly, it is a bit like reading they must appear in a symmetrical order. If you want to have one element inside another, then both its opening and closing tags must be inside the containing element. For example, the following is allowed:

```
<p> This paragraph contains some <em>emphasized text.</em></p>
```

Whereas the following is wrong because the closing </em> tag is not inside the paragraph element:

```
<p> This paragraph contains some <em>emphasized text. </p></em>
```

In other words, if an element is to contain another element, it must wholly contain that element.

A Few Words About JavaScript

Having addressed the differences between writing HTML and XHTML pages, and having learned how CSS can be used to style pages, a few words should be said about JavaScript. JavaScript is a type of programming language known as a *scripting language* that when used in a Web page allows you to control many features of how the browser behaves. JavaScript is supported by both IE and Netscape (as well as many other browsers that use the same core code as Netscape, such as Mozilla). You can embed JavaScript into your HTML and XHTML documents to achieve all manner of tasks, from practical applications such as performing calculations to visual effects such as creating rollover buttons that change image or color as users move their mouse over them.

One of the greatest strengths of JavaScript is that code can be programmed to run when an event fires. An event can be caused by something like a document loading or a window closing, or it can be caused by a user interacting with the site—for example pressing a key, moving a mouse over a particular element, or submitting a form. Indeed, you will see how XHTML features several event handler attributes (such as onMouseOver and onClick) so that scripts can be triggered when a user interacts with an element.

JavaScript can be a very powerful language in the right hands, and many books have been written on the subject. While there is not space to teach you JavaScript in great depth in this book, you can certainly get a taste for what it can do, and after reading Chapter 14, which introduces the language, and Chapter 15, which shows lots of example scripts, you should be able to incorporate JavaScripts into your Web pages—and thousands of free JavaScripts are available on the Web that you can use, too.

Tools for Writing Web Pages

Countless programs, or *tools*, are available to help you write Web pages. You may have heard of some of the common ones such as Macromedia Dreamweaver and Microsoft FrontPage. But you do not need to pay for one of these programs; you can just as easily write pages in any text editor such as Microsoft's Notepad on a PC or SimpleText on a Mac.

Web authoring tools often have what is known as a WYSIWYG interface, which stands for What You See Is What You Get. This means you have a graphical interface for creating Web pages (you never have to see the code if you don't want to). Even though some programs help you to write Web pages, and they can write much of the code for you, it is still very important to have a good understanding of what the code means, or you will soon find yourself quite limited by these programs.

Here are some of the reasons why:

- Using a graphical interface to write code for you means you do not learn how to code Web pages yourself; the tool generates the code for you and you are not encouraged to study or understand this code.

- Without understanding the code you will not be able to make fine adjustments to the way a page looks. Most experienced Web page authors who use WYSIWYG tools still change code by hand before they are satisfied with the appearance of a Web page.

- Tools do not help you select the best possible approach to solving a problem, particularly when it comes to laying out a Web page; you have to know the different ways to get text and images on a page in order to choose the best approach.

- Most authoring tools write code that deviates from the standards. They will often change capitalization, or order of elements and attributes, and leave out values for attributes.

- It is very easy to break a page using WYSIWYG editors when making alterations to a page.

- Once you have really learned to code in XHTML it is very easy to use any WYSIWYG editor to create Web pages. But it is not easy to write code if you just learn to use a WYSIWYG editor because you are not encouraged to understand the code behind it and your skills are locked into that tool.

This is not to say you should not use a tool if you have one, but do make sure that:

- You learn the meaning of the code that your tool generates

- The tool is not making alterations to the code each time you save it, or close and open the document. (Look out for missing quotes on attribute values and any capital letters in element or attribute names.)

Most professional Web designers and developers who use an authoring tool use the WYSIWYG interface only to help them write code, which they already understand, rather than write out every character manually.

Apart from helping you write code you already understand, the real strengths of an authoring tool such as Dreamweaver or FrontPage are their testing and document management features.

Whether you use a tool to create a Web page or not, I strongly recommend writing the content for your page before you start marking up your documents. A word processing application is ideal for this. It will also help to have a sketch on paper of how you want your page to look so that you can code your content to fit your design. Then you can either use a tool to help you create this layout or you can hand-code it.

Creating Your First Web Page

At last it is time to start creating your first Web page. It is going to be quite a simple page that tells viewers a bit about you and your interests. It might look a little basic, but don't let that put you off. As each chapter progresses, your pages will continue to get more impressive as you learn new features of the languages.

If you have a program you want to use for writing Web pages, then get it up and running now; otherwise simply fire up a text editor.

Try It Out   Creating Your First Page

In this example you are going to create a Web page about yourself. You will write this page in Transitional XHTML 1.0.

1. Start the program you are going to use to write your Web pages, whether this is a plain text editor or a dedicated Web page authoring tool. (If you are using an authoring tool, make sure that you are in the code view and delete any code it might have already entered for you.)

2. Enter the XML declaration and the DOCTYPE declaration for Transitional XHTML 1.0. Remember that the XML declaration should be the very first thing in your document; there should not even be a space before it:

```
<?xml version="1.0" ?>
<!DOCTYPE html PUBLIC "-//W3C//DTD XHTML 1.0 Transitional//EN"
"http://www.w3.org/TR/xhtml1/DTD/xhtml1-transitional.dtd">
```

3. Add in the opening <html> tag right after the DOCTYPE declaration and the closing </html> tag at the end. You will note that the opening <html> tag in this example carries an xmlns attribute. You look at this attribute in Chapter 2, but this is just another indication that the markup in this example is XHTML 1.0.

```
<?xml version="1.0" ?>
<!DOCTYPE html PUBLIC "-//W3C//DTD XHTML 1.0 Transitional//EN"
"http://www.w3.org/TR/xhtml1/DTD/xhtml1-transitional.dtd">

<html xmlns="http://www.w3.org/1999/xhtml">

</html>
```

4. Add the <head> and <body> elements inside the <html> element. You might remember that the <head> element contains information *about* the document, while the main part of the document lives in the <body> element:

```
<?xml version="1.0" ?>
<?xml version="1.0" ?>
<!DOCTYPE html PUBLIC "-//W3C//DTD XHTML 1.0 Transitional//EN"
"http://www.w3.org/TR/xhtml1/DTD/xhtml1-transitional.dtd"> <html
xmlns="http://www.w3.org/1999/xhtml">
  <head></head>
  <body></body>
</html>
```

5. Add in the <title> for the document inside the <head> element and don't forget to put your own name in there:

```
<head>
  <head>
    <title>Jon's Home Page</title>
  </head>
</html>
```

6. The main part of what users will see goes inside the <body> element. In this example, you will have a heading that welcomes people to your site and a couple of paragraphs of text about yourself:

```
<body>
  <h1>Welcome to Jon's Home Page</h1>
  <p>Jon has been creating Web sites for more than eight years. He has written
     several books on computer programming topics including HTML, XHTML, XML,
     and ASP. He also runs InPreparation Limited, a small Web solutions
     company based in London, with clients in the U.K., U.S., and
     Australia. </p>
  <p>When not sitting in front of a computer, Jon can usually be found
     listening to music or playing his guitar.</p>
</body>
```

7. Create a new folder called WebExamples that you can put your examples for this book in. Check that your file looks exactly like this, except the text about yourself, and save this page as MyFirstPage.html.

```
<?xml version="1.0" ?>
<!DOCTYPE html PUBLIC "-//W3C//DTD XHTML 1.0 Transitional//EN"
"http://www.w3.org/TR/xhtml1/DTD/xhtml1-transitional.dtd">
<html xmlns="http://www.w3.org/1999/xhtml">

  <head>
    <title>Jon's Home Page</title>
  </head>

<body>
  <h1>Welcome to Jon's Home Page</h1>
  <p>Jon has been creating Web sites for more than eight years. He has written
     several books on computer programming topics including HTML, XHTML, XML,
     and ASP. He also runs InPreparation Limited, a small Web solutions
     company based in London, with clients in the U.K., U.S., and
     Australia. </p>
  <p>When not sitting in front of a computer, Jon can usually be found
     listening to music or playing his guitar.</p>
</body>

</html>
```

8. Open the page in a Web browser. In Internet Explorer, choose File ➪ Open and then click Browse to find the file you want. If you are using Netscape, choose File ➪ Open File and find the page you just saved.

This shows how you can write and test Web pages on your computer; now you have only to put them on the Web when you are ready for others to see them.

If you are using a plain text editor and it tries to add the file extension .txt (or any other extension) rather than .html, try to save it again, but this time put the filename and extension in quotes like this: "contactUs.html". This should stop the program from saving the file with a .txt extension.

The page should look something like Figure 1-6.

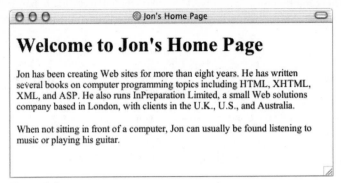

Figure 1-6

How It Works

Let's take another look at the example to make sure you are clear on how it works.

The first line of the example indicates that the document is an XML document (as all XHTML documents are). Following the XML declaration is the DOCTYPE declaration, which tells the Web browser which version of XHTML you are using. In this case the document is a Transitional XHTML 1.0 document. You can see the word "transitional" at the end of the first and second lines:

```
<?xml version="1.0" ?>
<!DOCTYPE html PUBLIC "-//W3C//DTD/ XHTML 1.0 Transitional//EN"
  "http://www.w3.org/TR/xhtml-transitional.dtd">
```

Remember that XML is a language that allows you to create your own markup languages, and because of its popularity, the W3C decided to rewrite HTML in XML, which is when it took the name XHTML (instead of HTML). Therefore, any XHTML document is, in fact, an example of an XML document, too.

The rest of the document is then contained within the <html> element. The first element after the opening <html> tag is always the <head> element.

The <head> element contains information about the document (rather than the content of the document). Inside the <head> element you can see a <title> element. (The title of the document tends to be displayed in the top bar of the browser window, and if you were to save it as one of your favorites, it would also be the name of the favorite item.)

```
<html xmlns="http://www.w3.org/1999/xhtml">

  <head>
    <title>Jon's Home Page</title>
  </head>
```

The <body> element follows the <head> element and contains the part of the page you see in the main portion of the browser window.

Inside the <body> element you should have given your page a heading. The <h1> element indicates that its content is a primary heading for the document. This should be followed by a couple of paragraphs.

The start of a paragraph is indicated with the opening <p> tag, while the end of the paragraph is noted with the closing </p> tag.

Finally, there is a closing </html> tag to indicate the end of the document.

```
<body>
  <h1>Welcome to Jon's Home Page</h1>
  <p>Jon has been creating Web sites for more than eight years. He has written
     several books on computer programming topics including HTML, XHTML, XML,
     and ASP. He also runs InPreparation Limited, a small Web solutions
     company based in London, with clients in the U.K., U.S., and
     Australia. </p>
  <p>When not sitting in front of a computer, Jon can usually be found
     listening to music or playing his guitar.</p>
</body>

</html>
```

The use of indenting on elements that are contained inside another element makes documents easier to read and can help you ensure that elements nest correctly.

Viewing the Source of Web Pages

Now that you have created your first Web page and have it running in a browser, it is time to learn one of the greatest tricks of the Web: viewing source code for pages. Both Internet Explorer and Netscape Navigator allow this.

Go back to the example you just wrote and look at it again in your browser. In IE, choose View ⇨ Source, or if you are using Netscape choose View ⇨ Page Source.

A new window should open up, and in this window you should see the code you wrote for your page (see Figure 1-7).

Many Web developers teach themselves techniques by looking at the source of their favorite Web sites. As you learn more about XHTML throughout this book, you can start to look at the source of some of your favorite sites and see how the sites work.

There are two things to remember when looking around at other people's source code:

❑   Other people have written and own the copyright to this code. You should use it only to learn how an effect was achieved; you should not copy code and just change the words or images on the page. You would not like it if someone stole your design and just changed a few words.

❑   Many people still write in HTML, and they do not obey the stricter rules of XHTML. You may see missing closing brackets, attribute values given without quotes, and all kinds of bad habits you should avoid. Browsers are very forgiving in that they often still display pages even if they have a lot of mistakes in them, but you should avoid relying on this or your pages might not work in newer XHTML-only browsers.

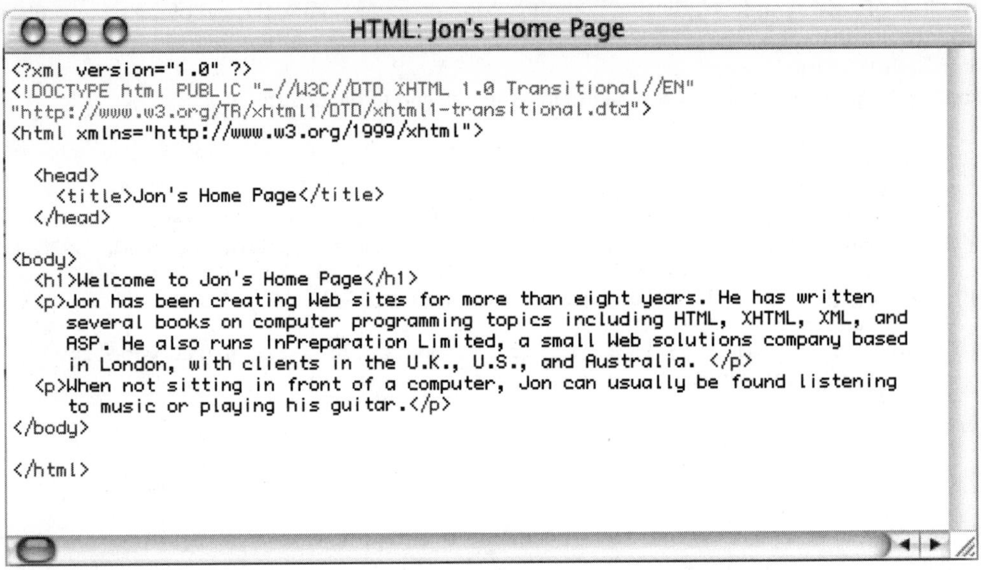

```
○ ○ ○                    HTML: Jon's Home Page
<?xml version="1.0" ?>
<!DOCTYPE html PUBLIC "-//W3C//DTD XHTML 1.0 Transitional//EN"
"http://www.w3.org/TR/xhtml1/DTD/xhtml1-transitional.dtd">
<html xmlns="http://www.w3.org/1999/xhtml">

  <head>
    <title>Jon's Home Page</title>
  </head>

<body>
  <h1>Welcome to Jon's Home Page</h1>
  <p>Jon has been creating Web sites for more than eight years. He has written
     several books on computer programming topics including HTML, XHTML, XML, and
     ASP. He also runs InPreparation Limited, a small Web solutions company based
     in London, with clients in the U.K., U.S., and Australia. </p>
  <p>When not sitting in front of a computer, Jon can usually be found listening
     to music or playing his guitar.</p>
</body>

</html>
```

Figure 1-7

As long as you are aware of these two points, you can learn a lot by looking at how other people write their Web sites.

Summary

In this chapter you have learned a bit about the different languages you will be using to write pages and how they fit together. You have seen that markup languages use tags, elements, and attributes to give added meaning to a document, and that the purpose of HTML and XHTML is largely to describe the structure of the document. The structure of documents on the Web often mirrors the structure of documents we meet every day, with paragraphs of text, forms, and tables, organized under headings.

You also now know that XHTML is like the latest version of HTML (not a completely different language), and that it uses most of the same elements as earlier versions of HTML, with a slightly stricter syntax and a few new rules. So, when you write XHTML pages, they will be compatible with most of the older browsers in use on the Web today.

The next six chapters of this book therefore teach you the elements and attributes that you can use to add structure to your documents. These will mainly be taken from Transitional XHTML 1.0 (with mentions of older syntax where it is particularly helpful). Again, Transitional XHTML still contains the deprecated elements from HTML 4.1, and where a feature has been deprecated you will see it clearly marked as such. This means that, if you want to write Strict XHTML 1.0 you need only to change your DOCTYPE declaration and avoid the deprecated markup.

In this chapter you also learned that CSS is the preferred method for indicating how a document should be styled; for example what color and typeface your text should be or the background color of pages. CSS rules will tend to live in separate documents; you will learn more about CSS in Chapters 9 and 10.

The combination of XHTML 1.0 and CSS will make your pages look great in the latest browsers while they continue to function well in older browsers, and will also teach you skills that will be relevant for a good many years to come.

In Chapter 2 you will start looking in detail at what goes into the body of XHTML pages and address how you can use markup to describe the structure of your text.

Exercises

The answers to all of the exercises are in Appendix A.

1. Look at the following HTML document and turn it into a Transitional XHTML document. There are some optional changes, as well as some required changes to make this document an XHTML document.

```
<html>
  <head>
    <TITLE>London</TITLE>
  </head>
  <body>
    <h1>Where I Live: London</h1>
    <p>London is the capital of England with a population of over
      seven million.
    <p>The Romans were the first to develop London as a port on the River
      Thames and as the main hub of their road network, although the banks
      of the Thames  had previously been inhabited by the Celts.
  </body>
```

2. Write the XHTML for the page shown in Figure 1-8.

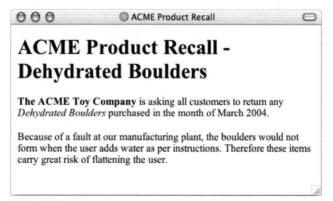

Figure 1-8

The Structure of a Page

Now that you've seen how to build a very basic Web page, and how the languages you will be learning in this book fit together, it is time to start looking at XHTML in depth. That means you must carefully look at the elements used to mark up a document and see what each can be used for. Then you must study the attributes each element can carry. While you are looking at these elements and attributes, you will see examples of how they can be used effectively to create Web pages.

This chapter starts by taking a close look at the four elements each XHTML document should contain: the `<html>`, `<head>`, `<title>`, and `<body>` elements, which provide the structure with which you can create XHTML pages. You can think of these elements as providing the skeleton on which you can flesh out your documents.

The next task is to look at some groups of attributes that nearly all XHTML elements can carry— the key word here being *nearly*, because not every element in XHTML will carry them. Still, it's important to learn about these attributes early so that you understand how each one functions with each element and so that you will not have to read about them each time they are mentioned.

The rest of the chapter then deals with all of the different types of text you will need to mark up, from headings and paragraphs and bulleted and numbered lists to quotations and citations. It will be in this section that you will really see how to add flesh to the bones of you XHTML documents.

In this chapter, then, you will learn:

- ❑ How the `<html>`, `<head>`, `<title>`, and `<body>` elements form the skeleton of a Web page
- ❑ The attribute groups that are common to many of the elements in XHTML
- ❑ How to structure your text so that the markup really describes its content

The really interesting part of this chapter will come when you start working on the text structures, but before you do that, it is important to really understand the skeleton of the document on which you build. So, bear with me as we look at the skeletal structure of a Web page again, this time in a little more detail.

Understanding the Basic Document Structure

As you saw in Chapter 1, XHTML documents are contained between the opening <html> and closing </html> tags (this <html> element is also known as the *root* element). Inside these tags, the document is split into two sections:

❑ The <head> element, which contains information *about* the document (such as a title or a link to a style sheet)

❑ The <body> element, which contains the real content of the document that you see.

This section takes a closer look at the four main elements that form the basic structure of every document: <html>, <head>, <title>, and <body>. These four elements should appear in every XHTML document that you write, and you will see them referred to throughout this book as the *skeleton* of the document.

Remember that before an opening <html> tag, an XHTML document can contain the optional XML declaration, and it should always contain a DOCTYPE declaration indicating which version of XHTML it uses.

The <html> Element

The <html> element is the containing element for the whole HTML or XHTML document. After the optional XML declaration and required DOCTYPE declaration, each XHTML document should have an opening <html> tag and each document should end with a closing </html> tag.

If you are writing Strict XHTML 1.0, the opening tag must also include something known as a *namespace identifier* (this indicates that the markup in the document belongs to the XHTML 1.0 namespace). Therefore the opening tag should look like this:

```
<html xmlns="http://www.w3.org/1999/xhtml">
```

While it is not strictly required in Transitional XHTML documents, it is a good practice to use it on all XHTML documents.

Only two elements appear as direct children of an <html> element: <head> and <body> (although the <head> and <body> elements will usually contain many more elements).

The <html> element can also carry the following attributes, which you will meet in the "Attribute Groups" section later in this chapter:

```
id dir lang xml:lang
```

You may sometimes come across the use of the version attribute in HTML 4.1 and earlier to indicate which version of HTML the document uses, although it is usually left off. XHTML documents should use the DOCTYPE declaration along with the xmlns attribute instead to indicate which version of XHTML they use.

The <head> Element

The <head> element is just a container for all other header elements. It should be the first thing to appear after the opening <html> tag.

Each <head> element should contain a <title> element indicating the title of the document, although it may also contain any combination of the following elements, in any order:

- ❑ <base>, which you will meet in Chapter 3.
- ❑ <object>, which is designed to include images, JavaScript objects, Flash animations, MP3 files, QuickTime movies and other components of a page. It is covered in Chapter 4.
- ❑ <link> to link to an external file, such as a style sheet or JavaScript file, as you will see in Chapter 9.
- ❑ <style> to include CSS rules inside the document; it's covered in Chapter 9.
- ❑ <script> for including script in the document, which you see in Chapter 14.
- ❑ <meta>, which includes information about the document such as keywords and a description, which are particularly helpful for search applications; this is covered in Chapter 16.

The opening <head> tag can carry the following attributes:

```
id dir lang xml:lang profile
```

The profile attribute is not actually in use yet, although it was included so it could be used in the future to specify a URL for something known as a profile that would describe the content of the document. The other attributes are covered in the "Attribute Groups" section later in this chapter.

The <title> Element

You should specify a title for every page that you write inside the <title> element (which is a child of the <head> element). It is used in several ways:

- ❑ At the very top of a browser window (as shown in Figure 2-1)
- ❑ As the default name for a bookmark in browsers such as IE and Netscape
- ❑ By search engines that use its content to help index pages

Therefore it is important to use a title that really describes the content of your site. For example, if you have a "contact us" page in your site, do not just use Contact Us for the title. Include your company or site name. Something like this would be more appropriate:

```
<title>Wrox Music: Contact Details</title>
```

Where possible, your title should describe the content of that page; for example, your home page should not just say "Home page." It should say what your site is about. For example:

```
<title>Wrox Music: Vintage Guitars, Keyboards, and Drums</title>
```

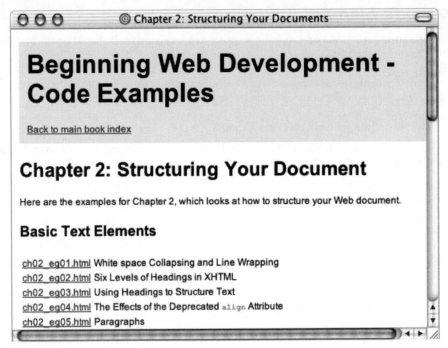

Figure 2-1

The test for a good title is whether a visitor can tell what she will find on that page just by reading the title, without looking at the actual content of the page.

The `<title>` element should contain only the text for the title; it may not contain any other elements. For example, you cannot add any instructions as to how the title should be formatted. Figure 2-1 shows how the content of the `<title>` element is displayed in the browser window and in the favorites in IE. (This example is taken from the code you can download for this chapter, and is the `index.html` file in the Chapter 2 code folder.)

The `<title>` element can carry the following attributes, which are covered in the "Attribute Groups" section later in the chapter:

```
id dir lang xml:lang
```

The `<body>` Element

The `<body>` element appears after the `<head>` element and contains the part of the Web page that you actually see in the main browser window, which is sometimes referred to as *body content*. It may contain anything from a couple of paragraphs under a heading to more complicated layouts containing forms and tables, and is likely to constitute the majority of any XHTML document. Most of what you will be learning in this and the following five chapters will be written between the opening `<body>` tag and closing `</body>` tag.

The <body> element may carry all of the attributes from the *attribute groups* you are about to meet in the next section. If you are using Transitional XHTML or HTML 4.1, you can use any of the following deprecated attributes on the <body> element (which are covered in Chapter 8):

```
background bgcolor alink link vlink text
```

There are also several browser specific attributes that you might see used on the <body> element; these also are covered in Chapter 8:

```
language, topmargin, bottommargin, leftmargin, rightmargin, scroll,
bgproperties, marginheight, marginwidth
```

Attribute Groups

As you saw in Chapter 1, attributes live on the opening tag of an element and provide extra information about the element that carries them. All attributes consist of a *name* and a *value*; the name reflects a property of the element the attribute is describing and the value is a value for that property. For example, the xml:lang attribute describes the language used within that element; a value such as EN-US would indicate that the language used inside the element is U.S. English. Many of the elements in XHTML can carry some or all of the attributes you will meet in this section.

There are three groups of attributes that many of the XHTML elements can carry (as you have already seen, the <html>, <head>, <title>, and <body> elements share some of these attributes). Because these attributes are common to so many of the elements, they are grouped together here to avoid having to repeat them each time they come up, so remember where you read this and you can keep referring back to them. The groups are:

- ❑ **Core attributes:** The class, id, and title attributes.
- ❑ **Internationalization attributes:** The dir, lang, and xml:lang attributes.
- ❑ **UI events:** Attributes associated with events onclick, ondoubleclick, onmousedown, onmouseup, onmouseover, onmousemove, onmouseout, onkeypress, onkeydown, and onkeyup (these are covered in more detail in Chapter 14).

> Together the core attributes and the internationalization attributes are known as the *universal attributes*.

Core Attributes

The four core attributes that can be used on the majority of XHTML elements (although not all) are:

```
id title class style
```

Where these attributes occasionally have special meaning for an element that differs from the description given here they will be visited again; otherwise their use can generally be described as you see in the subsections that follow.

The id Attribute

The id attribute can be used to uniquely identify any element within a page or style sheet. There are two primary reasons that you might want to use an id attribute on an element:

❑ If an element carries an id attribute as a unique identifier it is possible to identify just that element and its content (perhaps you want to link to a specific point in a document, to select one specific element's content, to associate a CSS style with a particular element, or identify that element using a script).

❑ If you have two elements of the same name within a Web page or style sheet, you can use the id attribute to distinguish between elements that have the same name (this is very likely, when you think most pages will contain at least two or more paragraphs of text).

The syntax for the id attribute is as follows (where *string* is your chosen value for the attribute):

```
id="string"
```

For example, the id attribute could be used to distinguish between two paragraph elements, like so:

```
<p id="accounts">This paragraph explains the role of the accounts
department.</p>
<p id="sales">This paragraph explains the role of the sales
department.</p>
```

Note that there are some special rules for the value of the id attribute; it must:

❑ Begin with a letter (A–Z or a–z) and can then be followed by any number of letters, digits (0–9), hyphens, underscores, colons, and periods (you may not start the value with a digit, hyphen, underscore, colon, or period).

❑ Remain unique within that document; no two attributes may have the same value within that XHTML document.

Before the id attribute was introduced, the name attribute served a similar purpose in HTML documents, but its use was deprecated in HTML 4.01, and now you should generally use the id attribute in XHTML documents. If you need to use the name attribute it is available in Transitional XHTML, but not Strict XHTML.

The title Attribute

The title attribute gives a suggested title for the element. They syntax for the title attribute is as follows:

```
title="string"
```

The behavior of this attribute will depend upon the element that carries it, although it is often displayed as a tooltip or while the element is loading.

Not every element that *can* carry a title attribute really needs one, so I will explain when this attribute is of particular use and will show you the behavior it has when used with that element.

The class Attribute

The class attribute is used to associate an element with a style sheet, and specifies the *class* of element. (You learn more about the use of the class attribute in Chapter 9, which introduces CSS.) The syntax of the class attribute is as follows:

```
class="className"
```

The value of the attribute may also be a space-separated list of class names. For example:

```
class="className1 className2 className3"
```

The style Attribute (deprecated)

The style attribute allows you to specify CSS rules within the element. For example:

```
<p style="font-family:arial; color:#FF0000;">Some text...</p>
```

As a general rule, however, it is best to avoid the use of this attribute. After all, one of the aims of XHTML was to remove stylistic markup from structural and semantic markup (as you learned in Chapter 1). This attribute is marked as deprecated in XHTML 1.0 (which means it will be removed from future versions of XHTML). If you want to use CSS rules to govern how an element appears, it is better to use the class attribute to associate the element with a CSS rule either in the <style> element or a separate style sheet instead. You will see each of these techniques in Chapter 9, which introduces CSS.

Internationalization

There are three internationalization attributes, which are available to most (although not all) XHTML elements.

Support even in the IE 6 or Netscape 7 browsers is still very patchy, and you are best off specifying a character set that will create text in the direction you require, although the xml:lang attribute could be used by other XML-aware applications.

```
dir lang xml:lang
```

Here is the Web address of a helpful W3C document that describes internationalization issues in greater detail:

```
http://www.w3.org/TR/i18n-html-tech/
```

The internationalization attributes are sometimes referred to by the rather odd name of the i18n attributes, named after the draft-ietf-html-i18n specification in which they were first defined.

The dir Attribute

The dir attribute allows you to indicate to the browser the direction in which the text should flow. When you want to indicate the directionality of a whole document (or the majority of the document) it should be used with the <html> element rather than the <body> element for two reasons: the <html> element has better support in browsers and it will then apply to the header elements as well as those in the body.

The dir attribute can also be used on elements within the body of the document if you want to change the direction of a small portion of the document.

The dir attribute can take one of two values, as you can see in the table that follows.

Value	Meaning
ltr	Left to right (the default value)
rtl	Right to left (for languages such as Hebrew or Arabic that are read right to left)

The lang Attribute

The lang attribute allows you to indicate the main language used in a document, but this attribute was kept in XHTML only for backwards compatibility with earlier versions of HTML. It has been replaced by the xml:lang attribute in new XHTML documents (which is covered in the next section). However, the XHTML recommendation suggests that you use both the lang and the xml:lang attributes on the <html> element in your XHTML 1.0 documents (to achieve maximum compatibility across different browsers).

The lang attribute was designed to offer language-specific display to users, although it has little effect in the main browsers. The real benefit of using the lang attribute is with screen readers (that might need to pronounce different languages in different ways), and with applications that can alert the user when they either do not support that language or it is a different language than their default language. When used with the <html> element it applies to the whole document, although it can be used on other elements, in which case it just applies to the content of those elements.

The values of the lang attribute are ISO-639 standard two-character language codes. If you want to specify a dialect of the language you can follow the language code with a dash and a subcode name. The table that follows offers some examples.

Value	Meaning
ar	Arabic
en	English
en-us	U. S. English
zh	Chinese

A list of language codes for most of the main languages in use today can be found in Appendix G.

The xml:lang Attribute

The xml:lang attribute is the XHTML replacement for the lang attribute. It is an attribute that is available in all XML languages (which is why it is prefixed by the characters xml:). The value of the xml:lang attribute should be an ISO-639 country code like those listed in the previous section; a full list appears in Appendix G.

While it has no effect in the main browsers, other XML-aware processors may use this information, and it is good practice to include the xml:lang attribute in your documents. When used with the <html> element it applies to the whole document, although it can be used on other elements, in which case it just applies to the content of those elements.

UI Events

The UI event attributes allow you to associate an *event*, such as a key press or the mouse being moved over an element, with a script (a portion of programming code that runs when the event occurs). For example, when someone moves a mouse over the content of a certain element you might use a script to make it change color.

You will meet the UI events in more detail in Chapter 14, although their names indicate quite clearly what event they are associated with; for example, onclick fires when a user clicks on that element's content, onmousemove fires when a mouse moves, and onmouseout fires when a user moves the mouse out of the content of a particular element.

There are ten events, known collectively as *common events*:

```
onclick, ondoubleclick, onmousedown, onmouseup, onmouseover, onmousemove,
onmouseout, onkeypress, onkeydown, onkeyup
```

The <body> and <frameset> elements also have the following events for when a page opens or is closed:

```
onload onunload
```

Finally, there are a number of events that work with forms only (which are mentioned in Chapter 6 and again in Chapter 14):

```
onfocus, onblur, onsubmit, onreset, onselect, onchange
```

Now that you have made your way through the preliminaries and learned about the elements that make up the skeleton of an XHTML document, it's time to get down to business marking up the text that will appear on your Web pages.

Basic Text Formatting

This section addresses the way in which you mark up text. Almost every document you create will contain some form of text, so this will be a very important section.

There are many elements that help you mark up your text, adding structural information to your documents. But remember that while one browser might display each of these elements in a certain way, another browser could display very different results. In particular, font sizes (and therefore the amount of space a section of text takes up) will change between browsers, as will the typefaces used; remember that you will not really be learning how to control the appearance (typefaces, colors, and font sizes) of text until Chapter 9.

In this section, you learn how to use what are known as *basic text formatting elements*:

❑   h1, h2, h3, h4, h5, h6

❑   p, br, pre

If you want people to read what you have written, then structuring your text well is even more important on the Web than when writing for print. People have trouble reading wide, long, paragraphs of text on Web sites unless they are broken up well (as you will see in Chapter 11), so getting into good habits from the start of your Web development career will help ensure that your pages get the attention they deserve.

Before you get started on the elements that you will use to mark up your text, it helps to know how text is displayed by default (it is up to you to tell the browser if you want it to treat text differently).

Whitespace and Flow

Before you start to mark up your text, it is best to understand what XHTML does when it comes across spaces and how browsers treat long sentences and paragraphs of text.

You might think that if you put several consecutive spaces between two words, the spaces would appear between those words onscreen, but this is not the case; by default, only one space will be displayed. This is known as *white space collapsing*. Similarly, if you start a new line in your source document, or you have consecutive empty lines, these will be ignored and simply treated as one space, as will tab characters. For example look at the following paragraph (taken from ch02_eg01.html):

```
<p>This    paragraph shows how    multiple spaces       between       words are
treated as a single space. This is known as white space collapsing, and
the big spaces between     some of the    words will not appear    in the
browser.



It also demonstrates how the browser will treat multiple carriage returns
(new lines) as a single space, too.</p>
```

As you can see in Figure 2-2, the browser treats the multiple spaces and several carriage returns (where text appears on a new line) as a single space.

This can be particularly helpful in allowing you to indent you code, something that I do throughout this book to make the code more readable.

As Figure 2-2 also shows, when a browser displays text it will automatically *wrap* the text onto new lines when it runs out of space. If you look again at the code for this example, and look at where each new line starts, the results are different on the screen than they are in the code. You can try this out for yourself, as all of the examples are available with the download code for this book; just try resizing the browser window (making it smaller and larger) and notice how the text wraps at new places on the screen.

It is therefore extremely important that you learn how to use the elements in the rest of this chapter to break up and control the presentation of your text.

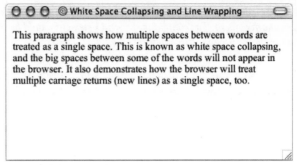

Figure 2-2

Creating Headings Using hn Elements

No matter what sort of document you are creating, most documents have headings in some form or other. Newspapers use headlines; a heading on a form tells you the purpose of the form; the title of a table of sports results tells you the league or division the teams play in, and so on.

In longer pieces of text, headings can also help structure a document. If you look at the table of contents for this book, you can see how different levels of headings have been arranged to add structure to the book, with subheadings under the main headings.

In XHTML you have six levels of headings, which use the elements <h1>, <h2>, <h3>, <h4>, <h5>, and <h6>. While browsers *can* display headings differently, they tend to display the <h1> element as the largest of the six and <h6> as the smallest, although CSS can be used to override the size and style of any of the elements. The levels of heading would look something like those in Figure 2-3 (ch02_eg02.html).

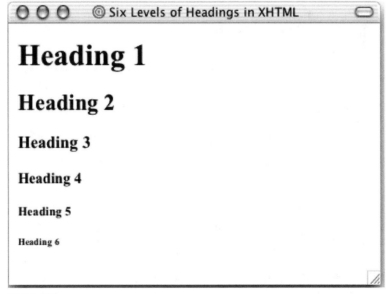

Figure 2-3

By default, most browsers display the contents of the <h1>, <h2>, and <h3> elements larger than the default size of text in the document. The content of the <h4> element would be the same size as the default text, and the content of the <h5> and <h6> elements would be smaller.

Here is another example of how you might use headings to structure a document (ch02_eg03.html), where the <h2> elements are subheadings of the <h1> element (this actually models the structure of this section of the chapter):

```
<h1>Basic Text Formatting</h1>
<p> This section is going to address the way in which you mark up text.
Almost every document you create will contain some form of text, so this
will be a very important section. </p>
<h2>Whitespace and Flow</h2>
<p> Before you start to mark up your text, it is best to understand what
XHTML does when it comes across spaces and how browsers treat long sentences
and paragraphs of text.</p>
<h2>Creating Headings</h2>
<p> No matter what sort of document you are creating, most documents have
headings in some form or other...</p>
```

Figure 2-4 shows how this will look.

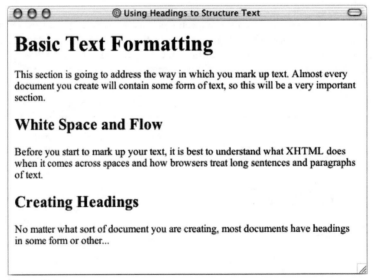

Figure 2-4

The six heading elements can all carry the universal attributes as well as a deprecated attribute called align.

```
align class id style title dir lang xml:lang
```

The align Attribute (deprecated)

The deprecated `align` attribute indicates whether the heading appears to the left, center, or right of the page (the default is the left). It can take the three values discussed in the table that follows.

Value	Meaning
left	The heading is displayed to the left of the browser window (or other containing element if it is nested within another element). This is the default value if the `align` attribute is not used.
center	The heading is displayed in the center of the browser window (or other containing element if it is nested within another element).
right	The heading is displayed to the right of the browser window (or other containing element if it is nested within another element).

I mention the `align` attribute here because you are still likely to see it used quite often. Here is an example of using the deprecated `align` attribute (`ch02_eg04.html`).

```
<h1 align="left">Left-Aligned Heading</h1>
    <p>This heading uses the align attribute with a value of left.</p>
<h1 align="center">Centered Heading</h1>
    <p>This heading uses the align attribute with a value of center.</p>
<h1 align="right">Right-Aligned Heading</h1>
    <p>This heading uses the align attribute with a value of right.</p>
```

Figure 2-5 shows the effect of the `align` attribute in a browser.

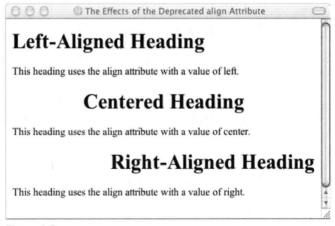

Figure 2-5

The `align` attribute has been replaced with the `text-align` property in CSS and the ability to float block level elements (as you will see in Chapter 9). The `align` attribute is covered in more detail in Chapter 8.

Creating Paragraphs Using the <p> Element

The <p> element offers another way to structure your text. Each paragraph of text should go in between an opening <p> and closing </p> tag, as in this example (ch02_eg05.html):

```
<p>Here is a paragraph of text.</p>
<p>Here is a second paragraph of text.</p>
<p>Here is a third paragraph of text.</p>
```

When a browser displays a paragraph it usually inserts a new line before the next paragraph and adds a little bit of extra vertical space, as in Figure 2-6.

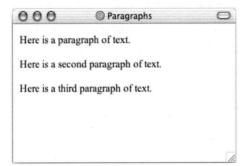

Figure 2-6

The <p> element can carry all of the universal attributes and the deprecated `align` attribute:

```
align class id style title dir lang xml:lang
```

*Creating Line Breaks Using the
 Element*

Whenever you use the <br /> element, anything following it starts on the next line. It is an example of an *empty element*, where you do not need opening *and* closing tags, as there is nothing to go in between them.

> *Note that the <br /> element has a space between the characters br and the forward slash. If you omit this space, older browsers will have trouble rendering the line break, while if you miss the forward slash character and just use <br> it is not valid XHTML.*

Most browsers allow you to use multiple <br /> elements to push text down several lines, and many designers use two line breaks between paragraphs of text rather than using the <p> element to structure text, as follows:

```
Paragraph one<br /><br />
Paragraph two<br /><br />
Paragraph three<br /><br />
```

While this creates a similar effect to using the paragraph element, if you do not use the <p> element itself then the document is no longer describing where each paragraph starts and finishes. Furthermore, in Strict XHTML the <br /> element can be used only within what are known as block level elements. These are elements such as the <p> element—elements that tend to naturally act as though they have a line break before and after them—you will see more about block level elements near the end of the chapter.

Avoid using <br /> elements just to position text; as it can produce results you might not expect because the amount of space created when you do so depends upon the size of the font.

Here you can see an example of the <br /> element in use within a paragraph (ch02_eg06.html):

```
<p>When you want to start a new line you can use the &lt;br /&gt; element.
So, the next<br />word will appear on a new line.</p>
```

Figure 2-7 shows you how the line breaks after the word "next."

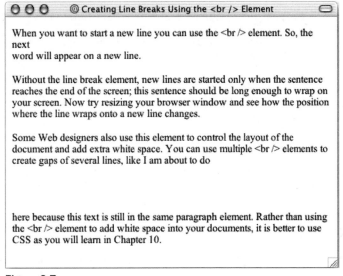

Figure 2-7

The <br /> element can carry the core attributes as well as an attribute called clear, which can be used with images, and is covered in Chapter 8.

```
clear class id style title
```

Creating Preformatted Text Using the <pre> Element

Sometimes you want your text to follow the exact format of how it is written in the XHTML document. You don't want the text to wrap onto the next line to fit the browser window's width; you want consecutive spaces preserved and line breaks where you wrote them.

Any text between the opening <pre> tag and the closing </pre> tag will preserve the formatting of the source document. You should be aware, however, that most browsers would display this text in a monospaced font by default.

Two of the most common uses of the `<pre>` element are to display tabular data without the use of a table (in which case you must use the monospaced font or columns will not align correctly) and to represent computer source code. For example, the following shows some JavaScript inside a `<pre>` element (`ch02_eg07.html`):

```
<pre>
function testFunction(strText){
    alert (strText)
}
</pre>
```

You can see in Figure 2-8 how the content of the `<pre>` element is displayed in the monospaced font, but more important, you can see how it follows the formatting shown inside the `<pre>` element—the whitespace is preserved.

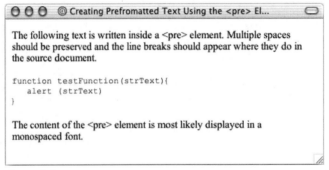

Figure 2-8

While tab characters do have an effect inside a `<pre>` element, with a tab stop representing eight spaces, the implementation of tabs varies across browsers, so it is advisable to use spaces instead.

You will come across more elements that can be used to represent code later in this chapter in the section "Phrase Elements," which covers the `<code>`, `<kbd>`, and `<var>` elements.

Both Netscape and IE support an extension to the XHTML recommendation that prevents line breaks, the `<nobr>` element. (This retains the normal style of its containing element and does not result in the text being displayed in a monospaced font.) Because it is an extension, it is not valid XHTML. The `<nobr>` element is covered in Chapter 8.

Try It Out   Basic Text Formatting

Now that you've seen the basic elements that you will be using to format your text—headings and paragraphs—it's time to try putting it to work.

In this example, you create a new page for a site about jazz legends, and this page tells people about Miles Davis. So, start up your text editor or Web page authoring tool and follow these steps:

1. You will be creating a Strict XHTML document, so add the XML declaration and a DOCTYPE declaration to indicate that you will be writing Strict XHTML:

```
<?xml version="1.0" encoding="UTF-8"?>
<!DOCTYPE html PUBLIC "-//W3C//DTD XHTML 1.0 Strict//EN"
    "http://www.w3.org/TR/xhtml1/DTD/xhtml1-strict.dtd">
```

2. Add the skeleton of the document: the `<html>`, `<head>`, `<title>`, and `<body>` elements. The root `<html>` element carries the `xmlns` attribute to indicate that the markup belongs to the XHTML namespace (namespaces are discussed in detail in Chapter 13).

```
<?xml version="1.0" encoding="UTF-8"?>
<!DOCTYPE html PUBLIC "-//W3C//DTD XHTML 1.0 Strict//EN"
    "http://www.w3.org/TR/xhtml1/DTD/xhtml1-strict.dtd">

<html xmlns="http://www.w3.org/1999/xhtml" lang="en">
  <head>
    <title>Jazz Legends - Miles Davis</title>
  </head>
  <body>

  </body>
</html>
```

3. Your page will have a main heading and some level 2 headings, which show the general structure of the page people will see:

```
<body>
  <h1>Jazz Legends - Miles Davis</h1>
  <h2>Styles of Miles</h2>
  <h2>Davis the Painter</h2>
</body>
```

4. You can now fill out the page with some paragraphs that follow the headings:

```
<body>
  <h1>Jazz Legends - Miles Davis</h1>
    <p>Miles Davis is known to many as one of the world's finest jazz musicians
    and an outstanding trumpet player. He also earned great respect in the
    world of music as an innovative bandleader and composer.</p>
  <h2>Styles of Miles</h2>
    <p>Miles Davis played and wrote in a variety of styles throughout his
    career, from tunes that have become jazz standards to his more
    experimental improvisational work. </p>
    <p>In the 1950s Miles was known for a warm, rich, wispy sound and was able
    to vary the color of his sound, pitch. He was also adept in using a Harmon
    mute. In the 1960s Miles began to play more in the upper register. In 1969
    he even incorporated the use of electronic instruments in his music.</p>
  <h2>Davis the Painter</h2>
    <p>Miles' love was not only for music; he is also considered a fine
    painter. Inspired by a Milan-based design movement known as Memphis,
    Miles painted a series of abstract paintings in 1988.</p>
  </body>
</html>
```

5. Save the file as `miles.html` and then open it in a Web browser. The result should look something like Figure 2-9.

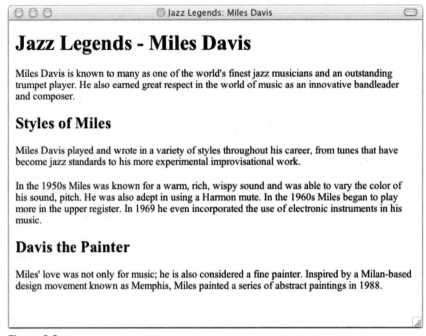

Figure 2-9

How It Works

The opening line of this page is the optional XML declaration. Because this document is a Strict XHTML document (and therefore is an XML document), it has been included here. The next line is the DOCTYPE declaration , which is required in Strict XHTML documents. The DOCTYPE declaration indicates which version of XHTML the document conforms to.

```
<?xml version="1.0" encoding="UTF-8"?>
<!DOCTYPE html PUBLIC "-//W3C//DTD XHTML 1.0 Strict//EN"
    "http://www.w3.org/TR/xhtml1/DTD/xhtml1-strict.dtd">
```

The whole of the page is then contained in the root `<html>` element. The opening `<html>` tag carries the namespace identifier, which is just another way of indicating that the markup your document contains is XHTML. The `<html>` element also carries the `lang` attribute, which indicates the language that the document is written in. Our Web page is written in English, so it uses the two-letter ISO code for English (the full list of country codes can be found in Appendix G). While the `lang` attribute has little practical use at the moment, it will help future-proof your documents.

```
<html xmlns="http://www.w3.org/1999/xhtml" lang="en" xml:lang="en">
```

The `<html>` element can contain only two child elements: the `<head>` element and `<body>` element. The `<head>` element contains the title for the page, and you should be able to tell from the title of the page the type of information the page will contain.

```
<head>
  <title>Jazz Legends: Miles Davis</title>
</head>
```

Meanwhile, the `<body>` element contains the main part of the Web page—the part that viewers will actually see in the main part of the Web browser. Note how this page contains headings to structure the information on the page just like you would find in a word processed document.

There are different levels of headings to help enforce structure. In this example there is a main heading introducing Miles Davis—the main topic for this page—and then subheadings each containing specific information about his music and other interests.

Don't forget the closing `</html>` tag at the end—after all, you must close every element correctly.

Presentational Elements

If you use a word processor, you are familiar with the ability to make text bold, italicized, or underlined; these are just three of the ten options available to indicate how text can appear in HTML and XHTML. The full list is bold, italic, monospaced, underlined, strikethrough, teletype, larger, smaller, superscripted, and subscripted text.

Technically speaking, these elements affect only the presentation of a document, and the markup is of no other use, but they remain in both Transitional and Strict XHTML 1.0. As you will see later in the chapter, there are dedicated elements for indicating things like emphasis within a piece of text, and these will result in a similar presentation of the information.

All of the following presentational elements can carry the universal attributes and the UI event attributes you met earlier in the chapter.

You should also be aware that you could use CSS to get similar results, as you will see in Chapter 9.

The `<b>` Element

Anything that appears in a `<b>` element is displayed in **bold**, like the word bold here:

```
The following word uses a <b>bold</b> typeface.
```

This does not necessarily mean the browser will use a boldface version of a font. Some browsers use an algorithm to take a font and make the lines thicker (giving it the appearance of being bold), while others (if they cannot find a boldface version of the font) may highlight or underline the text.

This `<b>` element has the same effect as the `<strong>` element, which you will meet later and is used to indicate that its contents have strong emphasis.

The `<i>` Element

The content of an `<i>` element is displayed in *italicized* text, like the word italic here:

```
The following word uses an <i>italic</i> typeface.
```

43

This does not necessarily mean the browser will look for an oblique or italicized version of the font. Some browsers use an algorithm to put the lines on a slant to simulate an italic font, while others (if they cannot find an italic version of the font) may highlight or underline the text.

The <i> element has the same effect as the <em> element, which you will meet later and is used to indicate that its contents have emphasis.

The <u> Element (deprecated)

The content of a <u> element is *underlined* with a simple line:

```
The following word would be <u>underlined</u>
```

The <u> element is deprecated in HTML 4 and XHTML 1.0, although it is still supported by Netscape and IE. The preferred method is to use CSS to achieve this effect, which you learn about in Chapter 9.

The <s> and <strike> Elements (deprecated)

The content of an <s> or <strike> element is displayed with a *strikethrough*, which is a thin line through the text (<s> is just the abbreviated form of <strike>).

```
The following word would have a <s>strikethrough</s>.
```

Both the <s> and <strike> elements are deprecated in HTML 4.1 and Transitional XHTML 1.0, and were removed from Strict XHTML 1.0, although they are still supported by Netscape and IE. The preferred method is to use CSS to achieve this effect, which you learn about in Chapter 9.

The <tt> Element

The content of a <tt> element is written in *monospaced* font. Most fonts are known as *variable-width fonts* because different letters are of different widths (for example, the letter m is wider than the letter i). In a monospaced font, however, each letter is the same width.

```
The following word will appear in a <tt>monospaced</tt> font.
```

The most popular example of a monospaced font is the Courier family of fonts, which is the font family used for the code in this book.

Figure 2-10 shows the use of the <b>, <i>, <u>, <s>, and <tt> elements (ch02_eg08.html).

The <sup> Element

The content of a <sup> element is written in *superscript*; the font size used is the same size as the characters surrounding it but is displayed half a character's height above the other characters.

```
Written on the 31<sup>st</sup> February.
```

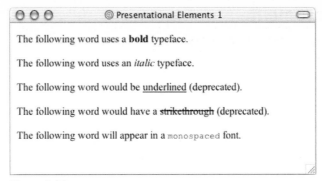

Figure 2-10

The <sup> element is especially helpful in adding exponential values to equations, and adding the *st*, *nd*, *rd*, and *th* suffixes to numbers such as dates.

The <sub> Element

The content of a <sub> element is written in subscript; the font size used is the same as the characters surrounding it, but is displayed half a character's height beneath the other characters.

```
The EPR paradox<sub>2</sub> was devised by Einstein, Podolsky, and Rosen.
```

The <sub> element is particularly helpful when combined with the <a> element (which you meet in the next chapter) to create footnotes.

The <big> Element

The content of the <big> element is displayed one font size larger than the rest of the text surrounding it. If the font is already the largest size, it has no effect. You can nest several <big> elements inside one another, and the content of each will get one size larger for each element.

```
The following word should be <big>bigger</big> than those around it.
```

In general, you should use CSS rather than the <big> element for formatting purposes.

The <small> Element

The content of the <small> element is displayed one font size smaller than the rest of the text surrounding it. If the font is already the smallest, it has no effect. You can nest several <small> elements inside one another, and the content of each gets one size smaller for each element.

```
The following word should be <small>smaller</small> than those around it.
```

In general, you should use CSS rather than the <small> element for formatting purposes.

The <hr /> Element

The <hr /> element creates a horizontal rule across the page. It is an empty element, rather like the <br /> element.

```
<br />
```

This is frequently used to separate distinct sections of a page where a new heading is not appropriate.

Figure 2-11 shows the use of the <sup>, <sub>, <big>, <small>, and <hr /> elements (ch02_eg09.html).

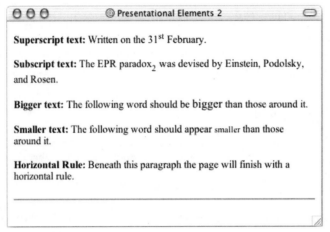

Superscript text: Written on the 31st February.

Subscript text: The EPR $paradox_2$ was devised by Einstein, Podolsky, and Rosen.

Bigger text: The following word should be bigger than those around it.

Smaller text: The following word should appear smaller than those around it.

Horizontal Rule: Beneath this paragraph the page will finish with a horizontal rule.

Figure 2-11

Phrase Elements

The following elements are not used as widely as the elements you have met so far. As the element names indicate, they are designed to describe their content:

- ❑ <em> and <strong> for emphasis
- ❑ <blockquote>, <cite>, and <q> for quotations and citations
- ❑ <abbr>, <acronym>, and <dfn> for abbreviations, acronyms, and key terms
- ❑ <code>, <kbd>, <var>, and <samp> for computer code and information
- ❑ <address> for addresses

While some of these phrase elements are displayed in a similar manner to the <b>, <i>, <pre>, and <tt> elements you have already seen, they are designed for specific purposes. For example, the <em> and <strong> elements give text emphasis and strong emphasis respectively and there are several elements for marking up quotes.

It is tempting to ignore these elements and just use the presentational elements you just met to create the same visual effect, but you should be aware of them and preferably get into the habit of using them where appropriate. For example, where you want to add emphasis to a word within a sentence you should use the <em> and <strong> elements rather than the presentational elements you just met; there are several good reasons for this, such as:

❑ Applications such as screen readers (which can read pages to Web users with visual impairments) could add suitable intonation to their voice so that users with visual impairments could hear where the emphasis should be placed.

❑ Automated programs could be written to find the words with emphasis and pull them out as keywords within a document, or specifically index those words so that a user could find important terms in a document.

As you can see, appropriate use of these elements adds more information to a document (such as which words should have emphasis, which are parts of programming code, and so on) rather than just saying how it should be presented visually.

All of the following phrase elements can carry the universal attributes and the UI event attributes you met earlier in the chapter.

The <em> Element Adds Emphasis

The content of an <em> element is intended to be a point of emphasis in your document, and it is usually displayed in italicized text. The kind of emphasis intended is on words such as "must" in the following sentence:

```
<p>You <em>must</em> remember to close elements in XHTML.</p>
```

You should use this element only when you are trying to add emphasis to a word, not just because you want to make the text appear italicized. If you just want italic text for stylistic reasons—without adding emphasis—you can use either the <i> element or CSS.

The <strong> Element Adds Strong Emphasis

The <strong> element is intended to show strong emphasis for its content; stronger emphasis than the <em> element. As with the <em> element, the <strong> element should be used only when you want to add strong emphasis to part of a document. Rather than being rendered in an italic font, most visual browsers display the strong emphasis in a bold font.

```
<p><em>Always</em> look at burning magnesium through protective colored
glass as it <strong>can cause blindness</strong>.</p>
```

Figure 2-12 shows how the <em> and <strong> elements are rendered in IE (ch02_eg10).

You need to remember that how the elements are presented (italics or bold) is largely irrelevant. You should use these elements to add emphasis to phrases, and therefore give your documents greater meaning, rather than to control how they appear visually. As you will see in Chapter 9, it is quite simple with CSS to change the visual presentation of these elements—for example to highlight any words inside an <em> element with a yellow background and make them bold rather than italic.

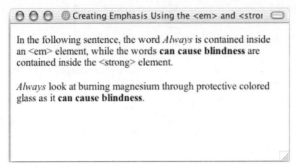

In the following sentence, the word *Always* is contained inside an <em> element, while the words **can cause blindness** are contained inside the <strong> element.

Always look at burning magnesium through protective colored glass as it **can cause blindness**.

Figure 2-12

The *<abbr>* Element Is for Abbreviations

You can indicate when you are using an abbreviated form by placing the abbreviation between opening <abbr> and closing </abbr> tags.

When possible, consider using a `title` attribute whose value is the full version of the abbreviations. If you are abbreviating a foreign word, you can also use the `xml:lang` attribute in XHTML (or the `lang` attribute in HTML).

For example, if you wanted to indicate that Bev was an abbreviation for Beverly, you could use the <abbr> element like so:

```
I have a friend called <abbr title="Beverly">Bev</abbr>.
```

At present, the major browsers do not change the appearance of the content of the <abbr> element. Note that this is strictly meant for abbreviations not acronyms, for which there is a separate element, which is covered next.

The *<acronym>* Element Is for Acronym Use

The <acronym> element allows you to indicate that the text between an opening <acronym> and closing </acronym> element is an acronym.

When possible use a `title` attribute whose value is the full version of the acronyms on the <acronym> element, and if the acronym is in a different language, include an `xml:lang` attribute in XHTML documents (or a `lang` attribute in HTML documents).

For example, if you wanted to indicate that XHTML was an acronym, you could use the <acronym> element like so:

```
This chapter covers marking up text in <acronym title="Extensible Hypertext
Markup Language">XHTML</acronym>.
```

At present, the major browsers do not change the appearance of the content of the <acronym> element.

The <dfn> Element Is for Special Terms

The <dfn> element allows you to specify that you are introducing a special term. Its use is similar to the words that are in italics in the midst of paragraphs in this book when new key concepts are introduced.

Typically, you would use the <dfn> element the first time you introduce a key term and only in that instance. Most recent browsers render the content of a <dfn> element in an italic font.

For example, you could indicate that the term "XHTML" in the following sentence is important and should be marked as such:

```
This book teaches you how mark up your documents for the web using
<dfn>XHTML</dfn>.
```

Figure 2-13 shows the use of the <dfn> element (ch02_eg11.html).

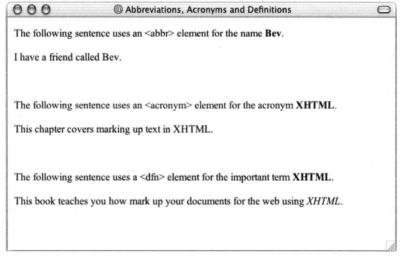

Figure 2-13

The <blockquote> Element Is for Quoting Text

When you want to quote a passage from another source, you should use the <blockquote> element. Note that there is a separate <q> element for use with smaller quotations, as discussed in the next section. Here's ch02_eg12.html:

```
<p>The following description of XHTML is taken from the W3C Web site:</p>

<blockquote> XHTML 1.0 is the W3C's first Recommendation for XHTML,
following on from earlier work on HTML 4.01, HTML 4.0, HTML 3.2 and HTML
2.0. </blockquote>
```

Text inside a <blockquote> element is usually indented from the left and right edges of the surrounding text, and sometimes uses an italicized font (although not in Figure 2-14 for IE 5.5 on a Mac).

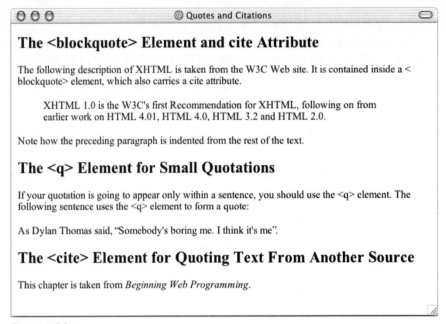

Figure 2-14

While `<blockquote>` is designed for use when quoting sections from another work, some designers use it for the effect on text, although it is possible to achieve the same look with CSS.

Using the cite Attribute with the <blockquote> Element

You can use the `cite` attribute on the `<blockquote>` element to indicate the source of the quote. The value of this URL should be a URL pointing to an online document, if possible the exact place in that document. Browsers will not actually do anything with this attribute, but it means the source of the quote is there should you need it in the future—it could also be used by other processing applications (`ch02_eg12.html`).

```
<blockquote cite="http://www.w3.org/markup/"> XHTML 1.0 is the W3C's first
Recommendation for XHTML, following on from earlier work on HTML 4.01, HTML
4.0, HTML 3.2 and HTML 2.0.</blockquote>
```

At the time of this writing, some validators had trouble with the `cite` attribute, such as the W3C validator, which does not recognize the presence of the `cite` attribute on the `<blockquote>` element.

The <q> Element Is for Short Quotations

The `<q>` element is intended to be used when you want to add a quote within a sentence rather than as an indented block on its own. Here's `ch12_eg04.html`:

```
<p>As Dylan Thomas said, <q>Somebody's boring me. I think it's me</q>.</p>
```

The HTML and XHTML recommendations say that the text enclosed in a <q> element should begin and end in double quotes. Netscape 6+ inserts these quotation marks for you, whereas IE does not. So, if you want your quote to be surrounded by quotation marks, be warned that inserting them in the document will result in two sets of quotes in Netscape. Neither IE nor Netscape changes the appearance of this element in any other way.

The <q> element (see Figure 2-14) can also carry the cite attribute. The value should be a URL pointing to the source of the quote.

The <cite> Element Is for Citations

If you are quoting a text, you can indicate the source placing it between an opening <cite> tag and closing </cite> tag. As you would expect in a print publication, the content of the <cite> element is rendered in italicized text by default (ch02_eg12.html).

```
This chapter is taken from <cite>Beginning Web Development</cite>.
```

If you are referencing an online resource, you should place your <cite> element inside an <a> element, which, as you see in Chapter 4, creates a link to the relevant document.

There are several applications that potentially could make use of the <cite> element. For example, a search application could use <cite> tags to find documents that reference certain works, or a browser could collect the contents of <cite> elements to generate a bibliography for any given document, although at the moment it is not widely enough used for either feature to exist.

You can see the <blockquote>, <q>, and <cite> elements in Figure 2-14.

The <code> Element Is for Code

If your pages include any programming code (which is not uncommon on the Web), the following four elements will be of particular use to you. Any code to appear on a Web page should be placed inside a <code> element. Usually the content of the <code> element is presented in a monospaced font, just like the code in most programming books (including this one).

Note that you cannot just use the opening and closing angle brackets inside these elements if you want to represent XHTML markup. The browser could mistake these characters for actual markup. You should use < instead of the left-angle bracket <, and you should use > instead of the right-angle bracket >. A list of all these character entities is in Appendix F.

Here you can see an example of using the <code> element to represent an <h1> element and its content in XHTML (ch02_eg13.html):

```
<p><code>&lt;h1&gt;This is a primary heading&lt;/h1&gt;</code></p>
```

Figure 2-15 shows you how this would look in a browser.

The use of the <code> element could theoretically allow search applications to look at the content of <code> elements to help them find a particular code segment. The <code> element is often used in conjunction with the <pre> element so that the formatting of the code is retained.

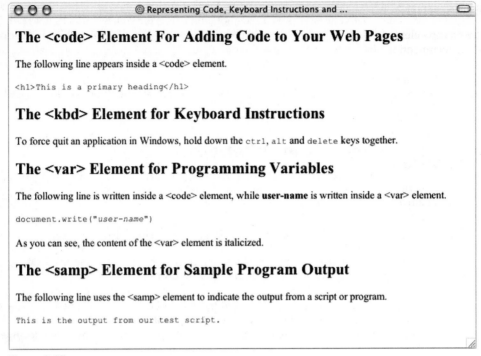

The <code> Element For Adding Code to Your Web Pages

The following line appears inside a <code> element.

<h1>This is a primary heading</h1>

The <kbd> Element for Keyboard Instructions

To force quit an application in Windows, hold down the ctrl, alt and delete keys together.

The <var> Element for Programming Variables

The following line is written inside a <code> element, while **user-name** is written inside a <var> element.

document.write("*user-name*")

As you can see, the content of the <var> element is italicized.

The <samp> Element for Sample Program Output

The following line uses the <samp> element to indicate the output from a script or program.

This is the output from our test script.

Figure 2-15

The <kbd> Element Is for Text Typed on a Keyboard

When you are talking about computers, if you want to tell a reader to enter some text, you can use the <kbd> element to indicate what should be typed in, as in this example (ch02_eg13.html):

```
<p>Type in the following: <kbd>This is the kbd element</kbd>.</p>
```

The content of a <kbd> element is usually represented in a monospaced font rather like the content of the <code> element. Figure 2-15 shows you what this would look like in a browser.

The <var> Element Is for Programming Variables

The <var> element is another of the elements added to help programmers. It is usually used in conjunction with the <pre> and <code> elements to indicate that the content of that element is a variable that can be supplied by a user (ch02_eg13.html).

```
<p><code>document.write("<var>user-name</var>")</code></p>
```

Typically the content of a <code> element is italicized, as you can see in Figure 2-15.

If you are not familiar with the concept of variables, they are covered in Chapter 14.

The <samp> Element Is for a Program Output

The <samp> element indicates sample output from a program, script, or the like. Again, it is mainly used when documenting programming concepts. For example:

```
<p>If everything worked you should see the result <samp>Test completed
OK</samp>.</p>
```

This tends to be displayed in a monospaced font, as you can see in Figure 2-15.

The <address> Element Is for Addresses

Many documents need to contain a snail mail address, and there is a special <address> element that is used to contain addresses. The address may also contain other contact information. For example, here is the address for Wrox, inside an <address> element, which is itself in a <p> element:

```
<address>Wrox Press, 10475 Crosspoint Blvd, Indianapolis, IN 46256</address>
```

A browser can display the address differently than the surrounding document, and Netscape and IE display it in italics, as you can see in Figure 2-16 (although you can override this with CSS).

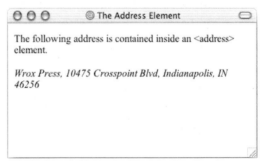

Figure 2-16

Indicating who wrote a document or who is responsible for it adds credibility to a document that is otherwise anonymous. The address <element> is a good way to add this at the end of the document. It can also help automated applications read addresses from documents.

That brings you to the end of the phrase elements, but not quite the end of all the text elements.

Lists

There are many reasons why you might want to add a list to your pages, from putting your five favorite albums on your home page to including a numbered set of instructions for visitors to follow (like the steps you follow in the Try It Out examples in this book).

You can create three types of lists in XHTML:

❑   **Unordered lists**, which are like lists of bullet points

❏ **Ordered lists,** which use a sequence of numbers or letters instead of bullet points

❏ **Definition lists,** which allow you to specify a term and its definition

I'm sure you will think of more uses for the lists as you meet them and start using them.

Using the <ul> Element to Create Unordered Lists

If you want to make a list of bullet points, you write the list within the <ul> element (which stands for unordered list). Each bullet point or line you want to write should then be contained between opening <li> tags and closing </li> tags (the li stands for *list item*).

You should always close the <li> element, even though you might see some HTML pages that leave off the closing tag. This is a bad habit you should avoid.

If you wanted to create a bulleted list you could do so like this (ch02_eg15.html):

```
<ul>
   <li>Bullet point number one</li>
   <li>Bullet point number two</li>
   <li>Bullet point number three</li>
</ul>
```

In a browser this list would look something like Figure 2-17.

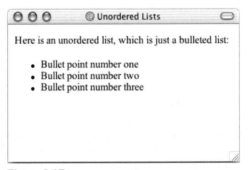

Figure 2-17

The <ul> and <li> elements can carry all the universal attributes and UI event attributes.

The <ul> element could also carry an attribute called compact in HTML 4.1—which is still allowed in Transitional XHTML but not in Strict XHTML 1.0—the purpose of which was to make the bullet points vertically closer together. Its value should also be compact, like so:

```
<ul compact="compact">
   <li>Item one</li>
   <li>Item two</li>
   <li>Item three</li>
</ul>
```

Ordered Lists

Sometimes, you want your lists to be ordered. In an ordered list, rather than prefixing each point with a bullet point, you can use either numbers (1, 2, 3), letters (A, B, C) or Roman numerals (i, ii, iii) to prefix the list item.

An ordered list is contained inside the <ol> element. Each item in the list should then be nested inside the <ol> element and contained between opening <li> and closing </li> tags.

```
<ol>
    <li>Point number one</li>
    <li>Point number two</li>
    <li>Point number three</li>
</ol>
```

The result should be similar to what you see in Figure 2-18.

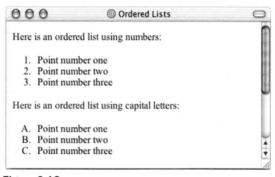

Figure 2-18

If you would rather have letters or Roman numerals than Arabic numbers, you must use the now-deprecated `type` attribute on the <ol> element.

Using the type Attribute to Select Numbers, Letters, or Roman Numerals in Ordered Lists (deprecated)

The `type` attribute on the <ol> element allows you to change the ordering of list items from the default of numbers to the options listed in the table that follows, by giving the `type` attribute the corresponding character.

Value for type Attribute	Description	Examples
1	Arabic numerals (the default)	1, 2, 3, 4, 5
A	Capital letters	A, B, C, D, E
A	Small letters	a, b, c, d, e
I	Large Roman numerals	I, II, III, IV, V
i	Small Roman numerals	i, ii, iii, iv, v

For example, here is an ordered list that uses small Roman numerals:

```
<ol type="i">
  <li>This is the first point</li>
  <li>This is the second point</li>
  <li>This is the third point</li>
</ol>
```

You can see what this might look like when combined with another attribute called `start` in Figure 2-19 (in the next section).

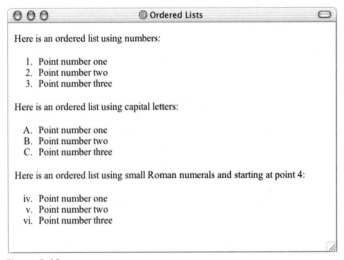

Figure 2-19

The `type` attribute was deprecated in HTML 4.1 in favor of the CSS `list-style-type` property; it will therefore work only in Transitional XHTML not Strict XHTML 1.0. The CSS replacement will work only in IE4+ and Netscape 4+ browsers.

You used to be able to use the `type` attribute on `<li>` elements, which would override the value in the `<ol>` element, but it was deprecated in HTML 4.1 and its use should be avoided. All of the universal attributes and UI event attributes can be used with the `<ol>` elements, and also a special attribute `start`, to control the number a list starts at.

Using the start Attribute to Change the Starting Number in Ordered Lists (deprecated)

If you want to specify the number that a numbered list should start at, you can use the `start` attribute on the `<ol>` element. The value of this attribute should be the numeric representation of that point in the list, so a D in a list that is ordered with capital letters would be represented by the value 4 (ch02_eg16.html).

```
<ol type="i" start="4">
  <li>Point number one</li>
  <li>Point number two</li>
</ol>
```

You can see the result in Figure 2-19.

The start attribute was deprecated in HTML 4.1 in favor of the CSS marker-offset property; it will therefore work only in Transitional XHTML 1.0 and not Strict XHTML 1.0.

Definition Lists

The definition list is a special kind of list for providing terms followed by a short text definition or description for them. Definition lists are contained inside the <dl> element. The <dl> element then contains alternating <dt> and <dd> elements. The content of the <dd> element is the term you will be defining. The <dt> element contains the definition of the previous <dd> element. For example, here is a definition list that describes the different types of lists in XHTML (ch02_eg17.html):

```
<dl>
  <dt>Unordered List</dt>
    <dd>A list of bullet points.</dd>
  <dt>Ordered List</dt>
    <dd>An ordered list of points, such as a numbered set of steps.</dd>
  <dt>Definition List</dt>
    <dd>A list of terms and definitions.</dd>
</dl>
```

In a browser, this would look something like Figure 2-20.

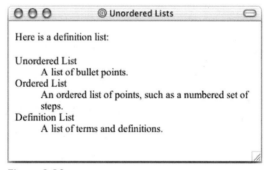

Figure 2-20

Each of these elements can carry the universal attributes and UI event attributes.

Nesting Lists

You can nest lists inside other lists. For example, you might want a numbered list with separate points corresponding to one of the list items. Each list will be numbered separately unless you specify otherwise using the start attribute. And each new list should be placed inside a <li> element:

```
<ol type="I">
  <li>Item one</li>
  <li>Item two</li>
  <li>Item three</li>
  <li>
```

```
    <ol type="i">
        <li>Item one</li>
        <li>Item two</li>
        <li>Item three</li>
     </ol>
   </li>
   <li>Item Five</li>
</ol>
```

In a browser, this will look something like Figure 2-21.

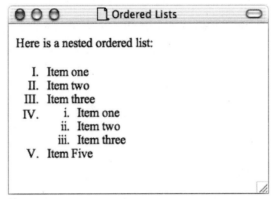

Figure 2-21

Try It Out **Using Text Markup**

Now that you've looked at the different elements and attributes you can use to mark up text, it is time to put them into practice. In this example, you use a mixture of the text markup to create a page that displays a recipe. So, open up your text editor or Web page authoring tool and follow these steps:

1. You will be writing this example in Transitional XHTML 1.0, so add in the optional XML declaration, and the DOCTYPE declaration:

```
<?xml version="1.0" encoding="UTF-8"?>
<!DOCTYPE html PUBLIC "-//W3C//DTD XHTML 1.0 Transitional//EN"
    "http://www.w3.org/TR/xhtml1/DTD/xhtml1-transitional.dtd">
```

2. Add in the skeleton elements for the document: <html>, <head>, <title>, and <body>. Don't forget to put the namespace identifier on the root element, along with an attribute to indicate the language of the document:

```
<html xmlns="http://www.w3.org/1999/xhtml" lang="en">
  <head>
    <title>Wrox Recipes - World's Best Scrambled Eggs</title>
  </head>
  <body>
  </body>
</html>
```

3.   Add some appropriate heading elements into the body of the document:

```
<body>
  <h1>Wrox Recipes - World's Best Scrambled Eggs</h1>
  <h2>Ingredients</h2>
  <h2>Instructions</h2>
</body>
```

4.   After the <h1> element there will be a bit of an explanation about the recipe (and why it is the World's Best). You can see that there are several of the elements you have met so far tucked away in these two paragraphs.

```
<h1>Wrox Recipes - World's Best Scrambled Eggs</h1>
  <p>I adapted this recipe from a book called
    <cite cite=" http://www.amazon.com/exec/obidos/tg/detail/-
    /0864119917/">Sydney Food</cite> by Bill Grainger. Ever since tasting
    these eggs on my 1<sup>st</sup> visit to Bill's restaurant in Kings
    Cross, Sydney, I have been after the recipe. I have since transformed
    it into what I really believe are the <em>best</em> scrambled eggs
    I have ever tasted.</p>
  <p>This recipe is what I call a <q>very special breakfast</q>; just look at
    the ingredients to see why. It has to be tasted to be believed.</p>
```

5.   After the first <h2> element, you will list the ingredients in an unordered list:

```
<h2>Ingredients</h2>
  <p>The following ingredients make one serving:</p>
  <ul>
    <li>2 eggs</li>
    <li>1 tablespoon of butter (10g)</li>
    <li>1/3 cup of cream <i>(2 3/4 fl ounces)</i></li>
    <li>A pinch of salt</li>
    <li>Freshly milled black pepper</li>
    <li>3 fresh chives (chopped)</li>
  </ul>
```

6.   Add the instructions after the second <h2> element; these will go in a numbered list:

```
<h2>Instructions</h2>
  <ol>
    <li>Whisk eggs, cream, and salt in a bowl.</li>
    <li>Melt the butter in a non-stick pan over a high heat <i>(taking care
    not to burn the butter)</i>.</li>
    <li>Pour egg mixture into pan and wait until it starts setting around
      the  edge of the pan (around 20 seconds).</li>
    <li>Using a wooden spatula, bring the mixture into the center as if it
      were an omelet, and let it cook for another 20 seconds.</li>
    <li>Fold contents in again, leave for 20 seconds, and repeat until
      the eggs are only just done.</li>
    <li>Grind a light sprinkling of freshly milled pepper over the eggs
      and blend in some chopped fresh chives.</li>
  </ol>
  <p>You should only make a <strong>maximum</strong> of two servings per
    frying pan.</p>
```

7. Save this example as `eggs.html`. When you open it in a browser you should see something like Figure 2-22.

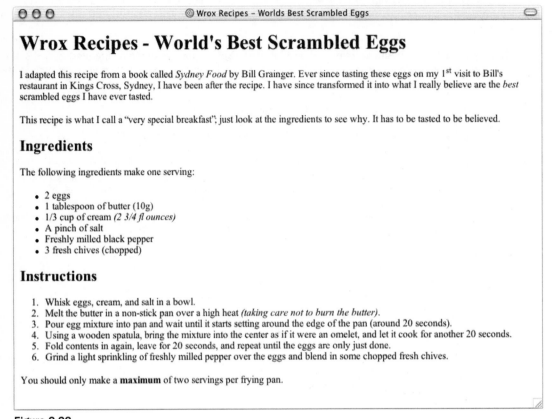

Figure 2-22

How It Works

You have seen the XML declaration and the skeleton of this document enough times already, so now it's time to focus on the new elements you have available to mark up text.

After the main heading for the document, which is contained in the `<h1>` elements, you can see two paragraphs of text. Start by looking at the first paragraph.

In the first sentence, the `<cite>` element has been used to indicate a reference to the book this recipe is adapted from. The next sentence makes use of the `<sup>` element so you can write "1st" and use superscript text—although you will note that this makes the gap between the first line and the second line of text larger than the gap between the second and third lines of text (as the superscript letters poke above the line). In the final sentence there is emphasis on the word "best," as these really are the *best* scrambled eggs I have ever tasted:

```
<h1>Wrox Recipes- World's Best Scrambled Eggs</h1>
  <p>I adapted this recipe from a book called
    <cite cite="http://www.bills.com.au">Sydney Food</cite> by Bill Grainger.
    Ever since tasting these eggs on my 1<sup>st</sup> visit to Bill's
    restaurant in Kings Cross, Sydney, I have been after the recipe. I have
    since transformed it into what I really believe are the <em>best</em>
    scrambled eggs I have ever tasted. </p>
```

You can see another new element at work in the second element; this is the <q> element for quotes that are sprinkled into a sentence:

```
<p>Although this recipe may be what I call a <q>very special breakfast</q>,
  just look at the ingredients to see why, it has to be tasted to be
  believed.</p>
```

The ingredients (listed under an <h2> element), contain an unordered list, and an italicized alternative measure for the amount of cream required:

```
<ul>
  <li>2 eggs</li>
  <li>10g butter</li>
  <li>1/3 cup of cream <i>(2 3/4 fl ounces)</i></li>
  <li>a pinch of salt</li>
  <li>freshly milled black pepper</li>
  <li>3 fresh chives (chopped)</li>
</ul>
```

The instructions for cooking the eggs (listed under the second <h2> element) contain a numbered list and a couple more paragraphs. You might note that the numbered list contains an italicized comment about not burning the butter, and the final paragraph contains a strong emphasis that you should cook no more than two batches of these eggs in a pan.

```
<h2>Instructions</h2>
  <p>The following ingredients make one serving.</p>
    <ol>
      <li>Whisk eggs, cream, and salt in a bowl.</li>
      <li>Melt the butter in a non-stick pan over a high heat <i>(taking care
        not to burn the butter)</i>.</li>
      <li>Pour egg mixture into pan, and wait until it starts setting
        around the edge of the pan (around twenty seconds).</li>
      <li>Using a wooden spatula, bring the mixture into the center as
        if it was an omelet, and let it cook for another 20 seconds.</li>
      <li>Fold contents in again, leave for 20 seconds, and repeat until
        the eggs are only just done.</li>
      <li>Grind a light sprinkling of freshly milled pepper over the eggs
        and blend in some chopped fresh chives.</li>
    </ol>
  <p>You should only make a <strong>maximum</strong> of two servings per
    frying pan.</p>
```

The page then finishes up as usual with closing </body> and </html> tags. I hope you will enjoy the eggs—go on, you know you want to try them now.

Editing Text

When working on a document with others, it helps if you can see changes that another person has made. Even when working on your own documents, it can be helpful to keep track of changes you make. There are two elements specifically designed for revising and editing text:

❑ The `<ins>` element for when you want to add text

❑ The `<del>` element for when you want to delete some text

Here you can see some changes made to the following XHTML (ch02_eg19.html):

```
<h1>How to Spot a Wrox Book</h1>
<p>Wrox-spotting is a popular pastime in bookshops. Programmers like to find
the distinctive <del>blue</del><ins>red</ins> spines because they know that
Wrox books are written by <del>1000 monkeys</del><ins>Programmers</ins> for
Programmers.</p>
<ins><p>Both readers and authors, however, have reservations about the use
of photos on the covers.</p></ins>
```

This example would look something like Figure 2-23 in a browser.

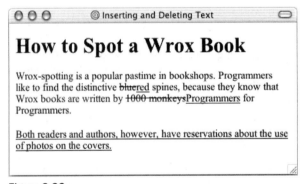

Figure 2-23

These features would also be particularly helpful in editing tools to note changes and modifications made by different authors.

If you are familiar with Microsoft Word, the `<ins>` and `<del>` elements are very similar to a feature called `Track Changes` *(which you can find under the Tools menu). The track changes feature underlines new text additions and crosses through deleted text.*

You must be careful using `<ins>` and `<del>` to ensure that you do not end up with a block-level element (such as a `<p>` or an `<h2>` element) inside an inline element such as a `<b>` or `<i>` element. You learn more about block-level elements and inline elements at the end of the chapter.

Using <ins> to Indicate New Additions to Text

Any text added to a document inside an <ins> element will be underlined to indicate that it is new text (refer to Figure 2-23).

```
<ins><p>This paragraph is contained inside an &lt;ins&gt; element.</p></ins>
```

You can use the cite attribute on the <ins> and <del> element to indicate the source or reason for a change, although this attribute is quite limiting as the value must be a URI.

You might also use the title attribute to provide information as to who added the <ins> or <del> element and why it was added or deleted; this information is offered to users as a tooltip in Netscape and IE.

The <ins> and <del> elements can also carry a datetime attribute whose value is a date and time in the following format:

```
YYYY-MM-DDThh:mm:ssTZD
```

This formula breaks down as follows:

- ❑ YYYY represents the year.
- ❑ MM represents the month.
- ❑ DD represents the day of the month.
- ❑ T is just a separator between the date and time.
- ❑ hh is the hour.
- ❑ mm is the number of minutes.
- ❑ ss is the number of seconds.
- ❑ TZD is the time zone designator.

For example, 2004-04-16T20:30-05:00 represents 8.30 pm on April 16, 2004 according to U.S. Eastern Standard Time.

> *The datetime attribute is likely to be entered only by a program or authoring tool, as the format is rather long to be entered by hand.*

Using <del> to Indicate Deleted Text

If you want to delete some text from a document, you can place it inside a <del> element to indicate that it is marked to be deleted. Text inside a <del> element will have a line or strikethrough (refer to Figure 2-23).

```
<del><p>This paragraph is contained inside a &lt;del&gt; element.</p></del>
```

The <del> element can carry the cite, datetime, and title attributes just like the <ins> element.

When you learn how to use CSS, you will see how it would be possible to show and hide the inserted and deleted content as required.

Using Character Entities for Special Characters

You can use most alphanumeric characters in your document and they will be displayed without a problem. There are, however, some characters that have special meaning in XHTML, and for some characters there is not an equivalent on the keyboard you can enter. For example, you cannot use the angle brackets that start and end tags, as the browser can mistake the following letters for markup. You can, however, use a set of different characters known as a *character entity* to represent these special characters. Sometimes you will also see character entities referred to as *escape characters*.

All special characters can be added into a document using the numeric entity for that character, and some also have named entities, as you can see in the table that follows.

Character	Numeric Entity	Named Entity
"	"	"
&	&	&
<	<	<
>	>	>

A full list of character entities (or special characters) is in Appendix F.

Comments

You can put comments between any tags in your XHTML documents. Comments use the following syntax:

```
<!-- comment goes here -->
```

Anything after <!-- until the closing --> will not be displayed. It can still be seen in the source code for the document, but it is not shown onscreen.

It is good practice to comment your code, especially in complex documents, to indicate sections of a document, and any other notes to anyone looking at the code. Comments help you and others understand your code.

You can even comment out whole sections of code. For example, in the following snippet of code you would not see the content of the <h3> element. You can also see there are comments indicating the section of the document, who added it, and when it was added.

```
<!-- Start of Footnotes Section added 04-24-04 by Bob Stewart -->
  <!-- <h2>Character Entities</h2> -->
  <p><strong>Character entities</strong> can be used to escape special
  characters that the browser might otherwise think have special meaning.</p>
<!-- End of Footnotes section -->
```

The <font> Element (deprecated)

You should be aware of the `<font>` element, which was introduced in HTML 3.2 to allow users more control over how text appears. It was deprecated in HTML 4.0, and has since been removed from XHTML. In its short life, however, it got a lot of use, and if you look at other people's code you will see it used a lot. If you want to read more about the `<font>` element, it is covered in Chapter 8. You might see the `<font>` element used like so:

```
<h3>Using the &lt;font&gt; element</h3>
<font face="arial, verdana, sans-serif" size="2" color="#666666">The
&lt;font&gt; element has been deprecated since HTML 4.0. You should now use
CSS to indicate how text should be styled. </font>
```

Understanding Block and Inline Elements

Now that you have seen many of the elements that can be used to mark up text, it is important to make an observation about all of these elements that live inside the `<body>` element because each one can fall into one of two categories:

- ❑ Block-level elements
- ❑ Inline elements

This is quite a conceptual distinction, but it will have important ramifications for other features of XHTML (some of which you are about to meet).

Block-level elements appear on the screen as if they have a carriage return or line break before and after them. For example the `<p>`, `<h1>`, `<h2>`, `<h3>`, `<h4>`, `<h5>`, `<h6>`, `<ul>`, `<ol>`, `<dl>`, `<pre>`, `<hr />`, `<blockquote>`, and `<address>` elements are all block level elements. They all start on their own new line, and anything that follows them appears on its own new line, too.

Inline elements, on the other hand, can appear within sentences and do not have to appear on a new line of their own. The `<b>`, `<i>`, `<u>`, `<em>`, `<strong>`, `<sup>`, `<sub>`, `<big>`, `<small>`, `<li>`, `<ins>`, `<del>`, `<code>`, `<cite>`, `<dfn>`, `<kbd>`, and `<var>` elements are all inline elements.

For example, look at the following heading and paragraph. These elements start on their own new line and anything that follows them goes on a new line, too. Meanwhile the inline elements in the paragraph do not require their own new line. Here is the code (`ch02_eg20.html`):

```
<h1>Block-Level Elements</h1>
  <p><strong>Block-level elements</strong> always start on a new line. The
  <code>&lt;h1&gt;</code> and <code>&lt;p&gt;</code> elements will not sit
  on the same line, whereas the inline elements flow with the rest of the
  text.</p>
```

You can see what this looks like in Figure 2-24.

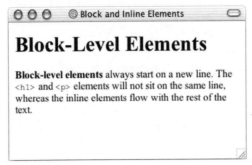

Figure 2-24

You should also be aware that in Strict XHTML block-level elements can contain other block-level elements, and inline elements. However, inline elements can appear only within block-level elements, and they may not contain block-level elements (so you should not have a <b> element outside of a block-level element).

Grouping Elements with <div> and <span>

The <div> and <span> elements allow you to group together several elements to create sections or subsections of a page. On their own, they will not affect the appearance of a page, but they are commonly used with CSS to allow you to attach a style to a section of a page (as you will see in Chapter 9). For example, you might want to put all of the footnotes on a page within a <div> element to indicate that all of the elements within that <div> element relate to the footnotes. You might then attach a style to this <div> element so that they appear using a special set of style rules.

The <div> element is used to group block-level elements together:

```
<div class="footnotes">
  <h2>Footnotes</h2>
  <p><b>1</b> The World Wide Web was invented by Tim Berners-Lee</p>
  <p><b>2</b> The W3C is the World Wide Web Consortium who maintain many Web
     standards</p>
</div>
```

The <span> element, on the other hand, can be used to group inline elements only. So, if you had a part of a sentence or paragraph you wanted to group together you could use the <span> element. Here you can see that I have added a <span> element to indicate which content refers to an inventor. It contains both a bold element and some text:

```
<div class="footnotes">
  <h2>Footnotes</h2>
  <p><span class="inventor"><b>1</b> The World Wide Web was invented by Tim
     Berners Lee</span></p>
```

```
    <p><b>2</b> The W3C is the World Wide Web Consortium who maintain many Web
        standards</p>
</div>
```

On its own, this would have no effect at all on how the document looks visually, but it does add extra meaning to the markup, which now groups together the related elements. This grouping could either be used by a processing application, or (as you will see in Chapter 9) could be used to attach special styles to these elements using CSS rules.

The <div> and <span> elements can carry all of the universal attributes and UI event attributes, as well as the deprecated align attribute (which is no longer available in Strict XHTML 1.0).

Summary

In this chapter you have met a lot of new elements and learned the attributes they can carry. You've seen how every XHTML document should contain at least the <html>, <head>, <title>, and <body> elements, and how the <html> element should carry a namespace identifier.

You then met some attributes: the core attributes (class, id, and title), the internationalization attributes (dir, lang, and xml:lang), and the UI event attributes, each of which will crop up regularly throughout the book, as most of the elements can support them.

The main part of this chapter dealt with elements that describe the structure of text:

- ❑ The six levels of headings: <h1>, <h2>, <h3>, <h4>, <h5>, and <h6>
- ❑ Paragraphs <p>, preformatted sections <pre>, line breaks <br />, and addresses <address>
- ❑ Presentational elements <b>, <i>, <u>, <s>, <tt>, <sup>, <sub>, <strike>, <big>, <small>, and <hr />
- ❑ Phrase elements such as <em>, <strong>, <abbr>, <acronym>, <dfn>, <blockquote>, <q>, <cite>, <code>, <kbd>, <var>, <samp>, and <address>
- ❑ Lists such as unordered lists using <ul> and <li>, ordered lists using <ol> and <li>, and definition lists using <dl>, <dt>, and <dd>
- ❑ Editing elements such as <ins> and <del>
- ❑ Grouping elements <div> and <span>

You will obviously use some of these elements more than others, but where an element fits the content you are trying to mark up, from paragraphs to addresses, you should try to use it. Structuring your text properly will help it last longer than if you just format it using line breaks and presentational elements.

You will come across many of these elements in later examples in this book starting with the next chapter, which introduces you to the very important topic of linking between documents (and linking to specific parts of a document).

Exercises

The answers to all of the exercises are in Appendix A.

1. Mark up the following sentence with the relevant presentational elements.

   The 1st time the **bold** man wrote in *italics*, he <u>underlined</u> several key words.

2. Mark up the following list, with inserted and deleted content:

   Ricotta pancake ingredients:

   - 1 ~~1/2~~ <u>3/4</u> cups ricotta
   - 3/4 cup milk
   - 4 eggs
   - 1 cup plain <u>white</u> flour
   - 1 teaspoon baking powder
   - ~~75g~~ <u>50g</u> butter
   - pinch of salt

Links and Navigation

What really distinguishes the Web from other mediums is the way in which Web pages can contain links that take you directly to other pages (and even specific parts of a given page). Known as *hyperlinks*, these links are often attributed to being the secret behind the Web's phenomenal success. Hyperlinks allow visitors to navigate between Web sites by clicking on words, phrases, and images.

The average Web site is a group of pages users navigate between using hypertext links. These pages often include links to other Web sites as well as to other pages in the same site.

In this chapter you learn how to create links between the different pages of your site, to specific points within pages of your sites, and how to link to other sites or (or *external sites*).

When you learn about links it is important to learn some of the key concepts regarding structuring your site into folders known as *directories*, and how you can use *relative URLs* to link between pages within your site.

In this chapter, then, you will learn:

❏   How to structure the folders on your Web site

❏   How to link between pages of your site

❏   How to link to specific parts of a page in your site

❏   How to link to other sites

> *This chapter covers only linking to Web pages; it does not cover the mechanisms for linking to and embedding other files; in particular the* <link> *element (which is covered in Chapter 9 on style sheets) or the* <img> *and* <object> *elements (which are covered in Chapter 4).*

Basic Links

In order to get started with links, you should see one basic example. Once you know the basics of linking, there is still a lot more to learn, but this one example will get you a long way.

A link is specified using the <a> element. Anything between the opening <a> tag and the closing </a> tag becomes part of the link a user can click in a browser. The following sections discuss linking to other documents and to e-mail addresses.

Linking to Other Documents

To link to another document, the opening <a> tag must carry an attribute called href, whose value is the page you are linking to.

As an example, here is the <body> of a document called ch03_eg01.html. This page contains a link to a second page called index.html:

```
<body>
    Return to the <a href="index.html">index page</a>.
</body>
```

As long as index.html is in the same folder as ch03_eg01.html, when you click the words "index page," the index.html page will be loaded into the same window, replacing the current ch03_eg01.html page. As you can see from Figure 3-1, the content of the <a> element forms the link.

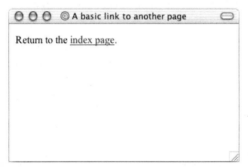

Figure 3-1

This is how the links for the download code for this chapter work. Remember that you can click the View menu in your browser and then select the View Source option at any time to see what is going on in an HTML or XHTML page.

While you can put all kinds of elements inside an <a> element, it is a good idea to make your links concise and to make the content of the <a> element actually describe what is at the other end of the link. Many people scan pages for links when they want to go to the next page without really reading the document. The content of the <a> element clearly sticks out more than the text around it (usually because it's presented in a different color). Users are less likely to stay on your site and follow your links if all of them just say "click here" because the link will not show them clearly and quickly where they are going.

A lot of Web designers also use images inside the <a> element, which is something you will see in the next chapter, but when you do use an image, make sure that the image makes it clear where the link will take you.

If you want to link to a different site, you can use the following syntax, where you specify a full URL (*Uniform Resource Locator*) to the page you want to link to rather than just the filename (you learn more about URLs later in the chapter):

```
<body>
    Why not visit the <a href="http://www.wrox.com/">Wrox Web site</a>?
</body>
```

This link points to the Wrox Web site. As you can see, the value of the `href` attribute is the same as you would type into a browser if you wanted to visit the Wrox Web site.

It is also good practice to use the `title` attribute on a link, as this will be displayed in a tooltip (a little bubble that appears stating the title) in most visual browsers when the user hovers over the link. This can help the visually impaired if they use a voice browser.

The value of the `title` attribute should be a description of what the link will take you to. They are especially important if you use an image for a link. For example, here is a link to the Google home page:

```
<a href="http://www.Google.com/" title="Search the Web with Google">Google</a>
is a very popular search engine.
```

Figure 3-2 shows the `title` attribute giving further information about the link to the user when the mouse is held over the link.

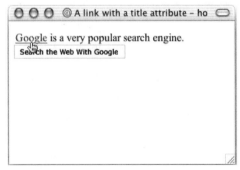

Figure 3-2

When you are linking to pages on your own Web site (as opposed to an external site), you can use a shorthand form called *relative URLs*. This not only saves you from having to type out the full URL but also has other advantages you will see when you learn about them later in the chapter.

You should be aware that everything inside the <a> element gets rendered as a link, including whitespace around the text or images, and therefore it is best to avoid spaces directly after an opening <a> tag or before the closing </a> tag. For example, look at the following link with opening and trailing spaces:

```
Why not visit the<a href="http://www.wrox.com/"> Wrox Web site </a>?
```

These spaces will be underlined in the default image, as shown in Figure 3-3.

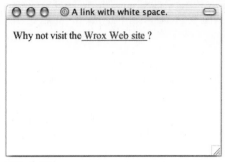

Figure 3-3

It is far better to use whitespace outside of these tags like so:

```
Why not visit the<a href="http://www.wrox.com/">Wrox Web site</a>?
```

Of course, you should still have spaces between words inside the <a> element; it's just best if they are not at the beginning or end.

Linking to E-mail Addresses

You've probably seen links on many sites that show an e-mail address, and you have probably noticed that clicking one of these links will opens a new e-mail in your default e-mail program, ready for you to send an e-mail to that address. Some even contain subject lines.

To create a link to an e-mail address you need to use the following syntax with the <a> element:

```
<a href="mailto:name@example.com">name@example.com</a>
```

Here, the value of the href attribute starts with the keyword mailto, followed by a colon, and then the e-mail address you want the mail sent to. As with any other link, the content of the <a> element is the visible part of the link shown in the browser, so you might choose to use the following:

```
<a href="mailto:name@example.com">E-mail us</a>.
```

Or, if you want users to see the e-mail address before clicking it, you can use the following:

```
For sales enquiries e-mail <a href="mailto:name@example.com">sales@example
.com</a>.
```

There is one drawback to using this technique, however: some less scrupulous inhabitants of the Web use little programs to automatically search Web sites for e-mail addresses. After they have found e-mail addresses on Web sites they will start sending spam (junk mail) to those addresses.

There are a few main alternatives to creating a link to an e-mail address:

❑   Use an e-mail form instead so that visitors fill in a form on your Web site to send you an e-mail. Once you have received the mail, you can then reply as normal because automated programs do not use contact forms to collect e-mail addresses. Use of an e-mail form requires either a CGI script or a server side scripting language such as ASP, JSP, or PHP. You will see an example of an e-mail form in Chapter 6.

❑   Write your e-mail address into the page using JavaScript (covered in Chapter 14). The idea behind this technique is that the programs that scour the Web for e-mail addresses cannot read the JavaScript version of an address.

❑   One technique that was used on the Web in the past was to insert the words nospam into an e-mail address, such as name@nospam.example.com—the idea being that users should remove the characters nospam before sending an e-mail. Any user that did not remove these characters would either have the e-mail bounced back to them or it would just go straight into a junk mail folder. This technique is not a very reliable one as it requires users to understand that they need to remove the nospam from the e-mail address. The result could be a lot of lost e-mails.

You have seen how to create the most basic types of links, and you are now ready to delve into the more in-depth topics regarding linking. In order to look at linking in depth, you need to get through a few pages that explain more about how you should organize the files in your Web site into folders, and also the anatomy of a URL (the address that identifies pages and other resources on your Web site).

Understanding Directories and Directory Structures

A *directory* is simply the name for a folder on a Web site. (In the same way your hard drive contains different folders, a Web site contains directories.) Usually you will find that a Web site contains several directories and that each directory contains different parts of a Web site. For example, a big site with several subsections will have a separate directory for each section of that site, and different types of files (such as images and style sheets) are usually kept in their own specific directory.

Just as you probably organize the files on your hard drive into separate folders, it is important to organize the files on your Web site into directories so that you can find what you are looking for more easily and keep control of all the files. As you can imagine, if all the files that were used in a Web site resided in the same folder, things would get complicated very quickly.

Figure 3-4 shows an example directory structure for a news site, with separate folders for each section and separate folders for different types of files. There are folders for images, scripts, and style sheets in the main folder. Note also how the Music section has its own folders for Images, Reviews, Articles, and MP3s.

Furthermore, a directory structure like this will help users navigate the site without knowing exact filenames; they can just pick the section they want, such as http://www.ExampleNewsSite.com/Business/ to get to the business news or http://www.ExampleNewsSite.com/Entertainment/Music/ to get to the music pages.

It is very important to keep any Web site well organized; it can be surprising how a small Web site can quickly grow and soon contain many more files than you initially imagined. Therefore, when you start to build any Web site you should create a good directory structure that can withstand high-speed growth.

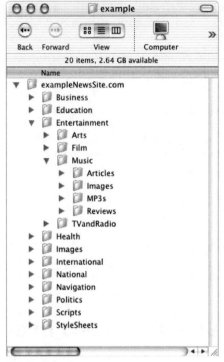

Figure 3-4

Before you continue to learn about linking it is important to learn some of the terms that are used in describing directory structures and the relationships between directories, so look back at Figure 3-4 to see an example directory structure:

❑ The main directory that holds the whole of you Web site is known as the *root folder* of your Web site; in this case it is called exampleNewSite.com.

❑ A directory that is within another directory is known as a *subdirectory*. Here, Film is a subdirectory of Entertainment.

❑ A directory that contains another directory is known as the *parent directory* of the subdirectory. Here, Entertainment is the parent directory of Film, TelevisionAndRadio, Arts, and Music.

What Are You Linking To?

At the start of this chapter you saw examples of creating links to pages in the same directory and to pages on different Web sites.

Now that you've seen how you should organize your site into separate folders, you need to look at how you can link to pages in different folders of your own site—for example how to link from the home page to a page in the Entertainment section, which will be in the Entertainment folder. You *can* use the full URL you would type into a Web browsers address bar—known as *absolute URLs*—for every link on your site, although it is better to use *relative URLs*, which are a kind of shorthand, to link between files in different folders of your site. Relative URLs specify where a file is *in relation* to the current one.

Before looking at how to create a relative URL and how it differs from an absolute URL, you need to understand the anatomy of a URL.

What a URL Is Made Up Of

A URL is made of up several parts, each of which offers information to the Web browser to help find the page you are after. It is easier to learn the parts of a URL if you look at the most common ones first. If you look at the example URL in Figure 3-5, there are three key parts: the scheme, the host address, and the file path. The following sections discuss each of these in turn.

Figure 3-5

The Scheme

The scheme identifies the type of URL you are linking to and therefore how the resource should be retrieved. For example, most Web pages use something called the *Hypertext Transfer Protocol* (HTTP) to pass information to you, which is why most Web pages start with `http://`, but you might have noticed other prefixes when doing banking online or downloading large files.

Here are the most common schemes:

Scheme	Description
`http://`	Hypertext Transfer Protocol (HTTP) is used to request pages from Web servers and send them back from Web servers to browsers.
`https://`	Secure Hypertext Transfer Protocol (HTTPS) encrypts the data sent between the browser and the Web server using a digital certificate.
`ftp://`	File Transfer Protocol is another method for transferring files on the Web. While HTTP is a lot more popular for viewing Web sites because of its integration with browsers, FTP is still commonly used to transfer large files across the Web and to upload source files to your Web server.
`file://`	Used to indicate that a file is on the local hard disk or a shared directory on a LAN.

The Host Address

The host address is where a Web site can be found, either the IP address (four sets of numbers between 0 and 258, for example 192.0.110.257) or more commonly the domain name for a site such as `www.wrox.com`.

As mentioned in Chapter 1, domain names are far easier to remember than IP addresses, but if a domain name is used, the browser will consult a domain name server (DNS) to find out the IP address associated with the domain name and then request files from the Web server using the IP address.

Note that "www" is not actually part of the domain name although it is often used in the host address—it has nothing to do with the protocol used.

The Filepath

The filepath always begins with a forward slash character, and may consist of one or more directory names (remember, a directory is just another name for a folder on the Web server); each directory name is separated by forward slash characters and the filepath may end with a filename at the end. Here `Overview.htm` is the filename:

```
/books/newReleases/BeginningWebDevelopment/Overview.htm
```

If a filename is not given, the Web server will either offer a list of files in that directory or return a default file.

Other Parts of the URL

A URL may, less commonly, contain a number of other parts.

Credentials are a way of specifying a username and password for a password-protected part of a site. The credentials come before the host address, and are separated from the host address by an @ sign. Note how the username is separated from the password by a colon. The following URL shows the username `administrator` and the password `letmein`:

```
http://administrator:letmein@www.wrox.com/administration/index.htm
```

Ports are like the doors to a Web server. A Web server often has several server programs running on the same machine, and each program communicates using a different port. For example, `http://` and `https://` by default use different ports (standard `http://` usually uses port 80 and `https://` usually uses port 443).

You will rarely have to specify a port, but if you do it comes after the domain name and is separated from it with a colon. For example, if you wanted to specify that a Web server was running on port 8080 you could use the following address:

```
http://www.wrox.com:8080/index.htm
```

Fragment identifiers can be used after a filename to indicate a specific part of the page that a browser should go to immediately. These are often used in long pages when you want to allow a user to get to a specific part of a page easily without scrolling through the whole page to find that point.

The fragment identifier is separated from the filename by a pound or hash sign:

```
http://www.wrox.com/newTitles/index.htm#HTML
```

You will learn more about fragment identifiers in the section of that name later in the chapter.

Path arguments are used to pass extra information to a server program. They are separated from the URL by a question mark and come in name/value pairs separated by the equal sign (they are rather like attributes without the quotation marks). Path arguments are commonly used to collect information from visitors and often to pass information to programs on the server that will tailor a page to you.

When you use a form on a Web page, such as a search form or an online order form, the browser can append the information you supply to the URL to pass information from you to the server—you do not type path arguments into a URL.

Here, the path arguments `searchTerm=HTML` are added to the URL to indicates the user is searching on the term `HTML`:

```
http://www.wrox.com/search.asp?searchTerm=HTML
```

You will learn more about path arguments in Chapter 5.

Absolute and Relative URLs

As you have already seen, a URL is used to locate a resource on the Internet. Each Web page and image—in fact every file on the Internet—has a unique URL, the address that can be used to find that particular file. No two files on the Internet share the same URL.

If you want to access a particular page of a Web site, you type the URL for that page into the address bar in your browser. For example, to get the page about film on the fictional news site you met earlier in the chapter you might type in the URL:

```
http://www.exampleNewsSite.com/Entertainment/Film/index.htm
```

An *absolute URL* like this one contains everything you need to uniquely identify a particular file on the Internet.

As you can see, absolute URLs can quickly get quite long, and every page of a Web site can contain many links. So it's about time you learned the shorthand for URLs that point to files within your Web site: relative URLs.

A *relative URL* indicates where the resource is in relation to the current page. For example, imagine you are looking at the index page for the entertainment section of the following fictional news site:

```
http://www.exampleNewsSite.com/Entertainment/index.htm
```

Then you want to add a link to the index pages for each of the subsections `Film`, `TVAndRadio`, `Arts`, and `Music`. Rather than including the full URL for each page, you can use a relative URL. For example:

```
Film/index.htm
TVAndRadio/TVAndRadio.htm
Arts/index.htm
Music/Music.htm
```

As I am sure you agree, this is a lot quicker than having to write out

```
http://www.exampleNewsSite.com/Entertainment/Film/index.htm
http://www.exampleNewsSite.com/Entertainment/TVAndRadio/TVAndRadio.htm
http://www.exampleNewsSite.com/Entertainment/Arts/index.htm
http://www.exampleNewsSite.com/Entertainment/Music/Music.htm
```

Although you might be interested to know that your Web browser still requests the full URL, not the shortened relative URL, it is the browser that is actually doing the work of turning the relative URLs into full absolute URLs.

Another key benefit to using relative URLs within your site is that it means you can change your domain name or copy a subsection of one site to a new site without having to change all of the links because each link is relative to other pages within the same site.

Note that relative URLs work only on links within the same directory structure; you cannot use them to link to pages on other servers.

The subsections that follow provide a summary of the different types of relative URLs you can use.

Same Directory

When you want to link to or include a resource from the same directory, you can just use the name of that file. For example, to link from the home page (index.html) to the contact us page (contactUs.htm), you could use the following:

```
contactUs.htm
```

Because the file lives in the same folder, you do not need to specify anything else.

Subdirectory

The Film, TVAndRadio, Arts, and Music directories from Figure 3-4 were all subdirectories of the Entertainment directory. If you are writing a page in the Entertainment directory, you can create a link to the index page of the subdirectories like so:

```
Film/index.htm
TVAndRadio/TVAndRadio.htm
Arts/index.htm
Music/Music.htm
```

You include the name of the subdirectory, followed by a forward slash character, and the name of the page you want to link to.

For each additional subdirectory, you just add the name of the directory followed by a forward slash character. So, if you are creating a link from a page in the root folder of the site, you use a relative URL like these to reach the same pages:

```
Entertainment/Film/index.htm
Entertainment/TVAndRadio/TVAndRadio.htm
Entertainment/Arts/index.htm
Entertainment/Music/Music.htm
```

Parent Directory

If you want to create a link from one directory to its parent directory (the directory that it is in), you use the ../ notation of two periods or dots followed by a forward slash character. For example, from a page in the Music directory to a page in the Entertainment directory, your relative URL looks like this:

```
../index.htm
```

If you want to link from the Music directory to the root directory, you repeat the notation:

```
../../index.htm
```

Each time you repeat the ../ notation, you go up another directory.

From the Root

It is also possible to indicate a file relative to the root folder of the site. So, if you wanted to link to the contactUs.htm page from any page within the site, you use its path preceded by a forward slash. For example, if the contact us page is in the root folder, you just need to enter:

```
/contactUs.htm
```

Alternatively, you could link to the Music section's index page from anywhere within that site using the following:

```
/Entertainment/Music/index.htm
```

The forward slash at the start indicates the root directory, and then the path from there is specified.

Default Files

You may have noticed on many Web sites that you do not need to actually specify the exact page that you want to view. For example, you might just enter the domain name or the domain name and a directory, such as:

```
http://www.exampleNewsSite.com/
```

or

```
http://www.exampleNewsSite.com/Entertainment/
```

This is because many Web servers allow their owners to send a default file to the visitor when they just specify a directory. So, http://www.exampleNewsSite.com/Entertainment/ will return the default file for the Entertainment directory, and if you specify http://www.exampleNewSite.com/ the server returns the default file for the root folder of the Web site. (Remember that the forward slash character can be used as an indicator of being relative to the root directory.)

Most servers use either index.html or default.html as the default HTML filename (although this might be different if you use a server side language such as ASP or PHP).

You might have noticed that both of these URLs end in a forward slash character. If you do not include the trailing slash at the end of the URL you request, it might look like this:

```
http://www.exampleNewsSite.com
```

or

```
http://www.exampleNewsSite.com/Entertainment
```

In these cases, the server tends to look for a file by these names, not find one, and tell the browser to request the same page with a slash character at the end. For example, if you enter the following into your browser without the trailing slash character:

```
http://www.wrox.com
```

most browsers read the following when you get to see the home page:

```
http://www.wrox.com/
```

Therefore, when you create links to folders within Web sites (rather than specific pages), it's a good idea to add a forward slash to the end of the URL:

If this did not happen, then relative URLs would not work from the page without the trailing slash.

The <base> Element

As I mentioned earlier, when a browser comes across a relative URL it actually transforms the relative URL into a full absolute URL. The <base> element allows you to specify a base URL for a page that all relative URLs will be added to when the browser comes across a relative URL. You specify the base URL as the value of the href attribute. For example, you might indicate a base URL for http://www.exampleSite2.com/ as follows:

```
<base href="http://www.exampleSite2.com/" />
```

In this case, a relative URL like this one:

```
Entertainment/Arts/index.html
```

ends up with the browser requesting this page:

```
http://www.exampleSite2.com/Entertainment/Arts/index.html
```

This is helpful when a page has been moved to a new server, but you still want all of the links to go back to the original site, or when there is no URL for the page itself (such as an HTML e-mail).

The only other attribute a <base> element can carry (apart from the href attribute) is the id attribute.

Creating Links with the <a> Element

You have already seen a couple of examples of using the <a> element at the start of the chapter. However, that was just a taste of what you can do with the <a> element. Now it is time to look at links in a little more depth.

All hypertext links on the Web take you from one part of the Web to another. You have already seen links that take you from one page to another (and this section covers them in more depth). You will also meet links that take you to a specific part of a page (either be a specific part of the same page or a different page).

Like all journeys, they have a starting point known as the *source*, and a finishing point known as the *destination*, which are both called *anchors*.

Each link that you see on a page that you can click is actually a *source anchor*, and each source anchor is created using the <a> element.

Creating a Source Anchor with the href Attribute

The source anchor is what most people think of when talking about links on the Web—whether the link contains text or an image. It is something you can click and expect to be taken somewhere else.

As you have already seen, any text that forms part of the link that a user can click is contained between the opening <a> tag and closing </a> tag, and the URL that the user should be taken to is specified as the value of the href attribute.

For example, when you click the words Wrox Press website (which you can see are inside the <a> element) the link takes you to http://www.wrox.com/:

```
Why not visit the <a href="http://www.wrox.com/">Wrox Press website</a> to
find out about some of our other books?
```

while the following link on the home page of the fictional news site would take you to the main Film page (note how this link uses a relative URL):

```
You can see more films in the <a href="Entertainment/Film/index.htm">film
section</a>.
```

By default, this link looks something like the one shown in Figure 3-6 underlined and in blue text.

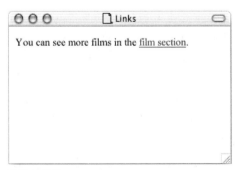

Figure 3-6

You need only to specify a destination anchor when you want to link to a specific part of a page, as described in the next section.

Creating a Destination Anchor Using the name and id Attributes (linking to a specific part of a page)

If you have a long Web page, you might want to link to a specific part of that page. You will usually want to do this when the page does not fit in the browser window and the user might otherwise have to scroll to find the relevant part of the page.

The *destination anchor* allows the page author to mark specific points in a page that a source link can point to.

Common examples of linking to a specific part of a page that you might have seen used on Web pages include:

❑ "Back to top" links at the bottom of long pages

❑ A list of contents for a page that takes the user to the relevant section

❑ Links to footnotes or definitions

You create a destination anchor using the <a> element again, but when it acts as a destination anchor it must carry either a name or id attribute.

You may remember from Chapter 2 that the name and id attributes were two of the universal attributes that most elements can carry. The name attribute was deprecated in the HTML 4 specification, and while you can still use it in Transitional XHTML 1.0 documents, Strict XHTML 1.0 permits only the use of the id attribute. Meanwhile the id attribute was introduced in HTML 4, which means it has the drawback that only version 4 browsers and later versions understand it as a method of creating destination anchors.

By way of an example, imagine that you have a long page with a main heading and several subheadings. This page does not all fit on the screen, so you want to add links to each of the main headings at the start of the document.

Before you can create links to each section of the page (using the source anchors), you have to add the destination anchors. Here you can see the subheadings of the page, each containing an <a> element with the name attribute whose value uniquely identifies that section:

```
<h1>Linking and Navigation</h1>
<h2><a name="URL">URLs</a></h2>
<h2><a name="SourceAnchors">Source Anchors</a></h2>
<h2><a name="DestinationAnchors">Destination Anchors</a></h2>
<h2><a name="Examples">Examples</a></h2>
```

With destination anchors in place, it's now possible to add source anchors to link to these sections, like so:

```
<p>This page covers the following topics:
  <ul>
    <li><a href="#URL">URLs</a></li>
    <li><a href="#SourceAnchors">Source Anchors</a></li>
    <li><a href="#DestinationAnchors">Destination Anchors</a></li>
    <li><a href="#Examples">Examples</a></li>
  </ul>
</p>
```

The value of the `href` attribute in the source anchors is the value of the `name` attribute preceded by a pound or hash sign (#). (You can see the full code for this example, and try it, with the download code for this chapter available from Wrox.com; the file is `ch03_eg06.html`).

Note that even a destination anchor should always have some content; otherwise some browsers will not find the destination. For example you should not use the following to indicate the top of the page:

```
<a name="top"></a>
```

Rather, you should put this around the main heading or some other content, like so:

```
<h1><a name="top">Linking and Navigation</a></h1>
```

In a long document, destination anchors are often placed just above the heading or section they link to so that the user sees a little whitespace above the appropriate section, making it easier to read the content. Because the <a> element should always have some content, a simple non-breaking space character   or line break element <br/> would suffice.

If someone wanted to link to a specific part of this page from a different Web site, she would add the full URL for the page, followed by the pound or hash sign and then the value of the `name` attribute, like so:

```
http://www.example.com/HTML/links.htm#SourceAnchors
```

> **The value of a name or id attribute should be unique within the page and source anchors should match the case of destination anchors.**

The `id` attribute works exactly the same as the `name` attribute, although its value must be unique within that document and must follow the rules that you met in Chapter 2.

If you want to create Strict XHTML, your pages must use the id attribute rather than the name attribute. But remember that the id attribute will not work as a destination anchor in IE 3.x or earlier and Netscape 3.x or earlier, so if your visitors are likely to use these browsers, you should use the name attribute and the Transitional XHTML. While you could use both attributes, the result will still not be valid Strict XHTML unless you make proper use of XML namespaces (which are discussed in Chapter 13).

The <a> Element's Other Attributes

The <a> element supports all of the universal attributes, the UI event attributes, and the following attributes:

```
accesskey charset cords href hreflang rel rev shape style tabindex target type
```

You have met many of these already, but here are the other attributes, including those with particular relevance to links.

The accesskey Attribute

The `accesskey` attribute provides a keyboard shortcut that can be used to activate a link. For example, you could make the T key an access key so that when the user presses either the Alt or Ctrl key on his keyboard (depending on his operating system) along with the T key, the link gets activated. This may either mean the browser immediately follows the link, or it may mean the link is highlighted and that the user then has to press the Enter (or Return) key for it to be followed.

The `accesskey` attribute should be specified on the source anchor. For example, if you want to follow a link to the top of the page when the user presses the T key on his keyboard (with either Alt or Ctrl) you use the `accesskey` attribute like so:

```
<a id="top" accesskey="t">Back to top</a>
```

Note that the key is case-insensitive. You will see more about the `accesskey` attribute (and some examples) when you look at forms in Chapter 6.

The charset Attribute

The `charset` attribute indicates the character encoding of the document the URL points to. The value must be a string that identifies the character set, such as UTF-8 or ISO-8859-1. (See Appendix F for the a list of character sets.)

The `charset` attribute is usually used on the source anchor, and typically only when the language is different than that of the main document containing the link. For example:

```
<a href="http://www.wrox.com/" charset="UTF-8">Wrox Web Site</a>
```

This is particularly useful when linking to foreign language sites written in encodings that some users might not be able to view.

The coords Attribute

The `coords` attribute is designed for use on a source anchor when it contains an image. It is designed so you can create an image map, which is where different parts of the image link to different documents or different parts of the same document. The `coords` attribute's value will be x and y coordinates that indicate which part of the image should follow this link.

You will learn more about using images as links in the Chapter 4.

The hreflang Attribute

The `hreflang` attribute specifies the language of the document a source link points to and can be used only when a value for the `href` attribute is given. For example:

```
<a href="http://www.wrox.com/" hreflang="en-US">Wrox Web Site</a>
```

The possible values are given in Appendix G.

The rel Attribute

The `rel` attribute is used on the source anchor to indicate the relationship between the current document and the resource specified by the `href` attribute. The major browsers do not at present make any use of this attribute, although it is possible that automated applications could. For example, the following link uses the rel attribute to indicate that its destination is a section of the document:

```
We shall come onto the <a href="#links" rel="section">links</a> section of our
chapter soon.
```

See the table that follows for possible values for rel.

Value	Description
toc (or contents)	A document that is a table of contents for the current document
index	A document that is an index for the current document
glossary	A document containing a glossary of terms that relate to the current document
copyright	A document containing the copyright statement for the current document
start	A document that is the first in a series of ordered documents, of which this is one document
next	A document that is the next in a series of ordered documents, of which this is one document
prev (or previous)	A document that is the previous in a series of ordered documents, of which this is one document
help	A document that helps users understand or navigate the page and or site
chapter	A document that acts as a chapter within a collection of documents
section	A document that acts as a section in a collection of documents
subsection	A document that acts as a subsection in a collection of documents
appendix	A document that acts as an appendix in a collection of documents

The rev Attribute

The rev attribute provides the same role as the rel attribute but is used on the destination anchor to describe the relation between the destination and the source.

The shape Attribute

If you want to create an image map, the shape attribute can be used to indicate the shape of an area that becomes a clickable *hotspot*. The shape attribute is covered in detail in Chapter 4, where you learn how to create image maps.

The tabindex Attribute

To understand the tabindex attribute, you need to know what it means for an element to gain *focus*. If the user clicks the Tab key on her keyboard when a page has loaded, the browser moves focus between certain parts of a page. The parts of the page that can gain focus include links and some parts of forms (such as the boxes that allow you to enter text). When a link receives focus, if the user presses Enter on the keyboard, the link is activated. You can see focus working on the Google Web site; if you repeatedly press the Tab key you should see focus pass between links on the page. After it has passed across each link in turn, it goes onto the box where you enter search terms, across the site's buttons, and usually ends up back where you typed in the URL. Then it cycles around the same elements again as you keep pressing Tab.

The `tabindex` attribute allows you to specify the order in which, when the Tab key is pressed, the links (or form controls) obtain focus. So, when the user clicks the Tab key, the focus may skip to the key items on the page that the user might have wanted to interact with.

The value of the `tabindex` attribute is a number between 1 and 32767. A link whose `tabindex` attribute has a value of 1 received focus before a link with a `tabindex` value of 20. Chapter 6 covers the `tabindex` attribute in more detail.

The target Attribute

The `target` attribute is used to indicate which window or frame the document contained in a link should open in. You learn more about frames in Chapter 7. The syntax is:

```
<a href="Page2.htm" target="main">Page 2</a>
```

When the user clicks the Page 2 link, the document `Page2.htm` loads in the window or frame called `main`.

The title Attribute

As mentioned at the start of the chapter, a `title` attribute is vital for any links that are images, and can also help provide additional information to visitors in the form of a visual text tooltip in most browsers or an auditory clue in voice browsers for the visually impaired. Figure 3-2 near the beginning of this chapter showed you what the title attribute looked like in IE when a user hovers over the link.

The type Attribute

The `type` attribute specifies the MIME type of the link. There is a list of MIME types in Appendix H. An HTML page would have the MIME type `text/html`, while a JPEG image would have the MIME type `img/jpeg`. Here is an example of the `type` attribute being used to indicate that the document the links points to is an HTML document:

```
<a href="index.htm" type="text/html">Index</a>
```

Theoretically the browser could use the information in the `type` attribute to either display it differently or indicate to the user what the format of the destination is, although none do use it at present.

Try It Out   Creating Links Within Pages

Now it's your turn to try making a long page with links between different parts of the page. In this example, you are going to create a page that is a restaurant menu. So open your text editor or authoring tool and follow these steps:

1. Start off with the XML declaration, DOCTYPE declaration, and the elements for the skeleton of the document: <html>, <head>, <title>, and <body>. Remember to give the document a title

and add in the namespace identifier on the root <html> element:

```
<?xml version="1.0" ?>
<!DOCTYPE html PUBLIC "-//W3C//DTD XHTML 1.0 Strict//EN"
    "http://www.w3.org/TR/xhtml1/DTD/xhtml1-strict.dtd">
<html xmlns="http://www.w3.org/1999/xhtml" lang="en">

<head>
  <title>A menu example</title>
</head>
<body>

</body>
</html>
```

2. Inside the <body> element, add the headings for the page. Each of these should have a destination anchor so that you can link directly to that part of the page. The main heading will be used for "Back to top" links, while each course of the menu will have an id attribute that describes its sections:

```
<body>
<h1><a id="top">Wrox Cafe Menu</a></h1>
<h2><a id="starters">Starters</a></h2>
<h2><a id="mains">Main Courses</a></h2>
<h2><a id="desserts">Desserts</a></h2>
</body>
```

3. Between the title and the starters, not only will there be an introductory paragraph, but also a menu linking to each of the courses. In order to be Strict XHTML the links at the top will go in a block level <div> element:

```
<h1><a id="top">Wrox Cafe Menu</a></h1>
<div id="nav"><a href="#starters">Starters</a> | <a href="#mains">Main
Courses</a> | <a href="#desserts">Desserts</a></div>

<p>Welcome to the Wrox Cafe, where we pride ourselves on good, honest home
cooked food at good, honest prices.</p>
<h2><a id="starters">Starters</a></h2>
```

4. At the bottom of the page you will have a description of vegetarian dishes. Links next to vegetarian items will point to this description, so it needs to have a destination anchor.

```
<p><a id="vege">Items marked with a (v) are suitable for vegetarians.</a></p>
```

5. Finally, you can just add in the items on the menu in a bulleted list. Note how the vegetarian items have a link down to the description of vegetarian dishes. Don't forget to add the "Back to top" links at the bottom of the page.

```
<h2><a id="starters">Starters</a></h2>
<ul>
  <li>Chestnut and Mushroom Goujons (<a href="#vege">v</a>)</li>
  <li>Goat Cheese Salad (<a href="#vege">v</a>)</li>
  <li>Honey Soy Chicken Kebabs</li>
  <li>Seafood Salad</li>
```

```
</ul>
<p><small><a href="#top">Back to top</a></small></p>
<h2><a id="mains">Main courses</a></h2>
<ul>
  <li>Spinach and Ricotta Roulade (<a href="#vege">v</a>)</li>
  <li>Beef Tournados with Mustard and Dill Sauce</li>
  <li>Roast Chicken Salad</li>
  <li>Icelandic Cod with Parsley Sauce</li>
  <li>Mushroom Wellington (<a href="#vege">v</a>)</li>
</ul>
<p><small><a href="#top">Back to top</a></small></p>
<h2><a id="desserts">Desserts</a></h2>
<ul>
  <li>Lemon Sorbet (<a href="#vege">v</a>)</li>
  <li>Chocolate Mud Pie (<a href="#vege">v</a>)</li>
  <li>Pecan Pie (<a href="#vege">v</a>)</li>
  <li>Selection of Fine Cheeses from Around the World</li>
</ul>
<p><small><a href="#top">Back to top</a></small></p>
```

6. Save your example as `menu.html` and take a look at in your browser. You should end up with something that looks like Figure 3-7.

Figure 3-7

How It Works

You have already seen the skeleton parts for the page (along with the declarations that come before it), so let's focus on the links.

There are three source anchors just under the first heading that form a simple navigation bar. When clicked these will take users to the appropriate section of the menu. These items are kept inside a <div> element because <a> elements should appear inside a block level element in Strict XHTML 1.0—although any earlier versions would allow you to leave this off.

```
<div id="nav"><a href="#starters">Starters</a> | <a href="#mains">Main courses
</a> | <a href="#desserts">Desserts</a></div>
```

The id attribute on the <div> element is just there to identify the purpose of this block-level grouping element. Because this element does not have a specific purpose like some of the other elements (such as <p> or <h2>), it helps to add this attribute as a reminder of what it is grouping.

Three additional source anchors are underneath each section of the menu to take you back to the top of the page.

```
<p><small><a href="#top">Back to top</a></small></p>
```

Finally, there are source anchors with the text v to indicate items are vegetarian, and to take you to a key at the bottom of the page that explains what the v stands for.

```
<li>Mushroom wellington (<a href="#vege">v</a>)</li>
```

The destination anchors are using the id attribute to indicate the potential targets of links. Each of the headings contains a destination anchor. The main menu heading requires an anchor so that the "Back to top" links will take the user to the top of the page, while the subheadings have anchors so that the navigation menu at the top can take them to that part of the page.

Remember that destination anchors must have some content—they cannot be empty or the browser might not recognize them, which is why they have been put inside the heading elements surrounding the actual heading name:

```
<h1><a id="top">Wrox Cafe Menu</a></h1>
<h2><a id="starters">Starters</a></h2>
<h2><a id="mains">Main courses</a></h2>
<h2><a id="desserts">Desserts</a></h2>
```

Similarly, the paragraph at the bottom that indicates what the (v) sign means contains a destination anchor, just like the heading.

```
<p><a id="vege">Items marked with a (v) are suitable for vegetarians.</a></p>
```

Advanced E-mail Links

As you saw at the beginning of the chapter, you can make a link open up the user's default e-mail editor, and address an e-mail to you—or any other e-mail address you give—automatically. This is done like so:

```
<a href="mailto:info@example.org">info@example.org</a>
```

You can also specify some other parts of the message, too, such as the subject, body, and people that it should be Cc'd or blind Cc'd to.

To add a subject to an e-mail, you follow the e-mail address with a question mark to separate the extra values from the e-mail address. Then you use the name/value pairs to specify the additional properties of the mail you want to control. The name and the value are separated by an equal sign.

For example, to set the subject to be XHTML, you would add the subject property name and what you wanted to be the subject, like so:

```
<a href="mailto:info@example.org?subject=XHTML">
```

You can specify more than one property by separating them using ampersands. Here you can see the subject and a Cc address have been added in:

```
<a href="mailto:info@example.org?subject=XHTML&cc=sales@example.org"></a>
```

The table that follows includes a full list of properties you can add like this:

Property	Purpose
subject	This adds a subject line to the e-mail; you can add this to encourage the user to use a subject line that makes it easier to recognize where the mail has come from.
body	This adds a message into the body of the e-mail, although you should be aware that users would be able to alter this message.
cc	This sends a carbon copy of the mail to the Cc'd address; the value must be a valid e-mail address. If you want to provide multiple addresses you simply repeat the property, separating it from the previous one with an ampersand.
bcc	This secretly sends a carbon copy of the mail to the Bcc'd address without any recipient seeing any other recipients; the value must be a valid e-mail address. If you want to provide multiple addresses you simply repeat the property, separating it from the previous one with an ampersand.

If you want to add a space between any of the words in the subject line, you should add %20 between the words instead of the space. If you want to take the body part of the message onto a new line you should add %0D%0A (where 0 is a zero, not a capital O).

It is common practice to add only the e-mail address in e-mail links. If you want to add subject lines or message bodies you are better off creating an e-mail form, like the one you will see in Chapter 6.

Summary

In this chapter you learned about links—the part of XHTML that puts the "hyper" in hypertext. Links enable visitors to your site to jump between pages and even between parts of pages (so that they don't have to scroll to find the place they need).

You have seen that you can use the <a> element to create source anchors, which are what most people think of when you mention links on the Web. The content of the source anchor is what users can click—and this should usually be an informative, concise description of what the target is (rather than text such as "click here"), or it can be an image (as you will see in Chapter 4).

You can also use the <a> element to create destination anchors. Destination anchors are a little like an index point or special marker because they allow you to create links that take you directly to that part of the page. Destination anchors should always have some content, and the old name attribute that HTML introduced for destination anchors has been replaced in Strict XHTML by the id attribute (although this works only in version 3+ browsers).

Along the way, you learned more about URLs, in particular the difference between an absolute URL like those that appear in the address bar of your browser and relative URLs, which describe where a resource is in relation to the document containing them. Learning the different ways in which relative URLs can be used will also be helpful as you head to the next chapter and learn about adding images and other objects into your documents.

Exercises

The answers to all of the exercises are given in Appendix A.

1. Look back at the Try It Out example where you created a menu, and create a new page that has links, like those at the top of the menu page, to each of the courses in the menu example. Then add a link to the main Wrox Press Web site (www.wrox.com). The page should look something like Figure 3-8.

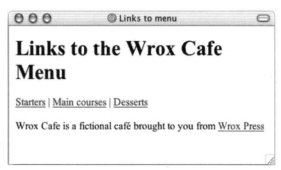

Figure 3-8

Chapter 3

2. Take the following sentence and place <a> elements around the parts that should have the link.

```
<p>To find out why advertising on our site works, visit the testimonials
page.</p>
```

3. What is wrong with the positioning of the <a> element here?

```
<p>You can read the full article <a>here</a>.</p>
```

Colors, Images, and Objects

In this chapter, you begin learning some aspects of Web design that will really breathe life into your Web pages. You'll start by learning how XHTML deals with color. You might remember from Chapter 1 that there were some odd six-character codes that represented colors, and in this chapter you learn what they mean so that you can use them wherever you have to deal with color. While we are looking at color, I will also introduce you to some key concepts behind creating colors and get you working with the color wheel to help you choose colors for your site. The authors of too many sites on the Web simply have not taken time to plan a good color scheme; and the result is that these sites look like they were built by amateurs (no matter how great the content). Learning a bit about color will really help make your pages look a lot more professional.

Next you will learn how to add images into your documents using the <img> element. You will see the difference between some of the main formats used for images on the Web and you will learn how to prepare your images for use on the Web. You will also learn how to make an image a link, and even how to divide an image up into sections so that different parts of the image link to different pages—this is known as an *image map*.

Finally you'll meet the <object> element that you can use to insert all manner of objects into pages, from MP3s and Flash movies to Active X controls and even images. In fact, the W3C sees the <object> element eventually replacing the <img> element, which is used to add images to your pages.

So, it's time to begin making your pages look a little more interesting, starting by adding color to them.

Adding Color to Your Site

When building almost any Web site, you will want to add color to your pages, and there are a lot of ways in which you can add color. As you will see later in the chapter, you can add color to your site through the use of images, but you are also likely to want to change the color of headings, paragraphs of text, page backgrounds, borders, and so on.

In Chapters 1 and 2 you've already come across some attributes that allow you to change the color of an element's contents, such as color and bgcolor. While attributes that specify color have been dropped from Strict XHTML 1.0 in favor of using CSS, they are still present in Transitional XHTML (although they are deprecated), and are used widely so you will more than likely come across them.

It is important to address color early on because color not only goes hand in hand with images but also has a very powerful effect on visitors, and creating a great color scheme is an important topic that deserves early attention.

The main issues you are going to look at in this section are therefore:

❑ How to specify which color you want

❑ Some key concepts behind creating color schemes

❑ How to choose a set of colors for your site

❑ Things that affect the appearance of colors

❑ Which colors and combinations of colors to avoid

> *Color is not the easiest topic to talk about in a book that is printed in black and white, but if you download the code examples for this book from www.wrox.com you get a lot more from this section—it contains color examples and color tools to help you along the way.*

Specifying the Color You Want

The first thing you need to learn about color is how to specify exactly the color you want; after all there are a lot of different reds, greens, and blues, and it is important you choose the right ones.

In XHTML there are two key ways of specifying a color:

❑ **Hex codes:** A six-digit code representing the amount of red, green, and blue that make up the color, preceded by a pound or hash sign # (for example, #333333).

❑ **Color names:** A set of names that represent over 200 colors, such as red, lightslategray, and fuchsia.

Appendix D contains a list of over 100 color names and their corresponding hex codes.

Using Hex Codes to Specify Colors

When you start using *hexadecimal codes* (or hex codes for short), they can appear a little daunting. The idea that colors are represented by a mix of numbers and letters might seem a little strange, but what follows the # sign is actually the amount of red, green, and blue that make up the color. The format for hex codes is:

```
# rrggbb
```

The table that follows shows some examples.

Color	Hexadecimal Code
Black	#000000
White	#FFFFFF
Red	#FF0000
Green	#008000
Blue	#0000FF
Purple	#800080

As you might already know, computer monitors work in a color space known as an *RGB color space*. When a computer monitor is not switched on, the screen is black because it is not emitting any color. To create the image you see onscreen, each of the pixels that makes up the screen emits different amounts of the colors red, green, and blue just like a television screen.

It is hardly surprising, therefore, that you specify colors in amounts of red, green, and blue that are required to make a given color. The values of red, green, and blue required to make a color are between 0 and 255, so when red, green, and blue all have a value of 0 you get black, whereas if each has a value of 255 you get white.

You may have seen that some software represents colors using three sets of numbers between 0 and 255. Figure 4-1 shows the color window in Adobe Photoshop.

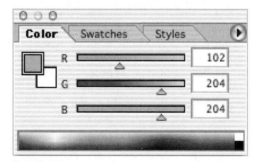

Figure 4-1

The hexadecimal codes used on the Web for color are a direct translation of these values between 0 and 255, except they use two characters not three to represent the numbers between 0 and 255. For example, FF represents 255 and 00 represents 0.

The best thing for really understanding how hex codes work is to take a quick look at how computers store information.

Understanding Hex Codes

You may have heard people say that computers store all their information in 0s and 1s, and while it may sound hard to believe, it's true! The smallest unit of information a computer stores in is known as a *bit*, and a bit can only have one of two values:

❏   0, which means off (or false)

❏   1, which means on (or true)

These two values on their own will not store much information, yet if you combine four bits together you can get 16 different values. For example, using combinations of four 0s and 1s, you can represent the digits 0–9 (and still have values to spare):

```
0000 0001 0010 0011 0100 0101 0110 0111 1000 1001 1010 1011 1100 1101 1110 1111
  0    1    2    3    4    5    6    7    8    9    –    –    –    –    –    –
```

Four bits can be replaced by a single hexadecimal digit. There are 16 digits in hexadecimal numbers to represent the 16 possible values of four 0s and 1s:

```
0000 0001 0010 0011 0100 0101 0110 0111 1000 1001 1010 1011 1100 1101 1110 1111
  0    1    2    3    4    5    6    7    8    9    A    B    C    D    E    F
```

0 is the smallest; F is the largest.

Still, computers need to work with more than 16 possible values, so they tend to store information in yet larger segments. A group of 8 bits is known as a *byte*. A byte can therefore be represented using just two hexadecimal digits. For example:

```
Binary          0100     1111
Hexadecimal       4       F
```

This gives 256 possible combinations of 0s and 1s, plenty for the characters of the English language, and yes, that is why colors are represented in numbers between 0 and 255 come in.

So, while hexadecimal codes for Web colors may appear a little complicated, I think you would agree that #4F4F4F is a lot easier to read than 010011110100111101001111. The following table shows some more hexadecimal codes and their corresponding decimal numbers.

Hexadecimal	Decimal
00	0
33	51
66	102
99	153
AA	170
BB	187
CC	204

Hexadecimal	Decimal
DD	221
EE	238
FF	255

Remember Appendix D holds a helpful table of over 200 colors for you to consult, and the download code features some handy color tools, too!

Using Color Names to Specify Colors

Rather than using hex values to specify colors, you can also use color names such as red, green, and white to specify the color you want. There are over 200 different color names supported by Netscape and IE, and there is a full list of these in Appendix D.

While names might sound a lot easier to understand than hex codes, some of the colors are easier to remember than others, and remembering which color each of the 200 names looks like is a tall order. Here is a sample of some of the color names:

```
aqua, beige, coral, darkcyan, firebrick, green, honeydew, indianred,
lavenderblush, maroon, navy, oldlace, palegreen, red, saddlebrown,
tan, white, yellow
```

Furthermore, if you do jobs for larger companies, such companies often want to specify very exact colors that represent their brand, and their color might not have an HTML name. Indeed, when clients specify the color they want, they usually specify a hex code.

Style guides are documents that larger companies often prepare when they employ other companies to perform marketing roles (such as advertising agencies and Web designers). Style guides can often be quite in-depth and contain brand-related information such as colors and fonts the company uses, photographic guidelines, and all manner of rules that govern how the company's brand is represented. The use of a strict style guide means that the client retains their unique look and feel even when several companies are producing marketing material for them.

Hex Codes versus Color Names

It may seem as though color names are more straightforward to use than hex codes; if you use colors such as red, orange, green, blue, black, and white, then they are simple to remember and use. However, remembering each color name and the color it gives you is very difficult.

In practice, you often end up referring to a color chart to find the color you want, whether you're working with hex codes or color names. Given that hex codes give you a lot more choices of shades, tints, and hues of colors than color names, and bearing in mind that a lot of companies ask for specific colors to represent their company, hex codes tend to be the choice of Web professionals.

If you are using either a graphics program or a Web page authoring tool, that program will usually generate the color code you need for you, and many graphics packages also have a color-picking tool to help you select the exact color you want. Figure 4-2 shows the color picker from Photoshop.

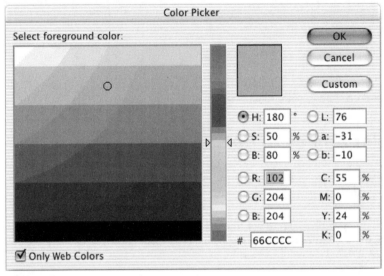

Figure 4-2

Note that the checkbox on the bottom left of this window indicates an option to use only Web safe colors. This is for a restricted color palette (containing a subset of all colors available) known as the Web Safe Color Palette, which you meet later in the chapter.

Choosing Your Colors for the Web

Now that you know how to specify a color, you need to think about choosing the colors for your site. If you look at the Web sites of any large international brands, you will see the colors you usually associate with that company. For example, you wouldn't expect the Coca Cola, Ferrari, or Virgin Web sites to be green. Big companies know the importance of using color to build a brand.

Color has a very strong influence on people and can affect how people view a company. So, when designing any Web site, color should be an important factor. A well-chosen color scheme is key to making any site attractive, and indeed well-chosen colors can mean the difference between an average looking site and a really attractive site.

In order to choose the colors you are going to use on the site you must have an understanding of the following:

❑ How colors are made up, and some key terms that describe colors

❑ What a color wheel is, and how it can help you choose your color schemes

❑ Different types of color scheme

❑ What the Web safe color palette is and why you can largely ignore it

❑ Factors that make colors look different on different computers

❑ Some issues regarding usability and color

While some of the following discussion of colors may be hard to follow in a black and white book, you will find color versions of many of the images used in this section in with the code examples for this chapter, which can be downloaded from www.wrox.com. Having these examples at hand while you read this section should make it easier to understand.

The Basics of Color

At school you probably learned that:

❑ There are three *primary colors*: red, yellow, and blue.

❑ Combining primary colors gives you *secondary colors* of green, orange, and purple.

❑ *Tertiary colors* are a combination of primary and secondary colors: red-orange, red-purple, blue-purple, blue-green, yellow-orange, and yellow green.

You now have a total of 12 colors. You can see these 12 colors in the color wheel illustrated in Figure 4-3. You may not be able to see all 12 colors clearly in this figure, but you can see a version on your own computer in ch04_eg01.html available with the code download for this chapter.

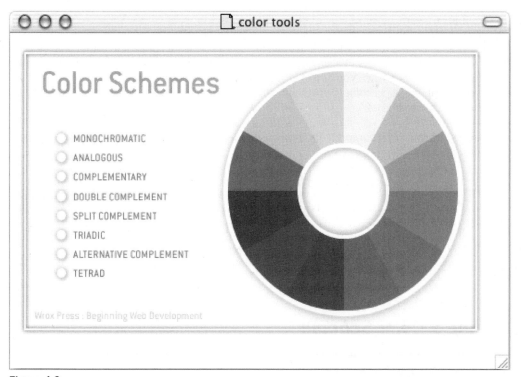

Figure 4-3

If you combine all of the colors in this basic color wheel you will end up with a more complex color wheel that shows every possible pure color (also known as a hue). Every color you use on the Web is either one of these pure colors, or what designers call a shade, tint, or tone of one of these colors (and seeing as designers like to use these terms it helps to know what each means):

❑ A *hue* is a pure color; it contains no black or white. It is the key part of a color that allows it to be identified as red, green, or blue.

❑ A *shade* is a hue with black added.

❑ A *tint* is a hue with white added.

❑ A *tone* is a hue with gray added.

❑ *Intensity* describes the intensity of a color, sometimes the terms *saturation* or *chromaticity* are used instead. In a hex code, for example, a blue with #0000FF would be an intense blue. Gray, meanwhile, has no identifiable hue, and is called *achromatic*.

You can see images that illustrate each of these color terms in the download code for this chapter (ch04_eg02.html); they will really help you understand these terms.

In order to specify these colors for the Web, you have seen that you can use hex codes. These indicate the amount of red, green, and blue required to make up that color. Before you turn it on, a computer screen is black. When you start to use your computer, however, color is created on the screen by emitting different amounts of red, green, and blue light.

You should be aware, however, that there are other ways to specify colors. For example, print designers usually specify colors using combinations of cyan, magenta, yellow, and black—often shortened to *CMYK*. (The *K* is used instead of black. If *B* were used for black people might think the **B** stood for blue.) Print designers specify colors this way because a plain sheet of paper is white (and it is white because it reflects all colors); then when you add cyan, magenta, or yellow ink to the page it subtracts from the light reflected, giving the paper color. Furthermore, black is present because cyan, magenta, and yellow together do not create black.

These two different ways of representing colors are known as *color spaces*. But why is this important? Consider the following:

❑ Most graphics programs will give you the option of preparing images in one of these two color spaces; you should prepare your graphics in RGB mode when creating work that will be displayed on screens and CMYK mode for print work.

❑ If you have worked in print, or moved from the Web to do a print job, you should be aware that CMYK has a smaller color space than RGB. Some of the colors in the RGB color space cannot be printed using CMYK because of the limitation of inks (your graphics program should indicate to you if a color cannot be printed).

Creating a Color Scheme

Now that you understand some of the key terms regarding color and how a color is specified, it is time to look at creating a color scheme—a selection of colors you will use in the design of your site. It is a good idea to start on this early on in the stages of planning your site because randomly selecting colors or just picking a few of your favorite colors will probably result in your site looking a lot less professional. Once you have decided upon your color scheme, it is then a lot easier to design the pages using those colors.

Your color scheme may be as simple as using black and white with one color to accent it. Or you may choose a complicated set of up to three to four colors to use with black and white. You should, however, avoid too many colors.

Some of the most popular color schemes are created by first choosing a key color and then selecting other colors based on their position in relation to the key color on the color wheel. For example, you might choose a color that is directly opposite your key color on the color wheel. The following descriptions of color schemes can give you a good idea of how to choose the colors for your site. To really see how the colors work together you need to look at the example code for this chapter (available as a download from www.wrox.com) as it will show you the actual colors (these are example ch04_eg03.html).

❑   A *monochromatic* color scheme uses one base color and then adds shades and tints of that color.

❑   An *analogous* color scheme selects colors adjacent to each other on the color wheel.

❑   A *complementary* color scheme uses colors on the opposite side of the wheel from one another. You should, however, avoid using one of these colors on top of the other.

❑   A *double complement* takes two sets of complementary colors.

❑   A *split complement* takes a color and the two colors adjacent to its complement.

❑   A *triadic* color scheme selects three colors from points of an equilateral triangle within a color wheel.

❑   An *alternate complement* adds another color from between two points of the triangle

If you are not given a set of colors to work with when creating a site, a good place to start is by picking a color scheme based upon the colors used in the logo. Another good backup is taking the main hues from any featured photographs or images used on the site. Failing that, open up the color wheels in the example code and spin them around until you find some colors you like.

If you want to find out the latest fashionable colors, fashion magazines and paint manufacturers' recent brochures tend to push the most popular colors of the day. However, choosing the latest "in" colors is not always a good solution for choosing brand colors because what is in fashion one day is out of fashion the next.

Contrast

Whichever colors you choose, you must ensure that there is sufficient contrast in the colors that readers can make out the text and images on your site. High contrast makes text easier to read. If there is not a lot of contrast between the text and background, users will struggle reading the text.

Black text on a white page is probably the most popular color scheme for documents we read each day; the contrast between them is high. If you look in the download folder for the code, you will see some examples of contrasting colors (ch04_eg04.html).

You should also be aware that your eyes can often play tricks on you when it comes to color; here are a couple points you need to be aware of:

❑   Complementary colors are sometimes known as *discordant colors* because they can play funny tricks on the eye, such as making one of the colors seem like it is moving. You should avoid using a discordant color on top of another one unless you are deliberately going after that effect. You can see an example of discordant colors in ch04_eg05.html with the download code for the chapter.

❑   A dark block of color with a slightly lighter block on top of it will make the lighter color seem lighter than it really is. You can see an example of this in ch04_eg06.html with the download code for the chapter.

Other Things That Affect Color

You should be warned that, once you have chosen your color scheme and come to look at the colors on a different screen or in a different program, you might find that the colors look very different. So, when you have decided upon your color scheme, it pays to test it out on a few different computers and in a few different programs to make sure you are still happy with it.

There are a lot of reasons why colors for a site will look different on one computer than the next:

❑   PCs and Macs have different gamma correction, which is a modification to the color saturation and brightness on your monitor. Hence, colors on Macs tend to appear lighter than they do on PCs.

❑   The color in LCD screens can vary when looked at from different angles, whereas CRT screens tend to have more even colors from different angles. Also, near-white colors can merge into each other more on CRT screens.

❑   Different software can render colors slightly differently.

So, don't be alarmed if your colors look slightly different in different situations, but if possible check your colors on a different setup to make sure they still work as you intended. (In particular, you may find grays, beiges, and greens look very different on a PC than on a Mac.) This does not mean you have to own different computers; you might be able to check them on a friend's computer or at your local library or Internet cafe.

Also, when creating your site and choosing colors in graphics programs, use the hex numbers you defined in your color scheme—do not just assume a color "looks right."

The Web Safe Color Palette

I should say a few words about something you may have heard of: the *Web safe color palette*. This is a selection of 216 colors that is sometimes said to be "safe" to use on the Web.

The Web safe color palette was actually devised back in 1994 for Netscape as a way to reduce problems of colors looking different on different systems. Back then a lot of computers used 8-bit technology, which (as you might remember from the introduction of hex codes) supports only 256 colors. Forty of those colors were reserved for use by the operating system, which meant that you had 216 colors left.

If a computer could not display a block of color it would try to recreate the color by having two alternating colors on pixels next to each other. This is a process known as *dithering*, and the resulting colors are not accurately replicated on different systems. Therefore, the 216 colors not used by the operating system became known as the Web safe color palette.

For a number of years it was suggested that Web designers pick their color schemes for Web sites from the 216 colors in this Web safe color palette. However, nowadays, statistics suggest that fewer than 5 percent of Web users still use 8-bit graphics cards, so you are quite safe to ignore this restriction.

When 16-bit graphics cards came along, they were the newest, greatest thing! However, these cards did not use a subset of the 24-bit true color palette. There are therefore slight differences in 194 of the supposed 216 "Web safe" colors. This resulted in some people claiming that there were only 22 truly Web safe colors that looked the same on each system. But such a restriction is extreme and is again safe to ignore.

In reality, the shift in colors will not affect your work too much, especially if you use blocks of colors. The only two pitfalls you really need to be aware of are:

❑ If the background color of your page will meet a flat area of color in a GIF image (for example the image features a flat orange—not textured—and your background is orange), some users might see a slight color shift between the two. It is better to make the GIF stretch the area you want to cover, or make a border.

❑ When designing a site, make sure that there is enough contrast between colors to make the text readable even if there is a slight shift in colors. For example, black against white is a good, safe contrast; yellow on orange is not, as already discussed in the *Contrast* section.

Final Words on Color

Color is a very powerful tool in the right hands, but can really turn visitors away when not given due care and attention.

What you have seen in this chapter simply scratches the surface of color theory, which in itself is a huge topic. You don't need to be an expert in color theory to make your site look good; you just need to think about color before you start designing the site.

If you have not been given a set of colors to work with, or you have been given only one color you need to work with (and told to use what other colors you like), take a look at those color wheels, which should prove a great help. And remember, you can always use different shades, tints, and tones of the colors you choose as accents. But try not to use every color in the rainbow and don't be afraid to ask your friend with the impeccable taste what he or she thinks of the colors before building your whole site in them.

Another interesting area of color that we do not have space to go into here is color psychology. Certain colors elicit different emotions, expectations, and reactions in your visitors. If you have found this section interesting, you will probably be fascinated to learn more about how we interpret colors.

Adding Images to Your Site

Images and graphics can really bring your site to life. In this section you will not only learn how to insert images and graphics into your pages, but also which image formats you can use and when you should choose which format.

You will see how careful you have to be when using images on the Web, as they can really slow down the speed of a site—and slow sites frustrate users. When you are writing a Web site and all of the images are on your computer, pages will appear to load very quickly. But as soon as you put your site on the Web, it will often slow down dramatically. So, choosing the right format for your images and saving them correctly will help make your site faster, and result in happier visitors. After all, even though many people access the Internet on fast connections there is still a large proportion of users who use dial-up modems.

For practice purposes, you can download images from other peoples sites by right-clicking the image (or Ctrl-clicking) and selecting either the download image to disk *or* save image as *options. Remember, however, that images are subject to copyright, and you could land yourself in legal trouble if you use other peoples' images on your site.*

Now that you've learned how to insert the right kind of images into your pages, you will then see how to turn them into links and even how to write code that divides them up so that when users click different parts of the image they get taken to different Web pages.

Types of Image Formats

To start off, you should look at how computers store and render pictures. There are two main ways in which graphics are created for computers:

❑ *Bitmapped graphics* divide a picture into a grid of pixels and specify the color of each pixel, rather like a computer tells a screen the color of each pixel. Broadly speaking, bitmaps are ideal for photographs and complicated graduations of shade and color. There are several different formats of bitmap; common ones include (the rather confusingly named) bitmap or BMP, JPEG, GIF, TIFF, and PNG. You will be learning more about JPEGs, GIFs, and PNGs later in the chapter.

❑ *Vector graphics* break the image into lines and shapes (like a wireframe drawing), and store the lines as coordinates. They then fill the spaces between the lines with color. Vector graphics are commonly used for line art, illustration, and animation. They often feature large areas of flat color (as opposed to textures, shades of colors, and photographic styles).

For a long time, bitmaps were the main image format for the Web, although more recently there are some formats on the Web that are making use of vector graphics, such as Flash and SVG.

Bitmap Images

Most static images on the Web will be bitmapped images. Browsers tend to support three common bitmap graphics formats, and most graphics programs will save images in these formats:

❑ **GIF:** Graphics Interchange format (pronounced either "gif" or "jif")

❑ **JPEG:** Joint Photographic Experts Group format (pronounced "jay peg")

❑ **PNG:** Portable Network Graphics (pronounced "ping" or "pee en gee")

We will take a quick look at each of these.

GIF Images

The GIF (or Graphics Interchange Format) used to be the standard for all Web graphics. GIF is an *indexed color format* that allows an image to select up to 256 colors from a range of over 16 million colors to recreate the picture; each pixel is one of these 256 colors. The file includes a lookup table and the pixels reference the detailed color information in the lookup table rather than each pixel having to specify this information. Figure 4-4 shows a GIF file and its color palette in Adobe Photoshop:

Figure 4-4

GIF images are particularly suited to images where there are large flat areas of color. A flat area of color is a section that is just one shade, for example a rectangle that is one green is a flat color whereas a picture of grass contains lots of different greens. The fewer colors the image uses, the smaller the GIF file is. A GIF containing less than 16 colors, also known as a 4-bit GIF, will take less than half the space of an 8-bit GIF using 256 colors. Therefore, if you are creating an image that uses less than 16 colors it is worth checking whether your program will automatically save your image as a 4-bit GIF because it would result in a smaller file that is quicker to download.

> *Note that if your text or lines are two colors (say black and white) and you have used anti-aliased edges to make them look smoother, your image will contain more than two colors because the edges use a variety of other colors to make them look smooth.*

Most graphics programs, when saving GIFs, will use a technique called *dithering* if they need to represent more than 256 colors. This means they use two or more colors in adjacent pixels to create an effect of a third color. Dithering has two drawbacks:

❑ It can result in some *banding* in colors that might appear flat to the eye in the original, but are actually very slightly different shades; this means that the colors that appeared the same color no longer have a smooth transition and changes in the shading become visible.

105

❑   If you place a flat color next to a dithered color you will be able to see where the change occurs (because the dithered color is really made up of more than one color).

Because GIFs support only 256 colors and have to use dithering to achieve any further colors, they are not really suitable for detailed photographs, which tend to contain more than 256 colors. If you have a photograph, gradient, or any image with similar shades of the same color next to each other, you are often better off using a JPEG, which can support unlimited colors, or sometimes a PNG—both of which you will meet shortly.

GIFs do have another handy feature: you can specify one color in a GIF to represent a *transparent background*—in parts of the image that are the specified color, the background will be allowed to show through. You should be aware, however, that each pixel is either on or off, opaque or transparent—there are not degrees of transparency, as there are in alpha-color transparency formats. This means that if you try to use it with curved corners, the corners may appear pixelated. To help overcome this problem you should try to make the transparency color as close to the background color as possible.

Figure 4-5 shows how a pixelated effect is created when a GIF is not created on a suitable background (notice the corners in particular).

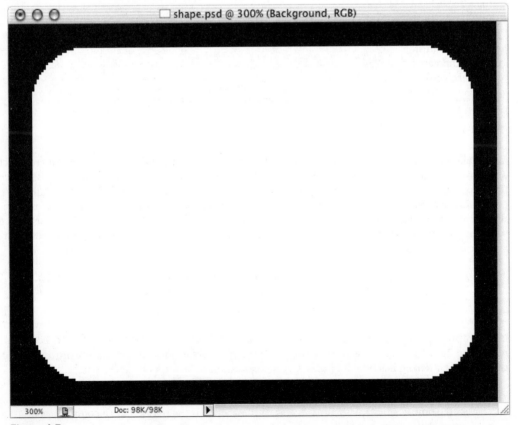

Figure 4-5

To make the GIF files smaller, they are compressed using a technique called *LZW compression* that scans rows of the image looking for consecutive pixels that share the same color, and when it comes across them it indicates that x number of pixels should be written from this point onwards using the same color.

LZW compression is known as a *lossless compression* technique because no data is lost and therefore there is no loss of quality (this is contrasted with *lossy compression* techniques where some of the data is discarded during compression and cannot therefore be recovered from the compressed file). However, when there are not many consecutive pixels of the same color, there is little saving in file size. This means that the format does not compress photographic images well because while the adjacent pixels may look the same in photographs, they tend to be very slightly different. Furthermore, if the picture uses complex dithering to achieve subtle coloring effects there is less chance of finding pixels of the same consecutive color, and therefore file size cannot be compressed.

Some programs will give you an option of saving the file as an *interlaced image*. *Interlacing* means that lines of the image are stored in a different order than they would appear in the image. This allows a browser to display every eighth row in turn and then fill in the lines between. The idea behind interlaced images was that, if you had a large file on a slow connection, the user would see something appearing early on, and the image would get progressively clearer. This can help users when the image is easily recognizable or for logos, but it is not ideal for images or text with a lot of detail. Interlaced GIFs are becoming less widely used on the Web as bandwidth rises.

Animated GIFs

GIF images can store more than one frame (or copy of the image) within a file, allowing the GIF to rotate between the versions/frames and create a simple animation. If you think of how a flip-book animation works, each page has some movement, and when a user flips the pages it looks like the images are moving. Compression for this technique is quite effective because only the changed pixels need storing with each frame, along with their positions.

> You should be very careful about the use of animated GIFs. A lot of sites offer animated GIFs, from cartoon characters doing something amusing to bouncing or flaming bullet points. Sure, they might be impressive or fun the first time you see a page, but they soon become tiresome, slow down the site, and distract users from the real content. While animated GIFs can be fun on a personal home page, you will not find such animations on the sites of large companies. If you are trying to create a professional looking site, you should use animated GIFs only if the animation gives additional information to the user.

JPEG Images

The JPEG image format was developed as a standard for storing and compressing images such as photographs with wide ranges of colors. When you save a JPEG, you can usually specify by how much, if at all, you want to compress an image—which depends upon the image quality you want. The process of compressing a JPEG involves discarding color data that people would not normally perceive, such as small color changes. However, because the image format discards this data when the image is compressed, some of the data is lost and the original cannot be recreated from a compressed version—hence it is known as *lossy compression*.

The amount of compression you apply will change from image to image, and you can judge how much to compress a JPEG by only by looking at it. Hence the size of the file varies depending upon how much you compress the image. When you are saving the image, you will often be asked for a percentage of quality to be used; 100 percent does not compress the picture at all, and around 60 percent is the most you can use for a photo (some programs use words such as excellent, very good, good, and so on instead).

A good image-editing program will allow you to compare the original image side by side with the compressed version as you choose how much compression to add. Figure 4-6 shows you how Adobe Photoshop lets you compare two versions of the image next to each other as you prepare to save the JPEG for the Web.

Figure 4-6

Because the JPEG format was designed to work with photo-realistic images, they do not work so well with images that have large amounts of flat color, or high-contrast hard edges (such as lettering and line drawings). As you increase compression in a JPEG you may also see banding start to show in colors that are very similar.

JPEG does support interlacing using the *Progressive JPEG*, allowing an initially blocky view of the image to download first, with greater detail being filled in as the rest of the image loads. The most helpful aspect of this is that it gives the user an idea of the size of the image that is being downloaded, and a rough idea of how complete it is. Because JPEGs tend to have a lot of detail, however, you often need a lot of the image to come through before you really get to see the intended picture.

PNG Images

The Portable Network Graphics format is the most recent format on the block. It was developed in the late 1990s because the company that owns the patent for GIFs (Unisys) decided to charge companies that developed software for creating and viewing GIFs a license fee to use the technology. While Web designers and Web surfers are not affected by this charge, the companies that make the software they use are.

The PNG format was designed for the same uses as GIF images, but while it was being created the designers decided to solve what they thought were some of the disadvantages with the GIF format. The result is two types of PNG. The 8-bit PNG has the same limitations as an 8-bit GIF—only 256 colors, and when transparency is used each pixel is either on or off. Then there is the enhanced PNG-24, a 24-bit version, which has the following advantages:

❑　The number of colors available for use in an image is not restricted, and so any color can be included without losing any data.

❑　A map (like the color map that indicates the color of each pixel in GIFs) is used to provide different levels of transparency for every pixel, which allows for softer, anti-aliased edges.

❑　The approach of sampling one in eight lines was replaced with a two-dimensional sample of pixels displaying a rough image using just $\frac{1}{64}$ of the file (whereas the GIF required $\frac{1}{8}$).

❑　PNG 24-bit files can contain gamma correction information to allow for slight differences in color between different monitors and platforms.

Furthermore, all PNGs tend to compress better than a GIF equivalent. The real drawback with the PNG format, however, is that support is limited. While the browser manufacturers introduced it into version 3 and 4 browsers, some of the more advanced features (such as transparency) still had problems in IE 5. As a result, most designers still use the GIF format.

Keeping File Sizes Small

You will often save the images for your site in the format that best compresses the image and therefore results in a smaller file size. This will not only make your pages quicker to load, but can also save you on the charges made for hosting your site.

Usually one or another format will be the obvious choice for you. The rule of thumb is:

❑　Use JPEGs for photo-realistic pictures with a lot of detail, or subtle shade differences you want to preserve.

❑　Use GIFs for images with flat color (rather than textured colors), and hard edges, such as diagrams, text, or logos.

You can also consider using PNGs if you do not need the advanced features such as transparency, or if you know the majority of your visitors will be using version 6 browsers.

If you look at the following images—one a photo of a forest, and the second, the logo of a fictional company called Color Wheels that uses only three colors—you can see the file size of each saved as a GIF and as a JPEG.

As you can see, the Color Wheels logo has areas of flat, plain color, whereas the photo of the forest uses lots of different shades. Therefore the logo is better suited to the GIF or PNG formats, while the photo of the forest with all its shadows is suited better to the JPEG format.

You should also make sure that your image resolution is no greater than 72 dots per inch (dpi) because this is the maximum resolution of computer monitors. While print designers usually work with images that are 300dpi, anything above 72 is not shown on computer screens.

Figure 4-7

Good image editing software is very helpful if you use a lot of images on your site. Adobe Photoshop is the most popular software used by professionals, although unfortunately it is very expensive. There is, however, a limited functionality version called Photoshop Elements that includes many of the common features—including the Save for Web options. Another popular image editing tool is Paint Shop Pro.

If you do have to include large complex photographic images on your site, it's good practice to offer users smaller versions first and then add a link to the larger version if it interests them. These smaller images are often referred to as *thumbnails*, and you will usually see them in image galleries or pages that contain summaries of information (such as the home pages of news sites and pages that list several products).

When creating the smaller version, scale the image down in an image-editing program; do not just alter the width *and* height *attributes of the* <img/> *or* <object> *elements you are about to meet or users will still have to download the full-sized image even though they are getting to see only a smaller version of it (which will take much longer to download). By creating a special thumbnail of any smaller images you use, your pages will load a lot quicker.*

Vector Images

Most illustration and animation software uses vector formats; for example, Macromedia Freehand and Adobe Illustrator both save images as vectors. As far as the Web goes, the champion of vector graphics is Macromedia Flash (which you will see on a lot of sites).

Because vector formats store information in terms of coordinates for lines and then colors inside those lines, it is very easy for vector formats to scale to different sizes. This has great potential for the Web, as it allows images to work with different resolution devices. Therefore you can expect to see an increasing adoption of vector image formats on the Web. Also, because vector technology is widely used for computer games, increasing amounts of work are being done on vector formats.

Browsers and XHTML do not, by default, support any vector graphics formats, although the main browsers now ship with the Macromedia Flash Player that is required to view Flash files, and as a result Flash is currently the most popular way of deploying vector graphics and animations on the Web. While the Macromedia Flash Player is free for download, and the browsers feature it, you should be aware that Macromedia charges for the software to create Flash files and doing so does require that you learn a whole new skill (which is outside the scope of this book).

As an alternative vector graphics format the W3C developed Scalable Vector Graphics (SVG), which (like XHTML) is written in XML, and means the two will be able to be integrated easily (furthermore it is an open standard, not the creation of an individual company like Macromedia Flash is). There are a number of tools that have recently emerged, and that are in development to support this format, and some of the latest browsers are supporting it, so you can expect it to grow significantly in the coming years.

Both Flash and SVG files tend to be included in pages using the more recent <object> element. (Indeed, the W3C would like to see all images included using this element in the long run, but for the moment images are more often added using the <img> element.)

Adding Images Using the <img> Element

Images are usually added to a site using the <img> element. It must also carry the src attribute indicating the source of the image and an alt attribute whose value is an alternate description for the image in case it does not load or the user has a visual impairment.

For example, the following line would add a logo to the page. In this case the image is in the same folder as the file, and is called logo.gif:

```
<img src="logo.gif" alt="Wrox logo" />
```

In addition to carrying all of the universal attributes and the UI event attributes, the <img> element can carry the following attributes

```
src alt align border height width hspace vspace ismap usemap longdesc name
```

The src Attribute

The src attribute is required to specify the URL of the image to load.

```
src="url"
```

The URL can be an absolute URL or a relative, just like the URLs when linking between pages that you met in Chapter 3, and use the same shorthand notations to indicate which folder an image is in.

It's a good idea to create a separate directory (or folder) in your Web site for images. If you have a very large site, with separate directories for each section, you can create an image folder for each section of the site.

> Generally speaking, images for your site should always reside on your server. It is not good practice to link to images on other sites because if the owner of the other site decides to move that image your users will no longer be able to see the image on your site.

The alt Attribute

The alt attribute is required to specify a text alternative for the image in case the browser cannot display the image (for any of a number of reasons). For example:

```
alt="Wrox logo"
```

Often referred to as *alt text*, the value of this attribute should really describe the image for users who cannot see it—either because the browser did not download the file correctly because the file cannot be found, or because the user has visual impairment that prevents him or her from seeing the image. The alt text should not just be the same as the filename. If you are using images for buttons then the button's alt text should usually be the same as what the button reads and describe what will happen if the user presses the button.

If your image is just used for layout and is not strictly visible (for example a block of color used to help position another element rather than something the user is supposed to see), then the `alt` attribute should still be used but given no value, as follows:

```
alt=""
```

The align Attribute (deprecated)

The `align` attribute is used to align the image within the page or the element that contains the image (such as a table cell).

```
align="right"
```

It can take one of the values in the table that follows.

Value	Purpose
top	The top of the image is aligned with top of the current line of text.
middle	The middle of the image is aligned with the current text baseline.
bottom	The bottom of the image is aligned with the baseline of the current line of text (the default), which usually results in images rising above the text.
left	The image is aligned to the left side of the containing window or element and any text flows around it.
right	The image is aligned to the right side of the containing window or element and any text flows around it.

You may come across the `absbottom`, `texttop`, `absmiddle`, and `baseline` values, but these are nonstandard extensions that can produce inconsistent results.

The border Attribute (deprecated)

The `border` attribute specifies the width of the border around the image in pixels:

```
border="2"
```

The default is value is 0, and if the attribute is not used there will not be a border unless the image is used as a link in which case you should specify `border="0"` (see the "Using Images as Links" section later in this chapter). This attribute has been replaced by the CSS `border` property.

The height and width Attributes

The height and width attributes specify the height and width of the image:

```
height="120" width="180"
```

The values can either be pixels as shown in the preceding code or a percentage of the page or containing element (in which case it will be followed with the percent sign).

Specifying the size of the image can help browsers lay out pages faster because they can allocate the correct amount of space to the image and continue to render the rest of the page before the image has finished loading.

If you want to scale an image, you can just provide the value for one of the attributes and the browser will maintain the correct ratio for the image (its width compared to the height). You can even distort images by providing a different width in relation to its height.

Figure 4-8 shows an image at its actual size (top: 100 pixels by 100 pixels), the image magnified (middle: the width attribute is given a value of 150 pixels), and the image distorted (bottom: the width attribute is given a value of 75 pixels and the height attribute a value of 125 pixels).

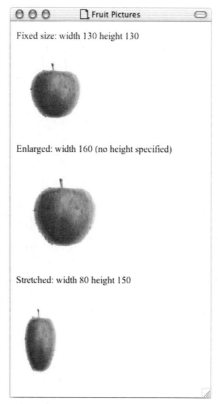

Figure 4-8

Here is the code for this example (ch04_eg07.html):

```
<p>Fixed size: width 130 height 130</p>
<img src="images/apple.jpg" alt="Photo of red apple" width="130"
height="130" />
<p>Enlarged: width 160 (no height specified)</p>
<img src="images/apple.jpg" alt="Photo of red apple" width="160" />
<p>Stretched: width 80 height 150</p>
<img src="images/apple.jpg" alt="Photo of red apple" width="80" height="150"/>
```

If you want to display the image a lot smaller than the original version rather than just specifying the smaller dimensions for the same image, you should resize the image in an image manipulation program to create the smaller version for use on the Web site. If you just reduce the size of the image using the height and width attributes the user will still have to download the full sized image, which will take longer than a special small version and use up more bandwidth.

The hspace and vspace Attributes (deprecated)

The hspace and vspace attributes are used to control the amount of whitespace around an image.

```
hspace="10"
vspace="14"
```

The value is the amount in pixels of whitespace that should be left around the image, and is like a white border. The hspace and vspace attributes are particularly helpful because text can flow around an image, and unless there is a gap between the text and the image, the text becomes hard to read and doesn't look as professional. Figure 4-9 illustrates this idea.

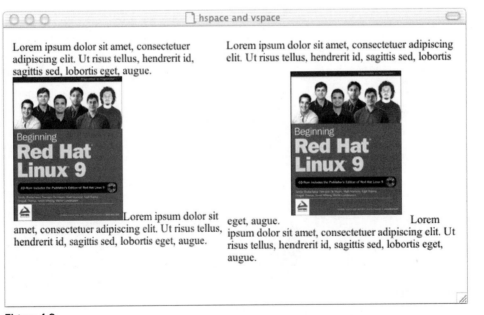

Figure 4-9

These attributes have been deprecated, and you can achieve the same result by using the border or margin properties in CSS.

The ismap and usemap Attributes

The ismap and usemap attributes are used with image maps. Image maps are covered in the "Image Maps" section later in the chapter.

The longdesc Attribute

The longdesc attribute is used to indicate the URL of a document containing a description for the image in more detail.

```
longdesc="../accessibility/profit_graphs.txt"
```

It is designed for users who cannot see the image, and for providing extra information that cannot be seen in the image. It would also be particularly helpful for providing explanations for things such as graphs and charts. Netscape 7 and IE 6 still do not support this attribute.

The name Attribute (deprecated)

The name attribute allows you to specify a name for the image so that it can then be referenced from script code. It is the predecessor to, and has been replaced by, the id attribute.

```
name="image_name"
```

Try It Out   Adding Images to a Document

In this example you're going to add some images to a document; they will be some brightly colored images of food accompanied by a description of each. So, open up your text editor or Web page authoring tool and follow these steps:

1. Start with the XML and DOCTYPE declarations and add the skeleton of the XHTML document, like so:

```
<?xml version="1.0" encoding="UTF-8"?>
  <!DOCTYPE html PUBLIC "-//W3C//DTD XHTML 1.0 Strict//EN"
     "http://www.w3.org/TR/xhtml1/DTD/xhtml1-strict.dtd">

<html xmlns="http://www.w3.org/1999/xhtml" lang="en">
<head>
  <title>Fruit Pictures</title>
</head>

<body>
</body>
</html>
```

2. Add the following to the body of the page. Pay particular attention to the <img> elements:

```
<h1>The Fruit Pictures Page</h1>
<p>The first image is an image of an apple.</p>
```

```
<img src="images/apple.jpg" alt="Photo of red apple" width="130" height=
"130" />
<p>The second image is an image of an orange cut in half.</p>
<img src="images/orange.jpg" alt="Photo of orange" width="130" height="130" />
<p>The third image shows a group of bananas.</p>
<img src="images/banana.jpg" alt="Photo of bananas" width="130" height="130"/>
```

3. Save the file as `fruit.html` and open it in your browser. You should end up with something that looks like Figure 4-10.

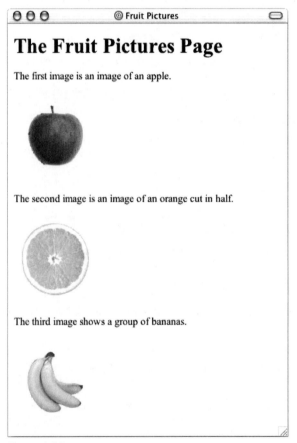

Figure 4-10

How It Works

You have met most of this code enough times already. But the parts to concentrate on are the `<img />` elements. Each `<img />` element adds a new image. There are three in the example.

```
<img src="images/apple.jpg" alt="Photo of red apple" width="130" height="130"
/>
```

The src attribute indicates the URL for the image. The URLs in this example are all relative URLs pointing to an images directory that is contained in the same directory as the example page. You might remember from Chapter 3 that I said that organizing your file structure was very important—you can here why this is the case.

The alt attribute should be used on every <img /> element you write. It will be shown if the browser cannot load the image and tells those who have vision impairments what the image is of.

The width and height attributes tell the browser how big the image should be displayed. By including these attributes the browser can lay out the page quicker because it can continue to display other items on the page without waiting for the image to download. While you can use these attributes to stretch or scale up an image, if you want to make the image smaller, you should save a new version of it rather than just using these attributes to save your viewers' time and bandwidth.

Adding Other Objects with the <object> Element

The W3C introduced the <object> element into HTML 4 with the intention that it be used to embed all media types into documents, not just graphics, but also MP3 files, Flash movies, QuickTime movies, JavaScript objects, Java applets, and so on. Note that, with formats that require a browser plug-in, you have to specify the program you expect to run files (for example the Macromedia Flash Player, Windows Media Player, the QuickTime Active X control, and so on).

The support for the <object> element in IE has been quite good for a while, except when it comes to including images, but Netscape really got up to speed only with the later releases of Netscape 6.1 (from late 2001 onwards).

The <object> element was initially introduced by Microsoft for support of their Active X technology (sometimes referred to as ActiveX plug-ins) so you may see older pages use it for this purpose.

Before the <object> element was introduced there was a range of elements browsers used to insert multimedia objects into pages, such as the <applet>, <embed> and <bgsound> elements, but these elements have been deprecated (they are covered in Chapter 13).

Because <object> elements often require an application such as a plug-in to be installed on the user's computer, you cannot be guaranteed every visitor to your site will be able to play the file. Furthermore, when it comes to large audio or movie files, you should give the visitor the option to download these large files (that can take a long time to download) if they want to. If you do not enable visitors to choose whether they download these files they will often leave a site.

The most common way of embedding moving graphics into Web pages without asking the user first is by using Macromedia Flash, which is not only installed on most computers but also uses vector graphics to create animations so it compresses them well (resulting in smaller file sizes). However, when Flash is used to add music to a page, it is widely considered good practice to offer a button to turn the music off.

If you are using Flash, you will most likely use the publishing tool (the Publish item on the File menu) to generate the code to insert a Flash movie into your page. Note, however, that Flash does not always generate XHTML code; it can use older HTML syntax, so you might need to add trailing slashes to the empty <param / > elements.

To embed an object into a page, you need to specify:

❑ The location of the code used to display or play the object (sometimes referred to as the *implementation* of the object)

❑ The actual data to be rendered

❑ Any additional values the object needs at run time

The first two are added using the `<object>` element while additional values are provided in the `<param>` element, which can be a child of the `<object>` element.

While the `<object>` element can contain a child `<param>` element, any other content of the `<object>` element should be displayed only if the browser cannot render the object:

```
<object>

Your browser does not appear to support the format used in this film clip,
for more details please look <a href="../help/video.htm">here</a>

</object>
```

You can nest `<object>` elements in order of preference in which they are viewed, so you can put an alternative format of object inside your preferred one. If neither is supported, the browser then displays the text content. To support older or different versions of browsers you might add older code, such as deprecated `<embed>` and `<applet>` elements inside the `<object>` element.

The *<object>* Element's Attributes

The `<object>` element can carry all of the universal attributes, the UI event attributes, and the following attributes:

```
archive border classid codebase codetype data declare height width hspace
vspace name standby tabindex usemap
```

The archive Attribute

The `archive` attribute is particularly of use with Java-based applications. It allows you to preload classes or collections of objects in an archive, for example when one class relies on others, and tends to be used to improve speed. The value should be one or more URLs to the resources in a space-separated list.

The border Attribute (deprecated)

The `border` attributes specifies the width of the border to appear around the object; the value is specified in pixels. You should use the `border` property in CSS instead.

The classid Attribute

The `classid` attribute is designed to specify the objects' implementation. When you are trying to include Flash or QuickTime files and a plug-in needs to be loaded, this value would indicate the application required to play or run the file. When you are working with Java, the value of this attribute is likely to be the Java class you want to include.

The value is supposed to be a URL according to the W3C, although IE for Windows tends to use it to store the registry key associated with that program, as shown here with a key for QuickTime movies:

```
classid="clsid:02BF25D5-8C17-4B23-BC80-D3488ABDDC6B"
```

A registry key is added to the registry whenever a new program is installed, and is a unique identifier for that program.

> Note that you should not go into the registry without backing it up first, and do not make any changes to values in there, or you might prevent your computer from working properly.

The codebase Attribute

The codebase attribute is supposed to give an alternative base URL for any relative URLs in the <object> element; otherwise the folder the page is in will be used. For example, if you were working with Java it might look like this:

```
codebase="http://www.example.org/javaclasses/"
```

However, when it comes to files such as QuickTime movies and Flash, IE uses it to specify where the program required to play or run the file can be found. For example, the QuickTime ActiveX control (required to play QuickTime movies) can be downloaded from here:

```
codebase="http://www.apple.com/qtactivex/qtplugin.cab"
```

It can also identify the version of the file that should be downloaded. If the object isn't installed on the machine loading the page, the browser should go to the URL specified to get it (although it will probably show users an alert first before starting to download).

The codetype Attribute

The codetype attribute specifies the MIME type expected by the browser. It is relevant only if a classid attribute has already been specified. For example, if you are working with Java, it might be:

```
codetype="application/java"
```

If you wanted to embed a QuickTime movie, you would use a value like this:

```
codetype="video/quicktime"
```

Browsers can use the codetype attribute to skip over unsupported media types without having to download unnecessary objects. Appendix H covers MIME types.

The declare Attribute

The declare attribute is used to declare an object without instantiating it. It could be used for forward references to objects, so they get loaded only if used, to create cross-references to other objects, or when you are using the object as a parameter within another object.

It is a Boolean attribute, and while it does not need a value in HTML, all attributes in XHTML require a value, so you would use:

```
declare="declare"
```

The data Attribute

If the object has a file to process or play, then the data attribute specifies the URL for that file. For example, here is a URL to an MP3:

```
data="http://www.example.com/mp3s/newsong.mp3"
```

The value can be a relative URL, which would be relative to the value provided in the codebase attribute if specified, otherwise relative to the page itself.

The height and width Attributes

The height and width attributes specify the height and width of an object. The values should be in pixels or a percentage of the containing element. It is treated just the like height and width attributes of the <img> element. The use of these attributes should make the page load faster because the browser can lay out the rest of the page without completely loading the object.

The hspace and vspace attributes (deprecated)

The hspace and vspace attributes specify the amount of whitespace that should appear around an object, just like when they are used with the <img> element. They have been replaced by the margin and border properties of CSS.

The name Attribute (deprecated)

The name attribute provides a name that can be used to refer to the object, in particular for use in scripts. It has been replaced by the id attribute in Strict XHTML.

The standby Attribute

The standby attribute specifies a text string that will be used when the object is loading.

```
standby="Trailer for Harry Potter 27 is loading"
```

The value should be a meaningful description of the object that is loading.

The tabindex Attribute

The tabindex attribute indicates the tab index of the object within a page. Tabbing order is discussed in Chapter 6.

The usemap Attribute

The usemap attribute indicates that the object is an image map containing defined areas that are hyperlinks. Its value is the map file used with the object. It can be a complete URL to an external file or a reference to the value of an inline <mapElement>'s mapName attribute. See the "Image Maps" section later in this chapter.

The <param> Element

The <param> element is the first thing inside an <object> element. It is used to specify the parameters that each object can take, and values for those parameters that are required at runtime.

For example, a QuickTime movie would accept a parameter with the name autoplay; this parameter would be used to indicate whether the movie should automatically start to play when the page loads, in which case the value could be true. Otherwise, if the user is expected to press a play button then the value specified would have to be false.

As well as the universal attributes and basic events, the <param> element can carry the following attributes:

```
name type value valuetype
```

The name and value Attributes

The name and value attributes act as a name/value pair (rather like attributes themselves). The name attribute provides a name for the parameter you are passing to the application, while the value gives the value of the parameter.

Here are a couple of examples, taken from a QuickTime movie. The first parameter indicates the source of the file being loaded to play, while the second indicates that the movie should start playing automatically as it is loading (without the user having to start it):

```
<param name="src" value="movieTrailer.movie" />
<param name="autoplay" value="true" />
```

If you were working with a Java applet, you could use the name and value attribute to pass values into a method.

The valuetype Attribute

If your object accepts parameters, then the valuetype attribute indicates whether the parameter will be a file, URL, or indeed another object. The table that follows shows the possible values.

Value	Purpose
data	The parameter value is a simple string—this is the default value.
ref	The parameter value is a URL
object	The parameter value is another object

The value Attribute

You do not need to specify a value attribute if you are just passing a string to an object as a parameter. However, if you are passing a URL or object, then you should use the value attribute. Its purpose is to tell the object the MIME type of the parameter it is being passed.

For example, you might want to specify that you were passing a Java object as a parameter, in which case you would use the value attribute like so:

```
value="application/java"
```

Using Images as Links

Images are often used to create graphical buttons or links to other pages. Turning an image into a link is as simple as placing the <img /> element inside an <a> element, like so:

```
<a href="../index.html" title="Click here to return to the home page">
<img src="images/banana.jpg" width="130" height="130" alt="Banana" border="0"
/></a>
```

Note the use of the deprecated border attribute. When you use an image inside an <a> element, the image will gain a border in IE for Windows, as shown in Figure 4-11.

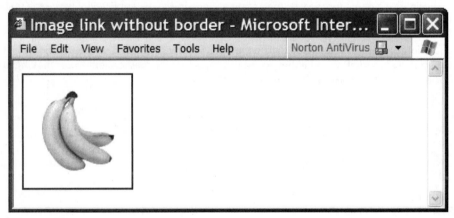

Figure 4-11

This border can be quite unsightly, so you either specify that the border should be 0 pixels wide, or set the border property of CSS for <img /> elements to be 0 (which you will learn how to do in Chapter 8).

This will also work when you want to include images using the <object> element, but not necessarily when you use the <object> element to include other objects, such as a Flash movie.

Putting a Flash movie inside <a> elements will rarely turn it into links. If you want a Flash movie to act as a link, you must put the link in the Flash file instead. A popular way of doing this to add a transparent layer as a button over the whole movie and use this to link to your chosen destination.

Image Maps

Image maps allow you to specify different areas of an image in your code, so that when users click different parts of the image, they get taken to different pages.

There are two types of image map:

❑   Server-side image maps

❑   Client side image maps

The difference between the two is how it is decided which link you should be taken to. With client-side image maps, the browser indicates which page you should be taken to based upon where the user clicks, whereas with server-side image maps the browser sends the server coordinates of where the user clicked and these are processed by a script file on the server that determines which page the user should be sent to.

Figure 4-12 shows a GIF that you will see turned into an image map. When users click the circle, they see what is on in the gallery; when they click the garden, they see the pages about the sculpture garden, and when they click the studios they see a page about the studios. Each of these sections is known as a clickable *hotspot*.

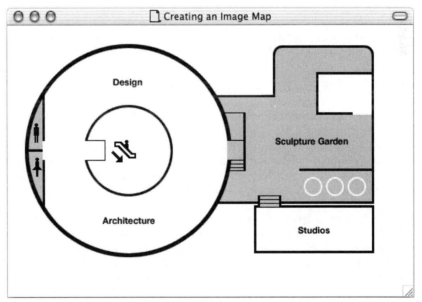

Figure 4-12

Image maps are particularly helpful when the image needs to be divided up in irregular shapes, such as maps. However, if the image can be divided up in a grid you might be better off chopping up an image manually and putting it together in a table, as you will see in Chapter 5.

These hotspots should not be too small; otherwise users might have difficulty in selecting the correct area they want. Users will soon get frustrated and leave your site if they click the wrong links on an image map.

While image maps are often the only way to turn irregular shaped images into links, you are far better off putting images in a table if your image can be divided into a grid. Image maps can also be difficult for people with motor control difficulties to navigate, so if for any reason you use image maps as the main method of navigation for your site you should offer text links at the bottom of the page (and indicate this in the alt text).

Server-Side Image Maps

With server-side images, the <img> element (inside an <a> element) carries a special ismap attribute, which tells the browser to send the server x, y coordinates representing where the user's mouse was when he or she clicked the image map. Then a script on the server is used to determine which page the user should be sent to based on the coordinates fed to it.

For example, look at the following link, where the <img> element carries the ismap attribute with a value of ismap (this is another attribute that did not require a value in HTML, and therefore uses its own name as a value in XHTML to make the attribute valid):

```
<a href="../location/map.asp"><img src="../images/states.gif" alt="map
of US States" border="0" ismap="ismap" /></a>
```

Now, if the user clicks the image 50 pixels to the right of the top-left corner of the image and 75 pixels down from the that same corner, the browser will send this information with the URL like so:

```
http://www.example.org/location/map.asp?50,75
```

You can see the coordinates appended at the end of the URL that is specified in the <a> element.

The thing about a server-side image map is that there needs to be a script, map file, or application on the server that can process the coordinates and know which page the user should then be sent to. The implementation of image maps will vary depending on what kind of server you are running on (whether it is a Windows server, or one of the many flavors of UNIX).

Because server-side image maps are processed on the server, the implementation of them is not covered by HTML or XHTML recommendations, and unfortunately there is not space to cover different possible implementations for each different platform here. If you want to learn about server-side image maps you should pick up a book that covers server-side scripting, such as a book on ASP, PHP, CGI, or JSP (which are discussed in Chapter 16). See the book list at Wrox.com for a list of books on topics such as these.

Client-Side Image Maps

Because server-side image maps rely on server technology, an alternative for the browser was introduced and client-side image maps were born. Client-side image maps use code within the HTML or XHTML page to indicate which parts of the image should link to which pages. Because the code that divides up the sections of the image is on the browser, it is possible for the browser to offer extra information to users either by showing them a URL in the status bar or as tooltip when the mouse is hovered over the image.

There are two methods of creating a client-side image map, using the <map> and <area> elements inside an <img> element, and more recently, using the <map> element inside the <object> element.

Client-Side Image Maps Using <map> and <area>

This earlier method of creating image maps has been supported for longer in browsers, going back to Netscape 4 and IE 4.

The image that is going to form the map is inserted into the page using the <img /> element as normal, except it carries an extra attribute called usemap. The value of the usemap attribute is the value of the name attribute on the <map> element, which you are about to meet, preceded by a pound or hash sign.

The <map> element actually creates the map for the image and usually follows directly after the <img /> element. It acts as a container for the <area> elements that actually define the clickable hotspots. The <map> element carries only one attribute, the name attribute, which is the name that identifies the map. This is how the <img /> element knows which <map> element to use.

The <area> element specifies the shape and the coordinates that define the boundaries of each clickable hotspot. Here's an example from the image map that was used for the image in Figure 4-12.

```
<img src="gallery_map.gif" alt="Gallery Map" width="500" height="300"
border="0" usemap="#gallery" />

<map name="gallery">
  <area shape="circle" coords="154,150,59" href="foyer.html" target="_self"
    alt="Foyer" >
  <area shape="poly" coords="272,79,351,79,351,15,486,15,486,218,272,218,292,
    166,292,136,270,76" href="sculpture_garden.html" target="_self"
    alt="Sculpture garden" />
  <area shape="rect" coords="325,224,488,286" href="workshop.html"
    target="_self" alt="Artists workshops" />
</map>
```

As you can see, the value of the usemap attribute on the <img /> element is #gallery, and this is used on the <map> element. Then the <area> elements actually define the sections of the image that are clickable.

If you have two areas that overlap each other, the first one in the code will take precedence.

The attributes that the <area> element can carry may look familiar from the <a> element. The ones that are relevant to image maps are covered here; otherwise see the "Adding Images Using the <img /> Element" section earlier in this chapter.

```
accesskey alt shape coords href nohref target tabindex taborder notab
```

The shape Attribute

The value of the shape attribute actually affects how the browser will use the coordinates specified in the coords attribute, and is therefore required. If you do not specify a shape attribute, IE usually assumes the area is a rectangle.

The table that follows shows the possible values of the shape attribute.

Value	Shape Created
default	The whole of the image not defined in an area (should be specified last)
rectangle or rect	Rectangle
polygon or poly	Polygon
circle or circ	Circle

You are better off using the abbreviated versions of the values as they are better supported in older browsers. The value default should be used last if you want to indicate any sections of the image not otherwise indicated by an <area> element—it's like a catch-all for the rest of the image.

The coords Attribute

The coords attribute specifies the area that is the clickable hotspot. The number of coordinates you specify depends on the shape you are creating (and have specified in the shape attribute).

❑ A rectangle contains four coordinates. The first two coordinates represent the top left of the rectangle, and the second two the bottom right.

❑ A circle contains three coordinates; the first two are the center of the circle, while the third is the radius in pixels.

❑ A polygon contains two coordinates for each point of the polygon. So a triangle would contain six coordinates, a pentagon would contain ten, and so on. You do not need to specify the first coordinate at the end again because the shape is automatically closed.

Some Web authoring and image editing programs will help work out the coordinates of an image map for you; they provide a tool that allows you to select the areas you want to turn into a map and use those shapes to create the coordinates for you. Figure 4-13 shows you Dreamweaver's Image Map tool—because each program is different, you should look in the help files for that program to see how yours creates an image map.

The href and nohref Attributes

The href attribute works just like the href attribute for an <a> element. Its value is the URL of the page you want to load when the user clicks that part of the image.

If you do not have an href attribute, you must use a nohref attribute indicating that the area will not take you anywhere.

The alt Attribute

The alt attribute specifies a text alternative for that section of the image and works just like the alt attribute on the <img /> element. It will actually override the alt text specified for the image when the user rolls over the area.

The target Attribute

The target attribute specifies which frame or window the page should be loaded into. Possible values are the same as for the target attribute of the <a> element.

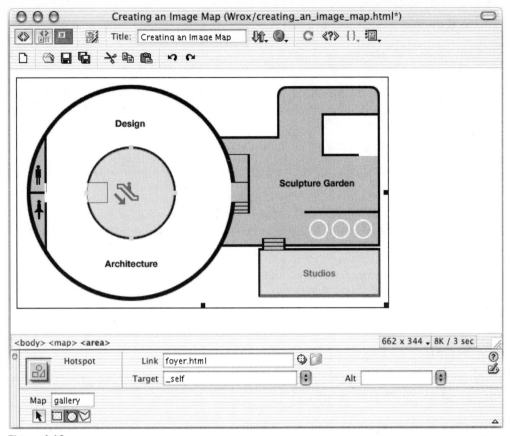

Figure 4-13

The tabindex Attributes

The tabindex attribute allows you to specify the order in which users can tab through items on a page. The value is a number between 1 and 32767. It is discussed in full in Chapter 7.

Client-Side Image Maps Using the \<object> Element

HTML 4 started to promote the use of the \<object> element rather than the \<map> element for adding image maps to your documents (although you can still use the \<map> element in Strict XHTML 1.0). The \<object> element takes a different approach to creating image maps.

It is the \<object> element that carries the usemap attribute (whose value is the value of the name attribute on the \<map> element preceded by the pound or hash sign). Inside the \<object> element you use the familiar \<map> element with the name attribute. But inside the \<map> element are standard \<a> elements.

The presence of the \<a> element in this context helps explain why it can carry attributes such as shape and coords.

```
<object data="gallery_map.gif" type="image/gif" alt="Gallery Map" width="500"
    height="300" border="0" usemap="#gallery" />

<map name="gallery">
  <a shape="circle" coords="154,150,59" href="foyer.html" target="_self">
Foyer</a>
  <a shape="poly" coords="272,79,351,79,351,15,486,15,486,218,272,218,292,166,
    292,136,270,76" href="sculpture_garden.html" target="_self">Sculpture
garden
    </a>
  <a shape="rect" coords="325,224,488,286" href="workshop.html"
target="_self">
    Artists workshops</a>
</map>
```

Rather than using `alt` attributes, you should put alt text (or a description of the link) inside the <a> element.

Unfortunately the support for this way of creating image maps is rather poor, so you are better off sticking to the old method for the moment.

Summary

In this chapter you have learned how to make your pages look a lot more exciting by adding color, images, and other multimedia objects.

First you saw how colors are specified in Web pages, using either color names or hexadecimal codes. While the hexadecimal codes can take a little getting used to, you can always use a reference to help you find the colors you want.

You then learned all about the different types of images used on the Web. While images add life to a page, you have to be careful with their sizes. If you have too many images or your images are too large they will slow down your site significantly. You therefore have to choose the format that will compress your image the best while retaining its quality. The GIF format is the format of choice for images with flat colors, while JPEGs are better for photographic images and graphics with gradients of the same color. Investing in good image-editing software that allows you to save images in these formats is a good idea if you use a lot of images on your pages.

While the < img /> element is the most common way of including an image in your document today, you also saw the <object> element which is going to be used more in the future. The <object> element is already widely used for embedding other types of files and code into your pages, from Flash or QuickTime movies to Java applets and JavaScript objects.

Finally, you saw how to divide up an image into clickable hotspots that turn different parts of the image into separate links. Another way of creating separate links in the one image is by chopping it up and putting the separate sections into different cells of a table; you'll learn about tables in Chapter 5.

Exercises

The answers to all of the exercises are given in Appendix A.

1. Add the images that describe a shade, a tint, and a tone to the following example. All of the images are provided in the images folder in the download code for Chapter 4.

```
<h1>Color Definitions and Examples</h1>
<p>A <b>hue</b> is a pure color; it contains no black or white. It is the key
part of a color that allows it to be identified as red, green or blue.</p>
<img src="images/hue.gif" alt="Color sample for hues" />
<p>A <b>shade</b> is a hue with black added</p>
   Add shade1.gif here
<br />
<p>A <b>tint</b> is a hue with white added</p>
   Add tint1.gif here
<p>A <b>tone</b> is a hue with gray added</p>
   Add tone1.gif here
```

Your finished page should look like Figure 4-14.

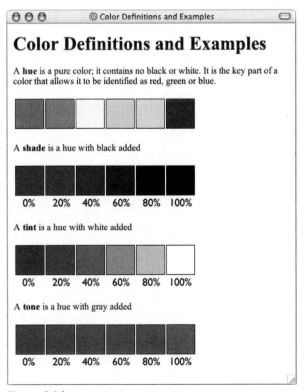

Figure 4-14

2. Look at the four images shown in Figure 4-15 and decide whether you are more likely to get smaller file sizes if you save them as JPEGs or GIFs.

Figure 4-15

Tables

In this chapter you learn how to put data into tables. As you will see, tables are used for a lot more than just displaying tabular data such as timetables, financial reports, or results from experiments. Web designers commonly use tables to format whole pages and create visually attractive layouts like those you might expect to see in a magazine.

This chapter begins with a discussion of the basic elements that are used to create all tables. Then I introduce some of the more advanced features of tables such as captions, headings, and more complicated table layouts. You will also learn about some formatting markup used with tables because, even though it is preferable to use CSS for presenting documents, you will sometimes need to resort to mixing style and content so that viewers with older browsers can view your documents. The chapter ends with a discussion of accessibility issues that relate to tables because they can have a serious effect particularly for users with visual impairments.

Introducing Tables

In order to work with tables, you need to start thinking in *grids*. Tables, just like spreadsheets, are made up of rows and columns, as shown in Figure 5-1.

Here you can see a grid of rectangles. Each rectangle is known as a *cell*. A *row* is made up of a set of cells on the same line from left to right, while a *column* is made up of a line of cells going from top to bottom.

By now you have understand that the names of elements in XHTML tend to refer to the type of markup they contain. So, you will hardly be surprised to know that you create a table in XHTML using the `<table>` element.

Inside the `<table>` element the table is written out row by row. A row is contained inside a `<tr>` element—which stands for *table row*. And each cell is then written inside the row element using a `<td>` element—which stands for *table data*.

Here is an example of a very basic table (ch05_eg01.html):

```
<table border="1">
  <tr>
```

```
      <td>Row 1, Column 1</td>
      <td>Row 1, Column 2</td>
   </tr>
   <tr>
      <td>Row 2, Column 1</td>
      <td>Row 2, Column 2</td>
   </tr>
 </table>
```

	Rows			
Column 1 Row 1	Column 2 Row 1	Column 3 Row 1	Column 4 Row 1	Column 5 Row 1
Column 1 Row 2	Column 2 Row 2	Column 3 Row 2	Column 4 Row 2	Column 5 Row 2
Column 1 Row 3	Column 2 Row 3	Column 3 Row 3	Column 4 Row 3	Column 5 Row 3
Column 1 Row 4	Column 2 Row 4	Column 3 Row 4	Column 4 Row 4	Column 5 Row 4
Column 1 Row 5	Column 2 Row 5	Column 3 Row 5	Column 4 Row 5	Column 5 Row 5

Columns

Figure 5-1

I always carefully indent table code so that it is easier to see the structure of the table, and start each row and cell on a new line. While this is just personal preference, leaving off just one ending tag or angle bracket in a table can prevent a whole table being displayed properly, and indenting helps you keep track of where you are when you come to look at the code (especially when you come to look at complicated nested tables later in the chapter).

This will look very basic in a Web browser, but gives you the idea of how a table is formed. You can see the result in Figure 5-2.

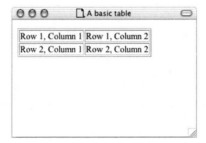

Figure 5-2

This is the basic structure that all tables will follow, although there are additional elements and attributes that allow you to control the presentation of tables.

Table headings have their own element, <th>, which is used in place of the table data or <td> element. The <th> element can be used for either column or row headers.

> Each cell must, however, have either a **<td>** or a **<th>** element in order for the table to display correctly even if that element is empty.

Here you can see a slightly more complex example of a table, which includes headings (ch05_eg02.html):

```
<table border="1">

  <tr>
    <th></th>
    <th>Outgoings ($)</th>
    <th>Receipts ($)</th>
    <th>Profit ($)</th>
  </tr>

  <tr>
    <th>Quarter 1 (Jan-Mar)</th>
    <td>11200.00</td>
    <td>21800.00</td>
    <td><b>10600.00</b></td>
  </tr>

  <tr>
    <th>Quarter 2 (Apr-Jun)</th>
    <td>11700.00</td>
    <td>22500.00</td>
    <td><b>10800.00</b></td>
  </tr>

  <tr>
    <th>Quarter 3 (Jul - Sep)</th>
    <td>11650.00</td>
    <td>22100.00</td>
    <td><b>10450.00</b></td>
  </tr>

  <tr>
    <th>Quarter 4 (Oct - Dec)</th>
    <td>11850.00</td>
    <td>22900.00</td>
    <td><b>11050.00</b></td>
  </tr>
</table>
```

As you can see, tables can take up a lot of space and make a document longer, but clear formatting of tables makes it much easier to see what is going on in your code, and no matter how familiar the code looks when you write it, you will be glad that you made good use of structure when you come back to it a year later.

In this example, the table shows a financial summary for a small company. Along the top in the first row you can see that there are headings for incomings, outgoings, and profit. The first cell is actually empty, but you must still add either a `<td>` or `<th>` element for it in the code; otherwise the first row would have less cells than all the others and the alignment of the columns would not match up as intended.

In each row, the first table cell is also a table heading cell (`<th>`) that indicates which quarter the results are for. Then the remaining three cells of each row contain table data, and are therefore contained inside the `<td>` elements. By default, most browsers render the content of a `<th>` element in bold text.

The figures showing the profit are also contained within a `<b>` element to display the profit figures in a bold typeface. This shows how any cell can, in fact, contain all manner of markup. The only constraint on placing markup inside a table is that it must nest within the table cell element (be that a `<td>` or a `<th>` element). You cannot have an opening tag for an element inside a table cell and a closing tag outside that cell—or vice versa.

Figure 5-3 shows what this table looks like in a Web browser.

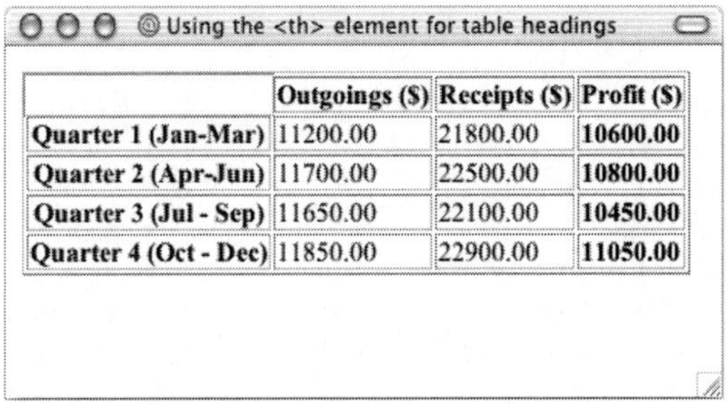

	Outgoings ($)	Receipts ($)	Profit ($)
Quarter 1 (Jan–Mar)	11200.00	21800.00	**10600.00**
Quarter 2 (Apr–Jun)	11700.00	22500.00	**10800.00**
Quarter 3 (Jul – Sep)	11650.00	22100.00	**10450.00**
Quarter 4 (Oct – Dec)	11850.00	22900.00	**11050.00**

Figure 5-3

It is worth noting that a lot of people, when creating tables, do not actually bother with the `<th>` element, and instead use the `<td>` element for every cell—including headers. However, it can help accessibility, and given that the element is there for a purpose, it is a good idea to use it. It can also help you present those cells differently when you style the table using CSS.

Basic Table Elements and Attributes

Now that you've seen how basic tables work, this section describes the elements in a little more detail, introducing the attributes they can carry. With these attributes, you can create more sophisticated table layouts.

The *<table>* Element Creates a Table

The `<table>` element is the containing element for all tables. It can carry the following attributes:

❑   All of the universal attributes

❑   Basic event attributes for scripting

The `<table>` element can carry the following deprecated attributes. Even though they are deprecated, you will still see many of them in use today:

```
align bgcolor border cellpadding cellspacing dir frame rules summary width
```

The align Attribute (deprecated)

Although it is deprecated, the `align` attribute is still frequently used with tables. When used with the `<table>` element, it indicates whether the table should be aligned to the `left` (the default), `right`, or `center` of the page. (When used with cells, as you will see shortly, it aligns the content of that cell.) The syntax is:

```
align="center"
```

If the table is contained within another element, then the `align` attribute will indicate whether the table should be aligned to the left, right, or center of that element.

If the table is aligned, text should flow around it. For example, here is a left-aligned table that is followed by some text (`ch05_eg03.html`):

```
<table border="1" align="left">
  <tr>
    <td>Row 1, Column 1</td>
    <td>Row 1, Column 2</td>
  </tr>
  <tr>
    <td>Row 2, Column 1</td>
    <td>Row 2, Column 2</td>
  </tr>
</table>
Lorem ipsum dolor sit amet, consectetuer adipiscing elit...
```

The text should flow around the table, as shown with the first table in Figure 5-4.

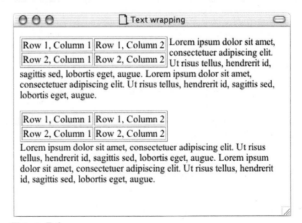

Figure 5-4

To prevent this flow you should place a line break after the table using the `clear` attribute (`<br clear="left" />`), which you can see in the second table of Figure 5-4.

```
</table>
<br clear="left" />
Lorem ipsum dolor sit amet, consectetuer adipiscing elit...
```

The clear attribute indicates how the browser should display the next line after the line break. With the value of left the text can begin only when there is nothing positioned on the left margin of the browser window (or if it were in a containing element, when nothing is positioned on the left margin of that element). The values clear attribute can take are all, left, right, or none; clear was covered in more detail in Chapter 2.

The bgcolor Attribute (deprecated)

The bgcolor attribute sets the background color for the table. The value of this attribute should be either a hex code or color name, as discussed in Chapter 4.

```
bgcolor="#rrggbb"
```

The border Attribute (deprecated)

If you use the border attribute, a border will be created around both the table and each individual cell. The value for this attribute is the width you want the outside border of the table to be in pixels. If you give this attribute a value of 0, or if you do not use this attribute, then you should not get any borders on either the table or any cells.

```
border="0"
```

> While this attribute is deprecated, it has been used in several of the examples in this chapter so that you can clearly see where the edge of each table cell is.

The cellpadding Attribute (deprecated)

The cellpadding attribute is used to create a gap between the edges of a cell and its contents. The value for this attribute can either be the amount of space or padding you want inside each wall of the cell in pixels or a percentage value (as a percentage of the width of the table).

As you can imagine, if two cells both contain writing, and there is no gap between the edge of the cells and the writing, the contents can become hard to read.

```
cellpadding="5" or cellpadding="2%"
```

The cellspacing Attribute (deprecated)

The cellspacing attribute is used to create a space between the borders of each cell. The value for this attribute can either be the amount of space you want to create between the cells in pixels or a percentage value (as a percentage of the width of the table).

```
cellspacing="6" or cellspacing="2%"
```

The dir Attribute

The `dir` attribute is supposed to indicate the direction of text that is used in the table. Possible values are `ltr` for left to right text and `rtl` for right to left (for languages such as Hebrew and Arabic).

```
dir="rtl"
```

If you use the `dir` attribute with a value of `rtl` on the `<table>` element, then the cells appear from the right first and each consecutive cell is placed to the left of that one.

The frame Attribute (deprecated)

The `frame` attribute is supposed to control the appearance of the outermost border of the whole table, referred to here as its *frame*, with greater control than the `border` attribute. If both the `frame` and `border` attributes are used, the `frame` attribute takes precedence. The syntax is:

```
frame="frameType"
```

The following table shows the possible values for *frametype*.

Value	Purpose
void	No outer border (the default)
above	A border on top only
below	A border on bottom only
hsides	A border on top and bottom
lhs	A border on left side of table
rhs	A border on right side of table
vsides	A border on left and right sides of table
box	A border on all sides
border	A border on all sides

Support for the `frame` attribute in Netscape 7 and IE 6 is not perfect, and better results can be achieved using CSS.

The rules Attribute (deprecated)

The `rules` attribute is used to indicate which inner borders of the table should be displayed, such as rows and columns. Here is the syntax; the default value is `none`.

```
rules="ruleType"
```

The following table shows the possible values for `ruleType`.

Value	Purpose
none	No inner borders (the default)
groups	Displays inner borders between all table groups (groups are created by the `<thead>`, `<tbody>`, `<tfoot>`, and `<colgroup>` elements)
rows	Displays horizontal borders between each row
cols	Displays vertical borders between each column
all	Displays horizontal and vertical borders between each row and column

Again, support in Netscape 7 and IE 6 is not perfect, and better results can be achieved using CSS.

The summary Attribute

The `summary` attribute is supposed to provide a summary of the table's purpose and structure for non-visual browsers such as speech browsers or Braille browsers. The value of this attribute is not rendered in Netscape or IE, but you should include it in your pages for accessibility purposes.

```
summary="Table shows the operating profit for the last four quarters. The
first column indicates the quarter, the second indicates outgoings, the
third indicates receipts, and the fourth indicates profit."
```

The width Attribute (deprecated)

The `width` attribute is used to specify the width of the table in pixels, or as a percentage of the available space. When the table is not nested inside another element, the available space is the width of the screen; otherwise the available space is the width of the containing element.

```
width="500" or width="90%"
```

There are also several browser-specific extensions to the `<table>` element covered in Chapter 8.

The <tr> Element Contains Table Rows

The `<tr>` element is used to contain each row in a table. Anything appearing within a `<tr>` element should appear on the same row. It can carry five attributes, four of which have been deprecated in favor of using CSS.

The align Attribute (deprecated)

The `align` attribute specifies the position of the content of all of the cells in the row.

```
align="alignment"
```

The table that follows lists the possible values for the `align` attribute.

Value	Purpose
left	Content is left-aligned.
right	Content is right-aligned.
center	Content is centered horizontally within the cell.
justify	Text within the cell is justified to fill the cell.
char	Cell contents are aligned horizontally around the first instance of a specific character (for example numbers could be aligned around the first instance of a decimal point).

By default, any `<td>` cells are usually left-aligned, while any `<th>` cells are usually centered. Unfortunately, only Netscape 6+ supports justified text, and neither IE nor Netscape supports the value `char`.

The bgcolor Attribute (deprecated)

The `bgcolor` attribute sets the background color for the row. The value of this attribute should be either a hex code or color value as discussed in Chapter 4.

```
bgcolor="#rrggbb"
```

The `bgcolor` attribute is commonly used on the `<tr>` element to shade alternate rows of a table different colors, therefore making it easier to read across each row.

The char Attribute

The `char` attribute is used to specify that the contents of each cell within the row will be aligned around the first instance of a particular character known as an *axis character*. The default character for this attribute in HTML was the decimal place, and the idea is that decimal figures would be aligned by the decimal point like so:

```
13412.22
  232.147
2449.6331
    2.12
```

The syntax is as follows:

```
char="."
```

Unfortunately, this potentially very helpful attribute is not supported at the time of writing, and there is no requirement for browsers to support it.

The charoff Attribute

The `charoff` attribute's name is an abbreviation of its purpose, to indicate a character offset. It is designed to indicate where characters that are aligned using the `char` attribute should be positioned in terms of either the number of characters used as the offset or a percentage of the length of the text. If this attribute is omitted, the default behavior is to make the offset the equivalent of the longest amount of text content that appeared before the character specified in the `char` attribute.

```
charoff="5"
```

Unfortunately, this attribute is not supported at the time of writing, and there is no requirement for browsers to support it.

The valign Attribute (deprecated)

The `valign` attribute specifies the vertical alignment of the contents of each cell in the row. The syntax is as follows:

```
valign="verticalPosition"
```

The table that follows shows the possible values of *verticalPosition*:

Value	Purpose
top	Aligns content with the top of the cell
middle	(Vertically) aligns content in the center of a cell
bottom	Aligns content with the bottom of the cell
baseline	Aligns content so that the first line of text in each cell starts on the same horizontal line

The <td> and <th> Elements Represent Table Cells

Every cell in a table will be represented by either a `<td>` element for cells containing table data or a `<th>` element for cells containing table headings.

By default the contents of a `<th>` element are usually displayed in a bold font, horizontally aligned in the center of the cell. The content of a `<td>` element, meanwhile, will usually be displayed left-aligned and not in bold (unless otherwise indicated by CSS or another element).

The `<td>` and `<th>` elements can both carry the same set of attributes, each of which applies just to that cell. Any effect these attributes have will override settings for the table as a whole or any containing element (such as a row).

In addition to the universal attributes and the basic event attributes, the `<td>` and `<th>` elements can also carry the following attributes:

```
abbr     align    axis     bgcolor   char      charoff   colspan   headers
height   nowrap   rowspan   scope     valign    widthThe  abbr      Attribute
```

The `abbr` attribute is used to provide an abbreviated version of the cell's content. If a browser with a small screen is being used to view the page, the content of this attribute could be displayed instead of the full content of the cell.

```
abbr="description of services"
```

While the major browsers do not currently support this attribute, it's likely to become more widely used by the increasing number of devices with small screens accessing the Internet.

The align Attribute (deprecated)

The `align` attribute sets the horizontal alignment for the content of the cell.

```
align="alignment"
```

The possible values for the `align` attribute are `left`, `right`, `center`, `justify`, and `char`, each of which was described in the "The align Attribute" subsection within the "The <tr> Element Contains Table Rows" section earlier in the chapter.

The axis Attribute

The `axis` attribute allows you to add conceptual categories to cells, and therefore represent n-dimensional data. The value of this attribute would be a comma-separated list of names for each category the cell belonged to.

```
axis="heavy, old, valuable"
```

Rather than having a visual formatting effect, this attribute allows you to preserve data, which then may be used programmatically, such as querying for all cells belonging to a certain category.

The bgcolor Attribute (deprecated)

The `bgcolor` attribute sets the background color for the cell. The value of this attribute should be either a hex code or a color name, as discussed in Chapter 4.

```
bgcolor="#rrggbb"
```

The char Attribute

The `char` attribute specifies a character, the first instance of which should be used to horizontally align the contents of a cell. (See the full description in the "The char Attribute" subsection within the "The <tr> Element Contains Table Rows" section earlier in the chapter.)

The charoff Attribute

The `charoff` attribute specifies the number of offset characters that can be displayed before the character specified as the value of the `char` attribute. (See the full description in the "The charoff Attribute" subsection within the "The <tr> Element Contains Table Rows" section earlier in the chapter.)

The colspan Attribute

The `colspan` attribute is used to specify how many columns of the table a cell will span across. The value of the `colspan` attribute is the number of columns the cell stretches across. (See the section "Spanning Columns Using the colspan Attribute" later in this chapter.)

```
colspan="2"
```

The headers Attribute

The `headers` attribute is used to indicate which headers correspond with that cell. The value of the attribute is a space-separated list of the header cells' `id` attribute values:

```
headers="income q1"
```

The main purpose of this attribute is in supporting voice browsers. When a table is being read to you it can be hard to keep track of which row and column you are on; therefore the header attribute is used to remind users which row and column the current cell's data belongs to.

The height Attribute (deprecated)

The height attribute allows you to specify the height of a cell in pixels or as a percentage of the available space:

```
height="20" or height="10%"
```

The nowrap Attribute (deprecated)

The nowrap attribute is used to stop text from wrapping onto a new line within a cell. You would only use nowrap when the text really would not make sense if it were allowed to wrap onto the next line (for example a line of code that would not work if it were spread across two lines). In HTML it was used without an attribute value, but that would not be allowed in Transitional XHTML. Rather, you would use the following:

```
nowrap="nowrap"
```

The rowspan Attribute

The rowspan attribute specifies the number of rows of the table a cell will span across, the value of the attribute being the number of rows the cell stretches across. (See the example in the section "Spanning Rows Using the rowspan Attribute" later in this chapter.)

```
rowspan="n"
```

The scope Attribute

The scope attribute can be used to indicate which cells the current header provides a label or header information for. It can be used instead of the headers attribute in basic tables, but does not have much support:

```
scope="range"
```

The table that follows shows the possible values of the attribute.

Value	Purpose
row	Cell contains header information for that row.
col	Cell contains header information for that column.
rowgroup	Cell contains header information for that rowgroup (a group of cells in a row created using the <thead>, <tbody>, or <tfoot> elements.
colgroup	Cell contains header information for that colgroup (a group of columns created using the <col> or <colgroup> element, both of which are discussed later in the chapter).

The valign Attribute

The `valign` attribute allows you to specify the vertical alignment for the content of the cell. Possible values are `top`, `middle`, `bottom`, and `baseline`, each of which is discussed more in the "The valign Attribute" section within the "The <tr> Element Contains Table Rows" section earlier in the chapter.

The width Attribute

The `width` attribute allows you to specify the width of a cell in pixels or as a percentage of the available space:

```
width="150" or width="30%"
```

You need to specify only the width attribute for the cells in the first row of a table, and the rest of the rows will follow the first row's cells' widths.

If you specify a `width` attribute for the `<table>` element, and the widths of individual cells add up to more that that width, most browsers will squash those cells to fit them into the width of the table.

Try It Out   **An Accessible Timetable**

In this example you create a timetable that is specifically designed to be accessible for those with visual impairments. Because you are likely to come across them in the real world, the example will contain some deprecated attributes.

1. Because this example contains deprecated attributes, you need to set up the skeleton ready to handle a Transitional XHTML 1.0 document.

```
<?xml version="1.0" encoding="UTF-8"?>
<!DOCTYPE html PUBLIC "-//W3C//DTD XHTML 1.0 Transitional//EN"
    "http://www.w3.org/TR/xhtml1/DTD/xhtml1-transitional.dtd">
<html xmlns="http://www.w3.org/1999/xhtml" lang="en">
<head>
  <title>An accessible timetable</title>
</head>
<body>
</body>
</html>
```

2. Next you can add in the main elements required to create a table with three rows and three columns. The left-most column and the top row will contain headings. While you are doing this, you'll add in some content for the table, too. The timetable will show a fictional weekend course on XHTML, with morning and afternoon sessions for Saturday and Sunday:

```
<body>
<table>
  <tr>
    <th></th>
    <th>Saturday</th>
    <th>Sunday</th>
  </tr>
  <tr>
```

143

```
    <th>Morning</th>
    <td>The structure of a document and how to mark up text.</td>
    <td>Adding tables and forms to pages. Splitting pages up into windows
        called frames.</td>
  </tr>
  <tr>
    <th>Afternoon</th>
    <td>Linking between pages and adding color images and objects to
        your pages.</td>
    <td>Using CSS to style your documents and make them look attractive.</td>
  </tr>
</table>
</body>
```

3. The next stage is to add `id` attributes to the `<th>` elements that have content, and `header` attributes to the `<td>` elements. The value of the `header` attributes should correspond to the values of the `id` attributes, indicating which headings correspond to each cell:

```
<table>
  <tr>
    <th></th>
    <th id="Saturday">Saturday</th>
    <th id="Sunday">Sunday</th>
  </tr>
  <tr>
    <th id="Morning">Morning</th>
    <td headers="Saturday Morning" abbr="Structure and markup">The
        structure of a document and how to markup text.</td>
    <td headers="Sunday Morning" abbr="Tables, forms and frames">Adding tables
        and forms to pages. Splitting pages up into windows called frames</td>
  </tr>
  <tr>
    <th id="Afternoon">Afternoon</th>
    <td headers="Saturday Afternoon" abbr="Links, color, images,
        objects">Linking between pages, and adding color images and
        objects to your pages.</td>
    <td headers="Sunday Afternoon" abbr="CSS">Using CSS to style your documents
        and make them look attractive.</td>
  </tr>
</table>
```

4. Save your file as `table.html`. The example in Figure 5-5 contains some CSS style rules that you learn more about in Chapter 9.

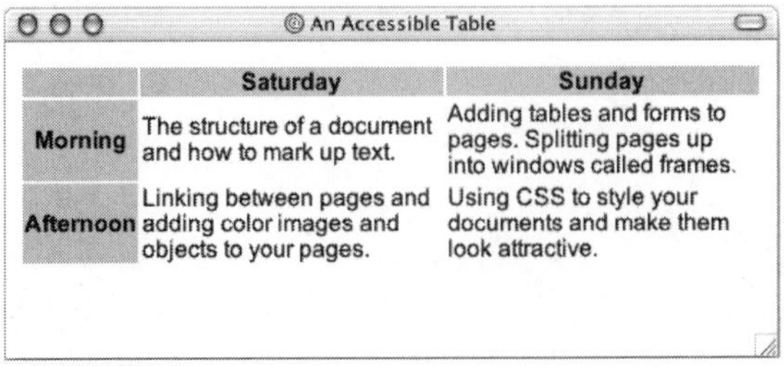

Figure 5-5

How It Works

The table is contained within the `<table>` element and its content is then written out a row at a time. Starting with the top row, you have three table heading elements. The first is empty because the top-left corner cell of the table is empty. The next two elements contain the headings for days. Remember that the id attributes will be used by individual table cells so they can indicate which headings correspond to them.

```
<table>
  <tr>
    <th></th>
    <th id="Saturday">Saturday</th>
    <th id="Sunday">Sunday</th>
  </tr>
  ...
</table>
```

Moving onto the next row of the table, the first cell is a heading for that row, indicating that this row shows times for morning sessions. The second two cells show table data. The headers attributes contain the values of the id attributes on their corresponding header elements:

```
<tr>
  <th id="Morning">Morning</th>
  <td headers="Saturday Morning" abbr="Structure and markup">The structure of
      a document and how to markup text.</td>
  <td headers="Sunday Morning" abbr="Tables, forms and frames">Adding tables
      and forms to pages. Splitting pages up into windows called frames</td>
</tr>
```

The final row uses the same structure as the first row:

```
<tr>
  <th id="Afternoon">Afternoon</th>
  <td headers="Saturday Afternoon" abbr="Links, color, images,
      objects">Linking between pages, and adding color images and
      objects to your pages.</td>
  <td headers="Sunday Afternoon" abbr="CSS">Using CSS to style your documents
      and make them look attractive.</td>
</tr>
```

As long as you accept that each row is written out in turn, you will have no problem creating quite complex tables.

To be honest, this example is quite a lot more complex than most tables you will come across. Not many people have gotten into the practice of using the id and header attributes on `<table>` elements, but it makes tables a lot easier to use for those with visual impairments, in particular when those tables have a lot of columns and rows. In fact, if you look at other people's code around on the Web at the moment, you are more likely to come across the use of lots of deprecated attributes rather than CSS rules.

Including attributes like these will set you apart from other coders who have not yet learned to make their tables more accessible. Furthermore, awareness of accessibility issues is being required in an increasing number of job positions, so you should learn how to use such attributes.

Advanced Tables

Now that you've seen the basics behind creating tables, it's time to look at some more advanced issues, such as the following:

❑   Splitting a table into three sections: a head, body, and foot

❑   Captioning tables

❑   Using the rowspan and colspan attributes to make cells stretch over more than one row or column

❑   Grouping columns using the <colgroup> element

❑   Sharing attributes between unrelated columns using the <col> element

Splitting up Tables Using a Head, Body, and Foot

Tables can be divided into three portions: a header, a body, and a foot. The head and foot are rather similar to headers and footers in a word-processed document that remain the same for every page, while the body is the main content of the table.

The separation of the parts of the table allows for the richer formatting of tables by browsers. For example, when printing a table, browsers could print the head and foot of a table on each page if the table spreads more than one side. Aural browsers could allow users to navigate between content and headers or footers with additional information easily. Indeed, Netscape 6 was the first browser that allowed you to create a table where the header and footer remain fixed while the body scrolls if the table does not fit on the page (unfortunately IE 6 does not support these attributes yet).

The three elements for separating the head, body, and foot of a table are:

❑   <thead> to create a separate table header

❑   <tbody> to indicate the main body of the table

❑   <tfoot> to create a separate table footer

A table may contain several <tbody> elements to indicate different "pages" or groups of data.

> Note that the **<tfoot>** element must appear before the **<tbody>** element in the source document.

Here you can see an example of a table that makes use of these elements (ch05_eg04.html):

```
<table>
  <thead>
    <tr>
      <td colspan="4">This is the head of the table</td>
```

```
      </tr>
    </thead>

    <tfoot>
      <tr>
        <td colspan="4">This is the foot of the table</td>
      </tr>
    </tfoot>

    <tbody>
      <tr>
        <td>Cell 1</td>
        <td>Cell 2</td>
        <td>Cell 3</td>
        <td>Cell 4</td>
      </tr>
      <tr>
        ...more rows here containing four cells...
      </tr>
    </tbody>

    <tbody>
      <tr>
        <td>Cell 1</td>
        <td>Cell 2</td>
        <td>Cell 3</td>
        <td>Cell 4</td>
      </tr>
      <tr>
        ...more rows here containing four cells...
      </tr>
    </tbody>
  </table>
```

Figure 5-6 shows what this example looks like in Netscape 7, which supports the thead, tbody, and tfoot elements. Note that this example uses CSS to give the header and footer of the table a background shade, and that the font used in these elements is larger; also the height of each <td> element has been set to 100 pixels to make the table larger.

All three elements carry the same attributes. In addition to the universal attributes, they can carry the following attributes:

```
align char charoff valign
```

The align Attribute

The align attribute is used to specify the horizontal positioning of the text and contained elements. The possible values for the align attribute are left, right, center, justify, and char, each of which was described in the "The align Attribute" subsection within the "The <tr> Element Contains Table Rows" section earlier in the chapter.

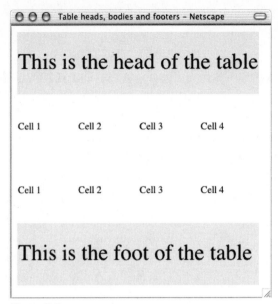

Figure 5-6

The char Attribute

The char attribute specifies a character, the first instance of which should be used to horizontally align the contents of each cell in the column group. (See the full description in the subsection "The char Attribute" within the "The <tr> Element Contains Table Rows" section earlier in the chapter.)

The charoff Attribute

The charoff attribute specifies the number of offset characters that can be displayed before the character specified as the value of the char attribute. (See the full description in the "The char Attribute" subsection within the section "The <tr> Element Contains Table Rows" earlier in the chapter.)

The valign Attribute

The valign attribute allows you to specify the vertical alignment for the content of the cells in each element. Possible values are top, middle, bottom, and baseline each of which is discussed more in the subsection "The valign Attribute" within the "The <tr> Element Contains Table Rows" section earlier in the chapter.

Adding a <caption> to a Table

To add a caption to a table you just use the <caption> element after the opening <table> tag and before the first row or header.

```
<table>
<caption>Spanning columns using the colspan attribute</caption>
  <tr>
```

By default, most browsers will display the contents of this attribute centered above the table, as shown in Figure 5-7 in the next section.

Spanning Columns Using the colspan Attribute

As you saw when looking at the <td> and <th> elements, both can carry an attribute that allows the table to span more than one column.

Remember that whenever you work with tables, you need to think in terms of grids. The colspan attribute allows a cell to stretch across more than one column, which means it can stretch across more than one rectangle horizontally in the grid. Take a look at the following example, which uses the deprecated border, width, height, and bgcolor attributes to illustrate a point visually (ch05_eg05.html):

```
<table border="1">
  <caption>Spanning columns using the colspan attribute</caption>
  <tr>
    <td bgcolor="#efefef" width="100" height="100"> </td>
    <td bgcolor="#999999" width="100" height="100"> </td>
    <td bgcolor="#000000" width="100" height="100"> </td>
  </tr>
  <tr>
    <td bgcolor="#efefef" width="100" height="100"> </td>
    <td colspan="2" bgcolor="#999999"> </td>
  </tr>
  <tr>
    <td colspan="3" bgcolor="#efefef" height="100"> </td>
  </tr>
</table>
```

You can see here that, for each extra column that a cell spans, you do not add in a cell for that row. So, if a table has three columns and one of the cells spans two columns, you have only two <td> elements in that row.

You might also have noticed the use of the non-breaking space character ( ) in the cells, which is included so that the cell has come content; without it some browsers will not display the background color (whether that color is specified using CSS or the deprecated bgcolor attribute).

Figure 5-7 shows what this example would look like in a browser.

Spanning Rows Using the rowspan Attribute

The rowpsan attribute does much the same thing as the colspan attribute, but it works in the opposite direction; it allows cells to stretch vertically across cells.

When you use a rowspan attribute, the corresponding cell in the row beneath it must be left out:

```
<table border="1">
  <caption>Spanning rows using the colspan attribute</caption>
  <tr>
```

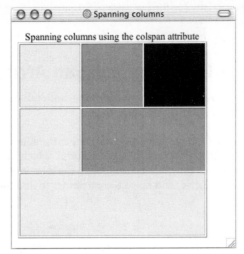

Figure 5-7

```
    <td bgcolor="#efefef" width="100" height="100"> </td>
    <td bgcolor="#999999" width="100" height="100"> </td>
    <td rowspan="3" bgcolor="#000000" width="100" height="100"> </td>
  </tr>
  <tr>
    <td bgcolor="#efefef" height="100"> </td>
    <td rowspan="2" bgcolor="#999999"> </td>
  </tr>
  <tr>
    <td bgcolor="#efefef" height="100"> </td>
  </tr>
</table>
```

You can see the effect of the rowspan attribute in Figure 5-8.

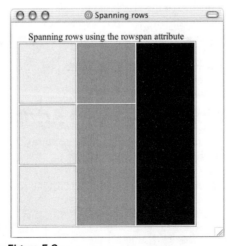

Figure 5-8

The rowspan and colspan attributes are particularly popular with designers who use tables to lay out pages; you will see examples of this in Chapter 11.

Grouping Columns Using the <colgroup> Element

If you are creating complex tables, you can group one or more adjacent columns together using the <colgroup> element. It is particularly helpful when two or more adjacent columns contain similar types of information. This allows you to apply formatting to the group of columns rather than having to style each column separately.

For example, in the following table, there are 12 columns. The first eight columns are in the first column group, the next two columns are in the second column group, and the final two columns are in the third column group:

```
<table>
  <colgroup span="8" width="75" class="mainColumns" />
  <colgroup span="2" width="50" class="subTotalColumns" />
  <colgroup span="2" width="80" class="totalColumns" />
  <tr>
    <td></td>
    ...
    <td></td>
  </tr>
</table>
```

As you can see, when the <colgroup> element is used, it comes directly after the opening <table> tag. The span attribute is being used to indicate how many columns the group contains, the width attribute sets the width of each column in the group (although in XHTML you should use CSS instead), and the class attribute could be used to attach further styles using CSS.

In addition to the universal attributes, the <colgroup> element can carry the following attributes:

```
align char charoff span valign width
```

Unfortunately, the support in Netscape 7 and IE 6 for grouping columns is currently limited.

The align Attribute

The align attribute is used to specify the horizontal positioning of the text in cells within a <colgroup> element. The possible values for the align attribute are left, right, center, justify, and char, each of which was described in the "The align Attribute" subsection within the section "The <tr> Element Contains Table Rows" earlier in the chapter.

The char Attribute

The char attribute specifies a character, the first instance of which should be used to horizontally align the contents of each cell in the column group. (See the full description in the "The char Attribute" subsection within the section "The <tr> Element Contains Table Rows" earlier in the chapter.)

The charoff Attribute

The charoff attribute specifies the number of offset characters that can be displayed before the character specified as the value of the char attribute. (See the full description in the "The charoff Attribute" subsection within the "The <tr> Element Contains Table Rows" section earlier in the chapter.

The span Attribute

The span attribute specifies how many columns a <colgroup> is supposed to stretch across.

```
span="5"
```

The valign Attribute

The valign attribute allows you to specify the vertical alignment for the content of the cell. Possible values are top, middle, bottom, and baseline, each of which is discussed more in the "The valign Attribute" subsection within the "The <tr> Element Contains Table Rows" section earlier in the chapter.

The width Attribute

The width attribute specifies the width of each cell in the column either in pixels or as a percentage of the available space. The width attribute can also take the special value "0*", which specifies that the column width should be the minimum width required to display all of the content of that column.

Columns Sharing Styles Using the <col> Element

The <col> element can be used to perform a similar role to the <colgroup> element, but without actually implying a structural group of columns. It can also be used to indicate that just one column needs special formatting different than the rest of the group.

The <col> elements are always empty elements, and are therefore used only to carry attributes, not content.

For example, the following table would have ten columns, and the first nine, while not a group, should be formatted differently than the last column.

```
<table>
  <colgroup span="10">
    <col span="9" width="100" id="mainColumns" />
    <col span="1" width="200" id="totalColumn" />
  </colgroup>
  <tr>
    <td></td>
    ...
    <td></td>
  </tr>
</table>
```

The attributes that the <col> element can carry are the same as for the <colgroup> element.

Unfortunately, the support in Netscape 7 and IE 6 for grouping columns is currently limited.

Accessibility Issues with Tables

Because tables are so widely used in page layout it is important to understand how they are dealt with by non-visual user-agents, such as voice browsers; otherwise, those with visual impairments might not be able to access your pages. In order to understand how to make tables accessible you first need to learn how tables *linearize* your page.

How Tables Linearize

To understand how a screen reader would read a table, look at the following simple table:

```
<table border="1">
  <tr>
    <td>Column 1, Row 1</td>
    <td>Column 2 Row 1</td>
  </tr>
  <tr>
    <td>Column 1, Row 2</td>
    <td>Column 2, Row 2</td>
  </tr>
</table>
```

Figure 5-9 shows what this simple table would look like in a browser.

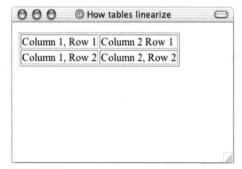

Figure 5-9

Screen readers tend to perform linearization on a table when they read it to a visitor. This means that they start at the first row and read the cells in that row from left to right, one by one, before moving on to the next row, and so on until they have read each row in the table. The order in which the cells in Figure 5-9 would be read is therefore:

- ❏ Column 1 Row 1
- ❏ Column 2 Row 1
- ❏ Column 1 Row 2
- ❏ Column 2 Row 2

Linearization of Tables Used for Layout

Web designers often use tables as a means for positioning text and images on a page where they want them to appear. Because the designer can control properties of the table, such as width of each individual cell, it is possible to create layouts that feature more than one column of text and to determine how wide each column should appear. Often the body of entire Web pages is contained within a table.

> While it is the W3Cs intention that tables should solely be used for tabular data and that CSS is the preferred mechanism for positioning elements on the page, until the support for CSS positioning in browsers improves (something you learn about in Chapter 9) and until more designers learn how to make best use of CSS positioning, it is likely that tables will still be used to control layout of Web pages.

You learn more about using both tables and CSS to control positioning of elements on a page in Chapters 9 and 10, but for now you should consider how pages that are written inside tables linearize for users of screen readers and be aware that you should consider using a table for layout only if you can make sure that it will linearize correctly.

As mentioned earlier in the chapter, you can include markup inside a table cell, as long as the whole element is contained within that cell. This means you can even place another whole table inside a table cell, creating what's called a *nested table*.

If you use nested tables, when a screen reader comes across a cell containing another table, the whole of the nested table must be linearized before the reader can move onto the next cell. For example, Figure 5-10 shows a common page layout.

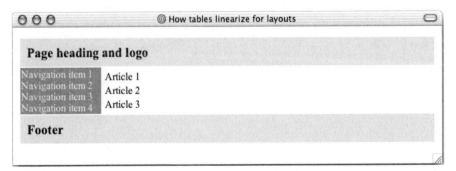

Figure 5-10

The layout in Figure 5-10 is created using a table with two columns and three rows:

- ❑   In the first row, the header and logo are in a cell that spans both columns.
- ❑   In the second row, the first cell contains the navigation bar, while the second cell contains a nested table with three rows and just one column
- ❑   In the third row, the cell spans both columns like the first one.

Here is the code for this page (note that there are also some CSS rules in the source document used to style this table, ch05_eg10.html):

```
<table>
  <tr>
    <td colspan="2" id="heading">Page heading and logo</td>
  </tr>

  <tr>
    <td id="navigation">Navigation item 1 <br />
        Navigation item 2 <br />
        Navigation item 3 <br />
        Navigation item 4 <br />
    </td>
    <td>

      <table>
        <tr>
          <td>Article 1</td>
        </tr>
        <tr>
          <td>Article 2</td>
        </tr>
        <tr>
          <td>Article 3</td>
        </tr>
      </table>

    </td>
  </tr>

  <tr>
    <td colspan="2" class="footer">Footer</td>
  </tr>
</table>
```

This example could have used the `<thead>` element for the first row and the `<tfoot>` element for the last row, but because the content of the table isn't really tabular data, it is not the intended use of the `<table>` element in the first place; I will rely only on the basic elements.

In this example, the order in which pages are read is as follows:

❑   Page heading and logo

❑   Navigation item 1

❑   Navigation item 2

❑   Navigation item 3

❑   Navigation item 4

❑   Article 1

❑   Article 2

❑   Article 3

❑   Footer

This is what you might expect, although there is quite a lot that is read before the user gets to the real content of the page. If the navigation links are the same for each page, the user might wish that she could skip to the real content rather than having to wait to hear the navigation for each page first. You can help users of aural browsers skip to the main content of the page very easily using a little trick discussed in Chapter 12.

Remember that if you are using tables to control layout you should use style sheets rather than markup to control how you want the text to appear in a table. (For example, do not use a <th> element just to get text centered and in a bold font; use it for headings only, and do not use the <em> element to get italicized text as a screen reader may add inflection to the voice to show emphasis.)

Ideally you would be testing your tables in a voice browser such as the IBM Home Page Reader (http://www.ibm.com/able/hpr.html).

There is also a table testing tool called Tablin that has been made available by the Web Accessibility Initiative of the W3C at http://www.w3.org/WAI/resources/Tablin/. This tool allows you to enter the URL of the page you want to test, and will return the text in the table as it would be linearized. You can see the result of using this tool with ch05_eg10.html in Figure 5-11.

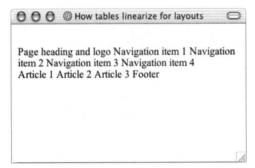

Figure 5-11

Linearization of Tables Used for Data

If you use tables to represent data, you should try to keep your tables simple, without cells spanning rows or columns, because they can make listening to a table very complicated. Here are some general guidelines for creating tables to hold data:

❑ Always try to use the <th> element to indicate a table heading. If you do not like their visual representation you can override this using CSS.

❑ If you cannot use the <th> element to indicate table headings, use the scope attribute with a value of row or col on all cells that are headings.

❑ Always put headings in the first row and the first column.

❑ If your table is complex and contains cells that span more than one cell, then use the headers attribute on those cells, and the next cell in the linearization process to clearly indicate which heading applies to that cell.

Summary

In this chapter you have seen how tables can be a powerful tool for Web developers. Tables are not only used to lay out tabular data, but are often used to control layout of pages, something you will learn more about in Chapter 11.

You have seen how all tables are based on a grid pattern and use the four basic elements: `<table>`, which contains each table; `<tr>`, which contains the rows of a table; `<td>`, which contains a cell of table data; and `<th>`, which represents a cell that contains a heading.

You have also seen how you can add headers, footers, and captions to tables. It is particularly helpful to add a `<thead>` and `<tfoot>` element to any table that may be longer than a browser window or sheet of printed paper, as they help a reader relate between the content and the information in headers or footers.

You can make cells span both columns and rows, although you should avoid doing this in tables that contain data, as it makes them harder for aural browsers to read to a user, and you can group columns together so that you can preserve structure and so they can share styles and attributes.

Finally, you saw some of the accessibility issues regarding use of tables. It is important to be aware of the process of linearization, which a screen reader performs before reading a table to a user, so that your sites are accessible to users with visual impairments. The chapter ended with some guidelines for making tables more accessible to all visitors.

In the next chapter you learn about frames as a way of dividing up page content.

Exercises

The answers to all of the exercises are in Appendix A.

1. Where should the `<caption>` element for a table be placed in the document, and by default where is it displayed?

2. In what order would the cells in Figure 5-12 be read out by a screen reader?

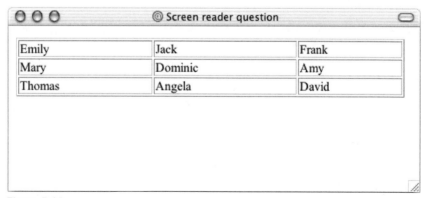

Figure 5-12

3. Create a table to hold the data shown in Figure 5-13. To give you a couple of clues, the document must be Transitional XHTML 1.0 because the `width` attribute is used on the cells of the first row of the table. You should also have seen examples of how the border is generated in this chapter, using another deprecated attribute, but this time on the `<table>` element rather than the cells.

Figure 5-13

Forms

Almost every time you want to collect information from a visitor to your site you need to use a *form*. You have probably used several different kinds of forms on different Web sites, from simple search boxes that allow you to enter keywords in order to find what you are looking for to complex forms that allow you to order groceries or book a holiday online.

Forms on the Web bear a strong resemblance to paper forms you have to fill out. On paper, there are areas to enter text, boxes to check (or cross), options to choose from, and so on. While on the Web, you can create a form by combining what are known as *form controls*, such as text boxes (to enter text into), checkboxes (to place a check in), select boxes and radio buttons (to choose from different options), and so on. In this chapter you learn how each of these different types of controls can be combined into a form.

In this chapter, then, you learn:

❑ How to create a form using the `<form>` element

❑ The different types of form control you can use to make a form—such as text input boxes, radio buttons, select boxes, and submit buttons

❑ What happens to the data a user enters

❑ How to make your forms accessible

❑ How to structure the content of your forms

By the end of the chapter you will be able to create all kinds of forms to collect information from visitors to your site.

> *What you do with the data that you collect depends upon the server your Web site is hosted on. XHTML is used only to present the form to the user; it does not allow you to say what happens with that data once it has been collected. To get a better idea of what happens to the data once it has been collected from a form, you will need to look at a book on a server-side language (such as ASP, PHP, or JSP). See the book list at Wrox.com for books on at least some of these topics.*

Introducing Forms

Any form that you create will live inside an element called <form>. Between the opening <form> and closing </form> tags, you will find the form controls (the text input boxes, drop-down boxes, checkboxes, a submit button and so on). A <form> element can also contain other XHTML markup just like the rest of a page.

Once the user has entered information into a form, the data is usually sent to a Web server. This usually happens when the user clicks what is known as a *submit button* (although the actual text on the button may say something different such as Search, Send, or Proceed).

Once the data that the user entered arrives at the server, a script or other program usually processes the data and sends a new Web page back to you. The returned page will usually respond to a request you have made or acknowledge an action you have taken.

As an example, you might want to add the search form shown in Figure 6-1 to your page.

Figure 6-1

You can see that this form contains a text box for the user to enter the keywords of what he or she is searching for, and a button with the word "Search." When the user clicks the Search button the information is sent the server. The server then processes the data and generates a new page for that user telling him or her what pages meet the search criteria (see Figure 6-2).

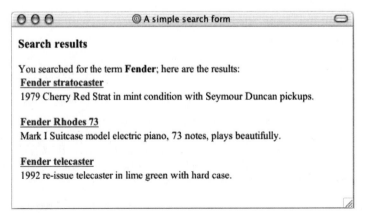

Figure 6-2

When a user fills in a form the data is sent to the server in *name/value* pairs. The *name* corresponds to the name of the form control, and the *value* is what the user has entered or the value of the option they have selected. (After all, if you have five text boxes on a form, you need to know which data corresponds to which text box.) The processing application can then process the information from each form control individually.

Here is the code for the simple search form shown in Figure 6-1:

```
<form action="http://www.example.org/search.asp" method="get">
    <h3>Search the site</h3>
    <input type="text" name="txtSearchItem" />
    <input type="submit" value="Search" />
</form>
```

The `<form>` element contains an attribute called `action` whose value is the URL of the page on the Web server that handles search requests. The `method` attribute meanwhile indicates which HTTP method will be used in getting the form data to the server. (You will learn that there are two methods you can use, `get` and `post`, later in the chapter.)

You will see some more complicated forms later in the chapter, but for now let's look in more detail at what makes up the form.

Creating a Form with the `<form>` Element

As you have already seen, forms live inside an element called `<form>`. The `<form>` element can also contain other markup such as paragraphs, headings, and so on. A `<form>` element must not, however, contain another `<form>` element.

Providing you keep your `<form>` elements separate from each other (and no one `<form>` element contains another `<form>` element), your page may contain as many forms as you like. For example, you might have a login form, a search form, and a form to subscribe to a newsletter all on the same page. If you do have more than one form on a page, users will be able to send the data from only one form at a time to the server.

Every `<form>` element should carry at least two attributes:

```
action method
```

A `<form>` element may also carry all of the universal attributes, the UI event attributes, and the following attributes:

```
enctype accept accept-charset onsubmit onreset
```

The action Attribute

The `action` attribute indicates which page or program on the server will receive the information from this form when a user presses the submit button.

For example, if you had a login form consisting of a username and password, the details the user enters may get passed to a page written in ASP (Active Server Pages) on the Web server called `checkLogin` `.asp`, in which case the `action` attribute would read as follows:

```
<form action="http://www.example.org/membership/checkLogin.asp">
```

Most browsers will accept only a URL beginning with `http://` as the value of the `action` attribute.

The method Attribute

Form data can be sent to the server in two ways, each corresponding to an *HTTP method*:

- ❑   The `get` method, which sends data as part of the URL
- ❑   The `post` method, which hides data in the HTTP headers

You learn more about these two methods later in the chapter, where you will learn what they mean and when you should use each method.

The id Attribute

The `id` attribute allows you to provide a unique identifier for the `<form>` element, just as it does for other elements.

It is good practice to give every `<form>` element an `id` attribute because many forms make use of style sheets and scripts, which require the use of the `id` attribute to identify the form.

> *As you will see in Chapter 15, it can help users if you automatically put the browser's cursor in the first text box on a form. This requires an `id` or `name` attribute to identify the form.*

The value of the `id` attribute should be unique within the document, and it should also follow the other rules mentioned in Chapter 1. I start the value of `id` and `name` attributes for forms with the characters `frm` and then use the rest of the value to describe the kind of data the form collects, for example `frmLogin` or `frmSearch`.

The name Attribute (deprecated)

As with most other attributes, the `name` attribute is the predecessor to the `id` attribute.

As with the `id` attribute, the value should be unique to the document. Starting the value with the characters `frm` followed by the purpose of the form can also be helpful (especially when you use script to access the form).

The onsubmit Attribute

If you have ever filled in a form on a Web site, and as soon as you have clicked the button to send the form data (even before the page is sent to the server) a message has appeared telling you that you have missed entering some data, or entered the wrong data, then the chances are you have come across a form that uses the onsubmit attribute to run a script function that checks the data you entered in the form.

When a user clicks a submit button, something called an *event* fires. It is rather like the browser raising its hand and saying "hey, I am sending this form data to the server." The idea behind these events is that a script (such as a JavaScript script) can be run before the data is sent to the server to ensure the quality and accuracy of the submitted data. The value of the onsubmit attribute should be a script function that would be used when this event fires.

So, an onsubmit attribute on the <form> element might look like this:

```
onsubmit="validateFormDetails();"
```

In this case, the validateFormDetails() function should have been defined in the document already (probably in the <head> element). So, when the user clicks the submit button this function will be called and run.

There are two key advantages to making some checks on the form before it is sent to the server:

❑ The user does not have to wait the extra time it would take for the page to be sent to the server and then returned if there are any errors

❑ The server does not have to deal with as much error checking as it would if the checks by the browser had not been performed.

In both cases it saves work on the server, which is especially important on very busy sites.

The onreset Attribute

Some forms contain a reset button that empties the form of all details although the button might say something like clear form instead; when this button is pressed an onreset event fires and a script can be run.

When the onreset attribute is used, its value is a script (just like the onsubmit attribute) that is executed when the user clicks the button that calls it.

The onreset event and attribute are used a lot less than onsubmit, although if you offer a Clear Form button it is good to confirm with users that they did intend to clear the form before performing the action (in case they pressed it by accident).

The enctype Attribute

If you use the HTTP post method to send data to the server, you can use the enctype attribute to specify how the browser encodes the data before it sends it to the server (to help make sure it arrives safely). Browsers tend to support two types of encoding:

❑ application/x-www-form-urlencoded, which is the standard method most forms use. It converts spaces to the plus sign and non-alphanumeric characters into the hexadecimal code for that character in ASCII text.

163

❑   mutlipart/form-data, which allows the data to be sent in parts, with each consecutive part corresponding the a form control, in the order they appear in the form. Each part can have an optional content-type header of its own indicating the type of data for that form control.

You are likely to use this attribute only if your form allows users to upload a file to the server or they are going to use non-ASCII characters, in which case the enctype attribute should be given the second value:

```
entype="multipart/form-data"
```

The accept-charset Attribute

The idea behind the accept-charset attribute is that it specifies a list of character encodings that a user may enter that the server can then process. However, Netscape 7 and IE 6 do not support this attribute. Values should be a space-separated or comma-delimited list of character sets (as shown in Appendix E).

For example, the following indicates that a server accepts UTF-8 encodings:

```
accept-charset="utf-8"
```

The main browsers will currently allow any character set to be entered.

The accept Attribute

The accept attribute is similar to the accept-charset attribute except it takes a comma-separated list of content types that the server processing the form can handle. Again, neither Netscape 7 nor IE 6 support this feature.

The idea is that a user would not be able to upload a file of a different content type other than those listed. Here you can see that the only types intended to be uploaded are images that are GIFs or JPEGs:

```
accept="image/gif, image/jpg"
```

The main browsers, however, currently still allow you to upload any file. A list of MIME types is shown in Appendix H.

The target Attribute

The target attribute is usually used with the <a> element to indicate which frame or browser window a new page should be loaded into. It also works with a form that generates a new page, allowing you to indicate which frame or window the page generated ends up in when the user submits the form.

Whitespace and the <form> Element

You should also be aware that, when a browser comes across a <form> element it often creates extra whitespace around that element. This can particularly affect your design if you want a form to fit in a small area, such as putting a search form in a menu bar. The only way to avoid this problem is through careful placement of the <form> element.

To avoid the extra space created, you can try either placing the <form> element near the start or end of the document, or, if you are using tables for layout purposes in a Transitional XHTML 1.0 document, between the <table> and <tr> elements. (You should be aware that this latter approach is a cheat, and therefore it might cause an error if you tried to validate the page; however, most browsers will still display the table and form as you intended.)

Form Controls

This section covers the different types of form controls that you can use to collect data from a visitor to your site. You will see:

- ❑ Text input controls
- ❑ Buttons
- ❑ Checkboxes and radio buttons
- ❑ Select boxes (sometimes referred to as drop-down menus) and list boxes
- ❑ File select boxes
- ❑ Hidden controls

Text Inputs

You undoubtedly have come across text input boxes on many Web pages. Possibly the most famous text input box is the one right in the middle of the Google home page that allows you to enter what you are searching for.

On a printed form, the equivalent of a text input is a box or line that you are allowed to write a response in or on.

There are actually three types of text input used on forms:

- ❑ **Single-line text input controls:** Used for items that require only one line of user input, such as search boxes or names. They are created using the <input> element.
- ❑ **Password input controls:** Single-line text input that mask the characters a user enters. They tend to either show an asterisk or a dot instead of each character the user types so that someone cannot simply look at the screen to see what a user types in. Password input controls are mainly used for entering passwords on login forms or sensitive details such as credit card numbers. They are also created using the <input> element.
- ❑ **Multi-line text input controls:** Used when the user is required to give details that may be longer than a single sentence. Multi-line input controls are created with the <textarea> element.

Single-Line Text Input Controls

Single-line text input controls are created using an <input> element whose type attribute has a value of text. Here is a basic example of a single-line text input used for a search box (ch06_eg02.html):

```
<form action="http://www.example.com/search.asp" method="get"
name="frmSearch">
```

```
Search:
  <input type="text" name="txtSearch" value="Search for" size="20"
maxlength="64" />
  <input type="submit" value="Submit" />
</form>
```

Figure 6-3 shows what this form looks like this in a browser.

Just as I try to start form names with the characters frm, I tend to start text input names with the characters txt to indicate that the form controls a text box. This is especially handy when working with the data on the server to remind you what sort of form control sent that data.

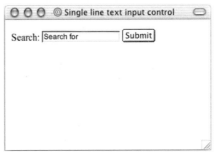

Search: Search for   Submit

Figure 6-3

The table that follows lists the attributes the `<input>` element can carry when creating a text input control.

Attribute	Purpose
type	Indicates the type of input control you want to create. The value for this attribute should be text when you want to create a single-line text input control. This is required because the `<input>` element is also used to create other form controls such as radio buttons and checkboxes.
name	Used to give the name part of the name/value pair that is sent to the server, representing each form control and the value the user entered. Each control needs to have a name so that the associated value (supplied or chosen by the user) can be retrieved individually at the other end.
value	Provides an initial value for the text input control that the user will see when the form loads. You need to use this attribute only if you want something to be written in the text input when the page loads (such as a cue for what the user should be entering); more often you are likely to leave it blank.
size	Allows you to specify the width of the text-input control in terms of characters so that the search box in the earlier example is 20 characters wide. The user is allowed to enter more characters than specified as the value of the length attribute (so in this case the user could search on words with more than 20 characters), in which case the browser should allow some way for the user to scroll along their entry; this is commonly done through the use of arrow keys.

Attribute	Purpose
maxlength	Allows you to specify the maximum number of characters a user can enter into the text box. Usually after the maximum number of characters has been entered, even if the user keeps pressing more keys, no new characters will be added.

When an <input> element's type attribute has a value of text, it can also carry the following attributes:

❑ All of the universal attributes

❑ disabled, readonly, tabindex, and accesskey, which are covered later in the chapter

Password Input Controls

If you want to collect sensitive data such as passwords and credit card information, you should use the password input. The password input masks the characters the user types on the screen by replacing them with either a dot or asterisk.

Password input controls are created almost identically to the single-line text input controls, except that the type attribute on the <input> element is given a value of password.

Here you can see an example of a login form that combines a single-line text input control and a password input control (ch06_eg03.html):

```
<form action="http://www.example.com/login.asp" method="post">
 Username:
 <input type="text" name="txtUsername" value="" size="20" maxlength="20" />
<br />
 Password:
 <input type="password" name="pwdPassword" value="" size="20"
maxlength="20" />
 <input type="submit" value="Submit" />
</form>
```

As you can see, I begin the name of any password with the characters pwd so that when I come to deal with the data on the server, I know the associated value came from a password input box.

Figure 6-4 shows you how this login form might look in a browser when the user starts entering details.

> **While passwords are hidden on the screen, they are still sent across the Internet as clear text. In order to make them secure you should use an SSL connection between the client and server.**

Multiple-Line Text Input Controls

If you want to allow a visitor to your site to enter more than one line of text, you should create a multiple-line text input control using the <textarea> element.

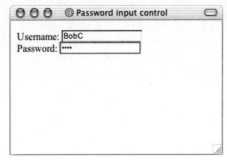

Figure 6-4

Here is an example of a multiple-line text input used to collect feedback from visitors to a site (ch06_eg04.html):

```
<form action="http://www.example.org/feedback.asp" method="post">
  Please tell us what you think of the site and then click submit:<br />
  <textarea name="txtFeedback" rows="20" cols="50">
Enter your feedback here.
  </textarea>
  <br />
  <input type="submit" value="Submit" />
</form>
```

Note that the text inside the `<textarea>` element is not indented. Anything written between the opening and closing `<textarea>` tags is treated as if it were written inside a `<pre>` element and formatting of the source document is preserved. If the words "Enter your feedback here" were indented in the code, they would also be indented in the resulting multi-line text input on the browser.

Figure 6-5 shows what this form might look like.

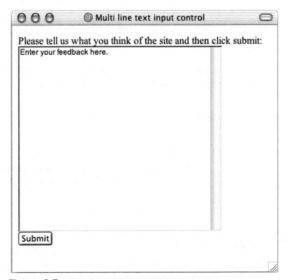

Figure 6-5

In the figure, you can see the writing between the opening <textarea> and closing </textarea> tags, which is shown in the text area when the page loads. Users can delete this text before adding their own text, and if they do not delete the text from the text box it will be sent to the server when the form is submitted. Users often just type after any text written in a <textarea> element, so you may choose to avoid adding anything in between the elements, but you should still have opening and closing <textarea> tags or earlier browsers may not render the element correctly.

The <textarea> element can take the attributes shown in the table that follows.

Attribute	Purpose
name	The name of the control. This is used in the name/value pair that is sent to the server.
rows	Used to specify the size of a <textarea>, it indicates the number of rows of text a <textarea> element should have and therefore corresponds to its height.
cols	Used to specify the size of a <textarea>; here it specifies the width of the box and refers to the number of columns. One column is the average width of a character.

The <textarea> element can also take the following attributes:

❑   All of the universal attributes

❑   disabled, readonly, tabindex, and accesskey, which are covered later in the chapter

❑   The UI event attributes

By default, when a user runs out of columns in a <textarea>, the text is wrapped onto the next line (which means it just flows onto the next line as text in a word processor does), but the server will receive it as if it were all on one line. Because some users expect the sentences to break where they see them break on the screen, both major browsers also support an extra attribute called wrap that allows you to indicate how the text should be wrapped. Possible values are:

❑   off (the default), which means scrollbars are added to the box if the user's words take up more space than the allowed width, and users have to scroll to see what they have entered

❑   virtual, which means that wherever the text wraps users see it on the new line but it is transmitted to the server as if it were all on the same line unless the user has pressed the Enter key, in which case it is treated as a line break

❑   physical, which means that wherever the user sees the text start on a new line, so will the server

The wrap attribute is not, however, part of the XHTML specification.

Buttons

Buttons are most commonly used to submit a form, although they are sometimes used to clear or reset a form and even to trigger client-side scripts. (For example, on a basic loan calculator form within the page a button might be used to trigger the script that calculates repayments.) You can create a button in three ways:

- ❑ Using an `<input>` element with a `type` attribute whose value is submit, reset, or button
- ❑ Using an `<input>` element with a `type` attribute whose value is image
- ❑ Using a `<button>` element

With each different method the button will look slightly different.

Creating Buttons Using the <input> Element

When you use the `<input>` element to create a button, the type of button you create is specified using the `type` attribute. The `type` attribute can take the following values:

- ❑ submit, which creates a button that automatically submits a form
- ❑ reset, which creates a button that automatically resets form controls to their initial values
- ❑ button, which creates a button that is used to trigger a client-side script when the user clicks that button

Here you can see examples of all three types of button (ch06_eg05.html):

```
<input type="submit" name="btnVoteRed" value="Vote for reds" />
<input type="submit" name="btnVoteBlue" value="Vote for blues" />
<br /><br />
<input type="reset" value="Clear form" /> <br /><br />
<input type="button" value="calculate" onclick="calculate()" />
```

Figure 6-6 shows what these buttons might look like in IE on a Mac (a PC will display them in a simple gray box).

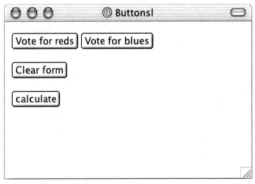

Figure 6-6

The table that follows shows the attributes used by the buttons.

In the same way that you can trigger a script when the user clicks a button, you can also trigger a script when the button gains or loses focus with the onfocus and onblur event attributes.

Attribute	Purpose
type	Specifies the type of button you want and takes one of the following values: submit, reset, or button.
name	Provides a name for the button. You need to add only a name attribute to a button if there is more than one button on the same form (in which case it helps indicate which button was clicked) although it can be seen as good practice to use it to provide an indication of what the button does.
value	Enables you to specify what the text on the button should read. If a name attribute is given, then the value of the value attribute is sent to the server as part of the name/value pair for this form control. If no value is given, then no name/value pair is sent for this button.
size	Enables you to specify the width of the button in pixels, although Netscape 7 and IE 6 still do not support this attribute.
onclick	Used to trigger a script when the user clicks the button; the value of this attribute is the script that should be run.

When an `<input>` element has a type attribute whose value is submit, reset, or button, it can also take the following attributes:

❑   All of the universal attributes

❑   disabled, readonly, tabindex, and accesskey, which are discussed later in the chapter

❑   The UI event attributes

If you do not use the title attribute for the submit button using the name attribute, you may find that a browser displays something inappropriate for the form. For example, IE displays the text Send Query.

Using Images for Buttons

You can use an image for a button rather than using the standard button that a browser renders for you. Creating an image button is very similar to creating any other button, but the type attribute has a value of image:

```
<input type="image" src="submit.jpg" alt="Submit" name="btnImageMap" />
```

Note how I start the value of a name attribute for a button with the characters btn , in keeping with the naming convention that I mentioned earlier. (When you come to refer to the name of the form control in other code, the use of this prefix will help remind you what type of form control the information came from.)

Because you are creating a button that has an image, you need to have two additional attributes, which are listed in the table that follows.

Attribute	Purpose
src	Specifies the source of the image file.
alt	Provides alternative text for the image. This will be displayed when the image cannot be found and also helps speech browsers. (It is supported only in IE 5 and Netscape 6 and later versions.)

If the image button has a name attribute, when you click it the browser sends a name/value pair to the server. The name will be what you provide for the name attribute and the value will be a pair of x and y coordinates for where on the button the user clicked.

In Figure 6-7 you can see a graphical submit button. Both Netscape and IE change the cursor as a cue for usability when a user hovers over such a button.

Figure 6-7

Creating Buttons Using the <button> Element

The <button> element was a more recent introduction that allows you to specify what appears on a button between an opening <button> tag and a closing </button> tag. So, you can include textual markup or image elements between these tags.

This element works only in IE 4 and Netscape 6 and later browsers, but the browsers that do support this element also offer a relief (or 3D) effect on the button, which resembles an up or down motion when the button is clicked.

Here are some examples of using the <button> element (ch06_eg06.html):

```
<button type="submit">Submit</button>
<br /><br />
<button type="reset"><b>Clear this form</b> I want to start again</button>
<br /><br />
<button type="button"><img src="submit.gif" alt="submit" /></button>
```

As you can see, the first submit button just contains text, the second reset button contains text and other markup (in the form of the <b> element), and the third submit button contains an <img> element.

Figure 6-8 shows what these buttons would look like.

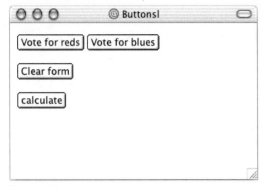

Figure 6-8

Checkboxes

Checkboxes are just like the little boxes that you have to check on paper forms. Like light switches, they can be either on or off. When they are checked they are on and the user can simply toggle between on and off positions by clicking the checkbox.

Checkboxes can appear individually with each having its own name, or they can appear as a group of checkboxes that share a control name and allow users to select several values for the same property.

Checkboxes are ideal form controls when you need to allow a user to:

❑   Provide a simple yes or no response with one control (such as accepting terms and conditions or subscribing to an e-mail list)

❑   Select several items from a list of possible options (such as when you want a user to indicate all of the skills they have from a given list)

A checkbox is created using the `<input>` element whose `type` attribute has a value of `checkbox`. Following is an example of some checkboxes that use the same control name (`ch06_eg07.html`):

```
<form action="http://www.example.com/cv.asp" method="get" name="frmCV">
Which of the following skills do you possess? Select all that apply.
  <input type="checkbox" name="chkSkills" value="html" />HTML <br />
  <input type="checkbox" name="chkSkills" value="xhtml" />XHTML <br />
  <input type="checkbox" name="chkSkills" value="CSS" />CSS<br />
  <input type="checkbox" name="chkSkills" value="JavaScript" />
JavaScript<br />
  <input type="checkbox" name="chkSkills" value="html" />ASP<br />
  <input type="checkbox" name="chkSkills" value="html" />PHP
</form>
```

As you can see, I start the name of checkboxes with the letters `chk`. Figure 6-9 shows how this form might look in a browser. Note how there is a line break after each checkbox so that it clearly appears on each line (if you have checkboxes side by side, users are likely to get confused between which label applies to which checkbox).

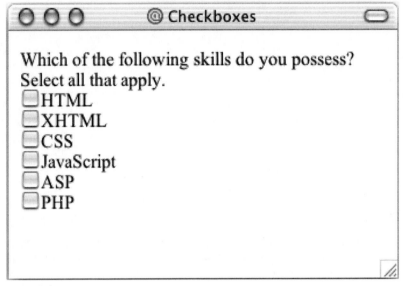

Figure 6-9

All of the selected skills will be sent to the processing application in the form of name/value pairs (so you could have several name/value pairs with the same name).

How you process multiple checkboxes with the same name depends on how you send the data to the server. If you use HTTP get to send the data, then the selected checkbox will be sent as part of the URL in the query string. If you use the HTTP post method, however, then you'll get an array that you can loop through representing the checked options.

As a contrast here is a single checkbox, acting like a simple yes or no option:

```
<form action="http://www.example.org/acceptTerms.asp" name="frmTandC"
method="get">
    <input type="checkbox" name="chkAcceptTerms" checked="checked" />
    I accept the <a href="terms.htm">terms and conditions</a>.<br />
    <input type="submit" />
</form>
```

Note how the <input> element that creates this checkbox does not carry a value attribute. In the absence of a value attribute, the value is on. You can also see an attribute called checked, with a value of checked, which indicates that when the page loads the checkbox is selected.

Before HTML 4.1, you could just provide the checked attribute without a value. This process is known as attribute minimization, and elements that carried the checked attribute without a value were considered to be on. In XHTML all attributes must have a value, so the name of these attributes is repeated as their value. Older browsers might ignore the value, but they still acknowledge the presence of the attribute.

The table that follows shows the attributes that an <input> element whose type attribute has a value of checkbox can carry.

Attribute	Purpose
type	Indicates that you want to create a checkbox.
name	Gives the name of the control (several checkboxes may share the same name—although if this is the case they should physically be placed together).
value	The value that will be used if the checkbox is selected (more than one checkbox should share the same name only if you want to allow users to select several items from the same list).
checked	Indicates that when the page loads, the checkbox should be selected.
size	Indicates the size of the checkbox in pixels (this does not work in IE 6 or Netscape 7).

Checkboxes can also carry the following attributes:

❑   All universal attributes

❑   disabled, readonly, tabindex, and accesskey which are discussed later in the chapter

❑   UI event attributes

Radio Buttons

Radio buttons are similar to checkboxes in that they can be either on or off, but there are two key differences:

❑   When you have a group of radio buttons that share the same name, only one of them can be selected. Once one radio button has been selected, if the user clicks another option, the new option is selected and the old one deselected.

❑   You should not use radio buttons for a single form control where the control indicates on or off because once a lone radio button has been selected it cannot be deselected again.

Therefore, radio buttons are ideal if you want to provide users with a number of options from which they can pick only one. In such situations, an alternative is to use a drop-down select box that allows users to select only one option from several. Your decision between whether to use a select box or a group of radio buttons depends on three things:

❑   **Users expectations:** If your form models a paper form where a user would be presented with several checkboxes, from which they can pick only one, then you should use a group of radio buttons.

❑   **Seeing all the options:** If users would benefit from having all the options in front of them before they pick one, you should use a group of radio buttons.

❑   **Space:** If you are concerned about space, a drop-down select box will take up far less space than a set of radio buttons.

If you wondered where the term "radio buttons" comes from, it is from old radios. On some old radios, you could press in only one button at a time to select the radio station you wanted to listen to from the ones that had been set. You could not press two of these buttons at the same time on your radio, and pressing one would pop the other out.

The `<input>` element is again called upon to create radio buttons, and this time the `type` attribute should be given a value of `radio`. For example, here radio buttons are used to allow users to select which class of travel they want to take (ch06_eg08.html):

```
<form action="http://www.example.com/flights.asp" name="frmFlightBooking"
    method="get">
  Please select which class of travel you wish to fly: <br />
    <input type="radio" name="radClass" value="First" />First class <br />
    <input type="radio" name="radClass" value="Business" />Business class <br />
    <input type="radio" name="radClass" value="Economy" />Economy class <br />
</form>
```

As you can see, the user should be allowed to select only one of the three options, so radio buttons are ideal. I start the name of a radio button with the letters `rad`. Figure 6-10 shows you what this might look like in a browser.

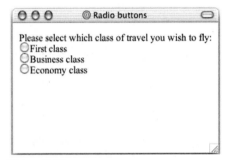

Figure 6-10

The table that follows lists the attributes for an `<input>` element whose `type` attribute has a value of `radio`.

Attribute	Purpose
type	To indicate that you want a radio button form control.
name	The name of the form control.
value	Used to indicate the value that will be sent to the server if this option is selected.
checked	Indicates that this option should be selected by default when the page loads. Remember that there is no point using this with a single radio button as a user can't deselect the option. If you use this attribute the value should also be checked in order for the attribute to be XHTML-compliant.
size	This attribute indicates the size of the radio button in pixels, but this attribute does not work in IE 6 or Netscape 7.

Radio buttons can also take the following attributes:

❑ All of the universal attributes

❑ All of the UI event attributes

❑ `disabled`, `tabindex`, and `accesskey`, which are covered later in the chapter

When you have a group of radio buttons that share the same name, some browsers will automatically select the first option as the page loads—even though they are not required to do so in the HTML specification. Therefore, if your radio buttons represent a set of values—say for a voting application—you might like to select a medium option so that, should some users forget to select one of the options, the results are not too biased by the browsers selection. To do this you should use the checked attribute.

Select Boxes

A drop-down select box allows users to select one item from a drop down menu. Drop-down select boxes can take up far less space than a group of radio buttons.

Drop-down select boxes can also provide an alternative to single-line text input controls where you want to limit the options that a user can enter; for example, you can use a select box to allow users to indicate which country or state they live in.

A drop-down select box is contained by a `<select>` element, while each individual option within that list is contained within an `<option>` element. For example, the following form creates a drop-down select box for the user to select a color (`ch06_eg09.html`):

```
<select name="selColor">
    <option selected="selected" value="">Select color</option>
    <option value="red">Red</option>
    <option value="green">Green</option>
    <option value="blue">Blue</option>
</select>
```

As you can see here, the text inside the `<option>` element is used to display options to the user, while the value that would be sent to the server if that option is selected is given in the `value` attribute. You can also see that the first `<option>` element does not have a value and that its content is `Select color`; this is to indicate to the user that she must pick one of the color choices. Finally, notice again that I use the letters `sel` at the start of the name of a select box.

Figure 6-11 shows what this would look like in a browser.

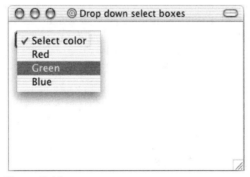

Figure 6-11

Note that the width of the select box will be the width of the longest option displayed to the user; in this case it will be the width of the text `Select color`.

The <select> Element

The <select> element is the containing element for a drop-down list box.

Attribute	Purpose
name	This is the name for the control.
size	This can be used to present a scrolling list box, as you will see shortly. Its value would be the number of rows in the list that should be visible at the same time.
multiple	Allows a user to select multiple items from the menu. If the attribute is not present, the user may select only one item. In earlier versions of HTML, this attribute did not have a value. However, to be valid XHTML it should be given the value of multiple (i.e., <select multiple="multiple">). Note that the use of this attribute will change the presentation of the select box, as you will see in the section "Selecting Multiple Options with the multiple Attribute" later in this chapter.

The HTML and XHTML recommendations indicate that a <select> element *must* contain at least one <option> element, although in practice it should contain more than one <option> element; after all, a drop-down list box with just one option might confuse a user.

The <option> Element

Inside any <select> element you will find at least one <option> element. The text between the opening <option> and closing </option> tags is displayed to the user as the label for that option. The <option> element can take the attributes shown in the table that follows.

Attribute	Purpose
value	The value that is sent to the server if this option is selected.
selected	Specifies that this option should be the initially selected value when the page loads. This attribute may be used on several <option> elements even if the <select> element does not carry the multiple attribute. Although earlier versions of XHTML did not require a value for this attribute, in order to be valid XHTML you should give this attribute a value of selected.
label	An alternative way of labeling options, using an attribute rather than element content. This attribute is particularly useful when using the <optgroup> element, which is covered a bit later in this chapter.

Creating Scrolling Select Boxes

As I mentioned earlier, it's possible to create scrolling menus where users can see a few of the options in a select box at a time. In order to do this, you just add the size attribute to the <select> element. The value of the size attribute is the number of options you want to be visible at any one time.

While scrolling select box menus are rarely used, they can give users an indication that there are several possible options open to them and allow them to see a few of the options at the same time. For example, here is a scrolling select box that allows the user to select a day of the week (ch06_eg10 .html):

```
<form action="http://www.example.org/days.asp" name="frmDays" method="get">
  <select size="4" name="selDay">
    <option value="Mon">Monday</option>
    <option value="Tue">Tuesday</option>
    <option value="Wed">Wednesday</option>
    <option value="Thu">Thursday</option>
    <option value="Fri">Friday</option>
    <option value="Sat">Saturday</option>
    <option value="Sun">Sunday</option>
  </select>
<br /><br /><input type="submit" value="Submit" />
</form>
```

As you can see from Figure 6-12, this clearly shows the user that he or she has several options while limiting the space used by showing only a few of the options.

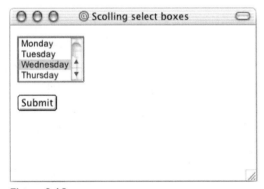

Figure 6-12

Note that the `multiple` attribute discussed in the subsection that follows is not used on this element.

Selecting Multiple Options with the multiple Attribute

The `multiple` attribute allows users to select more than one item from a select box. The value of the `multiple` attribute should be the word `multiple` in order for it to be valid XHTML (although earlier versions of HTML left it without a value).

The addition of this attribute automatically makes the select box look like a scrolling select box. Here you can see an example of a multiple-item select box that allows users to select more than one day of the week (ch06_eg11.html):

```
<form action="http://www.example.org/days.asp" method="get" name="frmDays">
  Please select more than one day of the week:<br />
  <select name="selDays" multiple="multiple">
    <option value="Mon">Monday</option>
    <option value="Tue">Tuesday</option>
```

```
      <option value="Wed">Wednesday</option>
      <option value="Thu">Thursday</option>
      <option value="Fri">Friday</option>
      <option value="Sat">Saturday</option>
      <option value="Sun">Sunday</option>
   </select>
<br /><br /><input type="submit" value="Submit">
</form>
```

The result is shown in Figure 6-13, where you can see that without the addition of the size attribute the select box is still a scrolling one.

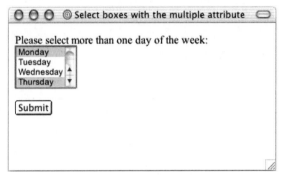

Figure 6-13

Grouping Options with the <optgroup> Element

If you have a very long list of items in a select box, you can group them together using the <optgroup> element, which acts just like a container element for all the elements you want within a group.

The <optgroup> element can carry a label attribute whose value is a label for that group of options. In the following example, you can see how the options are grouped in terms of type of equipment (ch06_eg12.html):

```
<form action="http://www.example.org/info.asp" method="get" name="frmInfo">
   Please select the product you are interested in:<br />
   <select name="selInformation">
     <optgroup label="Hardware">
       <option value="Desktop">Desktop computers</option>
       <option value="Laptop">Laptop computers</option>
     </optgroup>
     <optgroup label="Software">
       <option value="OfficeSoftware">Office software</option>
       <option value="Games">Games</option>
     </optgroup>
     <optgroup label="Peripherals">
       <option value="Monitors">Monitors</option>
       <option value="InputDevices">Input Devices</option>
       <option value="Storage">Storage</option>
     </optgroup>
</select>
<br /><br /><input type="submit" value="Submit" />
</form>
```

You will find that different browsers display `<optgroup>` elements in different ways. Figure 6-14 shows you how IE 5.5 on a Mac displays options held by `<optgroup>` elements, while Figure 6-15 shows you the result in Netscape 7 on a Mac.

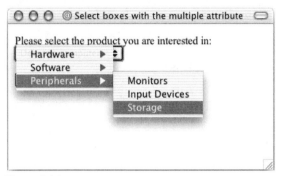

Figure 6-14

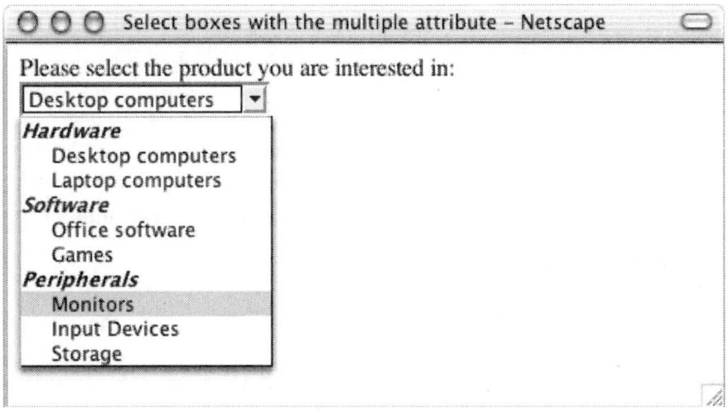

Figure 6-15

An alternative option for grouping elements is to add an `<option>` element that carries the `disabled` attribute, which you learn about shortly (`ch06_eg13.html`):

```
<form action="http://www.example.org/info.asp" method="get" name="frmInfo">
   Please select the product you are interested in:<br />
   <select name="selInformation">
     <option disabled="disabled" value=""> -- Hardware -- </option>
       <option value="Desktop">Desktop computers</option>
       <option value="Laptop">Laptop computers</option>
     <option disabled="disabled" value=""> -- Software -- </option>
       <option value="OfficeSoftware">Office software</option>
       <option value="Games">Games</option>
     <option disabled="disabled" value=""> -- Peripherals -- </option>
       <option value="Monitors">Monitors</option>
       <option value="InputDevices">Input Devices</option>
       <option value="Storage">Storage</option>
   </select>
<br /><br /><input type="submit" value="Submit" />
</form>
```

As you will see later in the chapter, the use of the `disabled` attribute prevents a user from selecting the option that carries it. With the careful use of a couple of dashes, the option groups become more clearly defined, as you can see in Figure 6-16.

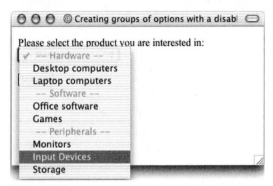

Figure 6-16

If you decide to use a select box as part of your navigation, for example to allow users to quickly jump to a particular section of a site, you should also include a submit button or go button. Avoid the temptation to use JavaScript to automatically take the user to the relevant page once he or she has selected an option. This is generally seen as an example of bad usability for several reasons. Many users can select the wrong section by accident. For example, if a user tries to select options using his or her up and down arrow keys, the script will fire as soon as he or she comes across the first option. Some browsers might not support the script, and it would need to be thoroughly checked on different platforms and for different browsers.

Attributes for Select Boxes

For completeness, here is the full list of attributes that the `<select>` element can carry:

- ❑ `name`, `size`, and `multiple`, all of which you have met
- ❑ `disabled` and `tabindex`, which are covered later in the chapter
- ❑ All universal attributes
- ❑ UI event attributes

Meanwhile the `<option>` element can carry the following attributes:

- ❑ `label`, which you have already seen
- ❑ `disabled`, which you learn about later in the chapter
- ❑ All universal attributes
- ❑ UI event attributes

File Select Boxes

If you want to allow a user to upload a file to your Web site from his computer, you will need to use a *file upload box*, also known as a *file select box*. This is created using the `<input>` element (again), this time giving the `type` attribute a value of `file` (ch06_eg14):

```
<form action="http://www.example.com/imageUpload.asp" method="post"
      name="fromImageUpload" enctype="multipart/form-data">

  <input type="file" name="fileUpload" accept="image/*" />

<br /><br /><input type="submit" value="Submit" />
</form>
```

When you are using a file upload box, the method attribute of the <form> element must be post.

There are some attributes in use here that you learned about at the beginning of the chapter:

❑ The enctype attribute has been added to the <form> element with a value of multipart/form-data so that each form control is sent separately to the server. This is required on a form that uses a file upload box.

❑ The accept attribute has been added to the <input> element to indicate the MIME types of the files that can be selected for upload. In this example, any image format can be uploaded as the wildcard character (the asterisk) has been used after the image/ portion of the MIME type. Unfortunately, this is not supported by Netscape 7 or IE 6.

In Figure 6-17 you can see that when you click the Browse button a file dialog box opens up enabling you to browse to a file and select which one you want to upload.

Figure 6-17

An <input> element whose type attribute has a value of file can take the following attributes:

❑ name, value, and accept, which you have already seen

❑ tabindex, accesskey, disabled, and readonly, which are covered later in the chapter

❑ All universal attributes

❑ UI event attributes

Hidden Controls

Sometimes you will want to pass information between pages without the user seeing it. Hidden form controls remain part of any form, but the user cannot see them in the Web browser. They should not, however, be used for any sensitive information you do not want the user to see because the user could see this data if she looked in the source of the page.

You may have come across forms on the Web that span more than one page. Long forms can be confusing; splitting them up can help a user, which means more forms will be filled out. In such cases, a Web site programmer often wants to pass values that a user has entered into the first form (on one page) onto the form in the second page, and then onto a further page. Hidden elements are one way in which programmers can pass values between pages.

You create a hidden control using the `<input>` element whose `type` attribute has a value of `hidden`. For example, the following form contains a hidden form control indicating which section of the site the user filled the form in from (`ch06_eg15.html`):

```
<form action="http://www.example.com/vote.asp" method="get" name="fromVote">
  <input type="hidden" name="hidPageSentFrom" value="home page" />
  <input type="submit" value="Click if this is your favorite page of our
site." />
</form>
```

So that a name and value can still be sent to the server for a hidden form control, the hidden control must carry `name` and `value` attributes.

Figure 6-18 shows that the hidden form control is not shown on the page, but it is available in the source for the page.

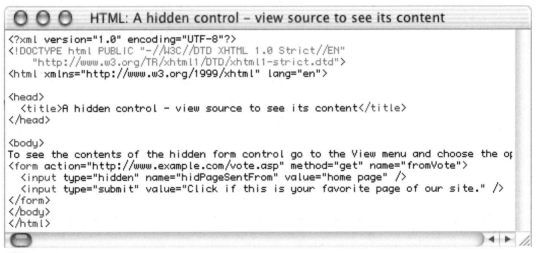

Figure 6-18

As you will see in Chapter 10, you can also hide form controls using the `display` and `visibility` properties.

Object Controls

The HTML 4.0 specification introduced the capability to use objects—embedded in an `<object>` element—as part of a form. To become successful controls they must appear inside the `<form>` element. For example, you may want to use an object that allows some kind of graphical interaction and store its value with the name of the object. However, this feature is not implemented in the main browsers at the time of writing.

Try It Out   Creating a Registration Form

In this example you are going to combine several of the form controls to make up a site registration form.

1. Create a new Transitional XHTML 1.0 document, with the skeleton in place. Then add a heading and introduction to what the user should be doing:

```
<?xml version="1.0" encoding="UTF-8"?>
<!DOCTYPE html PUBLIC "-//W3C//DTD XHTML 1.0 Transitional//EN"
    "http://www.w3.org/TR/xhtml1/DTD/xhtml1-transitional.dtd">
<html xmlns="http://www.w3.org/1999/xhtml" lang="en" xml:lang="en">

<head>
  <title>Registration</title>
</head>

<body>
  <h2>User Registration</h2>
  <p>Please complete the following form to register with our site:</p>
</body>
</html>
```

2. The form is going to be placed in a table with two columns so that the instructions are in the left column, and the form controls are aligned in the right column. (Without this, the form controls would look uneven across the page.) This is quite a common technique in writing forms.

In the first two rows you can add text inputs for username and password, and then leave a row blank for spacing out the page:

```
<table>
  <tr>
    <td>User Name:</td>
    <td><input type="text" name="txtUserName" size="20" /></td>
  </tr>
  <tr>
    <td>Password:</td>
    <td><input type="password" name="pwdPassword" size="20" /></td>
  </tr>
  <tr>
    <td> </td>
    <td> </td>
  </tr>
</table>
```

3. After the username and the password, add two radio buttons for the user to indicate his or her gender:

```
<tr>
  <td>Gender:</td>
  <td><input type="radio" name="radSex" value="male" />Male</td>
</tr>
<tr>
  <td></td>
  <td><input type="radio" name="radSex" value="female" />Female</td>
</tr>
<tr><td> </td><td> </td></tr>
```

4. Next you want to add a select box to indicate how the user heard about the Web site:

```
<tr>
  <td>How did you hear about us?:</td>
  <td>
    <select name="selReferrer">
      <option selected="selected" value="">Select answer</option>
      <option value="website">Another website</option>
      <option value="printAd">Magazine ad</option>
      <option value="friend">From a friend</option>
      <option value="other">Other</option>
    </select>
  </td>
</tr>
<tr><td> </td><td> </td></tr>
```

5. The last option for the user is whether they will subscribe to the newsletter on the site, which you accomplish with a checkbox. There is also the submit button for the form:

```
<tr>
  <td>Please select this box if you wish<br /> to be added to our mailing list
      <br /><small>We will not pass on your details to any third
      party.</small></td>
  <td><input type="checkbox" name="chkMailingList" /></td>
</tr>

<tr>
  <td></td>
  <td><input type="submit" value="Register now" /></td>
</tr>
</table>
```

6. Save the file as `registration.html` and open it up in your browser; it should look something like Figure 6-19.

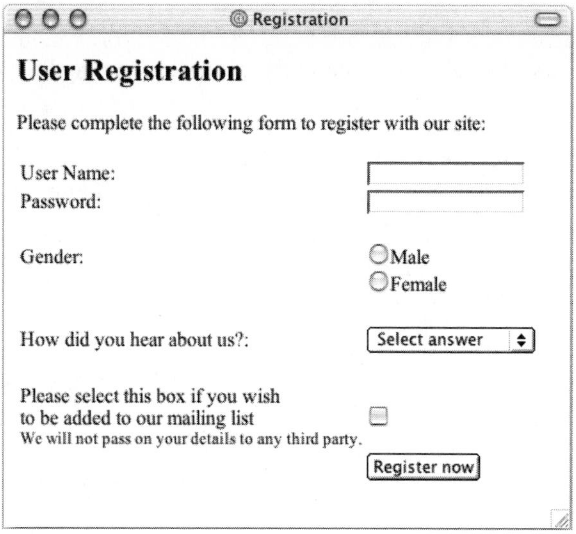

Figure 6-19

How It Works

This is an example of a form that makes use of several of the form controls, and you will just concentrate on those controls here.

First there were two text input boxes for the username and password. Because the password is sensitive information it used a password-type text input, which prevents anyone looking over the user's shoulder from seeing what the user is entering. Remember that the size attribute controls the width of the input box.

```
<tr>
  <td>User Name:</td>
  <td><input type="text" name="txtUserName" size="20" /></td>
</tr>
<tr>
  <td>Password:</td>
  <td><input type="password" name="pwdPassword" size="20" /></td>
</tr>
<tr>
```

Next the user has two radio buttons to indicate whether they are male or female. Both radio buttons have different names, making the selection mutually exclusive—you can pick only one of the two radio buttons. When the user selects one option, the value of the value attribute on that element is sent to the server.

```
<tr>
  <td>Gender:</td>
  <td><input type="radio" name="radSex" value="male" />Male</td>
</tr>
<tr>
  <td></td>
  <td><input type="radio" name="radSex" value="female" />Female</td>
</tr>
```

In the select box, the user has to choose how they heard about the site. The first option is automatically selected because it carries the `selected` attribute, which also acts as another hint to users that they must select one of the options. The value of the item selected will be sent to the server with the name `selRefferrer`.

```
<select name="selReferrer">
   <option selected="selected" value="">Select answer</option>
   <option value="website">Another website</option>
   <option value="printAd">Magazine ad</option>
   <option value="friend">From a friend</option>
   <option value="other">Other</option>
</select>
```

The user is finally presented with the option to subscribe to the newsletter, using a checkbox.

```
<tr>
   <td>Please select this box if you wish<br /> to be added to our mailing list
       <br /><small>We will not pass on your details to any third
       party.</small></td>
   <td><input type="checkbox" name="chkMailingList" /></td>
</tr>
```

In order to send the form, the user must click the `Register` now button. The words `Register` now appear because they have been given as the value of the `value` attribute:

```
<tr>
   <td></td>
   <td><input type="submit" value="Register now" /></td>
</tr>
```

Now that you've seen the basics of forms, it is time to look at some more advanced issues regarding their creation.

Creating Labels for Controls and the <label> Element

When you are creating a form it is absolutely vital that you provide good labeling so that the user knows what data he or she should be entering where.

Forms can be confusing enough at the best of times; I'm sure an insurance company or tax form has left you scratching your head at some point. So, unless your visitors are completely sure what information they should be providing and where that information should be, they will not be as inclined to fill in your forms.

Some form controls, such as buttons, already have labels. For the majority of form controls, however, you will have to provide the label yourself.

For controls that do not have a label, you should use the <label> element. This element does not affect the form in any way other than telling users what information they should be entering (ch06_eg16.html).

You can see that this form has been placed inside a table; this ensures that even if the labels are of different lengths the text inputs are aligned in their own column. If a list of text inputs has different indentations, it is very hard to use.

```
<form action="http://www.example.org/login.asp" method="post" name="frmLogin">
  <table>
    <tr>
      <td><label for="Uname">User name</label></td>
      <td><input type="text" id="Uname" name="txtUserName" /></td>
    </tr>
    <tr>
      <td><label for="Pwd">Password</label></td>
      <td><input type="password" id="Pwd" name="pwdPassword" /></td>
    </tr>
  </table>
</form>
```

As you can see here the `<label>` element carries an attribute called `for`, which indicates the form control the label is associated with. The value of the `for` attribute should be the same as the value of the `id` attribute on the corresponding form control. For example, the text box form control where a user enters his or her username has an `id` attribute whose value is `Uname`, and the label for this text box has a `for` attribute whose value is also `Uname`.

Figure 6-20 shows you what this login screen looks like.

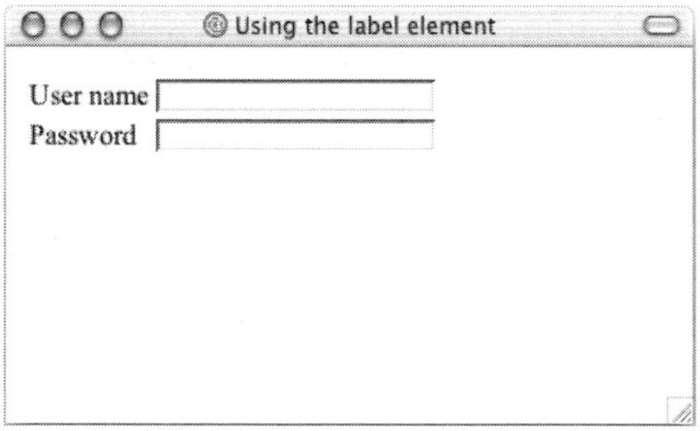

Figure 6-20

The label may be positioned before or after the control. For text boxes, it is generally good practice to have the label on the left, whereas for checkboxes and radio buttons it is often easier to associate the label with the correct form control if they are on the right.

> You should have a new **`<label>`** element for each form control.

Another way of to use the `<label>` element is as a containing element. This kind of label is sometimes known as an *implicit label*. For example:

```
<form action="http://www.example.org/login.asp" method="post" name="frmLogin">
  <label for="Uname"><input type="text" id="Uname" name="txtUserName"
```

```
/></label>
   <label for="Pwd"><input type="password" id="Pwd" name="pwdPassword"
/></label>
   </form>
```

The drawback with this approach is that you cannot control where the label appears in relation to the form control and you certainly cannot have the label in a different table cell than the form control as the markup would not nest correctly.

In the section "Focus" later in this chapter, you learn about giving form elements focus. When a label gains focus, the focus should be passed onto the associated control (although IE 5.5 for Mac has problems with this).

Structuring Your Forms with <fieldset> and <legend> Elements

Large forms can be confusing for users, so it's good practice to group together related form controls. The <fieldset> and <legend> elements do exactly this—help you group controls.

Both elements work only in IE 4 and Netscape 6 and later versions; however, older browsers will just ignore these elements, so you are safe to include them in all of your forms.

❑   The <fieldset> element creates a border around the group of form controls to show that they are related.

❑   The <legend> element allows you to specify a caption for the <fieldset> element, which acts as a title for the group of form controls. When used, the <legend> element should always be the first child of the <fieldset> element.

In the following example, you can see how a form has been divided into four sections: contact information, competition question, tiebreaker question, and enter the competition (ch06_eg17.html).

```
<form action="http://www.example.org/competition.asp" method="post"
name="frmComp">
 <fieldset>
  <legend><em>Contact Information</em></legend>
   <label>First name: <input type="text" name="txtFName"
size="20" /></label><br />
   <label>Last name: <input type="text" name="txtLName"
size="20" /></label><br />
   <label>E-mail: <input type="text" name="txtEmail"
size="20" /></label><br />
  </fieldset>
  <fieldset>
  <legend><em>Competition Question</em></legend>
   How tall is the Eiffel Tower in Paris, France? <br />
   <label><input type="radio" name="radAnswer" value="584" />584
    ft</label><br />
   <label><input type="radio" name="radAnswer" value="784" />784
```

```
  ft</label><br />
  <label><input type="radio" name="radAnswer" value="984" />984
  ft</label><br />
  <label><input type="radio" name="radAnswer" value="1184" />1184
  ft</label><br />
  </fieldset>
  <fieldset>
    <legend><em>Tiebreaker Question</em></legend>
      <label>In 25 words or less, say why you would like to win $10,000:
        <textarea name="txtTiebreaker" rows="10" cols="40"></textarea>
      </label>
  </fieldset>
  <fieldset>
    <legend><em>Enter competition</em></legend>
        <input type="submit" value="Enter Competition" />
  </fieldset>
</form>
```

You can see how the <fieldset> elements create borders around the groups of form controls, and how the <legend> elements are used to title the groups of controls. Remember that the <legend> element must be the first child of the <fieldset> element when it is used.

The <fieldset> element can take the following attributes:

❑   All of the universal attributes

❑   The basic event attributes

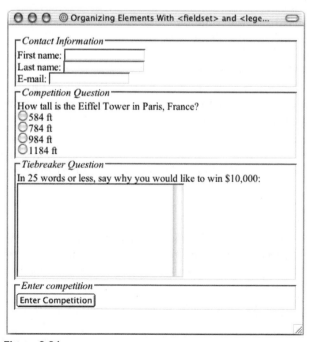

Figure 6-21

> Note that if you use a table to format your form, the **<table>** element must appear inside the **<fieldset>** element. If a **<fieldset>** resides within a table that is used to format the page, then the entire fieldset must reside within the same cell.

The <legend> element can take the following attributes:

❑ accesskey, which you will learn about in the next section

❑ align (which is deprecated—you should use CSS positioning instead)

❑ All of the universal attributes

❑ UI event attributes

Focus

When a Web page featuring several links or several form controls loads, you might have noticed that you are able to use your Tab key to move between those elements (or Shift+Tab to move backward through elements). As you move between them, the Web browser tends to add some form of border or highlighting to that element (be it a link or a form control). This is known as *focus*.

From what you have learned already about XHTML you know that not every element in the document receives this focus. In fact, it is only the elements that a user can interact with, such as links and form controls, that can receive focus. Indeed, if a user is expected to interact with an element, that element *must* be able to receive focus.

An element can gain focus in three ways:

❑ That element can be selected using a pointing device such as a mouse or trackball.

❑ The elements can be navigated between using the keyboard—often using the Tab key (or Shift+Tab to move backward through elements). The elements in some documents can be given a fixed *tabbing order*, indicating the order in which elements gain focus.

❑ Using a system such as a keyboard shortcut known as an *access key* to select a particular element. For example, on a PC you would likely press the Alt key plus an access key (such as Alt+E), whereas on a Mac you would press the Control key with an access key (such as Control+E).

Tabbing Order

If you want to control the order in which elements can gain focus you can use the tabindex attribute to give that element a number between 0 and 32767, which forms part of the tabbing order. Every time the user presses the Tab key the focus moves to the element with the next highest tabbing order (and again, Shift+Tab moves focus in reverse order).

The following elements can carry a tabindex attribute:

```
<a> <area> <button> <input> <object> <select> <textarea>
```

The `tabindex` attribute is supported by Netscape 6 and IE 4 and later versions, but older browsers just ignore this attribute, so it is safe to use it in all documents.

Once a user has tabbed through all elements in a document that can gain focus, then focus may be given to browser features (most commonly the address bar).

To demonstrate how tabbing order works, the following example gives focus to the checkboxes in a different order than you might expect (`ch06_eg18.html`):

```
<form action="http://www.example.com/tabbing.asp" method="get"
        name="frmTabExample">
    <input type="checkbox" name="chkNumber" value="1" tabindex="3" /> One<br />
    <input type="checkbox" name="chkNumber" value="2" tabindex="7" /> Two<br />
    <input type="checkbox" name="chkNumber" value="3" tabindex="4" /> Three<br />
    <input type="checkbox" name="chkNumber" value="4" tabindex="1" /> Four<br />
    <input type="checkbox" name="chkNumber" value="5" tabindex="9" /> Five<br />
    <input type="checkbox" name="chkNumber" value="6" tabindex="6" /> Six<br />
    <input type="checkbox" name="chkNumber" value="7" tabindex="10" />
Seven <br />
    <input type="checkbox" name="chkNumber" value="8" tabindex="2" /> Eight<br />
    <input type="checkbox" name="chkNumber" value="9" tabindex="8" /> Nine<br />
    <input type="checkbox" name="chkNumber" value="10" tabindex="5" /> Ten<br />
<input type="submit" value="Submit" />
</form>
```

In this example the checkboxes will receive focus in the following order:

```
4, 8, 1, 3, 10, 6, 2, 9, 5, 7
```

Figure 6-22 shows how IE 5.5 for Mac will, by default, give a blue outline to form elements as they gain focus.

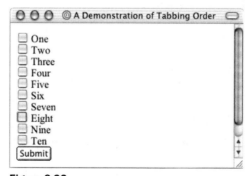

Figure 6-22

You should always start your `tabindex` values with 1 or higher, rather than 0, because elements that could gain focus yet do not have a `tabindex` attribute are given a value of 0 and are navigated in the order in which they appear after those with a `tabindex` have been cycled through. If two elements have the same value for a `tabindex` attribute, they will be navigated in the order in which they appear in the document.

Note that if an element is disabled, it cannot gain focus and does not participate in the tabbing order.

193

Access Keys

Access keys act just like keyboard shortcuts. The access key is a single character from the document's character set that is expected to appear on the user's keyboard. When this is used in conjunction with another key (such as Alt on Windows and Control on an Apple) the browser automatically goes to that section (exactly which key must be used in conjunction with the access key depends upon the operating system and browser).

The access key is defined using the `accesskey` attribute. The value of this attribute is the character (and key on the keyboard) you want the user to be able to press (in conjunction with the other key that is dependent upon the operating system and browser).

The following elements can carry an access key attribute:

```
<a> <area> <button> <input> <label> <legend> <textarea>
```

The `accesskey` attribute is supported by Netscape 6 and IE 4 and later versions, but older browsers just ignore these attributes, so it is safe to use them in all documents.

To see how access keys work, you can revisit the example of a competition form (`ch06_eg17.html`), which was covered in the section "Structuring Your Forms with <fieldset> and <legend> Elements" earlier in this chapter. Now the `accesskey` attributes can be added to the `<legend>` elements:

```
<legend accesskey="c"><u>C</u>ontact Information (ALT + C)</legend>
<legend>Competition Question</legend>
<legend accesskey="t"><u>T</u>iebreaker Question (ALT + T)</legend>
<legend>Enter competition</legend>
```

The new version of this file is `ch06_eg19.html` in the download code. (Extra `<br />` elements have been added to show how the screen scrolls to the appropriate section when an access key is used.) As a hint to users that they can use the access keys as shortcuts, information has also been added to the information in the `<legend>` element in two ways:

❑   In brackets after the title

❑   By underlining the access key itself

Figure 6-23 shows how this updated example looks in a browser.

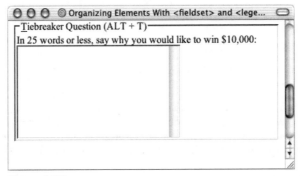

Figure 6-23

The effect of an access key being used depends upon the element that it is used with. With <legend> elements such as those shown previously, the browser scrolls to that part of the page automatically and gives focus to the first form control in the section. When used with form controls, those elements gain focus. As soon as the element gains focus, the user should be able to interact with it (either by typing in text controls or pressing the Enter or Return key with other form controls).

When using letters a–z, it does not matter whether you specify an uppercase or lowercase access key, although strictly speaking it should be lowercase.

Disabled and Read-Only Controls

Throughout the chapter you have seen that several of the elements can carry attributes called disabled and readonly:

❑ The readonly attribute prevents users from changing the value of the form control themselves, although it may be modified by a script. A name/value pair of a readonly control *will* be sent to the server. Its value should be readonly.

❑ The disabled attribute disables the form control so that users cannot alter it. A script can be used to re-enable the control, but unless a control is re-enabled the name/value pair will not be sent to the server. Its value should be disabled.

The readonly and disabled attributes work only in Netscape 6 and IE 5 and later versions, although older browsers ignore them, so you can add these attributes to all documents. You should be aware, however, that because older browsers ignore these attributes, users with older browsers would still be able to interact with form controls that have readonly or disabled attributes.

A readonly control is particularly helpful when you want to indicate to a user something that they have already said or that they are agreeing to, or when you want to stop them from changing a standard part of the form. You often see readonly controls for user agreements and in the body of e-mail forms that allow you to e-mail a link to a friend.

The disabled attribute is particularly helpful when preventing users from interacting with a control until they have done something else. For example, you might use a script to disable a submit button until all of the form fields contain a value.

The following table indicates which form controls work with the readonly and disabled attributes.

Element	readonly	disabled
<textarea>	Yes	Yes
<input type="text" />	Yes	Yes
<input type="checkbox" />	No	Yes
<input type="radio" />	No	Yes
<input type="submit" />	No	Yes

Continues

Element	readonly	disabled
<input type="reset"/ >	No	Yes
<input type="button"/ >	No	Yes
<select>	No	Yes
<option>	No	Yes
<button>	No	Yes

The following table indicates the main differences between the readonly and disabled attributes.

Attribute	readonly	disabled
Can be modified	Yes by script, not by user	Not while disabled
Will be sent to server	Yes	Not while disabled
Will receive focus	Yes	No
Included in tabbing order	Yes	No

Sending Form Data to the Server

You've already learned about the submit button, which the user presses to initiate the sending of form data to the server, but this book has not yet covered the difference between the HTTP get and HTTP post methods. You might remember that you can specify which of these two methods is used by adding the method attribute to the <form> element—just as all of the examples in this chapter have done.

The method attribute can take one of two values, either get or post, corresponding to the HTTP methods used to send the form data. If the <form> element does not carry a method attribute, then by default the get method will be used. If you are using a file upload form control you must choose the post method (and you must set the enctype attribute to have a value of mutlipart/form-data).

HTTP get

When you send form data to the server using the HTTP get method, the form data is appended to the URL specified in the action attribute of the <form> element.

The form data is separated from the URL using a question mark. Following the question mark you get the name/value pairs for each form control. Each name/value pair is separated by an ampersand (&).

For example, take the following login form, which you saw when the password form control was introduced:

```
<form action="http://www.example.com/login.asp" method="post">
  Username:
```

```
<input type="text" name="txtUsername" value="" size="20" maxlength="20"><br />
Password:
<input type="password" name="pwdPassword" value="" size="20" maxlength="20">
<input type="submit" />
</form>
```

When you click the submit button, your username and password are appended to the URL
`http://www.example.com/login.asp` like so in what is known as the *query string*:

```
http://www.example.com/login.asp?txtUserName=Bob&pwdPassword=LetMeIn
```

Note that, when a browser requests a URL with any spaces or unsafe characters (such as /, \, =, &, and +, which have special meanings in URL), they are replaced with a hex code to represent that character. This is done automatically by the browser, and is known as *URL encoding*. When the data reaches the server, it will usually un-encode the special characters automatically.

One of the great advantages of passing form data in a URL is that it can be bookmarked. If you look at searches performed on major search engines such as Google, they tend to use the get method so that the page can be bookmarked.

There are some disadvantages with the get method, however. Indeed, when sending sensitive data such as the password shown here, or credit card details, you should not use the get method because the sensitive data becomes part of the URL and is in full view to everyone.

You should not use the HTTP get method when:

❑   You are updating a data source such as a database or spreadsheet (because someone could make up URLs that would alter your data source)

❑   You are dealing with sensitive information, such as passwords or credit card details (because the sensitive form data would be visible as part of a URL).

❑   You have large amounts of data (because older browsers do not allow URLs to exceed more than 1,024 characters—although the recent versions of the main browsers do not have limits)

❑   Your form contains a file upload control (because uploaded files cannot be passed in the URL)

❑   Your users might enter non-ASCII characters such as Hebrew or Cyrillic characters

In these circumstances you should use the HTTP post method.

HTTP post

When you send data from a form to the server using the HTTP post method the form data is sent transparently in what are known as the *HTTP headers*. While you do not see these headers, they are sent in clear text and cannot be relied upon to be secure (unless you are sending data under a *Secure Sockets Layer*, or *SSL*).

If the login form you just saw was sent using the post method it could look something like this in the HTTP headers:

```
User-agent: MSIE 5.5
Content-Type: application/x-www-form-urlencoded
```

```
Content-length: 35
...other headers go here...
txtUserName=Bob&pwdPassword=LetMeIn
```

Note that the last line is the form data, and that it is in exactly the same format as the data after the question mark in the `get` method—it would also be URL-encoded if it contained spaces or any characters reserved for use in URLs.

There is nothing to stop you using the `post` method to send form data to a page that also contains a query string. For example, you might have one page to handle users that want to subscribe to or unsubscribe from a newsletter, and you might choose to indicate whether a user wanted to subscribe or unsubscribe in the query string. Meanwhile you might want to send their actual contact details in a form that uses the `post` method because you are updating a data source. In which case you could use the following `<form>` element as follows:

```
<form action="http://www.example.com/newsletter.asp?action=subscribe"
      method="post">
```

The only disadvantage with using the HTTP `post` method is that the information the user entered on the form cannot be bookmarked in the same way it can when it is contained in the URL. So you cannot use it to retrieve a page that was generated using specific form data as you can when you bookmark a page generated by most search engines.

Try It Out   The Registration Form Revisited

It is time to revisit the registration form from the earlier Try It Out section in this chapter. This time you add some more fields into it, and make it more usable.

1. Open the file `registration.html` that you made earlier in the chapter and save it as `registration2.html` so that you have a different copy to work with.

2. You should create `<label>` elements for all of the form controls. This involves putting the instructions for that control inside a `<label>` element. This element should carry the `for` attribute, whose value is the value of the `id` attribute on the corresponding form control, like this one:

```
<tr>
  <td><label for="userName">User name:</label></td>
  <td><input type="text" name="txtUserName" size="20" id="username" /></td>
</tr>
```

3. You have to label the two radio buttons individually:

```
<tr>
  <td>Gender:</td>
  <td><input type="radio" name="radSex" value="male" id="male" />
  <label for ="male">Male</label></td>
</tr>
<tr>
  <td></td>
  <td><input type="radio" name="radSex" value="female" id="female" />
  <label for="female">Female</label></td>
</tr>
```

If you remember the last chapter's discussion of table linearization for screen readers then this should work fine for most users. If, however, another column were to the right with unrelated information (such as ads) this could confuse readers, so the table for the form controls should hold only the controls and their labels.

4. Next you are going to add four new text boxes after the username and password. The first text input will be to confirm the password and then there will be an empty row. This will be followed by two text inputs: one for the user's first name and one for the user's last name. Then there will be another empty row, followed by an input for the user's e-mail address:

```
<tr>
  <td><label for="confPwd">Confirm Password:</label></td>
  <td><input type="password" name="pwdPasswordConf" size="20"
      id="confPassword" /></td>
</tr>
<tr><td> </td><td> </td></tr>
<tr>
  <td><label for="firstName">First name:</label></td>
  <td><input type="text" name="txtFirstName" size="20" id="firstName" /></td>
</tr>
<tr>
  <td><label for="lastName">Last name:</label></td>
  <td><input type="text" name="txtLastName" size="20" id="lastName" /></td>
</tr>
<tr><td> </td><td> </td></tr>
<tr>
  <td><label for="email">Email address:</label></td>
  <td><input type="text" name="txtEmail" size="20" id="email" /></td>
</tr>
```

5. Now it is time to split the form into two sections using the `<fieldset>` element. The first section will indicate that it is for information about the user (containing username, password, name, e-mail, and gender details), the second for information about the company (how the user found the site and if they want to be on the mailing list).

You might remember from last chapter that a table can contain any markup within a cell, or be contained by an element, but the markup cannot stretch across cells—it must nest properly. This means that the form has to be split into two tables (one for each section) in order for the `<fieldset>` elements to nest correctly.

Both `<fieldset>` elements will carry access keys. Here is the `<fieldset>` element for the second section of the form:

```
<fieldset>
    <legend accesskey="u">About <u>U</u>s (ALT + U)</legend>
<table>
  <tr>
    <td><label for="referrer">How did you hear about us?</label>:</td>
    <td>
      <select name="selReferrer" id="referrer">
        <option selected="selected" value="">Select answer</option>
        <option value="website">Another website</option>
        <option value="printAd">Magazine ad</option>
```

```
            <option value="friend">From a friend</option>
            <option value="other">Other</option>
      </select>
   </td>
 </tr>
 <tr><td> </td><td> </td></tr>

 <tr>
   <td><label for="mailList">Please select this box if you wish<br /> to be
       added to our mailing list
       <br /><small>We will not pass on your details to any third
       party.</small></label></td>
   <td><input type="checkbox" name="chkMailingList" id="mailList" /></td>
 </tr>

 </table>
 </fieldset>
```

This extended registration form is now a lot more usable. If you save the file again and open it in your browser, you should find something that looks like Figure 6-24.

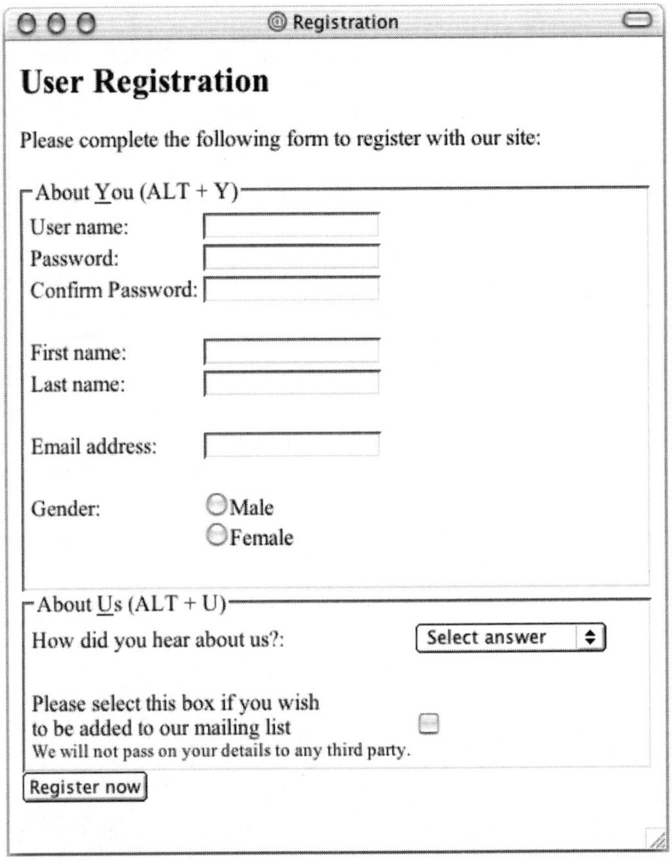

Figure 6-24

How It Works

You should be familiar with most of what is going on here, but let's just address a few key points.

❑ The form has been divided up into sections using the <fieldset> element. This added structure makes it easier to use the form, as the user knows what section he or she is in.

❑ The accesskey attributes, which provide keyboard shortcuts, are particularly helpful if you are creating long forms, so that users can immediately go to the relevant section. In reality the accesskey attributes are more likely to be of use when creating a site that people will use frequently, rather than a form that users will use only a few times. Users tend to use the shortcuts only if they are familiar with the form already and want to skip between the sections.

❑ As you will see in Chapter 12, if you are creating a particularly long form, it may be a good idea to split the form up into several pages.

❑ The <label> elements are of particular help to those who use screen readers. It ensures that the users know what they are supposed to be entering into which form control.

❑ When splitting up your page using the <fieldset> element, make sure that your elements nest correctly. You cannot just place <fieldset> elements between rows of a table.

Summary

This chapter has introduced you to the world of creating online forms, which are a vital part of many sites. In most cases when you want or need to directly collect information from a visitor to your site you will use a form, and you have seen several different examples of forms in this chapter. From simple search boxes and login pages to complex online order forms and registration processes, forms are a vital part of Web design.

You have learned how a form lives inside a <form> element and that inside a form there are one or more form controls. You have seen how the <input> element can be used to create several kinds of form controls, namely single line text input controls, checkboxes, radio buttons, file upload boxes, buttons, and hidden form controls. There are also the <textarea> elements for creating multiple line text inputs and the <select> and <option> elements for creating select boxes.

Once you have created a form with its form controls, you need to make sure that each element is labeled properly so that users know what information they should enter or which selection they will be making. You can also organize larger forms using the <fieldset> and <label> elements and aid navigation with tabindex and accesskey attributes.

Finally you learned when you should use the HTTP get or post methods to send form data to the server.

Next, it is time to look at the last of our core XHTML chapters, which covers framesets. You will see more about form design in Chapter 12, which covers some design issues that will make your forms easier to understand.

Exercises

The answers to all of the exercises are in Appendix A.

1. Create an e-mail feedback form that looks like the one shown in Figure 6-25.

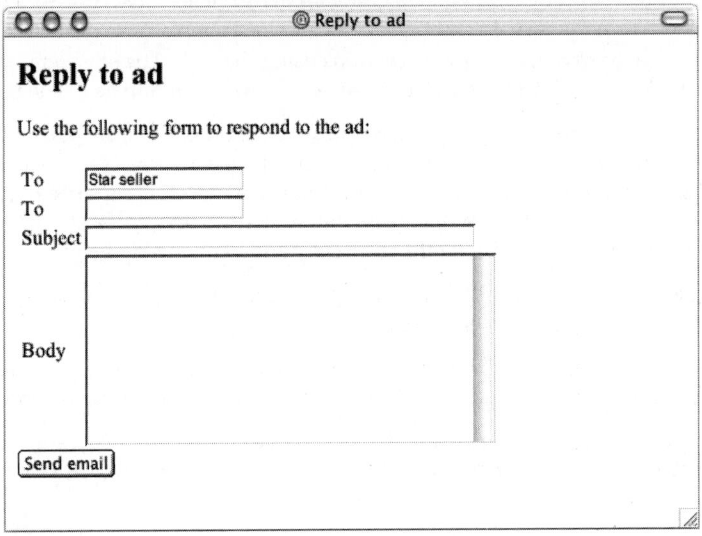

Figure 6-25

Note that the first text box is a `readonly` text box so that the user cannot alter the name of the person the mail is being sent to.

2. Create a voting or ranking form that looks like the one shown in Figure 6-26.

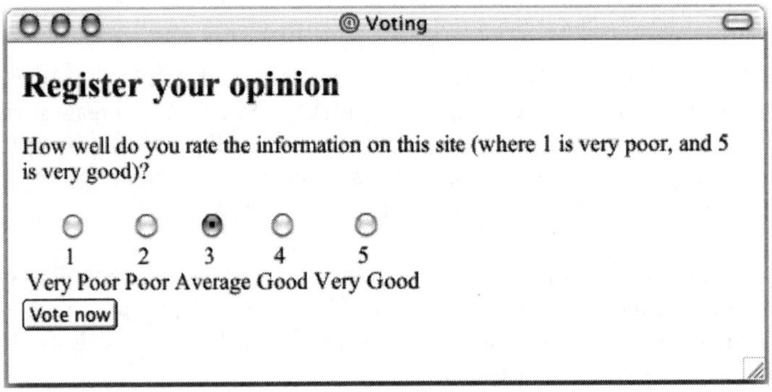

Figure 6-26

Note that the following `<style>` element was added to the `<head>` of the document to make each column of the table the same fixed width, with text aligned in the center (you see more about this in Chapter 8).

```
<head>
  <title>Voting</title>
  <style type="text/css">td {width:100; text-align:center;}</style>
</head>
```

Frames

Frames divide a browser window into several pieces or panes, each pane containing a separate XHTML page. One of the key advantages that frames offer is that you can then load and reload single panes without having to reload the entire contents of the browser window. A collection of frames in the browser window is known as a *frameset*.

The window is divided up into frames in a similar pattern to the way tables are organized: into rows and columns (although they are usually relatively basic in structure). The simplest of framesets might just divide the screen into two rows, while a complex frameset could use several rows and columns.

In this chapter you learn:

- ❑ How to create a frameset document with multiple frames
- ❑ How to create inline frames (single windows within a document that reloads)
- ❑ How to deal with users whose browsers cannot use frames

> I should warn you early on that there are actually very few cases in which I would consider using frames, although this is a matter of preference and I explain my reasons why in the first section of this chapter.

When to Use Frames

Before I show you what frames are capable of, I should mention that whether you use them is very much a matter of taste. A lot of beginners use frames in their sites, particularly creating one for navigation and the other for content. But then as they learn more about HTML and XHTML they tend to move toward using tables for layout (something you will learn more about in Chapter 10) and, increasingly, CSS.

Personally, there are very few circumstances in which I would suggest that you use frames in a page. The cases in which I think frames are useful include:

❏ When you want to create a (comparatively small) navigation bar, when the main content of the page must contain a lot of information and cannot be split into separate pages (so the user would have to scroll down a long way to see that section). In this case one frame acts like a table of contents to a very long document.

❏ When you have a lot of data in one part of the page that you do not want to reload, while another part of the page changes. Examples might include a photography site where you have lots of thumbnails in one frame, and the main picture in another. Rather than reloading the thumbnails each time a visitor wants to look at a new main picture, you can just reload the main picture.

For each frame you have in a layout, you need to have a file to be its content (each frame is essentially its own Web page), so the number of files in your site quickly grows. You therefore need to be particularly careful with your file structure so that you do not get lost in a sea of extra files.

A couple of other drawbacks you should be aware of with frames are as follows:

❏ Some browsers do not print well from framesets.

❏ Some smaller devices cannot cope with frames, often because their screen is not big enough to be divided up.

❏ If you design a page so that the content of a frame fits within the borders of a frame, users with a lower resolution monitor than you can end up seeing only a portion of what you intend them to see. Also, users with a higher resolution monitor than the designer may end up with large gaps around the edges of the frames.

❏ If you have a navigation frame loading different pages into a "main frame" it is hard to create a navigation bar that tells the user which page they are on (because the other frame loads the new page without telling the navigation bar).

❏ The browser's Back button might not work as the user hopes.

While you know my opinion on frames, if you think their advantages outweigh the disadvantages, then you should use them.

Introducing the Frameset

To help you understand frames, Figure 7-1 shows you a frameset document in a browser. This frameset divides the page into three and each separate part of the page is a separate XHTML document.

You may remember from Chapter 1 that, when writing a frameset document, you use a different DOCTYPE declaration. This is because frameset documents use a few elements in different ways than other XHTML documents.

To create a frameset document, first you need the <frameset> element, which is used instead of the <body> element. The frameset defines the rows and columns your page is divided into, which in turn specify where each individual frame will go. Each frame is then represented by a <frame> element.

You also need to learn the <noframes> element, which provides a message for users whose browsers do not support frames.

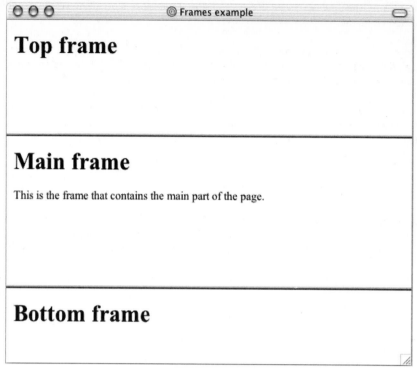

Figure 7-1

To get a better idea of how frames work, here is the code for the frameset shown previously in Figure 7-1 (ch07_eg01.html):

```
<?xml version="1.0" encoding="iso-8859-1"?>
<!DOCTYPE html PUBLIC "-//W3C//DTD XHTML 1.0 Frameset//EN"
  "http://www.w3.org/TR/xhtml1/DTD/xhtml1-frameset.dtd">

<html>
<head>
  <title>Frames example</title>
</head>

<frameset rows="150, *, 100">
    <frame src="top_frame.html" />
    <frame src="main_frame.html" />
    <frame src="bottom_frame.html" />
    <noframes><body>
      This site uses a technology called frames. Unfortunately, your
      browser does not support this technology. Please upgrade
      your browser and visit us again!
    </body></noframes>
</frameset>

</html>
```

In practical terms, the new DOCTYPE declaration does little more than allow you to use these frame-related elements.

You already know that there is no <body> element as it has been replaced with the <frameset> element; also, there should be no markup between the closing </head> tag and the opening <frameset> tag, other than a comment if you want to include one.

As you will see shortly, the <frameset> element must carry the two attributes rows and cols, which specify the number of rows and columns that make up the frameset. In our example there are just three rows, the first being 150 pixels high, the third just 100 pixels high, and the second taking up the rest of the page.

```
<frameset rows="150, *, 100">
```

Inside the <frameset> element are the empty <frames /> elements. The <frames /> elements indicate which page will be kept inside that frame using the src attribute. There is also a <noframes> element whose contents will be displayed if the user's browser does not support frames.

You see three pages in the browser window in this example:

❏   top_frame.html

❏   main_frame.html

❏   bottom_frame.html

You should be able to see which part of the window each of these pages corresponds to fairly easily in Figure 7-1, shown previously.

To give you another idea of how frames can work, look at Figure 7-2, which shows a site that uses horizontal and vertical frames. (This shows the similarity between the way in which simple tables divide up pages, and how frames can be used.)

> *Even though Netscape has supported frames since version 2, and IE introduced them in version 3, frames didn't make it into HTML until version 4.0.*

Now that you have a good idea of how a frameset document appears, it's time to look at the elements in a little more detail.

The <frameset> Element

The <frameset> element replaces the <body> element in frameset documents. It is the attributes of the <frameset> element that specify how the browser window will be divided up into rows and columns; these attributes are as follows:

❏   cols specifies how many columns are in the frameset

❏   rows specifies how many rows are in the frameset

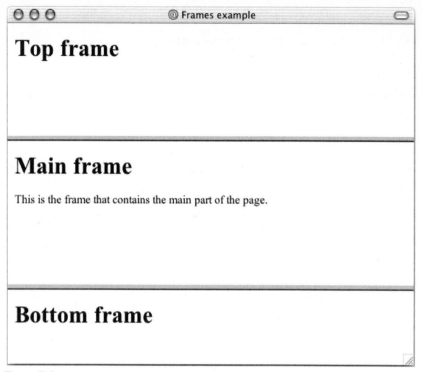

Figure 7-2

The `<frameset>` element contains a `<frame>` element for each frame of the document (or each cell of the grid constructed by the `<frameset>` element) and a `<noframes>` elements to indicate what should be displayed to the user if their browser does not load frames.

As well as the `rows` and `cols` attributes, the frameset element can also take the following attributes:

```
class id onload onunload rows style title
```

Netscape and IE also support the following well-used attributes (some of which are covered here because of their popularity). They are not, however, part of the W3C recommendation.

```
onblur onfocus border bordercolor frameborder framespacing
```

The cols Attribute

The `cols` attribute specifies how many columns are contained in the frameset and the size of each column. You have to provide a value to indicate the width for each of the columns in your frameset, and the number of values you provide (each separated by a comma) indicates how many columns there are in the document. For example, here there are three columns: the first takes up 20 percent of the width of the browser window, the second takes up 60 percent, and the third takes the last 20 percent:

```
cols="20%, 60%, 20%"
```

Because there are three values, the browser knows that there should be three columns.

You can specify the width of each column in one of four ways:

❑ Absolute values in pixels

❑ A percentage of the browser window (or parent frame if you are nesting framesets)

❑ Using a wildcard symbol

❑ As relative widths of the browser window (or parent frame)

You can mix and match these different ways of specifying column widths, but note the precedence they take (discussed after the four methods).

If you do not specify a `cols` attribute then the default value is 100 percent, so, if you do not specify a `cols` attribute then there will be one column that takes up 100 percent of the width of the browser.

Absolute Values in Pixels

To specify the width of a column in pixels, you just use a number. (You do not need to use px or any other characters after the number.) For example, here are three columns: the first is 100 pixels, the second is 500 pixels, and the third takes up the remainder of the page (using the wildcard symbol *).

```
cols="100, 500, *"
```

If you use absolute values only, and the width of the window is less or more than the specified values, then the browser will adjust the width of each column in proportion to the width of the browser window. So, if you want three columns of 100 pixels, you might specify it like this:

```
cols="100, 100, 100"
```

However, if the browser window were 600 pixels wide, you would end up with three columns of 200 pixels. Therefore if you really want to specify fixed absolute widths that won't grow, use a wildcard character after the third column and either make the content of the fourth frame blank or do not include a `<frame />` element for it:

```
cols="100, 100, 100, *"
```

Interestingly, if you have four columns 200 pixels wide, and the browser window is only 600 pixels wide, your columns would all be squashed proportionately to 150 pixels wide; the window will not use scrollbars to make the page 800 pixels wide.

A Percentage of the Browser Window or Parent Frame

To specify the width of a column as a percentage of a window (or, if you use nested frames, which you will meet later in the chapter, a percentage of the parent frame) you use a number followed by the percent sign. For example, the following attribute value specifies two columns, one of 40 percent and another of 60 percent of the browser window:

```
cols="40%, 60%"
```

If you specify widths as percentages, but they are more or less than 100 percent, the browser will adjust widths proportionately.

The Wildcard Symbol

The asterisk, or wildcard symbol, indicates the "rest of the window," when used with an absolute value or percentage. Here the first column is 400 pixels wide and the second frame takes up the remainder of the browser window:

```
cols="400, *"
```

Relative Widths Between Columns

As an alternative to percentages, you can use relative widths of the browser window, which are best illustrated with an example. Here the window is divided into sixths: the first column takes up half of the window, the second takes one third, and the third takes one sixth:

```
cols="3*, 2*, 1*"
```

You can tell that the window is divided up into sixths by adding up the values of the relative widths.

Value Priorities and Resizing Windows

Absolute widths always take priority over relative widths. Look at the following example with three columns:

```
cols="250, *, 250"
```

If the window is only 510 pixels wide, then the center frame will be only 10 pixels wide. You have to be careful when designing frames so that your users will be able to see what you intend them to see.

Furthermore, if the user resizes his or her window to less than 500 pixels wide, the browser will try to show as much of the columns defined using absolute widths as possible, ignoring any columns defined using relative widths.

Whenever a user resizes his or her window, relative widths and percentages are recalculated, but absolute widths remain the same.

If you specify too many columns for the number of frames you want, the rightmost column ends up being a blank space; if you specify too many frames, the extra ones will be ignored.

The rows Attribute

The rows attribute works just like the cols attribute and can take the same values, but it is used to specify the rows in the frameset. For example, the following rows attribute will specify three rows: the top row should be 100 pixels tall, the second should be 80 percent of the screen, and the bottom row should take up the screen that is left (if anything):

```
rows="100, 80%, *"
```

The default value for the rows attribute is 100 percent so, if you do not specify a rows attribute, one row will take up 100 percent of the height of the browser.

Browser-Specific Extensions to the <frameset> Element

Both Netscape and IE added some very important extensions to the <frameset> element that really deserve mention here. As you might have noticed in the first example, by default a frame creates a border and you will likely want to control the appearance of this border. While you can now use CSS to control these properties, you are likely to come across them if you look at older code.

The border Attribute

The border attribute specifies the width of the border of each frame in pixels. It was introduced in Netscape 3 and IE 4.

```
border="10"
```

If you do not want a border, you can give this attribute a value of 0. Figure 7-2 shows what the example in Figure 7-1 would look like with a 10-pixel border (ch07_eg02.html):

When you are first creating a frameset document it can be a good idea to set this attribute to have a value of 1, even if you do not want borders, as it makes the frames clear when you are building the site; you can easily remove them by altering this one attribute on the <frameset> element.

Note that if you nest framesets (as you will see how to do later in the chapter) Netscape pays attention only to the border attribute on the outermost <frameset> element.

The frameborder Attribute

The frameborder attribute specifies whether a three-dimensional border should be displayed between frames. The following indicates that there should not be any borders (which is the same as if the border attribute is given a value of 0):

```
frameborder="0"
```

The table that follows shows possible values for the frameborder attribute.

Value	Purpose
1 or yes	Indicates borders should be shown, the default value (yes is not part of HTML 4 but is still supported by IE and Netscape)
0 or no	Indicates borders should not be shown (no is not part of HTML 4 but is still supported by IE and Netscape)

Figure 7-3 shows what the frames would look like without a border—you cannot see where one frame ends and another begins—unless you have different images or background colors for the pages in the frames (ch07_eg04.html).

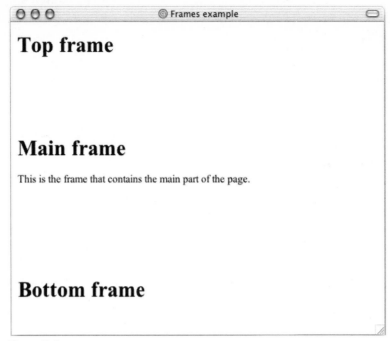

Figure 7-3

The framespacing Attribute

The framespacing attribute specifies the amount of space between frames in a frameset. The value should be given in pixels and the default value is 2 if not otherwise specified.

```
framespacing="10"
```

Figure 7-4 shows what the example from Figure 7-1 would look like with a framespacing attribute indicating a 5-pixel gap between frames (ch07_eg05.html).

You will have all Netscape 3 and above and IE 3 and above browsers covered if you use the border, frameborder, and framespacing attributes together, each with a value of 0.

```
border="0" frameborder="0" framespacing="0"
```

Several other browser-specific attributes are covered in Chapter 8.

The <frame> Element

The <frame> element indicates what goes in each frame of the frameset. The <frame> element is always an empty element, and therefore should not have any content, although each <frame> element should always carry one attribute, src, to indicate the page that should represent that frame.

The <frame> element can carry any of the universal attributes, and the following attributes:

```
frameborder marginwidth marginheight noresize scrolling longdesc src name
```

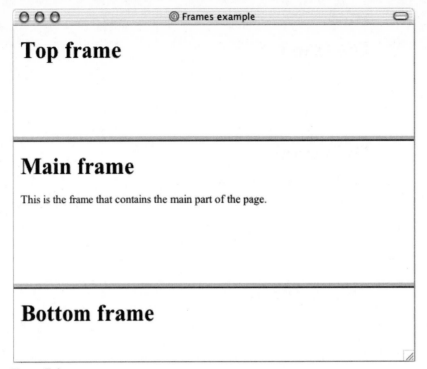

Figure 7-4

Note that there are no CSS styles related to the <frame> element.

The src Attribute

The src attribute indicates the file that should be used in the frame.

```
src="main_page.html"
```

The value for the src attribute is a normal XHTML page so you must have a corresponding page for each <frame /> element.

While the value of this attribute will generally be a file on your server, its value can be any URL, so you could use the src attribute to specify another site.

You might find that some search engines on the Internet (such as the Google search feature on Netscape.com) will create a frameset whereby the top of the page remains the search site and the bottom of the page will be the page you requested.

Personally, I find this use of frames frustrating; it feels as though a Web site using this tactic is trying to keep me on their site longer than I want to be there. If you use a frame like this, it is good practice to offer a link that will close the top frame and allow the viewer to view just the content of the main frame (as Netscape does).

The name Attribute

The name attribute allows you to give a name to a frame; it is used to indicate which frame a document should be loaded into. This is especially important when you want to create links in one frame that load pages into a second frame, in which case the second frame needs a name to identify itself as the target of the link. You will see more about making links between frames later in the chapter.

```
name="main_frame"
```

You should note that the name attribute has not been replaced by the id attribute in XHTML (as with some other elements); even in Strict XHTML the value of the name attribute is used to identify that frame.

The frameborder Attribute

The frameborder attribute specifies whether or not the borders of that frame are shown; it overrides the value given in the frameborder attribute on the <frameset> element if one is given, and the possible values are the same. The table that follows shows the possible values of the frameborder attribute.

Value	Purpose
1 or yes	Indicates borders should be shown, the default value (yes is not part of HTML 4 but is still supported by IE and Netscape)
0 or no	Indicates borders should not be shown (no is not part of HTML 4 but is still supported by IE and Netscape)

The marginwidth and marginheight Attributes

The margin is the space between the three-dimensional border of a frame and its contents.

The marginwidth attribute allows you to specify the width of the space between the left and right of the frame's borders and the frame's content. The value is given in pixels.

The marginheight attribute allows you to specify the height of the space between the top and bottom of the frame's borders and its contents. The value is given in pixels.

```
marginheight="10" marginwidth="10"
```

The noresize Attribute

By clicking and dragging on the borders of a frame you are usually able to resize that frame. For users, this is helpful if they cannot read everything in a frame, but it does make it harder for the designer to control the layout of the page.

The noresize attribute prevents a user from being able to resize the frame. It used to be a minimized attribute without a value in HTML 4, but now it should take a value of noresize.

```
noresize="noresize"
```

Bear in mind that users with lower resolution monitors than you might have trouble seeing the content of a frame you see on a high resolution monitor. If you use the noresize *attribute, users that couldn't see the entire content of a frame would have no way of resizing the frames to view the missing material.*

The scrolling Attribute

If the content of a frame is too big for the space it has been allocated, the browser will likely provide the user with scrollbars so she can read the rest of the content for that frame.

You can control the appearance of the scrollbars that appear on the frame using the scrollbar attribute:

```
scrolling="yes"
```

This attribute can take one of three possible values listed in the table that follows.

Value	Purpose
yes	Indicates that the frame must always contain a set of scrollbars whether or not they are required, although IE just shows a vertical scrollbar and Netscape acts as if it were just set to auto.
no	Indicates that the frame must not contain a set of scrollbars even if the content does not fit into the frame.
auto	Indicates that the browser should include scrollbars when the content does not fit in the frame but otherwise not to show them.

The longdesc Attribute

The longdesc attribute allows you to provide a link to another page containing a long description of the contents of the frame. The value of this attribute should be the URL pointing to where that description will be found.

```
longdesc="framedescription.html"
```

Note that the W3C indicates that the value of this URL must not be an anchor within the same page.

The <noframes> Element

If a user's browser does not support frames (an increasingly rare eventuality these days), the contents of the <noframes> element should be displayed to the user.

In XHTML you must place a <body> element inside the <noframes> element because the <frameset> element is supposed to replace the <body> element, but if a browser does not understand the <frameset> element it should understand what is inside the <body> element contained in the <noframes> element.

You should think very carefully about how you phrase the contents of this element. You should bear in mind that the average user who gets to see the content of this element probably doesn't actually know what a frame is, so you should *not* just write something like this element:

```
<noframes><body>This site requires frames.</body></noframes>
```

This will make little sense to the average user—after all, their browser is likely pretty old by now, and they are unlikely to have studied HTML or XHTML and know what frames are. Rather you should offer a more descriptive example content, along these lines:

```
<noframes><body>This site makes uses of a technology called frames.
Unfortunately the browser you are using does not support this technology. We
recommend that you update your browser. We apologize for any inconvenience
this causes.</body></noframes>
```

You can use other XHTML markup within the `<noframes>` element if you want to present your message nicely.

While ideally you would have a non-frames version of the site for those users who have browsers that do not support frames, this takes a lot of work. Another helpful alternative is to provide links to the pages that make up the frames so that the user can still see the content of the site.

Creating Links Between Frames

One of the most popular uses of frames is to place navigation bars in one frame and then load the pages with the content into a separate frame. This is particularly helpful in three situations:

❑   When your navigation bar is rather large in size (such as thumbnails of photographs in a gallery). By using frames, the user does not need to reload the navigation bar each time she views a new page.

❑   When your main document is very long and the navigation bar provides shortcuts to parts of the main document.

❑   When you do not want to reload the whole page.

As you have already seen, each `<frame>` element can carry the `name` attribute to give each frame a name. This name is used in the links to indicate which frame the new page should load into. Consider this very simple example:

```
<frameset cols="200, *"
  <frame src="frames/linksNav.html" />
  <frame src="frames/linksMain.html" name="main_page" />
</frameset>
```

There are two columns in this example. The first is 200 pixels wide and will contain the navigation bar. The second column or frame will contain the main part of the page. The links on the left side navigation bar will load pages into the right side main page.

The links in the `linksNav.html` file look like this:

```
<a href="http://www.wrox.com" target="main_page">Wrox Press</a><br /><br />
<a href="http://www.google.com" target="main_page">Google</a><br /><br />
<a href="http://www.microsoft.com" target="main_page">Microsoft</a><br /><br />
<a href="http://news.bbc.co.uk/" target="main_page">BBC News</a><br /><br />
```

Note that this technique for creating navigation bars makes it very hard to indicate which page the user is on, as you would need to either use JavaScript or pass information to the navigation bar from the main page each time a new page was loaded.

Figure 7-5 shows what this example might look like in a browser.

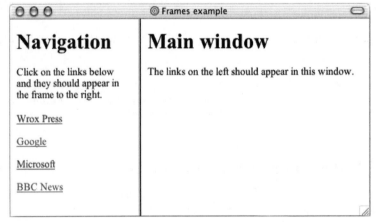

Figure 7-5

As you can see, you will need to use the `name` attribute for any frame you might want to load a new page into—it is the key to getting new content into that frame.

The `target` attribute can also take the attribute values listed in the table that follows.

Value	Purpose
_self	Loads the page into the current frame.
_blank	Loads a page into a new browser window—opening a new window (same as using a target that doesn't exist).
_parent	Loads the page into the parent window, which in the case of a single frameset is the main browser window (and the page will replace all the frames), or in nested frames it replaces the frame that frameset lives inside.
_top	Loads the page into the browser window, replacing any current frames.

If you are creating links to external pages, you should usually use the _top value for the target attribute so that the external site replaces your whole site; after all, your users probably don't want to view external pages just in frames of your site. The other option is to open external sites in new windows.

> Forgetting to add the **name** attribute to the **<frame>** element and the **target** attribute to the **<a>** element are the most common reasons why beginners have problems creating Web sites that use frames. If either is missing, the browser just loads the link in that frame.

Setting a Default Target Frames Using the <base> Element

You can set a default target frame using the <base> element in any page that contains links that should open in another frame. The <base> element should carry an attribute called target, whose value is the name for the frame you want the content to be loaded into. So, you could add the following to linksNav.html to specify a default frame target:

```
<head>
  <base target="main_page" />
</head>
```

Nested Framesets

You have seen that a single frameset gives you a fixed grid-like structure of rows and columns just like a table. If you want to create a more complex design, you might choose to use a nested frameset.

You create a nested frameset by using a new <frameset> element in the place of the <frame> element that would have represented the cell where the nested frame should appear. Take a look at the following example (ch07_eg07.html):

```
<frameset rows="*, 300, *">
  <frame src="frames/top_frame.html" />

  <frameset cols="*, 400, *">
    <frame src="frames/blank.html" />
    <frame src="frames/main_frame.html" />
    <frame src="frames/blank.html" />
  </frameset>

  <frame src="frames/bottom_frame.html" />
</frameset>
```

This example creates a set of three rows. A nested frameset with three columns is in the middle row. You can see that the two side columns actually share the same file. Figure 7-6 shows what this example looks like in a browser.

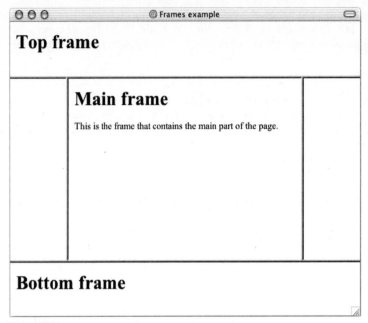

Figure 7-6

Try It Out   A Frame-Based Book Viewer

In this example you are going to create a frame-based viewer for previewing details about books. It could quite easily be a Web site design of its own if there were more pages.

The idea behind the viewer is that you have three books in a frame at the top of the page, which forms a navigation pane. This frame does not resize or scroll. Then you have a second frame that contains the details of all the new book releases. The third frame just contains a copyright and privacy policy notice like those you see at the bottom of a lot of Web sites.

Before you start to build the example it would help to have a look at what you are going to create. You can see the page in Figure 7-7.

There are actually four files that make up this example:

❑   books.html, which contains the frameset for the whole document

❑   nav.html, which is the top frame

❑   newBooks.html, which is the page with all the book details

❑   footer.html, which is the page containing the footer image

You will work through these pages in this order.

1.   Start your text editor or Web page editor and create a skeleton of a frameset document, remembering that this will be slightly different than the documents you have been creating so far. This is the file books.html:

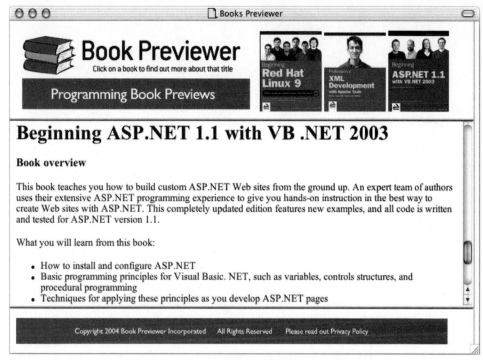

Figure 7-7

```
<?xml version="1.0" encoding="iso-8859-1"?>
<!DOCTYPE html PUBLIC "-//W3C//DTD XHTML 1.0 Frameset//EN"
"http://www.w3.org/TR/xhtml1/DTD/xhtml1-frameset.dtd">
<html xmlns="http://www.w3.org/1999/xhtml">
  <head>
    <title>Books Previewer</title>
  </head>
</html>
```

2.   Divide the page up into the relevant frames. While it might have looked like there were just three frames in the screenshot, if you look carefully, the edge of the middle frame does not touch the right side of the browser window. I wanted to make the page a fixed width.

As you can see, this example contains two `<frameset>` elements. The first divides the page into two columns: the first is 750 pixels wide and the second takes up the remaining page (if the window is set to wider than 750 pixels).

Within the first column you can see the second `<frameset>` element, which holds the real content of the page. Three `<frame>` elements are within this nested frameset, which you can see clearly in Figure 7-7.

```
<frameset cols="750, *">
  <frameset rows="150, *, 70" frameborder="1" noresize="noresize" >
    <frame src="frames/nav.html" scrolling="no" />
```

```
          <frame src="frames/newBooks.html" name="main_page" />
          <frame src="frames/footer.html" scrolling="no" />
      </frameset>
  </frameset>
   <noframes><body>
          This site uses a technology called frames. Unfortunately, your
          browser does not support this technology. Please upgrade your
          browser and visit us again!
  <body></noframes>
```

You can now see the three `<frame />` elements, each of which points to its own file.

3. Create a new file called nav.html to form the content of the navigation frame at the top of the window. This is just a normal XHTML document, so start the skeleton as you usually would. You also need to add a `<style>` element into the `<head>` element to prevent the images that are links from having a border around them. (You learn more about this in Chapter 9, but for now just copy it out.)

```
<?xml version="1.0" encoding="iso-8859-1"?>
<!DOCTYPE html PUBLIC "-//W3C//DTD XHTML 1.0 Transitional//EN"
"http://www.w3.org/TR/xhtml1/DTD/xhtml1-transitional.dtd">
<html xmlns="http://www.w3.org/1999/xhtml">

<head>
  <title>Navigation</title>
  <style type="text/css">img {border-style:none; border-width:0px;}</style>
</head>

<body>

</body>
</html>
```

4. In the actual page, there is one image on the left of the navigation bar that is the title of the page and then there are three images that are links to the different parts of the page in the main frame:

```
<img src="../images/nav_left.gif" width="390" height="125" alt="Books
Preview" />

<a href="../frames/newBooks.html#linux" target="main_page">
   <img src="../images/543784.jpg" width="100" height="125" /></a>
<a href="../frames/newBooks.html#xml" target="main_page">
   <img src="../images/543555.jpg" width="100" height="123" /></a>
<a href="../frames/newBooks.html#asp" target="main_page">
   <img src="../images/557076.jpg" width="100" height="126" /></a>
```

You can see that the `<a>` elements have both the href and target attributes. Remember that the target attribute is the one that indicates which frame the page should appear in. Meanwhile the href attribute points not only to the page that should be loaded but also the specific part of that page.

5. Next you have the newBooks.html file. The skeleton of the page, and indeed the basic text markup are quite straightforward; you can see those in the code download for the chapter if you

want to. In this otherwise normal XHTML page, it's important to note the <a> elements acting as target anchors so that the links in the navigation pane show the user the appropriate part of the page.

The <a> elements sit inside the <h1> elements and contain the heading. (Remember that if the target anchor element is empty some browser will not recognize them.) Here you can see the heading elements:

```
<h1><a name="xml">Professional XML Development with Apache Tools: Xerces,
     Xalan,FOP, Cocoon, Axis, Xindice</a></h1>
<h1><a name="linux">Beginning Red Hat Linux 9</a></h1>
<h1><a name="asp">Beginning ASP.NET 1.1 with VB .NET 2003</a></h1>
```

6. Finally you come to footer.html, which is a rather simple plain XHTML page with an image inside it:

```
<?xml version="1.0" encoding="iso-8859-1"?>
<!DOCTYPE html PUBLIC "-//W3C//DTD XHTML 1.0 Transitional//EN"
"http://www.w3.org/TR/xhtml1/DTD/xhtml1-transitional.dtd">
<html xmlns="http://www.w3.org/1999/xhtml">
<head>
  <title>Footer</title>
</head>
<body>
  <img src="../images/footer.gif" alt="Copyright and privacy statement"
       width="700" height="40" />
</body>
</html>
```

You have already seen what this frameset looks like in Figure 7-7, so you should just look at some of the key points again.

How It Works

At first this example looked like it just contained three frames. On closer inspection, in order to get a fixed width, the three frames were contained within another frameset. The containing frameset has one column fixed to 750 pixels wide, and rather than having a corresponding <frame> element, it has the <frameset> element. Because the second column is blank, it does not need a <frame> element either.

```
<frameset cols="750, *">
  <frameset rows="150, *, 70" frameborder="1" noresize="noresize" >
    <frame src="frames/nav.html" scrolling="no" />
    <frame src="frames/newBooks.html" name="main_page" />
    <frame src="frames/footer.html" scrolling="no" />
  </frameset>
</frameset>
```

You can see that the nested frameset then divides the page up into the three obvious rows, each with its corresponding <frame> element. The nested <frameset> element carries the noresize attribute to prevent users from resizing the different frames that make up each of the rows.

Also note how the first and last <frame> elements carry the scrolling attribute with a value of no to prevent these frames from being given scrollbars.

This example shows how frames can be used to allow users to navigate between what would otherwise be very long single documents. It also illustrates how you end up with quite a few files for a single page, and how you have to be careful to keep track of those pages and remember which one appears in which frame. You can see that the <a> elements in the navigation frame got more complicated, indicating which element frame is the target frame as well as having to provide the source of the document.

```
<a href="../frames/newBooks.html#linux" target="main_page">
    <img src="../images/543784.jpg" width="100" height="125" /></a>
<a href="../frames/newBooks.html#xml" target="main_page">
    <img src="../images/543555.jpg" width="100" height="123" /></a>
<a href="../frames/newBooks.html#asp" target="main_page">
    <img src="../images/557076.jpg" width="100" height="126" /></a>
```

While these links are not too complicated, you can imagine that, if there were three frames each with links to one another, it could get rather more complicated. This example does, however, illustrate how the frameset works.

Floating or Inline Frames with <iframe>

Another special kind of frame is known as an *inline* or *floating frame* because it can appear anywhere within an HTML or XHTML page. (It does not need to appear either in a <frameset> element or even in a document that uses the frameset document type declaration.)

The floating frame is created using the <iframe> element, and, rather like an image, the inline frame can have text flowing around it and you can set borders and margins around the floating frame.

Here is a simple example of a floating frame (ch07_eg07.html):

```
<body>
<h1>Floating frame</h1>
<p>Lorem ipsum dolor sit amet, consectetuer adipiscing elit. Ut risus
tellus, hendrerit id, sagittis sed, lobortis eget, augue.
  <iframe src="frames/iframe.html">
    Error! You should be seeing our news in this window.
    This site uses a technology called frames which is not supported by older
    browsers. If you are using a version of Internet Explorer older than
    version 3 or a version of Netscape older than version 6 you might need
    to upgrade yourbrowser.
  </iframe>
 Lorem ipsum dolor sit amet, consectetuer adipiscing elit. Ut risus tellus,
hendrerit id, sagittis sed, lobortis eget, augue.</p>
</body>
```

Note that between the opening <iframe> tag and the closing </iframe> tag is a message for those whose browsers do not support <iframes>.

Even if you do not add a message between the opening <iframe> and closing </iframe>, you should not make it an empty element; otherwise it might not display correctly in some browsers. Rather, you should still have both the opening and closing tags but no content.

You can see what this page looks like in Figure 7-8.

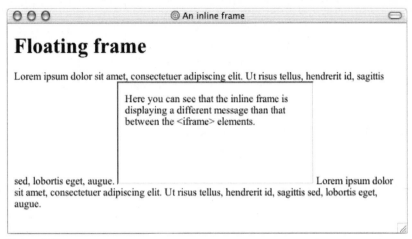

Figure 7-8

While the <iframe> element wasn't introduced until HTML 4.0, it first appeared in version 3 of IE, although Netscape didn't bring in the tag until version 6.

The <iframe> Element

The <iframe> element sits in the middle of a normal XHTML to create an inline frame. The only attribute it has to carry is the src attribute, whose value is the URL of the page to be included (wherever the <iframe> element is in the document). Remember that this element does not have to be part of the frameset document type.

In addition to the universal attributes, the <iframe> element can carry these attributes:

```
align height width frameborder longdesc marginwidth marginheight name
scrolling src
```

Note that there are no CSS styles or events particular to the <iframe> element.

The src Attribute

The src attribute is required on the <iframe> element as it indicates where the browser can find the file with the content for that frame, just as it does on the <frame> element.

The align Attribute (deprecated)

The align attribute indicates how the text that is outside of the floating frame will appear. It should take one of the values listed in the table that follows.

Value	Purpose
left	The frame will be aligned with the left margin of the page, allowing the text to flow around it to the right.
right	The frame will be aligned with the right margin of the page, allowing the text to flow around it to the left.
top	The top of the frame will be inline with the text around it.
middle	The middle of the frame will be inline with text around it.
bottom	The bottom of the frame will be inline with the text around it (the default setting as you can see from Figure 7-8).

The height and width Attributes

The height and width attributes allow you to specify the height and width of a frame just as you would with an image.

```
height="250" width="500"
```

The value of the height and width attributes can be given in pixels (as in the preceding line of code) or in percentages of the browser (as in the line of code that follows) or parent element if it is contained by another element.

```
height="20%" width="40%"
```

Keep in mind, however, that users with different screen resolutions will see different amounts of the screen. If you do not specify a height or width, the browser works out a size based on the full size of the screen.

The frameborder Attribute

The frameborder attribute specifies whether the borders of the frame are shown.

```
frameborder="0"
```

The longdesc Attribute

The longdesc attribute allows you to specify a link to another page where there is a description in text of what would otherwise be in the frame. This is particularly helpful if you are putting images in the frame, as they make your site accessible to those with visual impairments. It can also be used if the user is having trouble loading the frame.

```
longdesc="../textDescriptions/iframe1.html"
```

The marginheight and marginwidth Attributes

The marginheight and marginwidth attributes allow you to specify the distance in pixels between the border of the frame and the content of the frame.

```
marginwidth="8" marginheight="8"
```

The marginwidth attribute allows you to specify the distance between left and right borders and the content, while the marginheight attribute specifies the distance between top and bottom borders and the content.

The scrolling Attribute

The scrolling attribute specifies whether a frame should have scrollbars (just as it does for the <frame> element).

Try It Out   **Using an Inline Frame**

In this example you create a simple page for children to learn about fruit. The page allows the child to click a link and load the corresponding image into the inline frame without the rest of the page changing.

1.   Create the skeleton of a standard Transitional XHTML document, as follows:

```
<?xml version=\"1.0\" encoding=\"iso-8859-1\"?>
<!DOCTYPE html PUBLIC "-//W3C//DTD XHTML 1.0 Transitional//EN"
"http://www.w3.org/TR/xhtml1/DTD/xhtml1-transitional.dtd">
<html xmlns="http://www.w3.org/1999/xhtml">
<head>
    <title>Iframe example</title>
</head>

<body>
</body>
</html>
```

2.   Add a heading and then the <iframe> element, which must have a name attribute. In this case you should use the scrolling attribute to prevent the frame from having scrollbars. You should also set a size for the frame:

```
<h1>Learn your fruit</h1>
  <iframe name="iframe" height="150" width="150" scrolling="no">Pictures of
    fruit will appear here</iframe>
```

3.   Add the links that will load the images into the inline frame. As with the other type of frames, if you want the links to load the page into another frame, the links must carry the target attribute whose value is the name of the iframe.

```
<p>Click on the name of the fruit to see an image of it appear.</p>
<p>The <a href="images/orange.jpg" target="iframe">orange</a> is an
    orange colored fruit.</p>
<p>This <a href="images/apple.jpg" target="iframe">apple</a> is red
    and crunchy.</p>
<p>The <a href="images/banana.jpg" target="iframe">banana</a> is
    long and yellow.</p>
```

Your example should look something like Figure 7-9.

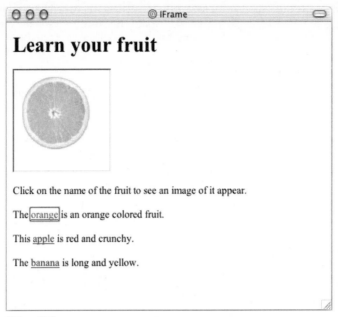

Figure 7-9

How It Works

The `<iframe>` element can be very useful as it allows you to refresh just one portion of the page without reloading the whole page, and it can also be part of a normal XHTML document.

Once you have added the `<iframe>` element to the page, you just create links on the page that load new content into the inline frame. In this example there was no initial content in the iframe when the page loaded, although you could have used the `src` attribute to indicate a file that should go there by default when the page loaded.

Remember that the `<iframe>` element should not be an empty element, and between the opening and closing tags you should have what you want the user to see if the frame cannot be loaded.

Summary

In this chapter you learned about frames, which allow you to divide a browser window into separate panes. Each of these panes contains a discrete XHTML document that can be loaded and reloaded separately from the other frames.

Frames are particularly helpful if part of your page's content remains the same while the main body changes—for example, when either the main body is long in length (and you want the navigation to remain in view) or the navigation takes a long time to load (and you do not want to reload it for each page).

The chapter covered two types of frames:

❑ The more traditional frameset document, which uses the <frameset> element to divide the screen into rows and columns. The <frameset> element then contains a <frame> element corresponding to each part of the window. These frames belong to the frameset document type and require a different DOCTYPE declaration than other XHTML documents because the <frameset> element replaces the <body> element.

❑ The more recent inline or floating frame, which lives in a normal XHTML page, and allows only the content of the frame to be reloaded. Inline frames can appear anywhere within the document.

As I have already mentioned, rather than immediately using frames to divide up the page, you will learn in Chapter 11 how you can use tables to create effective layouts, too.

Exercises

The answers to all of the exercises are in Appendix A.

1. Re-create the frameset document shown in Figure 7-10, where clicking a fruit loads a new page in the main window. When the page loads it will carry the details for the appropriate fruit.

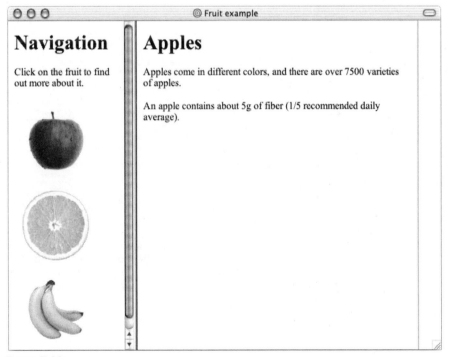

Figure 7-10

2. Re-create the <iframe> element shown in Figure 7-11.

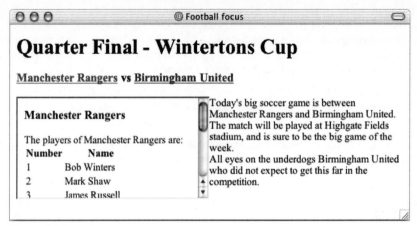

Figure 7-11

3. Here is the new exercise code; the only change is to the text:

```
<?xml version="1.0" encoding="iso-8859-1"?>
<!DOCTYPE html PUBLIC "-//W3C//DTD XHTML 1.0 Transitional//EN"
"http://www.w3.org/TR/xhtml1/DTD/xhtml1-transitional.dtd">

<html xmlns="http://www.w3.org/1999/xhtml">
<head>
  <title>Football focus</title>
</head>

<body>
  <h1>Quarter Final - Wintertons Cup</h1>
  <h3>
    <a href="frames/teamA.html" target="iframe">Manchester Rangers</a>
      vs
    <a href="frames/teamB.html" target="iframe">Birmingham United</a>
  </h3>

  <p><iframe name="iframe" width="300" height="150" src="frames/clickForTeams
.html"
align="left"></iframe>
      Today's big soccer game ise between Manchester Rangers and Birmingham
      United.<br />The match will be played at Highgate Fields stadium, and
      is sure to be the big game of the week. <br /> All eyes on the underdogs
      Birmingham United who did not expect to get this far in the competition.
  </p>
</body>
</html>
```

Deprecated and Browser-Specific Markup

With the changes between versions of HTML and XHTML, quite a lot of markup has been *deprecated*, which means it has either already been removed from XHTML specifications or that it will be removed in coming versions. While you will still be able to use much of this markup with Transitional XHTML, Strict XHTML 1.0 has already removed most of the elements, attributes, and styles you learn about in this chapter.

You may be wondering why you should read any further if this markup is deprecated or out of date. The answer is because you are likely to come across it in other people's code, and sometimes you might need to resort to some of it in order to get a specific job done. Why would you need to use it to get a job done? Because some clients want their sites to look the same in every browser possible (including IE 3 and Netscape 3), and some of these browsers will not support what you want to do with CSS.

In addition to deprecated markup, you will also see some of the browser-specific markup that you may well come across. This is markup that Microsoft or Netscape (and in some cases both companies) added to their browsers to allow users to do more things than their competitors—but these elements and attributes never made it into the HTML recommendations, and are therefore referred to as *browser-specific markup*.

So, not only does this chapter help you deal with markup that you come across that has been deprecated, but also you might use some techniques to get the result you want. This chapter covers the following:

- ❏　Elements and attributes that have been deprecated in recent versions of HTML and XHTML
- ❏　How to specify font appearances without using CSS
- ❏　How to control backgrounds without using CSS
- ❏　Ways to control presentations of links, lists, and tables without using CSS
- ❏　Elements and attributes that control the formatting of a document

❏   Elements, attributes, and styles that Microsoft added to IE (but are not supported by other browser manufacturers)

❏   Elements, attributes, and styles that Netscape added to Navigator (but are not supported by other browser manufacturers)

Before you look at any of this markup, however, a quick word on why a good part of a chapter is deprecated markup.

Why Deprecated Markup Exists

In the first chapter, I explained how XHTML 1.0 was created after its predecessor (HTML) had reached version 4.01. With each version of HTML, new elements and attributes are added or old ones removed. But these changes have been necessary, not only because Web page authors have wanted to create increasingly complicated pages, but also because the types of browsers (also known as *clients*) accessing the Internet have changed.

While you used to be able to browse the Web only on desktop computers, lots of new devices are going online, and these new devices are part of the reason why markup that describes the content of a document (headings, paragraphs, and so on) has been separated from the presentation rules. This separation of style from content is one of the biggest sources of deprecated markup, as CSS takes the place of elements and attributes that controlled how a document should appear. The new devices that are accessing the Web along with the aim of separating style from content led to XHTML, which will make it possible to deliver Web content to all manner of devices, each potentially with different style sheets that format the content especially for that type of device.

Unfortunately, the older browsers that were built before CSS and other more recent markup simply will not understand the newer ways of doing things, and if you ever have to create a Web site for IE 3 or Netscape 3 you will have to think very carefully about whether you use CSS (which they barely understand, if at all) or whether you use these deprecated elements and elements.

While these earlier browsers will not use the CSS rules to style HTML or XHTML documents, they will be able to render the content of elements without styling. So, where possible, my preference is to use CSS for most of the presentational styles and resort to deprecated elements and attributes only if the page would not be laid out correctly if the browser cannot show the CSS—which generally means I avoid things like CSS positioning (which you learn about in Chapter 11) unless the site is for those with the latest browsers.

The result of these changes will be greater operability in the long run, as well as an improved way of writing code.

Older Pages Break Many Rules

You should be aware that a lot of the pages you see on the Web probably break a lot of the rules you have learned in this book so far. You will see element and attribute names in upper- and lowercase, you will see missing quotation marks on attribute values, even attributes without values, and you will see elements that do not have closing tags. You will see pages without DOCTYPE declarations and pages littered with deprecated markup. Keep in mind, however, that many of the pages that break the rules you have learned might have been written when the rules were not as strict, and at the time of writing the code may have been perfectly acceptable.

Even if a page with bad or deprecated markup renders fine in your browser, it's still wise to avoid bad habits at all costs; otherwise your pages will not be viewable by as many browsers in the future. Some of the techniques you will see were not wrong at the time the page was designed and built. Best practices have changed over time, and my goal is to show you what in my opinion are best practices for today. In five to ten years, these may well change, too. But bad habits are far easier to pick up than put down.

Even authoring tools such as Microsoft FrontPage and Macromedia Dreamweaver, until the later releases, would generate code that had strange capitalization, missing quotation marks, and featured attributes without values. This certainly does not make it okay to follow their lead. These first versions of these programs were written before XHTML came along with its stricter rules (which were discussed in Chapter 1). Older browsers are very forgiving of code that is not written correctly and have been designed to render a page anyway. But that is one of the main reasons why browsers have been increasing in size—future browsers will not be so forgiving.

You have been warned that you are going to see some odd things, but if you remember to stick to the principles you have learned in this book (and don't miss quotes, attribute values, and closing elements or follow the bad habits others have) your pages will be available for many more people and your skills will be more marketable. So, on with the deprecated markup.

Fonts

In this section you learn about several elements (and their attributes) that affect the appearance of text and fonts, all of which have been deprecated.

The <font> Element

The `<font>` element was introduced in HTML 3.2 and deprecated in HTML 4.0, but is still widely used today. It allows you to indicate the typeface, size, and color of font the browser should display between the opening `<font>` and closing `</font>` tags. You could probably find many sites littered with `<font>` tags, one for each time you see the style of text change on the page.

The table that follows shows the three attributes the `<font>` element relies upon.

Attribute Name	Use	Values
face	Specify the typeface that should be used	Name of the typeface to use (can include more than one name in order of preference).
size	Specify the size of the font	A number between 1 and 7 where 1 is the smallest font size and 7 is the largest font size.
color	Specify the color of the font	A color name or hex value (see Appendix D).

Here is an example of how the `<font>` element would have been used (`ch08_eg01.html`). You can see that there are three occurrences of the `<font>` element:

```
<html>
  <head>
    <title>Example of &lt;font&gt; Element</title>
  </head>
  <body>
    <p>This is the browser's default font.</p>
    <font face="arial, verdana, sans-serif" size="2">
      <h1>Example of the &lt;font&gt; Element</h1>
        <p><font size="4" color="darkgray">Here is some size 3 writing
        in the color called darkgray. The typeface is determined by the
        previous &lt;font&gt; element that contains this paragraph.</font></p>
        <p><font face="courier" size="2" color="#000000">Now here is a courier
            font, size 2, in back</font></p>
    </font>
  </body>
</html>
```

The result of this example is shown in Figure 8-1.

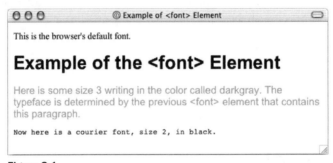

Figure 8-1

As you can see from Figure 8-1, all of the writing within a `<font>` element follows the rules laid down in the attributes of the opening `<font>` tag. The first paragraph is in the browser's default font (which is probably a size 3 Times family font in black). The first `<font>` element appears directly after this paragraph, and contains the rest of the page. This first `<font>` element acts like a default setting for all but the first paragraph in this page. The element is not closed until just before the closing `<body>` tag, and therefore the remainder of the document should be in an Arial typeface.

As you can see, the name of the Arial typeface is followed by the typeface Verdana; this is supposed to be a second choice if Arial is not available. Then if Verdana is not available, the browser's default sans-serif font should be used (you learn more about the types of fonts in Chapters 9 and 10):

```
<font face="arial, verdana, sans-serif" size="2">
```

This `<font>` element also indicates that the default size of the text in the rest of the document should be size 2. Note that this `<font>` element does not override the size of the `<h1>` element, but it does affect the typeface used—the heading is written in Arial.

While this <font> element is acting as a default for most of the page, if you want a particular part of the page to have any other font properties, you can indicate so in another <font> element.

You can see in the second paragraph that the color and size of font is changed to dark gray and size 4.

```
<p><font size="4" color="darkgray">Here is some size 4 darkgray
     writing</font></p>
```

The third paragraph then uses a different typeface, a smaller size, and black:

```
<p><font face="courier" size="2" color="#000000">Now here is a courier
     font, size 2, in back</font></p>
```

Note that you may have to use <font> elements inside <td> and <th> elements, as the styles specified outside tables are not inherited by the text inside cells. Figure 8-2 shows you the different font sizes from 1 to 7 (ch08_eg02.html).

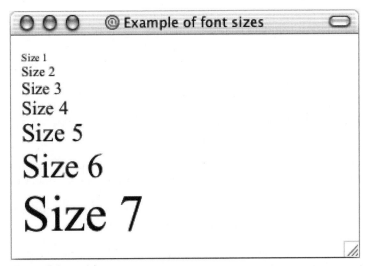

Figure 8-2

Font sizes can change slightly from browser to browser, so you should not use them to create layouts judged to the pixel as they appear on your screen.

The preferred method with CSS would be to use the font-family, font-size, and color properties on the element containing the text that you wanted to style. You learn about these CSS properties in the next chapter.

The text Attribute

The text attribute is used on the <body> element to indicate the default color for text in the document, it was deprecated in HTML 4. Its value should be either a color name or a hex color. For example (ch08_eg03.html):

```
<body text="#999999">
  This text should be in a different color than the next bit
    <font color="#000000">which is black</font>, and now back to gray.
</body>
```

You can see the result in Figure 8-3.

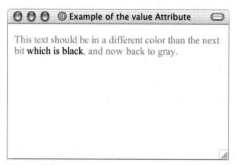

Figure 8-3

The <basefont> Element

The `<basefont>` element is supposed to set a default font size, color, and typeface for any parts of the document that are not otherwise contained within a `<font>` element. You can then use the `<font>` elements to override the `<basefont>` settings.

The attributes that the `<basefont>` element takes are exactly the same as for the `<font>` element, which you've just seen. And again, elements such as the heading elements will retain their own size.

You can also set the size of fonts relative to the size of the `<basefont>` by giving them a value of +1 for a size larger or -2 for two sizes smaller (on the same scale from 1 to 7).

You can see these effects by revisiting the last example, and making some changes—the changes are highlighted (ch08_eg04.html):

```
<html>
  <head>
    <title>Example of &lt;basefont&gt; Element</title>
  </head>
  <body>
    <basefont face="arial, verdana, sans-serif" size="2" color="#ff0000">
    <p>This is the page's default font.</p>
      <h2>Example of the &lt;basefont&gt; Element</h2>
      <p><font size="+4" color="darkgray">Here is some darkgray text
          four sizes  larger</font></p>
      <p><font face="courier" size="-1" color="#000000">Here is a courier
          font, a size smaller, in black</font></p>
  </body>
</html>
```

You can see the result in Figure 8-4.

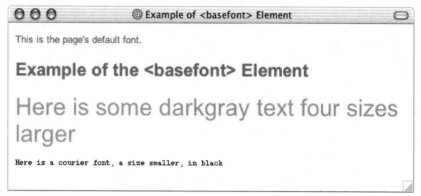

Figure 8-4

As you can see, the default font now takes on the properties specified in the `<basefont>` element; it is red, size 2, and uses the Arial typeface.

The paragraph after the `<h2>` element uses a font size four sizes larger than the default size and is gray text, whereas the following paragraph uses a font one size smaller than the default font—you can also see that the color of this font is black (overriding the default).

Because this element was deprecated in HTML 4, the preferred option is to use CSS styles attached to the `<body>` element to set default font properties for the document.

The `<s>` and `<strike>` Elements

Both the `<s>` and `<strike>` elements were added to HTML in version 3.2 and deprecated in version 4. They indicate that their content should have a strikethrough style. For example (`ch08_eg05.html`):

```
<s>This text will have a line through it</s>
<strike>This text will also have a line through it.</strike>
```

You can see the results in Figure 8-5.

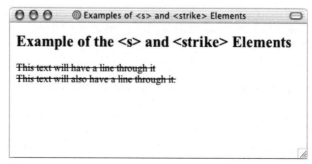

Figure 8-5

You should now use the text-decoration property in CSS, with a value of strikethrough, unless you are trying to indicate deleted content, in which case you should use the <del> element.

The <u> Element

The <u> element renders its content underlined. It was introduced in HTML 3.2 and deprecated in version 4.

```
<u>This text should be underlined.</u>
```

You can see the effect in Figure 8-6.

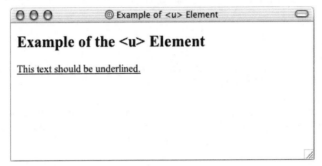

Figure 8-6

You should now use the text-decoration property in CSS with a value of underline unless you are trying to indicate added content (when a document has been revised), in which case you should use the <ins> element.

The <listing>, <plaintext>, and <xmp> Elements

These three elements are all obsolete; they were introduced in HTML 2 and removed from HTML 4. They are included here only because you may come across them in old examples.

All three elements display text in a monospaced font as the <pre> element does.

The <xmp> element was designed for a short snippet of example code, and cannot contain any other markup; any characters such as angle brackets in element names get displayed as if they are text, so you do not need to use escape characters for them. You should also be aware that it imposes a maximum limit of 80 characters on any one line.

The <listing> element meanwhile has a limit of 132 characters, and tends to display text in a small font.

The <plaintext> tag indicates that *anything* following it should appear as plain text, even markup. Because everything following the <plaintext> element is displayed as normal text, including tags, there is no closing tag (if you tried to use a </plaintext> tag, it too would be displayed as normal text).

Here is an example of these three elements (ch08_eg07.html):

```
<body>
  <h2>Example of the &lt;listing&gt;, &lt;plaintext&gt;, and &lt;xmp&gt;
      Elements</h2>
  <listing>These words are written inside a &lt;listing&gt; element.</listing>
  <xmp>These words are written inside an <xmp> element.</xmp>
  <plaintext>These words are written inside a <plaintext>
      element.
</body>
```

You can see the result in Figure 8-7. Note how the escape characters in the <xmp> element are ignored and not escaped (this could also contain angle brackets and they would display normally). You will also see the closing </body> and </html> tags because anything after the opening <plaintext> tag is treated as plain text:

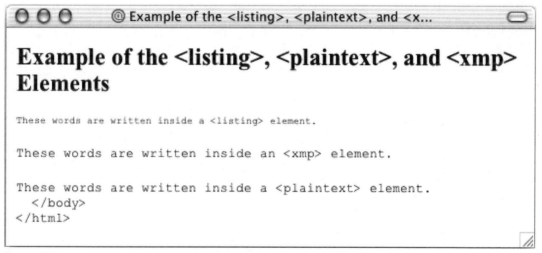

Figure 8-7

The replacements in XHTML are <pre> and <samp>.

Backgrounds

There were two attributes in HTML that would allow you to change the background of a whole page or part of it:

❑   bgcolor, which allowed you to specify a background color on the <body> and various table elements

❑   background, which allowed you to specify a background image on the <body> element

The bgcolor Attribute

The bgcolor attribute allowed you to specify a background color for the whole document, or just part of it. It could be used on the following elements:

```
<body> <table> <tr> <th> <td>
```

The value of the attribute should be a color name or hex color, as described in Chapter 4 and Appendix D.

Here is an example of a document using some different background colors (ch08_eg08.html):

```html
<html>
  <head>
    <title>Example of bgcolor Attribute</title>
  </head>
  <body bgcolor="#efefef">
      <h2>Example of the bgcolor Attribute</h2>
      <table bgcolor="#999999">
        <tr>
          <th bgcolor="#cccccc">Heading One</th>
          <th bgcolor="#cccccc">Heading Two</th>
        </tr>
        <tr bgcolor="#f2f2f2">
          <td>Cell One</td>
          <td>Cell Two</td>
        </tr>
        <tr>
          <td>Cell Three</td>
          <td>Cell Four</td>
        </tr>
      </table>
  </body>
</html>
```

You can see this page in Figure 8-8.

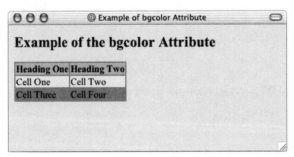

Figure 8-8

The page has a very light gray background color specified on the <body> element. The table then has a background color, which you can see on the bottom row and all around the edges of the table—this is the default color for the table. Then you can see that the bgcolor attribute is used both on the <th> element (the table headings) and the following <tr> element in the first row.

The preferred method of changing background colors now is to use the background-color property in CSS.

The background Attribute

The background attribute allowed you to specify a background image for the whole page, and its value should be the URL to the background image (which can be an absolute or relative URL). Netscape and Microsoft also allowed this attribute to be used on tables to create a background image for the tables.

Here you can see an example of the background attribute being used (ch08_eg09.html):

```
<html>
  <head>
    <title>Example of background Attribute</title>
  </head>
  <body background="images/background_large.gif" bgcolor="#f2f2f2">
      <h2>Example of the background Attribute</h2>
  </body>
</html>
```

Note that the bgcolor attribute has also been used on the <body> element, which will be used if the image cannot be found. You can see the result in Figure 8-9.

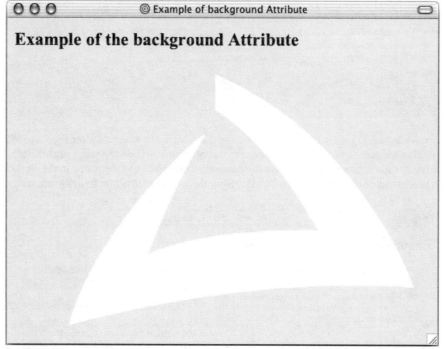

Figure 8-9

Formatting

The next set of elements and attributes help you format and position elements and their content on the page.

The *<center>* Element

The <center> element was introduced by Netscape to allow authors to center content on a page. Anything between the opening and closing <center> tags will be centered horizontally in the middle of the page or the containing element. It was added to the HTML 3.2 specification and deprecated in HTML 4.

Here is an example of how the <center> element was used. The example also contains a table because of the interesting way in which tables are dealt with inside a <center> element (ch08_eg10.html).

```
<body>
  <h2>Example of the &lt;center&gt; Element</h2>
  <center>
    Anything inside a &lt;center&gt; element is centered on the page, or within
    its containing element.<br /><br />
    <table width="600" border="1">
      <tr>
        <td>Cells whose content is written inside a &lt;center&gt; will be
            centered within the cell, like the one to the right.</td>
        <td><center>This cell's content should be centered.</td>
      </tr>
      <tr>
        <td><center>This cell's content should be centered.</td>
        <td>Cells whose content is written inside a &lt;center&gt; will
            be centered within the cell, like the one to the left.</td>
      </tr>
    </table>
  </center>
</body>
```

In this example (see Figure 8-10) you can see how the <center> tag (just after the <h1> element) centers the content of the rest of the page. Interestingly, it centers any text on the page, and the table itself, but it does not center the text in the cells unless they contain <center> elements inside the <td> elements. (The table in this example has been given a border using the border attribute to illustrate where its edges lie.)

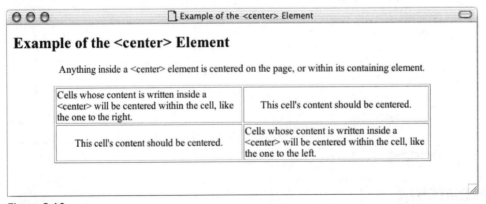

Figure 8-10

The preferred method of aligning text content is to use CSS properties such as text-align.

The align Attribute

The align attribute is used with many elements to indicate positioning of an element within the browser or its containing element. It was deprecated in HTML 4.01.

The possible values for the align attribute are shown in the table that follows. Note that the value justify works with text only, and that top, middle, and bottom are less supported than left, right, and center.

Value	Purpose
left	Aligns element with the left side of the page or containing element
right	Aligns element with the right side of the page or containing element
center	Centers the element within the page or containing element
justify	Justifies words across the page or containing element so that the left and right side of the text touches the container
top	Aligns element with the top of the browser window or containing element
middle	Vertically aligns element in the middle of the browser window or containing element
bottom	Aligns element with the bottom of the browser window or containing element

Here are the elements that could carry the align attribute:

```
<caption> <applet> <iframe> <img> <input> <object> <legend> <table> <hr>
<div> <h1> <h2> <h3> <h4> <h5> <h6> <p>
```

The following example contains a few examples of how the align attribute can be used (ch08_eg11.html).

```
<body>
  <h2 align="center">Example of the align Attribute</h2>

    <table width="600" align="center" border="1">
      <tr>
        <td align="left">This cell's content should be left-aligned.</td>
        <td align="right">This cell's content should be right-aligned.</td>
      </tr>
      <tr>
        <td align="center">This cell's content should be centered.</td>
        <td width="300" align="justify">This cell's content should be
        justified, but it needs to spread across more than one line to
        show it working.</td>
      </tr>
    </table>
</body>
```

You can see here that the `<h1>` and `<table>` elements are both centered and then each cell in the table uses a different kind of alignment.

In order for text to be justified it needs to wrap onto more than one line (which is why the `<td>` element carries a `width` attribute in this example). The last line of a justified paragraph does not have to stretch to the left and right borders of the browser or its containing element like the other lines do.

Figure 8-11 shows what this page looks like.

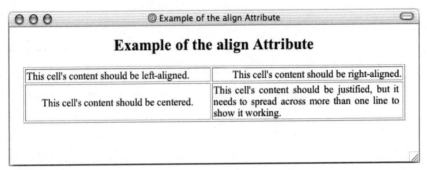

Figure 8-11

The preferred method of aligning content in CSS are the `text-align` and `vertical-align` properties and `float` positioning.

The width Attribute

The `width` attribute sets the width of an element in pixels. It could be used with the following elements:

```
<td> <th> <table> <hr> <applet>
```

The `width` attribute is still commonly used today, especially among those who use tables for layout. Sites that rely on tables for positioning content need the width to be fixed for the page to display properly and make sense to the reader, and while few visitors would have browsers that are version 3 or older, those few that do would not be able to view the site properly without the fixed width tables because they do not support the CSS `width` property. (You learn more about this in Chapter 11.)

Here you can see an example of the `width` attribute on a table and an `<hr />` element (ch08_eg12.html):

```
<body>
    <h2>Example of the width Attribute</h2>

    <table width="600" border="1">
      <tr>
        <td width="200">This cell should be 200 pixels wide.</td>
        <td width="400">This cell should be 400 pixels wide.</td>
      </tr>
```

```
    <tr>
      <td width="200">This cell should be 200 pixels wide.</td>
      <td width="400">This cell should be 400 pixels wide.</td>
    </tr>
  </table>

  <br /><br />

  <hr width="300" />

</body>
```

You can see what this looks like in a browser in Figure 8-12.

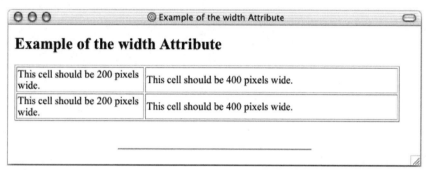

Figure 8-12

The preferred method of setting the width for these elements is the width property in CSS.

The height Attribute

The height attribute sets the height of an element in pixels. It was used with the <td> <td> and <applet> elements. Here you can see the height attribute used on the <td> element (ch08_eg13.html):

```
<body>
  <h2>Example of the height Attribute</h2>

  <table width="600" border="1">
    <tr>
      <td width="300" height="300">This cell should be 300 pixels high.</td>
      <td width="300" height="300">This cell should be 300 pixels high.</td>
    </tr>
  </table>

</body>
```

As you can see from Figure 8-13, these table cells are square.

The preferred method of setting the height for these elements is the height property in CSS.

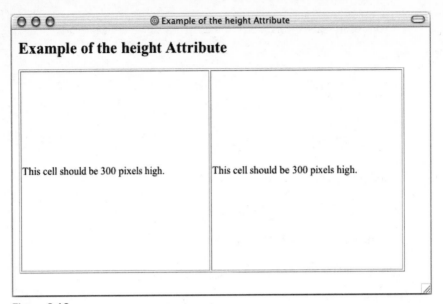

Figure 8-13

The vspace Attribute

The vspace attribute specifies the amount of whitespace or padding that should appear above or below an HTML element. Its value is given in pixels.

The following example shows how the vspace attribute on the <img> element makes sure that there are 20 pixels above and beneath the image to separate it from the text (ch08_eg14.html):

```
<body>
    <h2>Example of the vspace Attribute</h2>

    <p>Lorem ipsum dolor sit amet, consectetur adipisicing elit, sed
do eiusmod  tempor incididunt ut labore et dolore magna aliqua. Ut enim
ad minim veniam,  quis nostrud exercitation ullamco laboris nisi ut
aliquip ex ea commodo  consequat. Duis aute irure dolor in reprehenderit
in voluptate velit esse  cillum dolore eu fugiat nulla pariatur. Excepteur
sint occaecat cupidatat  non proident, sunt in culpa qui officia deserunt
mollit anim id est laborum.
    <img src="images/logo_small.gif" alt="wrox logo" vspace="20" border="1" />
    Lorem ipsum dolor sit amet, consectetur adipisicing elit, sed do eiusmod
tempor incididunt ut labore et dolore magna aliqua. Ut enim ad minim veniam,
quis nostrud exercitation ullamco laboris nisi ut aliquip ex ea commodo
consequat. Duis aute irure dolor in reprehenderit in voluptate velit esse
cillum dolore eu fugiat nulla pariatur. Excepteur sint occaecat cupidatat
non proident, sunt in culpa qui officia deserunt mollit anim id est
laborum.</p>

</body>
```

You can see the result in Figure 8-14.

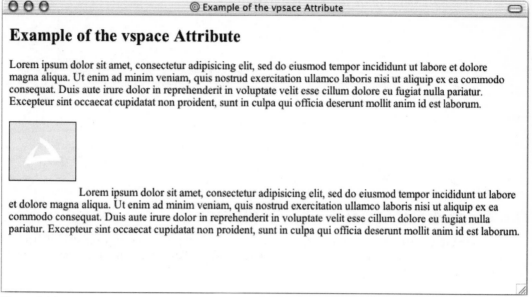

Figure 8-14

This has been replaced by the `padding` properties in the CSS box model.

The hspace Attribute

The `hspace` attribute is the horizontal equivalent of the `vspace` attribute and ensures that there is padding or whitespace to the left and right of an element.

Here you can see that the `hspace` attribute is used to create 40 pixels of padding to the left and right of the image (`ch08_eg15.html`):

```
<body>
  <h2>Example of the vspace Attribute</h2>

  <p><img src="images/logo_small.gif" alt="wrox logo" hspace="40"
border="1" />
    There should be 40 pixels between the image and the edge of the window, and
    another 40 pixels between the edge of the image and this text.</p>

</body>
```

You can see the result in Figure 8-15.

This has been replaced by the `padding` properties in the CSS box model.

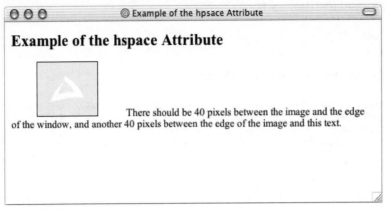

Figure 8-15

The clear Attribute (on <br /> element)

The `clear` attribute used on a line break element `<br />` indicates how the browser should display the line after the `<br />` element. The values it can take are `left`, `right`, `all`, and `none`. Its use is best explained by way of an example (`ch08_eg16.html`):

```
<body>
    <img src="images/logo_small.gif" alt="wrox logo" align="left" border="1" />
    The text after this image will be displayed next to the image and wrap
    to the next line until you see the line break element.<br clear="left"> Now
    it should be on a new line underneath (not next to) the image.
</body>
```

If the `clear` attribute is used on a `<br />` element then the text or element that follows it will not be displayed until the border indicated as a value of the `clear` attribute is clear. In this case, because the `<br />` element has a `clear` attribute whose value is `left`, the text after the `<br />` element will not be shown until there is nothing to the left of it (within the containing element or box). In this example the text does not continue until after the image, which was to the left of this text.

You can see the result in Figure 8-16—and note how the text continues under the image. If it were not for the `clear` attribute this text would simply appear on then next line.

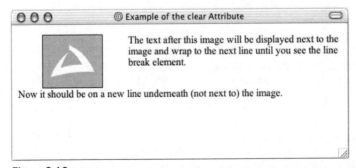

Figure 8-16

If the value `all` is given, there must not be anything to the `left` or `right` of the text or element.

CSS has its own `clear` property to replace this attribute.

Links

You may have noticed on some Web sites, that the colors of links change when you have visited a page or when you click the link. As you can see in the table that follows, there are three attributes that allow you to change the colors of links: `alink`, `link`, and `vlink`. Each should be specified on the `<body>` element.

Attribute	Use	Values
alink	Specify the color of an active link or selected link	A hex code or color name
link	Specify the default color of all links in the document	A hex code or color name
vlink	Specify the color of visited links	A hex code or color name

The following is an example of the how these attributes affect the colors of links (ch08_eg17.html):

```
<body alink="0033ff" link="#0000ff" vlink="#333399">
    <h2>Example of the Link Attribute</h2>
    <p>This example contains some links, which you should play with to see how
        they behave:</p>
    <ul>
        <li>The <a href="http://www.wrox.com/">Wrox Web site</a> tells you about
            existing and forthcoming Wrox books.</li>
        <li>The <a href="http://www.w3.org/">W3C Web site</a> is the home of the
            XHTML and CSS recommendations.</li>
        <li>The <a href="http://www.google.com/">Google Web site</a> is a popular
            search engine.</li>
    </ul>

</body>
```

In this example, there are different shades of blue for links that have not yet been visited and those that the user has already been to. This helps users navigate a site because they can identify links they have already visited (which helps them find a page again by following a trail of links they have already been to), while also helping them not go to the same page twice if they do not want to.

Usually the colors for links that have and have not been visited are quite similar, as you can see with these links in Figure 8-17. For a better idea of how this example works, try it out for yourself (it is available for download along with the rest of the code for this chapter).

Lists

Several elements and attributes relate to lists and are deprecated or no longer permitted, from attributes that helped order and style lists to other elements that created visual effects similar to lists.

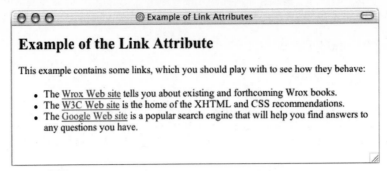

Figure 8-17

The start Attribute

The start attribute is used on the <ol> element of ordered lists to indicate at what number a browser should start numbering a list. The default is, of course, 1. For example (ch08_eg18.html):

```
<body>
  <ol start="4">
    <li>This list should start at four</li>
    <li>Therefore this item should be five</li>
    <li>And this item should be six</li>
  </ol>
</body>
```

You can see the result of this in Figure 8-18.

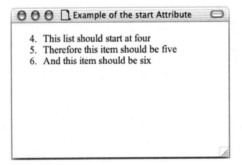

Figure 8-18

This has been replaced by CSS counters and the counter-reset property. However, these CSS counters are not well supported in browsers yet, so you will probably have to use this attribute if you want a list to start with a number other than 1.

The value Attribute

The value attribute was designed to be used on the <li> element to indicate what number that line item should be in numbered lists and therefore allows you to create numbered lists that leave out numbers or are out of sequence. Here you can see an example:

```
<body>
  <ol>
    <li value="3">one</li>
    <li value="7">two</li>
    <li value="1">three</li>
    <li value="9">four</li>
    <li value="4">five</li>
  </ol>
</body>
```

You can see the result and how the points are numbered out of sequence in Figure 8-19.

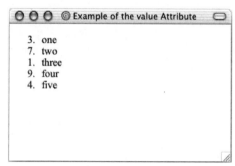

Figure 8-19

The type Attribute

The type attribute controls the type of bullet point or numbering (also known as the *marker*) that is used on lists. This attribute can be used on the <li>, <ol>, and <ul> elements.

The table that follows shows different types of markers for bullet points and numbering systems.

Value	Description
disc	A solid circle
square	A solid square
circle	An empty circle
1	Numbers 1, 2, 3, 4
a	Lowercase letters a, b, c, d
A	Uppercase letters A, B, C, D
i	Lowercase Roman numerals i, ii, iii, iv
I	Uppercase Roman numerals I, II, III, IV

The default for unordered lists is the disc, and the default for ordered lists is Arabic numerals such as 1, 2, 3, and so on. Here you can see these values for the type attribute in use (ch08_eg20.html):

```
<body>
  <ul>
    <li type="disc">Disc bullet point</li>
    <li type="square">Square bullet point</li>
    <li type="circle">Circle bullet point</li>
  </ul>

  <ol>
    <li type="1">Numbers</li>
    <li type="a">Lowercase letters</li>
    <li type="A">Uppercase letters</li>
    <li type="i">Lowercase Roman numerals</li>
    <li type="I">Uppercase Roman numerals</li>
  </ol>

</body>
```

You can see each of these in Figure 8-20.

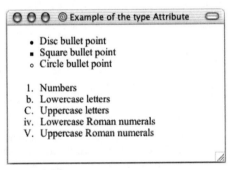

Figure 8-20

The <dir> and <menu> Elements

The <dir> and <menu> elements were added in the HTML 2.0 specification, and are used to create unordered bulleted lists and nested lists. They are almost exactly the same as each other and the <ul> element (ch08_eg21.html).

```
<dir>
  <li>Item 1</li>
  <li>Item 2</li>
  <li>Item 3</li>
  <li>Item 4</li>
  <dir>
    <li>Item 4.1</li>
    <li>Item 4.2</li>
    <li>Item 4.3</li>
```

```
      <li>Item 4.4</li>
   </dir>
</dir>

<menu>
   <li>Item 1</li>
   <li>Item 2</li>
   <li>Item 3</li>
   <li>Item 4</li>
   <menu>
      <li>Item 4.1</li>
      <li>Item 4.2</li>
      <li>Item 4.3</li>
      <li>Item 4.4</li>
   </menu>
</menu>
```

You can see the result of each of these elements in Figure 8-21.

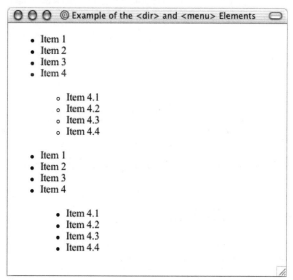

Figure 8-21

The <dir> element was initially intended to list files in a directory, while the <menu> element was devised for a menu of links and can therefore be displayed a little bit more compactly in some browsers than the content of <ul> and <dir> elements. You should simply use the <ul> element instead of either of these deprecated elements.

Tables

There are a couple of attributes that have been deprecated that were previously allowed on the <table> element—notably the align and bgcolor attributes, which you have already met, and the nowrap attribute, which is covered next.

The nowrap Attribute

The nowrap attribute used to be available on the `<td>` and `<th>` elements, and prevented the text from wrapping within that table cell. For example:

```
<table width="200">
  <tr>
    <td nowrap>This text should not wrap even though the table is only
        supposed to be 200 pixels wide.</td>
  </tr>
</table>
```

As you can see in Figure 8-22, although the table is supposed to be only 200 pixels wide, it actually stretches for as long as the line—the text does not wrap.

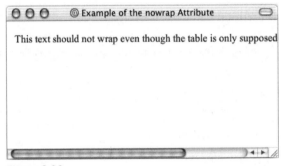

Figure 8-22

The replacement for the nowrap attribute is the white-space property in CSS with the value of nowrap.

Miscellaneous Attributes

This section describes a selection of other elements and attributes that have been deprecated but do not easily fit into one of the preceding sections.

The border Attribute

The border attribute specifies the thickness of a border around an element in pixels. For example, here is an `<img>` element with a border attribute (ch08_eg23.html):

```
<body>
    <img src="images/logosmall.gif" border="4" alt="wrox logo" />
</body>
```

You can see the result in Figure 8-23.

This attribute has been replaced by the border-width property of CSS.

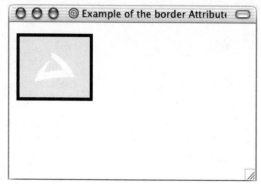

Figure 8-23

The compact Attribute

The compact attribute tells the browser to show text with less height between lines than normal. It does not take a value (although if it were used with Transitional XHTML 1.0 it would require a value of compact).

The default value is false. This attribute has been replaced by letter-spacing and word-spacing properties.

The language Attribute

The language attribute is supposed to indicate what scripting language should be used for an HTML element—most commonly the <script> element. For example:

```
<script language="JavaScript">
```

The language attribute has been replaced with the type attribute, whose value is a MIME type (for example type="text/JavaScript").

The version Attribute

The version attribute specifies which version of the HTML DTD the document is written according to.

This has been dropped because it duplicates information that should be provided by the DOCTYPE declaration.

The <applet> Element

The <applet> element was used to embed Java applets into an HTML page. The element and its attributes were introduced in HTML 3.2 and have been replaced by the <object> element, which was discussed in Chapter 4.

The table that follows shows the attributes that `<applet>` can carry.

Attribute	Use
code	The filename of the Java applet's compiled code. The path to the applet file specified by the code is relative to the codebase of the applet (not a URL or absolute path).
codebase	Specifies the directory for the Java applet code. If the codebase attribute is not specified, the applet files are assumed to be in the same directory as the HTML file.
object	Specifies the filename of the Java applet's compiled code that stores a serialized representation of an applet's state. The path to the file should be relative only to the codebase of the applet (not a URL or absolute path).
name	Specifies the name of the element so that scripts can communicate with it (only deprecated for use with the `<applet>` element).
archive	A space-delimited set of URLs with multiple Java classes or other resources that will be loaded into the browser to improve applet performance. (Only deprecated for use with the `<applet>` element.)
width	The width of the applet in pixels.
height	The height of the applet in pixels.

The <embed> Element

The `<embed>` element was used before the `<object>` element was introduced into HTML as a way of including a file that required a special plug-in application. For example, it was used to include Flash animations in pages.

The object to be included would be identified using the `src` attribute—just like an image. You indicate the type of content to be included using the `type` attribute, whose value is a MIME type for that resource (or just leave the browser to work it out itself).

The attributes that the <embed> element can take are listed in the table that follows.

Attribute	Use
align	Specifies the alignment of the object within the page or its containing element.
border	Specifies the width of the border for the object in pixels.
height	Specifies the height of the object (in pixels).
hidden	Hides the object from the user (making it 0 pixels wide and 0 pixels high). This is particularly useful for audio.
hspace	Specifies the horizontal space that should be left to the left and right of the object (in pixels).

Attribute	Use
name	As with the name attribute on other elements, this is used to label the element.
palette	In IE, the value is a pair of hexadecimal color values separated by a vertical bar. The first is the foreground color and the second is the background color. In Netscape the palette attribute is either foreground *or* background, indicating which palette of window system colors the plug-in should use.
pluginspage	Specifies the URL of a Web page from which you can download the plug-in required to use the file. (Netscape only.)
src	The URL of the object you want to embed.
type	Indicates the MIME type of the object to be included in the page (which determines the plug-in used to view the object).
units	Allows you to change the units of measurement that indicate the height and width of the embedded object from the default of pixels to the relative en unit (half of the width of the text's point size).
vpsace	Specifies the amount of vertical space that should be left to the top and bottom of the object (in pixels).
width	Specifies the width of the object in pixels.

The <embed> element can also carry attributes that are specific to the plug-in required to view them. You should refer to the documentation for the particular plug-in you need to use for documentation on these attributes as there are too many to list here.

If you are using Macromedia Flash to include graphics in your pages, you will find that the publishing tool that gives you the HTML code to include Flash animations in your pages not only uses the <object> element to include the animation in the page, but also provides the <embed> element for any browser that is older and does not understand the <object> element.

The <isindex> Element

The <isindex> element was introduced in HTML 2.0 to create a single-line text field without the need for a <form> element (the user's entry would be sent using the HTTP get method). When the user presses the Enter (or Return) key the form is submitted and spaces are replaced with a + character. (A program or page on the server would then have to respond to, or act upon, the data sent.

When it is displayed the text box will have a horizontal rule above and beneath it.

While you can use several <isindex> tags, only the last one with content will be sent to the server. It can also carry the prompt attribute, which allows you to provide a hint to users as to what they should be entering into the box. For example, here is an <isindex> element used to create a search box (ch08_eg24.html):

```
<body>
    <isindex prompt="search">
</body>
```

You can see the result of this with its horizontal lines in Figure 8-24.

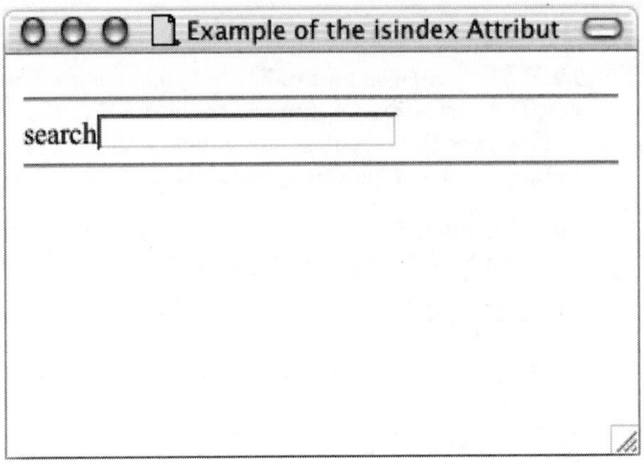

Figure 8-24

The <nobr> Element

Both Netscape and IE support an extension to the XHTML recommendation that prevents line breaks: the <nobr> element. (This retains the normal style of its containing element and does not result in the text being displayed in a monospaced font.) If you choose to use the <nobr> element it can contain another child element called <wbr> to indicate where a break can occur within a <nobr> element, although this is an extension as well.

IE-Specific Elements

The table that follows lists five elements that IE supports that are not part of the HTML recommendations. You should generally avoid these elements unless you are providing different pages for different browsers or you know all your visitors will be using IE.

Element	IE Versions	Purpose
<bgsound>	2, 3, 4, 5, 6	Plays a sound file in the background (replaced by the <object> element)
<marquee>	2, 3, 4, 5, 6	Renders text in a scrolling fashion
<ruby>	5, 6	Provides pronunciation support
<rt>	5, 6	Provides pronunciation support
<xml>	5, 6	Creates an XML data island, embedding an XML recordset into the page

IE-Specific Attributes

The following table lists IE-specific attributes.

Attribute	Purpose
atomicselection	Specifies whether the grouping element and its content must be selected as a whole.
balance	The balance of audio between the left and right speakers (used with `<bgsound>`).
behavior	Specifies how content of a `<marquee>` element scrolls.
bgproperties	Sets a fixed background image for a page; also known as a watermark.
bordercolordark	Specifies the darker of the colors used when cells in a table are rendered with 3D borders. Used on the `<table>` element.
bordercolorlight	Specifies the lighter of the colors used when cells in a table are rendered with 3D borders. Used on the `<table>` element.
bottommargin	Specifies the bottom margin for the page in pixels. Used on the `<body>` element.
contenteditable	Determines whether the content of a grouping element can be edited by a user.
dataformatas	Sets or retrieves whether data contained by the grouping element should be displayed as text or HTML.
datalfd	Used in databinding when the browser is connected to a server-side database (see a reference on ASP for more information).
datasrc	Used in databinding when the browser is connected to a server-side database (see a reference on ASP for more information).
datapagesize	Used in databinding when the browser is connected to a server-side database (see a reference on ASP for more information).
direction	Indicates the direction of scrolling text within a `<marquee>` element.
dynsrc	Used for embedding movies into client-side caches.
framespacing	Specifies the amount of space between frames in a frameset in pixels.
hidefocus	Used to prevent a visible line showing around an element when it is in focus.
leftmargin	Specifies the left margin for the page in pixels. Used on the `<body>` element.
rightmargin	Specifies the right margin for the page in pixels. Used on the `<body>` element.

Continues

Attribute	Purpose
loop	Specifies the number of times the content of a `<marquee>` element should scroll.
lowsrc	Allows you to specify a low-resolution version of an image on an `<img>` element that should be loaded first.
scrollamount	Specifies the number of pixels the text scrolls each time the `<marquee>` element is redrawn; the value is in pixels and it must be a positive integer.
acrolldelay	Specifies the time delay in milliseconds between each drawing of the `<marquee>` element. (The default is that it is redrawn every 60 milliseconds.)
topmargin	Specifies the top margin for the page in pixels. Used on the `<body>` element.
truespeed	A Boolean attribute indicating whether the `scrolldelay` value should be used. Default is `false`; if true the `<marquee>` element will use the values that are indicated in `scrollamount` and `scrolldelay` attributes. (Any value under 60 milliseconds is ignored.)
unselectable	Indicates an element cannot be selected.
volume	Indicates the volume at which the content of a `<bgsound>` element should be played, with values from –10000 to 0 (default is 0, which is full volume).

Note that when a table is being used to control the whole layout of a page and the page appears in the very top-left corner of IE without a white border around the edge, it sometimes uses the topmargin and leftmargin attribute on the `<body>` element to indicate that there should be no margin around the edges.

```
<body topmargin="0" leftmargin="0" border="0">
```

You can safely use the topmargin and leftmargin attributes in Transitional XHTML, as Netscape and other browsers should simply ignore the attributes they do not understand, although they would not be valid as they are not part of the markup. (Validation is discussed in Chapter 16.)

IE-Specific CSS Styles

You learn about CSS in the next two chapters, but the table that follows lists some styles that are supported only by IE.

Property	IE Versions	Purpose
`behavior`	5, 6	Determines how text in a `<marquee>` element scrolls.
`ime-mode`	5, 6	Allows input of Chinese, Japanese, and Korean characters when used with an input method indicator.
`layout-grid`	5, 6	Shorthand for other layout-grid properties.
`layout-grid-char`	5, 6	Specifies size of character grid for rendering text (similar to `line-height` property).
`layout-grid-charspacing`	5, 6	Specifies spacing between characters (similar effect to `line-height`).
`layout-grid-line`	5, 6	Specifies grid line value used to render text (similar to `line-height`).
`layout-grid-mode`	5, 6	Specifies whether the grid uses one or two dimensions.
`layout-grid-type`	5, 6	Specifies the type (if any) of page layout grid to be used when rendering an element's content.
`line-break`	5, 6	Specifies rules for when a line should break in Japanese.
`ruby-align`	5, 6	Specifies horizontal alignment of the text in an `<rt>` element.
`ruby-overhang`	5, 6	Specifies whether text in the `<rt>` element will hang over the edge of non-ruby content if wider than it.
`ruby-position`	5, 6	Specifies the position of the text specified in the `<rt>` element (above or inline).
`text-autospace`	5, 6	Controls the autospacing and narrow space width adjustment behavior of text; of particular use with ideographs used in Asian languages.
`text-justify`	5, 6	Justifies text in an element.
`text-kashida-space`	5.5, 6	Controls the ratio of kashida expansion to whitespace expansion when justifying text in an element. A kashida is a typographic effect that justifies lines of text by elongating certain characters in specific points; often used in Arabic.

Continues

Property	IE Versions	Purpose
text-underline-position	5.5, 6	Specifies how far an underline should appear beneath the text when the text-decoration property is used.
word-break	5, 6	Controls line breaking within words; of particular use with documents containing multiple languages.
word-wrap	5.5, 6	Controls where a long word should break if it is too large for its containing element.
writing-mode	5.5, 6	Controls horizontal and vertical direction of flow of content in object.
zoom	5.5, 6	Specifies magnification scale of an object.

The layout-grid properties are used with Asian languages that often employ page layout for characters in order to format text using a one- or two-dimensional grid.

There are also several CSS styles that are particular to the presentation of a scrollbar. It does not hurt to add these properties to any CSS style sheet, as browsers that do not understand these properties will just ignore them. All colors can be specified as a color name, hex code, or RGB value (as with all colors in CSS).

Property	IE Versions	Purpose
scrollbar-3dlight-color	5.5, 6	Color of top-left edges of scroll box and scroll arrows on the scrollbar.
scrollbar-arrow-color	5.5, 6	Color of the arrows on a scroll arrow.
scrollbar-base-color	5.5, 6	Color of main elements of a scrollbar, which includes the scroll box, track, and scroll arrows.
scrollbar-darkshadow-color	5.5, 6	Color of the gutter of a scrollbar.
scrollbar-face-color	5.5, 6	Color of the scroll box and scroll arrows of a scrollbar.
scrollbar-highlight-color	5.5, 6	Color of the top-left edges of the scroll box and scroll arrows of a scrollbar.
scrollbar-shadow-color	5.5, 6	Color of the bottom and right edges of the scroll box and scroll arrows of a scrollbar.

Netscape-Specific Elements and Attributes

The table that follows shows the elements that are supported by Netscape only. The versions of Netscape that support these elements are given in the Versions column of the table.

Element	Versions	Use
`<blink>`	2, 3, 4, 6, 7	Makes the content of the element blink on and off. (CSS2 `text-decoration` property has a value of `blink` that does not work in current browsers.)
`<ilayer>`	4	Creates an inline layer that can contain a different page from the one currently in view in a separate section of the HTML document. The `<iframe>` element in HTML 4 can create similar effects. It differs from the `<layer>` tag in that it is relatively positioned—not absolutely positioned.
`<keygen>`	2, 3, 4, 6, 7	Used to generate an encryption key for forms submitted from an HTML document (lives inside the form, creates a select list of available encryption key sizes, requires that the client has a certificate installed, and uses proprietary Netscape encryption schemes).
`<layer>`	4	Creates a layer that can contain a different page from the one currently in view in a separate section of the HTML document. The `<div>` element in HTML 4 can create similar effects.
`<multicol>`	2, 3, 4	Allows the user to define multiple column formatting—like newspaper-style columns. You use a table or CSS positioning to create a similar effect in XHTML.
`<noembed>`	2, 3, 4, 6, 7	Renders HTML text for browsers unable to support the `<embed>` element.
`<nolayer>`	4	Renders HTML text for browsers unable to render the content of a `<layer>` element.
`<spacer>`	3, 4	Renders whitespace in an HTML document.

Netscape-Specific Attributes

The following table contains the attributes that are supported by Netscape only.

Attribute	Netscape Versions	Purpose
`above`	4	Indicates which layer should appear on top of the other if two layers overlap. Used on `<layer>` and `<ilayer>` elements. (Like "bring to top" in a desktop publishing program.)
`below`	4	Indicates which layer should appear on bottom of the other if two layers overlap. Used on `<layer>` and `<ilayer>` elements. (Like "send to back" in a desktop publishing program.)

Continues

261

Attribute	Netscape Versions	Purpose
challenge	2	Used on the <keygen> element to specify the string value that the encrypted key value is packed into.
clip	4	Specifies an area in pixels that should be clipped so that the browser shows only the indicated content, which is specified using four values representing the x, y positions from the top-left corner and bottom-right corner. Used on <layer> and <ilayer> elements.
gutter	3, 4	Used on <multicol> element to indicate the number of pixels between each column.
hidden	4	Used with the <embed> element to indicate that an object should not be visible to the viewer. Other items in the page should flow around it normally. Typically used for embedding sound files into a page where you do not want the user to see the object.
left	4	Specifies the horizontal offset of the parent element within the document. Value given in pixels. Used with <layer> and <ilayer> elements.
mayscript	3, 4, 6, 7	Boolean attribute used on the <applet> element to indicate whether the Java applet will be able to access JavaScript features. Must be set to yes if an applet accesses JavaScript—otherwise the browser will crash.
pagex	4	Specifies the horizontal position of the layer in relation to the page (given in pixels). Used with <layer> and <ilayer> elements.
pagey	4	Specifies the vertical position of the layer in relation to the page (given in pixels). Used with <layer> and <ilayer> elements.
pluginspage	4, 6, 7	Used on the <embed> element to indicate the URL of a Web page that allows users to download an embedded object if they do not have it installed.
point-size	4, 6, 7	Specifies the size of a font in points.
top	4	Specifies the vertical offset from the parent element. Value given in pixels. Used with <layer> and <ilayer> elements.
weight	4, 6, 7	Specifies the weight of a font (normal or bold).
z-index	4	Indicates which layer should be on top of, or underneath, others when they overlap. The value is a number above 0; the higher the number the nearer the top the layer is.

Summary

In this chapter you've seen several elements and attributes that have either been removed from the XHTML recommendation or were never in it in the first place (and were implemented only by Netscape and Microsoft in their browsers).

You will undoubtedly come across some of these elements and attributes if you look at other people's code, and now you know what they do. You might actually find yourself looking at other people's code more often than you expect. Because viewing the source of other people's pages is actually one of the best ways to learn how a layout was achieved, most Web designers look at other people's code quite often—it's a great way to learn new tricks.

You should generally try to avoid using deprecated elements unless you need to support older browsers and the page will not render well without them. Fonts, colors, backgrounds, and link specifications are completely cosmetic, and users whose browsers do not support CSS will not lose any of the meaning of the page, only the look.

Unless you are prepared to create different pages for different browsers, you should generally stick well clear of browser-specific attributes. The only exceptions to this rule are as follows:

❑ You can use some of the extended style sheet rules, such as those for the colors of scrollbars, which only add to the appearance of a page on IE. (For Netscape users there is no equivalent yet.)

❑ When you are developing an intranet (a Web site for use within a company) or other kind of site where you *know* all users will have a particular browser.

Creating pages using browser-specific elements requires a lot more maintenance, and generally causes more headaches than finding an alternative way around the design issues.

Still, you are now equipped to deal with deprecated and browser-specific elements and attributes that you are likely to come across.

Exercises

The answers to all of the exercises are in Appendix A.

1. The following is an old HTML page that contains a fictional listing of files a user might be able to download. Your task is to re-create it using XHTML.

```
<html>
  <head>
    <title>Example of the value Attribute</title>
  </head>
  <body>
  <h1>Code Download</h1>
  The code download folder contains the following files and folders:

    <dir>
      <li>index.html</li>
```

```
            <li>sampleCode</li>
            <li>images</li>
        </dir>

    </body>
</html>
```

2. Take the following code sample and turn it into XHTML. It contains only a few lines of code, but there are a few things you need to watch out for.

```
<HTML>
  <HEAD>
    <TITLE>Exercise 2</TITLE>
  </HEAD>
  <BODY>
    <H1>The &lt;title&gt; Element</H1>
    The following line shows the title of a document:
    <XMP><title>Exercise 2</title></XMP>
  </BODY>
</HTML>
```

Cascading Style Sheets

In this chapter you are going to begin taking control of the style of your pages, including the colors and size of fonts, the width and colors of lines, and the amount of whitespace between items on the page. The cascading style sheets specification, or CSS for short, allows you to specify rules for how the content of elements within your document appears. In fact, you can set different rules to control the appearance of every element in your page so that your pages start to look a lot more interesting.

As you have seen throughout the book so far, several elements and attributes were marked as deprecated in HTML 4.0, and many of these have been replaced by the use of CSS. For example, the old HTML <font> element, and the align, bgcolor, and color attributes, have all been replaced by CSS rules. As you saw in Chapter 1, the W3C (which oversees the development of Web technologies) decided that the HTML and XHTML languages should no longer contain rules that indicated how the document appears, rather that CSS should be used to control the appearance of Web pages.

There are actually two versions of CSS released by the W3C. The properties and features you will learn in this chapter are taken from CSS1 and CSS2. You will see mention where more recent browsers still fail to support properties, and Appendix C contains information on which versions of IE and Netscape first supported each property so you know which browser a CSS property works with and which it does not. One helpful thing about CSS is that users should still be able to read the document even if the CSS properties are not implemented by the browser—it just won't look quite as you intended.

In this chapter you learn the following:

❑   What makes up a CSS rule

❑   How to place CSS rules within your document, and how to link to an external CSS document

❑   How properties and values control presentation of different elements within your document

❑   How to control the presentation of text using CSS

❑   How CSS is based on a box model, and how you set different properties for these boxes (such as width and styles of borders)

By the end of the chapter you should be confidently writing CSS style sheets, and have learned many of the properties you can use to affect the presentation of any document using the style sheet.

In Chapter 10 you will go on to learn the rest of the properties from CSS1 and CSS2, as well as learning how CSS can be used to position the content of elements within a page.

Since the introduction of the Web, those building pages have desired the same control over their pages that print designers have over a printed page. There are, however, some inherent differences in the Internet as a medium when compared with print media. For example, a printed page in a book is always the same size in every copy of the book; the viewers do not need to own a font in order to view the page as they generally do on the Web or have the option of printing the page themselves. These are issues that you learn more about in Chapters 11 and 12 when you look at page layout and design issues.

Introducing CSS

CSS works by allowing your associate *rules* with the elements that appear in the document. These rules govern how the content of those elements should be rendered. Figure 9-1 shows you an example of a CSS rule, which as you can see is made up of two parts:

❑ The *selector*, which indicates which element or elements the declaration applies to. (If it applies to more than one element, you can have a comma-separated list of several elements.)

❑ The *declaration*, which sets out how the elements should be styled.

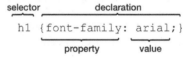

Figure 9-1

The rule in Figure 9-1 applies to all `<h1>` elements and indicates that they should appear in the Arial typeface.

The declaration is also split into two parts, separated by a colon:

❑ A *property*, which is the property of the selected element(s) that you want to affect, in this case it is the `font-family` property.

❑ A *value*, which is a specification for this property; in this case it is the `Arial` typeface.

This is very similar to the way elements can carry attributes in HTML where the attribute controls a property of the element, and its value would be the setting for that property. In this case, however, rather than the having to specify the attribute on each instance of the element, the selector indicates which elements the rule applies to and the rule changes the properties of those elements.

Here is an example of a CSS rule that applies to several elements (in this example the `<h1>`, `<h2>`, and `<h3>` elements): a comma separates the name of each element that this rule will apply to. The rule also specifies several properties for these elements with each rule separated by a semicolon. Note how all the properties are kept inside the curly braces:

```
h1, h2, h3 {
  color:#000000;
  background-color:#FFFFFF;
  font-family:arial, verdana, sans-serif;
  font-weight:bold;}
```

This should be fairly straightforward; the content of each heading element will be written in a bold, Arial font (unless the computer does not have it, in which case it will look for Verdana and then any sans serif font), in black with a white background.

While you do not need to add a semicolon at the end of a single declaration, as you can see in the preceding example, a declaration can consist of several property-value pairs, and each property-value pair within a rule must be separated by a semicolon. Therefore, it is good practice to start adding semicolons every time you write a rule in case you want to add another rule later; if you forget to add the semicolon, any further property-value pairs will be ignored.

A Basic Example

This following example is going to use quite a number of CSS rules. The purpose of most of these rules should be clear by their name. After this example, you will look at different aspects of CSS, and how to control text, tables, whitespace and backgrounds.

Before starting, take a look at the XHTML document without the CSS rules attached. Figure 9-2 shows you what the document looks like without styling.

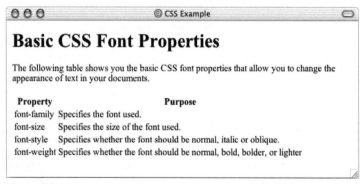

Figure 9-2

The following document (ch09_eg01.html) contains a heading, a paragraph, and a table. Notice the use of the <link> element inside the <head> element, which tells the browser that this document should be styled with the style sheet shown inside the <link> element.

```
<?xml version="1.0" encoding="iso-8859-1"?>
<!DOCTYPE html PUBLIC "-//W3C//DTD XHTML 1.0 Strict//EN"
    "http://www.w3.org/TR/xhtml1/DTD/xhtml1-strict.dtd">
<html xmlns="http://www.w3.org/1999/xhtml" lang="en">
```

```
<head>
  <title>CSS Example</title>
  <link rel="stylesheet" type="text/css" href="ch09_eg01.css" />
</head>

<body>

<h1>Basic CSS Font Properties</h1>
<p>The following table shows you the basic CSS font properties that allow you
to change the appearance of text in your documents.</p>

<table>
  <tr>
    <th>Property</th>
    <th>Purpose</th>
  </tr>
  <tr>
    <td class="code">font-family</td>
    <td>Specifies the font used.</td>
  </tr>
  <tr>
    <td class="code">font-size</td>
    <td>Specifies the size of the font used.</td>
  </tr>
  <tr>
    <td class="code">font-style</td>
    <td>Specifies whether the font should be normal, italic or oblique.</td>
  </tr>
  <tr>
    <td class="code">font-weight</td>
    <td>Specifies whether the font should be normal, bold, bolder,
    or lighter</td>
  </tr>
  </table>

</body>
</html>
```

Figure 9-3 shows what this document looks like with a style sheet attached.

Now, let's take a look at the style sheet used with this document ch09_eg01.html. You should be able to create a CSS style sheet in the same editor you are using to create your HTML pages. CSS files are just simple text files (so you can create them in SimpleText on Mac or Windows Notepad). They are saved with the file extension .css.

The style sheet is split up here so that you can see what each rule does, but the document as a whole is made up of just these rules. The first line is a comment; anything between the opening /* and closing */ will be ignored by the browser and therefore will not be shown:

```
/* Style sheet for ch09_eg01.html */
```

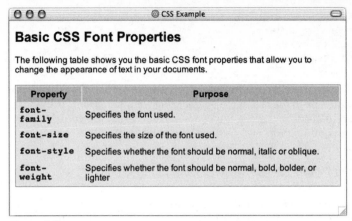

Figure 9-3

The next rule applies to the <body> element. It specifies that the default color of any text and lines used on the page will be black, that the background of the page should be in white, and that the typeface used throughout the document should be Arial. If Arial is not available, Verdana will be used instead; failing that, any sans-serif font will be used.

```
body {
    color:#000000;
    background-color:#ffffff;
    font-family:arial, verdana, sans-serif; }
```

I always specify a `background-color` *property for the body of a document because some people change the default background color of their computers (so that it is not a glaring white), and if you do not set this property the background of the browser will be whatever color the user has as his or her background screen color.*

The next two rules simply specify the size of the contents of the <h1> and <p> elements respectively:

```
h1 {font-size:18pt;}
p {font-size:12pt;}
```

Next it is time to add a few settings to control the appearance of the table—first to give it a light gray background, and then to draw a 1-pixel dark gray border around the edge.

```
table {
    background-color:#efefef;
    border-style:solid;
    border-width:1px;
    border-color:#999999;}
```

Within the table, the headings should have a medium gray background color, appear in a bold font, and have a padding of 5 pixels. You look at the padding in a moment.

```
th {
    background-color:#cccccc;
    font-weight:bold;
    padding:5px;}
```

The individual table data cells have 5 pixels of padding all around them; otherwise the text in one column might run up right next to the text in the neighboring column. *Padding* is the space between the edge of a box and the content inside it. Adding this space makes the text much easier to read. Padding is covered more in the "The padding Property" section later in this chapter.

```
td {padding:5px;}
```

Finally, you might have noticed that the CSS properties in the table were in a Courier font. This is because the table cells that contained these CSS properties carried a class attribute whose value was code. On its own, this attribute does not change the display of the document, as you can see from Figure 9-2, shown previously. The class attribute does, however, allow you to make a more specific selector, so the following rule applies only to <td> elements that carry a class attribute whose value is code, not to all <td> elements:

```
td.code {
    font-family:courier, courier-new, serif;
    font-weight:bold;}
```

There you have the first example. The code for this example is with the download code for the rest of the book. If you want to view a style sheet like this from a Web site you can simply type the URL for the style sheet into the browser and you will see the text. You can try it with the download code to see how it is displayed; to do so, when looking at the example in a browser, remove the filename ch09_eg01.html and replace it with the filename ch09_eg01.css and you will see the CSS rules appear in your browser.

Inheritance

One of the powerful features of CSS is that many of the properties that have been applied to one element will be *inherited* by child elements (elements contained within the element that the rules were declared upon). For example, once the font-family property had been declared for the <body> element in the previous example, it applied to all of the elements inside the <body> element (all of the <body> element's child elements).

If a more specific rule comes along, the more specific rule will override any properties associated with the <body> element, or any other containing element. In the preceding example, most of the text was in an Arial typeface, as specified in the rule associated with the <body> element. There were a few table cells that used a Courier typeface. The table cells that were different had a class attribute whose value was code:

```
<td class="code">font-size</td>
```

Here you can see the rule associated with these elements:

```
td.code {
    font-family:courier, courier-new, serif;
    font-weight:bold;}
```

This rule takes precedence over the one associated with the <body> element because the selector is more specific about which element it applies to.

The way in which some properties inherit saves you from having to write rules and all the property-value pairs out for each element and makes for a more compact style sheet. Appendix C contains a handy reference to CSS properties and tells you which ones do and do not inherit if you need to check.

Where You Can Add CSS Rules

The example that you saw at the beginning of the chapter used a separate style sheet, or *external style sheet*, to contain the CSS rules. This involved the use of the <link /> element in the header of the XHTML document to indicate which style sheet should be used to control the appearance of the document.

CSS rules can also appear in two places inside the HTML or XHTML document:

❑　Inside the <head> element, contained with a <style> element

❑　As a value of a style attribute on any element that can carry the style attribute

When the style sheet rules are held inside a <style> element in the head of the document, they are referred to as an *internal style sheet*.

```
<head>
  <title>Internal Style sheet</title>
  <style type="text/css">
  body {
    color:#000000;
    background-color:#ffffff;
    font-family:arial, verdana, sans-serif; }
  h1 {font-size:18pt;}
  p {font-size:12pt;}
</style>
</head>
```

When style attributes are used, they are known as *inline style rules*. For example:

```
<td style="font-family:courier; padding:5px; border-style:solid;
border-width:1px; border-color:#000000;">
```

Here you can see that the properties are added within the style attribute. There is no need for a selector here (because the style is automatically applied to the element that carries the style attribute), and there are no curly braces. You still need to separate each property from its value using a colon and each of the property-value pairs from each other using a semicolon.

The style attribute was deprecated in Transitional XHTML and is not allowed in Strict XHTML 1.0 because it mixes stylistic markup with the semantic and structural markup.

271

The <link> Element

As you have already seen, the `<link />` element can be used to create a link to CSS style sheets. The `<link />` element is always an empty element that describes the relationship between two documents. It can be used in several ways, but when used with style sheets the relationship indicates that the CSS document contains rules for the presentation of the document containing the `<link />` element.

When the `<link />` element is used to attach a style sheet to a document, it creates a very different kind of link than the kind of link created with an `<a>` element because the style sheet is automatically associated with the document, so the user does not have to click anything to activate the link.

> *The `<link />` element was also originally supposed to be able to be used to create navigation between an ordered sequence of pages. However the major browsers ignore the `<link />` element when used in this context.*

The `<link />` element is most commonly used for linking CSS style sheets to documents. When used with style sheets, the `<link />` element must carry three attributes: `type`, `rel`, and `href`.

```
<link rel="stylesheet" type="text/css" href="../style sheets/interface.css" />
```

In addition to the core attributes, the `<link />` element can also take the following attributes:

```
charset dir href hreflang media rel rev style target type
```

You have met many of these already, so the more important ones are discussed in the following sections along with some of the less common ones.

The rel Attribute

The `rel` attribute is required and specifies the relationship between the document containing the link and the document being linked to.

The key value for working with style sheets is `stylesheet`.

```
rel="stylesheet"
```

The other possible values for this element are discussed in Chapter 3.

The type Attribute

The type attribute specifies the MIME type of the document being linked to:

```
type="text/css"
```

The other MIME types are listed in Appendix H.

The href Attribute

The href attribute specifies the URL for the document being linked to.

```
href="../stylesheets/interface.css"
```

The value of this attribute can be an absolute or relative URL.

The hreflang Attribute

The hreflang attribute specifies the language that the resource specified is written in. Its value should be one of the language codes specified in Appendix G.

```
hreflang="en-US"
```

The media Attribute

The media attribute specifies the output device that is intended for use with the document:

```
media="screen"
```

Although it is not used much at present, this attribute will have increasing impact as more people access the Internet in different ways. See the table that follows for the possible values.

Value	Uses
screen	Non-paged computer screens
tty	Media with a fixed-pitch character grid, such as teletypes, terminals, or portable devices with limited display capabilities
tv	TV devices with low-resolution, color screens, and limited ability to scroll down pages
print	Printed documents, which are sometimes referred to as *paged media* (and documents shown onscreen in print preview mode)
projection	Projectors
handheld	Handheld devices, small screens, bitmapped graphics, and limited bandwidth
braille	Braille tactile feedback devices
aural	Speech synthesizers
all	Suitable for all devices

The <style> Element

The <style> element is used inside the <head> element to contain style sheet rules within a document, rather than linking to an external document. It is also sometimes used when a document needs to contain just a few extra rules that do not apply to the other documents that share the same style sheet.

For example, here you can see a style sheet attached to the XHTML document using the `<link />` element you just learned about, as well as a `<style>` element containing an additional rule:

```
<head>
  <title>
  <link rel="stylesheet" type="text/css" href="../styles/mySite.css" />
  <style type="text/css">
    h1 {color:#FF0000;}
  </style>
</head>
```

The `<style>` element takes the following attributes:

```
dir lang media title type
```

Some browsers also support the `id` and `src` attributes although they are not part of any W3C recommendation.

> *Many document authors add comment marks inside the `<style>` elements so that all CSS rules appear between the `<!--` and the `-->` marks when they appear as an internal style sheet. The idea is that this will hide the code from older browsers that will not understand CSS. The drawback with this technique is that more modern browsers can strip out the content of an XHTML comment and not process their contents; therefore some browsers could ignore all of the style rules. Indeed, a server is also allowed to strip out comments and not send them to the client. In practice, the number of browsers that are likely to visit your site and have a problem viewing it because the style rules are included without a comment is so few that you are better off leaving them off altogether as shown previously.*

Advantages of External CSS Style Sheets

If two or more documents are going to use a style sheet, you should always aim to use an external style sheet (although you may sometimes resort to an internal style sheet to override rules in the external style sheet).

There are several advantages to using external CSS style sheets rather than internal style sheets or inline style rules, including:

❑ The same style sheet can be use by all of the Web pages in your site, which means you can *reuse* the same style sheet with many different XHTML documents. This saves you from including the stylistic markup in each individual document.

❑ Because the style rules are written only once, rather than appearing on every element or in every document, the source documents are smaller. This means that, once the CSS style sheet has been downloaded with the first document that uses it, subsequent documents will be quicker to download (because the browser retains a copy of the CSS style sheet and the rules do not have to be downloaded for every page). This also puts less strain on the server (the computer that sends the Web pages to the people viewing the site) because the pages it sends out are smaller.

❑   You can change the appearance of several pages by just altering the style sheet rather than each individual page; this is particularly helpful if you want to change your company's colors, for example, or the font used for a certain type of element wherever that element appears across the whole site.

❑   The style sheet can act as a style template to help different authors achieve the same style of document without learning all of the individual style settings.

❑   Because the source document does not contain the style rules, different style sheets can be attached to the same document. So you can use the same XHTML document with one style sheet when the viewer is on a desktop computer, another style sheet when the user has a handheld device, another style sheet when the page is being printed, another style sheet when the page is being viewed on a TV, and so on. You reuse the same document with different style sheets for different visitors' needs.

❑   A style sheet can import and use styles from other style sheets, making for modular development and good reuse (see Chapter 10.)

❑   If you remove the style sheet, the site should be a lot more accessible for those with visual impairments because it does not have restrictions of fonts.

It is fair to say, therefore, that whenever you are writing a whole site, you should be using an external style sheet to control the presentation, although as you will see in the next chapter you might use several external style sheets for different aspects of the site.

CSS Properties

Having learned the background of CSS, how to write CSS rules, and where you can place them, it is time to start looking at all of the properties you can use to affect the presentation of your documents. Much of the rest of this chapter looks at examples of CSS properties and how you can use them to specify the intended appearance of your documents. In particular you will learn the `font`, `text`, `border`, `padding`, and `margin` properties. The following table shows the main properties available to us from CSS1 and CSS2.

You will be meeting each of these properties over the next two chapters, and they will be covered in the groupings you can see here.

Some other properties are not covered in these two chapters, but you can find them on one of the following Web sites:

❑   `http://www.w3.org/style/css/`

❑   `http://www.devguru.com/Technologies/css/quickref/css_index.html`

❑   `http://www.w3schools.com/css/css_reference.asp`

The topics not covered are those with less support, or those that are a lot less common, such as the properties for aural style sheets. To find full coverage of these, pick up a book dedicated to CSS.

FONT	BORDER	PADDING	TABLE
font	border	padding	border-collapse
font-family	border-bottom	padding-bottom	border-spacing
font-size	border-bottom-color	padding-left	caption-side
font-size-adjust	border-bottom-style	padding-right	empty-cells
font-stretch	border-bottom-width	padding-top	table-layout
font-style	border-color		
font-variant	border-left	DIMENSIONS	LIST and MARKER
font-weight	border-left-color	height	list-style
	border-left-style	line-height	list-style-image
TEXT	border-left-width	max-height	list-style-position
color	border-right	max-width	list-style-type
direction	border-right-color	min-height	marker-offset
letter-spacing	border-right-style	min-width	
text-align	border-right-width	width	GENERATED
text-decoration	border-style		CONTENT
text-indent	border-top	POSITIONING	content
text-shadow	border-top-color	bottom	counter-increment
text-transform	border-top-style	clip	counter-reset
unicode-bidi	border-top-width	left	quotes
white-space	border-width	overflow	
word-spacing		right	CLASSIFICATION
	MARGIN	top	clear
BACKGROUND	margin	vertical-align	cursor
background	margin-bottom	z-index	display
background-	margin-left		float
attachment	margin-right	OUTLINES	position
background-color	margin-top	outline	visibility
background-image		outline-color	
background-position		outline-style	
background-repeat		outline-width	

Controlling Fonts

There are several properties that allow you to control the appearance of text in your documents. These can be split into two groups:

❑   Those that directly affect the font and its appearance

❑   Those that have other formatting effects upon the text

The table that follows lists the properties that directly affect the font.

Property	Purpose
font	Allows you to combine several properties into one
font-family	Specifies the family of font to be used (the user must have this installed on his or her computer)

Property	Purpose
`font-size`	Specifies the size of a font
`font-weight`	Specifies whether the font should be normal, bold, or bolder than the containing element
`font-style`	Specifies whether the font should be normal, italic, or oblique (an oblique font is the normal font on a slant rather than a separate italic version of the font)
`font-stretch`	Allows you to control the width of the actual letters in a font (not spaces between them)
`font-variant`	Specifies whether the font should be normal or smallcaps
`font-size-adjust`	Allows you to alter the aspect ratio of the size of characters of the font

Before you start looking at fonts, it's important to understand a few issues. Perhaps most importantly, a font is not the same thing as a typeface:

❏   A *typeface* is a family of fonts, such as the Arial family.

❏   A *font* is a specific member of that family, such as Arial 12 point bold.

You will often see the terms used interchangeably, but it is helpful to be aware of the distinction.

Typefaces tend to belong to one of two groups: serif and sans-serif fonts. Serif fonts have extra curls on letters. For example the following l contains a *serif* on the top of the letter leaning back and at the bottom of the letter, whereas sans-serif fonts have straight ends to the letters. The third example is of a monospaced serif font. Every letter in a monospaced font is the same width, whereas most fonts have different widths for different letters (as you can see in serif and sans-serif fonts, the l tends to be narrower than the m). See Figure 9-4 for an example.

serif font

sans-serif font

monospaced font

Figure 9-4

In general print theory, serif fonts are easier to read for long periods of text. However, on the Internet this does not hold true; many people find sans-serif fonts easier to read onscreen because they are not so detailed.

To study the properties that affect fonts, most of the examples will follow a similar structure using paragraphs of text; each <p> element carries a `class` attribute with a different value:

```
<p class="one">Here is some text.</p>
<p class="two">Here is some text.</p>
<p class="three">Here is some text.</p>
```

The use of the `class` attribute allows you to add different styles to different elements that share the same name.

The font-family Property

The `font-family` property allows you to specify the typeface that should be used. There is a big restriction with this property; the person viewing the page must have this font on his or her computer, otherwise they will not see the page in that font. You can, however, specify more than one font so that, if the user does not have your first choice of font, the browser looks for the next font in the list (`ch09_eg02.css`).

```
p.one {font-family:arial, verdana, sans-serif;}
p.two {font-family:times, "times new roman", serif;}
p.three {font-family:courier, "courier new", serif;}
```

If a font name contains spaces, such as `times new roman` *or* `courier new`, *you should place the name in double quotation marks.*

Figure 9-5 shows what this example would look like in a browser; you can see the different types of font used for each paragraph (`ch09_eg02.html`).

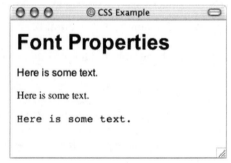

Figure 9-5

The comma-separated list of fonts you can use should end with either serif or sans-serif, so that the computer can use its default serif or non-serif font if it cannot find any of the typefaces you specify.

One thing to bear in mind when choosing fonts is that they can each be of different heights or widths, so you will probably want to choose a similar sized font as an alternative for your first choice. For example Courier New is a lot shorter and wider than Impact (which is quite tall and narrow).

When designers want to use a specific typeface that is not likely to be on the majority of users computers, they tend to use a GIF image for that text. It is generally frowned upon to use images for large sections of text, but for logos or headings and other small amounts of text, this is a good solution. If you do this, remember that you must provide the text that would be seen in the image as the value of the `alt` attribute.

There are several efforts to allow you to use fonts that others are not likely to have on their computer that involve downloading the font in question; however most fonts are copyrighted and—like software—cannot simply be distributed by the purchaser. In addition, many users are wary of downloading files from Web sites, so this cannot be relied upon as a technique for achieving the look you require.

The font-size Property

The `font-size` property allows you to specify a size for the font. There are several ways in which you can specify a value for this property:

- ❑ Absolute size
- ❑ Relative size
- ❑ Length
- ❑ Percentage (in relation to parent element)

An absolute size would be one of the following values:

```
xx-small x-small small medium large x-large xx-large
```

A relative size would be one of the following two values:

```
smaller larger
```

Length can be any unit of length:

```
px em ex pt in cm pc mm
```

You will see what each of these different units means later in the chapter under the heading named after the measurements of lengths (as they are used in conjunction with several properties. Probably the most common is px for pixels.

A percentage is calculated as a proportion of the element that contains the text.

```
2% 10% 25% 50 % 100%
```

For example:

```
p.one {font-size:xx-small;}
p.twelve {font-size:12px;}
p.cithirteen {font-size:3pc;}
p.cifourteen {font-size:10%;}
```

Figure 9-6 shows you how some of these different font sizes work in the browser (ch09_eg03.html and ch09_eg03.css contain several examples of different ways of specifying size and compares how they look).

The font-weight Property

Most fonts have different variations, such as bold and italic. While many good fonts have completely different versions of each character for bold text, browsers tend to use an algorithm to calculate and add to the character's thickness when it is supposed to be bold. Because it uses an algorithm it means you can also create a lighter version of fonts, too. This is what the `font-weight` property is for.

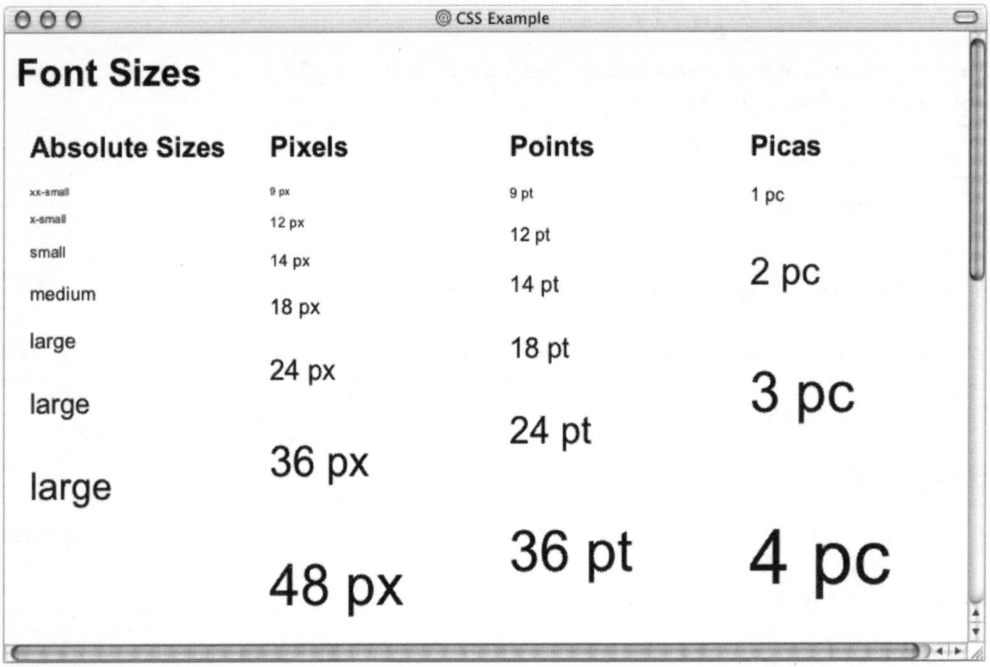

Figure 9-6

The possible values for font-weight are:

```
normal bold bolder lighter 100 200 300 400 500 600 700 800 900
```

So you assign a bold font like so (ch09_eg04.css):

```
p.one {font-weight:normal;}
p.two {font-weight:bold;}
p.three {font-weight:bolder;}
p.four {font-weight:lighter;}
p.five {font-weight:100;}
p.six {font-weight:200;}
```

Figure 9-7 shows you how these values appear in the browser (ch09_eg04.html).

Of these values, bold is most commonly used although you might also come across the use of normal (especially if a large body of text is already in bold and an exception has to be created).

The font-style Property

The font-style property allows you to specify that a font should be normal, italic, or oblique, and these are the values of the font-style property; for example:

```
p.one {font-style:normal;}
p.two {font-style:italic;}
p.three {font-style:oblique;}
```

Figure 9-7

Figure 9-8 shows you how these values appear in the browser (from ch09_eg05.css):

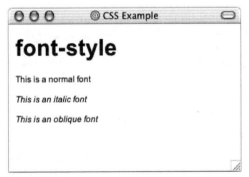

Figure 9-8

The font-variant Property

There are two possible values for the font-variant property: normal and small-caps. A small caps font looks like a smaller version of the uppercase letterset.

For example, look at the following paragraph, which contains a <span> with a class attribute (ch09_eg06.html):

```
<p class="one">This is a normal font, but then <span class="smallcaps">there
are some small caps</span> in the middle.</p>
```

Now look at the style sheet (ch09_eg06.css):

```
p {font-variant:normal;}
span.smallcaps {font-variant:small-caps;}
```

As you can see from Figure 9-9, the rule associated with the <span> element indicates that its content should be shown in small caps.

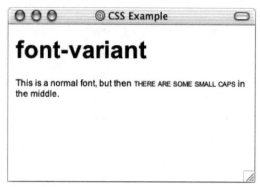

Figure 9-9

The font-stretch Property

The font-stretch property sets the width of the actual letters in a font (not the space between them). It can take either relative or fixed values. The relative values are as follows:

```
normal wider narrower
```

The fixed values are as follows:

```
ultra-condensed extra-condensed condensed semi-condensed semi-expanded
expanded extra-expanded ultra-expanded
```

For example, you could make a condensed Arial font using the following syntax:

```
p {font-family:arial; font-stretch:condensed;}
```

Unfortunately, however, this property is not supported by either IE 6 or Netscape 7.

The font-size-adjust Property

As I mentioned earlier in the chapter, fonts can be different heights and widths. A font's *aspect value* is the ratio between the height of a lowercase letter x in the font and the height of the font. The font-size-adjust property allows you to alter the aspect value of a font.

For example, Verdana has an aspect value of 0.58 (which means that, when the font's size is 100 px, its x-height is 58 pixels). Times New Roman has an aspect value of 0.46 (which means that, when the font's size is 100 px, its x-height is 46 pixels). This makes Verdana easier to read at smaller sizes than Times New Roman. By altering a font's aspect value you can, therefore, change its height.

Unfortunately, neither Netscape 7 nor IE 6 support this property.

Text Formatting

In addition to the font properties, you can use several properties to affect the appearance or formatting of your text. They are listed in the table that follows.

Property	Purpose
color	Specifies the color of the text
text-align	Specifies the alignment of the text within its containing element
vertical-align	Vertical alignment of text within containing element and in relation to containing element
text-decoration	Specifies whether the text should be underlined, overlined, strikethrough, or blinking text
text-indent	Specifies an indent from the left border for the text
text-transform	Specifies that the content of the element should all be uppercase, lowercase, or capitalized
text-shadow	Specifies that the text should have a drop shadow
letter-spacing	Controls the width between letters (known to print designers as *kerning*)
word-spacing	Controls the amount of space between each word
white-space	Specifies whether the whitespace should be collapsed, preserved, or prevented from wrapping
direction	Specifies the direction of text (similar to the dir attribute)
unicode-bidi	Allows you to create bidirectional text

The color Property

The color property allows you to specify the color of the text. The value of this property can either be a hex code for a color or a color name, as you saw in Chapter 4.

For example, the following rule would make the content of paragraph elements red:

```
p {color:#ff0000;}
```

See Appendix D for a list of over 150 color names and corresponding hex codes.

The text-align Property

The text-align property works like the deprecated align attribute would with text. It aligns the text within its containing element or the browser window. See the table that follows or possible values.

Value	Purpose
left	Aligns the text with the left border of the containing element
right	Aligns the text with the right border of the containing element
center	Centers the content in the middle of the containing element
justify	Spreads the width across the whole width of the containing element

For example, you can see how these work in a table that is 500 pixels wide. Here are the rules for each row (ch09_eg08.html):

```
td.leftAlign {text-align:left;}
td.rightAlign {text-align:right;}
td.center {text-align:center;}
td.justify {text-align:justify;}
```

Figure 9-10 shows you how these work.

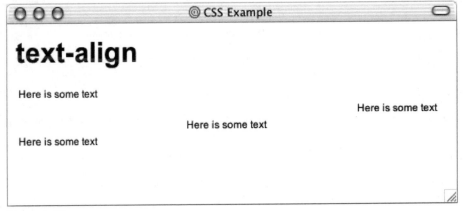

Figure 9-10

The vertical-align Property

The vertical-align property is useful when working with inline elements, in particular images and portions of text. It allows you to control their vertical positioning within the containing element.

```
span.footnote {vertical-align:sub;}
```

It can take several values, as you can see in the table that follows.

Value	Purpose
baseline	Everything should be aligned on the baseline of the parent element (this is the default setting).
sub	Makes the element subscript. With images, the top of the image should be on the baseline. With text, the top of the font body should be on the baseline.
super	Makes the element superscript. With images, the bottom of the image should be level with the top of the font. With text, the bottom of the descender (the part of letters such as g and p that go beneath the line of text) should align with the top of the font body.
top	The top of the text and the top of the image should align with the top of the tallest element on the line.
text-top	The top of the text and the top of the image should align with the top of the tallest text on the line.
middle	The vertical midpoint of the element should be aligned with the vertical midpoint of the parent.
bottom	The bottom of the text and the bottom of the image should align with the bottom of the lowest element on the line.
text-bottom	The bottom of the text and the bottom of the image should align with the bottom of the lowest text on the line.

This property may also accept a length and a percentage value.

You can try out all of these in your browser using Ch09_eg09.html. Figure 9-11 shows you some of these values.

The text-decoration Property

The text-decoration property allows you to specify the values shown in the table that follows.

Value	Purpose
underline	Adds a line under the content
overline	Adds a line over the top of the content
line-through	Like strikethrough text, with a line through the middle. In general, this should be used only to indicate text that is marked for deletion.
blink	Creates blinking text (which is generally frowned upon and considered annoying)

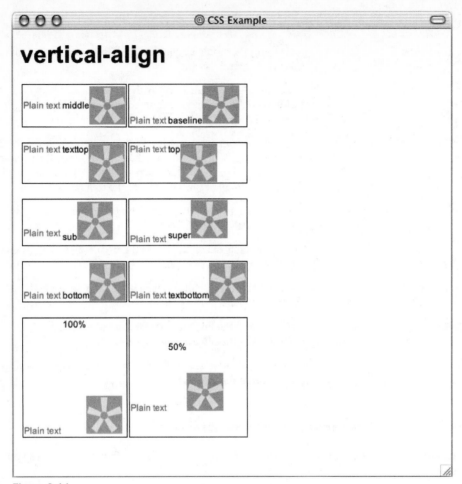

Figure 9-11

For example, here are these properties used on separate paragraphs:

```
p.underline {text-decoration:underline;}
p.overline {text-decoration:overline;}
p.line-through {text-decoration:line-through;}
p.blink {text-decoration:blink;}
```

Figure 9-12 shows you these properties that are demonstrated in Ch09_eg10.html. Note that the blink property works in Netscape 4 only.

The text-indent Property

The text-indent property allows you to specify how much the content of a block-level element should be indented from the left side of the browser window or the left side of its containing element. For

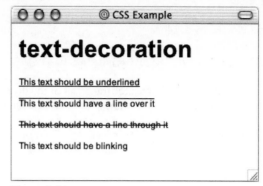

Figure 9-12

example, here you can see that the second paragraph has been indented. First, here is the XHTML in
ch08_eg11.html:

```
<p>This paragraph should be aligned with the left-hand side of the browser. </p>
<p class="indent">The content of this paragraph should be indented by 3 em. </p>
```

Now, here is the rule that indents the second paragraph (ch08_eg11.css):

```
.indent {text-indent:3em;}
```

You can see what this looks like in Figure 9-13.

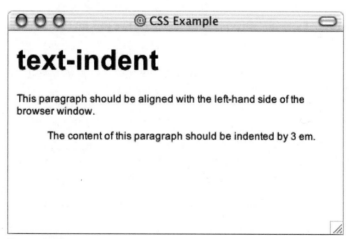

Figure 9-13

The text-shadow Property

The text-shadow property is supposed to create a *drop shadow*, which is a dark version of the word just
behind it and slightly offset. This has often been used in print media, and its popularity has meant that is

has gained its own CSS property in CSS2. The value for this property is quite complicated, as it can take three lengths, optionally followed by a color:

```
.dropShadow { text-shadow: 0.3em 0.3em 0.5em black}
```

The first two lengths specify X and Y coordinates for the offset of the drop shadow, while the third specifies a blur effect. This is then followed by a color, which can be a name or a hex value.

Unfortunately this property does not work in IE 6 or Netscape 7 although an example has been provided with the download code in ch09_eg12.html and ch09_eg12.css.

The text-transform Property

The text-transform property allows you to specify the case for the content of an element. The possible values are shown in the table that follows.

Value	Purpose
none	No change should take place
capitalize	The first letter of every word should be capitalized
uppercase	The entire content of the element should be uppercase
lowercase	The entire content of the element should be lowercase

Look at the following four paragraphs, all of which look like this (but with different values for the class attribute):

```
<p class="none"><i>The Catcher in the Rye</i> was written by J.D. Salinger</p>
```

Here you can see the four different values for the text-transform property in use (ch09_eg13.css):

```
p.none {text-transform:none;}
p.Capitalize {text-transform:Capitalize;}
p.UPPERCASE {text-transform:UPPERCASE;}
p.lowercase {text-transform:lowercase;}
```

Figure 9-14 shows you how the paragraphs would appear in a browser with these styles applied.

The letter-spacing Property

The letter-spacing property is supposed to control something that print designers refer to as *kerning*; the gap between letters. Loose kerning indicates that there is a lot of space between letters, whereas tight kerning refers to letters being squeezed together. No kerning refers to the normal gap between letters for that font.

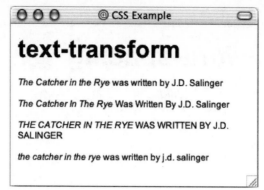

Figure 9-14

The possible values are `normal` or a unit of length (which is the next topic). For example (`ch09_eg15 .css` which is used with `ch09_eg15.html`):

```
span.wider {letter-spacing:50px;}
```

Figure 9-15 gives you an indication of what this looks like.

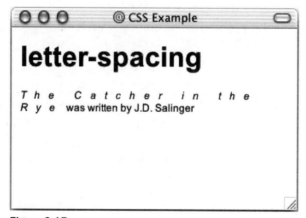

Figure 9-15

The word-spacing Property

The `word-spacing` property is supposed to set the gap between words. Its value should be a unit of length. For example (`ch09_eg15.css` used with `ch09_eg15.html`):

```
span.wider {word-spacing:20px;}
```

Figure 9-16 gives you an indication of what this looks like.

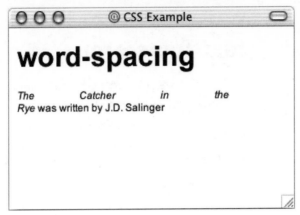

Figure 9-16

The white-space Property

The white-space property controls whether or not whitespace is preserved within and between block level elements. By default a browser makes any double spaces a singe space, and makes any carriage returns a single space, too. The white-space property offers the same results as the XHTML <pre> element and nowrap attribute. See the table that follows for the possible values for this property.

Value	Meaning
normal	Normal whitespace collapsing rules are followed.
pre	Whitespace is preserved just as in the <pre> element of XHTML, but the formatting is whatever is indicated for that element, not just a monospaced font.
nowrap	Text is broken onto a new line only if explicitly told to with a element, otherwise text does not wrap.

For example, you could use the white-space property like so (ch09_eg16.css):

```
.pre {white-space:pre;}
.nowrap {white-space:nowrap;}
```

Unfortunately, the value of pre does not work in IE 6, although it does work in Netscape 4 and later. The nowrap property works in IE 6 and Netscape 4 and later. You can see both of these properties working in Figure 9-17.

The direction Property

The direction property is rather like the dir attribute and specifies the direction in which the text should flow. The possible values are:

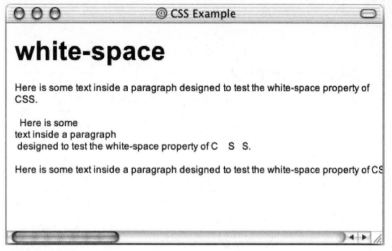

Figure 9-17

Value	Meaning
ltr	The text flows from left to right.
rtl	The text flows from right to left.
inherit	The text flows in the same direction as its parent element.

For example, here are rules for two paragraphs indicating different directions for the text (ch09_eg17 .css used with ch09_eg17.html):

```
p.ltr {direction:ltr;}
p.rtl {direction:rtl;}
```

In practice, both IE and Netscape use this property much like the align attribute is used. The value rtl will simply right-align text, as you can see in Figure 9-18. Note however, that the period (or full stop) is to the left of the sentence in the paragraph that is supposed to be running right to left.

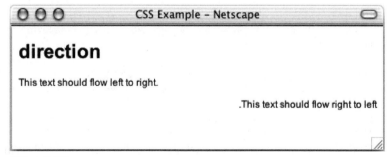

Figure 9-18

Do not use this property instead of the text-align property, as it will break when new browsers fully support this property.

The unicode-bidi Property

This is a property designed for internationalization purposes, and the bidi part in the name is short for *bi-directional*. It allows words to appear in the direction that would be inferred by the Unicode standard and for authors to specify a change in direction of the elements' content contrary to the Unicode standard. See the table that follows for possible values.

Value	Purpose
normal	No directional embedding will be enabled.
embed	The element opens an additional level of embedding, and the intending Unicode direction will be followed.
bidi-override	Overrides the default directional values of an inline element in order to allow the direction property to set the direction in the element (overrides the Unicode settings).

It is particularly helpful for inline elements that should be facing a different direction than the rest of the containing element—for example if you were using a word that was written in a different direction because the embed value allows your text to flow in the opposite direction from the rest of the containing element. If you want to stop this from happening you can use the bidi-override value.

Text Pseudo-Classes

While you are learning about text, there are two very helpful pseudo-classes that can help you work with text. These pseudo-classes allow you to render either the first letter or the first line of an element in a different way than the rest of that element. Both of these are commonly used when laying out text.

The first-letter Pseudo-Class

The first-letter pseudo-class allows you to specify a rule just for the first letter of an element. This is most commonly used on the first character of a new page, either in some magazine style articles or in children's books.

Here is an example of the first-letter pseudo-class being applied to a <p> element carrying a class attribute whose value is pageOne (ch09_eg18.css which is used with ch09_eg18.html):

```
p.pageOne:first-letter {font-size:42px;}
```

You can see the effect of this first-letter pseudo-class in Figure 9-19 (which also shows the next pseudo-class).

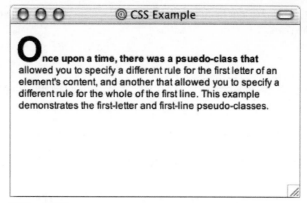

Figure 9-19

The first-line Pseudo-Class

The `first-line` pseudo-class should allow you to render the first line of any paragraph differently than the rest of the paragraph. Commonly this might be in a bold font so that the reader can clearly see an introduction (for articles) or the first line (for poems or hymns).

The name of the pseudo-class is separated from the element it should appear on by a colon:

```
p:first-line {font-weight:bold;}
```

Note how, if you resize the window so that there is less text on the first line, only the first line of text in the browser will be given this new style. You can see the first-line `pseudo-class` in action in Figure 9-19, which also demonstrates the `first-letter` pseudo-class.

Try It Out   **A Font Test Page**

Now that you've learned about using CSS to format text, it is time to try putting what you have learned into practice by creating a font test page. You will be able to use this page to test whether a browser supports a font or not.

1.   Create a new XHTML document, with the skeleton you are used to creating by now:

```
<?xml version="1.0" encoding="iso-8859-1"?>
<!DOCTYPE html PUBLIC "-//W3C//DTD XHTML 1.0 Transitional//EN"
    "http://www.w3.org/TR/xhtml1/DTD/xhtml1-transitional.dtd">
<html xmlns="http://www.w3.org/1999/xhtml" lang="en">

<head>
  <title>Font test</title>
</head>

<body>
</body>
</html>
```

2. Add a `<link />` element to an external style sheet. The name of the style sheet will be `font-test.css`.

```
<head>
  <title>Font text</title>
<link rel="stylesheet" type="text/css" href="font-test.css" />
</head>
```

3. Add a `<div>` element like this one and then copy and paste that line ten times:

```
<div class="">The quick brown fox jumped over the lazy dog.</div>
```

4. Add the name of some typefaces as the value of the class attributes and add the name of the typeface at the beginning of the sentence like so:

```
<div class="arial">Arial The quick brown fox jumped over the lazy dog.</div>
<div class="helvetica">Helvetica The quick brown fox jumped over the lazy dog.
</div>
<div class="TimesNewRoman">Times New Roman The quick brown fox jumped over the
lazy dog.</div>
<div class="MrsEaves">Mrs Eaves The quick brown fox jumped over the lazy dog.
</div>
```

5. Save this file as `font-test.html`.

6. Create a new document in the editor you are using and save the file as `font-test.css`.

7. Add the selectors for each of the `<div>` elements you added to your XHTML document:

```
div.arial
div.helvetica
div.TimesNewRoman
div.MrsEaves
```

8. Add `font-family` properties to each of these, and give the value of the typeface specified:

```
div.arial {font-family:arial;}
div.helvetica {font-family:Helvetica;}
div.TimesNewRoman {font-family:"Times New Roman";}
div.MrsEaves {font-family:"Mrs Eaves";}
```

9. Add another typeface after the one you want to view, and separate the two with a comma. Note that this second typeface should be very different than the ones you are hoping to see. I am using Courier, a monospaced font, as the second choice, so it will be clear whether or not the browser supports the font I have named.

```
div.arial {font-family:arial, courier;}
div.helvetica {font-family:Helvetica, courier;}
div.TimesNewRoman {font-family:"Times New Roman", courier;}
div.MrsEaves {font-family:"Mrs Eaves", courier;}
```

10. Add the following rule to make sure that there is adequate space between each line to look at the fonts:

```
div {line-height:28px;}
```

11. Save this CSS file and open the XHTML page in your browser. You should end up with something like Figure 9-20.

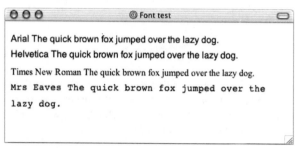

Figure 9-20

As you can see from this example, the computer this screenshot was taken on does not have the Mrs Eaves typefaces.

One of the exercises at the end of the chapter expands upon this example.

How It Works

The first thing to note about this example is the presence of the `<link />` element in the source XHTML document, which indicates that it should be styled using the `font-test.css` style sheet.

```
<link rel="stylesheet" type="text/css" href="font-test.css" />
```

This line features three attributes, all of which are required to indicate the relationship between the document containing the link and the document it is linking to, and so that the document can be located.

The browser should now use the style sheet to lay out the example as specified in `font-test.css`. Each `<div>` element in the XHTML document carried a `class` attribute, which is used by CSS to identify that particular element's content and style it differently than other `<div>` elements. The value of the `class` attributes is the typeface to be checked.

It is the selectors in a CSS rule that determine which elements a rule applies to, and the class selector was used in the style sheet to individually identify each `<div>` element so that different rules could be applied to each one. For example, the text to be displayed in an Arial typeface was identified like so:

```
div.arial
```

The properties were then added inside curly braces that followed the selector. The `font-family` property allows you to specify the typeface you want to use for the content of the selected elements (and their children—because this property is inherited by child elements). A second font that is *not* similar in appearance was then specified as the second option if the browser could not find the requested font; this makes it clear if the browser does not support a font. I used Courier because it is clearly identifiable as a monospaced font.

```
div.arial {font-family:arial,courier;}
```

Finally, the `line-height` property added extra height between each line of text to make the examples more readable. This property was specified using one selector for every `<div>` element rather than repeating it for each `<div>` element. Also a rule was added so that the content of the whole document would have a white background—this property was attached to the `<body>` element.

Selectors

You should be starting to get the hang of writing rules in style sheets that indicate how an element should appear, but before you look at more of the properties that you can use to affect the layout of a document, you need to look at some more of the fundamentals, starting with a look at the different ways in which you can select which element or elements a rule applies to.

You can select elements in several ways, not just by using their name as you have seen in this chapter (which is, incidentally, known as a *simple selector*), or using the value of the class attribute in the document the sheet is styling. You can create selectors that are a lot more specific. In addition to providing the element name as a selector, you can use the following as selectors.

Universal Selector

The *universal selector* is an asterisk; it is like a wildcard and matches all element types in the document.

```
*{}
```

If you want a rule to apply to all elements you can use this selector. Sometimes it is used for default values, such as a `font-family` and `font-size`, that will apply to the whole of the document (unless another more specific selector indicates an element should use different values for these same properties).

It is slightly different than applying default styles to the `<body>` element, as the universal selector applies to every element, and does not rely on the property being inherited.

The Type Selector

The *type selector* matches all of the elements specified in the comma-delimited list. It allows you to apply the same rules to several elements. For example, the following would match all `page`, `heading`, and `paragraph` elements.

```
page, heading, paragraph {}
```

If you have the same rules that apply to several elements, this technique can lead to a smaller style sheet, saving bandwidth and load on your server (the computer sending your Web pages to those that request them).

The Class Selector

The *class selector* allows you to match a rule with an element carrying a class attribute whose value you specify in the class selector. For example, imagine you had a `<p>` element with a class attribute whose value was BackgroundNote, like so:

```
<p class="BackgroundNote">This paragraph contains an aside.</p>
```

You can use a class selector in one of two ways here: first you could simply assign a rule that applies to any element that has a class attribute whose value is BackgroundNote, like so, simply preceding the value of the class attribute with a period or full stop:

```
.BackgroundNote {}
```

Or you can create a selector that selects only the `<p>` elements that carry a class attribute with a value of BackgroundNote (not other elements) like so:

```
p.BackgroundNote {}
```

If you have several elements that can all carry a class attribute with the same value (for example a `<p>` element and a `<div>` element could both use the class attribute with the same value) *and* you want the content of these elements to be displayed in the same manner you will want to use the former notation. If the class is specific to that element (perhaps a `<code>` element), then you should use the latter notation.

The ID Selector

The *id selector* works just like a class selector, but works on the value of id attributes. But rather than using a period or full stop before the value of the id attribute, you use a hash or pound sign (#). So, a `<p>` element with an id attribute whose value is abstract could be identified with this selector.

```
p.#abstract
```

Because the value of an id attribute should be unique within a document, this selector should apply only to the content of one element.

The Child Selector

The *child selector* matches an element that is a direct child of another. In this case it matches any `<b>` elements that are direct children of `<td>` elements:

```
td > b {}
```

This would enables you to specify a different style for `<b>` elements that are direct children of the `<td>` element rather than for `<b>` elements that appear elsewhere in the document.

Note, however, that this selector applies only to a `<b>` element that is a direct child of the parent element. The following selector does not really make sense because the `<b>` element should not be a direct child of a `<table>` element:

```
table > b {}
```

The Descendent Selector

The *descendent selector* matches an element type that is a descendent of another specified element, at any level of nesting not just a direct child. In this case the selector matches any `<b>` element that is a child of the `<table>` element, which means it would apply to `<b>` elements both in `<td>` and `<th>` elements.

```
table b {}
```

This is a contrast to the child selector because it applies to all of the children of the `<table>` element, rather than just the direct children.

The Adjacent Sibling Selector

An *adjacent sibling selector* matches an element type that is the next sibling of another. For example, if you want to make the first paragraph after any level 1 heading a different style you can use the adjacent sibling selector like so:

```
h1 + p {}
```

Both elements must have the same element, and this will apply only to the `<p>` element directly after a heading.

Sometimes the descendent selector, child selector, and adjacent selectors are collectively referred to as *contextual selectors* because they allow you to associate rules that indicate that an element should appear in a different way depending upon where it appears in the document. For example, you might want to make the content of a `<strong>` element appear in a different way if it is inside a `<p>` element than when it appears in a `<td>` element. Remember that the more specific a rule, the greater precedence it has over other rules.

Attribute Selectors

Attribute selectors allow you to use the attributes that an element carries in the selector. There are several ways in which you can use attribute selectors. For example, look at the following paragraph that carries an `id` attribute:

```
<p id="important" class="XHTML attributes">You must place all attributes
in double quotes.</p>
```

The table that follows lists the attribute selectors and what they would match in this example.

Unfortunately, none of these work in IE 6, and only the first two work in Netscape 6 and later. When they do become supported, however, they will be powerful tools for allowing you to apply a style to an element based on the presence of, or value of, an attribute.

Selector	Matches
paragraph[id]	An element called paragraph carrying an attribute called id
paragraph[id="important"]	An element called paragraph carrying an attribute called id whose value is important
paragraph[class~="XHTML"]	An element called paragraph carrying an attribute called class, whose value is a list of space-separated words, one of which is exactly the same as XHTML
paragraph[class|="XHT"]	An element called paragraph carrying an attribute called class whose value begins with XHT

Another feature is the ability to use regular expressions in selectors. However, the use of regular expressions in selectors is not yet supported in any of the major browsers. Furthermore, regular expressions are a complicated topic, and you are better off getting used to the selectors named here before you consider learning about regular expressions.

HTML was not fussy over capitalization of selectors and would apply all of the following selectors to the <body> element:

```
Body{}
body{}
BODY{}
```

Indeed, Transitional XHTML will allow you to get away with this, but remember that XHTML is written in XML, and XML is case-sensitive. (This was one of the differences I mentioned between HTML and XHTML back in Chapter 1.) Therefore your selectors should match the case of the element and attribute names used in documents (which should all be lowercase).

Lengths

ou have already seen that some of the properties' values are given as *lengths* (size of fonts, height of lines of text), and you will come across the need to specify lengths in several more CSS properties. It is helpful to take a look at these now because the next section relies on lengths for several properties.

Lengths can be measured in one of three ways in CSS:

- ❑ Absolute units
- ❑ Relative units
- ❑ Percentages

Absolute Units

The following table shows the *absolute units* that you can use in CSS.

Unit	Full Name
pt	A point
in	An inch
cm	A centimeter
pc	A pica
mm	A millimeter

I shouldn't really need to clarify inches, millimeters, or centimeters, but the other two are more interesting. A point is $\frac{1}{72}$ of an inch (the same as a pixel in most computer screen resolutions), and a pica is $\frac{1}{12}$ of an inch (12 points). Typographers tend to use points to measure font sizes and leading (the gaps between lines), while picas are used to measure line lengths.

Relative Units

Relative units and percentages can be very useful, but they also bring their own issues that you need to be aware of for two reasons:

❑ They can adjust size with the kind of media that the document is being shown on.

❑ Users can increase and decrease the size of fonts on a Web browser and the rest of the page will scale to fit.

px

A *pixel* is the smallest unit of resolution, and the size of a layout that uses pixels as a unit of measurement *can* depend upon the viewing medium (keep reading to see why I say "can").

Most computer screens have a resolution of 72 dots per inch (dpi), but you will find that most modern laser and bubble jet printers are set with a higher resolution—my current printer runs at 300 dpi. In contrast, mobile phones and PDAs can have an even lower resolution than computer screens.

So, a table that is 500 pixels wide could be 9.9444 inches wide on a 72 dpi screen, 1.666 inches wide at 300 dpi, or 13.888 pixels wide on a 32 dpi screen (and a screen with such low resolution is very unlikely to be that wide).

In reality, when you print a Web page from IE or Netscape it will adjust the pixels to present a readable version of the document. In fact, CSS recommends that user agents rescale pixel units so that reading at arms length 1 pixel would correspond to about 0.28 mm or $\frac{1}{90}$ th of an inch. This does, however, stop a pixel from being a relative unit any more, and makes it an absolute unit.

Most powerful programming languages have a function that allows programmers to adjust images to the screen resolution, but unfortunately this is not possible in CSS.

em

An *em* unit corresponds directly to the font size of the *reference* element, which will be either that element or the containing element.

The term *em* is often thought to come from the width of a lowercase *m*, although it is generally considered the height of the font. (Note that an *en* is half an *em*.)

ex

The *ex* should be the height of a lowercase *x*. Because different fonts have different proportions, the ex is related to the font size and the type of font. In Figure 9-21 you can see the *x* in the Courier typeface is smaller than the *x* in the Impact typeface.

courier   **impact**

Figure 9-21

Percentages

Percentages give a value in relation to another value (the value depends upon the property in question). Note that when a percentage value is inherited, it is the value that is set by the percentage that is inherited (not the percentage).

Coming to Grips with the Box Model

Now that you've seen how to specify properties, learned more about selectors, and looked at some of the basic units of length, it is almost time to continue looking at properties that you can use to control the presentation of element content. But before you do, you need to understand how CSS is based upon a *box model*.

Every element gets treated as a *box* in CSS, and remembering this will really help you understand how to create attractive layouts with CSS.

As you can see in the table that follows, every box has three properties you must be aware of.

Property	Description
border	Even if you cannot see it, every box has a border. This separates the edge of the box from other boxes.
margin	The margin is the distance between the edge of a box and the box next to it.
padding	This padding is the space between the content of the box and its border.

You can get a better idea of these properties in Figure 9-22, which shows the various parts of the box (the black line is the border).

Figure 9-22

You can use CSS to individually control the top, bottom, left, and right margin border and padding; you can specify a different width and color for each one.

The padding and margin properties are especially important in creating whitespace, which is the space between parts of the page, in your designs. For example, if you had text inside a box with a border, you would want to have some padding so that the edge of the text does not touch the border. (If text actually touches a border of the same color it makes it much harder to read.) Meanwhile, if you had two boxes with borders, if there were not a margin between them the borders would run into each other.

There is, however, an interesting issue with margins: when a bottom margin of one element meets the top margin of another, only the larger of the two will show (if they are the same size, then the margin will be equivalent to the size of just one of the margins). Figure 9-23 shows the vertical margins of two adjacent boxes collapsing.

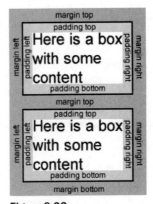

Figure 9-23

To really understand how the box model works with elements, take a look at the example in the next section.

An Example Illustrating the Box Model

To illustrate the box model with a real page, it is as if the <body> element creates a box that contains the whole page, and then each heading, paragraph, image, or link creates another box within the page.

Each box can have different properties that affect the appearance of its contents. Take a look at the following XHTML (09_19.html):

```
<?xml version="1.0" ?>
<!DOCTYPE html PUBLIC "-//W3C//DTD XHTML 1.0 Transitional//EN"
    "http://www.w3.org/TR/xhtml1/DTD/xhtml1-transitional.dtd">
<html xmlns="http://www.w3.org/1999/xhtml" lang="en" xml:lang="en">

<head>
  <title>Understanding the Box Model</title>
  <link rel="stylesheet" type="text/css" href="ch09_eg19.css" />
</head>

<body>
  <h1>Thinking Inside the Box</h1>
  <p class="description">When you are styling a web page with CSS page you
  must start to think in terms of <b>boxes</b>.</p>

  <p>Each element is treated as if it generates a new box. Each box can have
  new rules associated with it.</p>

  <img src="images/boxmodel.gif" alt="How CSS treats a box" />

  <p>As you can see from the diagram above, each box has a <b>border</b>.
  Between the content and the border you can have <b>padding</b>, and
  outside of the border you can have a <b>margin</b> to separate this box
  from any neighboring boxes.</p>
</body>
</html>
```

Each element involved with the body of the document—<body>, <h2>, <p>, <img>, and <b>—gets treated as if it were in a separate box. You can see this by creating some CSS rules to add a border around each of these elements using some new properties here, which you will meet shortly (ch09_eg19.css).

```
body {
    color:#000000;
    background-color:#ffffff;
    font-family:arial, verdana, sans-serif;
    font-size:12px;}

body, h1, p, img, b {
    border-style:solid;
    border-width:2px;
    border-color:#000000;
    padding:2px;}

h1, b {background-color:#cccccc;}
```

This gives you an even better idea of how all styling with CSS involves selecting an element and then setting different properties with appropriate values.

Figure 9-24 shows you how this page looks in a browser. While it is not too attractive, it shows you how the boxes are created for each element. The line is actually the border of the box created for that element. In addition to each element having a border, the <h1> and <bold> elements also have a gray background to help distinguish them.

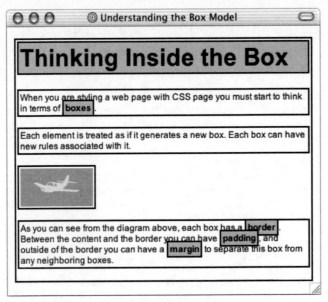

Figure 9-24

You may remember from Chapter 1 that I told you there was a difference between *block level elements* and *inline elements*; the difference becomes quite important when working with CSS because it determines how each box is treated. This example illustrates the point well; if you look at the <h1> element, its box takes up the full width of the browser, whereas the boxes around the <b> elements sit in the middle of the rest of the paragraph rather than taking up a whole line.

The <h1> element is a block level element, as are the <body> and <p> elements. It is treated as if it creates a separate block on its own and it appears on its own new line. The <b> element, meanwhile, is an inline element, flows within its containing element, and does not have to appear on a new line of its own. A block element will also by default take up the full width of the page (or the element it is contained within), while an inline element will take up only as much space as it needs.

The <img /> element may look like it is a block level element although it is actually an inline element. You can tell this because, while it looks as thought it is on its own line, the border around it takes up only the width of the image; if it were a block level element, the border would reach the full width of the browser. The image is on its own line only because the elements on either side of it *are* block level elements (and therefore the surrounding elements appear on their own lines).

In Strict XHTML this image element should be placed inside a block level element, as you are supposed to have block level elements only as children of the <body> element. While it does not matter in Transitional XHTML, you could simply fix this issue by putting the element inside a <div> element (which you might remember is a grouping element).

The Border Properties

The border properties allow you to specify how the border of the box representing an element should look. There are three properties of a border you can change:

❑ border-color to indicate the color a border should be

❑ border-style to indicate whether a border should be solid, dashed line, double line, or one of the other possible values

❑ border-width to indicate the width a border should be

The border-color Property

The border-color property allows you to change the color of the border surrounding a box. For example:

```
p {border-color:#ff0000;}
```

The value can be a hex code for the color or a color name like those you learned about in Chapter 4. It can also be expressed as values for red, green, and blue; between 0 and 255; or percentages of red green and blue. See the table that follows for examples.

Color Name	hex	RGB Values	RGB Percentages
red	#ff0000	rgb (255, 0, 0)	rgb (100%, 0, 0)
green	#00ff00	rgb (0, 255, 0)	rgb (0, 100%, 0)
blue	#0000ff	rgb (0, 0, 255)	rgb (0, 0, 100%)

You can individually change the color of the bottom, left, top and right sides of a box's border using the properties:

❑ border-bottom-color

❑ border-right-color

❑ border-top-color

❑ border-left-color

The border-style Property

The border-style property allows you to select one of the following styles of border:

```
p {border-style:solid;}
```

The default value for this property is none, so no border shows automatically. The table that follows shows the possible values.

Value	Description
none	No border. (Equivalent of border-width:0;)
solid	Border is a single solid line.

Continues

Value	Description
dotted	Border is a series of dots.
dashed	Border is a series of short lines.
double	Border is two solid lines; the value of the border-width property creates the sum of the two lines and the space between them.
groove	Border looks as though it is carved into the page.
ridge	Border looks the opposite of groove.
inset	Border makes the box look like it is embedded in the page.
outset	Border makes the box look like it is coming out of the canvas.
hidden	Same as none, except in terms of border-conflict resolution for table elements. (See section on tables.)

Figure 9-25 shows an example of what each of these would look like (taken from ch09_eg20.html). Note that even though the last four examples in Figure 9-25 look very similar, they are different, and you can try them for yourself with the download code for this example.

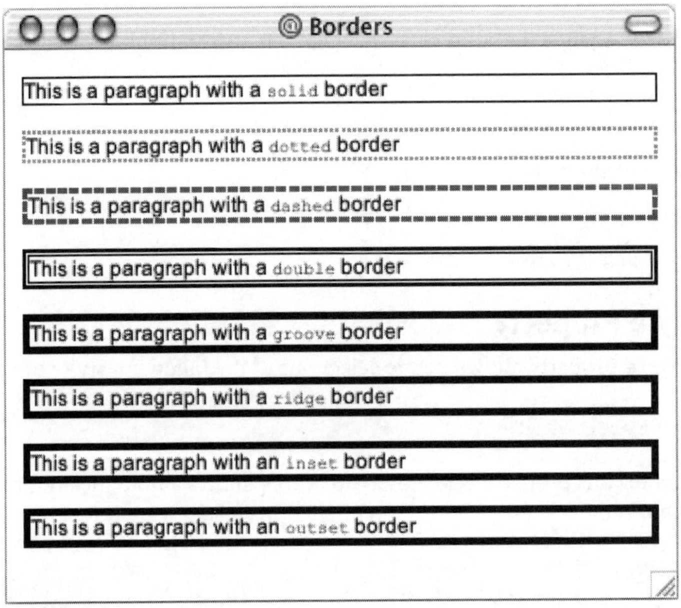

Figure 9-25

You can individually change the style of the bottom, left, top, and right borders of a box using the properties:

- ❏ border-bottom-color
- ❏ border-right-color
- ❏ border-top-color
- ❏ border-left-color

The border-width Property

The border-width property allows you to set the width of your borders.

```
p {border-style:solid; }
    border-width:4px; }
```

The value of the border-width attribute cannot be a percentage; it must be a length (as discussed in the "Lengths" section earlier in the chapter) or one of the following values:

- ❏ thin
- ❏ medium
- ❏ thick

The width of these values is not specified in the CSS recommendation in terms of pixels; the actual width is dependent on the browser.

You can individually change the width of the bottom, top, left, and right borders of a box using the following properties:

- ❏ border-bottom-color
- ❏ border-top-color
- ❏ border-left-color
- ❏ border-right-color

Expressing Border Properties Using Shorthand

The border property allows you to specify color, style, and width of lines in one property:

```
p {border: 4px solid red; }
```

If you use this shorthand, the values should not have anything between them. You can also specify the three properties on any of the following properties in the same way:

- ❏ border-bottom
- ❏ border-top
- ❏ border-left
- ❏ border-right

The padding Property

The `padding` property allows you to specify how much space should appear between the content of an element and its border:

```
td {padding:5px;}
```

The value of this attribute should be either a length, a percentage, or the word `inherit`. If the value is `inherit` it will have the same padding as its parent element.

If a percentage is used, the percentage is of the containing box. So, if the rule indicates the padding on the `<body>` element should be 10 percent, 5 percent of the browser window's width will be inside the content of the `<body>` element on each side as padding. Alternatively, if the rule indicated a `<td>` element should have a 10 percent padding in a cell that is 100 pixels square, there will be a 5-pixel padding around each side of the square inside the border.

The padding of an element will not inherit, so if the `<body>` element has a padding property with a value of 50 pixels, this will not automatically apply to all other elements inside it.

- ❑ `padding-bottom`
- ❑ `padding-top`
- ❑ `padding-left`
- ❑ `padding-right`

The `padding` attribute is especially helpful in creating whitespace between the content of an element and any border it has. (Even if the border is not visible, padding prevents the content of two adjacent boxes from touching.) Take a look at the following two paragraphs in Figure 9-26.

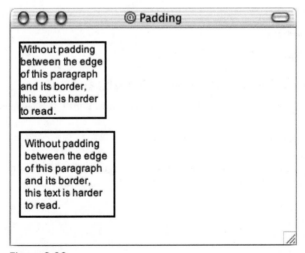

Figure 9-26

If you look at the CSS rules for these two paragraph elements, you can see that by default the first paragraph has no padding; it must be specified if you want this gap (`ch09_eg21.css`).

```
.a, .b {border-style:solid;
   border-color:#000000;
   border-width:2px;
   width:100px;}

.b {padding:5px;}
```

I'm sure you can imagine that when you have a table with lots of adjacent cells, this `padding` property becomes very valuable.

The margin Property

The `margin` property is the gap between boxes, and its value is either a length, a percentage, or `inherit`, each of which has exactly the same meaning as it did for the `padding` property you just saw.

```
p {margin:20px;}
```

As with the `padding` property, the values of the `margin` property are not inherited by child elements. But remember that the adjacent vertical margins (top and bottom margins) will collapse into each other so that the distance between the blocks is not the sum of the margins, but only the greater of the two margins (or the same size as one margin if both are equal).

You can also set different values for the margin on each side of the box using the following properties:

- ❑ `margin-bottom`
- ❑ `margin-top`
- ❑ `margin-left`
- ❑ `margin-right`

If you look at the following example (see Figure 9-27 and `ch09_eg22.html`), you can see three paragraphs with taller margins on the top than the bottom, and therefore the bottom margin is collapsed when it meets a top margin. Again, this is not the most attractive example, but it illustrates both block and inline boxes using margins.

The words in the paragraphs that are emphasized using the `<em>` element have `margin-left` and `margin-right` properties set. Because these elements also have a background color set, you can really see how the margins to the left and the right separate the words from the surrounding words.

Here are the rules from `ch09_eg22.css`:

```
body {
   color:#000000;
   background-color:#ffffff;
   font-family:arial, verdana, sans-serif;
   font-size:12px;}

p {
   margin-top:40px;
   margin-bottom:30px;
```

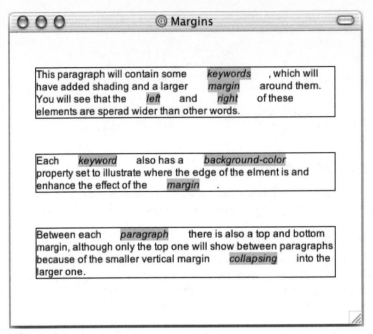

Figure 9-27

```
    margin-left:20px;
    margin-right:20px;
    border-style:solid;
    border-width:1px;
    border-color:#000000;}

em {
    background-color:#cccccc;
    margin-left:20px;
    margin-right:20px;}
```

Dimensions

Now that you've seen the border that surrounds every box, the padding that can appear inside each box and the margin that can go around them, it is time to look at how you can change the dimensions of boxes.

The table that follows shows the properties that allow you to control the dimensions of a box.

Property	Purpose
height	Sets the height of a box
width	Sets the width of a box
line-height	Sets the height of a line of text (like leading in a layout program)

Property	Purpose
max-height	Sets a maximum height that a box can be
min-height	Sets the minimum height that a box can be
max-width	Sets the maximum width that a box can be
min-width	Sets the minimum width that a box can be

The height and width Properties

The height and width properties allow you to set the height and width for boxes. They can take values of a length, a percentage, or the keyword auto (the default value being auto).

Here you can see the CSS rules for two paragraph elements, the first with a class attribute whose value is one and the second whose class attribute has a value of two (ch09_eg23.css):

```
p.one {
   width:200px; height:100px;
   padding:5px; margin:10px;
   border-style:solid; border-color:#000000; border-width:2px;}

p.two {
   width:300px; height:100px;
   padding:5px; margin:10px;
   border-style:solid; border-color:#000000; border-width:2px;}
```

As you can see in Figure 9-28, the first paragraph will be 200 pixels wide and 100 pixels high, while the second paragraph will be 300 pixels wide and 100 pixels high.

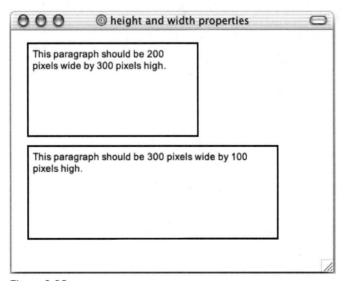

Figure 9-28

The line-height Property

The line-height property is one of the most important properties in laying out text. It allows you to increase the space between lines of text (known in the publishing industry as *leading*).

The value of the line-height property can be a number, a length, or a percentage. It is a good idea to specify this property in the same measurement in which you specify the size of your text.

Here you can see two rules setting different line-height properties (ch09_eg24.css):

```
p.one {
    line-height:16px;}

p.two {
    line-height:28px;}
```

As you can see in Figure 9-29, the first paragraph does not have a line-height attribute, while the second and third paragraphs correspond to the preceding rules.

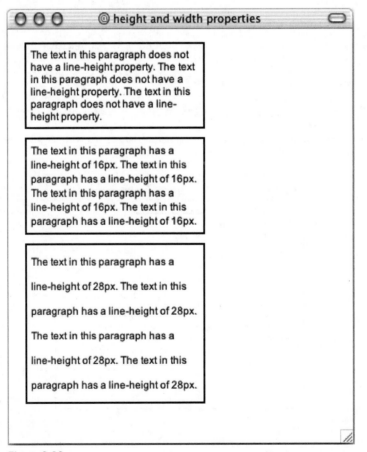

Figure 9-29

The max-height and max-width Property

The `max-height` and `max-width` properties allow you to specify maximum height and width for a box. The value of these properties can be a number, a length, or a percentage.

```
p {max-height:300px; max-length:300px;}
```

These properties will be particularly useful when supported because they will allow you to specify a maximum area an element's content can take up when you create templates for pages whose content can vary.

Unfortunately, they do not work in either Netscape 7 or IE 6.

The min-width and min-height Property

The `min-width` and `min-height` properties correspond with the `max-height` and `max-width` properties, but specify a minimum width and height for the box.

The value of these properties can be a number, a length, or a percentage.

```
P {min-width:100px; min-height:100px;}
```

These properties, when supported, will also be very helpful when creating style sheets that are templates for pages whose content is unknown. The `min-width` and `max-width` properties will ensure that a box takes up at least a certain space—which can be very important for aligning boxes correctly.

Try It Out   **A Style Sheet for Code**

I often find the need to display code online. So I wrote the following style sheet to enable me to define styles very similar to those you see in this book, for showing code on the Web. As you will see in the next chapter, this code can then be included in other style sheets when needed. It is a reusable style sheet.

The style sheet features several styles for block and inline elements. The table that follows shows the styles you will be creating.

Style Name	Inline or Block	Use
codeInText	Inline	For a bit of code written in the middle of a sentence, shown in a monospace font.
codeForeground	Block	Highlighted code in a monospace font for showing examples.
codeBackground	Block	Like codeForeground, but not highlighted because it has been seen before, or is not the key point of the example.
keystroke	Inline	Keys a user should enter on the keyboard, distinguishable because it is italic.

Continues

Style Name	Inline or Block	Use
`importantWords`	Inline	The first use of a key term; helps users scan the document because it appears in a bold font.
`boxText`	Block	Creates a block of important or key notes that is in a box and has background shading.
`Background`	Block	Creates a block of italic text that has an aside or interesting note.

1. The first thing to do is create class selectors for each of these styles. Element names are not used for several of the styles here because the styles could apply to different elements (for example, box text could be in a `<p>` element or a `<div>` grouping other elements). The selectors that do use elements are the ones representing code.

```
code.codeInText{}
code.codeForeground {}
code.codeBackground {}
.keystroke {}
.importantWords {}
.boxText {}
.background {}
```

2. Now it's time to start adding declarations to each selector inside the curly brackets. First is the `codeInText` style for words that appear in the middle of a sentence or paragraph that represent code. In the same tradition as most written matter on programming, the code will be displayed in a monospaced font. The first choice of typeface—specified using the `font-family` property—is Courier, failing which the browser should try to find Courier New, and if it cannot find that typeface, it will use its default monospaced font (although most computers do have Courier or Courier New installed).

To make the code easier to read, this font will appear in bold text, as indicated using the `font-weight` property.

```
.codeInText {font-family:courier, "courier new", monospace; font-weight:bold;}
```

3. The second style is the `codeForeground` style. This style uses the same kind of font as the `codeInText` style.

Here a few things to take note of:

❑ The `codeForeground` style should always be displayed as a block level element, but just in case it is used with an inline element the `display` property is used with a value of `block` to ensure that it is displayed as a block (you will see more of this property in Chapter 10).

❑ You will also see that the letter-spacing property has been used with a negative value because monospace fonts tend to take up quite a bit of width on the page. So, to help get as many characters as possible on the same line, it is given a negative value of .1 of an em (or 10 percent of a font's height).

❑ The background color of the codeForeground style is gray. This helps the code stand out and makes it more readable. A one and a half em-sized padding has been added inside the box so that the text does not go right to the edge of the background color—this also makes the code easier to read.

❑ The margin ensures that the box does not touch any other boxes or paragraphs. It has a smaller margin on the bottom than the top, as do all of the styles in this style sheet that use the margin property.

```
.codeForeground {
  font-family:courier, "courier new", monosapce; font-weight:bold;
  letter-spacing:-0.1em;
  display:block;
  background-color:#cccccc;
  padding:0.5em;
  margin-bottom:1em; margin-top:1.5em;}
```

4. The codeBackground style is identical to the codeForground style except that the background-color is white:

```
.codeBackground {
  font-family:courier, "courier new", monosapce; font-weight:bold;
  letter-spacing:-0.1em;
  display:block;
  background-color:#ffffff;
  padding:0.5em;
  margin-bottom:1em; margin-top:1em;}
```

5. The keystroke style is in a Times typeface, or Times New Roman if Times is not available, failing which the default serif typeface for the browser. The keystroke style should be italicized as follows:

```
.keyStroke {
  font-family:times, "Times New Roman", serif;
  font-style:italic;}
```

6. The importantWords style is simply bold:

```
.importantWords {font-weight:bold; }
```

7. The boxText style has a bold font, a very light gray background, and the thing that really differentiates it is that it has a border. Like the codeForeground style, boxText has some padding so that the text does not reach the border—which makes it easier to read—and it has a margin to inset it from the left and right as well as vertically to separate it from other elements. Note that the bottom margin is slightly smaller than the top margin.

```
.boxText {
  font-weight:bold;
  background-color:#efefef;
  width:90%;
```

```
    padding:1em;
    margin-left:3em; margin-right:3em; margin-bottom:1em; margin-top:1.5em;
    border-style:solid; border-width:1px; border-color:#000000;}
```

8. The final style is the `background` style. This style is italic and has the same amount of padding and margins as the `boxText` style.

```
.background {
    font-style:italic;
    width:90%;
    padding:1em;
    margin-left:3em; margin-right:3em; margin-bottom:1em; margin-top:1em;}
```

9. For this example I also included a rule for the `<p>` element and a rule for the `<body>` element:

```
body {
    color:#000000;
    background-color:#ffffff;
    font-family:arial, verdana, sans-serif;
    font-size:12px;}

p {margin-bottom:1em; margin-top:1.5em;}
```

10. Save this file as `codeStyles.css`. Then take a look at the following XHTML file, which makes use of this style sheet. As you can see, the `<link />` element indicates that this is the style sheet to be used for this example. You can then see the elements with the `class` attributes that relate to these styles:

```
<?xml version="1.0" ?>
<!DOCTYPE html PUBLIC "-//W3C//DTD XHTML 1.0 Transitional//EN"
    "http://www.w3.org/TR/xhtml1/DTD/xhtml1-transitional.dtd">
<html xmlns="http://www.w3.org/1999/xhtml" lang="en">

<head>
  <title>CSS Example</title>
  <link rel="stylesheet" type="text/css" href="codeStyles.css" />
</head>

<body>
<p>You are about to see some <code class="codeInText">codeInText</code>
followed by some <span class="importantWords">importantWords</span>, and the
font for a <span class="keystroke">keystroke</span>.</p>

<p>Next you will see some foreground code:</p>
<code class="codeForeground">p {font-family:arial, sans-serif;
font-weight:bold;}</code>

<p>Next you will see some background code:</p>
<code class="codeBackground">p {font-family:arial, sans-serif;
font-weight:bold;}</code>
```

```
<p class="boxText">This is some boxed text for important statements.</p>
<p class="background">Here is a background comment or aside.</p>
</body>
</html>
```

If you look at this example in the browser, it should look like the screenshot in Figure 9-30.

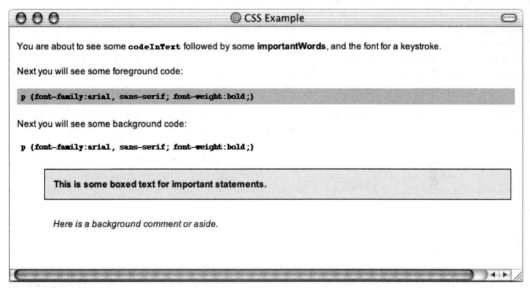

Figure 9-30

How It Works

You've read through this chapter so you should have a good idea of how this example works. But I will bring up some of the key points here.

The style sheet is linked to the example XHTML document using the <link /> element in the head of that document.

```
<link rel="stylesheet" type="text/css" href="codeStyles.css" />
```

The point behind the style sheet was that it would be able to be used with several documents, which is why the style rules were not put inside a <style> element in the XHTML document.

Notice that several of the styles used margin properties, and when they did, the top margin was larger than the bottom margin. I tend to keep bottom margins a little bit smaller than top margins, so that if adjacent vertical margins collapse I know which one it is more likely to be. This is especially helpful because you cannot actually see the edge of a margin in the same way you can use the border property to see the edge of a box.

```
.codeBackground {
   font-family:courier, "courier new", monospace; font-weight:bold;
   letter-spacing:-0.1em;
```

```
display:block;
background-color:#ffffff;
padding:0.5em;
margin-bottom:1em; margin-top:1em;}
```

The margins were greater to the left and the right in these examples so that the boxes were indented. If the text-indent property had been used only the first line would have been indented.

In the block boxes of code, two properties were not anywhere else on the style sheet. The letter-spacing property is used to make more letters fit on the same line than otherwise would. You cannot, however, set them too narrowly or the user will not be able to read the words (one-tenth of an em is the maximum here). There was also the display property with a value of block to ensure that codeForeground and codeBackground styles get treated as block level elements.

The boxText and background styles were indented from the margins to the left and the right so that they were clearly separate from the text around them and to make them stand out more.

You might have noticed that all lengths in the style sheet were specified in ems so that they relate to the default size of the text in the document. If some of these elements were given in absolute sizes, they might have suddenly appeared a lot smaller or larger than the surrounding text if their lengths were not relative.

Summary

In this chapter you learned how to write a CSS style sheet. You have seen that a CSS style sheet is made up of rules that first select the element or elements to which the rules will apply, and then contain property-value pairs that change the appearance of the element's content.

You have learned how you can change the appearance of fonts and text.

You now know that CSS manages to render a document by treating each element as if it were a separate box and then using the properties to style that box, and you have learned how to set the dimensions and borders, padding, and margins for each box.

In the next chapter you not only learn some more properties, you also see how you can use CSS to position elements, which is intended to replace the use of tables for layout purposes. You even see how you can insert content from a style sheet into a document, deal with bulleted lists, create counters, and more.

Exercises

1. Go back to the first Try It Out example in this chapter and add styles to show what bold and italic versions of each font would look like. You should end up with something looking like Figure 9-31.

    You are allowed to use only <span> and <br /> elements in the source document and class selectors in the style sheet. You also need to add a top margin to the content of the <div> elements to separate them from each other.

2. Take a look at the following XHTML page:

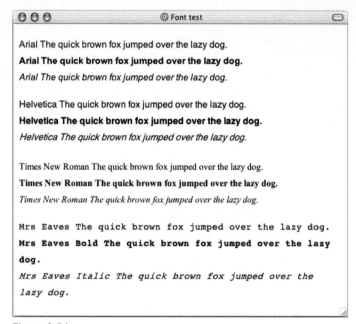

Figure 9-31

```
<?xml version="1.0" encoding="iso-8859-1"?>
<!DOCTYPE html PUBLIC "-//W3C//DTD XHTML 1.0 Transitional//EN"
    "http://www.w3.org/TR/xhtml1/DTD/xhtml1-transitional.dtd">
<html xmlns="http://www.w3.org/1999/xhtml" lang="en">

<head>
  <title>Font test</title>
  <link rel="stylesheet" type="text/css" href="tableStyles.css" />
</head>

<body>
<table>
  <tr>
    <th>Quantity</th>
    <th>Ingredient</th>
  </tr>
  <tr class="odd">
    <td>3</td>
    <td>Eggs</td>
  </tr>
  <tr>
    <td>100ml</td>
    <td>Milk</td>
  </tr>
  <tr class="odd">
    <td>200g</td>
    <td>Spinach</td>
```

```
      </tr>
      <tr>
        <td>1 pinch</td>
        <td>Cinnamon</td>
      </tr>
    </table>
  </body>
</html>
```

Now create the `tableStyles.css` style sheet that makes this example look like it does in Figure 9-32.

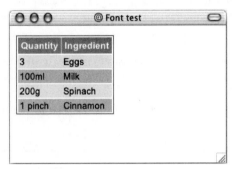

Figure 9-32

Don't worry about getting the sizes exactly the same as the screenshot, but do make sure you have padding in the cells and a border around the outside. Just to let you know, the white border is created by default in IE and you find out how to remove this in Chapter 10.

More Cascading Style Sheets

In this chapter you learn more about working with CSS. You will start by working through many of the remaining properties from CSS1 and CSS2 that allow you to control presentation of links, backgrounds, list styles, table styles, and outlines around boxes (which are different than borders). You then learn about the :before and :after pseudo-classes that allow you to add content that was not in the source document before or after an element. Finally, you see how CSS can be used to position boxes on the page—and therefore be used to create layouts instead of using tables.

By the end of the chapter you will know how to control the following:

❏ Presentation of links

❏ Backgrounds of document

❏ Styles of bullet points and numbered lists

❏ Appearance of tables

❏ Outlines around boxes

❏ Boxes that can gain focus or are active

❏ Addition of content to the XHTML document before or after an element

❏ The three positioning schemes that allow you to determine where on a page a box will appear—something that prepares you to use CSS to create layouts

By the end of the chapter you will be even better equipped to design pages than people who rely on deprecated HTML elements and attributes to style pages.

Some of the features you learn about in this chapter are not yet widely supported in browsers. They are, however, worth learning about so that you are aware of the direction that CSS is going in, as it is destined to take over from the deprecated HTML elements and attributes that control styles.

Links

You can control the presentation of your links using keywords reserved for use with links. These keywords, shown in the table that follows, allow you to indicate different styles for links.

Keyword	Purpose
link	Styles to be used for links in general
visited	Styles to be used for links that have already been visited
active	Styles to use for links that are currently active (being clicked)

You can also use the :hover pseudo-class to control the presentation of a link when the user hovers over it.

There are three properties you are likely to want to use with these keywords and the pseudo-class:

❑ **color:** Changes the colors of the links. This is often used to display a slightly different color for links that have already been visited than those not yet visited—this helps users see where they've been.

❑ **text-decoration:** Controls whether the link is underlined or not. Links always used to be underlined on the Web, although since the late 1990s it has been more popular to not underline links. Using the text-decoration property you can specify that your links should not be underlined unless the user hovers over or selects one.

❑ **background-color:** Highlights the link, as if it had been highlighted with a highlighter pen. It is most commonly used when the user hovers over a link.

Here is an example that will change the styles of links as users interact with them (ch10_eg01.css):

```
body {background-color:#ffffff;}

a {
  font-family: arial, verdana, sans-serif;
  font-size:12px;
  font-weight:bold;}

a:link {
  color:#0000ff;
  text-decoration:none;}

a:visited {
  color:#333399;
  text-decoration:none;}

a:active {
  color:#0033ff;
  text-decoration:underline;}

a:link:hover {
  background-color:#e9e9e9;
  text-decoration:underline;}
```

Figure 10-1 gives you an idea of how this will look, although it is rather hard to see the full effect of this in print, with the links changing as the user rolls the mouse over links and visits the sites, so try the example out with the downloaded code for this chapter.

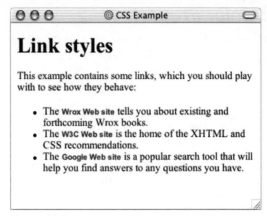

Figure 10-1

There are also two pseudo-classes called `:focus` and `:active` that alter the style of an element as it gains focus or becomes active. You learn about these pseudo-classes later in the chapter.

Backgrounds

The table that follows lists the six properties in CSS that allow you to specify how the background of either the whole browser window or any single box should appear.

Property	Purpose
background-color	Specifies a color that should be used for the background of the page or box
background-image	Sets an image to be in the background of a page or box
background-repeat	Indicates whether the background image should be repeated across the page or box
background-attachment	Indicates a background image should be fixed in one position on the page, and whether it should stay in that position when the user scrolls down the page or not
background-position	Indicates where an image should be positioned in either the window or the containing box
background	A shorthand form that allows you to specify all of these properties

Note that the shorthand `background` property is better supported in some browsers than the individual properties, but you need to learn what values the properties can take before going on to use the shorthand.

The background-color Property

The background-color property allows you to specify a single solid color for the background of your pages and the inside of any box created by CSS.

The value of this property can be a hex code, a color name, or an RGB value. For example:

```
body {background-color:#cccccc; color:#000000;}
b {background-color:#FF0000; color:#FFFFFF;}
p {background-color: rgb(255,255,255);}
```

When the background-color property is set for the <body> element it affects the whole document, and when it is used on any other element it will use the specified color inside the border of the box created for that element, as you can see in Figure 10-2.

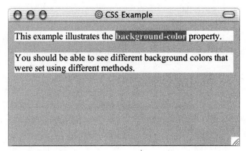

Figure 10-2

I add a rule for the <body> element to set the background-color property for nearly every style sheet I write for the simple reason that some people set their computers to have a background other than plain white (often because it causes less strain on their eyes). When the background color of an operating system is changed, the background color of the Web browser is usually that color (as are applications such as word processors). If you do not specify this property you cannot guarantee that the visitor to the site has the same background color as you.

The background-color property is the CSS replacement for the bgcolor attribute that was available in HTML.

Appendix D covers over 150 color names and their hex values, while RGB values were discussed in the last chapter.

The background-image Property

As its name suggests, the background-image property allows you to add an image to the background of any box in CSS and its effect can be quite powerful. The value it takes is as follows, starting with the letters url, and then holding the URL for the image in brackets:

```
body {background-image: url(images/background.gif); }
```

The background-image property overrides the background-color property. It is good practice, however, to supply a background-color property with a value that is similar to the main color in the image even when you want to use a background image because the page will use this color while the page is loading or if it cannot load the image for any reason.

Here is an example of using a single background image. The background image is only 200 pixels wide and 150 pixels high, and the `background-color` property is given the same value as the background color of the color for this image so that the image does not look so small (`ch10_eg03.css`):

```css
body {
    background-image: url(images/background.gif);
    background-color: #cccccc;}
```

Figure 10-3 shows you an image used for a background; by default this image is repeated all across the page.

Figure 10-3

This is not a great example of a background image, but it makes an important point. The problem is that there is not enough contrast between the colors used in the background image and the text that appears on top of it, which makes the text harder to read.

You must make sure that there is sufficient contrast between any background image and the writing that appears on top of it. In Chapter 4 I mentioned how you should use carefully chosen contrasting colors when selecting a color scheme for your site. Using background images is no different. The color of your font must be sufficiently contrasted from the background of the page if you are going to use an image. Low-contrast images that use similar colors make better backgrounds.

Figure 10-4 shows an improved example of the background image, which uses lighter colors and therefore increases the contrast with the image. This time I have also used a larger image (`ch10_eg03b .html`).

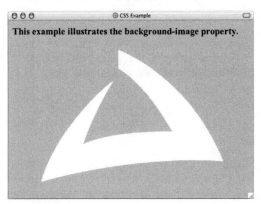

Figure 10-4

You should note that there is no way of expressing the intended width and height of the image, and it is not able to have an `alt` attribute (alternate text for those not able to see the image for any reason); therefore a background image should never be used to convey any important information because it is not accessible to those unable to see the image for any reason.

You should also be wary of using large files as background images because they can be slow to load. The larger the file size of the image, the longer it takes to load and render.

The `background-image` property works well with most block level elements, although there can be difficulties with using background images in tables.

The `background-image` property replaces the `background` attribute in HTML.

The background-repeat Property

By default, the background-image property repeats across the whole page, creating what is affectionately known as *wallpaper*. The wallpaper is made up of one image that is repeated over and over again, and which (if the image is designed well) you will not see the edges of; therefore it is important that any patterns should *tessellate*, or fit together, well. Wallpaper is often made up of textures such as paper, marble, or abstract surfaces, rather than photos or logos.

If you do not want your image to repeat all over the background of the page, you should use the `background-repeat` property, which has four helpful values, as you can see in the table that follows.

Value	Purpose
repeat	This causes the image to repeat to cover the whole page.
repeat-x	The image will be repeated horizontally across the page (not down the whole page vertically).
repeat-y	The image will be repeated vertically down the page (not across horizontally).
no-repeat	The image is displayed only once.

These different properties can have interesting effects. It is worth looking at each in turn. You have already seen the effect of the repeat value, so the next one to look at is `repeat-x`, which creates a horizontal bar following the browser's x-axis (`ch10_eg04.css`):

```
body {
    background-image: url(images/background_small.gif);
    background-repeat: repeat-x;
    background-color: #ffffff;}
```

You can see the result of using this property in Figure 10-5.

The `repeat-y` value works just like `repeat-x` but in the other direction: vertically following the browser's y-axis (`ch10_eg05.css`):

Figure 10-5

```
body {
    background-image: url(images/background_small.gif);
    background-repeat: repeat-y;
    background-color: #ffffff;}
```

In Figure 10-6 you can see the result with the sidebar coming down the left.

Figure 10-6

The final value was no-repeat, leaving one instance of the image that by default will be in the top-left corner of the browser window (ch10_eg06.css):

```
body {
    background-image: url(images/background_small.gif);
    background-repeat: no-repeat;
    background-color: #f2f2f2;}
```

You can see the result in Figure 10-7.

The background-position Property (for fixing position of backgrounds)

When the background-color property is the same as the background color of the image, you cannot see the edge of the image (as in Figure 10-7). However, you may want to alter the position of this image,

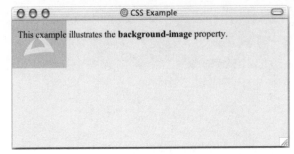

Figure 10-7

and you can do so using the `background-position` property, which takes the values shown in the table that follows.

Value	Meaning
x% y%	Percentages along the x (horizontal) and y (vertical) axis.
x y	Absolute lengths along the x (horizontal) and y (vertical) axis.
left	Show to the left of the page or containing element.
center	Show to the center of the page or containing element.
right	Show to the right of the page or containing element.
top	Shown at the top of the page or containing element.
center	Shown at the center of the page or containing element.
bottom	Shown at the bottom of the page or containing element.

Here is an example of fixing the position of the image (`ch10_eg07.css`):

```
body {
    background-image: url(images/background_small.gif);
    background-position: 50% 20%;
    background-repeat: no-repeat;
    background-color: #f2f2f2; }
```

This image will be 50 percent of the way in from the left side of the screen and 20 percent of the way down from the top of the whole document. As you can see in Figure 10-8, because the text stretches over more of the page than the background image, the logo looks like it's more than 20 percent of the way down the page (the position of the image can even shift a bit in IE when the text is longer than the window, unless you use one of the values `top`, `center`, or `bottom`).

The background-attachment Property (for watermarks)

The `background-attachment` property allows you to specify an image known as a *watermark*. The key difference with this setting is that the background image can stay in the same position even when the user

Figure 10-8

scrolls up and down a page or scrolls with all of the other elements of the page. The background-attachment property can take two values, as you can see from the table that follows.

Value	Purpose
fixed	The image will not move if the user scrolls up and down the page.
scroll	The image stays in the same place on the background of the page. If the user scrolls up or down the page, the image moves, too.

Here is an example where the image will stay in the middle of the page even when the user scrolls further down (ch10_eg08.css):

```
body {
    background-image: url(images/background_small.gif);
    background-attachment: fixed;
    background-position: center;
    background-repeat: no-repeat;
    background-color: #f2f2f2; }
```

Figure 10-9 shows that the user has scrolled halfway down the page and the image remains in the center.

Figure 10-9

The background Property (the well-supported shorthand)

The `background` property allows you to specify all five of the background properties at once. If you do not supply one of the values the default value will be used. The values can be given in any order:

❑   background-color

❑   background-image

❑   background-repeat

❑   background-attachment

❑   background-position

For example, you can just write:

```
body {background: #cc66ff; url(images/background_small.gif) fixed
no-repeat center;}
```

This creates exactly the same effect as the example shown in Figure 10-9.

Lists

You learned about lists in Chapter 2. Lists are very helpful in conveying a set of either numbered or bulleted points, and it is simple enough to use the `<ul>` and `<li>` elements to create unordered lists, or the `<ol>` and `<li>` elements to create ordered lists, but CSS allows you great control over how they are presented.

Note that the bullet point, or number in the case of numbered lists, is referred to as the *marker*.

In this section you learn about the list properties shown in the table that follows.

Property	Purpose
list-style-type	Allows you to control the shape or appearance of the marker (bullet point or number).
list-style-position	Specifies whether a long point that wraps to a second line should align with the first line or start underneath the start of the marker.
list-style-image	Specifies an image for the marker rather than a bullet point or number.
list-style	Serves as shorthand for the preceding properties.
marker-offset	Specifies the distance between a marker and the text in the list.

The list-style-type Property

The list-style-type property allows you to control the shape or style of bullet point (also known as a *marker*) in the case of unordered lists, and the style of numbering characters in ordered lists. The table that follows shows the standard styles for an unordered list.

Value	Marker
none	None
disc (default)	A filled-in circle
circle	An empty circle
square	A filled-in square

The table that follows lists the popularly supported values for ordered lists.

Value	Meaning	Example
decimal	Number	1, 2, 3, 4, 5
decimal-leading-zero	0 before the number	01, 02, 03, 04, 05
lower-alpha	Lowercase alphanumeric characters	a, b, c, d, e
upper-alpha	Uppercase alphanumeric characters	A, B, C, D, E
lower-roman	Lowercase Roman numerals	i, ii, iii, iv, v
upper-roman	Uppercase Roman numerals	I, II, III, IV, V

The list-style property can either be used on the <ul> and <ol> elements or on the <li> element. Here is an example that demonstrates all of these styles (ch10_eg09.html):

```
li.a {list-style:none;}
li.b {list-style:disc;}
li.c {list-style:circle;}
li.d {list-style:square;}
li.e {list-style:decimal;}
li.f {list-style:lower-alpha;}
li.g {list-style:upper-alpha;}
li.h {list-style:lower-roman;}
li.i {list-style:upper-roman;}
```

You can see the result with examples of each kind of bullet in Figure 10-10.

The list-style-position Property

The list-style-position property indicates whether the marker should appear inside or outside of the box containing the bullet points.

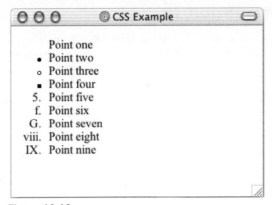

Figure 10-10

The real difference comes when a bullet points wraps onto more than one line because this property sets whether the text on the new line wraps underneath the bullet point or in line with the position of the first line of text. There are two values for this property, as you can see in the table that follows.

Value	Purpose
inside	If the text goes onto a second line, the text will wrap underneath the marker. It will also appear indented to where the text would have started if the list had a value of outside.
outside	If the text goes onto a second line, the text will be aligned with the start of the first line (to the right of the bullet).

Here you can see how this property is written; in this case it is given on the `<ul>` or `<ol>` elements (ch10_eg10.css):

```
ul {list-stlye-position:outside; }
ol {list-style-position:inside; }
```

Figure 10-11 shows you what this would look like in a browser.

You can see here that the list-style position property with the value outside creates bullet points to the left of the text, whereas the inside value starts the list item where the writing would have started if the value had been outside and adds the marker to the text rather than keeping it separate.

The list-style-image Property

The list-style-image property allows you to specify an image so that you can use your own bullet style. The syntax is as follows, similar to the background-image property with the letters url starting

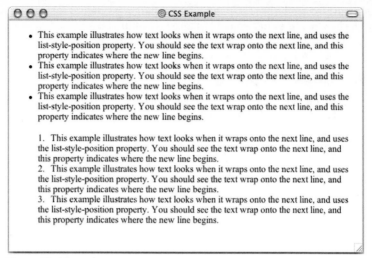

Figure 10-11

the value of the property followed by the URL in brackets (ch10_eg11.css):

```
li {list-style-image: url(images/bulletpoint.gif);}
```

You can see an example of some triangular bullet points in Figure 10-12.

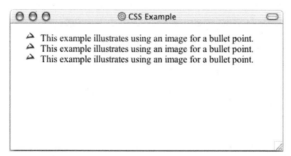

Figure 10-12

If the image cannot be displayed the browser should just display a dot rather than a broken image symbol.

If you are using nested lists, this value will inherit from its parent element. To prevent this happening you can give the property a value of none.

The list-style Property (the shorthand)

The list-style property is a way of expressing the other three properties at once. They can appear in any order. For example:

```
ul {list-style: inside circle;}
```

Remember, you can also set the border, padding, and margin properties for <ul>, <ol>, <li>, <dl>, <dt>, and <dd> elements, as each element has its own box in CSS.

The marker-offset Property

The marker-offset property allows you to specify the distance between the marker and the text relating to that marker. Its value should be a length, as follows:

```
ol {marker-offset:2em;}
```

Unfortunately, however, this property is not supported in IE 6 or Netscape 7.

Tables

In the last chapter, you saw a couple of examples that use CSS with tables. Properties that are commonly used with the <table>, <td>, and <th> elements include the following:

❑   padding to set the amount of space between the border of a table cell and its content—this property is very important to make tables easier to read

❑   border to set the properties of the border of a table

❑   text and font properties to change the appearance of anything written in the cell

❑   text-align to align writing to the left, right, or center of a cell

❑   vertical-align to align writing to the top, middle, or bottom of a cell

❑   width to set the width of a table or cell

❑   height to set the height (often used on a row as well)

❑   background-color to change the background color of a table or cell

❑   background-image to add an image to the background of a table or cell

You should be aware that, apart from the background-color and height properties, it is best to avoid using these properties with <tr> elements, as browser support for these properties on rows is not as good as for individual cells.

Take a look at the table in Figure 10-13; it might look familiar because you saw it at the beginning of the last chapter, but this time it has an added <caption> element (ch10_12.html).

Now take a look at the style sheet for this table (ch10_eg12.css):

```
body {color:#000000; background-color:#ffffff;}
h1 {font-size:18pt;}
p {font-size:12pt;}

table {
    width:350px;
```

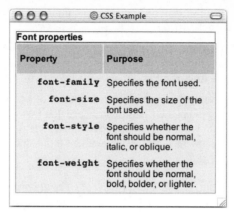

Figure 10-13

```
      background-color:#efefef;
      font-family:arial, verdana, sans-serif;
      border-style:solid; border-width:1px; border-color:#999999;}

caption {
   font-weight:bold;
   text-align:left;
   border-style:solid; border-width:1px; border-color:#666666;}

th {
   height:50px;
   font-weight:bold;
   text-align:left;
   background-color:#cccccc;}

td, th {padding:5px;}

td.code {
   width:150px;
   font-family:courier, courier-new, serif;
   font-weight:bold;
   text-align:right;
   vertical-align:top;}
```

Here are some key points to note about this example, some of which you will be altering with new table properties you are about to meet:

❑   The <table> element has a width property to fix the width of the table to 350 pixels; otherwise it would take up as much of the screen as needed to show as much text as possible on one line.

❑   The <table> element also has a border property set, which creates a single pixel border all around the table. Note, however, that none of the other cells in the table inherit this property.

❑   The <caption> element has its font-weight, border, and text-align properties set. By default the text would be normal (not bold), aligned in the center, and have no border.

335

❏ The <th> element has a height of 50 pixels specified, and the text is aligned left (rather than centered, which is the default).

❏ The <th> and <td> elements both have a padding property set to 5px (5 pixels) so that the content of the cells does not reach where the border of those cells would be. Creating space around the cells is very important and makes the table more readable.

❏ The <td> elements whose class attribute has a value of code are given a width property whose value is 150 px (150 pixels) This makes sure that the content of this whole column remains on one line. Unfortunately there is no way to assign a style to a column, but in the case of the width property, once it has been set on one element it does not need to be set on all of the others in the column.

Support for styling tables with CSS is still a bit patchy in different browsers; for example, while you can set border *properties for a caption, you cannot set a* height *for it, so you should try out your examples in as many styles as possible.*

You should make note of the gap between the two columns (which is apparent between the table header cells). By default a border is created between each cell of the table—to create a bit of space between each cell in case there are no rules specified to create this essential gap. You can, however, remove this gap using a property called border-spacing, which you learn about in the next section.

Table-Specific Properties

Several properties relate to tables only; these are listed in the table that follows. There are also some special values the border-style property can carry, and when learning about borders it is particularly helpful to learn how borders are rendered using one of two models declared using the border-collapse property.

Property	Purpose
border-collapse	Indicates whether the browser should control the appearance of adjacent borders that touch each other or whether each cell should maintain its style.
border-spacing	Specifies the width that should appear between table cells.
caption-side	Specifies which side of a table the caption should appear on.
empty-cells	Specifies whether the border should be shown if a cell is empty.
table-layout	Allows browsers to speed up layout of a table by using the first width properties it comes across for the rest of a column (rather than having to load the whole table before rendering it).

The border-collapse Property

The border-collapse property specifies whether the browser should display every border—even if there are two cells with different border properties in adjacent cells—or whether the browser should automatically decide which border to display based upon a built-in complex set of rules. The table that follows shows the possible values for the border-collapse property.

Value	Purpose
collapse	Horizontal borders will be collapsed and vertical borders will abut one another. (There are complex rules about conflict resolution for different border rules in the recommendation, but you should try them out and see how they work.)
separate	Separate rules are observed and different properties are available to further control appearance.

Here you can see two tables: the first has a border-collapse property with a value of collapse, the second has a value of separate, and both tables contain adjacent cells with dotted and solid lines:

```
table.one {border-collapse:collapse;}
table.two {border-collapse:separate;}

td.a {border-style:dotted; border-width:3px; border-color:#000000; padding:
10px;}
td.b {border-style:solid; border-width:3px; border-color:#333333; padding:
10px;}
```

Figure 10-14 shows you how, with a value of collapse, the browser collapses borders into each other so that the dotted border takes precedence over the solid border. This, of course, wouldn't look as odd if the borders were both solid, but it does illustrate the point well.

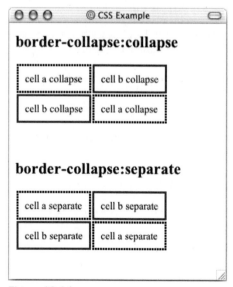

Figure 10-14

You may remember that at the beginning of this section you saw a table that had a light gray gap between the table heading cells. It would be this property that you would change to get rid of that gap.
Figure 10-15 shows you the example from the beginning of the chapter with the borders collapsed.

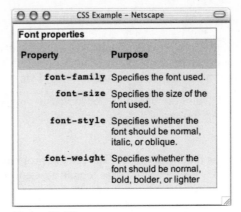

Figure 10-15

If you use the value of separate for this property, there are two further properties that control border presentation:

❑   border-spacing

❑   empty-cells

The following sections discuss these properties.

The border-spacing Property

The border-spacing property specifies the distance that separates adjacent cells' borders. It can take either one or two values; these should be units of length.

If you provide one value it will applies to both vertical and horizontal borders:

```
td {border-spacing:2px;}
```

Or you can specify two values, in which case the first refers to the horizontal spacing and the second to the vertical spacing:

```
td {border-spacing:2px; 4px;}
```

Unfortunately, this property does not work in Netscape 7 or IE 6.

The caption-side Property

The caption-side property allows you to specify where the content of a <caption> element should be placed in relationship to the table. The table that follows lists the possible values.

For example, here you can see the caption being set to the bottom of the table:

```
caption {caption-side:bottom}
```

Value	Purpose
top	The caption will appear above the table (the default).
right	The caption will appear to the right of the table.
bottom	The caption will appear below the table.
left	The caption will appear on the left side of the table.

Unfortunately, IE does not support this property, and Netscape 6 and later supports only the top and bottom values. But Figure 10-16 shows you the caption-side property at work.

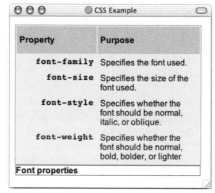

Figure 10-16

The empty-cells Property

The empty-cells property indicates whether a cell without any content should have a border displayed. It can take one of three values, as you can see in the table that follows.

Value	Purpose
show	Borders will be shown even if the cell is empty (the default in Netscape).
hide	Borders will be hidden if cell is empty (the default in IE).
inherit	Will obey the rules of the containing table (only of use in nested tables).

If you want to explicitly hide or show borders you should use this attribute because IE and Netscape treat empty cells differently.

Here you can see a table with two empty cells: an empty <th> element and an empty <td> element (ch10_eg16.html):

```
<table>
  <tr>
```

```
      <th></th>
      <th>Title one</th>
      <th>Title two</th>
   </tr>
   <tr>
      <th>Row Title</th>
      <td>value</td>
      <td>value</td>
   </tr>
   <tr>
      <th>Row Title</th>
      <td>value</td>
      <td></td>
   </tr>
</table>
```

Here is the `empty-cells` property used to hide borders of empty cells in the `<table>` element (`ch10_eg16.css`):

```
table {
   background-color:#efefef;
   width:350px;
   border-collapse:separate;
   empty-cells:hide;}

td {padding:5px;
   border-style:solid;
   border-width:1px;
   border-color:#999999;}
```

You can see what the table without borders for empty cells looks like in Figure 10-17.

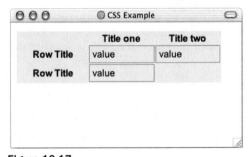

Figure 10-17

Whether or not you use this property is a matter of taste, and if you have specified no borders anyway it will, of course, be irrelevant.

The table-layout Property

The `table-layout` property is supposed to help you control how a browser should render or lay out a table (although support in browsers is weak). See the table that follows for the three possible values this property can take.

Value	Purpose
fixed	The browser will calculate the layout by taking the first width specified for a column (if any are given) and use that to calculate the width of all other cells in that column. This speeds up rendering if you have a large table and you specify the widths on the first row.
auto	The browser looks at each cell before rendering the table and then calculates the size based upon the settings for all cells. This is slower at rendering, but more useful if you do not know the exact size of each column. This is the default value.
inherit	Will obey the rules of the containing table (only of use in nested tables).

Unless your tables are very large or contain a lot of images that will be slow to load, you can avoid using this property.

There are also several properties that allow you to specify rules for groups of elements, although support for these is patchy. They are as follows:

- ❑ IE 5 and later supports table-header-group and table-footer-group.
- ❑ Netscape 6 and later supports inline-table, table-row, table-column-group, table-column, table-row, and table-cell.

Outlines

Outlines are similar to the borders that you met in the last chapter, but there are two crucial differences:

- ❑ An outline does not take up space.
- ❑ Outlines do not have to be rectangular.

The idea behind the outline properties is that you might want to highlight some aspect of a page for the user; this will allow you to do that without affecting the flow of the page (where elements are positioned) in the way that a physical border would take up space. It is almost like the outline style sits on top of the page after it has been rendered.

Unfortunately, the outline properties are not supported by IE 6 or Netscape 7; they are, nevertheless introduced here for when they are supported.

The table that follows lists the four outline properties.

Note that the outline is always the same on all sides; you cannot specify different values for different sides of the element.

Property	Purpose
outline-width	Specifies the width of the outline
outline-style	Specifies the line style for the outline
outline-color	Specifies the color of the outline
outline	Shorthand for above properties

The outline-width Property

The outline-width property specifies the width of the outline to be added to the box. Its value should be a length or one of the values thin, medium, or thick—just like the border-width attribute:

```
input {border-width:2px;}
```

The outline-style Property

The outline-style property specifies the style for the line (solid, dotted, or dashed) that goes around the box. Its value should be one of the values used with the border-style property you learned about in Chapter 9; for example:

```
input {outline-style:solid;}
```

The outline-color Property

The outline-color property allows you to specify the color of the outline. Its value should either be a color name, a hex color, or an RGB value, as with the color and border-color properties you learned about in Chapter 9; for example:

```
input {outline-color:#ff0000;}
```

The outline Property (the shorthand)

The outline property is the shorthand that allows you to specify values for any of the three properties discussed previously in any order you like. For example:

```
input {outline: ##ff0000 thick solid;}
```

The outline properties discussed in the previous section will be of particular use with the :focus and :active pseudo-classes, which are covered next, to indicate which element is currently active or has focus.

The :focus and :active Pseudo-Classes

You may remember that in Chapter 6 when talking about forms, the topic of focus came up. An element needs to be able to gain focus if a user is going to interact with it; typically such elements would be form controls and links.

When an element gains focus, it tends to have a slightly different appearance, and the :focus pseudo-class allows you to associate extra rules with an element when it gains focus. Meanwhile the :active pseudo-class allows you to associate further styles with elements when they are activated—such as when a user clicks a link.

Here is an example of a rule that will add a different background-color to any form <input> element that gains focus:

```
input:focus {background-color:#33FFFF;}
```

Unfortunately, the :focus pseudo class does not work in IE 6 on Windows, although Figure 10-18 shows you what a text input box would look like with this style when it gains focus in IE 5.5 on a Mac.

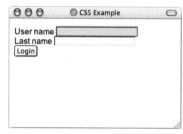

Figure 10-18

As you can see, this can really help users know which item they should currently be filling in as they work their way through a form.

Generated Content

CSS2 introduced a powerful way in which you could add content into a XHTML document that was not part of the initial XHTML document that was being styled. This content could appear only before or after an element that is specified using a selector, and is added by the use of the :before and :after pseudo-elements. The content property is then used with these pseudo-elements to specify what should be inserted into the document.

The :before and :after pseudo-elements work to a limited degree in Netscape 6 and later, and not at all in IE 6.

The :before and :after Pseudo-Elements

The :before and :after pseudo-elements allow you to add text before or after each instance of an element or elements defined in a selector. For example, the following CSS rule adds the words "You need to register to read the full article" before each instance of a <p> element that carries the abstract attribute (ch01_eg18.css):

```
p.abstract:after {content: "You need to register to read the full
article.";
  color:#ff0000;}
```

Here you can see the pseudo-element :after is used at the end of the selector and is separated from it using a colon. Then, inside the declaration you can see the content property; the text in quotes will be added to the end of the element. There are a number of types of content the content property can add to the document, not just text, which you will see in the next section.

The default styles for the parent element will be adopted if no other declarations are added to the rule, although in this case the added content was written in red. You can see this pseudo-element in use in Figure 10-19.

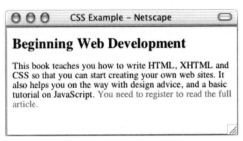

Figure 10-19

Unfortunately this only works in IE 5 for Mac and later and Netscape 6 and later.

By default the element created using these pseudo-classes will be inline unless you use the display property with a value of block, but if the element identified in the selector is an inline element you cannot use the display property with a value of block.

The content Property

The content property is used with the :before and :after pseudo-elements to indicate what content should be added to the document. The table that follows lists the values it can take; each value inserts different types of content into the XHTML document it is supposed to be styling.

Value	Purpose
A string	To insert plain text, this may not include quotes, and therefore cannot include XHTML markup that carries attributes (the term "string" refers to a set of alphanumeric characters).
A url	The URL can point to an image, text file, or HTML file to be included at this point.
A counter	A numbered counter for elements on the page (discussed in the next section).
atrr(x)	The value of an attribute named x that is carried on that element (this is of more use to languages other than XHTML).
open-quote	Inserts the appropriate opening quote symbol (see the "Quotation Marks" section later in this chapter).

Value	Purpose
close-quote	Inserts the appropriate opening quote symbol (see the "Quotation Marks" section later in this chapter).
no-open-quote	Do not use any opening quotes.
no-close-quote	Do not use a closing quote (of particular use in prose where one person is speaking for a long while and style dictates the quote is closed only on the last paragraph).

Counters

You have already seen how you can add numbered bullets to a page, so the concept of automatic numbering is not new. But the counter() function is designed to allow you to create a counter that increments each time a browser comes across any specified element—not just a <li> element. Unfortunately, Netscape 7 and IE 6 still do not support this function.

The idea is particularly helpful if you want to create automatically numbered subsections of a document without them appearing as part of an ordered list (which use the <ol> and <li> elements).

To review the use of the counter() function, look at the following sample XHTML (this example is not in the download code because the function is not supported—this example is only to demonstrate what will be possible when counters are supported by browsers):

```
<body>
<h1> Introducing Web Technologies</h1>
   <h2>Introducing HTML</h2>
   <h2>Introducing CS</h2>
   <h2>Introducing XHTML</h2>
<h1> Structure of Documents</h1>
   <h2>Text</h2>
   <h2>Lists</h2>
   <h2>Tables</h2>
   <h2>Forms</h2>
</body>
```

The example is going to contain two counters: one called chapter and the other called section. Each time an <h1> element comes up, the chapter counter will be incremented by 1, and each time the <h2> element comes up, the section counter will be incremented by 1.

Furthermore, each time the browser comes across an <h1> element it will insert the word Chapter and the number in the counter before the content of the <h1> element. Meanwhile, each time the browser comes across an <h2> element it will display the number of the chapter counter, then a period or full stop, and then the value of the section counter.

The result should look something like Figure 10-20 (which is only a simulation of the counter).

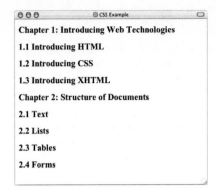

Figure 10-20

Now, here are the CSS rules using the `:before` pseudo-class to insert the automatic numbering of section:

```
h1:before {
    content: "Chapter " counter(chapter) ". ";
    counter-increment: chapter;
    counter-reset: section;}

h2:before {
    content: counter(chapter) ". " counter(section) " ";
    counter-increment: section;}
```

The `counter-increment` property indicates that a counter is supposed to be incremented each time the browser comes across the element specified in the selector. In this case, every time the browser comes across an `<h1>` element of the `chapter`, the counter is incremented by 1.

The `counter-reset` property indicates which counter should be reset, so in the case of the `section` counter, every time the browser comes across an `<h1>` element the subsections should start from 1 again.

Note that if the `display` property has a value of `none`, this counter will not be incremented.

If you want to use the `:before` pseudo-element to add content before or after an `<li>` element rather than a different element of your choosing (such as the `<h1>` element), you can use the `display` property with a value of `marker` to allow the value of the `content` property to replace what would have been the bullet point or other marker.

Quotation Marks

CSS2 introduced the `quote` property to let you apply context-sensitive quotations to your documents. You use this property to specify the appropriate quotation marks for each level of quotation (so an initial quote may use double quotation marks and then a quote within that would use single quotation marks). It can also help you create the right quotation marks for the language you are writing in.

Unfortunately these features are not supported in Netscape 7 or IE 6. But, by way of an example, if you were writing in English you could specify that outer quotes should be displayed with the double quotation marks, while inner quotes should use single quotation marks.

```
q:lang(en) { quotes: '"' '"' "'" "'" }
```

If you were writing in French you might chose something more like this:

```
q:lang(fr) { quotes: "<<" ">>" "<" ">" }
```

Then when you want to use a quote, inside the <q> element you use the :before and :after pseudo-elements to add the quotes with the content property set using the appropriate values:

```
q:before { content: open-quote }
q:after  { content: close-quote }
```

Miscellaneous Properties

There are a few other properties that you should be aware of that have not yet been covered, and these will be addressed in the following sections:

❑   The cursor property

❑   The display property

❑   The visibility property

The cursor Property

The cursor property allows you to specify the type of cursor that should be displayed to the user. One popular use for this property is in using images for submit buttons on forms. By default, when a cursor hovers over a link, the cursor changed from a pointer to a hand. For a submit button on a form, however, this does not happen. Therefore, using the cursor property to change the cursor to a hand whenever someone hovers over an image that is a submit button. This provides a visual clue that they can click it.

The table that follows shows possible values for the cursor property.

Value	Description
auto	Shape of the cursor depends on the context area it is over (an I over text, a hand over a link, and so on)
crosshair	A crosshair or plus sign
default	Usually an arrow
pointer	A pointing hand (in IE 4 this value is hand)
move	A grasping hand (ideal if you are doing drag-and-drop DHTML)
e-resizene-resizenw-resizen-resizese-resizesw-resizes-resizew-resize	Indicate that an edge can be moved. For example, if you were stretching a box of image with the mouse, the se-resize cursor is used to indicate a movement starting from the southeast corner of the box.

Continues

Value	Description
text	The I bar
wait	An hour glass
help	A question mark or balloon, ideal for use over help buttons
<url>	The source of a cursor image file

You should try to use only these values to add helpful information for users, and in places they would expect to see that cursor. For example, using the crosshair when someone hovers over a link can confuse visitors.

The display Property

The display property forces an element (or box) to be a different type of box than you might expect it to be. You might have noticed that it was used in the last chapter to make an inline box appear like a block box.

```
display:block;
```

Apart from this use you will have little reason to use this property. The other values this property can take are for use with languages other than XHTML.

Visibility of Boxes

A property called visibility allows you to hide a box from view, although it still affects the layout of the page (even though its contents are not seen). You may choose to use the visibility property to hide error messages that are only displayed if the user needs to see them, or to hide answers to a quiz until the user selects an option.

The visibility property can take the values listed in the table that follows.

Value	Purpose
visible	The box and its contents are shown to the user.
hidden	The box and its content are made invisible, although they still affect the layout of the page.
collapse	This is for use only with dynamic table columns and row effects, which are not covered in this chapter because they are outside the scope of this book and are poorly supported.

For example, here are four paragraphs of text (ch10_eg19.html):

```
<body>
  <p>Here is a paragraph of text.</p>
```

```
    <p>Here is a paragraph of text.</p>
    <p class="invisible">This paragraph of text should be invisible.</p>
    <p>Here is a paragraph of text.</p>
</body>
```

Note that the third paragraph has a class attribute whose value indicates that it's part of the invisible class. Now, look at the rule for this class (ch10_eg19.html):

```
p.invisible {visibility:hidden;}
```

You can see from Figure 10-21 that the invisible paragraph still takes up space, but it is not visible to the user.

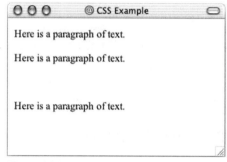

Figure 10-21

Remember that the source code will still contain whatever is in the invisible paragraph, so you should not use this to hide sensitive information such as credit card details or passwords.

Additional Rules

You should consider the following three rules before moving on to positioning using CSS.

❑   @import imports another style sheet into the current style sheet.

❑   @charset indicates the character set the style sheet uses.

❑   !important indicates that a user-defined rule should take precedence over the author's style sheets.

The @import Rule: Modularized Style Sheets

The @import rule allows you to import styles from another style sheet. It should appear right at the start of the style sheet before any of the rules, and its value is a URL. It can be written in one of two ways:

```
@import "mystyle.css";
@import url("mystyle.css");
```

Either works fine. The significance of the @import rule is that it allows you to develop your style sheets with a modular approach. You can create separate style sheets for different aspects of your site. This is the concept I started to introduce in the last chapter when you created a style sheet for code styles. Now if you want to include those styles in any other style sheet you write—rather than repeating them—you just use the @import rule to bring those rules into the style sheet you are writing.

Here is an example of a style sheet that imports the codeStyles.css style sheet from the last chapter (for convenience, this has been copied into the folder for the code download for this chapter). This example is ch10_eg20.css:

```
@import "codeStyles.css"

body {
  background-color:#ffffff;
  font-family:arial, verdana, Helvetica, sans-serif;}

h1 {font-size:24pt;}
```

As you can see, it does not contain many rules itself; the code styles have all been taken from the imported style sheet. Figure 10-22 shows a page that uses this style sheet that has located the styles for the code (ch10_eg20.html):

Figure 10-22

Another example of a modular style sheet you might consider developing would be a forms style sheet for any pages or sites that use a lot of forms. This would enable you to create nicer presentation for form controls.

The @charset Rule

If you are writing your document using a character set other than ASCII or ISO-8859-1 you might want to set the @charset rule at the top of your style sheet to indicate what character set the style sheet is written in.

The @charset rule must be written right at the beginning of the style sheet without even a space before it. The value is held in quotes and should be one of the language codes specified in Appendix G.

```
@charset "iso-8859-1"
```

!important

As you know, part of the aim of CSS and the separation of style from content was to make documents more accessible to those with visual impairments. So, after you have spent your valuable time learning about CSS and how to write your style sheets to make your sites attractive, I have to tell you users can create their own style sheets, too!

In reality, very few people do create their own CSS style sheets to view pages how they want, but the ability is there, and was designed for those with disabilities. By default your style sheet should be viewed rather than theirs; however the user's style sheet can contain the !important rule, which says "override the site's style sheet for this property." For example, a user might use the rule like so:

```
p {font-size:18pt !important;
   font-weight:bold !important;}
```

There is nothing you can do to force the user to use your style sheet, and in practice a very small percentage (if any) of your visitors will create their own style sheet, so you should not worry about it—it's covered here only so that you understand what the rule is and why you may come across it.

> Note that in CSS1, the !important rule allowed authors to overrule users' style sheets, but this was switched over in the second version.

Positioning with CSS

Up to this point, you have learned how the content of each element is represented in CSS using a box and you've seen many of the properties you can use to affect the appearance of the box and its content. Now it's time to look at how to control where the content of an element appears on the page by specifying where that box should be positioned within a page.

Before CSS, tables were often used to control precisely where the content of a page appeared, and the content was displayed in the order it appeared in the XHTML document. Using CSS positioning, however, you can lay out your pages without the use of tables and even present information in a different order than it appeared in the XHTML document.

In CSS2 there are three types of positioning to help control layout of a page: *normal, float,* and *absolute* positioning; in the following sections you'll be seeing how you can use each of these positioning schemes to indicate where the content of an element should appear on the page.

> In practice tables are still commonly used for positioning elements on the page—you will be looking at page layout in more depth in Chapter 11. However, XHTML is moving toward using CSS for positioning, and it does make your content a lot more reusable—as soon as a page resorts to using tables for layout, it generally confines the page to the medium it was originally designed for. As more devices with different capabilities access the Internet you are likely to see the use of CSS for positioning increase, allowing layouts to scale to the screen and enabling different style sheets to be used with the same document.

Normal Flow

By default, elements are laid out on the page using what is known as *normal flow*. In normal flow, the block level elements within a page will flow from top to bottom and inline elements will flow from left to right.

For example, each heading and paragraph should appear on a different line, whereas the contents of elements such as <b>, <em>, and <span> do not start on new lines.

Remember that normal flow can occur within another block level element; for example, you can have a <td> element that contains headings and paragraphs, in which case these elements are on new lines within that table cell.

Figure 10-23 illustrates three paragraphs with normal flow, each of which contains an inline <b> element (ch10_eg21.html).

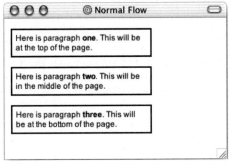

Figure 10-23

If you want the content of elements to appear in other places than where they would in normal flow, you have two properties to help you: position and float.

The position Property

The position property allows you to specify a position for a box. It can take the four values listed in the table that follows.

Value	Meaning
static	This is the same as normal flow, and is the default so you will rarely (if ever) see it specified.
relative	The position of the box can be offset from where it would be in normal flow.
absolute	The box is positioned exactly from the position in the containing element using x and y coordinates from the top-left corner of the containing element.
fixed	The position is calculated from a fixed point; in the case of the browser this point is the top-left corner of a browser window and does not change position if the user scrolls the window.

You will see how these are used in the coming sections.

Box Offset Properties

As you shall see in the coming sections, when boxes have a position property whose value is relative, absolute, or fixed they will also use *box offset* properties to indicate where these boxes should be positioned. The table that follows lists the box offset properties.

Property	Meaning
top	Offset position from the top of the containing element
right	Offset position from the right of the containing element
bottom	Offset position from the bottom of the containing element
left	Offset position from the left of the containing element

Each can take a value of a length, a percentage, or auto. Relative units, including percentages, are calculated with respect to the containing boxes' dimensions or properties.

Relative Positioning

Relative positioning positions an element in relation to the element's position in normal flow. It is displaced from that position by an amount given using the box offset properties.

To come back to the example of normal positioning, you can reposition the second paragraph using relative positioning, as shown in Figure 10-24.

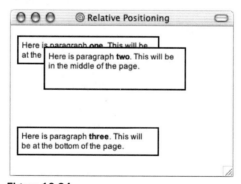

Figure 10-24

The second paragraph in this example is offset from where it would be in normal flow (where it was in the last example) by 40 pixels from the left and 40 pixels from the top—note the minus sign, which raises it above its position in normal flow (ch10_eg22.css).

```
p {border-style:solid;
   border-color:#000000;
   border-width:2px;
   padding:5px;
```

353

```
      width:200px;
      background-color:#FFFFFF;}

  p.two {
    position:relative;
    left: 40px;
    top: -40px;}
```

The value of the box offsets (in this case top and left) can be a length, a percentage, or `auto`. If it is an absolute length it can be a negative value.

You should specify only a left or right offset and a top or bottom offset. If you specify both left and right or both top and bottom, one must be the absolute negative of the other (for example top:3px; bottom:-3px;). If you have top and bottom or left and right, and they do not have absolute negative values of each other, the right or bottom offset will be ignored.

When you are using relative positioning, you can end up with some boxes overlapping others, as in the previous example. Because you are offsetting a box relative to normal flow, if the offset is large enough, one box will end up on top of another. This may create an effect you are looking for; however, there are a couple of pitfalls you should be aware of:

❑   Unless you set a background for a box (either a background color or image) it will be transparent by default, making any overlapping text an unreadable mess. In the preceding example I used the `background-color` property to make the background of the paragraphs white and thereby prevent this from happening.

❑   The CSS specification does not say which element should appear on top when relatively positioned elements overlap each other, so there can be differences between browsers.

Absolute Positioning

Absolute positioning completely removes an element's content from normal flow, allowing you to fix its position.

You can specify that an element's content should be absolutely positioned by giving it the `position` property with a value of `absolute`; then you use the box offset properties to position it where you want.

The box offsets fix the position of a box relative to the containing block—a containing block being an element with the position property set to `relative` or `fixed`.

Take a look at the following style sheet. This style sheet is for use with three paragraphs again, but this time the paragraphs are held within a `<div>` element that also uses absolute positioning (`ch20_eg23.css`):

```
  div.page {
    position:absolute;
    left:50px;
```

```
   top: 100px;
   border-style:solid; border-width:2px; border-color:#000000;}

p {
   background-color:#FFFFFF;
   width:200px;
   padding:5px;
   border-style:solid; border-color:#000000; border-width:2px;}

p.two {
   position:absolute;
   left:50px;
   top: -25px;}
```

Figure 10-25 shows you what this would look like in a browser; as you can clearly see, the element has been taken out of normal flow because the third paragraph is now in the place where the second paragraph would have been if it participated in normal flow. Furthermore, it even appears before the first paragraph!

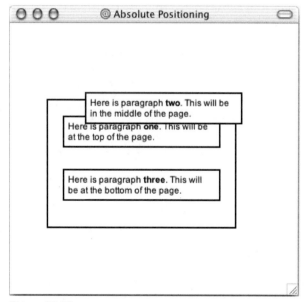

Figure 10-25

The presence of the <div class"page"> element here is to show that the paragraph is being positioned according the containing block—the absolutely positioned <div> element.

Absolutely positioned elements always come out above relatively positioned elements like you see here unless the z-index property (which you learn about later in this chapter) is used.

It is also worth noting that, because absolutely positioned boxes are taken out of normal flow, even if two vertical margins meet their margins do not collapse.

Fixed Positioning

The final value for the `positioning` property you need to be aware of is the value `fixed`. This value specifies that the content of the element should not only be completely removed from normal flow, but also that the box should not move when users scroll down the page.

Netscape 6.1 and later supports fixed positioning as does IE 5.5 on a Mac, but IE 6 on Windows has yet to support it.

To demonstrate fixed positioning, here is a sample of XHTML from `ch10_eg24.html`; this example continues with several more paragraphs so that you can see the page scrolling while the content of the `<div>` element remains fixed at the top of the page:

```
<div class="header">Beginning Web Development</div>
<p class="one">This page has to contain several paragraphs so you can see
the effect of fixed positioning. Fixed positioning has been used on the
header so it does not move even when the rest of the page scrolls.</p>
```

Here you can see the style sheet for this example (`ch10_eg24.css`). The header has the `position` property with the value `fixed` and is positioned to the top left of the browser window:

```
div.header {
  position:fixed;
  top: 0px;
  left:0px;
  width:100%;
  padding:20px;
  font-size:28px;
  color:#ffffff; background-color:#666666;
  border-style:solid; border-width:2px; border-color:#000000;}

p {
  width:300px;
  padding:5px;
  color:#000000; background-color:#FFFFFF;
  border-style:solid; border-color:#000000; border-width:2px;}

p.one {margin-top:100px; }
```

This last rule is supposed to make the first paragraph drop down from the top of the page so that it's in view, but unfortunately it does not work in this context.

Figure 10-26 shows you what this fixed header element looks like even though the user has scrolled halfway down the page.

The z-index Property

Absolutely positioned elements have a tendency to overlap other elements. When this happens the default behavior is to have the first elements underneath later ones. This is known as *stacking context*. If you have boxes that are absolutely positioned, you can control which of the absolutely positioned boxes appears on top using the z-index property to alter the stacking context. If you are familiar with graphic design packages, the stacking context is similar to using the "bring to top" and "send to back" features.

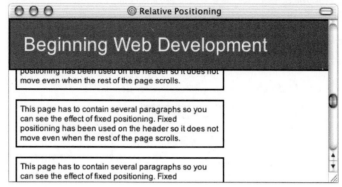

Figure 10-26

The value of the z-index property is a number, and the higher the number the nearer the top that element should be displayed.

To illustrate z-index, take a look at another example of absolute positioning—this time there are just three paragraphs:

```
<p class="one">Here is paragraph <b>one</b>. This will be at the top of the
page.</p>
<p class="two">Here is paragraph <b>two</b>. This will be underneath the other
elements.</p>
<p class="three">Here is paragraph <b>three</b>. This will be at the bottom of
the page.</p>
```

Each of these paragraphs shares common width, background-color, padding and border properties. Then each paragraph is positioned separately using absolute positioning. Because these paragraphs now all overlap, the z-index property is added to control which one appears on top; the higher the value, the nearer the top it ends up (ch10_eg25.css):

```
p {
    width:200px;
    background-color:#ffffff;
    padding:5px; margin:10px;
    border-style:solid; border-color:#000000; border-width:2px; }

p.one {
    z-index:3;
    position:absolute;
    left:0px; top:0px; }

p.two {
    z-index:1;
    position:absolute;
    left:150px; top: 25px; }
```

```
p.three {
    z-index:2;
    position:absolute;
    left:40px; top:35px;}
```

Figure 10-27 shows how the second paragraph now appears to be underneath the first and third paragraphs, and the first one remains on top.

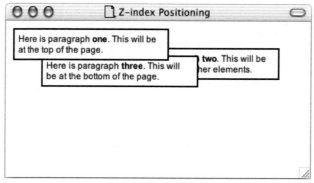

Figure 10-27

Floating Using the float Property

The float element allows you to take an element out of normal flow and place it as far to the left or right of a containing box as possible within that element's padding. (Its vertical margins, however, will not be collapsed above or below it like block boxes in normal flow can; rather, the floated box will be aligned with the top of the containing box.)

To indicate that you want a box floated either to the left or the right of the containing box you set the float property, which can take one of the values listed in the table that follows.

Value	Purpose
left	The box is floated to the left of the containing element and the content of the containing element will flow to the right of it.
right	The box is floated to the right of the containing element and the content of the containing element will flow to the left of it.
none	The box is not floated and remains where it would have been positioned in normal flow.
inherit	The box takes the same property as its containing element.

Whenever you specify a float property, you should also set a width property indicating the width of the containing box that the floating box should take up; otherwise it will automatically take up 100 percent of the width of the containing box leaving no space for things to flow around it, therefore making it just like a plain block level element.

Look at the following XHTML (ch10_eg26.html) and note how there is a <span> element at the beginning of the first paragraph:

```
<body>
   <h1>Heading</h1>
   <p><span class="pullQuote">Here is the pullquote. It will be removed from
normal flow and appear on the right of the page.</span>
   Here is paragraph <b>one</b>. This will be at the top of the page. Here is
   paragraph <b>one</b>. This will be at the top of the page. Here is paragraph
   <b>one</b>. This will be at the top of the page. Here is paragraph
   <b>one</b>. This will be at the top of the page. Here is paragraph <b>one
   </b>. This will be at the top of the page.</p>

   <p>Here is paragraph <b>two</b>. This will be at the bottom of the page.</p>
</body>
```

Even the inline <span> element can be floated, taking it away from its containing element. It will be taken out of the normal flow and placed to the right of the containing <p> element using the float property with a value of right (ch10_eg26.css):

```
p {
   border-style:solid;
   border-color:#000000;
   border-width:2px;
   padding:5px;
   background-color:#FFFFFF;
   width:500px;}

.pullQuote {
   float:right;
   width:150px;
   padding:5px;
   margin:5px;
   border-style:solid;
   border-width:1px; }
```

You can see how the content of the <span> element with the class attribute whose value is pullQuote ends up to the right of the page with the rest of the paragraph flowing to the left and then underneath it, as shown in Figure 10-28.

The clear Property

The clear property, rather like the HTML clear attribute, will prevent content floating to the left of the box created by the float and push it underneath it. The table that follows lists the four values the clear property can take.

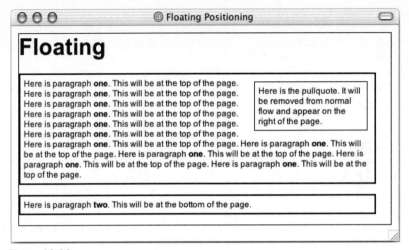

Figure 10-28

Value	Purpose
left	The content of the element with the `clear` property is cleared from the left side of a float (it cannot appear to the left of a floating element).
right	The content of the element with the `clear` property is cleared from the right side of a float (it cannot appear to the right of a floating element).
both	The content of the element with the `clear` property is cleared from either side of a float (it cannot appear to either side of a floating element).
none	Allows floating on either side.

Look at this slightly different example (`ch10_eg27.html`) where the `pullQuote` is not contained in the paragraph:

```
<h1>Floating</h1>

    <div class="pullQuote">Here is the pullquote. It will be removed from
    normal flow and appear on the right of the page.</div>

    <p>Here is paragraph <b>one</b>. This will be at the top of the page. Here is
    is paragraph <b>one</b>. This will be at the top of the page. </p>
```

The following style sheet will float the pull quote to the right, but the paragraph element uses the `clear` property to prevent any floated content appearing to the right of it (`ch10_eg27.css`):

```
p {
  clear:right;
  background-color:#FFFFFF; }
```

```
div.pullQuote {
  float:right;
  padding:5px;
  margin:5px;
  width:150px;
  border-style:solid; border-width:1px; }
```

Figure 10-29 shows you how the `clear` property works in this example.

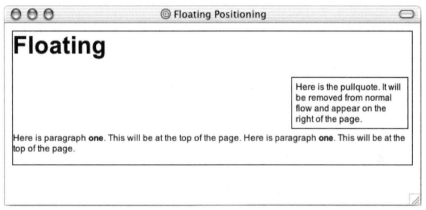

Figure 10-29

Overflow

Occasionally an element's content might be larger than the amount of space allocated to it; perhaps the width and height properties did not allow enough room or a `<pre>` element contains a very long line.

When a nested element needs more room to be displayed than the surrounding element offers, the `overflow` property specifies how the browser should deal with the content. It can take one of the four values listed in the table that follows.

Value	Purpose
`visible`	Allows the content to overflow the borders of its containing element.
`hidden`	The content of the nested element is simply cut off at the border of the containing element.
`scroll`	The size of the containing element does not change, but the scrollbars are added to allow the user to scroll to see the content.
`auto`	The purpose is the same as `scroll`, but the scrollbar will be shown only if the content does overflow.

In the next example, which just contains a paragraph and a heading, you can see an example of the `auto` value being used to create scrollbars for the paragraph that is too long to fit in the 150 pixel by 100 pixel container (`ch10_eg28.css`):

```
p {
overflow:auto;
width:150px;
height:100px;
background-color:#FFFFFF;}
```

You can see the scrollbar created in Figure 10-30.

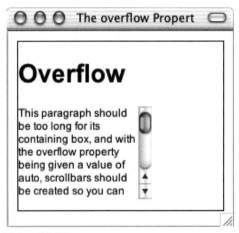

Figure 10-30

Try It Out A Sample Layout

In this example you are going to create a sample page layout that uses a combination of the techniques you learned in this chapter to present an article using CSS rather than tables.

The page you are going to work with is shown in Figure 10-31 without the style sheet attached.

```
<body>

<h1>Cascading Style Sheets</h1>

   <div class="nav"><a href="../index.htm">Examples index</a>
       <a href="">Chapter 10 Code</a></div>

<h2>CSS Positioning</h2>

   <p class="abstract"><img class="floatLeft" src="images/background.gif"
       alt="wrox logo" />This article introduces the topic of laying out
       Wweb pages in CSS using a combination of positioning schemes.</p>
```

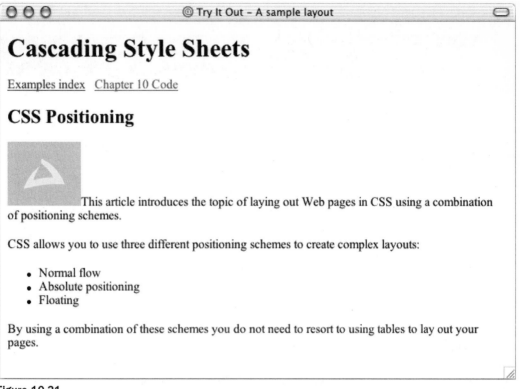

Figure 10-31

```
    <p>CSS allows you to use three different positioning schemes to create
        complex layouts:</p>

    <ul>
      <li>Normal flow</li>
      <li>Absolute positioning</li>
      <li>Floating</li>
    </ul>

    <p>By using a combination of these schemes you do not need to resort to
        using tables to lay out your pages.</p>

  </body>
```

This example is a good illustration of the state of play with CSS—only some of the latest browsers support enough of the features to really make it work for your sites. While you can design your site in such a way that it will work with most browsers, few people like to (or are able to) design with the limits of technology.

The resulting page is going to look like Figure 10-32 in Netscape 6 and later (although this screenshot was taken in Netscape 7).

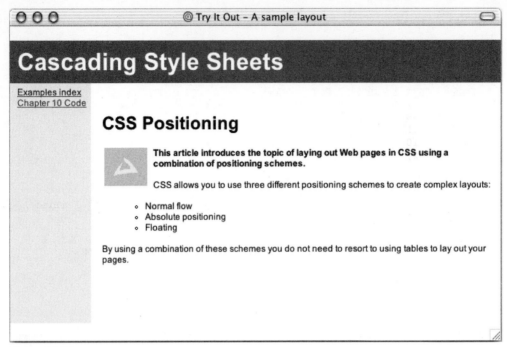

Figure 10-32

To start working on the CSS file for this page, start up your Web page editor and follow these steps:

1. Create a file called `samplePage.css` and add the elements from the XHTML page and use class selectors where appropriate to identify each type of element. You should end up with a list like the one that follows; then you will be able to look at the rule for each element in turn.

```
body {}
h1 {}
div.nav {}
h2 {}
p {}
p.abstract {}
img {}
ul {}
```

2. First comes the rule for the `<body>` element, which just sets up some defaults for the page:

```
body {
    color:#000000;
    background-color:#ffffff;
    font-family:arial, verdana, sans-serif;
    font-size:12px;}
```

3. Next is the header for the site, which uses fixed positioning to anchor it to the top of the page even if the user scrolls. It also has a `z-index` property to ensure that this heading remains on top of the navigation.

```
h1 {
    position:fixed;
    top:0px; left:0px;
    width:100%;
    color:#ffffff; background-color:#666666;
    padding:10px;
    z-index:2;}
```

4. The navigation is removed from normal flow because it is absolutely positioned. It is positioned 60 pixels from the top so that the links will not disappear underneath the page's heading when the page first loads. The navigation is placed in a box that is 100 pixels wide and 300 pixels high with a light gray background, and it has a `z-index` of 1 to make sure that it goes underneath the heading for the page (which you just saw with a `z-index` of 2).

```
div.nav {
    z-index:1;
    position:absolute;
    top:60px;
    left:0px;
    width:100px;
    height:300px;
    padding-left:10px; padding-top:20px; padding-bottom:10px;
    background-color:#efefef;}
```

5. You may have noticed that the navigation bar contains the word "Navigation," which was not in the original HTML file. This style sheet uses the CSS `:before` pseudo-class to add this word in. You can see here that it also has other styles associated with it.

```
div.nav:before {
    content: "Navigation ";
    font-size:18px;
    font-weight:bold;}
```

6. Next is the rule for the `<h2>` element, which needs to be indented from the left because the navigation takes up the first 110 pixels to the left of it. It also has padding at the top to bring the text underneath the heading.

```
h2 {
    padding-top:80px;
    padding-left:115px;}
```

7. Next are the two rules for paragraphs, the first for all paragraphs, and the second one to make sure that the abstract of the article is in bold. Like the `<h2>` element, all paragraphs need to be indented from the left.

```
p {padding-left:115px;}
p.abstract{font-weight:bold;}
```

8. The image that sits in the first paragraph is floated to the left of the text. As you can see, the text in the paragraph flows around the image. It also has a 5-pixel padding to the right.

```
img {
    float:left;
    width:60px;
    padding-right:5px;}
```

9. Finally you have the rule for the unordered list element, which needs to be indented further than the paragraphs or level 2 heading. It also specifies the style of bullet to be used with the list-style property.

```
ul {
    clear:left;
    list-style:circle;
    padding-left:145px;}
```

10. Save your style sheet and try loading the samplePage.html file that is going to use it. You have already seen the result in Netscape, but what does it look like in IE? Figure 10-33 gives you an idea of what you will see in IE.

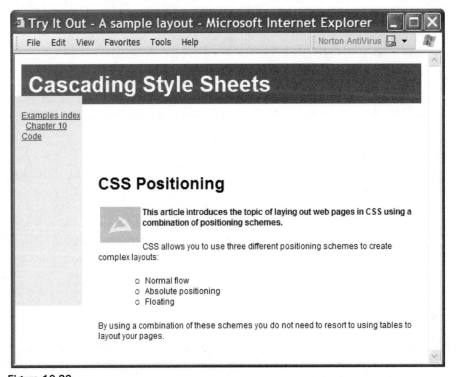

Figure 10-33

How It Works

It's important to note that not all of the rules in this example work in all browsers, and that is a problem that is holding up CSS's deployment by Web developers. However, you can get a good idea of what this example should look like in newer versions of Netscape (version 6 and later). So, the following discussion focuses on the result you saw in Figure 10-32 in Netscape 6.

Starting with the fixed heading, the `<h1>` element is taken out of normal flow and fixed to the top of the browser window (note that the whitespace above the heading should not really appear). Absolutely positioned elements always stay on top, so this would cover other content on the page if those elements (namely the navigation and the paragraphs) did not use padding to prevent them from overlapping.

The navigation bar not only uses the `padding-top` property to bring it down beneath the heading, but it also uses the `z-index` property. The `z-index` property is there to ensure that, if there is any overlap between the navigation and the title, the title will appear on the top. You cannot rely on pixel-perfect positioning from CSS, and if the navigation bar were to appear on top, it would look a little odd.

The headings, paragraphs, and unordered list that make up the body of the article all have to have padding to bring them in off the left side of the browser, where they would otherwise overlap with the navigation (which you may remember has been taken out of normal flow because it is absolutely positioned). These paragraphs and other elements that remain in normal flow therefore must move out of the way of the absolutely positioned elements.

The image inside the first paragraph is floated within the block level paragraph container and has a `padding-right` property set to 5 pixels so that the writing does not run right to the edge of it.

Finally, the unordered list has to be moved further in from the left margin than the paragraph or heading because it has bullet points to the left of where the text starts. If the unordered list were given a `padding-left` property with a value of 115 like the heading or paragraph, the text would start 115 pixels in from the left, but the markers (the bullet points) would be even further to the left. Hence this property is set to 145 so that it remains further indented than the text.

Summary

In this chapter you have learned the CSS properties that allow you to control lists, links, tables, outlines, and backgrounds with CSS. You then saw how CSS allows you to add content from the style sheet into the document (when browsers catch up and support it). The `:before` and `:after` pseudo-classes allow you to add content before or after an element specified in the selector. This includes text, an image, or content from a file. It even allows for automatic numbering or counting of any element using the `counter()` function and can manage complex sets of quotation marks.

You also learned how to use the `@import` rule to include rules from other style sheets into the current one and create modularized style sheets and re-use rules from different sections of sites, while the `@charset` rule indicates which character set is being used in the style sheet.

Finally, this chapter looked at the three main positioning schemes in CSS: normal flow (and its offshoot relative positioning), absolute positioning (and its offshoot fixed positioning), and floating. These are powerful tools for controlling where the content of a document should appear; they complete the picture of separating style from content as you don't have to use tables to control the layout of documents.

As the examples through this chapter, and in particular the longer example at the end, have shown, support for CSS, even in the latest browsers, is still not complete. Bearing in mind that the CSS2 recommendation was completed in 1998, it is a pity that browser manufacturers have not made a better attempt at implementing it.

The lack of support for some of the main features, particularly in IE for Windows, is what is holding many Web designers and developers back from creating a true separation of style from content. They are still forced to use tables instead of CSS positioning to create the layouts their clients expect.

With careful attention, it is possible to create pages that use CSS for layouts, yet there is still the problem that older browsers will not support these layouts. As a result, most designers will use a combination of older techniques for page layout and CSS for some of the styling.

Exercises

The answers to all of the exercises are in Appendix A.

1. In this exercise you will create a linked table of contents that will sit at the top of a long document in an ordered list and link to the headings in the main part of the document.

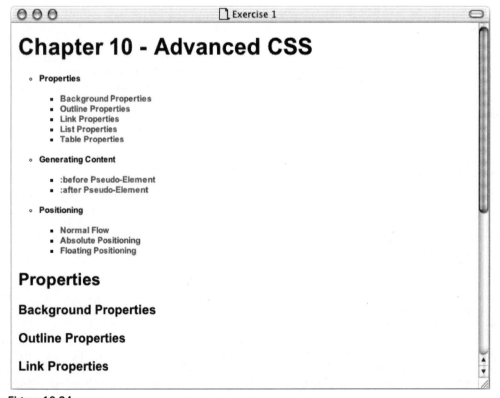

Figure 10-34

The XHTML file, example1.html, is provided with the download code for this book ready for you to create the style sheet. Your style sheet should do the following:

- ❑ Set the styles of all links including active and visited links
- ❑ Make the contents of the list bold
- ❑ Make the background of the list light gray and use padding to ensure the bullet points show
- ❑ Make the width of the links box 250 pixels wide
- ❑ Change the styles of heading bullet points to empty circles
- ❑ Change the style of link bullet points to squares

Your page should look something like Figure 10-34.

2. In this exercise you will test your CSS positioning skills. You should create a page that represents the links to the different sections of the chapter in a very different way. Each of the sections will be shown in a different block, and each block will be absolutely positioned in a diagonal top left to bottom right direction. The middle box should appear on top as is shown in the Figure 10-35.

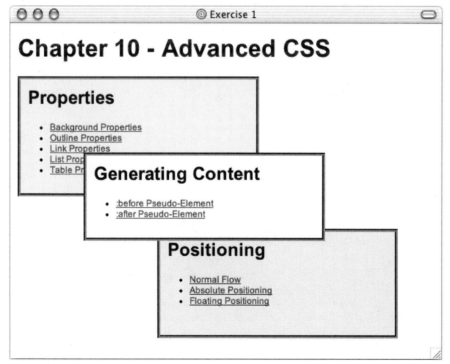

Figure 10-35

You can find the source XHTML file (exercise2.html) with the download code for this chapter.

Page Layout

This chapter is the first of two chapters about design issues. This chapter addresses designing and constructing *layouts* for Web pages. Although there is no rule book that says how you should design your page, there are some important factors that you should consider regarding the appearance of a page, and it is these issues you learn about in this chapter.

No one can tell you how to make an attractive page—that is a matter of taste. What you will see in this chapter is a discussion about the aims of the site, the size of your page, what should appear on the page, and where each item should go on that page. You also need to know how to make these designs work in code. This chapter is broadly grouped into four sections to reflect these topics:

❑   Understanding the aims of the site correctly

❑   Looking at a page as a whole and addressing the question of how big you should make the page

❑   Knowing the elements that make up each page such as logos, headings, links, and possibly ads

❑   Positioning the various elements within the page

Once you have looked at the overall layout of the page in this chapter, see Chapter 12 for some more specific issues of design within the page, such as design of menus, forms, links, and text.

Understanding the Site

Whether you are going to create a Web site for yourself or you are hoping to create sites for clients, you must have a good understanding of the site you want to create before you can start designing it. There are some fundamental questions you need to be asking to make sure you understand the aims and audience for the site; specifically, you need to be sure that you know:

❑   Who you expect to visit the site

❑   How often you expect them to visit

❑   What sort of information you think they would expect to find at your site

❑   What *you* want your site to do for your visitors

Without being clear on these items you cannot design an effective site.

The following sections will help you answer these questions before you start working on the site.

Understanding a Site's Aims

Before you can even start working on a site, you must ensure that you have clearly defined two things:

❑   The aims of the site

❑   Who you expect to visit it (known in publishing as the site's *target audience*)

Consider the goal of the site you are going to work on. Are you trying to promote a product or a service and make people aware of it, explain a product or service to new customers in depth, sell a product or service directly from the site, or get potential customers to speak to a sales person? Perhaps the site you are working on is not designed to push a product or service; you may be trying to teach new skills; create a community; post a resume; create a portfolio; publish information about a hobbies/interests; support a publication, radio show, TV program, or other form of media; or publish your opinion on a topic.

If you intend to start creating Web sites for companies, you may come across clients who think they need a Web site (or an update to their existing Web site) but are not sure what they should be putting on it. In an ideal world clients would know exactly what they wanted on their Web site, and they would have the content ready for you before you started work on it, but, particularly when you are building sites for small- and medium-sized companies, you often have to help the client understand what a Web site can do for their business before you start work on it.

Often your site will have more than one aim. For example, a manufacturer might want to provide more than just information about its product; it probably also wants to let people know how to get in touch with the company and where to visit the company, or it may want to offer a form for customers to e-mail to company. You may want to tell visitors more about your company and its background to build up trust in you. Companies with investors may want to put quarterly reports or information about the board of directors. There might be events that you want to list of interest to those visiting your site, such as trade exhibitions, film release dates, or stars' birthdays. The varieties of purposes a Web site can have are near endless.

You should make sure you list all of the aims of the site at this stage. After all, you will want the design and the site to address all of these aims. You also need to ensure that you have the same understanding of the aims and purposes of the site as the client.

> *If you are working on a site for a client, it is good to get them to agree to the aims of the site when you have defined them. Many clients can decide they want extra functionality added to a site during the development of the site, so pinning down the aims from the start is important. If the client wants to then extend on these aims you can re-negotiate terms for these extra features (such as extra development time and extra payment).*

Who You Expect to Visit

Throughout the design process, you must keep one thing in mind: You need to design the page for your target audience. Whether you are choosing where to position an element of the site or deciding whether to use a technology or feature (such as sound or animation), the major influence for your decisions should always be what your target audience would want. So, naturally, it's very important to understand your target audience.

Unfortunately, some companies ask designers to push messages that the leadership thinks are most interesting or important instead of putting themselves in the position of their visitors. For example, some companies put information for investors on their front page, such as quarterly reports or information about the board of directors. This says to me that the site is aimed at the companies' investors, not its customers. If the intention is to aim the site at investors rather than customers, this may be the correct decision. But as a customer I don't want to be reminded about how much profit a company is making if I'm about to hand over my hard-earned money! Instead, the site should have a link to the section of the site that is just for the small number of visitors that are investors, and instead use the valuable space on the front page for links that customers will be interested in.

So you need to ask yourself the following:

❑ Who will be visiting your site and what information will they be looking for? Will your visitors be potential customers (members of the public or other companies), press and media, those interested in the general topic, hobbyists, or investors?

❑ Why are they coming? How many of the visitors want to buy a product or service; learn a new skill; perform their job; find out more about your company, service, or area of interest; decide whether you are a good investment; or find out when you are open, where you are located, and what your phone number is?

❑ How many visitors are just coming out of interest, for entertainment, or because something related to your site is in the news at the moment? You may decide that you expect 50 percent of your visitors to come for one reason, and another 50 percent to come for another reason.

❑ What do you know about these visitors? You may have an idea of the demographic of people usually interested in the product or service you supply or the topic you are covering. Things such as age, gender, and technical ability may affect some of your design decisions.

New Content

Another important question is whether people are going to spend any time developing and maintaining the content of the site after it has been launched. There is a very simple reason for asking this: If the content of your site does not change, how can you can expect visitors to come back to your site more than once?

Some sites, such as those containing helpful reference information, may be visited numerous times by the same people, but the average site for a small company that explains that company's products or services will not generate a lot of return viewers.

Some sites do not need to change often; for example if you are a roofer it is unlikely that visitors will come back after they have had their roof recovered. (They might come in the first place to see samples of your work, but after the roof has been replaced, they have little incentive to visit regularly again.) If you are creating a site about books or music, however, there will likely be new information you could post regularly that might attract visitors back at regular intervals.

So, you need to question how often you expect these same people to come back to your site. If you want them to come back regularly, you are going to have to provide them with an incentive to come back. You may also decide that your expectations fall somewhere in between, such as a clothing site that showcases new clothing lines either semi-annually or quarterly.

The problem with keeping content fresh is that it takes a lot of time, and someone has to be responsible for updating the site on a regular basis.

Defining Your Site's Content

Now that you have a good idea of the goals of your site, who it is aimed at, and how often the content is going to change, you can take a closer look at what is going to be the actual content of your site.

You need to put yourself in the position of each of your potential visitors and think about what they might want to know. It is best to first list every possibility and then trim it back to the best ones. When generating the potential content of your site you should treat it like a brainstorming session—don't hold back! Remember, your site must address the needs of your visitors and what they will expect from the site, not just what you want your visitors to see.

This list could include things such as information about products and services the company offers, including photos or examples of work; how these products and services can be attained; contact details; and information about the company. (Customers often like to know a bit of the background behind a company that trades on the Internet; it helps reassure them that it is safe to hand over their money.) Don't forget to drill down further. For example, what information are you going to include about a product or service? A product could have a photo, description, dimensions, information about how and where it is made, typical uses for it, and so on. A service might require descriptions of the work involved, how long it takes to complete, what is required so the service can be performed, who will be performing the service, and how they are qualified to perform the service.

If you sell something, you should always try to offer a price—if the price varies (for example, a roofer might charge different amounts for different types and sizes of roof) adding a price guide for a product or service results in a higher level of inquiries than a site that gives no indication of price.

You should also look at other sites that address a similar topic—the competition—and look at what they do and don't do well and whether these sites meet the needs of the people you expect to visit your site. One of the key points to think about here is what you can do differently or better; after all there is little point in just doing the same thing and re-inventing the wheel.

Don't forget that you will want to add things such as your logo or branding to most pages, maybe a search form, and possibly advertising. You should also remember some boring yet necessary features such as a copyright notice, terms and conditions, and a privacy policy (if you collect information about users or use a technology known as *cookies* for storing information on the user's computer).

Once you have every possible thing your customers might want to know on your list you can trim your ideas back to what you are actually going to do for this Web site. Remember that all unused ideas can always be used in a future update of the site.

Grouping and Categorization

Now you can start to group together the ideas of what you want to cover. If the site is advertising several products or services, these may be placed together in related groups of products or services, which can be split into subgroups. For example:

❑   You might group the information about how the company was formed and its history along with information about the company today: a general "about us" section.

❑   The different ways in which people can get in contact with you (phone, e-mail, fax, opening hours of a store, maybe a map, and so on) could all be put in one "contact us" group.

❑   If a company has outside investors and is floated on the stock market, you might want to create a section for the investors with company reports, information on the board of directors, and so on.

For most sites, you should try to create no more than six or seven primary groups, categories, or sections for your site. These sections will form the *primary navigation* items of your site or the main menu, which are also known as the *global navigation*. For example, you might have sections such as Product Catalogue, Local Stockists, Trade Enquiries, About Us, and Contact Us. You will also have a home page (which is not included in the six or seven primary groups). This method of grouping the site will make it much easier to navigate and understand.

Some of the sections will likely contain subsections with several pages of their own, and there may be more than seven subsections in each category. For example, a publisher might have more than seven books in a book category, or a cookery site may have more than seven recipes. On larger sites it would be possible to add another level of subcategories. A publisher might add subcategories for each book topic, while a recipe site might split recipes into starters, main courses, dinners, light meals and so on. If there were subsections these would form *secondary* or *category navigation*.

Remember that your grouping should reflect what you expect the visitors to your site will want to do and the customers' understanding of your products, services, or subject. For example, if your customers were looking for a product on your site, would they be looking within a list of manufacturers or would they be looking in a list of types of product?

These categories and subcategories are like a table of contents and will form the basis of the navigation for your site—the sections will each need to take part in the main menu while the subsections will often form their own submenus. This organization is very important on Web sites because they do not have the linear order a book does; users are far more likely to take different routes through a Web site. The better organized your site, the more chance users will find what they are looking for.

Creating a Site Map

By now you should be getting a good idea of the sections and pages that are going to make up your site so you should start drawing up a site map, which should look something like either a family tree or folder list in Windows Explorer. It should start with the home page for the site and all of the main categories at the top of the tree.

If any of the categories contains subcategories or more than one page, these pages should appear as children of the first page. For example, if one of your main categories is "products" then you might have this split into several subsections with a page about each item in that category, or you might just have two or three products to list off that page—and each of those may then have its own page in the position of a grandchild of the product.

You can see an example of a site map in Figure 11-1; you could draw this either vertically as done here or horizontally (more like a family tree).

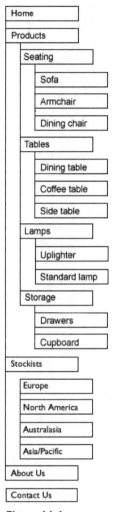

Figure 11-1

Once you have created a site map you will know the following:

❑   How many pages are on your site

❑   What information will appear on each of those pages

❑   What links will appear on each page (and where those links point to)

Identifying Key Elements for Every Page

Before you can start to really design a page, you need to perform one last step. You need to identify the key items or *elements* that should appear on the page. These elements will include things such as branding or logos, primary navigation, category navigation (on the relevant category pages), headings, the main content of the page, a search box, and space for self-promotions or for advertising other companies' products and services.

> You should create the list of the key elements of each page before you even start thinking about where to position them, although it is very helpful if you have an idea of how much space each element will take.

These elements will reflect the aims of the site. But be warned: Many clients will want to put everything on every page. You must show them how the organization and planning you have done here will lead to a good design and simple navigation that avoids the need to put everything on each page. (You learn more about navigation in Chapter 12.) A site that is less cluttered yet easy to navigate is better than a site that has everything on each page (because it is harder to find what you want on a page where there is too much).

Page Size (and Screen Resolution)

Now that you know what should go on each page, you are ready to start looking at designing the pages themselves. In the same way that an artist must decide on the size of canvas before he or she can start painting, so you must decide what size of page you are going to use for your site.

Unfortunately, different visitors to your site will have different size monitors working at different resolutions. Therefore, your canvas will not look the same size to everyone that visits your site, and you cannot design something that looks good on your monitor and just expect it to look good on someone else's computer. Several factors affect how big your "canvas" should be. Consider the following:

❑   Different computers have different screen resolutions (640×480, 800×600, and 1024×768 are the most popular)

❑   Different users have different sized monitors (15, 17, 19, 21+ inch monitors)

❑   People tend not to browse with the whole of the screen showing—they tend to have toolbars and other applications showing

If you do not use sensible dimensions for a page when you start to design and build your site, you could end up rebuilding the whole thing when one of your clients gets home and notices that what looked great on the computer at work simply doesn't fit on a monitor at home.

The issue of screen resolution refers to the number of pixels that make up a picture on a monitor screen. A screen that has a 640×480 resolution will be 640 pixels wide by 480 pixels tall, a screen that is 800×600 will be 800 pixels wide and 600 pixels tall, and so on.

Therefore, if you design a page that is 850 pixels wide it will not all fit into a 640 × 480 resolution or 800 × 600 resolution screen without the user having to scroll horizontally. While it is quite normal to have pages that scroll vertically, you should not expect users to scroll horizontally—this is used only rarely as a novelty on sites.

Most operating systems allow you to change the resolution of your monitor, so you can try altering the resolution of your monitor to get an idea of how different it can look for different users. On a PC you will find this in the Windows Control Panel under the Displays option; on a Mac it is in System Preferences under the Screen option.

The following table shows you statistics for screen resolutions from a site called theCounter.com. The statistics are taken from visitors to the site in the month of January over five years, and they show the percentage of visitors that had different screen resolutions. You can view these statistics on an ongoing basis at `http://www.theCounter.com/`.

Month/Year	640 × 480	800 × 600	1024 × 768	1152 × 864	1280 × 1024
Jan 2004	1 percent	37 percent	49 percent	3 percent	6 percent
Jan 2003	2 percent	46 percent	40 percent	3 percent	4 percent
Jan 2002	4 percent	52 percent	34 percent	2 percent	3 percent
Jan 2001	7 percent	54 percent	30 percent	2 percent	2 percent
Jan 2000	11 percent	56 percent	25 percent	2 percent	2 percent

As you can see, in January 2004 less than 1 percent of users had 640 × 480 resolution, although 37 percent still used 800 × 600. Remembering that you should be designing your sites for your customers, even if you or your client uses a 21-inch monitor at 1280 × 1024 resolution you should make sure that your design works well on an 800 × 600 screen.

Given the fact that many users like to browse with a little gap around the edge of their browser window so that they can see part of other open applications, you should really leave a little space for this as well by taking off up to another 40 pixels for the edge of the browser window itself.

As a result, I tend to make the main content of a page no wider than 700 pixels wide. The 1 percent of users who have 640 × 480 resolution monitors may have to scroll horizontally to see all of the content, but chances are that they will be used to having to do this on many other sites, too.

> **While you should generally avoid expecting users to scroll horizontally, you can safely expect them to scroll vertically. Visitors should, however, be able to tell what the page is about without scrolling, so make sure that the main parts are in view when the page loads. Generally speaking, you should at least be able to see the company logo or branding, the main heading for any page, as well as the first few items of primary navigation.**

Vertically you should account for the fact that a lot of users will have a menu or taskbar (such as the taskbar on Windows or the dock on Mac OS X) that will take up part of the screen's vertical height. You also have to consider the various toolbars that can appear in a browser window. Therefore you should make the key points of a page that identify what that page is about appear in the top 450 pixels or so of the browser window.

Fixed-Width versus Liquid Designs

Although I said that you should make the content fit within a page that is 700 pixels wide and that a user should be able to understand what a page is about from the top 450 pixels of the screen, you might have noticed some designs stretch to fit the whole page. This is known as a *liquid design*. By contrast, designs that force a page to a certain height or width are known as *fixed-width designs*.

> *It is interesting to note that users with higher resolution monitors tend to leave larger gaps around the edge of the window they browse in, exposing more of their desktop and other applications that are running. So, even when users have high resolutions their browser windows are rarely as big as you might imagine.*

One of the most common misconceptions I have come across when working on Web sites for clients is that they think every Web page takes up the whole screen. That is simply not true!

Of course, some sites stretch to fit the whole browser window. In these cases, parts of the page stretch and shrink depending upon the size of the browser, and if the user resizes his or her browser, the page will usually change size with the window. Figure 11-2 shows a fictional news site that uses a liquid design to take up the whole page. With this Web site, the navigation bar on the left stays the same width but the main part of the page stretches. (Note that the browser windows in the next three figures are all the same width.)

Figure 11-2

Many sites, however, have a fixed width and are either aligned to the left or the center of the page. These sites should take into account the limited width of a browser window (as discussed earlier). The key difference with this approach (compared with the liquid designs) is that the designer has much greater control over the layout of a page because she knows how large it will be. It also means that the designer can limit the width of things like columns of text (which can be especially helpful on the Web as users often find it difficult to read wide paragraphs on a computer screen). An example of a fixed-width design is shown in Figure 11-3; when the user increases the size of the browser window the page stays the same size but gains whitespace on the right (the browser window in this figure is the same width as it was in Figure 11-2).

Figure 11-3

Other sites combine the two designs and have a fixed width in the middle, but the top and bottom of the page stretch to the edge of the sides of the window. This helps prevent large gaps appearing all around pages but keeps the main content to a fixed width. An example of such a site is shown in Figure 11-4 (again, the browser window in this figure is the same width as it was in Figures 11-2 and 11-3).

Now that you've seen the three types of page design (liquid, fixed-width, and mixed), the following sections show you how to create them in code.

Liquid Design

A liquid design can stretch to fit the page. In order to do so, you specify proportions of a page using percentage values in tables or CSS. For example, you might decide your page takes up 95 percent of the width of the browser so that there is always a small gap around the edge. Figure 11-5 shows a page that takes up 95 percent of the window. If the user increases the size of the browser window, the page increases in size but retains the border around the outside.

Figure 11-4

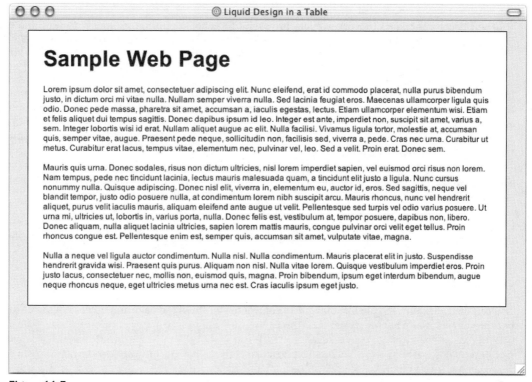

Figure 11-5

Here (ch11_eg01.html) you can see how this effect can be created using a table; the <table> element is given a width attribute with a value of 95%:

```
<body>
  <table width="95%" align="center">
    <tr>
      <td>

        <!-- CONTENT OF PAGE GOES HERE -->

      </td>
    </tr>
  </table>
</body>
```

Before CSS, the use of tables was the easiest way to control positioning of content on pages, and the only way to create more than one column in a single page. (The only other approach would be to use frames and separate pages.) Strictly speaking this is not a correct use of the <table> element. A train timetable, for example, is real tabular data containing many rows and columns and therefore it should be placed in a table, but a page is not a single cell of tabular data. For years, however, designers relied upon tables as the only way of accurately positioning elements upon a page, and this clever misuse of the <table> element is still very common today.

There are at least two common reasons for the use of tables for layout:

❑ Clients want pages to work in every browser. CSS is not supported in older browsers, and there are even major bugs in some of the more recent browsers' CSS support, such as IE 6 on Windows.

❑ Many designers have not yet learned how to use CSS to control the layout of pages.

If you would rather use CSS to control the size of a page, you can use the <div> element to contain all of the markup for that page. The <div> element was very briefly introduced in Chapter 2 as a grouping element, and this is a great example of how it can be used to group all of the elements that make up a page together in one block. Once the elements are inside the <div> element, CSS rules can be applied to that group of elements as a whole.

The page would now sit inside the one <div> element (rather than inside <table>, <tr>, and <td> elements) like so (ch11_eg02.html):

```
<body>
  <div id="page">
      <!-- CONTENT OF PAGE GOES HERE -->
  </div>
</body>
```

You can then attach a CSS rule like this one to control the width of the page and other styles such as the background color and border styles:

```
div#page {
  width:95%;
  background-color:#ffffff;
```

```
border-style:solid; border-width:1px; border-color:#666666;
padding:20px;
font-size:12px;}
```

When you look at this in a browser, however, you can come across some slightly strange effects even in version 6 and 7 browsers. Unfortunately, in both IE and Netscape you might find the page ends up with a little more space on the right side of the page than on the left, as you can see in Figure 11-6.

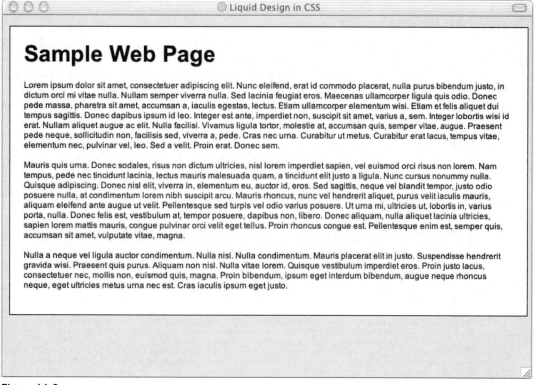

Figure 11-6

As with each of the designs (liquid, fixed-width, and mixed), there are advantages and disadvantages to this approach.

The advantages are as follows:

❑ The page expands to fill the browser window and therefore does not leave large spaces around the page when there is a large window.

❑ If the user has a small window open in his or her browser, the page can contract to fit that window.

❑ The design is tolerant of users setting font sizes larger than the designer intended as the page layout can stretch.

The disadvantages are as follows:

- ❑ If you do not control the width of sections of your page, your design can be thrown out and you can get unsightly gaps around certain elements.

- ❑ If the user has a very wide window, lines of text can become very long, and these become hard to read.

- ❑ If the user has a very narrow window, words may be squashed too small and you could end up with just a word or two on each line.

Fixed-Width Design

Fixed-width designs use lengths to indicate the dimensions of the page, such as pixels, ems, and centimeters. Fixed-width designs allows designers much greater control over how their page appears because they know the size of the canvas; it cannot stretch and shrink as the users resize their windows. Even though a design might look a slightly different size on different resolution monitors, the proportions of elements on the page can remain the same. You can see an example of a fixed-width page in Figure 11-7. The code for this page (ch11_eg03.html) follows shortly.

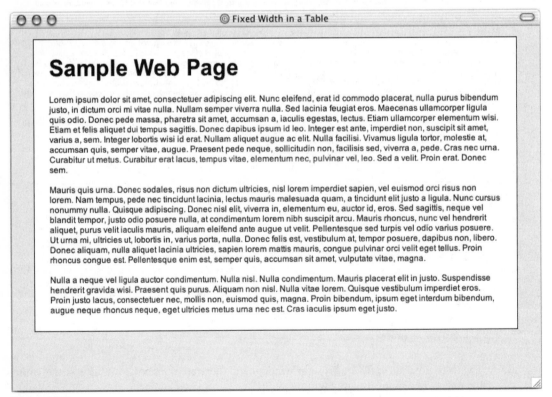

Figure 11-7

While Figure 11-7 may look similar to Figures 11-5 and 11-6, if you try out the corresponding code that is provided with the download code for the rest of the book from www.wrox.com you will find that this example does not stretch to take up more of the browser window, unlike the previous example of a liquid layout.

Fixed-width designs often place the whole page inside a table. Usually, the width attribute is used on the <table> element rather than using the width property in CSS to ensure that the width works with browsers that do not support CSS or cannot load the style sheet. When the width attribute is used on a <table>, no matter how big the user's browser is, the table (and therefore the main content of the page) remains that size. If the user's browser is narrower than the table, horizontal scrollbars will appear, whereas if the window is wider than the table there will be space to the side of the table (or both sides if it's centered).

The value of the width attribute is most often given in pixels in a fixed-width design. As you can see in ch11_eg03.html, the <table> element not only carries the width but also the align attribute to make sure that the table appears in the center of the page. While these attributes are deprecated, they are often used on tables that are used for layout.

This page contains some sample text and a background color for the body to illustrate the point better:

```
<body>
  <table width="700" align="center">
    <tr>
      <td>

      <!-- CONTENT OF PAGE GOES HERE -->

      </td>
    </tr>
  </table>
</body>
```

Note that fixed-width designs that use pixels look smaller on higher-resolution monitors because when the same size monitor is set with a higher resolution more pixels are visible on the screen.

When you are using tables with dimensions given in pixels, you are confining the use of the site to a browser on a desktop computer. It will not be accessible to those with smaller-screened devices such as PDAs or mobile phones, and it probably will not work on TV set top boxes because TVs have lower resolutions than computer screens (320 × 240 in the U.S. if you're curious).

Rather than using a table to contain the page, you can use a <div> element to contain the elements that make up the content of the page and then use CSS to control the width of the page (just like the example of using CSS that you saw in the previous section). The <div> element need only carry the id or class attribute to identify it. Then you can attach rules to that element, like this one associated with the <div> element whose id attribute has a value of page (ch11_eg04.css):

```
div#page {
  width:700px;
  background-color:#ffffff;
  border-style:solid; border-width:1px; border-color:#666666;
  padding:20px;
  font-size:12px; }
```

You can see the result in Figure 11-8; even if you increase or decrease the size of the browser window, the width of the site does not increase or decrease.

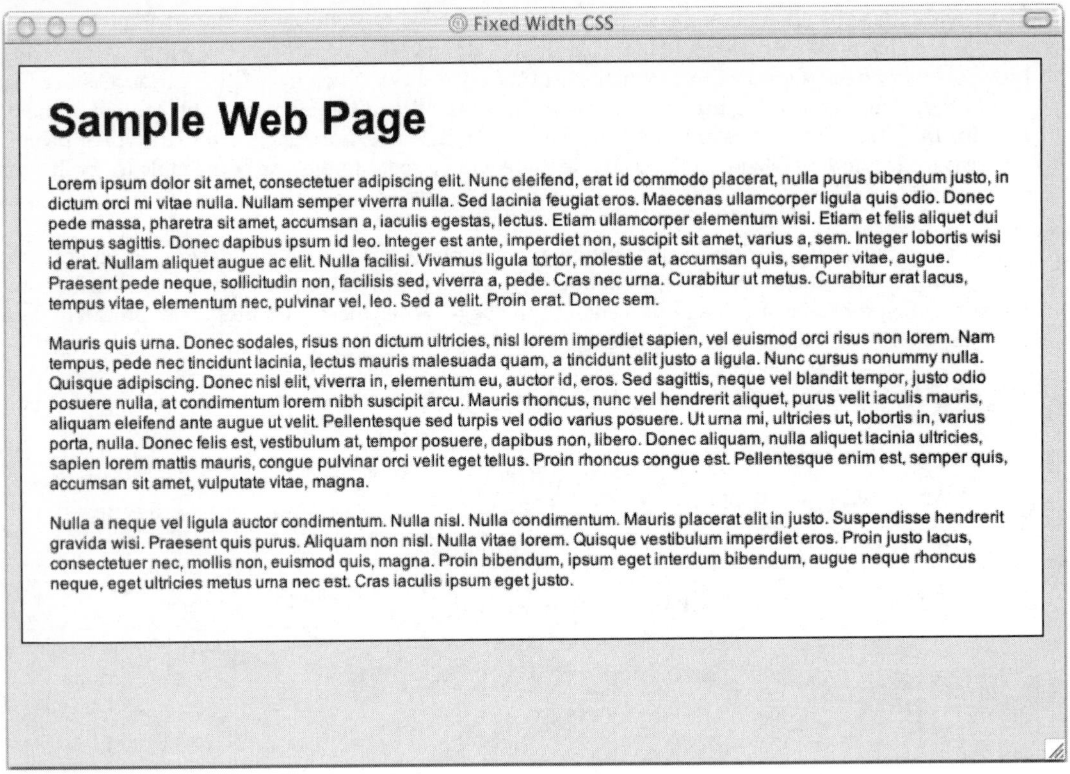

Figure 11-8

As with the liquid design, there are both advantages and disadvantages to the fixed-width page approach.

The advantages are as follows:

❑ Pixel values are accurate at controlling width and positioning of elements.

❑ The designer has far greater control over the appearance and position of items on the page.

❑ The size of an image will always remain the same relative to the page.

❑ You can control the lengths of lines of text regardless of the size of the user's window.

The disadvantages are as follows:

❑ Your code can end up with lots of nested tables, which makes it complicated to see the content in between the table's tags; therefore it is easy to break the page when you are editing it.

❑ If a user has font sizes set to a larger value, the text might not fit as intended in the table.

❑ If the user browses at higher resolution than it was designed, the page can look smaller on their screen and can therefore be hard to read.

❑ The design works only on devices that have similar size and resolution of screens as desktop computers (likely ruling out use of the page by mobile phones or PDAs, for example).

❑ You can have a page sitting in the middle of a window with big gaps around it.

Mixed Design

A mixed design combines fixed and liquid designs; part of the page will stretch, while the other part of the page remains a fixed width. This helps prevent large gaps around the edge of a page, but fixes the size of some of the elements.

One approach to the mixed design is to make just the heading of a page stretch across the whole page, while the main body of the page stays the same size.

This approach requires two `<table>` or `<div>` elements. The first is the header that takes up 100 percent of the width of the page, while the second is a fixed width, as you can see here in `ch11_eg05.html`:

```
<body>
  <table width="100%">
    <tr>
      <td>
        <h1>Branding and Masthead</h1>
      </td>
    </tr>
  </table>

  <br />
  <table width="700" align="center">
    <tr>
      <td>
      <!-- MAIN PAGE CONTENT GOES HERE -->
      </td>
    <tr>
  </table>
</body>
```

You will also find that many sites add a table into the first table (representing the heading of the page) in order to make it the same width as the main page. Any text, logo, or branding will be placed in this nested table that is set to the same width as the page, while the table that stretches the full width of the page contains a background image or color that matches the header and can stretch across the full width of the page.

You can see what this example looks like in Figure 11-9.

The advantages are as follows:

❑   You can control the size of the parts of pages that you want.

❑   You do not get large amounts of whitespace all around a page.

The disadvantages are as follows:

❑   You can end up with part of the page looking out of proportion to another part of the page.

❑   You can have a lot of `<table>` or `<div>` elements.

Now that you've seen how to control the size of a page, you should look at designing the content of the pages.

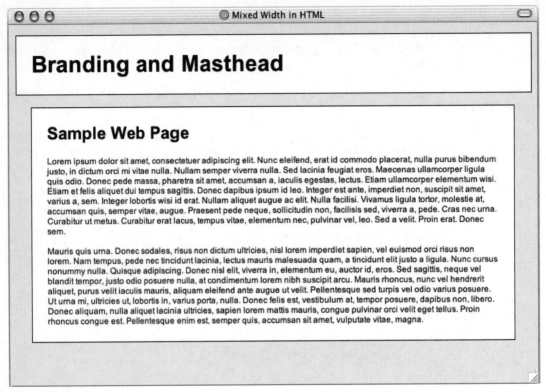

Figure 11-9

Designing Pages

By now you should know how many pages you have, which pages link to which other pages, what the main elements of each page are (elements here means items on the page such as navigation, branding, articles/products, and so on, rather than the individual markup elements), and whether your page will be a fixed size or whether it will stretch. Now it's time to work out how the content is going to fit onto the page, which elements should be grouped together, and where they should be positioned on the page. All of this should happen before you start building your page.

Before you even start to design a site, however, it can often help to ask your client what their favorite Web sites are and what they like about each of these sites. This will give you an idea of their tastes and what they find attractive.

Sketching the Placement of Elements

Now it's time to start getting a feel for the way this information will work on a page, and where each of the elements should go on a page. At this point you should just be using text and lines to sketch out where each element (such as the heading or link) goes on the page and how much space it gets; you should not be thinking about colors, fonts, backgrounds, images, or other design issues yet.

While it might seem strange (and difficult at first) not to add visual presentation at this stage, it is important that you just focus on making sure you include every item the user can interact with and give it the necessary space. This process is sometimes referred to as *wireframing*.

Once you have created a wireframe model, you can then go back to the list of target visitors you expect to visit your site and make sure that they can easily find what you think they will come to the site for. You can see from this simple model where the links go, and you get a good idea of the functionality of the site without getting distracted by the issues surrounding the look of the page. This is particularly important for two reasons:

❑   When you show users and clients a prototype of the fully designed site, they tend to focus on the visual elements rather than the proposed function. So, a skeletal model ensures that the client focuses on the function and structure of the content and not its appearance.

❑   If you do need to make changes, you can do so before the design or programming starts, which can save you from rewriting and/or redesigning much of the site later on.

An important point at this stage in the process is deciding which of these elements is most important and should go at the top of the pages. Chances are that not all of the content of your pages will fit onto the screen at once—or at least not on all resolutions.

Assuming that for the longer pages users will have to scroll vertically, you will want to make sure that the most important elements are at the top of the page.

The general rule is that the most used functions should always take priority on a site, rather than what the marketing department wants to push this week or month. It all comes back to designing your site with your visitors in mind. If you do not keep the visitors happy, they will not make your site a success.

Generally speaking, you want the following items to be visible as the page loads:

❑   Branding.

❑   Global navigation (a link to the home page and the main sections of the site—note that the Home page should almost always be the first item of navigation).

❑   Subsection navigation (if you are in one of the subsections of the site, the subsection navigation should contain links to the sections within that section).

❑   Page heading.

❑   Enough of the content that users can tell what the page is about.

❑   Search.

❑   Promotions/Advertising (self or others).

When you have both global and local navigation on the screen, the whole of the menu does not need to fit onto the screen when it loads, but it helps if there is enough for the user to see that there are other options.

The items that do not need to appear on the portion of the page that is visible when the page loads are as follows:

❑   The rest of the content of the page (information about a product/service/article or whatever the main point of the page is)

❑ Links to related information or other sites (things that are not essential to the use of this site)

❑ Advertising

❑ Bottom navigation—Copyright, Terms and Conditions, Privacy Policy (these are things that are generally required, but rarely used, and can therefore go at the bottom of the page)

❑ Text version of navigation

It is also helpful to know that users (except in cases where the user's language is a right-to-left language, such as Arabic) tend to scan a page in the general order of a letter *z*, from top left to top right of a page, and then down to bottom left and across to bottom right, as you can see in Figure 11-10.

Figure 11-10

This means that putting your primary navigation at the top right of a page may not be the best place; sometimes under the logo is better. (Again, languages such as Arabic and Hebrew might be better off starting from the top right.) Figure 11-11 shows you an example of placing navigation at the top right of a page, where the user is not going to immediately see it as clearly as they would under the logo.

If you are designing a site for a company that is likely to want to change the main feature on a site regularly, you are best off creating a part of the page for the company to control. You may give a proportion of the home page (or home pages of the subcategories) to them for regularly changing features. For example, a shop might change the main section of a page every time there is an upcoming

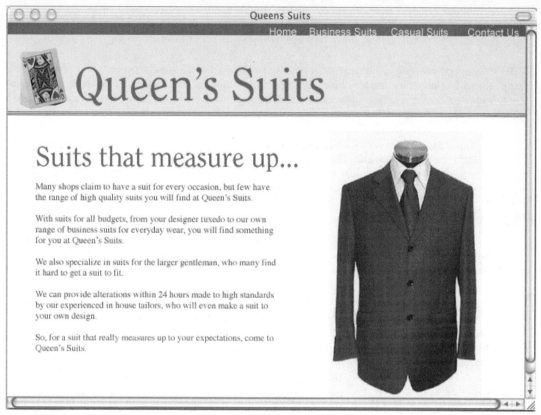

Figure 11-11

occasion it wants to market such as religious holidays, New Year's, Valentine's Day, Mother's Day, Father's Day, start of school terms, and so on.

As you will see in the section "Structuring Pages" later in this chapter, there are two models you can use for laying out content within a page—either a grid model if you are going to use tables or a box model if you use CSS. Once you have looked at the options for positioning content in that section, you will be able to plan and sketch the layout of your document better.

Introducing the Style

Now that you have an idea of what the site looks like in terms of text and simple lines you can start adding the style or character of the page—playing with colors and fonts, backgrounds and images—and create a page that is visually appealing.

Now that you know where each of the elements should appear on the page this can be a much easier task.

If you decide to use a designer to design the site, some designers will have serious problems with being forced to design a site where all of the elements have already been placed on the page and being told the rough amount of space those element can take up. It's like asking them to color in a picture rather than draw the picture. So, you may well ask the designer to do the wireframe as well, although a designer may also find this difficult, as it requires a very different approach than what most designers are used to.

The size and positioning of elements on a page is a valid part of the design process (not only the visual appearance but also the interface or interaction design—how the site handles). However, the process of wireframing a design will help the user or client focus on what their site actually does and will help you finalize the functionality before starting to design the page.

If you use a designer to work on Web pages you will often have to strike a balance and sometimes allow the designer to completely reposition the elements that you have already positioned on each page and change the amount of space for items. Just make sure that the necessary items fit in the part of the page that is viewable when the page loads. You will most likely find your own balance as you work on a few sites.

What Is Already Done for You?

As with any form of marketing, creating an easily identifiable style will help re-enforce a brand. If a company has a logo, you should use that logo, if they have company colors you should feature those colors in the site's color scheme. Otherwise, it is up to you to design something that is visually attractive.

> **Unless a client specifically asks you to redesign the company logo you should avoid doing so because it is part of the brand they have built up, and it probably appears on things such as stationery and signs for the company.**

You should ask your client if they have a digital copy of their logo (rather than scanning it in from a brochure). If they have had an ad or leaflet in print, either the client or the people who designed it should have an electronic version you can use.

I have worked in the past with clients that have terrible logos that really bring down the look of the site, yet they are unwilling to change them. If you are unfortunate enough to come across such a logo, you are best off keeping the actual size of the logo relatively small; then you can rely on the company's colors to maintain the identity, and sometimes even re-write the company name in a plain font.

You should also ask the company for any materials they are supposed to provide such as photographs of products or work done for previous customers, along with any text they are supposed to be supplying. If the client can supply good photographs for the site, it can make a site look a lot more professional.

Common Page Elements

In most cases, there should be some degree of consistency across all of the pages within a site that, like any form of branding, helps visitors identify the site from its look. The first step in designing your pages should therefore be to look at the elements that will appear on every page, and this will usually mean starting with the branding and the primary navigation.

The branding and primary navigation should be in the same place on every page. For example, if you decide to put your primary navigation under the logo stretching from left to right, it should be under the logo stretching from left to right on each page. You may then choose to place the subnavigation in a different part of the page, say down the left side, but when elements appear on more than one page, they should appear in the same place on each page so that the user can learn how to use the site more quickly.

Similarly, if your site dedicates a page to each product or service you offer, or each article or story you publish, then each of these pages should follow a consistent design. For example, if you are creating an online store, you will want the information for each product to be laid out in a similar way so that the information (such as the size or price of a product) is easy to find. Similarly, if you are doing an article/news-based site, the layout of articles is likely to be similar.

If the bottom of the page contains links to other pages such as the copyright, privacy policy, and terms and conditions pages, it should also look the same across the bottom of all pages.

You will often hear the terms *header* and *footer* used in relation to pages. The term "header" is generally used to describe the heading of any page on a site that tends to be consistent across the site and features the logo and often the primary navigation. The footer, meanwhile, is anything that appears on the bottom of every page. Between the header and the footer is the content or body of the page.

Images' Influence on Design

The use of images often has a strong influence on visitors' perceptions of a site. Great logos, graphics, and photographs can make the difference between an average site and a good site, while a bad logo or a poor photo on the front page can discourage a user from looking through the site no matter how good the content is.

Increasingly, sites are featuring high quality photographs shot especially for that company, and often these are not just photos of products; they are images that represent a lifestyle or image the company is trying to associate with the brand. These images may tie in with (or be taken from) other marketing efforts from a company.

The quality of photographs often depends on the budget for the site. If your client has photos taken by a professional for its marketing material, you should consider using these. Or if the client's budget is large enough, you can hire a photographer to take appropriate shots. It is actually quite hard to find examples of sites for multinational companies and popular brands that do not contain impressive graphics.

While a lot of free clip art is on the Web, this tends to look quite amateurish. It's fine for a hobby site, but not ideal for a company Web site.

You can use a number of stock photo sites to obtain images rather than hiring a photographer, but be warned that you usually need to pay to use the images, and the fees can be quite expensive. Some examples of stock photography sites are http://www.gettyimages.com and http://www.corbis.com. Two sites that (at the time of writing) were offering photos you could use freely were http://www.istockphoto.com and http://www.stockxchng.com, although the quality of the free images is generally not as high as those of the paid-for site.

> You should always make sure that you have the necessary copyright to use an image. If you do not you could end up with either a court case, a heavy fine, or at the very least a letter telling you to remove the image, which would require you to redesign the site and explain your mistake to the client.

Grouping Elements

You can use the following methods to make it clear to a user that several elements of a page are related; for example, you might want to group together links for new products, the elements of a registration form, or summary details for a product:

❑ **Location:** Making sure that similar elements of the design are near to each other

❑ **Color:** Using both foreground and blocks of background colors can make it clear which items relate to each other

❑ **Borders and padding:** Creating a gap between one group of elements and other items on the page to indicate which are grouped together

❑ **Styles:** Such as using similar buttons for navigation items

Figures 11-2, 11-3, and 11-4, which show the fictional news site near the beginning of the chapter, illustrate the use of buttons that are close together forming the navigation bar for the site. All these buttons follow a similar style. The navigation, header, and footer also use background colors to group their respective information together. There are gaps in the main page between each of the articles that make it clear which text belongs to which picture and a border around the edge of the whole page to group that information together.

Navigation

Placement of your navigation is likely to be one of the early decisions you make when working with any design.

How you design your navigation will largely depend on how many items you need to have in that menu. You should already have a good idea of the structure of the site, and you should have created a navigation hierarchy when you created the site map—remember that you should ideally be looking to fit your site into a maximum of about seven sections. You should certainly avoid having more than ten primary links on the page.

In the subsections of the site you can have more than seven subheadings and links, and the sub-navigation or secondary navigation sometimes appears in a different position on the page than the primary navigation.

Top Navigation

Placing navigation directly under a header is a very popular option. This is usually either aligned to the left side of the page or to the center of the page.

Apple and Amazon.com are examples of sites that use top navigation in the center of the page. The secondary navigation is then left underneath this. Figure 11-12 gives you an example of navigation at the top of the page.

Left Navigation

Placing your navigation bar on the left is also a very common option. Some sites place all of their navigation on the left side of the page, as you can see in Figure 11-13.

Figure 11-12

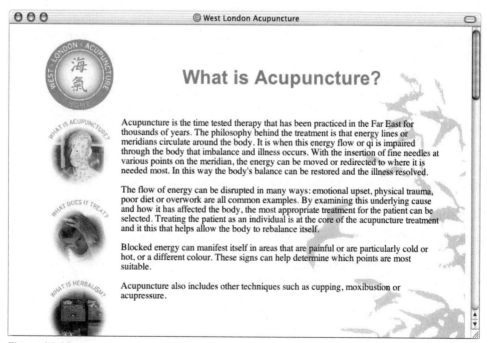

Figure 11-13

Other sites keep primary navigation at the top and then place secondary navigation on the left side of the page, as you can see in Figure 11-14.

Figure 11-14

Bottom Navigation

You should generally avoid putting your primary navigation links at the bottom of the page because you can't guarantee that they will be in view when the page loads without using either frames (which complicate the writing of pages—I recommend you use frames only if the content really requires them) or by using CSS positioning properties that are supported only in the very latest browsers.

It is common, however, to place links of lower importance at the bottom of the page—for example, links to a copyright statement, privacy policy, and terms and conditions. These are items that you might want to appear on every page, but which you do not want to take up valuable space on the screen when the page first loads.

You will also find that some sites place a text-only version of a navigation bar at the bottom of the page if the main navigation bar is created using complicated images (and things such as rollover images). This is done to help those using screen readers access the links faster and more easily.

Right Navigation

It is rare that you will see a site with a right side navigation bar, although it is not unheard of. The disadvantage of putting your primary links on the right side of a page is that users with a narrow browser window might not see the link when they load the site; it's not as likely to be on immediate display as a left side navigation bar or top navigation.

Sometimes right-hand columns are used for additional content and links to other parts of the site that are not vital to a user's navigation. For example, an e-commerce store might have a right column containing a set of links to related products or the latest items added to the store; these are added features for the users of the site that are not essential to navigation.

Home Pages

First impressions do count, so your front page is very important. Unless you are working on a site for a company or subject that is a household name, it's important that a visitor should be able to ascertain the main purpose of your site easily from the front page.

> I've said this before, but it's crucial to remember that your front page should not only cover what a company's marketing department wants it to cover that week or month—it's not just some advertising billboard they can use as they fancy—it must also address the needs of the majority of visitors to the site. For example, the marketing department may want to push a new product, whereas most customers visiting the site want to find out about an older, more established one. If those users cannot find the information they came to the site looking for, the marketing department will not have as large an audience for the things they want to push. Balancing what the users and what the company wants is extremely important—and users should take priority.

Over the life of the Web, several types of front door pages have contained logos, animations, and so on. They are seen before the user actually gets to see the real home page of the site. You should generally avoid these types of pages and let the user get straight to what they came for. While some sites have very impressive animations written in Macromedia Flash, most visitors want to see this animation only once, if that; after the first time it gets in the way of their access to the real content of the site. Meanwhile, other visitors simply will not wait to download an animation and will be on their way to another site before even entering yours. One exception to this rule is if you have adult content—in which case you might need a page before the content for users to indicate their age and in some cases a verification check.

Content Pages

Content pages are the meat of most sites; for example, on news sites they can contain articles and on e-commerce sites they contain details of a product. A content page should display the content in a way that makes it easy for the user to read the information.

As mentioned earlier, if you have several products or services, the information that you offer should be consistent for each item. If you are dealing with clothes, a visitor should quickly and easily be able to tell the color and sizes a garment is available in. For food, the flavors, food ingredients, health information, and serving sizes should be found in the same place on each page.

You should not make a page too busy; a clean presentation allows users to focus on the content. Even if you have a lot of information to fit on a page, make sure there is plenty of space between different elements.

Images should be relevant to the product, service, or topic in question and will usually look better if they are left- or right-aligned with the text flowing around them. There should also be a gap between any images and the text that flows around them (set using either the padding or margin properties in CSS).

You should also avoid filling any commercial site with clip art and animated gifs, although you may use them on a personal site if you want to. While that dancing cat might appear very cute at first, if it has nothing to do with the topic you are trying to get across to the users it will only distract them from the real content.

If you are dealing with products a company sells, these pages need to be action-oriented—for example, they must allow you to locate or select an item, find the information you want about it, and then, most likely, allow you to buy it.

When you have to present large amounts of text, make sure that your text does not spread too widely across the page. Many people have difficulty reading wide lines of text on computer screens; therefore, specifying a physical rather than percentage width of a page will make text more readable.

A lot of companies think that simply advertising their product or service on the Web will get them new business and that customers will contact them if they want a price. They seem to think that speaking to the person will make it easier to close a sale. In my experience, sites have gained more inquiries once they have added a price to the site. (If the price of every product/service you offer varies it is good practice to offer sample prices of work you have done.) Remember, getting an e-mail inquiry for a price will not make it easier to close the deal (unless the user provides telephone or land-mail contact details), as the customer is still anonymous to you.

Structuring Pages

You have already seen how to control the size of a page and how you design Web pages. Now you have to translate these designs into code.

If you want anything other than the normal flow of elements down a page where each element just appears in the order it was written, you are going to either have to look at positioning elements on a page using either tables or CSS. One of the most common effects designers want to create is a layout that has more than one column—for example, a narrow column for the navigation on the left followed by a second column that contains the main content of the page (and then sometimes more than one column to the right).

How you approach the layout of your pages will largely depend upon whether you are using tables or CSS to position elements. If you use tables to position elements on a page you need to think in terms of grids—rows and columns. For example, Figure 11-15 shows you how a page can be divided into rows and columns (the thick black lines separate rows and columns).

These rows and columns may be of different heights and widths, but there is a grid there nevertheless. You can even nest tables to create complex layouts where some elements are positioned within a table cell.

Tables enable the designer to control the layout of a page with pixel accuracy, but they also have the restriction that the design will work only on screens that are a similar size and resolution.

If you think of designing in CSS, however, you must think in terms of boxes, which are positioned according to one of the positioning schemes you met in the last chapter. Normal flow is how the page would be laid out without CSS positioning, but you can change the position of any box in relation to its containing box using relative and fixed positioning.

When you work with CSS for layouts you must remember that this is a very different approach than using tables because the properties of each box can be different and are affected less by the grid structure of a table. Figure 11-16 demonstrates a page layout that uses CSS.

Unfortunately, because of the poor support for some key features of CSS in recent browsers (in particular IE) few sites are designed using CSS positioning. But before you ignore CSS positioning and get to work

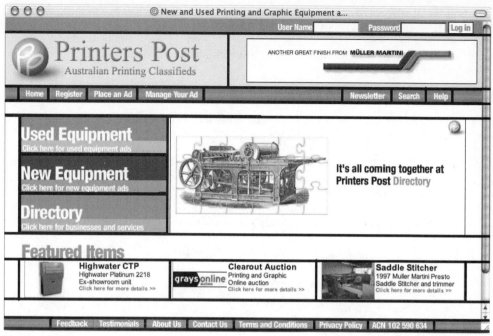

Figure 11-15

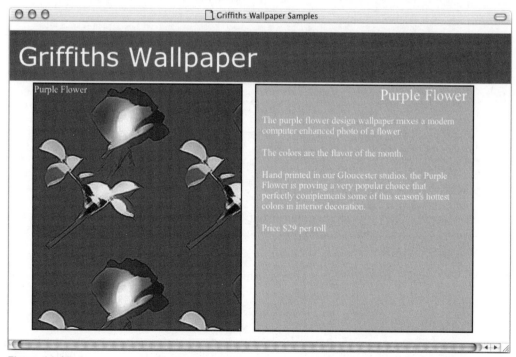

Figure 11-16

on layouts that use tables (because they work in most of the browsers that access the Web today), let's take look at some examples of both table and CSS positioning.

In the following sections you will learn how to create multicolumn layouts.

Single-Column Layouts

The single-column layout is one of the easiest and is often ideal for smaller sites. Single-column sites tend to have three or four rows.

If you look at Figure 11-17 you can see how the outline for this site is based on a fixed-width table with one column and three rows. Looking at the rows in turn, the first contains the logo or branding, the second contains the navigation, and the third contains the content. Each of these rows has a different background color to help you distinguish them. (If there is a fourth row, it tends to contain a copyright notice, links to terms and conditions or privacy policy and other required links that few users will use.)

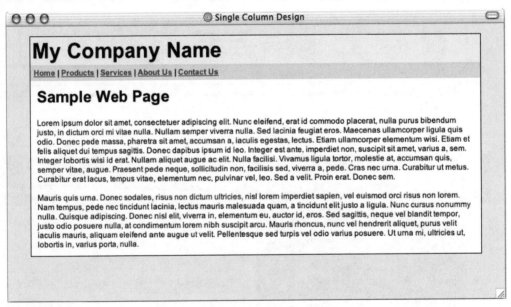

Figure 11-17

Remember that on this kind of site you should control the width of the text. If the width of this table had not been fixed and were allowed to stretch across the full width of the browser, you could end up with some very long lines of text.

Here you can see the code that generates this structure (ch11_eg06.html):

```
<body>
  <table width="700" align="center" cellpadding="0" cellspacing="0">

    <tr>
      <td class="header">
      <!-- heading goes here -->
```

```
        </td>
      </tr>

      <tr>
        <td class="nav">
        <!-- navigation goes here -->
        </td>
      </tr>

      <tr>
        <td class="content">
        <!-- content goes here -->
        </td>
      </tr>

    </table>
  </body>
```

Note the use of the `cellpadding` and `cellspacing` attributes on the `<table>` element. If these were not used, the table would end up looking like Figure 11-18.

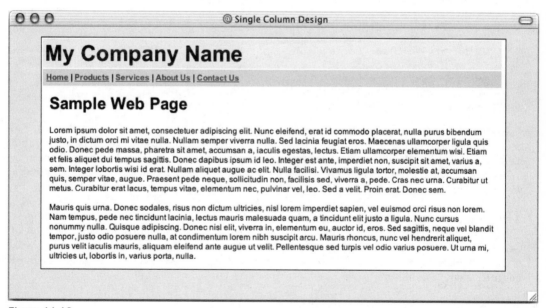

Figure 11-18

If you wanted to create something similar in CSS you could use separate `<div>` elements for each of the rows in the previous example. You would end up with an XHTML document that looked something like this (`ch11_eg07.html`):

```
  <body>
    <div class="page">
      <div class="header"><h1>My Company Name</h1></div>
```

```
        <div class="nav">
          <!-- MAIN PAGE CONTENT GOES HERE -->
        </div>

        <div class="content">
        <!-- MAIN PAGE CONTENT GOES HERE -->
        </div>

      </div>
    </body>
```

It starts to get interesting when you put this into CSS. In theory you should be able to use a style sheet like this one. The main point to note here is that a `width` property has been set for the `page` class, along with `margin-left` and `margin-right` properties.

```
body {background-color:#efefef;
    font-family:arial, verdana, sans-serif;}

.page {
    width:700px;
    margin-left:auto;
    margin-right:auto;
    font-size:12px;
    background-color:#ffffff;
    border-style:solid; border-width:1px; border-color:#666666;}

.header {background-color:#f3f3f3; padding:3px;}
.nav {font-weight:bold; background-color:#e3e3e3; padding:5px;}
.content {padding:10px;}
```

According to the CSS recommendation, any block level element (in this case the <div> element) that has equal margins on both the left and right sides should be displayed in the center of the page. As you might have guessed by the "should" in that last sentence, this does not work in many browsers. It doesn't work in IE except in IE 6 on Windows (and only then if the document has a recent DOCTYPE declaration), and it works only in Netscape version 6 and later.

A simple trick, however, can help you get around this problem by adding two `text-align` properties. The first is added to the containing element (in this case the <body> element) and is given a value of `center` to center the elements inside it, and then the <div> element whose `class` element has a value of `left` to prevent the text inside that element from being centered is added. The result is something like this (`ch11_eg07.css`):

```
body {background-color:#efefef;
    font-family:arial, verdana, sans-serif;
    text-align:center;}
.page {
    margin-left:auto;
    margin-right:auto;
    text-align:left;
    width:700px;
    font-size:12px;
    background-color:#ffffff;
    border-style:solid; border-width:1px; border-color:#666666;}
```

```
.header {background-color:#f3f3f3; padding:3px;}
.nav {font-weight:bold; background-color:#e3e3e3; padding:5px;}
.content {padding:10px;}
```

The fact that you need little "hacks" like this one to get the page to display correctly has held back the adoption of CSS as a presentation format.

Two-Column Layouts

Two-column layouts tend to be used where one column contains navigation and the other contains the main content of the page. In these designs the page will still usually have a heading that spans both of the columns. More often than not it is the column on the left that contains the navigation, while the right column holds the content.

You can see an example of a two-column layout in Figure 11-19.

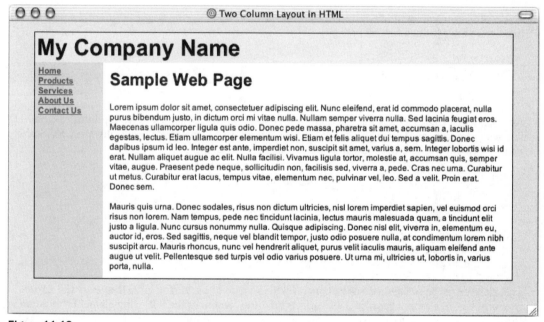

Figure 11-19

Here you can see the XHTML for this page (ch11_eg08.html):

```
<body>
  <table width="700" align="center" cellpadding="0" cellspacing="0">
    <tr>
      <td class="header" colspan="2">
        <!-- heading goes here -->
      </td>
    </tr>
    <tr>
```

```
        <td class="nav" valign="top" width="100">
        <!-- navigation goes here -->
        </td>
        <td class="content" valign="top">
        <!-- content goes here -->
        </td>
      </tr>
    </table>
</body>
```

Note the `valign="top"` attribute on the columns containing the navigation and the main content. This is there because, by default, content is vertically centered. If the one column contained less information than the other (which is most likely) then it would not necessarily appear in view when the page loads and generally would not look as attractive.

You should also note how the width of the navigation column has been set in the table. This makes the navigation column a fixed width.

You could easily adjust the design so that it stretches and takes up the whole width of the page (simply make the width of the table 100 percent):

```
<body>
  <table width="100%" align="center" cellpadding="0" cellspacing="0">
    <tr>
```

Again, when it comes to creating a similar design in CSS, you face some interesting hurdles. The XHTML is exactly the same as it was in ch11_eg08.html, but the CSS changes. Specifically, the CSS for the `<div>` element whose `class` attribute had a value of nav changes:

```
.nav {
   float:left;
   width:100px;
   height:30em;
   font-weight:bold;
   background-color:#e3e3e3;
   padding:5px; }
```

This element needs to have a `float` property with a value of `left`. You have to specify the `float` property on this element because it also affects how the content of the following element should be rendered. Also, whenever you specify a `float` property you should also specify a width for that block; otherwise it takes up the full width of its containing block.

The most interesting property in this rule is the `height` property. If this were not here, the navigation would not take up a whole column—rather it would just take up the height of the links and then the content would wrap underneath it.

Unfortunately, you cannot give the `height` property a value of `100%` to indicate that it should take up 100 percent of the height of the containing element. Rather, you have to give it a fixed value. In this case the value is `30em` (which is relative to the size of the font). When you specify a value like this, you should also specify it for the containing element. Otherwise you can end up with the navigation bar overlapping the rest of the page.

This also means that if the content of the page is shorter than the side bar, it will have a lot of whitespace beneath it, or, if it's longer than the length of the page it will not all fit into the containing element (which might result in it overlapping the containing element, depending upon the behavior of the browser).

Three-Column Layouts

Three-column layouts tend to have navigation on the left, the main content in the center, and then additional content such as related links, further items of interest, advertisements, and so on in the right column. You can see an example of a three-column layout in Figure 11-20.

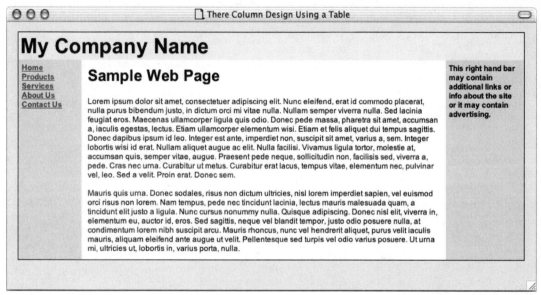

Figure 11-20

The following example shows you how to create this layout in XHTML using a table with three columns, each of which is a fixed width (ch11_eg10.html):

```
<body>
  <table width="700" align="center" cellpadding="0" cellspacing="0">
    <tr>
      <td class="header" colspan="2">
      <!-- heading goes here -->
      </td>
    </tr>
    <tr>
      <td class="nav" valign="top" width="100">
      <!-- navigation goes here -->
      </td>
      <td class="content" valign="top" >
      <!-- content goes here -->
      </td>
      <td class="right" valign="top" >
```

```
    <!-- right hand column content goes here -->
      </td>
    </tr>
  </table>
</body>
```

Again, the valign attribute is used on the cells to make sure that their content sits at the top of the cell rather than being vertically aligned in the center of the page as would be the default; after all, it's very unlikely that each would be the same length.

If you wanted to re-create this design in CSS, you could easily do so with absolute positioning—but be aware that versions of IE before version 6 will have problems with pixel-perfect positioning and can be off by three pixels. While some people get around this problem using floats, as you saw in the last chapter, floats restrict the order in which the content can appear.

First, here is the XHTML structure for this example (ch11_eg11.html). Note how the <body> element carries leftmargin and topmargin attributes:

```
<body leftmargin="0" topmargin="0">
  <div class="header">
    <!-- heading goes here -->
  </div>
  <div class="nav">
    <!-- navigation goes here -->
  </div>
  <div class="content">
    <!-- content goes here -->
  </div>
  <div class="right">
    <!-- third column content goes here -->
  </div>
</body>
```

The trick with the layout this time is to first position the heading using absolute positioning and then to position the left and right columns underneath either side of the browser. First, here are the rules for the body and the header. As you can see, the header is positioned absolutely at the top left of the page and is supposed to take up 100 percent of the width of the page. In addition it should be 60 pixels high.

```
body {
  background-color:#efefef;
  font-family:arial, verdana, sans-serif;}

.header {
  position:absolute;
  top:0px; left:0px;
  width:100%;
  background-color:#f3f3f3;
  height:60px;}
```

Next, here are the left and right columns. Each of these is absolutely positioned 60 pixels from the top, and both are positioned next to the edge of the page—the navigation is to the left and the extra column to the right (the navigation box also specifies a height):

```
.nav {
  position:absolute;
  left:0px; top:60px;
  width:100px;
  font-weight:bold;
  background-color:#e3e3e3;
  padding:5px;
  height:30em;}

.right {
  position:absolute;
  right:0px; top:60px;
  font-weight:bold;
  background-color:#e3e3e3;
  padding:5px;
  width:100px;}
```

Now you can see how the center content box stretches to fit the rest of the page because its margins to the left and the right are the width of the boxes to the left and the right.

```
.content {
  padding-top:40px;
  margin-left: 208px;
  margin-right:208px;}
```

You can see the result in Figure 11-21.

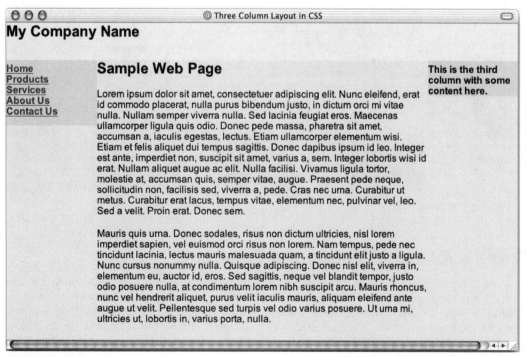

Figure 11-21

Sacrificial Columns

An increasing number of sites that use fixed-width tables aligned to the left side of the page are adding extra columns to the right for those with higher resolution monitors and wider windows. The extra column always goes on the right, and is known as a *sacrificial column* because its content is not vital to the readers' understanding of the site. (It is content that can be sacrificed.) Only those users whose browsers and screens are wide enough to see the entire page see the extra column. Other users could scroll to see the sacrificial column, but the page design tends to make it clear that you are seeing all of the main content of the page.

If a user's browser does not show the sacrificial column within the width of the window, the user should not lose any meaning from the page and its main content should be no harder to comprehend, although the user may miss out on extra information or advertising that is off-screen.

Figure 11-22 shows an example of a design using a sacrificial column.

Figure 11-22

Fixing a Minimum Width of a Column

If you are creating a liquid layout, you might want to specify a minimum width for a column of a table so that if a user shrinks down her browser window very small the page doesn't shrink below a certain sensible width. To do this you can use a single-pixel transparent GIF image in each column you want to set the minimum width for; you then set the width property of the <img> element to be the minimum width you want the column to be. Because the image is transparent, the user cannot see it, but the column containing the image will be at least the width of the GIF image, whose width property specifies it should be 400 pixels wide; therefore the column will be at least this wide.

In the following example you can see that the table is supposed to take up only 50 percent of the browser window. But, as you make the window smaller, the table should remain 440 pixels wide (400 pixels for the image and 20 pixels of padding to the left and right):

```
<body>
  <table width="50%" align="center">
    <tr>
      <td>

        <img src="images/1px.gif" width="400" height="1" alt="" />

        <!-- CONTENT OF PAGE GOES HERE -->

      </td>
    </tr>
  </table>
</body>
```

You can also use a single pixel that is the same color as the background, but the idea of the transparent single-pixel GIF is that it will work on any background. You can find a single-pixel transparent GIF called 1px.gif in the images folder of the download code for this chapter.

Of course, if your table contained an image that was already wider than the specified image, the minimum width of the table would be the width of that image.

Nesting Tables Inside Tables

In addition to using tables for columns in a page, nested tables are often used to create far more complex layouts; for example, it is not uncommon to use a separate table for laying out navigation elements. In the following example you can see how nested tables create a far more complex layout. This page will take up the whole of the browser window and the header and footer will be made to look like they stretch to take up the whole screen, while the real content lives in nested tables that are a fixed width of only 700 pixels wide. You can see the page in Figure 11-23.

One table holds the whole of this page: the header is in one row of this table, the main content of the page in the second, and the footer in the third. In each row are nested tables that contain the header in the first row, the main content in the second, and the footer in the third.

The use of nested tables allows the page to look like it stretches across the whole browser window, but at the same time allows you to control the width of the content itself. The background color of the top and the bottom of the page can stretch the width of the browser, while the text and images live in the nested tables that can have a fixed width.

In this design the outermost table stretches the full width and height of the browser window; within this table the first row contains the header, the second the main content, and the third the footer. Inside these rows are nested tables with fixed widths that ensure the content of the page remains the same width.

Here is the XHTML for this page (ch11_eg12.html). Note how the opening <body> tag carries the proprietary IE leftmargin and topmargin attributes; IE will otherwise leave a blank margin around the whole page. Luckily Netscape will simply ignore these attributes.

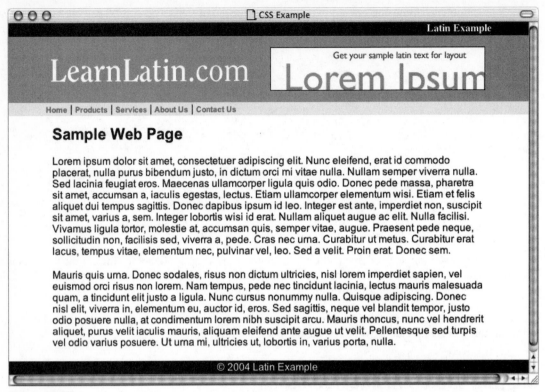

Figure 11-23

```
<html xmlns="http://www.w3.org/1999/xhtml" lang="en" xml:lang="en">
<head>
  <title>Nested Tables</title> <link rel="stylesheet" type="text/css"
href="ch11_eg12.css" />
</head>
<body leftmargin="0" topmargin="0">
```

The first table is the outermost table that will contain the whole page and make sure that it stretches the full height and width of the browser window (note that the `height` attribute is an extension to the XHTML recommendation supported by both IE 4 and later and Netscape 3 and later):

```
<table width="100%" height="100%" border="0" cellpadding="0" cellspacing="0">
  <tr valign="top"><td valign="top">
```

Inside the first row you find another table that holds the heading for the page. This nested table in this first row is slightly different than the other two rows (which hold the main content and the footer) because the header actually features three shades within the three separate rows that make up the header:

- ❑   The first is black and says "Latin Example" to the right

- ❑   The second is mid gray and contains the logo and a banner ad

- ❑   The third is light gray and contains the navigation bar

So the header lives in a nested table that also contains three rows and stretches the full width of the browser. Each row has a different class that corresponds with a CSS rule to indicate the appropriate background color. The content of these rows, however, stays the same width: 700 pixels. That is because the real content is in another nested table with a fixed-width table.

```
<table width="100%" border="0" cellpadding="0" cellspacing="0">
  <tr class="topBar">
    <td height="20">
      <table width="700" border="0" align="center" cellpadding="0"
             cellspacing="0">
        <tr>
          <td class="TM">Latin Example</td>
        </tr>
      </table>
    </td>
  </tr>


  <tr>
    <td height="100" class="masthead">
      <table width="700" border="0" align="center" cellpadding="0"
             cellspacing="0">
        <tr>
          <td>LOGO</td>
          <td>banner ad</td>
        </tr>
      </table>
    </td>
  </tr>


  <tr>
    <td height="20" class="nav">
      <table width="700" border="0" align="center" cellpadding="0"
             cellspacing="0" class="nav">
        <tr>
          <td><a href="">Home</a> | <a href="">Products</a> |
              <a href="">Services</a> | <a href="">About Us</a> |
              <a href="">Contact Us</a> </td>
        </tr>
      </table>
    </td>
  </tr>
</table>
</td></tr>
```

This is the end of the header and the end of the first row of the table that contains the whole page.

In the next row is another nested table that holds the main content of the page.

```
<tr valign="middle"><td valign="middle">
  <table width="700" border="0" align="center" cellpadding="0"
  cellspacing="10">
   <tr>
     <td valign="top" width="100%">
```

```
        <h2>Sample Web Page</h2>
        <p><!-- Latin text goes here --></p>
      </td>
    </tr>
  </table>
</td></tr>
```

In the final row you get the footer of the page, which looks like it stretches across the whole page just like the header did. This effect is created by giving the whole row the same background color and then nesting a table inside this row with a fixed width that contains the footer:

```
<tr valign="bottom" class="footer">
  <td valign="bottom">
    <table width="700" border="0" align="center" cellpadding="0"
    cellspacing="0">
      <tr>
        <td height="20" class="footer">&copy; 2004 Latin Example</td>
      </tr>
    </table>
  </td>
</tr>
</table>
</body>
</html>
```

You must remember when working with tables that a cell must wholly contain any other element—elements are not allowed to straddle two table cells.

Rethinking Design for CSS

While CSS is very popular in styling content of elements—with properties that affect fonts, colors, and padding commonly used on Web sites—CSS positioning is a long way behind, primarily because browsers have poor support for CSS positioning.

You have seen a few of the smaller issues with CSS positioning in the previous section, and indeed more were encountered in Chapter 10. When you consider these difficulties and the issues regarding which browser supports which property, it's no wonder that tables are still widely used to position elements on a page.

I hope this situation changes as browsers develop because using CSS to position elements is the final step in removing styling from presentation.

Throughout this book I have been extolling the virtues of keeping presentational rules out of the XHTML documents. But when it comes to positioning elements on a page, tables are still the easiest way to get results in all but the latest of browsers—and few people can expect all of their visitors to have the latest browsers.

The idea of using tables for page layout may seem to negate the benefits of separating style from content, and you may be tempted to use lots of the other deprecated elements and attributes and write only Transitional XHTML documents. But getting into bad habits today will make it harder to change your ways tomorrow.

As more devices access the Web, the delivery of pages must change, too, and there is a lot of work going on to help make the Web accessible to lots of devices for many different purposes. Separating style from content is one of these issues, and being able to do so will make your skills more marketable in the long run.

As more and more browsers support the CSS model, more imaginative and complex layouts that use CSS will flourish. While we wait for the browsers to catch up with these standards, here are some sites that have been taking the lead in using and teaching how to use CSS for layouts:

❑   http://www.bluerobot.com/web/layouts/

❑   http://www.positioniseverything.net/

❑   http://www.meyerweb.com/eric/css/edge/

❑   http://www.alistapart.com/topics/css/

❑   http://www.thenoodleincident.com/tutorials/box_lesson/boxes.html

Before the end of the chapter, I want to leave you with one example of CSS positioning that it is not possible to recreate solely using HTML or XHTML. The following example has several elements that will come together as the page shrinks and then stretch out as the browser window increases. This may sound like a liquid design written in a table, but there are some very different things about this design:

❑   The text flows neatly around the pull quote without gaps appearing as the page is resized. If this were in a table, the amount of text that could appear next to the pull quote would be fixed.

❑   The page elements overlap each other so that you can see how many pages there are for this article.

❑   Because the layout is done with CSS, the page could still be used with different types of browsers.

You can see this page in Figure 11-24.

You really need to try this one out with the code that you can download for this chapter to see how it stretches and shrinks, and you need to try it in Netscape 6 or later and IE 6. But even from this figure, you get a much better idea of how layout in CSS is a question of dealing with the position of boxes rather than the splitting up of a page into grids.

To see how this works, here is an XHTML page (ch11_eg13.html). Note how it uses <div> elements to mark the various sections of the page: the header, the different pages of the article (all of which you will be able to see on the screen as if laid out on a table), the navigation bar, and a footer that allows you to go to the next page of the article.

```
<html>
<head>
  <title>CSS Positioning</title>
  <link rel="stylesheet" type="text/css" href="ch11_eg13.css" />
</head>
<body>

<div class="header"><h1>CSS Demonstration</h1></div>

<div class="nav">
```

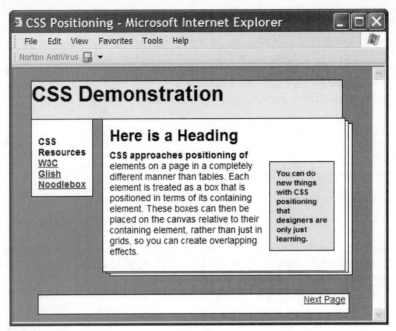

Figure 11-24

```
  CSS Resources<br>
  <a href="http://www.w3.org">W3C</a><br>
  <a href="http://www.glish.com">Glish</a><br>
  <a href="http://www.noodlebox.com">Noodlebox</a><br>
</div>

<div class="page">
  <h2>Here is a Heading</h2>

  <p class="Article"><span class="pullQuote">You can do new things with CSS
positioning that designers are only just learning.</span>CSS approaches
positioning of elements on a page in a completely different manner than
tables. Each element is treated a as box which is positioned in terms of its
containing element. These boxes can then be placed on the canvas relative to
their containing element, rather than just in grids, so you can create
overlapping effects.</p>
</div>

<div class="page2">This would be page 2</div>
<div class="page3">This would be page 3</div>

<div class="bottom"><a href="">Next Page</a></div>
</body>
</html>
```

Now, onto the style sheet (ch11_eg13.css) to see how the CSS positioning is really working. To start off, the <body> element has a background-color and font-family property set. These act as defaults for the whole document. The `<div>` element, whose `class` attribute has a value of `header`, is the first of the boxes that will be positioned. This box is positioned relative to its containing element, which in this case is the `<body>` element and therefore represents the browser window. The header takes up 90 percent of the width of the page and is positioned 5 percent down from the top of the window and 5 percent in from the left:

```
body {
   background-color:#999999;
   font-family:arial, verdana, sans-serif; font-size:14px;}

div.header {
   position:absolute; top:5%; left:5%;
   width:90%; height:14%;
   background-color:#f2f2f2;
   border-style:solid; border-width:1px; border-color:#000000;}
```

The next box is the `<div>` element whose `class` attribute has a value of `nav`. This box will take up 15 percent of the width of the page—as specified in the width property—and will be 5 percent in from the left of the window and 20 percent from the top.

```
div.nav {
   position:absolute; left:5%; top:20%;
   width:15%;
   font-weight:bold;
   background-color:#ffffff;
   padding-top:25px; padding-left:10px; padding-right:10px;
   padding-bottom:10px;
   border-style:solid; border-width:1px; border-color:#000000;}
```

The first part of the page (the `<div>` element with the `class` attribute whose value is `page`) takes up 60 percent of the width of the screen. It sits next to the navigation because both are absolutely positioned in terms of their containing element (or the browser window). The `z-index` property ensures that this page sits on the top of the other two in the document because it has a higher value than they do:

```
div.page {
   position:absolute; left:25%; top:20%;
   width:70%; height:60%;
   background-color:#ffffff;
   border-style:solid; border-width:1px; border-color:#000000;
   z-index:5; }
```

The rules for the `<h2>` element and the paragraphs are fairly straightforward. The relative positioning of the `<p>` element, whose class attribute is `article`, indicates that it should be higher than it would in normal flow to close the gap between it and the heading. This certainly would not be possible with a table-based layout as the content of the elements could not overlap. This is a far more subtle effect than the overlaps you see between pages.

```
h2 {position:relative; top:10px; left:10px;}
p {padding:10px;}
p.article {position:relative; top:-12px;}
p.article:first-line {font-weight:bold;}
```

415

The pull quote is a floated element and the content of the paragraph flows around this element, changing with the width of the page:

```
span.pullQuote {
    float:right; width:100px;
    padding:10px; margin:6px;
    font-size:11px; font-weight:bold;
    border-style:solid; border-width:1px; border-color:#000000;
    background-color:#efefef;}
```

The second and third pages that you can see sitting behind the first page are simply offset and have a different z-index value. Again, this would not be possible with a table-based layout:

```
div.page2 {
    position:absolute; left:26%; top:21%;
    width:70%; height:60%;
    background-color:#ffffff;
    border-style:solid; border-width:1px; border-color:#000000;
    z-index:2;}

div.page3 {
    position:absolute; left:27%; top:22%;
    width:70%; height:60%;
    background-color:#ffffff;
    border-style:solid; border-width:1px; border-color:#000000;
    z-index:1;}
```

Finally there is the footer of the page, which takes up the bottom 11 percent of the screen—it is 3 percent from the bottom of the window and is 8 percent of the total window height.

```
div.bottom {
    position:absolute; bottom:3%;
    width:90%; height:8%;
    margin-left:5%; margin-right:5%;
    text-align:right;
    padding-right:5px;
    background-color:#ffffff;
    border-style:solid; border-width:1px; border-color:#000000;}
```

This is just an example of how CSS positioning will allow very different features than table layouts, and is an indication that we have more interesting designs to come from CSS as support in major browsers becomes more widespread.

Summary

This chapter has covered the basics of page layout. Every designer learns new tricks as they create more sites and try out more complex techniques. This chapter has given you the basic skills you need to make a practical start at designing pages.

This chapter has been concerned with more than the physical appearance of pages; it has also covered how you approach the design of a site. Before sketching out any designs, you need to make sure you have a good idea of what the site's aims are, who you expect to visit the site, and what you expect visitors to want from your site. You can then decide what kind of information you will need to put on the pages and organize that into sections. These sections should reflect the structure the site will take, and you can create a site map.

One of the first real design decisions should be whether you are using a fixed width or liquid layout—whether your page should always stay the same size or expand and contract to fit the browser window.

When you know the overall structure of your site, the size of the pages, and what will appear on each page, you can create a wireframe design of the site that uses only lines and text—holding back on the style until the client understands and agrees with the type of content that should be on the site and how the visitors should achieve what they came to the site for.

Having waited so long, you can start to add the style to your pages—fonts, colors, images, positioning, and so on. Once you decide how your page should look, you can use tables or CSS to position these elements on the page. While poor support for CSS positioning in browsers means that tables are still commonly used for positioning, you saw how CSS will open up new possibilities when more users can finally view pages properly.

I hope the practical advice in this chapter will make it easier for you to design your Web sites, as well as help you deal with those people or organizations you might be creating sites for.

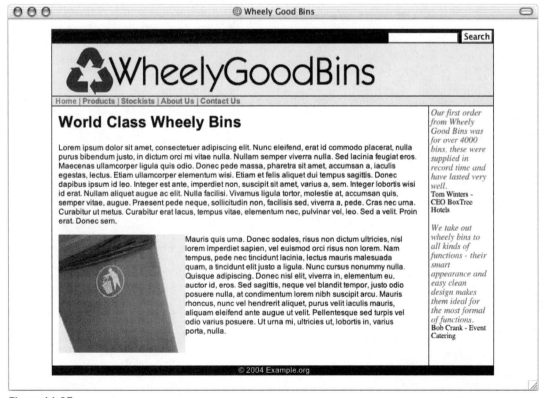

Figure 11-25

Exercises

The answers to all of the exercises are in Appendix A.

1. Take a look at the page shown in Figure 11-25. List all of the different elements on the page that would have been listed in the design stage, and put them together in their relevant grouping or categories.

For example, for the search box you might list the following:

```
Search Box
   Text input
   Search button
```

2. Look again at Figure 11-25 and use tables to create a layout similar to this one. In order to help you, try working out where the grid of the table might be. Hint: One table contains the whole page, and the search bar, logo and branding, navigation, main page, and footer each live in their own rows. Two tables (one inside the other) are nested in the main page.

Design Issues

This chapter looks at design issues that affect specific parts of pages—text, menus, tables, and forms. Each is addressed in its own section, and each section contains helpful tips that will help make your pages not only look more attractive, but also available to more users.

First you'll look at text and how to align it, space it out, and control the width of columns of text. You will then look at choosing fonts and font sizes, and you also learn how background images can affect readability of text.

Next you look at navigation. This topic covers three areas: menus, links, and search features. Almost every site has a menu that helps the user navigate between sections of the site. If your menu is not clear, people will not be able to explore your site and they will not look at as much of it. So you need to be aware of some key points in designing menus so that they are clear for the user to understand and simple to use. Most sites also feature links in other parts of the page than just the menu, and you need to make it clear to users what the links are on your site so that they know where they can click. You can use techniques such as color, underlining, and change of cursor icon to indicate links to the user. Finally, a search option can help users find what they want on a site rather than having to navigate, or if they have tried navigating but can't find what they came for.

Next you look at tables. In Chapter 11, you saw how to use tables to control the layout of pages as a whole into grids. This section takes up the topic again, this time focusing on how tables are used within pages. I also introduce some helpful techniques to make sure that the tables you use to position elements within a page show up as you intend them to.

Finally you look at creating usable forms. Forms are the most common way to gather information from a user; however, most people do not like filling out forms so a well-designed form significantly increases your chances that users will fill them out and—just as importantly—that they fill out the right information.

While this chapter can't teach you how to be a great Web page designer—that requires creativity, a good eye, and flair—it will teach you how to achieve some of the effects that contribute to good design and introduce you to some guidelines you can use when approaching a design that will help you improve both the look and usability of your site.

You will see throughout this chapter mentions of programs called screen readers. *Screen readers are programs that read a page to a user. While screen readers are commonly used by those with visual impairments, they are likely to become more popular in other Web-based scenarios, such as for those who want to access information while they are driving or doing something else that prevents them from actually reading a screen.*

Text

In this section you be looking at some issues surrounding the positioning of text on a page. First you will look at issues regarding the placement and spacing of text; then you will look at issues regarding fonts. In all you will see how:

❑ Adding whitespace helps make pages more attractive.

❑ Careful alignment of text makes it easier to read.

❑ Wide columns of text are harder to read (and are best not used for summaries).

❑ Background images can make text hard to read (because of low contrast).

❑ Fonts must be carefully chosen.

❑ Fixed font sizes will appear different sizes on screens that are different resolutions

Whitespace Helps Make More Attractive Pages

You should always give your text space to breath. A page that is too cramped is not only hard to read, it also looks less attractive, whereas a page with space between navigation, text, images, and other items on the page will be easier to read and more attractive. This space between the elements of a page is what designers refer to as *whitespace*.

Two key allies will help you create whitespace on your page: padding and margins. You should note here that whitespace need not be white; it just refers to the space between elements of a page such as writing, images, form controls, table borders, and links. (It is usually the same color as the background of the page.)

You can also change the background color of a table cell or CSS box to help separate an element from others on the page. By giving just one part of the page a slightly different shade of background, it helps it stand out from other items that are nearby. Again, the elements that have a background color should also use padding and margins to create a gap around the edge of them.

Take a look at Figure 12-1 where there are small gaps or no gaps between the navigation, text, images, and tables on the page (ch12_eg01.html).

Now compare that with Figure 12-2. By adding space between the elements of the page it is instantly more readable and more attractive, while the background colors help distinguish items from their neighbors (ch12_eg02.html).

Notably, the items in the navigation are not so close to the picture—they have a background color and padding around them, which makes them easier to read. A nice space between the picture and the text that appears next to it is created by giving the image a margin. Finally, the table at the bottom uses a combination of background colors and padding for cells to add space between the cells.

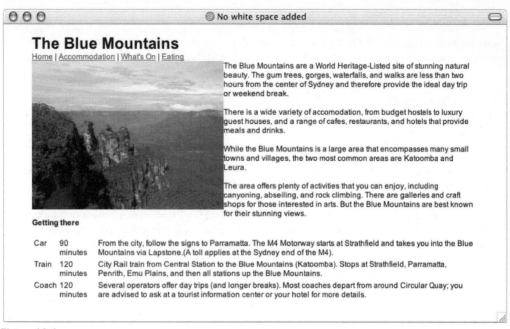

Figure 12-1

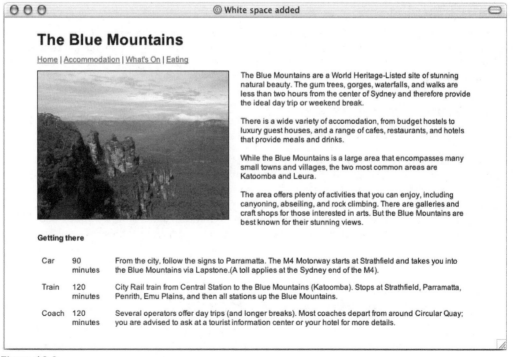

Figure 12-2

This extra space was added to the page using CSS. You saw in Chapter 9 how CSS works on a box model, whereby each element in the XHTML document is represented by a box, and how each box has a border with a margin outside the border to separate this box from adjacent ones and padding to separate the content from the border. It is the `border` and `margin` properties that have been used to add whitespace to this page.

The first CSS rule that changed the appearance of this example applied to the `<td>` element. This indicated that the content of each table cell should have 5 pixels of padding and that the contents should be vertically aligned with the top of the cells.

```
td {font-size:12px;vertical-align:top; padding:5px;}
```

This rule most notably adds padding to the navigation, to the two cells that separate the text from the image in the top half of the page, and each of the table cells in the "Getting there" section.

You can see the padding in effect better as soon as the table cell that contains the navigation is given a background color. Now you can see where the border of the cell would be, and how there is a gap between the navigation items and the edge of that cell:

```
.navigation {background-color:#efefef; }
```

The `<img>` element was also given a margin on the right side to increase the distance between it and the text next to it. As you can see from Figure 12-1, it is harder to read text that comes right up to the edge of an image:

```
img {margin-right:8px; border-style:solid; border-width:1px; border-color:
#000000;}
```

Finally, you might have noticed that the different cells in the table at the bottom of the page have different background shadings, which, along with the gaps between the cells, help to make the content more readable. The padding for each table cell in the page has also added a gap between the text and the border of these cells, which again adds to readability.

```
.transport {background-color:#efefef;}
.duration {background-color:#f2f2f2;}
.description {background-color:#efefef;}
```

You might remember that there were two attributes that could be used on a table called `cellpadding` and `cellspacing`. The `cellpadding` attribute gave padding to each cell, whereas the `cellspacing` attribute specified the space between cells. Because some earlier browsers automatically created gaps in and between cells, I tend to set both of these attributes to 0 on a table that is used for layout, and then rely on CSS for creating the whitespace I want. I also tend to indicate that a table's `border` should be 0. You can see these three attributes in use on the opening `<table>` element for these examples:

```
<table width="700" align="center" cellpadding="0" cellspacing="0">
```

Carefully Aligned Text Is More Readable

How you align your text determines how readable it is. Most commonly, text is left-aligned (this is the default). However, you can also center text, have it right-aligned or justified, or it can be put out of line by other elements on the page.

Generally speaking, if you have a paragraph of text it will be much easier to read if it is left-aligned. While you might think a paragraph of text looks good centered, it will be harder to read. Centered text is best left for headings (and, occasionally, very short paragraphs).

If you like the use of justified text, you should make sure that the column is wide enough to support it without looking like there are large gaps between some words—justification can look rather odd in narrow paragraphs.

Figure 12-3 shows an example of three paragraphs of text: the first is centered, the second is left-aligned, and the third is justified (ch12_eg03.html).

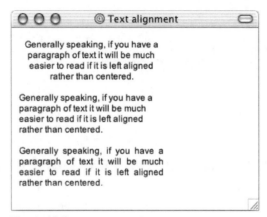

Figure 12-3

Wide Columns of Text Are Harder to Read

Most people find it hard to read long lines of text on a computer screen. As the lines of text become wider it becomes harder for the user to follow onto the correct line—and this problem is exacerbated when users are scanning a page rather than carefully reading it. Therefore it can help to limit the width of your columns of text.

How wide your columns are depends upon their content. If you are creating a page for a whole article, your columns are likely to be wider than if you are creating a page that contains snippets of several articles that many users will be skimming through quickly. After all, when users decide that they want to read something they will put more effort into following the text correctly than they will if they are just skimming a front page.

This is a particularly important issue for liquid designs where a page stretches to fill the browser. In such cases users with higher resolution displays can end up with very wide pages, and therefore it can be hard to follow the text onto the next line. You can see an example of this in Figure 12-4 (eg12_04.html).

You can control the width of text using the width attribute on a table or table cell or you can use the CSS width property on any block level element—in this example it was used on the <p> element.

You will also find that authors tend to write shorter paragraphs for online formats than when writing for print, as these are easier to read. If you have to write a very long piece, it is often good practice to split it up into several distinct pages rather than having one long page the user has to scroll through.

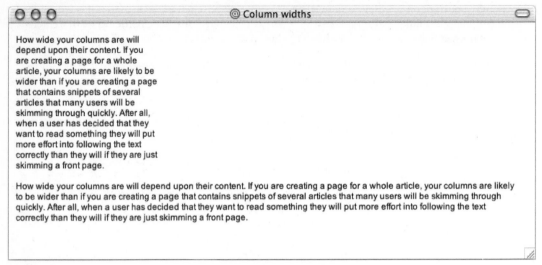

Figure 12-4

Background Images Can Make Text Hard to Read

If you want to use a background image behind any text, you should make sure that the text clearly stands out from it. I have seen many Web sites—in particular those that use background images as wallpaper for the whole page—where a background image has been chosen because the user likes the image and *not* because it makes a good background.

Photos tend to make poor choices of background images because they have varying contrasts across the picture, which makes the text harder to read. If you must use an image for a background it should be low contrast—for example a texture—rather than a photo. Remember also that background images should be small files; otherwise they will take longer to load. Remember also that you should set a background color similar to the main color of the photo in case the background color shows while the page loads.

Choose Fonts Carefully

It is a generally held belief that serif fonts are easier to read for extended periods of time. There is some evidence that we do not need to read as much of each character in a serif font in order to understand the sentence (compared with a sans-serif font). In fact, when reading books and long articles in a language with which we are familiar, good readers don't need to look at the whole of each character so carefully, either focusing on the top half of characters or sometimes just on the general shape of familiar words.

On the Web, however, the evidence is not so clear. Many people find it easier to read san-serif fonts on the Web because the serifs on the font (the tops, tails and curls) actually make the characters less clear (primarily because the resolution of screens is lower than the resolution at which pages are printed). In reality, you are safe using either serif or sans-serif fonts as long as they are large enough to read, but the arguments for using a serif font for longer blocks of text does not translate from print to the Web.

When choosing which fonts (or typefaces) to use on a page, you should make sure that users will have some of the fonts you expect them to have; if users don't have your desired font installed on their computer, your Web site won't show up in that font. Unfortunately you are quite limited in the fonts you can expect users to have. You can safely assume that most users will have Arial, Verdana, Courier or Courier New, and Times or Times New Roman typefaces installed, but not too much beyond these (especially when your visitors use different operating systems).

You are able to supply alternatives in case users do not have your first choice of font. If the computer does not have your first choice of font the browser will look for the next one in the list, then the next, and so on.

When supplying a list of fonts in order of preference in CSS you use the `font-family` property like so:

```
font-family: Geneva, Arial, Helvetica, sans-serif;
```

You can also specify values in a similar way in the deprecated `<font>` element:

```
<font face="Geneva, Arial, Helvetica, sans-serif">This is some text.</font>
```

Here are some common lists of fonts that are applied:

- ❑ **Sans-serif:** Arial, Helvetica
- ❑ **Sans-serif:** Verdana, Arial, Helvetica
- ❑ **Serif:** Times New Roman, Times
- ❑ **Monospace:** Courier New, Courier
- ❑ **Sans-serif:** Geneva, Arial, Helvetica

Indeed, the majority of users will have many more typefaces installed; it's just that you cannot be sure that users will have the same fonts that you have installed. For example, not many users will have ITC New Baskerville, but its appearance is not that dissimilar to Times so you can put ITC New Baskerville as your preferred font and then rely on Times for those who do not have it installed.

The disadvantage with this approach is that ITC New Baskerville is a wider font so it will take up more space than Times would in a layout—you need to be aware of differences in sizes of fonts when designing a page or such differences can throw off the intended look of the page.

While there are technologies for downloading fonts to a user's computer, if the users do not have that font installed there are some drawbacks to these technologies:

- ❑ They require that you have permission to distribute the font (which, like CDs, are usually copyrighted).
- ❑ They do not work in all browsers.
- ❑ It takes longer for the page to render.
- ❑ People do not tend to like downloading files just to view a page.

If you have a specific font you need to use, such as for a logo, you should use a GIF image of the writing. However, it is considered bad practice to use images for large sections of text, and you should put the text as the value of the `alt` attribute for those who cannot see the image.

You should also make sure that you choose a typeface that gets across the image that you want to portray. For example, if you are trying to put across a professional image you should avoid fonts such as Comic Sans MS, which is more of a "fun" font.

If you want to look into this topic in more detail, there is some interesting information on the usability of various fonts at `http://psychology.wichita.edu/surl/usabilitynews/3S/font.htm`.

Fixed Size Fonts Are Affected by Screen Resolution

You should be aware that, if you use fixed font sizes such as pixels or points, the size they appear on screen will depend on the user's monitor. For example, a font that is 12 pixels high will look much smaller on a $1,280 \times 1,024$ monitor than on an 800×600 monitor that is the same physical size because there are 40 percent more pixels on the screen.

Using fixed-size fonts also makes it harder for users to change the size of the font if they are having difficulty reading the text.

Navigation

One of the most interesting things about navigation is that no matter how well you plan your site, different people will use it in their own individual way. For example, even if you expect people to start their visit to your site on its home page, once the site has been launched you might find that another site links to a different page within your site and you get a lot of visitors who come to your site via another page.

When designing a site, therefore, it is your job to help people find the information they want as quickly and easily as possible.

A user will navigate your site in one of three highly common ways:

❑   Using a menu that you provide

❑   Browsing through links provided in the middle of text (and other parts of the page than the menu)

❑   Searching for relevant items of information

In this section you learn how to make it easier for users to get around your site using these three methods.

Menus

A menu is a key part of *any* Web site that features more than one page. It allows users to see the sections of your site quickly and easily and allows them to get where they want.

As you saw in Chapter 11, a site may have more than one menu; you may have primary navigation in one menu and secondary navigation in a submenu or separate menu. Usually menus appear on the top of a site (above or below the logo) or on the left side of the page.

The menu tends to be the main way in which users will navigate between sections of a site, and good menu design makes a huge difference in the following:

❑ Whether or not users achieve what they wanted to when they came to your site

❑ How long they will spend at your site

There are eight guiding rules I'll introduce you to in this section:

❑ Menus must focus on what users want to achieve.

❑ Menus must be concise.

❑ If you use icons, make sure they are easy to understand and add a text link, too.

❑ Grouping of menu items must be logical.

❑ Menus must quick and easy to read.

❑ Menu items must be easy to select.

❑ Menus must load quickly.

❑ Menus must be consistent across a site.

Menus Must Focus on What Visitors Want to Achieve

For 99 percent of Web sites the main priority of a menu should be satisfying the user—especially commercial sites. Ask yourself the following questions:

❑ **What do users come to my site to find out?** Do they really come to find profiles of who set the company up and the board of directors, or do they come to find out about a product/service you offer?

❑ **How do I best describe this information in concise terms they will understand?** For example, if you use jargon, the visitor might not understand your terms and will not click the link that would have given them the information they came for.

❑ **What is the most important of these items?** The prominence of each link should reflect the number of visitors who come to your site for that information. For example, if you are working on a site for a music store that sells a lot more guitars than drums, your first menu item (after the home button) should be for guitars not drums (even if you want to build up the business in drums).

This will give you a better idea of the order of items on a menu and what each should say.

Menus Must Be Clearly Separated from Content

When you design your page, a menu must be immediately identifiable as the way to navigate the site. You can achieve this using a number of techniques:

❑ You can use a different size font for the menu compared with the main content (generally the menu text should be larger than the main text on a page).

❑ You can add extra space around the menu (as you saw in the example of whitespace earlier in this chapter).

❑ Place the menu in a box or use a line to separate it from the main content

While using images often makes a menu very distinct from content, you must be careful that your images are not so large that they slow down the loading of the site. Figure 12-5 shows an example of a site that uses images for navigation within a separate box.

Figure 12-5

You should take a closer look at how this menu was created; it is contained within a table and the table is given a background image that is only 1 pixel wide and 20 pixels high, but this image stretches across the whole table because it is a background image. A background color is also used for those browsers that do not support the `background` attribute with the value of an image URL.

Inside the table each menu item has its own image that is contained in an `<a>` element to make it a link. Because these images are links they should have a `border` property set to 0; otherwise they can get unsightly lines around them in some browsers (including IE on Windows).

Between each image is a spacer image that is a darker line to separate the links if they are butted up next to each other.

```
<table>
  <tr>
    <td height="20">
      <table width="700" border="0" align="center" cellpadding="0"
             cellspacing="0">
        <tr>
          <td width="2"><img src="../images/navigation_divider.gif" alt=""
              width="2" height="16" border="0" /></td>

          <td width="48">
            <a href="default.asp" title="Home page">
              <img src="../images/navigation_home.gif" alt="Home" width="38"
                   height="16" border="0" />
            </a>
          </td>

          <td width="2"><img src="../images/navigation_divider.gif" alt=""
              width="2" height="16" border="0" /></td>

          <td width="80">
            <a href="prodList.asp" title="Home page">
              <img src="images/navigation_stock_list.gif" alt="Stock List"
                   width="70" height="16" border="0" />
```

```
            </a>
          </td>

          <td width="2"><img src="images/navigation_divider.gif" alt=""
             width="2" height="16" border="0" /></td>

          <td width="64">
            <a href="prodWanted.asp" title="Equipment wanted">
              <img src="images/navigation_wanted.gif" alt="Wanted"
                 width="54" height="16" border="0" />
            </a>
          </td>

          <td width="2"><img src="images/navigation_divider.gif" alt=""
             width="2" height="16" border="0" /></td>

          <td width="85">
            <a href="contactUs.asp" title="Contact us">
              <img src="images/navigation_contact_us.gif" alt="Contact Us"
                 width="75" height="16" border="0" />
            </a>
          </td>

          <td><img src="images/navigation_divider.gif" alt="-" width="2"
                 height="16" border="0" /></td>
        </tr>
      </table>
    </td>
  </tr>
</table>
```

Because all of these images are fairly small they should not add too much time when downloading the page.

If you want to ensure that the menu takes up the same size in each browser window you should set the width of each cell. And if you want to ensure that there is no gap between images and the edges of the cells, just set the width of the cell to be the same as the width of an image.

> When the code for table cells are written on new lines, or have spaces between them, some browsers will leave gaps between each cell when it is rendered in the browser. If this happens to one of your tables just remove the spaces between the `<td>` elements first, and if this does not fix the problem remove the spaces between and `<tr>` elements.

If You Use Icons to Represent a Link, Make Sure Everyone Will Understand Them

Many Web sites use images for links that are known as icons. These icons are images such as a magnifying glass to indicate a search feature. If you are going to use icons. make sure that your target audience will understand these images; otherwise users will not click them.

Many users are familiar with the following icons:

❑   A house to indicate the home page

❑   A magnifying glass to indicate a search feature

❑   An envelope to indicate an e-mail address or link

❑   A question mark to indicate help files

If you use icons that are less common, it's a good idea to add the link in words as well as using the image. (Don't expect that users will hover over a link to find a tooltip that tells them more about that link.)

Menus Must Be Quick and Easy to Read

When browsing Web pages, most visitors do not really read them—they scan them. Making your menu distinct from the main part of a page (and using bold, a different color, or underlined text for links within the body of a page) will help users scan and register the navigation items more easily.

Any words or images you use in a menu must be large enough to read (even for users that have high screen resolutions that make text appear smaller), and text must contrast well with its background.

Links should also be short and concise. For example, a link that just reads "Home" is a lot easier to read and understand than a link that says "Front door." Having said that, a couple of simple words are always better than one word of jargon.

Grouping of Menu Items Must Be Logical

If you have a lot of pages, you might well decide to create submenus. If so, it's very important that you group menu items so that visitors will understand where to look for something without having to search through several sections or categories.

If you do use submenus, you should make sure that they are clearly distinguishable from the main menu, and that it is clear which items belong to which section. Submenus often make use of a smaller font, an indented position, or an alternate color to show they are distinct from the main menu.

For example, if you are creating a site for a computer store, you might create a grouping something like this with three main sections, each containing their own subsections:

❑   **Computers:** Desktop computers, laptop computers

❑   **Software:** Business software, games

❑   **Peripherals:** Printers, scanners

This would be easier to navigate than a simple alphabetized menu.

Menus Items Must Be Easy to Select

If a menu item is too small or there is not enough space between menu items, it can be very difficult for some users to select the correct menu item. A user with a dodgy mouse, poor eyesight, or difficulties with motor control may have trouble hitting a small or tight target, and even those most able to control a pointing device will find it easier to hit larger targets. Furthermore, most users can find moving targets either irritating or hard to hit—and they are best avoided in most designs.

When you are creating a menu, you need to make sure it will work on all of the main browsers. As the Web has grown up, there have been many menus (particularly drop-down menus that use JavaScript) that do not work even on some of the more common browsers.

There are two ways around this problem:

- ❏ Test your menu on many different types of browsers (particularly older versions).
- ❏ Avoid complex code in menus.

Drop-down or pop-up menus, which make new items appear as you hover your mouse over a heading, tend to be particularly problematic for two reasons:

- ❏ They are often written in JavaScript, which is implemented slightly differently in the various browsers—particularly the older ones—so, while a menu might appear to work fine in the designer's browser, some other visitors will simply not be able to navigate the site.
- ❏ They can be too sensitive or move too quickly for users to select the item they require.

I have come across many sites that have attempted to implement drop-down menus that simply do not work in my browser. As a result, and for usability reasons, I now avoid these menus completely.

Recently, designers have been playing with more experimental types of menu (particularly in Macromedia Flash) that often require quite dexterous control—these menus often move and slide between items as the user moves the mouse to the left or right when hovering over an item. While such menus that require fine control of a pointing device often look great on experimental sites, they can exclude those who do not have excellent control over their pointing device, and are therefore best left to the realms of experimental sites.

Menus Must Load Quickly

When creating a menu you should not expect that every visitor to your site has a fast Internet connection—many visitors may still be on a dial-up connection. Although these numbers are constantly dropping, your menu should load within the first couple of seconds. If your menu takes longer than around eight seconds to load many users will think that the page is not loading or that the browser has frozen—they will try to reload the page or, even worse, click their Back button or go to another page.

The loading speed is a particularly important for designers who use graphics or Flash in their menus, and if you want an image to change when the user rolls his mouse over an image to make it appear highlighted then your loading time can double (as a second image is required for each image that the user rolls over).

Note that some browsers require the content of a table to completely load before displaying the table, so if you are putting images in a table users might have to wait quite a while for a page to load.

Menus Must Be Consistent Across a Site

The more pages a site contains, the more navigation items you are going to require and the harder it is for a navigation system to be consistent across all pages, but the navigation system is important nonetheless.

The menus in each section of your site should have a similar look and feel so that users know exactly where to go to navigate the site. And, while your primary navigation might be at the top of the page under the logo and your subnavigation could be on the left of the page, the navigation items for each section of the site should be in a similar location for each page.

Links

In addition to menus your visitors will be using to navigate the site, many Web pages contain other hyperlinks in the text that makes up the body of the document. This short section addresses two topics regarding links that are not part of the main menu:

❑ Text links

❑ Images as links

Text Links

By default, text links tend to be blue and underlined. Some experts on usability suggest that all links should be left to their default appearance. However, from your experience of the Web, you probably know that by using a color that is clearly different from the main text it is easy to tell what text makes up a link.

As you saw in Chapter 9, you can change the appearance of links as a user hovers over them and when a user has already visited them. Here is a quick reminder of how you change the appearance of links using CSS:

```
a {font-weight:bold; color:#ff0000; text-decoration:none;}
a:hover {color:#FF9900; text-decoration:underline; background-color:#f9f0f0;}
a:visited {color:#990000;}
```

As users hover over links they will be underlined, change color, and gain a background color. The visited links will be in a different shade reminding users where they have been. You can see this best if you run the example available with the download code for the chapter.

Note that it is generally a bad idea to use a different weight of text when a user hovers over a link because this changes the width of the font making it hard to read and changing the width of the line.

Images as Links

Images are often used as links in menus, advertisements, photos to click on, graphical icons, and so on. Whenever you use an image as a link you should use three attributes on the image:

❑ **border="0":** If you don't use this you will get a border around the image in many browsers, which can look unsightly.

❑ **alt ="description of image or text on image":** Use this to tell users who cannot see the image what the image is of or what it says.

❑ **title="where the link will take the user":** Use this to show users a tooltip that says where the link will take them; this is also used by screen readers.

You saw an example of using images as links earlier in the chapter (ch12_eg05.html). In Chapter 15 you will see an example of using JavaScript to create what are known as *rollover images*, or images that change as the user hovers over them.

Site Search Features

The third way a user can navigate your site is by using a search feature. A search feature allows users to immediately look for a keyword (or words) that relate to the information they are trying to find from your site. Searching can save users from having to learn your scheme for navigating the site and offers another way to find the information if they are having difficulty finding what they came for.

Search Features Make Sites More Usable

Search features are increasingly important as your sites grow. If you have only a few pages then your menu should be rather easy to understand anyway. Larger sites, however, which might incorporate submenus where not all options are featured on every page, can really benefit from this addition.

There are many ways in which you can implement a search feature on your site. While some methods require fairly advanced programming experience, there are ways in which you can add a fairly simple search feature.

Some larger commercial sites use either a special indexing application to index the site to make the search facilities available, or, if the content of the site is stored in a database (which is common in larger sites), they use programming commands called *queries* to ask the database which pages contain the terms the user searched for.

For sites that do not use databases or indexing tools, the easiest way to add a search feature to your site is to use a third-party search utility to index your site for you. These services also give you the code to create a search box that will send queries to their site. When visitors to your site use a search box, their query gets sent to the server of the company offering the search service and the server will then return the answers to the user on your behalf. The best of these services will allow you to add your own styling to the results.

The best-known company to offer this kind of service is Google, which offers this service for free at the time of this writing. (Google makes its revenue from supplying ads in with the search results—but as you can see from Figure 12-7 they are not intrusive; they appear only on the right side of the results page, as they do when you send a query to Google.com.)

Adding a Google Search to Your Site

Google, which is currently the most widely used search engine on the Internet, offers a very powerful and flexible service whereby you can use its search engine to provide a search feature on your own site. At the time of this writing you have to register in order to use the service; however the instructions and setup on the site are quite simple and the service is free.

Figure 12-6 shows you how an arts and music site called `Neumu.net` has a small search box underneath the navigation bar.

When a visitor to this site searches the Neumu site, the request is sent to Google, which then generates a page with items from Neumu containing those words and sends it to the user. Obviously, the results point back to the Neumu site, as you can see in Figure 12-7.

You can see the code for the search box by selecting View Source on the menu.

> Remember that you cannot just copy this code; you need to register for the service yourself.

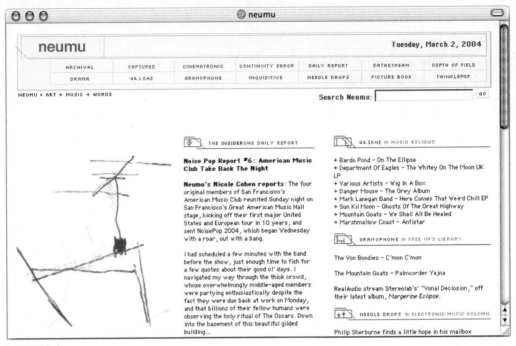

Figure 12-6

Figure 12-7

Another site that offers a free search service for a limited number of pages is http://www.Atomz.com/, although they do charge for larger sites.

Tables

In the last chapter you saw how you can use tables to control the layout of a page. In this section you learn some tricks you can use with tables that you might use within a section of the page, just for a small part of the content.

Don't forget that in this chapter you have already seen the following:

❑ That it is important to give tables padding when they contain text to make them easier to read

❑ How to use a table to contain images and links in a navigation bar

In this section you will see how to use tables to do the following:

❑ Shade alternate rows, making long tables easier to read

❑ Create a custom box with rounded corners, like a frame

❑ Create a drop shadow for an image—especially helpful when adding drop shadows to many images without needing to alter the images themselves

Shading Multiple Rows of a Table

When you have a table that contains multiple rows of information it will make it easier to follow the rows if you alternate the background color of the rows very slightly, thereby making it easier to distinguish which line the information corresponds to. Figure 12-8 shows you an example of a table that has alternating colors for each row.

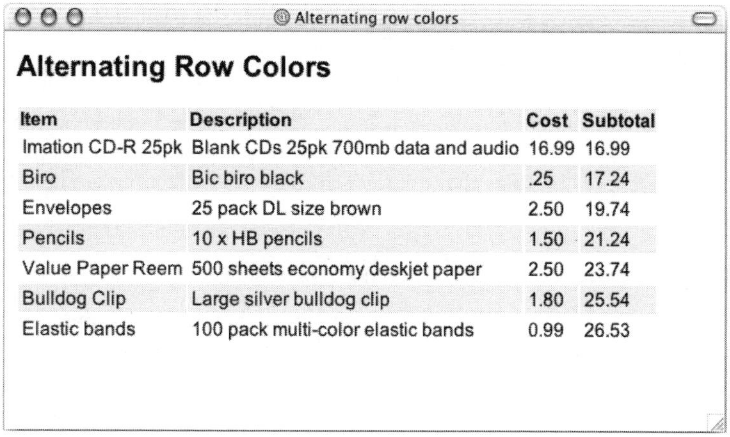

Alternating Row Colors

Item	Description	Cost	Subtotal
Imation CD-R 25pk	Blank CDs 25pk 700mb data and audio	16.99	16.99
Biro	Bic biro black	.25	17.24
Envelopes	25 pack DL size brown	2.50	19.74
Pencils	10 x HB pencils	1.50	21.24
Value Paper Reem	500 sheets economy deskjet paper	2.50	23.74
Bulldog Clip	Large silver bulldog clip	1.80	25.54
Elastic bands	100 pack multi-color elastic bands	0.99	26.53

Figure 12-8

This was achieved using odd and even classes on rows like so (ch12_eg08.html):

```
<table>
  <tr>
    <th>Item</th>
    <th>Description</th>
    <th>Cost</th>
    <th>Subtotal</th>
  </tr>
  <tr class="even">
    <td>Imation CD-R 25pk</td>
    <td>Blank CDs 25pk 700mb data and audio</td>
    <td>16.99</td>
    <td>16.99</td>
  </tr>
  <tr class="odd">
    <td>Biro</td>
    <td>Bic biro black</td>
    <td>.25</td>
    <td>17.24</td>
  </tr>
  <tr class="even">
    <td>Envelopes</td>
    <td>25 pack DL size brown</td>
    <td>2.50</td>
    <td>19.74</td>
  </tr>
</table>
```

Here is the CSS that goes with this example:

```
body{
  color:#000000; background-color:#ffffff;
  font-family:arial, verdana, sans-serif; font-size:12pt;}

th {font-weight:bold; text-align:left; background-color:#fff336;}
.odd {background-color:#efefef;}
.even {background-color:#ffffff;}
```

Remember that whatever background colors you use, there must be a good contrast between the background and the text in order for the user to be able to read it easily. The very light gray in this example is a good example of a color that does not dramatically affect the readability of the table itself.

Creating a Custom Frame with Tables

Sometimes tables can be used with graphics to create a special frame for some content. The combination of images and pixel-accurate table layouts allows you to create a wide range of effects. You can see an example in Figure 12-9.

This is created using a table with three rows and three columns. The 3 × 3 grid holds eight separate images—one for each edge—and then has the content in the middle. Figure 12-10 shows you the images separated out into the grid.

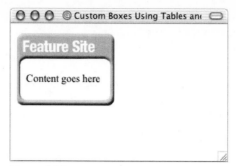

Figure 12-9

Figure 12-10

Here you can see the table used to create this example (`ch12_eg09.html`). Note how the `border`, `cellpadding`, and `cellspacing` attributes are set on the opening `<table>` tag to ensure that no browser will impose its default border or leave gaps between the table elements.

```
<table border="0" cellpadding="0" cellspacing="0">
  <tr>
    <td><img src="images/featured_topLeft_14x48.gif" alt="" height="48"
          width="14" /></td>
    <td><img src="images/featured_top_121x48.gif" alt="" height="48"
          width="121" /></td>
    <td><img src="images/featured_topRight_15x48.gif" alt="" height="48"
          width="15" /></td>
  </tr>
  <tr>
    <td><img src="images/featured_left_14x1.gif" alt="" height="40"
          width="14" /></td>
    <td>Content goes here</td>
    <td><img src="images/featured_right_15x1.gif" alt="" height="40"
          width="15" /></td>
  </tr>
  <tr>
    <td><img src="images/featured_bottomLeft_14x20.gif" alt="" height="20"
          width="14" /></td>
    <td><img src="images/featured_bottom_1x20.gif" alt="" height="20"
          width="121" /></td>
```

```
      <td><img src="images/featured_bottomRight_15x20.gif" alt="" height="20"
             width="15" /></td>
  </tr>
</table>
```

Note also how in this example I have used the size of the images in their names. This can be a helpful technique for remembering the size of image you create. It is especially helpful if you are creating images for other people to use so that they know the size the image is intended to be.

In order to make this quicker to load, the images in the cells in the middle of the left and right columns are only 1 pixel high and the image in the middle at the bottom is only 1 pixel wide. (Remember you can see the dimensions of the image in its name in this example.) The `height` property of the images on the left and right is then stretched to the desired dimensions for the content, while the width of the bottom image is set to the same width as the image at the top in the middle, which is 121 pixels.

This technique can be used to create all kinds of similar effects. As you might imagine, if you want a box with curved corners but not the three-dimensional effect used in these images, you would just use flat images. If you wanted curved corners at the top (and square edges at the bottom), you would just use curved images in the top row. If you wanted to make the content look like it was on a TV screen, you would make an image that looked like a TV screen and cut out the edges so they could go into the table.

As with all tables, the secret is to think in grids. Sketch out the design you want, and then impose a grid over the top of it to see where you have to cut up the images and create tables.

Creating a Drop Shadow with a Table

If you have several images and you want to add a drop shadow to each of them, here is a handy trick that saves you from having to open each image, add the drop shadow, and then save the image again. This technique uses a drop shadow in a background image for a table and then places the image that is supposed to have the drop shadow in the foreground.

You can see the effect you are going to create in Figure 12-11.

Around the edge of the photo of my cat, you can see the gray drop shadow. The trick is that the image used in the background is slightly larger than the image in the foreground.

You can see the image that is going to be used as the background on its own in Figure 12-12; it's 400 pixels wide and 360 pixels tall (whereas the photo of the cat is 390 pixels wide by 350 pixels tall).

Here is the code that makes this example work (ch12_eg10.html):

```
<table border="0" cellpadding="0" cellspacing="0"
       background="images/drop_shadow.gif"
       width="400" height="360" bgcolor="#ffffff">
  <tr>
    <td valign="top">
      <img src="images/jasper.jpg" alt="Jasper (cat)" width="390" height=
"350" />
    </td>
</table>
```

Figure 12-11

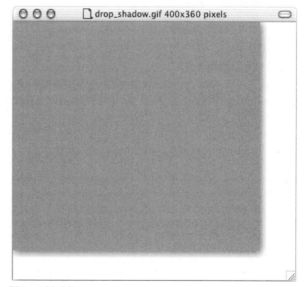

Figure 12-12

This code is quite simple, although you can see lots of attributes hanging off the elements, and the use of these attributes does not fit with the aims of separating style from content.

You should note a couple of points here:

❑ You must specify the width and height of the table to be the same size as the background image (although you could provide all of these details in a CSS style sheet).

❑ The cell containing the foreground image must have the valign="top" attribute so that the image is not in the vertical middle of the page, which is the default (but cannot be specified in the CSS style sheet).

Forms

I have yet to meet anyone who enjoys filling in forms—especially on the Web. Therefore, if your site must include a form, good design is essential or people will not fill them in (and if you are an online shop that is your core business).

In this section you are going to learn about the following:

❑ What to do before designing the form

❑ How to design a form, select the right form controls, group them correctly, and label them

❑ How best to lay out a form

To work through the points in this section you will see an example of a basic form that users have to fill in before they can register for an online service.

Before Designing the Form

Before you address how a form should really look you need to do some preparation—this is just like the preparation you need to do before you start designing a site, although it should take less time.

Listing Required Information First

When designing a form, you should start out by creating a complete list of the information you require from a user. You might start with a general list with items such as login details, name, mailing address, and e-mail address, but you need to make sure for each item that you know what makes up these requirements. For example, do you need to get a user's first name and last name separately? If so these are going to be separate items on the form. What makes up the address: house number/name, street name, suburb, ZIP Code, and so on? Which of these needs to be separated from each other?

Here is a list of the information that is needed for our registration form:

❑ Login information

❑ User's name

❑ User's address

❑ User's contact details

When this is broken down the exact information that is needed is as follows:

❑ **Login information:** username and password

❑ **Name:** First name, last name

❑ **Land address:** Street address, suburb, ZIP Code

❑ **Contact information:** E-mail address, area code, phone number

Generally, there are two types of information you must collect:

❑ You must capture the information you need in order to get a job done, and you shouldn't ask for information you don't need. For example, you should not ask for a fax number unless you are going to need it.

❑ You might need to capture information for the purposes of research and marketing. When you start thinking about this type of information, it is often tempting to collect as much information as possible. However the longer a form is, the less likely the user is to complete it. Furthermore, there are some questions (about topics such as income and possessions) that users do not like to answer—and if you ask them, visitors might question whether they can trust you. Unless you have a good reason for collecting the data, you should not collect it.

If you want to collect lots of non-essential information (for example to get a better idea of the demographic of visitors to your site), consider offering users an incentive to give it such as a prize drawing or an offer of premium content.

> Note that when collecting and storing information about customers, you must also ensure that you meet the data protection laws of your country.

Group-Related Information

Once you know what information you want to collect from a visitor to you site, you need to look to see if there is a logical grouping to the information you require from visitors to help them understand the form.

If you find such a grouping in related information you should make sure that these items go together in the form. In the example for this section you need three groups of information:

❑ Login details

❑ Name and e-mail address

❑ Other contact details

In this example, the grouping is the same as the initial list of required information before it was broken down, but sometimes the grouping can be quite different.

Model Paper Forms Users Are Familiar With

If you are creating an online application that requires a form that would previously have been filled in on paper *and* that your users would be familiar with, then you should make sure that your online form reflects that paper form. (Note that if the form would not have been familiar to users this is not necessary.) If the goal of your application is to put existing software online then it could also be modeled on the software.

The reason for modeling your form on something that the user is familiar with is quite obvious; it makes it easier for the user to fill in. That is not to say that the layout of the form should be exactly the same (often paper forms cram too many questions into a small space). Rather, you should be asking similar questions in a similar order and grouping.

Are Users Going to Provide the Same Information Each Time?

Will users have to provide the same information each time they visit the site? Or will some data be stored in a database (or other application) and retrieved when they log in again? For example, if you are working on an online store, once the user has logged in will the application remember the user's name, address, and contact details?

If you are going to store information about users—in particular their credit card details—you must make sure that you are abiding by your country's laws on storage of such information.

You also should consider how your form is going to be processed. If it is going to be processed by a human, the human can interpret the data the user enters, whereas if it goes straight into a database, users must be a lot more precise about the information they enter. This may affect your choice of form control required to collect the information.

What Else Needs to Appear on the Form?

Several forms contain extra information, such as price lists, details of a shopping cart, legal notices, and so on. Before you start designing the form you should be aware of all the information that might be put on it, not just the form controls themselves.

Designing the Form

Now that you know what information must be captured by the form, you can start to design it. You can start by selecting the appropriate type of control and then group the controls together and label them. You can then put final touches to the layout of the form to control its presentation.

Selecting the Type of Form Control

You learned about the different types of form controls that you can use in Chapter 6. It's important that you choose the correct type of form control for the information that you are trying to collect. Once you have decided on which form control to use for each piece of information you'll have an idea of the possible length and layout of the form.

Entering text:

- ❑ If there is just one line of text you use an `<input>` element whose `type` attribute has the value of `text`.
- ❑ If you want the user to enter more than one line of text you use the `<textarea>` element.
- ❑ If the information is sensitive (such as a credit card or password) use an `<input>` element whose `type` attribute has a value of `password`.

Giving the user a limited choice of options:

- ❑ If the user can select only one option (from several) use a group of radio buttons (with the same name) or a select box.
- ❑ If the user can select multiple items use checkboxes or a multiple select box.

Also consider how visitors would be used to giving this kind of information. For example, use a set of text inputs for each line of an address rather than, say, using a combination of a text input for the street name and a select box to indicate whether the street is a street, road, avenue, or close for the first line of the address.

Remember that each form control should use a name that describes its content. Rather than just arbitrary names such as input1 and input2, it's good practice to give the names a prefix that describes what kind of form control they relate to as well:

- ❑ txt*Name* for text boxes and text areas
- ❑ rad*Name* for radio buttons
- ❑ chk*Name* for checkboxes
- ❑ sel*Name* for select boxes

Radio Buttons and Checkboxes

Although radio buttons and checkboxes take up more room than select boxes, they tend to be easier for visitors to use because users can see all of the options at once.

If there are only three or four options, and the user is allowed to pick only one, then radio buttons are usually a better choice than select boxes because all are visible. An exception to this rule would be if the design contained several select boxes (in which case the consistency of design is more important).

If there are only three or four options, and the user is allowed to pick several, then the use of checkboxes for multiple selections is almost better than multiple select boxes—no matter how much space they take—not only because they are more common, but also because if you use a multiple select box you should tell the user that they can select multiple items and how to go about this.

Checkboxes are also ideal if the user has to indicate that they agree to or have read something, such as terms and conditions. It is important to use a checkbox in these cases rather than a radio button because, when you have selected a radio button, while you can change your choice to a different radio button, there is no way to deselect all of the radio buttons in a group.

> Note that you should never use a programming language (such as JavaScript) to change the intention of radio buttons or checkboxes. In other words, you should never make checkboxes mutually exclusive (like radio buttons are) and you should not allow a user to select more than one radio button from a group because this will confuse users who expect radio buttons and checkboxes to follow their normal default behavior. Also, be careful not to repeatedly mix radio buttons and checkboxes in the same form or you will confuse users.

Radio buttons and checkboxes also allow you to provide more information to the user than a select box. A radio button or checkbox can have a long description next to it, whereas, if you use a long description in a select box the whole box grows wider. You can see an example of a long drop-down (which goes off the screen) and a set of radio buttons in Figure 12-13 (ch12_eg11.html).

If your radio buttons represent an optional question, you should not automatically select one item by default. You cannot deselect all radio buttons by clicking them again as you can checkboxes; you can make only an different choice. It is also often helpful to give users an "other" option if they might not choose one of the options you have given.

443

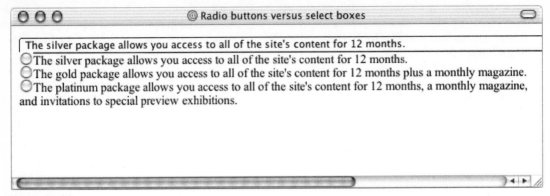

Figure 12-13

Select Boxes

Select boxes, also known as drop-down list boxes, save space on the screen, especially when there are lots of options, although as Figure 12-13 showed they do not look very good with long descriptions for each option. Indeed the width of a select box is the width of the widest option in it.

You should remember when providing a select box to include options for all users; for example, if you use a drop-down for U.S. states and you have visitors from outside the U.S. you should have at least one option for those who do not live in a U.S. state, even if the option is just "Outside U.S."

The order of items in a select box should reflect users' experience; for example, if you use month names, put them in chronological order, whereas if you use states or countries alphabetical lists are easier to use.

If one (or a few options) within a long list are more popular or are more likely to be chosen than other options, then you should put these at the top of the select box so that the user comes to those first.

Text Boxes

Text boxes tend to be the most natural way for users to offer the majority of information. Generally speaking, text areas should be large enough for users to enter what they want without having scrollbars appearing (unless they are very long, such as the body of an e-mail or an article for a Web site).

Be aware that users often take the size of the text box to be an indication of the length of text that they should provide. This can be especially helpful for things like dates, as you can see in Figure 12-14, where you want the user to enter four digits for a year.

Grouping Controls

Once you've decided what form controls you are going to use, you can start to put them on the page. As I already mentioned, these should be grouped together into related items of information—and that these groups should reflect the users' understanding of the topic.

You can group form elements in the following ways:

- ❑ Fieldsets
- ❑ Labels
- ❑ Splitting the form into several pages

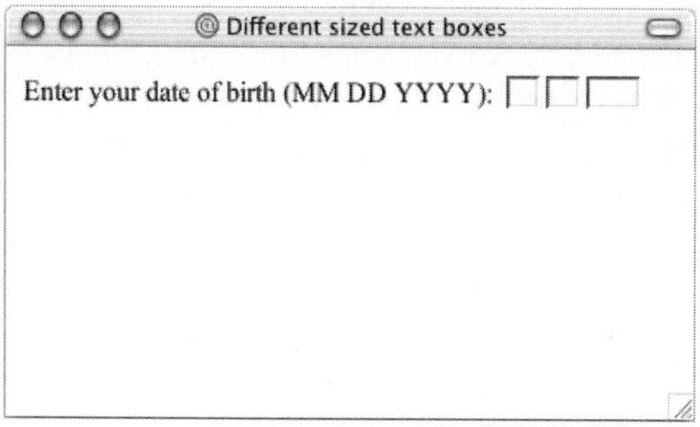

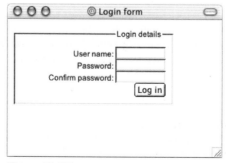

Figure 12-14

You can also use padding and shading as you saw in the first section of this chapter, which covered whitespace.

Using <fieldset> Elements

You already learned about the `<fieldset>` element in Chapter 6; it allows you to group sections of a form between the opening `<fieldset>` and closing `</fieldset>` tags. The form can also carry a `<legend>` element to indicate a caption for the box.

For example, here is a form for a user to enter their login details (`ch12_eg13.html`):

```
<form name="frmLogin" action="login.asp" method="post">
  <fieldset>
    <legend>Login</legend>
      User name: <input type="text" size="12" name="txtUserName" /><br />
      Password: <input type="password" size="12" name="txtPassword" /><br />
      Confirm password: <input type="password" size="12"
              name="txtPasswordConfirmed" /><br />
      <input type="submit" value="Log in" />
  </fieldset>
</form>
```

Fieldsets were introduced in IE 4 and Netscape 6. Older browsers just ignore the `<fieldset>` and `<legend>` buttons if they do not understand them, so you can safely add these elements to all forms. You can see what this example looks like in Figure 12-15.

Figure 12-15

You may also choose to use an alternative to fieldsets to group together parts of a form, such as line breaks, background colors, or a table with associated style rules, but fieldsets have specifically been introduced for grouping form elements, and you can associate styles with the <fieldset> element, as was done in this example:

```
fieldset {
    width:250px;
    padding:10px;
    font-size:12px;
    text-align:right;}
```

Note here how the width property has been set in the style sheet. This is particularly helpful to add to <fieldset> elements because they will otherwise stretch to the width of the browser window (or containing element).

Splitting a Form into Separate Pages

Long forms not only put off users but also make the form harder for the user to fill in. And if you are writing validation and error handling (such as the error messages to say a form field has not been filled in or contains the wrong sort of information) then this code becomes more complicated as a form gets longer. Therefore, if you have a long form you can split it up into several pages. The reasons you might do this include:

❑　Smaller forms are less intimidating.

❑　When related information is put on the same page, it is easier to digest.

As a general guide, your form should be not much more than a "screen full" (at 800 × 600 resolution) so the user does not have to scroll much.

If you split a form into separate pages you should clearly indicate to the users how far they are through the form. You can see in Figure 12-16 a form that has been split up into four pages and a confirmation page.

Splitting a form into several pages can introduce new complexities into the programming because the program has to remember what a user has entered between each form; however, there are several ways of doing this with a little extra effort. You will generally want users to go through these steps in order rather than allowing them to go between each page at random, so avoid links that allow them to jump to any page.

Number Questions

If you have a lot of questions, such as an application form or an online test, you should number questions so that the users know where questions start and end. This can also be a help if you want to indicate to a user that he or she should jump to another section of the form because you can explicitly indicate which number question they should be going to.

Layout of Forms

Ideally, a layout of a form should reflect what a user would expect to see when dealing with such data. Layout is related to the user's experiences with paper forms or software equivalents. You can even consider an everyday experience such as how a user writes out his or her address. (We usually write our address on a few separate lines as opposed to using drop-down boxes.)

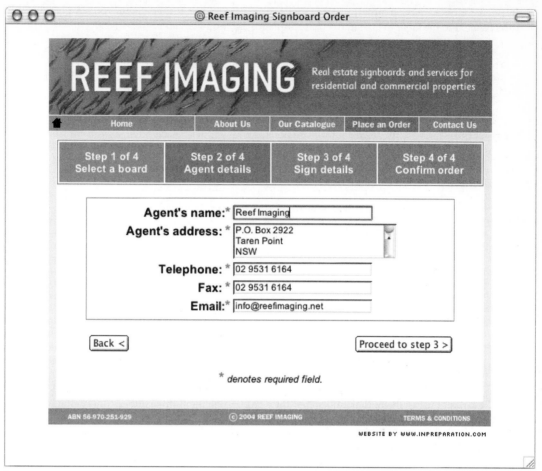

Figure 12-16

Labelling Controls

The first issue concerned with layout of forms is the labelling of controls. It's very important that each control is clearly labelled so that users know what information they should be adding and where. There are two types of labels:

❑ Implicit labels that are normal text and markup next to the control
❑ Explicit labels that use the `<label>` element

You should consider the following as guidelines for where the label for an element should generally appear:

❑ **Text entry fields:** To the left of the input or directly above
❑ **Checkboxes and radio buttons:** To the right of the checkbox or radio button
❑ **Buttons:** On the button itself—its value

Implicit controls are the simplest way to label a control; to add an implicit label you simply add text directly next to the label in question. For example (ch12_eg14.html):

```
First name: <input type="text" name="txtFirstName" size="12" /> <br />
Last name: <input type="text" name="txtLastName" size="12" /> <br />
E-mail address: <input type="text" name="txtEmail" size="12" /> <br />
```

The disadvantage with this approach is that the presentation is not very attractive—and gets worse with longer forms—because the form controls are not aligned well with each other, as you can see in Figure 12-17.

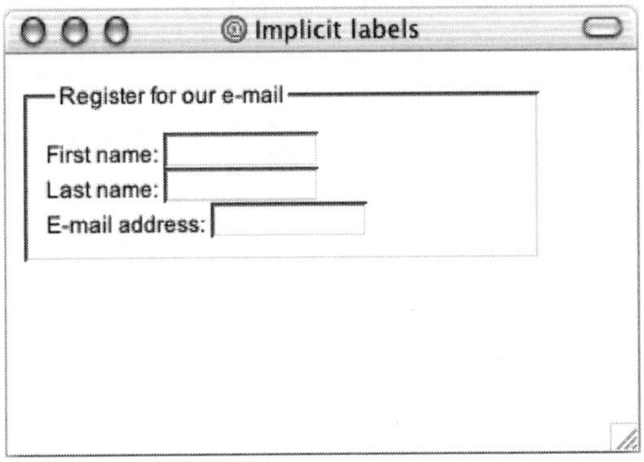

Figure 12-17

While `<label>` elements do require a little extra programming effort, it is generally a good idea to get into the habit of using them. Remember that the `<label>` element must either contain the form control or use the `for` attribute whose value is the value of the `id` attribute on the form control:

```
<label for="firstName">First name: </label>
<input type="text" name="txtFirstName" size="12" id="firstName" />

<label for="lastName">Last name: </label>
<input type="text" name="txtLastName" size="12" id="lastName" />

<label for="email">E-mail address: </label>
<input type="text" name="txtEmail" size="12" id="email" />
```

Unfortunately, this will look just the same as the previous example shown in Figure 12-17, but the `<label>` element does have advantages:

❑ It makes it easier for screen readers to associate a control with its label. In particular, you can associate labels with form controls even when the label is not next to that item—for example, in a table the label might be in a row above the form control.

❑ Labels can increase the clickable area of a radio button or checkbox, which some users find hard to accurately click on, because the user can click on the label.

Unfortunately, labels are supported only in IE 4 and Netscape 6 and later versions; however older browsers just ignore the `<label>` element and display their contents, so you are safe to use them on any form.

Here you can see the example of a form that allows you to indicate how you heard about a company. When the users click the label, the radio button associated with that form will be selected (ch12_eg15.html):

```
<form name="frmExample" action="" method="post">
  <fieldset>
    <legend>How did you hear about us?</legend>

    <input type="radio" id="referrer1" name="radReferrer" value="Mouth" />
    <label for="referrer1" >Word of Mouth</label><br />

    <input type="radio" id="referrer2" name="radReferrer" value="Google" />
    <label for="referrer2" >Google Search</label><br />

    <input type="radio" id="referrer3" name="radReferrer"
  value="Magazine Ad" />
    <label for="referrer3" >Magazine Ad</label><br />

    <input type="radio" id="referrer4" name="radReferrer" value="Other" />
    <label for="referrer4" >Other</label>  
    <input type="text" value="txtOther" size="12" /><br />

    <input type="submit" value="Submit" />
  </fieldset>
</form>
```

You can see this form in Figure 12-18.

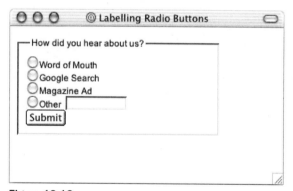

Figure 12-18

Remember that when choosing the prompt or the label for a form you must choose words that will really mean something to users. What might be obvious to you might not be so clear to a visitor that is not as familiar with the topic as you—for example a productId *number might be a unique identifying number for a product, but a customer can't be expected to know this or where to find it.*

Using Tables for Layout

As you saw in Chapter 11, many designers and programmers use tables for layout and positioning of elements on their Web pages. You must, however, remember how tables linearize in a screen reader (as discussed in Chapter 5).

To remind you how a screen reader would linearize a simple table, look at the following table.

Row 1 Column1	Row 1 Column 2
Row 2 Column 1	Row 2 Column 2
Row 3 Column 1	Row 3 Column 3

The cells of this table would generally be read row by row in the following order:

```
Row 1 Column 1, Row 1 Column 2, Row 2 Column 1, Row 2 Column 2,
Row 3 Column 1, Row 3 Column 2.
```

So, the correct way to lay out the previous example in a table would be as shown here (ch12_eg16 .html). Note that this example does not use the <label> elements so that you can understand the order in which elements are read without the use of this <label> element:

```
<table>
  <tr>
    <td class="formPrompt">First name: </td>
    <td><input type="text" name="txtFirstName" size="12" /></td>
  </tr>
  <tr>
    <td class="formPrompt">Last name: </td>
    <td><input type="text" name="txtLastName" size="12" /></td>
  </tr>
  <tr>
    <td class="formPrompt">E-mail address: </td>
    <td><input type="text" name="txtEmail" size="12" /></td>
  </tr>
</table>
```

This will order the elements correctly and users with a screen reader will understand the form. Note that the class="formPrompt" on the <td> elements that are labels is associated with a CSS style sheet rule that indicates the text should be right-aligned in the table, which makes for a much neater display on the pages and prevents large gaps between a label and its associated control. You can see the result in Figure 12-19.

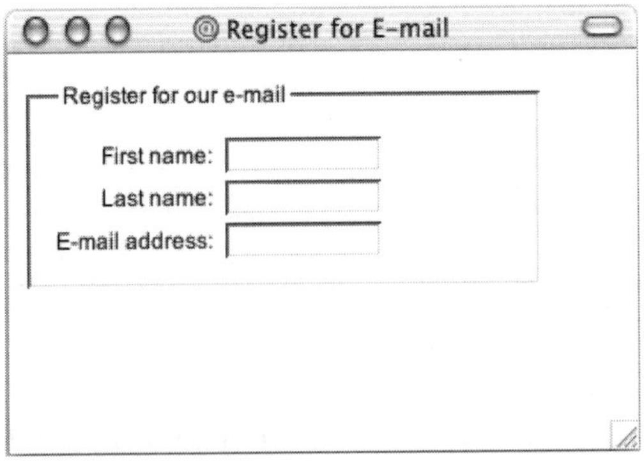

Figure 12-19

Tables that get more complex than this need a lot of consideration. For example, take a look at Figure 12-20.

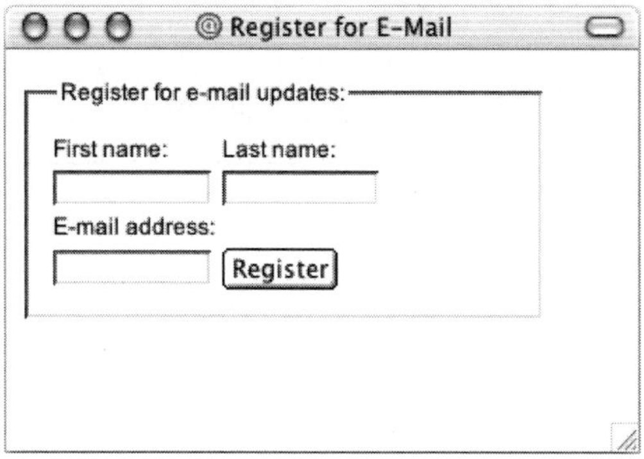

Figure 12-20

Here there are two columns of form controls and the labels are above the elements. This design would necessitate the use the `<label>` element; otherwise a screen reader would read the labels on the first row and then the two form controls on the second (ch12_eg17.html):

```
<table>
  <tr>
    <td><label for="fname">First name:</label></td>
    <td><label for="lname">Last name:</label></td>
  </tr>
  <tr>
    <td><input type="text" name="txtFirstName" id="fname" size="12" /></td>
    <td><input type="text" name="txtLastName" id="lname" size="12" /></td>
  </tr>
  <tr>
    <td><label for="email">E-mail address:</label></td>
    <td></td>
  </tr>
  <tr>
    <td><input type="text" name="txtEmail" id="email" size="12" /></td>
    <td><input type="submit" value="Register" /></td>
  </tr>
</table>
```

Generally, however, it is better to stick to a single column of form controls. While printed forms often use more than one column of questions, it is not a good idea to have more than one column of form controls on the Web for these reasons:

❑   You do not know the size of the user's screen, and the user might not be able to see the second column (especially the small percentage of users that browse at 640 × 480 resolution).

❑   It is more likely that users would miss one of the items on the form.

❑   You will have to employ a complex table layout that may confuse those with screen readers.

Keeping Relevant Information Next to or Above Form Controls

By now you are getting the idea of how vital good labelling is to a user's understanding, so here are a couple of examples where the position of a label requires extra care. Take a look at the example in Figure 12-21, which is for a telephone number.

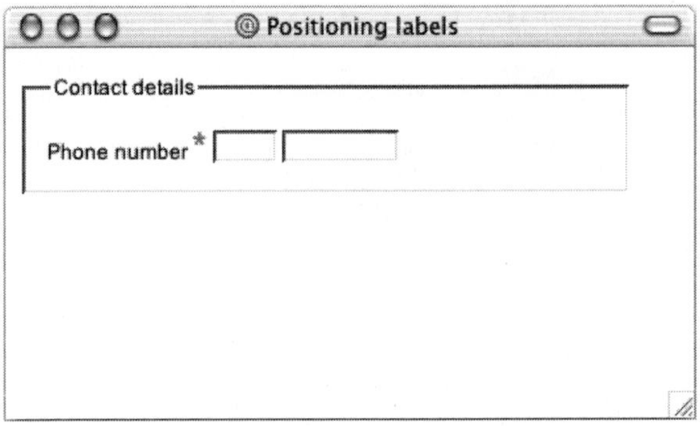

Figure 12-21

As you can see here, there is no indication what the separate boxes are for. While you or I might guess that one box is for the area code and the other for the main part of the number, users with screen readers are likely to be more confused by what the second box is for as they can only listen to the form, not see it. Some users, especially those in a hurry, might try to put the whole number in just one text box.

A far better approach to this example would be to indicate labels for the area code and the number, as shown in Figure 12-22.

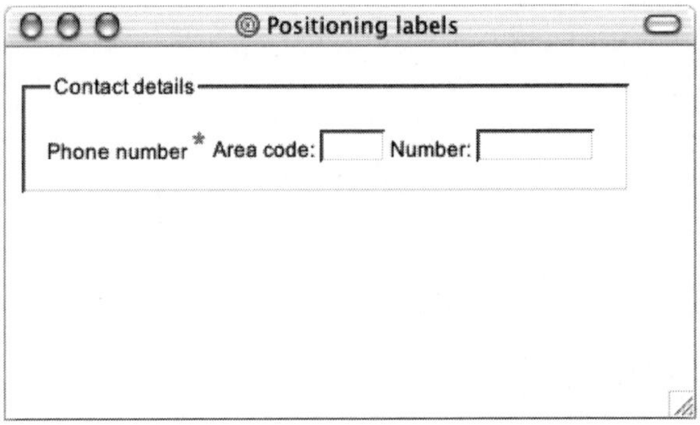

Figure 12-22

This is much clearer for all, and you can see the code here (ch12_eg18.html):

```
<table>
  <tr>
    <td class="label">Phone number <span class="important">*</span></td>
    <td>Area code<input type="text" name="txtTelAreaCode" size="5" />
        Number<input type="text" name="txtTelNo" size="10" /></td>
  </tr>
</table>
```

Proper labelling is also very important when you have radio buttons or multiple choice buttons that express an option or rating. You can see a problematic example in Figure 12-23.

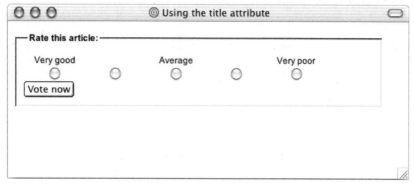

Figure 12-23

The code for this example puts the radio buttons and labels in a table. The problem with this example is not that the labels are not related to the correct radio buttons—as you can see the `<label>` element is used and associate with the correct table cells in the following code—the problem is that those with screen readers will hear labels for only three options, whereas there are really five options to choose from. You should be offering labels for each.

```
<table>
  <tr>
    <td><label for="VeryGood">Very good</label></td>
    <td></td>
    <td><label for="Average">Average</label></td>
    <td></td>
    <td><label for="VeryPoor">Very poor</label></td>
  </tr>
  <tr>
    <td><input type="radio" name="radRating" value="5" id="VeryGood"
    /></td>
    <td><input type="radio" name="radRating" value="4" id="Good" /></td>
    <td><input type="radio" name="radRating" value="3" id="Average" /></td>
    <td><input type="radio" name="radRating" value="2" id="Poor" /></td>
    <td><input type="radio" name="radRating" value="1" id="VeryPoor" /></td>
  </tr>
</table>
```

If you really do not want to offer a text alternative for each of these items, a rather drastic alternative is to use a single-pixel transparent GIF with alt text inside the `<label>` element, which will not show up in the browser (`ch12_eg19.html`) that explains each option for those with screen readers, as follows:

```
<table>
  <tr>
    <td><label for="VeryGood">Very good</label></td>
    <td><label for="Good"><img src="images/1px.gif" alt="This option
has no label its value is good" /></td>
```

```
    <td><label for="Average">Average</label></td>
    <td><label for="Poor"><img src="images/1px.gif" alt= "This option
has no label its value is poor" /></td>
    <td><label for="VeryPoor">Very poor</label></td>
  </tr>
  <tr>
    <td><input type="radio" name="radRating" value="5" id="VeryGood" /></td>
    <td><input type="radio" name="radRating" value="4" id="Good" /></td>
    <td><input type="radio" name="radRating" value="3" id="Average" /></td>
    <td><input type="radio" name="radRating" value="2" id="Poor" /></td>
    <td><input type="radio" name="radRating" value="1" id="VeryPoor" /></td>
  </tr>
</table>
```

You cannot actually see the difference between this example and the previous one, but you would be able to hear a difference if you could not see it and were relying on a screen reader.

Required Information

A form will often include questions that a user must answer in order for it to be processed correctly. If a form control must be filled in, you should tell a user this. It's common practice to use an asterisk (*) to indicate required fields and of course to include a note on the page that acts as a key indicating what the asterisk means. Furthermore, it is common to put the asterisk in a different color (such as red) than the main text next to it so users can see it is important.

```
First name <span class="required">*</span>:
<input type="text" name="txtFirstName" size="12" />
```

The required class could be used with a CSS rule like this:

```
span.required {
    font-weight:bold;
    font-size:20px;
    color:#ff0000;}
```

You can see an example of this in Figures 12-22 and 12-23, the screenshots of the telephone number example.

Careful Placement of Buttons

You should be very careful about where you place buttons on a page. They should be close to the relevant part of the form; for example, in an online store they should be close to the product, as in Figure 12-24.

If you use "Next," "Proceed," or "Submit" buttons on a form—for example to link between different pages of the form to indicate that a user should go on to the next step—these buttons should be on the right side of the page; "Back" buttons should be on the left side. This mirrors the user's experience with the Back and Forward buttons on a browser window (with Back being the first button on the left and Forward being to the right of it). It also follows the direction of the text that visitors will be reading in languages where the text flows from left to right (so as users come to the end of a form, they should be reading from left to right). You can see an example of this in Figure 12-25.

Figure 12-24

Note that, if you use a Reset or Clear form button, it should be to the left of the Submit or Next button because it reflects previous experience of Web users.

Providing title Text for Form Controls

One way of adding extra information for users is to add a `title` attribute to the form control. When users put their cursor over the form control, the value of the `title` attribute appears as a tooltip. This is particularly helpful for clarifying the type of information that a user has to enter.

For example, here is a text input that requires a user to enter an authorization code. The `title` attribute clarifies where the authorization code comes from (`ch12_eg20.html`):

```
<form name="frmExample" action="" method="post">
  <fieldset>
    <legend>Enter your authorization code</legend>
    Code: 
```

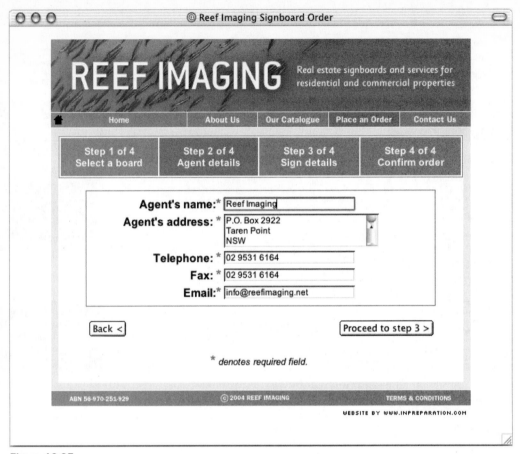

Figure 12-25

```
        <input type="text" name="txtAuthCode" title="Enter the authorization
        code that was e-mailed when you registered." /></td>

  </fieldset>
  </form>
```

You can see the result in Figure 12-26, with the tooltip showing as the user hovers over the text input.

Tab Index

Once you have created your form you should check the tabbing order of form elements. Users should be able to use the Tab key on their keyboard to move between the form controls. If the order in which the form controls gain focus is not the order in which you would expect to fill out the form, you should use the tabindex attribute, which can take a value of 1 to 32,767 (Chapter 6 covered this attribute).

The tabindex attribute can be used on the following elements:

```
<a> <area> <button> <input> <object> <select> <textarea>
```

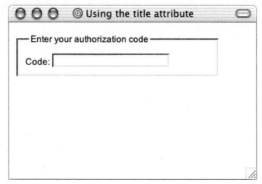

Figure 12-26

In Chapter 15 you will see an example of how you can automatically give focus to a form element when the page loads. You will also see how to affect the appearance of the form controls that currently have focus.

Don't Rely on Color to Convey Information

While color can be a very powerful tool in aiding the understanding of forms, you should never rely on a color alone to convey information, and you must ensure that there is enough contrast between colors to make the distinction clear.

For example, you should not just use color to indicate required fields on a form. In Figure 12-27 the form uses color to indicate which fields are required, but because this book is printed in black and white and the form uses color to convey information you cannot see which items must be filled in.

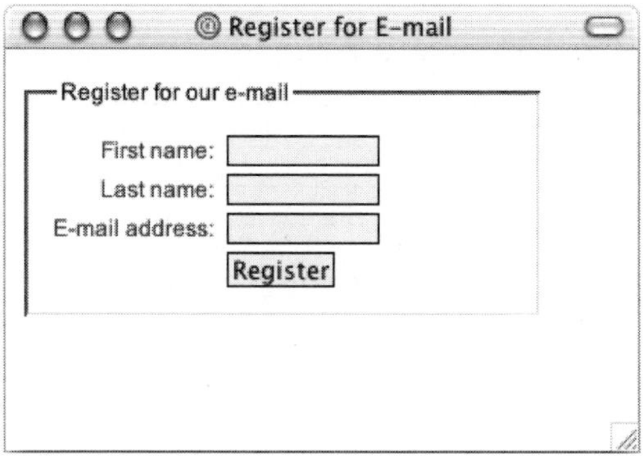

Figure 12-27

> This is an important issue because a fair number of people have some form of color blindness.

You can, however, resolve the problem easily. As you can see in Figure 12-28 the fields that are mandatory use the asterisk as well as color.

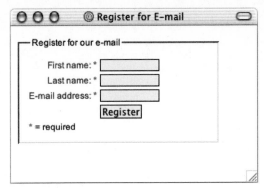

Figure 12-28

A good way to test whether you are relying on color too much is to change the settings of your monitor so that they are showing in grayscale (on Windows use the Display Properties in the Control Panel and on a Mac use the Display settings in the System Preferences). If information is lost when the page is grayscale then you are relying on color too much.

Using CSS with Form Elements

IE 5 and Netscape 6 and later versions allow you to associate CSS styles with some form controls. While the support for all form controls is rather patchy you can easily change things such as borders and background colors of text inputs, text areas, and submit buttons to create more of a styled form than you could create with plain HTML.

Figure 12-29 shows a form whose text inputs have solid black borders and very light gray backgrounds.

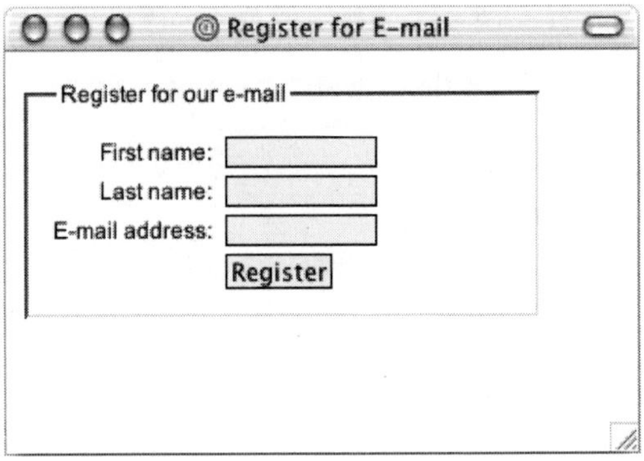

Figure 12-29

Here is the CSS style that is associated with the `<input>` elements (ch12_eg21.html):

```
input {
  border-style:solid;
  border-color:#000000;
  border-width:1px;
  background-color:#f2f2f2;}
```

If you use styles with form elements you just have to make sure that you do not make the form harder to fill in by adding unnecessary style. As with any kind of text, if you do not have good contrast for text controls, they will be hard to read and users might enter the incorrect information.

Testing the Form

Once you have laid out your form, you then need to test the form. You will see more about testing a site in Chapter 16. Briefly, however, it is very helpful to watch people using your form once you have designed it to see how they interact with it.

The most important thing while doing this, and which you must remember, is that if you can see that a user is going to make a mistake, don't interrupt him; watch what he does, as it will teach you more about how the user expected the form to work.

Try It Out   A Site Registration Form

In this example you are going to create a simple registration form for a Web site. You will have to collect the information listed in the table that follows using the form controls listed.

Information	Form control	Required
First name	Text input	Yes
Last name	Text input	Yes
E-mail address	Text input	Yes
Password for accessing the site	Password text input	Yes
Confirmation of Password	Password text input	Yes
Register	Submit button	N/A

Figure 12-30 shows you what the form will look like when you are finished.

1. First set up the skeleton of the document, as you are probably used to by now. Don't forget the link to the CSS style sheet called `registration.css`. You can also add a `<form>` element:

```
<html>
  <head>
    <title>Try it out</title>
    <link rel="stylesheet" type="text/css" href="registration.css" />
  </head>
  <body>

  <form name="frmExample" action="" method="post">
  </form>

  </body>
</html>
```

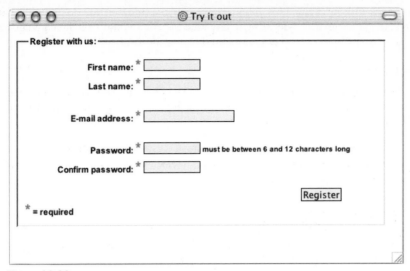

Figure 12-30

2. The form contains only five text inputs so it does not need splitting into separate groups, but it would be a good idea to put the whole thing in a `<fieldset>` element with a `<legend>`:

```
<form name="frmExample" action="" method="post">
<fieldset>
  <legend>Register with us:</legend>

</fieldset>
</form>
```

3. The rest of the form lives inside a table within the `<fieldset>` element. The table has two columns, one for labels and the other for form controls, and the cells in each column need to have a separate `class` attribute.

The value of the `class` attribute on the cells that contain labels will be `label`, while the value of the `class` attribute in the cells that contain a form control will be `form`. Each form element's label will use a `<label>` element. And each form control is required so you can add a required notice next to the labels.

The first row will contain a text input for the user's first name. You can add it like this:

```
<table>
  <tr>
    <td class="label">
      <label for="fname">First name: <span class="required">*</span></label>
    </td>
    <td class="form">
      <input type="text" name="txtFirstName" id="fname" size="12" />
    </td>
  </tr>
</table>
```

4. Add the text input for the last name and the e-mail address. You can make the size of the e-mail address text input a little larger than the other text inputs as this is likely to be longer:

```
<tr>
  <td class="label">
    <label for="lname">Last name:
    <span class="required">*</span></label>
  </td>
  <td class="form">
    <input type="text" name="txtLastName" id="lname" size="12" />
  </td>
</tr>

<tr><td> </td><td> </td></tr>

<tr>
  <td class="label">
    <label for="email">E-mail address:
    <span class="required">*</span></label>
  </td>
  <td class="form">
    <input type="password" name="txtEmail" id="email" size="20" />
  </td>
</tr>
<tr><td> </td><td> </td></tr>
```

An empty row of the table has been added above and below the e-mail address row to space out the form a bit more. If you just have a long list of form controls, the form can seem longer and more complicated than if the rows are split up a little, although in this case they do not need to be split up into distinct sections.

5. The final two controls users will have to fill in allow them to provide a password for the site and to confirm it. Both `<input>` elements have a `type` attribute whose value is `password`. In order to explain that the password should be between 6 and 12 characters long, a message has been added after the first password box in the right column. The reason for adding the note to the right of the password input is that it would throw out alignment of labels on the left if it were placed on the same side.

```
<tr>
  <td class="label">
    <label for="pwd">Password: <span class="required">*</span></label>
  </td>
  <td class="form">
    <input type="password" name="txtPassword" id="pwd" size="12" />
    <span class="small"> must be between 6 and 12 characters long</span>
  </td>
</tr>

<tr>
  <td class="label">
    <label for="pwdConf">Confirm password:
    <span class="required">*</span></label>
```

```
    </td>
    <td class="form">
      <input type="password" name="txtPasswordConf" id="pwdConf" size="12" />
    </td>
  </tr>
```

6. A Submit button has to be added to the end of the form. You put this in a `<div>` so that it can be positioned to the right side of the form. This is followed by the key to explain the purpose of the asterisk.

```
<div class="submit"><input type="submit" value="Register" /></div>
<span class="required">*</span> = required
```

7. Save this form as `registration.html`, and when you open this page up in a browser you should see a page that looks like page shown previously in Figure 12-30.

Here is the CSS style sheet used with this example (`registration.css`):

```
body{color:#000000; background-color:#ffffff;
  font-family:arial, verdana, sans-serif; font-size:12pt;}

fieldset {font-size:12px; font-weight:bold; padding:10px;
  width:500px;}

td {font-size:12px;}
td.label {text-align:right;
  width:175px;}
td.form {width:350px;}

div.submit {width:450px; text-align:right; padding-top:15px;}

span.small {font-size:10px;}
span.required {font-weight:bold; font-size:20px; color:#ff0000;}

input {border-style:solid; border-color:#000000; border-width:1px;
  background-color:#f2f2f2;}
```

How It Works

This example is fairly straightforward, but here are some things to note about the example:

❑ The form labels and form controls are aligned using a two-column table and CSS. This makes the form much neater and easier to read compared with a table where form elements are not aligned.

❑ Each form control is labelled with a `<label>` element.

❑ A screen reader should easily be able to read the correct information to the user because of the way the table linearizes the content.

❑ The form is contained in a `<fieldset>` element to show the boundary and size of the form, and this is given a `<legend>` to describe the purpose of the form.

❑ Required information is indicated with a red asterisk that uses color and a symbol to indicate some extra meaning (remember that you should not rely on color alone to convey meaning).

❑ Whitespace is added to either side of the e-mail input to make the layout more attractive and less intimidating.

❑ The Submit button is moved to the right of the form with the use of a `<div>`. Putting submission buttons to the right follows the way the eye scans a page and indicates moving forward not backward—and coincides with users' experience of how the forward button is positioned to the right of the Back button on a browser menu.

❑ The text inputs and submit button were given CSS styles to give them outlines and backgrounds, a more stylized presentation than plain XHTML form controls.

Summary

In this chapter you have learned a lot more about Web page layout. In Chapter 11, you looked at the general layout or structure of a page. In this chapter, you learned about issues regarding particular parts of pages: text, navigation, tables and forms—the bits that fill in that structure. From adding whitespace between elements on a page, such as text and images, to aligning parts of a form inside a table, you've seen lots of handy hints that will help you design better pages.

You have to remember, however, that there are no set rules that will make you a good designer; whether you have the eye for Web design depends on how artistic and creative you are. It's a bit like being an artist in that it requires a skill, patience, and practice. It's a little like being well-dressed in that having good taste in clothes is hard to explain, or like being an interior decorator in that you have to know how things will work together. It's also a bit like being an architect in that you need to ensure that everyone is able to access the site. It's a bit like being a brand consultant in that you need to choose the right colors and select fonts that work well with the aims and values of your site.

What you have learned in this chapter is how to make the designs you might sketch on paper come to life, as well as tips and tricks on how to make them work.

The only real restrictions you should impose upon yourself when designing a Web page surround what your audience would find attractive and easy to use. Remember that if you want your site to attract a lot of visitors, don't design the site just for yourself, and don't just design it for your clients; design it for expected visitors to the site.

Exercises

The answers to all of the exercises are in Appendix A.

1. In this exercise you should add a second page to the Try It Out form at the end of the chapter (`registration.html`). The table that follows shows the new items you must add to the form.

You should also add the following:

❑ An indication at the top of the page as to how much of the form the user has completed

❑ A Back button and a Proceed button at the bottom (instead of the Submit button)

Information	Form control	Required
Address 1	Text input	Yes
Address 2	Text input	No
Town/Suburb	Text input	No
City/State	Text input	Yes
ZIP Code	Text input	Yes

When you have finished the page should look something like Figure 12-31 (`registration2.html`).

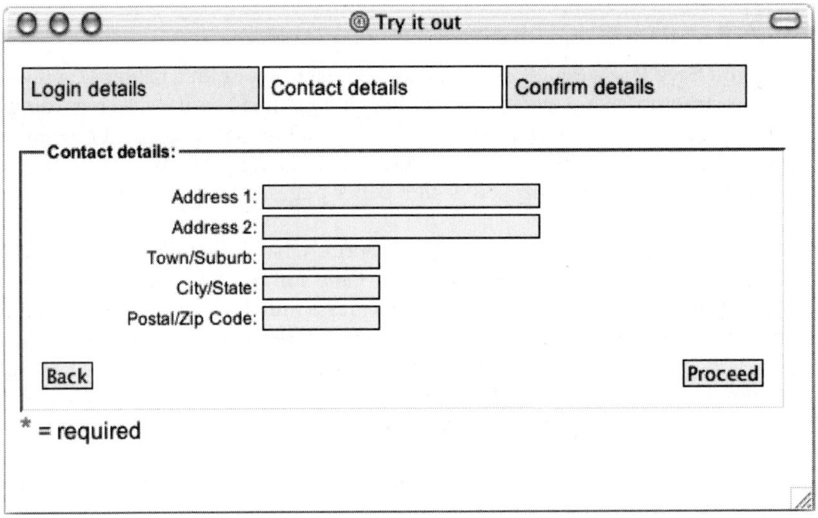

Figure 12-31

Modularized XHTML and Serving Multiple Devices

In this chapter you look into the future and learn where XHTML and Web development are heading. While you don't *need* to know what you will learn in this chapter in order to start building Web pages, this chapter teaches you how XHTML can help you write pages that will last longer, and which won't have to be rewritten again when technologies change and when you really do find the new breed of Internet-enabled devices—other than desktop PCs—accessing the Web.

Throughout this book I have made many references to other devices that can access the Internet such as phones, PDAs, even fridges and microwaves. I have indicated how voice browsers not only have the potential to help those with vision impairments to access the Web, but also car drivers or anyone on the move. All of this might sound a little far fetched today. But in this chapter you will see that it's a lot closer than you think.

Despite marketing hype about mobile phones being able to access the Web, relatively few people use them for this purpose compared with those that access the Web via desktop computers. But times are changing; an increasing amount of services are becoming available on mobile phones. Furthermore, wireless networks mean you no longer need a wire to your modem in order to access the Web; you can have access in every room in your house. You can even find wireless *hot spots* in some cafes in the major cities of the world. The next step will be devices that really take advantage of this freedom. When a Web-enabled microwave costs only $50 more than a standard microwave, you might just work out that it is the price of only a couple of cookbooks and decide to use the Web for recipes instead of paper. Suddenly these technologies are not quite so far fetched.

But why does this matter for you? Consider the following:

❑ There will be many more browsers than the dominant IE and Netscape, and you will want your pages to work in all of them.

❑ Different devices will have different capabilities, depending upon the screen size, memory, and power available to them.

So, in this chapter you learn all about how the technologies you have learned so far in this book will adapt to these new various devices.

Introducing Modularized XHTML

Modularized XHTML is the next logical step from XHTML 1.0 (which you have been learning in this book) and will help you develop Web pages that work on all different kinds of browsers.

In this chapter you learn the following:

❑ How XHTML has been split into separate modules, each with related functionality, making it easier to support various devices

❑ How XHTML 1.0's successor XHTML 1.1 is actually made from a selection of these modules

❑ About XHTML MP, a language created for use with mobile devices that uses a subset of the modules used in XHTML 1.1 that reflect the capabilities of smaller devices

❑ Why XHTML and separation of style from content really are advantages if you end up creating different versions of sites for different devices

❑ How XHTML plays well with other emerging technologies, such as SVG and MathML

❑ An example of a Web site that works on a desktop PC and a mobile phone

This doesn't mean you have to learn lots of new markup—almost all of the markup is the same as it was in Strict XHTML 1.0—rather, this chapter explains the theory behind splitting up XHTML and what it means in terms of how Web sites are developed today and how they will be developed in the future. As you will see, reading this chapter now could save you a lot of time in the future and give you an edge over Web developers that are not keeping an eye on where the technology is headed.

Where We Are Today

So far in this book you have been learned to write Web pages in XHTML 1.0. Throughout the book, and particularly in Chapter 9, you have also seen some older markup from previous versions of HTML that is still widely used today. As you learned in Chapter 1, this older markup can be used in the Transitional XHTML 1.0 document type but not in the Strict XHTML document type.

So, you should have a good balance of skills. You know the latest techniques and have the ability to write code that follows best practices such as closing all tags properly, using lowercase characters for element and attributes names, and putting all attribute values in quotes. All of these techniques help make your pages XHTML-compliant. But you have also seen that some of the older ways of doing things are still the best or only ways of getting a job done—for example, some layouts are going to look better in many users' browsers if you use tables rather than CSS positioning. It's important to know these older techniques so that your skills are practical today in a market where not everyone's browsers support the latest W3C recommendations and so that you can read code in pages that does not adhere to the stricter principles of XHTML.

I hope, then, that you will not be too concerned when I tell you that Modularized XHTML is already a W3C recommendation and has the same status as XHTML 1.0. It shouldn't worry you because you will learn all about it in this one chapter. When designing pages for browsers that run on desktop PCs most of the differences are conceptual; there are only a couple of real changes to the code itself. However, Modularized XHTML really steps out into the spotlight when creating new document types—in particular, hybrid documents that contain markup from different languages and in creating languages for different devices.

As you will see in this chapter Modularized XHTML has already been used to create a version of XHTML for use on mobile phones that is already being used by many large companies such as Nokia.

Modularizing XHTML

While not everyone uses them yet, there are already various devices on the market that will access the Internet. If you have the money you can go and buy mobile phones, PDAs, TVs, digital book readers, and even refrigerators that are Web-enabled.

But some of these devices have different capabilities; for example:

❑   Some have monochrome displays, while others are color.

❑   Different devices have different screen sizes (and different shapes—some are wider or taller than others).

❑   Different screens have different resolutions.

❑   Not all of the HTML 4 specification is relevant to all devices; for example, book readers do not need to know about the colors or sizes of fonts that they are reading.

❑   Different devices will need different added functions that are not part of the HTML 4 specification. Phones might need to respond to events such as a call or receipt of an SMS message, while a TV might respond to the end of a program.

❑   Some devices have more power available to them than others (some run off mains while others have limited battery life).

❑   Some devices have very little memory available to them; others have plenty.

Trying to fit a complex Web site onto a phone's screen can be like putting a whole magazine on a postage stamp. Even if the screen could support a table that was 700 pixels wide it would be too small to read. And given that some screens are a mere 128 pixels wide, you cannot assume every device has the same size canvas.

Furthermore, some devices just don't have the same power source or memory available to them to run the whole XHTML specification. The browsers have to be a lot smaller than the versions of IE 6 or Netscape 7 that run on your desktop (for example Netscape 7.1 requires 52MB of hard drive space and 64MB of RAM).

When mobile phones that accessed the Internet first became a big thing, around 1999–2000, the industry came up with different specifications devised to address the needs of these devices (with smaller screens, less memory, and so on). Their specifications included:

❑   WML (Wireless Markup Language), more commonly known as being part of the WAP (wireless access protocol) group of specifications

❑   HDML (Handheld Device Markup Language)

❑   cHTML (Compact HTML)

❑   HTML 4.0 Guidelines for Mobile Access

But if you look at these competing languages that have sprung up to support the different devices, you can see that they share common features. Each language allows users to mark up the following types of information:

❑ Basic text, including headings, paragraphs, and lists

❑ Hyperlinks and links to related documents

❑ Basic forms

❑ Basic tables

❑ Images

❑ Metainformation (information *about* the Web page, rather than the content itself)

The W3C understood that the various devices that can now access the Internet were no longer able to be served by one single language: HTML. Therefore, rather than have several competing languages for every new type of device, the W3C thought it would be much better if XHTML was split into modules, with each module covering some common functionality (such as basic text or hyperlinks).

Splitting XHTML into modules has two key advantages:

❑ The modules could be used as building blocks for different variations of XHTML developed for different devices (rather than using completely different markup language for each type of device).

❑ If a new document type is created it should either support a module completely or not at all. That way a document type could simply list the modules it supports and developers would have a head start on understanding it.

Instead of reinventing the wheel, as WML, cHTML and HDML did, all new languages could be built from these same basic building blocks. The new document types would be based on what is known as an *XHTML Host Language*, which can then be extended with other modules that will fit the needs of that particular device—for example a phone could add features so that it could respond to events such as phone calls and messages as they are received or ended.

The 32 Abstract Modules

The first step of modularizing XHTML was to define a set of abstract modules that could be used as the building blocks of languages that belonged to the XHTML family. Each of these modules would contain related functionality. Then languages could be built from these basic modules. The XHTML 1.0 recommendation was therefore split into 32 abstract modules, which you learn about in a moment.

As you will see from the following table, the XHTML 1.1 DTD (*Document Type Definition*, the document that contains the rules for what markup can appear in a document and where that markup can appear within a document) contains 21 of these modules, which cover the functionality of the XHTML 1.0 Strict DTD. (You will learn more about DTDs in the next section.)

Later in the chapter, you learn about another document type called XHTML Basic, which was designed as a host language for use on smaller devices. As you will also see from the table, XHTML Basic uses just 11 of the modules. This gives you a much better idea of how languages can be created using these modules as the building blocks.

So, the following table shows the full list of XHTML Abstract Modules, and you can see which ones belong to three different groups:

- ❑ The core modules are the modules that must be supported in order for a language to be part of the XHTML family. This is the minimum requirements list.

- ❑ XHTML Basic is a cut down version of XHTML designed for use on small devices.

- ❑ XHTML 1.1 is the modularized version of XHTML (and corresponds to Strict XHTML 1.0).

Module Name	Core Module	XHTML Basic	XHTML 1.1
Structure	X	X	X
Text	X	X	X
Hypertext	X	X	X
List	X	X	X
Applet			
Object		X	X
Presentation			X
Edit			X
Bidirectional text			X
Frames			
IFrame			
Basic forms		X	
Forms			X
Basic tables		X	
Table			X
Image		X	X
Client-side image map			X
Server-side image map			X
Intrinsic events			X
Metainformation		X	X
Scripting			X
Stylesheet			X
Style attribute (deprecated)			X

Continues

Module Name	Core Module	XHTML Basic	XHTML 1.1
Link		X	X
Target			
Base		X	X
Ruby annotation			X
Name identification			
Legacy			

Note that the legacy module can be used to support elements that have been deprecated from earlier versions of HTML and XHTML and is therefore helpful in writing code that supports older devices, but these do not belong to the XHTML 1.1 recommendation.

How Modules Are Implemented Using Schemas

When you create a language in XML, such as XHTML or XHTML Basic, you have to define rules for it; you say what markup it can contain (the names of the elements and attributes), where they can appear in the document, and so on. These rules are written in a special document called a *schema*.

The two most common formats of schemas are *DTDs* and *XML Schemas*. DTDs (Document Type Definitions) use a strange notation called Extended Backus Naur Form (EBNF), whereas XML Schemas are a more recent addition and are written in XML. You certainly do not need to worry about learning about DTDs and XML Schemas unless you start creating your own languages or using languages that have not been documented. But it helps to know that each of these modules has its own schema that says what makes up that module.

The schema for each module of XHTML is known as the module implementation—after all, that is the document that says what markup makes up that module. Implementations of these modules have been written as DTDs and XML Schema documents. So, anyone that wants to create a language based on these modules incorporates the rules of their chosen modules in a new language.

XHTML 1.1

As I mentioned earlier in the chapter, XHTML 1.1 contains 21 of the XHTML abstract modules. These correspond with the functionality of Strict XHTML 1.0. As you will see, there is little difference between writing an XHTML 1.1 document and a Strict XHTML 1.0 document. The fact that the language is based on modules makes little difference until you start developing sites for different devices.

In this section you will:

❑ See which elements belong to the modules that make up XHTML 1.1 (and some of the key attributes)

❑ Learn the differences between an XHTML 1.1 document and a Strict XHTML 1.0 document.

After looking at XHTML 1.1 you will see a little bit more about XHTML Basic and then you will see how both can be applied to an example site.

Looking at XHTML 1.1's Modules

It's now time to meet the modules that are used in XHTML 1.1. Because each module corresponds to a set of functionality, their names are often quite similar to the topic and section headings in this book that introduced the corresponding functionality. You will also see the elements that make up each of the modules, and notable attributes where relevant.

You have already learned about nearly all of the elements in XHTML 1.1. There is no new markup to learn; the only element you have not seen yet in this book will be covered in Chapter 16. So this section teaches you how the elements (which were covered earlier in the book) are grouped together.

Structure Module

The structure module contains the main elements for the skeleton of a document:

```
<body>, <head>, <html>, <title>
```

Text Module

The text module contains elements that allow you to mark up text so that the elements describe their content and the structure of the document. You learned about these elements in Chapter 2.

```
<abbr>, <acronym>, <address>, <blockquote>, <br>, <cite>, <code>,
<dfn>, <div>, <em>, <h1, <h2>, <h3>, <h4>, <h5>, <h6>, <kbd>, <p>, <pre>,
<q>, <samp>, <span>, <strong, <var>
```

Hypertext Module

The hypertext module contains just one element for creating links, which you learned about in Chapter 3.

```
<a>
```

List Module

The list module allows you to create the three types of lists you learned about in Chapter 2: unordered lists, ordered lists, and definition lists:

```
<ul>, <li>, <ol>, <dl>, <dt>, <dd>
```

Object Module

The object module contains the `<object>` element, which is used for including all kinds of objects into a document. You learned about `<object>` in Chapter 3, along with `<param>`, the other element in this module that can pass parameters to the object.

```
<object>, <param>
```

Presentation Module

The presentation module contains the elements that you learned about in Chapter 2 for marking up text that affect how it is presented.

```
<b>, <big>, <hr>, <i>, <small>, <sub>, <sup>, <tt>
```

Edit Module

The edit module contains the two elements you need to indicate which parts of a document have been added to or removed in different versions as users modify the document.

```
<del>, <ins>
```

Bidirectional Text Module

The bidirectional text module contains the one element for handling bidirectional text, which is very important for browsers that will work with languages that are read in more than one direction.

```
<bdo>
```

Forms Module

The forms module allows you to include forms in a page and contains elements to create the form controls you learned about in Chapter 6.

```
<button>, <fieldset>, <form>, <input>, <label>, <legend>, <select>,
<optgroup>, <option>, <textarea>
```

Table Module

The table module is strictly intended for use in displaying tabular data. If you are going to develop true XHTML 1.1 applications (or indeed Strict XHTML 1.0 applications) you should not be using the `<table>` element as a method of controlling the appearance of a document or the layout of a page.

```
<caption>, <col>, <colgroup>, <table>, <tbody>, <td>, <tfoot>, <th>,
<thead>, <tr>
```

However, as you saw in Chapter 11, tables are still commonly used on sites designed primarily for desktop computers, as they are the most accurate way of controlling a layout that will work in the majority of browsers.

Image Module

The image module, for including images, contains the one element you learned about in Chapter 4:

```
<img>
```

Client-Side Image Map Module

The client-side image map module is used solely for creating client-side image maps (which were discussed in Chapter 4) and has two elements:

```
<area>, <map>
```

Server-Side Image Map Module

The server-side image map module is used solely for creating server-side image maps (which were discussed in Chapter 4). It contains only one attribute used on the `<img>` element:

```
ismap
```

Intrinsic Events Module

Intrinsic events are attributes that are used with elements that fire events when certain actions are performed by a user. If the module defining the elements listed here is selected, then they can carry the attributes listed in the table that follows:

Elements	Attributes	Corresponding Modules
`<a>`	`onblur, onfocus`	Hypertext (which is a core module)
`<area>`	`onblur, onfocus`	Client-side image map
`<frameset>`	`onload, onunload`	Frames
`<form>`	`onreset, onsubmit`	Basic forms or forms
`<body>`	`onload, onunload`	Structure (which is a core module)
`<label>`	`onblur, onfocus`	Forms
`<input>`	`onblur, onchange, onfocus, onselect`	Basic forms or forms
`<select>`	`onblur, onchange, onfocus`	Basic forms or forms
`<textarea>`	`onblur, onchange, onfocus, onselect`	Basic forms or forms
`<button>`	`onblur, onfocus`	Forms

Metainformation Module

The Metainformation module contains the one element, which you learn about in Chapter 16, that allows you to add information about the document: the `<meta>` element. This can include a title and keywords that will be used by search engines (and other applications) to determine the content of a document.

```
<meta>
```

Scripting Module

The scripting element contains the two elements that are used to contain a script and indicate what happens if the browser does not support the identified scripting language:

```
<noscript>, <script>
```

Stylesheet Module

The `<style>` element is used to include CSS rules within a document, inside the `<head>` element.

```
<style>
```

Style Attribute (Module Deprecated)

The style attribute is the one you met in Chapter 11 and allows you to specify inline CSS style rules. Because content is supposed to be separated from stylistic rules, this has been deprecated.

```
style="CSS rules"
```

Link Module

The link module contains just one element that allows you to describe links between documents, such as a document and a style sheet or a JavaScript—in both of these cases the file that is linked to is used with the file.

```
<link>
```

Base Module

The base module contains the base element that is used in conjunction with links to indicate a base URL for pages. You learned about this element in Chapter 3.

```
<base>
```

Ruby Annotation Module

XHTML also uses the Ruby Annotation module as defined in the W3C's Ruby recommendation:

```
<ruby>, <rbc>, <rtc>, <rb>, <rt>, <rp>
```

Ruby is a term for a run of small character annotations that are sometimes added to the characters of an ideographic script such as Japanese to clarify the pronunciation (and/or the meaning) of those characters. In vertical text they are usually added in a very small font along the side of the ideogram, while in horizontal text they are used on the top.

The Differences Between XHTML 1.0 and XHTML 1.1

The modules used give the same functionality that we found in Strict XHTML 1.0. The only changes you have to make from writing a Strict XHTML 1.0 document are:

❑ The DOCTYPE declaration must precede the root element. The public identifier, if present, should be represented like so:

```
<!DOCTYPE html PUBLIC "-//W3C//DTD XHTML 1.1//EN"
    "http://www.w3.org/TR/xhtml11/DTD/xhtml11.dtd">
```

❑ The root element should carry the xmlns attribute indicating the namespace for the document.

❑ The lang attribute on each element has been removed; you should use the xml:lang attribute instead.

❑ The name attribute on the <a> and <map> elements has been removed; you should use the id attribute instead.

❑ The ruby collection of elements has been added.

❑ The style attribute has been deprecated.

Here is an example of an XHTML 1.1 conforming document (ch13_eg01.html):

```
<?xml version="1.0" encoding="UTF-8" ?>
<!DOCTYPE html PUBLIC "-//W3C//DTD XHTML 1.1//EN"
    "http://www.w3.org/TR/xhtml11/DTD/xhtml11.dtd">

<html xmlns="http://www.w3.org/1999/xhtml" xml:lang="en" >
  <head>
    <title>Example 1</title>
  </head>
  <body>
    <p>This document conforms to XHTML 1.1.</p>
  </body>
</html>
```

XHTML Basic

As I have already mentioned, the memory and power that would be required to implement the full HTML specification would be too high for some smaller devices. So, rather than create a whole new language for these devices from scratch, XHTML Basic was designed to be a *host language* document type that supports content authoring for small devices such as mobile phones, PDAs, and set top boxes.

What Is XHTML Basic?

The idea with XHTML Basic being a host language for small devices is that, if you are going to create a new document type for a small device, it should be based on XHTML Basic and support all of its features. Then, where necessary, it can build upon these features. For example, some devices may require extra events that trigger when a phone call or SMS message is received.

XHTML Basic is made up of the core modules of XHTML (structure, text, hypertext, and list) and the basic forms, basic tables, image, object, metainformation, link, and base modules. Any language that uses XHTML Basic as a host language will support all of the features of these modules.

The advantages of this approach are as follows:

❑ Document authors know that there is a set of features that they can expect all small devices that use XHTML Basic as a host language to support. This makes authoring pages for these devices easier.

❑ The same content will be available to more devices and more content will be available to all devices.

❑ It is easier to learn new languages for devices because the core set of modules remains the same.

When a host language such as XHTML Basic is extended, if the features are available in another of XHTML's abstract modules, that module should be added. For example if you wanted to add scripting or CSS support then the scripting and CSS modules should be used (rather than re-creating them).

The following table provides a quick summary of the modules and elements available in XHTML Basic.

Module	Markup
Structure*	body, head, html, title
Text*	abbr, acronym, address, blockquote, br, cite, code, dfn, div, em, h1, h2, h3, h4, h5, h6, kbd, p, pre, q, samp, span, strong, var
Hypertext*	a
List*	dl, dt, dd, ol, ul, li
Basic forms	form, input, label, select, option, textarea
Basic tables	table, tr, td, th, caption
Image	img
Object	object, param
Metainformation	meta
Link	link
Base	base

* = core module.

Later in the chapter you will see an example of a language for mobile phones that was developed using XHTML Basic as a host language. It is this kind of subsetting and extending of XHTML that makes it a strong foundation for all document types required by new devices of the future.

What XHTML Basic Includes and Leaves Out

You have already seen that HTML 4 contained features that not every device could support and that several competing markup languages for mobile devices re-created common functionality. You also know it will be a base for further extensions. So, here are some of the things that were left behind and why:

❑ The <style> element was left out because you can use the link element to link to external style sheets to style a document for different types of client. Therefore, browsers that support style sheets can download them, but they are not required to display information.

❑ The <script> and <noscript> elements are not supported because small devices might not have the memory and CPU power to handle execution of scripts or programs. Indeed, as scripting languages have developed they have become very powerful in themselves, but the power has come at the cost of the size of, and memory required by, scripting engines. It was deemed that documents for these devices should be readable without requiring scripts.

❑ Event handler attributes, which are used to invoke scripts, are not supported because events tend to be device-dependent. For example, a TV might have an onChannelChange event, whereas a phone might have an incomingCall event, neither of which applies to the other device. Ideally, it would be better to use a generic event handling mechanism than hardwiring event names into the DTD.

❑ While basic XHTML forms are supported, more complex form functions are not applicable to all small devices. For example, if a device does not have a local file system it will not be able to use the file and image input types in forms. This is why only the basic XHTML forms module is included.

❑ As with forms, only basic tables are supported. Tables can be difficult to display on small devices, so features of the tables module will not apply to all small devices; for example, the nesting of tables is left out. Furthermore, tables should be created only for representing tabular data, not for layout purposes.

So, while XHTML Basic can be used as is, the intention is that it be used as a host language. Extra features could be added in a particular implementation that would support the requirements of the target device. Adding markup from other languages results in a new document type that is an extension of XHTML Basic.

Understanding XML Namespaces

When you create any new language in XML (such as an extension of XHTML) it will have its own namespace. You might remember the term "namespace" from earlier chapters, but it is time to have a closer look at namespaces.

As you already know, XHTML is written in XML. The idea behind XML is that it is a language in which you create different markup languages. So, XHTML is an example of a language written in XML. All languages written in XML look very similar; they all have elements (words contained between angle brackets) and these elements can carry attributes. What really changes between each language written in XML are things such as the words between the brackets, what attributes those elements can carry, and the order in which elements are allowed to appear in documents written in that language.

XML is used for all kinds of markup languages with different purposes—from languages for displaying information such as XHTML, SVG (Scalable Vector Graphics, a graphics format), and MathML (for writing complex mathematical formulas) to languages that convey program data or set up files or that form electronic receipts or purchase orders between businesses.

One of the key points about a language written in XML is that the element names should describe their content; for example, a `<table>` element contains table data. But with so many different languages being written in XML, it is likely that more than one language will make use of an element called `<table>`. For example, a group of furniture manufacturers might use an element called `<table>` to indicate a kitchen or dining table. A language written for sports might use a `<table>` element to indicate the position of teams in a league table.

If documents contained markup from only one language and programs were written to understand only that one language, this probably would not be a problem. However, it is possible for an XML document to contain markup from more than one language, and many programs have to work with many different languages. For example, an XHTML document could contain a graph or animation in SVG. In this case it is important for the browser to know which language each element belongs to.

Indeed, it is not only individual documents that can contain markup from two languages, but whole new document types can be created by combining parts of two different languages. These are known as *hybrid document types*.

So that processing applications (such as browsers) know to which language an element belongs, every time a language is created it is given a namespace. The namespace is a URI that just acts as a unique identifier for the language; you do not need to find a DTD or schema at that URI (the set of rules for what elements and attributes the document can contain); it just has to be reserved for the namespace (so nothing else should be found at that URI—such as an XHTML page).

The namespace that you have seen throughout this book for XHTML has been given on the root <html> element, as you can see in the highlighted line of the following example:

```
<?xml version="1.0" encoding="UTF-8"?>
<!DOCTYPE html PUBLIC "-//W3C//DTD XHTML 1.0 Transitional//EN"
    "http://www.w3.org/TR/xhtml1/DTD/xhtml1-transitional.dtd">
<html xmlns="http://www.w3.org/1999/xhtml" lang="en">

<head><title>A simple page</title></head>

<body>
  <h3>Welcome to a Test page</h3>
  <p>This is just a test page to illustrate a namespace.</p>
</body>
</html>
```

The namespace for XHTML is http://www.w3.org/1999/xhtml, but if you tried to go there you would not actually find anything because it is a conceptual unique identifier that allows the program to tell that the elements and attributes in this document belong to that namespace—so these elements will not be mistaken for elements from a different language with the same name.

When a namespace is declared on the root element of a document, it indicates that it is the default namespace for the document and that all of the elements in that document belong to the specified namespace. However, if there is another namespace declared on one of the child elements, it (and any elements it contains) belong to that namespace.

Namespaces are inherited by child elements just as CSS styles are inherited. They apply to all child elements unless there is a more specific rule or namespace.

In the following snippet of a document, the default namespace is the XHTML namespace—it is on the root <html> element. However, there is also an <svg> element that contains a <rect> element. The <svg> element has the SVG namespace and contains a rectangle with rounded corners written in Scalable Vector Graphics (you learn about this language in the next section). The namespace on this <svg> element means that it and the <rect> element belong to the SVG namespace, although the rest of the document belongs to the XHTML namespace (ch13_eg02.html).

```
<html xmlns="http://www.w3.org/1999/xhtml">
<head><title>A Page with Two Namespaces</title></head>
<body>
    <p>Here is a rectangle in SVG.</p>
    <svg xmlns="http://www.w3.org/2000/svg" width="5cm" height="2.5cm">
      <rect width="150px" height="100px" rx="15" ry="15"
            style="fill: #FF0000; stroke: #0000FF" stroke="2">
      </rect>
    </svg>
</body>
</html>
```

You can see this page working in a browser in Figure 13-1. Unfortunately, neither of the main two browsers support SVG at the time of this writing so you need to view this in an XHTML- and SVG-compliant browser, such as the W3C's Amaya, which can be downloaded from `http://www.w3.org/`.

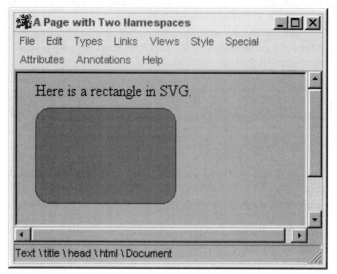

Figure 13-1

With the exception of this example, all of the other examples that you have seen in the book contain markup from the XHTML namespace so that when the namespace has been declared on the root element of the document it has applied to all elements. However, in the next section you'll see a document that contains markup from not just two but three namespaces.

Hybrid Document Types

Because XHTML was modularized, it is possible to create whole new document types that mix parts of XHTML with other languages written in XML. For example, it's possible to extend XHTML Basic with parts of the SVG language to create a special language for financial reports, with text and basic tables of data in XHTML and graphs and charts in SVG.

The result is known as a *hybrid document type*. Indeed, when new versions of XHTML come out, extensions to the language can take the form of new modules.

The XHTML plus MathML plus SVG profile developed by the W3C integrates XHTML 1.1, MathML 2.0, and SVG 1.1 using the XHTML Modularization framework to create such a hybrid document type.

> Unfortunately, the support for MathML and SVG is poor in mainstream browsers. However, the W3C has developed its own browser called Amaya that supports both of these languages; you can download Amaya for free from the W3C site (`http://www.w3c.org`). While you cannot expect many people to use Amaya, it's a great tool for testing standards conformance.

Obviously you already know what XHTML is, but you may not know what the other two are for:

❑ SVG (or Scalable Vector Graphics) is a language written in XML that allows you to create vector graphics. Vector graphics were discussed in Chapter 4; they are similar to those generated by Macromedia Flash. As the name suggests, one of the great advantages with SVG is that the graphics do scale and can therefore stretch and shrink with the device they are used upon. From logos and diagrams to graphs and illustrations, SVG has a very bright future—although it is likely that a tool will generate the SVG code for you rather than you having to manually write the code (as you will see in the next section).

❑ MathML is another XML language used for displaying complex mathematical equations that aren't supported by normal character sets and layout methods. Previously such equations had to be included in documents as graphics; this method has major disadvantages because it cannot be read by a screen reader or indeed an automated program for analyzing or collecting equations, and it cannot be reused in other documents as readily.

The combination of XHTML for hypertext documents (consisting of text, images, links, tables, and forms) enhanced with graphics from SVG and mathematical and scientific equations in MathML helps create a document type that can cope with the requirements of most documents.

You can read more about this hybrid document type at http://www.w3.org/TR/ XHTMLplusMathMLplusSVG/. It does assume you know the three constituent languages, but once you do, it is very simple to put them together into a hybrid document type.

You could therefore have a document containing a description of a complex equation, with diagrams and a logo in SVG. The following example uses this hybrid document type to create a document containing parts of the MathML and SVG languages. Unfortunately they are both large topics in their own right, so I will only highlight where the markup from each of these languages is (rather than trying to explain each language).

This document uses XHTML 1.1 as the host language and then extends it with MathML and SVG, although it is possible to use either MathML or SVG as the host language. For example, you might make SVG the host language of your new document type if your documents mainly consist of SVG graphics but you want to include just a few modules from XHTML markup.

First take a look at the document in full; then I will point out the different parts of the document (ch13_eg03.html).

```
<?xml version="1.0"?>
<!DOCTYPE html PUBLIC
     "-//W3C//DTD XHTML 1.1 plus MathML 2.0 plus SVG 1.1//EN"
     "http://www.w3.org/2002/04/xhtml-math-svg/xhtml-math-svg.dtd">
<html xmlns="http://www.w3.org/1999/xhtml" xml:lang="en">
   <head>
     <title>An XHTML Document  Containing MathML plus SVG</title>
   </head>
   <body>
     <h1>A Hybrid Document Type</h1>
     <p>This document will contain a mix of XHTML, MathML and SVG. Unfortunately
     it will not work in many browsers, but you can try it out in the
     W3C's Amaya.</p>
```

```
      <math xmlns="http://www.w3.org/1998/Math/MathML">
        <mroot>
          <mrow>
            <mi>x</mi>
            <mo>+</mo>
            <mn>1</mn>
          </mrow>
          <mn>3</mn>
        </mroot>
      </math>
      <p>This is a very simple equation, but if you look at the source of the
      code, you will see that it is written in MathML.</p>
      <p>Finally, here is a rectangle in SVG.</p>
      <svg xmlns="http://www.w3.org/2000/svg" width="5cm" height="2.5cm">
        <rect width="150px" height="100px" rx="15" ry="15"
              style="fill: #FF0000; stroke: #0000FF" stroke="2">
        </rect>
      </svg>
    </body>
</html>
```

You can see what this page looks like in Figure 13-2 (which shows the W3C's Amaya browser).

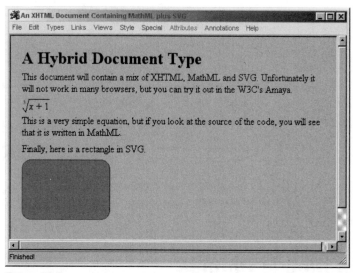

Figure 13-2

The first point to note about this example is that it uses the XHTML plus MathML plus SVG DTD in the DOCTYPE declaration:

```
<!DOCTYPE html PUBLIC
    "-//W3C//DTD XHTML 1.1 plus MathML 2.0 plus SVG 1.1//EN"
    "http://www.w3.org/2002/04/xhtml-math-svg/xhtml-math-svg.dtd">
```

On the root element, however, it indicates the XHTML namespace. Remember that this is the default namespace, and unless another element declares itself to be from another namespace then the elements belong to the XHTML namespace.

```
<html xmlns="http://www.w3.org/1999/xhtml" xml:lang="en">
```

After the <head>, and a title and paragraph, you see the <math> element. This part of the document contains MathML—and the <math> element (just like the <html> element) indicates that its content is written in MathML. The MathML namespace on this element also applies to the children of this element. So, you can see the <mroot>, <mrow>, <mi>, <mo>, and <mn> elements belong to this namespace.

```
<math xmlns="http://www.w3.org/1998/Math/MathML">
  <mroot>
    <mrow>
      <mi>x</mi>
      <mo>+</mo>
      <mn>1</mn>
    </mrow>
    <mn>3</mn>
  </mroot>
</math>
```

As you can see from Figure 13-2, this inserts a mathematical equation.

Soon after this in the document is the <svg> element with the SVG namespace, which contains a <rect> element that is part of the SVG namespace and draws the simple rectangle with rounded corners.

```
<svg xmlns="http://www.w3.org/2000/svg" width="5cm" height="2.5cm">
  <rect width="150px" height="100px" rx="15" ry="15"
        style="fill: #FF0000; stroke: #0000FF" stroke="2">
  </rect>
</svg>
```

This kind of hybrid document and the ability to extend a technology using modules of a language makes it much easier to create languages that will fulfill the needs of future clients using existing technologies and therefore will make it easier to develop for these devices.

XHTML on Mobile Phones

You have seen how the elements and attributes that made up XHTML were split into several abstract modules, which were then combined into XHTML 1.1 and XHTML Basic by the W3C. Now it's time to look at an example of how XHTML Basic has been used as a host language in a widely used application.

Modularized XHTML has already made a real impact in the mobile phone industry, giving the companies involved a chance to create a more unified solution for bringing the Web to mobile phones rather than creating several different languages. This means more people will be able to develop mobile applications and that these applications will be available to more users.

The Background

When a company (originally called Unwired Planet, later changing its name first to Phone.com and then again to Openwave) wanted to allow access to the Internet over a mobile phone, it devised a language called HDML (Handheld Device Markup Language). This company joined with Nokia and a number of other companies to create the WAP Forum (now known as the Open Mobile Alliance) with the aim of creating a common standard for wireless Internet access.

Using HDML as a basis for its work, they created WML (Wireless Markup Language), which is a language used on early WAP-compatible phones. WML is actually just one part of the WAP (Wireless Application Protocol) group of specifications.

Meanwhile, in Japan, a company called NTT DoCoMo created a service called iMode, which ran on cHTML (Compact HTML). This was a proprietary technology. iMode was much more successful than WAP and WML, partly because it did not pretend to offer the whole Web on a phone (which is what some marketers touted WAP to be); rather it was sold as information on your phone.

Both iMode and WML incorporate features that are not found in HTML and would not be needed with desktop computers. For example, they allow links to making a voice call. WML also allowed phones scroll controllers and soft keys to control the content of the screen (not just relying on hyperlinks).

One disadvantage with WML was that it was rendered in lots of different ways on different phones—in particular pop-up lists were notoriously rendered in various ways (some horizontally, some vertically, some with new pages, and so on). As a result, developers either had to pick a browser to support (which meant people with other phones would suffer poor usability) or develop different versions for different phones.

While the phone companies had been developing their own solutions, the W3C had developed XHTML and split it into modules. Of particular note was XHTML Basic, a set of basic modules that were designed for small devices. One of the key advantages of XHTML Basic was that it could use CSS to control display.

Then the two main players—NTT DoCoMo and WAP Forum—joined forces to create a new standard. They combined the features of iMode and WML with those of XHTML Basic to create a solution that would meet all users' needs.

With XHTML Basic at the heart of this new language and CSS for rendering, it was hoped that the convergence between wireless and desktop experiences could be accelerated.

The new language was to be known as the *XHTML Mobile Profile* (or *XHTML MP* for short) and it contained added functions from cHTML and WML that was not in XHTML, along with markup that was not in XHTML Basic but was in full XHTML (such as `<acronym>`, `<address>`, `<br>`, `<big>`, `<small>`, `<hr />`, `<i>`, `<fieldset>`, and `<optgroup>`).

Nokia and NTT DoCoMo then added features of WML that couldn't be found in XHTML at all—things such as alternative ways to control navigation along with new events that suit the mobile devices and other features.

This was a great solution because:

❑   The markup is very similar to XHTML.

❑   It meets more requirements for usability.

- ❑ While CSS controls layout, the phone controls navigation and cache.
- ❑ You can have different multiple non-link commands on a page.

Unfortunately, however, Nokia and NTT DoCoMo decided to use a different namespace than Openwave. Nokia decided to use XHTML MP with no namespace; Openwave used the suggested namespace. Meanwhile, most other browsers (such as the successor to iMode) support only XHTML Basic without the extended features of XHTML MP (so usability suffers).

Having got so close to agreeing on the standards, implementation has been inconsistent. Still, there is hope that there will again be convergence.

Mobile Access Today

Things look promising for the future, with mobiles sharing a common language with their larger desktop brothers and sisters. However, the reality at the time of this writing is that these there are still lots of mobiles out there that do not support XHTML MP—these phones are a couple of years older, have monochrome displays, and support only WAP and WML. In addition, a lot of the newer phones still support WML for backward-compatibility.

Therefore, at the time of this writing, a lot of the sites that were making content available to mobile phones were doing so in WML. This is slightly more complicated than serving XHTML to phones because WML requires a WAP gateway to be installed on the server.

The more advanced of the sites serving mobile content detect the capabilities of the phone and then serve appropriate content for that device. This means generating even more versions of the site. Such sites will generate simple text WML content for the more basic phone browsers and XHTML MP styled with CSS and containing images for the latest phones with color screens.

While creating different versions of sites for different devices sounds like a lot of extra work, when different versions of sites are generated for different devices, the pages do not tend to be written by hand, but rather tend to be automatically generated from a database using special code on the Web server and template pages.

Creating Sites for Different Platforms

I've talked about the technologies that allow you to offer content to different devices so now it is time to take a look at the more practical side of serving Web pages to different devices.

When you start to look at the services aimed at devices other than desktop PCs, such as services for mobile phones, PDAs, and set top boxes, you find that few sites offer exactly the same content for each device.

If the content is not the same for each device, and you are going to have to create different pages for each device, you may well ask why it should be an issue whether you develop for different devices in the same language or whether you use different languages for each platform. You may even ask why it's so important to separate content from style if the page is just being styled for that medium. There are three simple reasons for using XHTML that will be expanded on in this section:

- ❑ Different versions of the site are often created from content within the same database.

- ❑ It is possible to transform XHTML into XHTML MP using another language called XSLT.
- ❑ Learning new languages is easier if the languages share the same basic components.

So, in this section you will learn more about the content that is served to different types of sites and how some sites go about generating pages suited to each device. By the end of this section not only will you know how larger sites are developed so that they can serve content to different devices, but you will also see why it is important to be careful when writing your XHTML code.

Of course, if you need any other reason for using Strict XHTML wherever possible, the answer is that it is very hard to get out of bad habits that you have learned. I've seen more than one author say that they find it hard to code in XHTML because they've been writing with bad habits for so many years. Remembering to add closing tags when you're used to leaving them off, or write element names in lowercase when you have used capitals for several years, or using quotes when you never have before—all of these things can be very hard to get used to. In my experience, however, learning to code Strict XHTML all the time is much easier than learning to code in Strict XHTML some of the time.

Working with (not Against) the Constraints of a Device

One of the central issues when developing content for different types of devices is that each can have very different capabilities. Mobile phones and PDAs obviously have far smaller screens than desktop PCs and are not as able to carry as much information on the screen at once, while set top boxes tend to work with TVs that have a lower resolution than computer monitors.

In fact, some devices are so different from desktop PCs that you can think of them as completely different mediums. The physical limitations of these devices, along with the situations in which they are used often mean that users actually *want* different types of content from different devices—users don't necessarily want the same information that is on a Web site they access on their PC to be the same as the information available on a mobile.

For example, it would be hard to imagine reading a whole chapter of a book on a mobile phone screen—even the average news article can be too long for a mobile phone. Therefore, a news site might decide to just offer the headlines to a mobile phone, possibly with a synopsis of the story, but phone users wouldn't want something the length of a page of this book on their mobile phone.

Then there is the issue of the kind of information that you are likely to want when using a small device on the move. While you're out on the town you are far more likely to want to know what film is on at the cinema near you rather than wanting to read biographical information about one of the movie's stars. You are more likely to want to know where the nearest sushi restaurant is than to read up on techniques for how to create the perfect sushi roll. And you are more likely to want to check the time of your next train home than to learn about the history of the Orient Express.

For some sites and businesses there would be little advantage to having a presence for mobile phones other than their contact details and full Web site address. For example, few people are going to book a photographer, landscape gardener, or luxury cruise via their mobile phone, at least not without seeing photos or finding out more information than you can easily read on your mobile phone. And those sites that have content that mobile users will want to read might find that they offer quite a different presentation on a site designed for desktop users.

So, you only need to develop content for different platforms if users will want to access that information on different platforms. If you decide it is worth having your site available to different devices then, rather than struggling to work out how to get the same content on a different device you need to be thinking what users will want on this kind of device.

Why Use XHTML if Content or Sections of Sites Are Different?

Why then, you may well ask, has there been so much talk of writing pages so that they can be accessed by all kinds of different devices if you are likely to want different content? It is not only the service and text that may differ from device to device; obviously, a small device will not handle logos that are 500 pixels wide or tables used to lay out pages designed for a computer screen, so the pages will be very different for different devices. So, why even bother developing content that can be used on different devices and why bother separating style from content? The answer to this is that a lot of larger sites do not hand-code pages in the way you have been doing in this book.

Also, as has already been mentioned (more than once), it's far easier to learn a new language if it is based on the same elements as one you already know. If you want developers to adopt a new document type quicker, then knowing parts of the language already will make it easier to learn. It can also help manufacturers of new devices because they will automatically have a base of developers who can supply content for their platform; and this is important because one of the reasons why WAP did not achieve better success in Europe was the lack of good mobile content that was helpful to users.

Database-Driven Web Sites

When you start to look at developing larger sites where the content changes regularly, such as with news sites, you do not want to hand code every XHTML page. Rather, you will put your content in a database and then files on the Web server will create pages for you; this is known as a *database-driven Web site*.

Database-driven Web sites became very popular in the late 1990s with the advent of what are known as *server-side scripting languages* such as ASP (Active Server Pages), PHP (Personal Home Pages), and JSP (JavaServer pages).

The ability to store the content of Web pages in a database and to then access this information using scripting languages on the server meant the following:

❑   It was far easier and quicker to create and maintain content for the Web. If you were publishing articles every day, you would not have to manually code an HTML page each day. So, database-driven sites allowed you to enter the text (and markup) into an HTML form and then add that content to the database. When visitors wanted to access the story, a template page would be used to display it in the correct way for that device and the content would fit inside the page.

❑   Different people could add information to the database using the same forms, without all of them having to learn how to code the pages in the same way.

❑   It was possible to create pages that specifically answered users' queries, such as what time trains go from London to Edinburgh on Sundays around 12:00. Users enter details of the information that they want to know into a form and this information is turned into something known as a *database query*. The database then returns information relevant to that query and it is formatted in a template page and returned to the user. After all, when you are creating a Web site to show a train timetable you would not want to create a page for every possible journey from and to every stop on the line.

To get a better sense of what I mean, take a look at Figure 13-3. In this diagram you can see five steps:

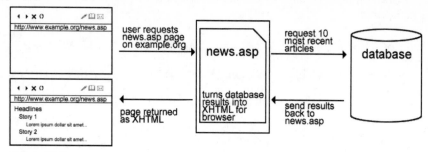

Figure 13-3

❑ A visitor to the site enters the URL http://www.example.org/news/news.asp.

❑ An ASP file on the server asks the database for the headline and summary of the last ten items of news along with a unique number for that article (each article in the database would have a separate article).

❑ The database returns these items to the ASP file.

❑ The ASP file puts the information from the database into an XHTML template that is served back to the user.

When the user wants to see one of the articles from the news, he or she clicks the link to that article and this will request the ASP page that is the template for all articles; here is what happens when the user clicks the link requesting the article page (see Figure 13-4):

❑ User requests http://www.example.org/news/article.asp?Article_ID=1234. This is asking for the article.asp page, and is saying that the user wants to view article number 1234.

❑ The article.asp page on the server asks the database for the content of article 1234.

❑ The database returns the information for article 1234.

❑ The article.asp page formats the page in XHTML using a template.

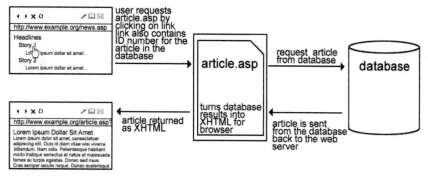

Figure 13-4

To understand this a little better, have a look at the following table, which shows how the articles might be stored in a database. Relational databases store information in tables, which are just like spreadsheets or the tables created in Chapter 5. For example, a news site may use a table like this one for its articles (you have to imagine that this table has lots more articles and that the full title, summary, and text of the article is in the table cell).

ID	Title	Summary	Text	Author	Date	Img	Section
57549	Soap Star Guilty	In a long running	Since June 2001 <b>Tony	B.R.Tardy	1/5/04:08	TDraper.jpg	Ents
57550	Cure For Hayfever	<b>Dr. Clarence	A team of scientists at <a>	T.G.Summers	1/5/04:08	Field12.jpg	Science

Each time a new article is added to the database it is automatically given a new ID, which is a unique identifier for that article. You can see from this table that this number increments by 1 for each new article.

It is very important to note here how the content in the database can contain simple XHTML markup. You can see the <b> element used and the start of an <a> element. You will see more about this shortly.

So, when the user visits the news page for the site, the ASP file on the server would ask the database to tell it the ID, title, and summary of the latest ten articles and the database would return these details. The ASP page would then take the database results and format them as an XHTML page to the browser, which would allow it to be displayed as shown in Figure 13-5.

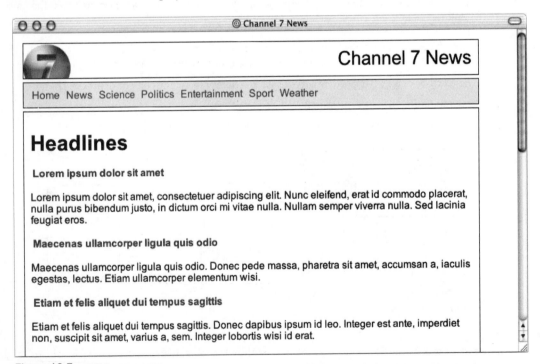

Figure 13-5

The page on the server has not only formatted the titles and summaries of the articles, but it has also generated links to the full story using the ID, which is a number that uniquely identifies that article. So, each time a new article is added to the Web site, rather than manually writing a new front page, the server asks the database for the ten most recent articles, which are then returned to the user.

As I will discuss in Chapter 16, learning a language such as ASP, PHP, or JSP is something you might like to consider when you are comfortable writing XHTML pages, but the concept here is very helpful to understand even if you cannot write your own database-driven site yet. Also, you can see how you need to know XHTML before you can start developing a database-driven site because that is still what is getting sent to the browser.

Here is an idea of the XHTML code that the news.asp file might be generating (ch13_eg04.html):

```
<?xml version="1.0" encoding="UTF-8"?>
<!DOCTYPE html PUBLIC "-//W3C//DTD XHTML 1.0 Transitional//EN"
    "http://www.w3.org/TR/xhtml1/DTD/xhtml1-transitional.dtd">
<html xmlns="http://www.w3.org/1999/xhtml" lang="en">
<head>
  <title>Channel 7 News</title>
  <link rel="stylesheet" type="text/css" href="ch13_eg04.css" />
</head>
<body>

<div class="heading">Channel 7 News</div>
<div class="nav">
  <a href="">Home</a> | <a href="">News</a> | <a href="">Science</a> |
  <a href="">Politics</a> | <a href="">Entertainment</a> | <a href="">Sport</a>
  <a href="">Weather</a>
</div>

<div class="page">
  <h1>Headlines</h1>

  <h3><a href="http://www.example.com/news/viewArticle.asp?Article_ID=1239">
    Lorem ipsum dolor sit amet
  </a></h3>
  <p>Lorem ipsum dolor sit amet, consectetuer adipiscing elit. Nunc eleifend,
  erat id commodo placerat, nulla purus bibendum justo, in dictum orci
  mi vitae nulla. Nullam semper viverra nulla. Sed lacinia feugiat eros.</p>

  <h3><a href="http://www.example.com/news/viewArticle.asp?Article_ID=1238">
    Maecenas ullamcorper ligula quis odio
  </a></h3>
  <p>Maecenas ullamcorper ligula quis odio. Donec pede massa, pharetra
  sit amet, accumsan a, iaculis egestas, lectus. Etiam ullamcorper
  elementum wisi. </p>

  <h3><a href="http://www.example.com/news/viewArticle.asp?Article_ID=1237">
    Etiam et felis aliquet dui tempus sagittis
  </a></h3>
  <p>Etiam et felis aliquet dui tempus sagittis. Donec dapibus ipsum id leo.
  Integer est ante, imperdiet non, suscipit sit amet, varius a, sem. Integer
  lobortis wisi id erat. </p>
```

All ten articles on this page would follow this same template: the headline is contained in a link to the article. This is then followed by the summary of the article.

```
        </div>
      </div>
    </body>
    </html>
```

Similarly, rather than creating a page for each story individually, the `article.asp` page acts as a template for all articles and this page just requests the one article it has been asked to display using the ID to identify it. The actual story might therefore look like the page in Figure 13-6.

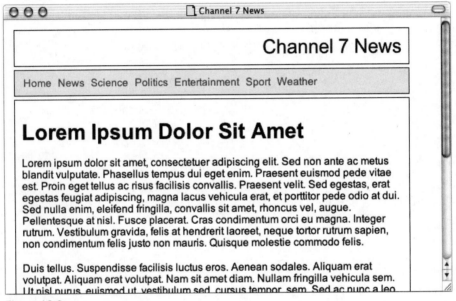

Figure 13-6

So, you've seen how the one page on the server can be used to generate different content on the front page every time a new article is added without having to constantly rewrite the front page. Also you have seen how one template page can be used to control the layout of each article.

Therefore, it should not be too hard for you to make the leap to the idea that the same database can be used to serve content to a mobile phone. When users visit the mobile page for a site they might just get the headlines of the ten latest stories, and if they want to find out any more another page will deliver them to the summary rather than the full article.

The beauty of this approach is that you need to develop only template pages that generate the content for each type of device from the same set of data in the database. These templates will govern how much of the content is shown to the user, how it is displayed, and even which style sheet should be used with that page. But the key to this approach is that the content, which is stored in the database, is XHTML. And if you want to serve content to a mobile device, it should only XHTML Basic for links and essential formatting.

Figure 13-7 shows you a screenshot of a mobile phone simulator that is displaying the headlines from this news site.

Figure 13-7

This mobile phone simulator was created by Nokia. You can download it from `http://www.nokia` `.com` (ch13_eg05.html):

```
<?xml version="1.0" charset="iso-8859-1"?>
<!DOCTYPE html PUBLIC "-//WAPFORUM//DTD XHTML Mobile 1.0//EN"
  "http://www.wapforum.org/DTD/xhtml-mobile10.dtd">
<html xmlns="http://www.w3.org/1999/xhtml">
<head>
  <title>Channel 7 News</title>
  <link rel="stylesheet" type="text/css" href="article.css" />
</head>
<body>
<h1>7 Headlines</h1>

<ul>
  <li>
    <a href="http://www.example.org/mobile/articleSummary.asp?ID=1239">
    Lorem Ipsum Dolor
    </a>
  </li>
```

```
<li>
  <a href="http://www.example.org/mobile/articleSummary.asp?ID=1238">
  Mauris quis urna.
  </a>
</li>

<li>
  <a href="http://www.example.org/mobile/articleSummary.asp?ID=1237">
   Donec nisl elit, viverra in.
  </a>
</li>
```

Again, all ten titles follow the same structure, with the title of the article being a link to the synopsis and each title being a separate bullet point.

```
    </ul>
  </body>
</html>
```

Note how XHTML MP uses the same XHTML namespace, but has a different public identifier and DTD specified in the DOCTYPE declaration. The rest of the page just uses simple XHTML markup.

Obviously, if the information in the database contained styling or formatting it would not necessarily be available to all devices. By using only simple XHTML in the content that is in the database, and not using features such as tables to control layout, it really is possible to use the same content for several different devices. Furthermore, it means that the people writing the content need to learn only a few very basic markup elements in order to add formatting such as headings, bold text, and links to the site.

So, the separation of the style from content and the use of common building blocks in different document types make the content you write work on many more devices. And if someone comes up with a new device that accesses the Web tomorrow, you need only write a new set of templates to offer the whole of the site to that device. And knowing that the device uses a language based on XHTML modules your content, there's far less to learn in order to write the template.

Transforming Pages Using XSLT

I should briefly mention another technology that is being used to transform documents from one XML language to another. This technology is Extensible Stylesheet Language—but do not be deceived by the use of the word "stylesheet" in the name; it is not like CSS.

Some people use this technology to create different versions of a page from the one source page. The part of this language that is used to help serve content to different devices is XSLT, Extensible Stylesheet Language Transformations. This allows you to take each element from the source document and indicate how it should look in a new transformed document. For example a full XHTML page can be transformed into a page for mobile devices using XHTML MP.

Therefore, XSLT can be used to take a full XHTML document and strip parts of it out so that it can be served to a mobile phone.

If you wanted to generate pages for older desktop browsers that did not support XHTML and CSS, you could do a different type of transform that inserts the appropriate deprecated code instead of newer features. For example, you might have an XHTML document where there are <span> elements whose class attribute have a value of instruction. This could be used to associate a CSS style that affects the way this element's text is rendered.

```
<span class="instruction">Press the Alt key</span>
```

An XSLT style sheet could contain a rule that says, each time you come across a <span> element whose class attribute has a value of instruction, replace the opening <span> element with the <font> and <i> elements, like so:

```
<font face="arial, verdana, sans-serif" size="2"><i>
```

And then replace the closing </span> element with the closing </i> and </font> elements.

XSLT is a huge topic in itself and is beyond the scope of this book. However, to give you a taste of what it looks like, here is the XSLT rule that would transform the <span> elements as just described; if the <span> element has a class attribute whose value is important, then the old HTML <font> element and an <i> element will be written into the document to replace the <span> element, and if the <span> element does not have a class attribute with this value it will just write out the content of the <span> element on its own:

```
<xsl:template match="span">
  <xsl:choose>
    <xsl:when test="@class = 'important'">
      <font face="arial, verdana, sans-serif" size="2" color="#000000"><b>
        <xsl:apply-templates select="." />
      </b></font>
    </xsl:when>
    <xsl:otherwise>
      <xsl:apply-templates select="." />
    </xsl:otherwise>
  </xsl:choose>
</xsl:template>
```

This is just a single rule that you might find in a style sheet, and your average XSLT style sheet would probably contain many, many rules, so you can see that XSLT can get quite complicated. If you want to learn more about XSLT, you should pick up a copy of *Beginning XSLT 2.0* by Jeni Tennison.

You should also note how this example demonstrates the importance of closing each element and nesting it correctly; if the elements in the document you are going to transform are not closed then the XSLT processor will not be able to tell where a corresponding closing element is for any given opening element and will not be able to transform the page.

Complementary Services for Different Devices

The mobile phone is the other extreme from the desktop PC in terms of capabilities. A browser in a fridge or microwave would not have restrictions of power because they both run from the mains. They can also have larger screens than a mobile phone, but a user might want them to be able to read text and respond to voice commands. After all, if you're in the kitchen you might not be able to look at the screen if you are concentrating on your own ingredients and your hands might be covered in food that you would not want to get on your browser or a pointing device.

Similarly, a voice browser or book reader can handle long pages much better than a mobile phone and would be capable of reading large amounts of text to a user. While it does not require any visual formatting, it could make use of the various aural properties that are in CSS2 (which I did not cover because they are not supported by any major browser yet), allowing you to control the type of voice and its position between stereo speakers (to the left or right).

So, while there are likely to be a huge range of devices that will be able to access the Internet, not every device will be used to access all sites and not all sites will suit all devices. (How many people would watch a movie on a microwave or mobile phone?) You certainly won't want to access all the features of every site on every device.

Some of the best sites that cater to different devices at the moment focus on different aspects of the site for different platforms—and these tend to complement each other. For example, a news site may offer you headlines to your mobile phone, and maybe a synopsis of the story if it was requested, but if you want to read the full article you have to go to the site. A classified ads site may send a message to your phone when a new ad is placed that contains a keyword you asked it to watch for, but if you want to browse ads you are expected to use a desktop PC. Alternatively, a music site may just feature a small section of the site for access by mobile phones that allows users to download ringtones whereas a desktop version might allow you to download whole songs, create your own compilations, and so on.

More to Come...

In the future, you are likely to see different applications and complementary uses of technologies; a cookery site may make ingredients for recipes available to smaller devices (so you can get the right ingredients) but then show the recipe only on a larger screen. A browser in a fridge might require a new variation on XHTML that supports SVG so that you can see a graphical representation of how long food will last or a chart of nutritional content of a meal.

The content that is served is not a one size fits all. When you are developing for different devices you need to bear in mind what your audience will be doing and what users will want to find out using each type of device. Different media and the aspects of varying devices can complement each other. Here you can see how the use of a database to contain the content is very powerful. In order for this to work, however, any markup that you have in the database or that you want to be transformed using XSLT, those emphasized words and links, must be written in XHTML and should not contain any styling.

Summary

In this chapter you have seen a glimpse of the future of XHTML—how it has been modularized (or split up into sections) for development of other languages. This is vital because, as the example with mobile phones demonstrated, if HTML had not become more flexible it would no longer have been suitable for the different types of devices that access the Web. We might have been faced with the necessity of learning a new language for each type of device. Not only would this have been more work for developers, but it would also mean that less content was available for the devices because it would be harder to deploy.

The use of the different abstract modules of XHTML as building blocks for other languages also means that documents can easily integrate features of XHTML with other languages such as SVG and MathML to create documents that are very sophisticated. Rather than relying on images to carry equations or logos it is possible to use code—which can therefore be read and processed by other applications.

The lessons of the mobile phone industry are valuable ones as we look to the future. Those developing sites for mobile devices today are still dealing with the legacy of solutions that came along before XHTML MP, and while XTHML looks set to replace languages such as WML, these languages serve as a reminder to us of the benefits of following standards set by organizations such as the W3C.

Toward the end of the chapter you also had a brief overview of two ways in which content can be served to different devices. While you would need to learn another language to collect your content from a database, or to perform transformations on your documents, you can see why it is important to learn to code correctly from the start and how your content can be re-purposed for different devices. Before you start learning these languages, however, you are about to learn about JavaScript in the next chapter.

Exercises

The answers to all of the exercises are in Appendix A.

1. Take a look at the XHTML page for a cookery site shown in Figure 13-8.

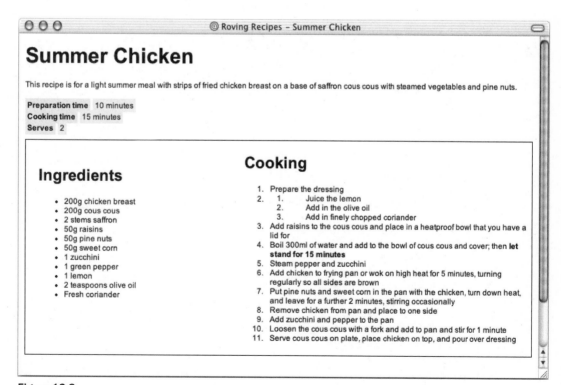

Figure 13-8

The following is the code for this page. Create a cut-down version that shows only the name and ingredients in XHTML MP that a shopper can see on his or her phone in the supermarket. You might want to leave on the preparation time and cooking time, and as a hint, all of the element names are still available in XHTML MP.

```
<?xml version="1.0" encoding="UTF-8"?>
<!DOCTYPE html PUBLIC "-//W3C//DTD XHTML 1.0 Transitional//EN"
    "http://www.w3.org/TR/xhtml1/DTD/xhtml1-transitional.dtd">
<html xmlns="http://www.w3.org/1999/xhtml" lang="en">

<head>
   <title>Roving Recipes - Summer Chicken</title>
   <link rel="stylesheet" type="text/css" href="exercise1.css" />
</head>

<body>

<h1>Summer Chicken</h1>
   <p>This recipe is for a light summer meal with strips of fried
      chicken breast on a base of saffron cous cous with steamed
      vegetables and pine nuts.</p>

   <div>
      <span class="leftColumn">Preparation time</span>
      <span class ="rightColumn">10 minutes</span>
   </div>
   <div>
      <span class ="leftColumn">Cooking time</span>
      <span class ="rightColumn">15 minutes</span>
   </div>
   <div>
      <span class ="leftColumn">Serves</span>
      <span class ="rightColumn">2</span>
   </div>

   <div class="page">
      <div class="ingredients">

         <h2>Ingredients</h2>
           <ul>
             <li>200g chicken breast</li>
             <li>200g cous cous</li>
             <li>2 stems saffron</li>
             <li>50g raisins</li>
             <li>50g pine nuts</li>
             <li>50g sweet corn</li>
             <li>1 zucchini</li>
             <li>1 green pepper</li>
             <li>1 lemon</li>
             <li>2 teaspoons olive oil</li>
             <li>Fresh coriander</li>
           </ul>

      </div>
      <div class="cooking">
```

```
        <h2>Cooking</h2>
        <ol>
          <li>Prepare the dressing</li>
            <li><ol>
              <li>Juice the lemon</li>
              <li>Add in the olive oil</li>
              <li>Add in finely chopped coriander</li>
            </ol></li>
          <li>Add raisins to the cous cous and place in a heatproof bowl
              that you have a lid for</li>
          <li>Boil 300ml of water and add to the bowl of cous cous and cover;
              then <b>let it stand for 15 minutes</b></li>
          <li>Steam pepper and zucchini</li>
          <li>Add chicken to frying pan or wok on high heat for 5 minutes,
              turning regularly so all sides are brown</li>
          <li>Put pine nuts and sweet corn in the pan with the chicken, turn
              down heat, and leave for a further 2 minutes, stirring
              occasionally</li>
          <li>Remove chicken from pan and place to one side</li>
          <li>Add zucchini and pepper to the pan</li>
          <li>Loosen the cous cous with a fork and add to pan and stir for
              1 minute</li>
          <li>Serve cous cous on plate, place chicken on top, and pour over
              dressing</li>
        </ol>
      </div>
    </div>

</body>
</html>
```

Learning JavaScript

In the previous chapters, you have learned about markup languages and style sheet languages. While you can think of learning these languages as starting to program, most seasoned programmers would make a distinction between marking up documents and proper "programming" where calculations are performed on data and decisions are made programmatically based upon some input the program receives. In this chapter you really are going to start learning to program; you will be learning the basics of a programming language called JavaScript. JavaScript is a lightweight programming language, often referred to as a scripting language, but is capable of teaching you many of the basic concepts of programming.

It's not possible to teach you everything there is to learn about JavaScript in one or two chapters, but what you will learn in this chapter and the next should be enough to help you understand the thousands of free scripts that are available on the Web and allow you to incorporate them into your Web pages—you should even be able to customize these scripts and write some of your own based upon what you will learn in this and the following chapter. In addition, it will give you an idea of what programming is really about.

So, this chapter is going to cover the basics of JavaScript; then in Chapter 15 you are going to see lots of examples that should both act as a library of helpful scripts that you can use in your own pages and also clarify how the basic concepts you learned in this chapter work in practice.

As you will see, JavaScript gives Web developers a programming language for use in Web pages and allows them to do the following:

❑ Read elements from documents and write new elements and text into documents

❑ Manipulate or move text

❑ Create pop-up windows

❑ Perform mathematical calculations on data

❑ React to events, such as a user rolling over an image or clicking a button

❑ Retrieve the current date and time from a user's computer or the last time a document was modified

❑   Determine the user's screen size, browser version, or screen resolution

❑   Perform actions based upon conditions such as alerting users if they enter the wrong information into a form or if they press a certain button.

JavaScript was first introduced into the browser in Netscape 2.0—although it was known as LiveScript at the time. The idea behind it was to add interactive features to documents on the Web, which up to that point had been static. Back then you could only enter a URL or click a link and read the page and view the images. JavaScript allowed Web page authors to access and manipulate features and content of the document and browsers used to view them.

> **You should note that JavaScript is not the same as Java, which is a bigger programming language (although there are some similarities).**

You might need to read through this chapter more than once to get a good grasp of what you can do with JavaScript, and once you have seen the examples in the next chapter you should have a better idea of its power. There is a lot to learn but these two chapters should get you well on your way.

What Is Programming About?

As you will see in this chapter, programming is largely about performing calculations upon data. Examples of the tasks you can perform include:

❑   Mathematical calculations on numbers such as addition, subtraction, multiplication, and division.

❑   Checking if a value matches another (whether a user enters some specific text or a number).

❑   Finding a subsection of text, such as the third and fourth letters of a word or the first or last words of a sentence.

❑   Checking how long a piece of text is, or where the first occurrence of the letter "t" is within a section of text.

❑   Checking whether two values are different, or whether one is longer or shorter than the other.

❑   Performing different actions based upon whether a condition (or one of several conditions) is met—for example if a user enters a number less than 10, a program can perform one action; otherwise it will perform a different action.

❑   Repeating an action a certain number of times or until a condition is met (such as a user pressing a button).

These actions might sound quite simple, but they can be combined so that they become quite complicated and powerful. Different sets of actions can be performed in different situations different number of times.

In order to mean anything the programming language first requires an environment to work within. In this case we will be looking at using JavaScript with Web documents in the browser (JavaScript may also reside in other applications or on a Web server). So, the values used to perform calculations will largely come from the Web documents that are loaded into the browser. For example, you might check whether a user has entered a password into a form field and if the user has not entered anything you can ask him to provide his password before submitting the form to the server; otherwise you will submit the form as normal.

To make it easier for applications to work with programming languages there are things called *Application Programming Interfaces* or *APIs* that indicate how an application can work with a programming language. The API for Web documents is known as the *DOM* or *document object model*. The DOM defines what properties of a document can be retrieved and changed and the methods that can be performed. For example, you can retrieve properties such as the value of the `height` attribute of any image, the `href` attribute of any link, or the length of a password entered into a text box in a form. Meanwhile, methods allow you to perform actions such as the `reset()` or `submit()` methods on a form that allow you to reset or submit a form.

For example, when you are creating an image that changes as a mouse moves over it (known as a *rollover image*) you will want to use the DOM to access the `src` property of that image and change the value of the `src` property (so it points to another image) using a script. You will then want it to change back to the original value when the user's mouse pointer is no longer over the image. To react to a user moving the mouse over an image like this, you also need to know about *events*.

A programming language needs to be able to respond to events, such as a user moving a mouse over an element, clicking a mouse button, pressing a key on his keyboard, or clicking the submit button on a form. When any of these actions occur an event *fires*. When an event fires, it can be used to trigger a specific part of a script (such as the rollover script for an image such as that discussed previously).

Another common example of a script that is triggered by an event is when a user submits a form. Often a script on the browser will check that a user has entered appropriate data into the form; if the values do not meet conditions set in the script an error message warns the users that they have to enter appropriate data.

So, the DOM specifies how JavaScript (and other programming languages) can be used to access information about a document. Then you can perform calculations and decisions based on the values retrieved from the document using JavaScript. Your scripts may even invoke methods and change some of the properties of the document. You may also use events to trigger certain scripts. Now that you know what a script can do, you need to learn how to add one to your Web page.

How to Add a Script to Your Pages

Rather like CSS rules, JavaScript can either be embedded in a page or placed in an external script file. But in order to work in the browser, the browser must support JavaScript *and* must have it enabled (most browsers allow you to disable JavaScript). Bearing in mind that a user might not have JavaScript enabled in her browser or might be using an older browser that does not support JavaScript, you should generally use JavaScript only to enhance the experience of using your pages, not make it a requirement in order to use or view the page.

You should also be aware that there are several versions of JavaScript, and the older browsers tend not support the latest features, but in this chapter you will mainly be focusing on features supported by IE 3 and Netscape 2 and later versions.

You add scripts to your page inside the `<script>` element. The `type` attribute on the opening `<script>` tag indicates what scripting language will be found inside the element. There are several other scripting languages (such as VBScript or Perl), but JavaScript is by far the most popular for use in a browser. Here you can see a very simple script that will write the words "My first JavaScript" into the page (`ch14_eg01.html`):

```
<html>
<body>
```

```
<p>
  <script type="text/javascript">
    document.write("My first JavaScript")
  </script>
</p>
</body>
</html>
```

The JavaScript uses the `write()` method to write text into the document. The text is outputted where it is written. Figure 14-1 shows what this simple page would look like.

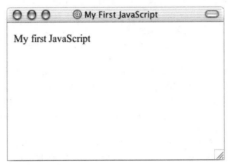

Figure 14-1

Where you put your JavaScript within a page is very important. If you put it in the body of a page—as in this example—then it will run (or execute) as the page loads.

Sometimes, however, you will want a script to run only when an *event* triggers; an event can be something like a key being pressed or a submit button being clicked. This will usually result in something known as a *function* being called. Functions are put inside `<script>` elements that live in the `<head>` of a page to ensure that they load before the page is displayed and are therefore ready for use immediately when the page has loaded. A function also allows you to reuse the same script in different parts of the page.

You can also write JavaScript in external documents that have the file extension `.js`. This is a particularly good option if your script is used by more than one page—because you do not need to repeat the script in each page that uses it, and if you want to update your script you need only to change it in one place. When you place your JavaScript in an external file you need to use the `src` attribute on the `<script>` element whose value is an absolute or relative URL pointing to the file containing the JavaScript. For example:

```
<script type="JavaScript" src="scripts/validation.js" />
```

So there are three places where you can put your JavaScripts—and a single XHTML document can use all three because there is no limit on the number of scripts one document can contain:

❑   **In the `<head>` of a page:** These scripts will be called when an event triggers them.

❑   **In the `<body>` section:** These scripts will run as the page loads.

❑   **In an external file:** If the link is placed inside the `<head>` element the script is treated like an element in the head of the document waiting for an event to trigger it, whereas if it is placed in the `<body>` element it will act like a script in the body section and execute as the page loads.

Some early browsers did not support JavaScript, and therefore you will sometimes see JavaScript written inside an HTML or XHTML comment so that older browsers can ignore the script, which would otherwise cause errors, as shown here. Newer browsers will just ignore these comments in the `<script>` element:

```
<script type="text/javascript">
  <!--
    document.write("My first JavaScript")
  //-->
</script>
```

Note how two forward slash characters (`//`) precede the closing characters of the XHTML comment. This is actually a JavaScript comment that prevents the JavaScript compiler from trying to process the `-->` characters.

You should note, however, that XHTML allows browsers and other applications processing XHTML documents to ignore comments—a server could even strip them out before sending them to a client, so they should preferably be left out unless you know you have to deal with very old browsers.

In addition, in order to create well-formed XHTML you have to be very careful about how you include scripts in your documents because JavaScript contains characters (such as the angle brackets < and >) that should not be used outside of something known as a *CDATA section* in Strict XHTML. The CDATA section indicates to any program processing the document that this section of code does not contain markup (and therefore should not be processed as such). This effectively allows you to use characters that cannot otherwise appear in the document. Also, XHTML comments should not contain double dashes and there are JavaScript operators that use such symbols—for example a counter that is decrementing in a loop.

Unfortunately, including scripts inside the CDATA section—as you should with XHTML—can cause problems for early browsers that do not understand XML. However, it is possible to combine JavaScript comments with CDATA sections for backward compatibility, like so:

```
<script type="text/javascript">
//<![CDATA[
  ...
]]>
</script>
```

A good alternative to worrying about browsers that cannot support scripts, however, is to use external scripts because if the browser cannot process the `<script>` element it will not even try to load the document containing the script.

Comments in JavaScript

There are two ways to add comments to your JavaScript code. The first, which you have just seen, allows you to comment out anything on that line after the comment marks. Here, anything on the same line after the two forward slash characters is treated as a comment:

```
<script type="text/javascript">
document.write("My first JavaScript") // comment goes here
</script>
```

You can also comment out multiple lines using the following syntax, holding the comment between an opening pair of characters /* and a closing pair of characters */ like so:

```
\* This whole section is commented
out so it is not treated as a part of
the script. */
```

This is similar to comments in CSS.

As with all code it's good practice to comment your code clearly, even if you are the only person likely to be using it because what might have seemed clear when you wrote a script may not be so obvious when you come back to it later. Adding variable name descriptions and explanations of functions and their parameters are good examples of where comments make code easier to read.

The <noscript> Element

The <noscript> element offers alternative content for users whose browsers do not support JavaScript or have it disabled. It can contain any XHTML content that the author wants to be seen in the browser if the user does not have JavaScript enabled.

Strictly speaking, the W3C's recommendations say only that the content of this element should be displayed when the browser does not support the scripting language required; however, the browser manufacturers have decided that it should also work when scripting is disabled. The only exception is Netscape 2, which would show the content even when scripting is supported—although very few people still use this browser.

Try It Out   **Creating an External JavaScript**

You have already seen a basic example of a JavaScript that writes to a page. In this example you will move that code to an external file. The external file is going to be used to write some text to the page.

1. Open your editor and type in the following code:

```
document.write("Here is some text from an external file.")
```

2. Save this file as external.js.

3. Open a new page in your editor and add the following. Note how the <script> element is empty this time, but it carries the src attribute whose value is the JavaScript file:

```
<html>
<body>
  <script src="external.js" type="text/JavaScript"></script>
  <noscript>This only shows if the browser has JavaScript turned off.
  </noscript>
</body>
</html>
```

4. Save this example as ch14_eg02.html and open it in your browser. You should see something like Figure 14-2.

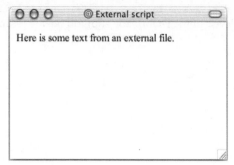

Figure 14-2

How It Works

When the `<script>` element in an XHTML document carries an `src` attribute, the element is used to load an external JavaScript file. The `src` attribute indicates the source of the file—where it can be found. This may be a relative or full URL.

You can use this approach to include external JavaScripts in either the `<head>` or the `<body>` of a document. If you place them in the body of the document they are executed as the page loads—just as if the script were actually in the page there—as in this example. If you place them in the head then they will be triggered by an event.

I tend to use external JavaScript files for most functions and place the `<script>` element in the head of the document. This allows me to re-use scripts on different sites I develop and ensures that the XHTML documents focus on content rather than being littered with scripts.

The Document Object Model

As I mentioned at the start of the chapter, JavaScript by itself doesn't do much more than allow you to perform calculations. In order make a document more interactive the script needs to be able to access the contents of the document and know when the user is interacting with it.

In this section you will be focusing on three objects: the document object, the forms collection (and its children), and the images object. You will meet other objects nearer the end of this chapter.

Introducing the Document Object Model

The *document object model* explains what *properties* of a document a script can retrieve and which ones it can alter; it also defines some *methods* that can be called upon the document. As you will see in this chapter the properties of a document often correspond with attributes that are carried by XHTML elements in the document, while methods generally perform some sort of task.

For example, the document object model specifies how you can retrieve values users have entered into a form. Once you have retrieved these values, you can use JavaScript to ensure the user has entered an appropriate value for that form control. JavaScript is the programming language doing the calculations—in this case checking the values a user has entered—and the document object model or DOM explains how to access the document.

Figure 14-3 shows you an illustration of the Level 0 HTML Document Object Model (as you will see shortly there are different levels of the DOM). You should note the resemblance in structure to a family tree.

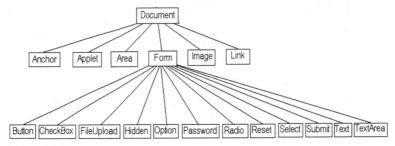

Figure 14-3

Note that the DOM is not part of JavaScript, it just explains how all programming languages should be able to access the properties of a document; other languages can access the properties of the document in the same way.

Figure 14-3 shows you how the elements of a page are made available in scripts as *scriptable objects*. The Document object represents the whole document and then each of the child objects represents a *collection* of similar tags within that document:

❑ The *forms* collection contains all of the `<form>` tags in the document.

❑ The *image* collection represents all of the images in a document.

❑ The *link* collection represents all of the hyperlinks within a page.

❑ The *anchor* collection represents all of the anchors in a document (`<a>` elements with a name or id attribute rather than an href attribute).

❑ The *area* collection represents all of the image maps that use an `<area>` element in the document.

❑ The *applet* collection represents all of the applets within a document

The forms collection also has child objects to represent each of the different types of form control that can appear on a form: Button, CheckBox, FileUpload, Hidden, Option, Password, Radio, Reset, Select, Submit, Text, and TextArea.

To better understand how to access the document using the DOM take a look at the following simple document, which contains one form and two links:

```
<h1>User Registration</h1>
<form name="frmLogin" action="login.asp" method="post">
  Username <input type="text" name="txtUsername" size="12" /> <br />
  Password <input type="password" name="pwdPassword" size="12" /> <br />
  <input type="submit" value="Log In" />
</form>
<p>If you are a new user <a href="register.asp">Register here</a> |
    If you have lost your password you can <a href="lostPassword.asp">retrieve
    your password here</a>.</p>
```

The DOM would therefore make the content of the form available for use in the script as part of the forms collection and the links as part of the links collection.

There are two ways to access values from this document—both involve indicating the part of the document you are interested in by using a *dot notation*. This involves using a period or full-stop character between each object in the object model and the best way to explain this is with an example.

In order to access the first link in the document, you could use something like this:

```
document.links[0].href
```

There are four parts of this statement, each separated by periods, to get to the first link:

❑   The word document indicates I am accessing the document object.

❑   The word links corresponds to the links collection (after all this example is to retrieve the value of the first link in the document).

❑   The [0] indicates that I want the first link in the document—rather confusingly the items of a collection are numbered from 0 rather than 1, which means the second link in the links collection is represented using [1].

❑   I have indicated that I want to retrieve the href property for this link.

Each object has different properties that correspond to that type of element; for example links have properties such as the href property that accesses the value of the href attribute on this <a> element. Similarly, a <textarea> object has properties such as cols, disabled, readOnly, and rows, which correspond with the attributes on that element.

An alternative approach is to use the names of elements to navigate a document. For example, the following line requests the value of the password box:

```
document.frmLogin.pwdPassword.value
```

Again there are four parts to this statement:

❑   The document comes first again as it is the top-level object.

❑   Next you can see the name of the form frmLogin.

❑   This is followed by the name of the form control pwdPassword.

❑   Finally the property I am interested in is the value of the password box, and this property is called value

Both of these approaches allow you to navigate through a document, choosing the elements and properties of those elements you are interested in, and then you can retrieve those values, perform calculations upon them, and provide alternative values.

There is also a second type of object model, the Browser Object Model, *that makes features of the browser available to the programmer, such as the window object that can be used to create new pop-up windows. You learn about the window object later in the chapter.*

The trickiest thing about the document object model is that, like many of the W3C recommendations, it is implemented differently in different browsers. Indeed the object model you are dealing with in this chapter is not a W3C recommendation. Rather, I will be mainly focusing on the objects that belong to what is generally referred to as DOM Level 0 or the original DOM, which is available from Netscape 2 and IE 3 (and later) and corresponds with aspects of the W3C DOM Level 1 HTML. The W3C has released DOM Level 1, 2 and 3—each consisting of more than one part, and each having different features and different levels of support in different browsers. Much of the DOM proposed by the W3C deals with authoring whole documents programmatically and accessing all documents written in XML (not just those for use in browsers). But for the purpose of learning, DOM Level 0 is a good start because it works in most browsers and has crossover with the basic W3C recommendation.

Objects, Methods, and Properties

As you saw in Figure 14-3, an object model (such as the document object model) is made up of several objects, each of which can have *properties* and *methods*:

❑   A property tells you something about an object.

❑   A method performs an action.

Once you understand how to work with one object it makes it much easier to work with all kinds of objects—and you will come across many different types of object when you start programming. For example, look at the document object; following are some of the properties and methods for the document object.

Properties of the Document Object

In the following table you can see the properties of the document object. Several of these properties correspond to attributes that would be carried by the <body> element—which contains the document.

Many properties you can set as well as read. If you can set a property it is known as a read/write property (because you can read it or write to it), whereas the ones you can only read are known as read only. You can see which properties can be read and which can be written to in the last column of the table.

Property Name	Purpose	Read/Write
alinkColor	The alink attribute on the <body> element (deprecated)	Read/write
bgcolor	The bgcolor attribute on the <body> element (deprecated)	Read/write
fgcolor	The text attribute of the <body> element (deprecated)	Read/write
lastModified	The date the document was last modified (this is usually sent by the Web server in things known as HTTP headers that you do not see)	Read only

Property Name	Purpose	Read/Write
linkColor	The link attribute of the <body> element (deprecated)	Read/write
referrer	The URL of the HTML page that the user came from if they clicked a link. Empty if there is no referrer.	Read only
title	The title of the page in the <title> element	Read only (until IE 5 and Netscape 6 and later versions)
vlinkColor	The vlink attribute of the <body> element (deprecated)	Read/write

The deprecated properties have been dropped in favor of using CSS to style text, links, and backgrounds.

For example, you can access the title of a document like so:

```
document.title
```

Or you could find out the date a document was last modified like so:

```
document.lastModified
```

Note that, if the server does not support the lastModified property, Netscape will display 1 January 1970 and IE will display the current date.

Methods of the Document Object

Methods perform actions and are always written followed by a pair of brackets. Inside the brackets of some methods you can sometimes see things known as *parameters* or *arguments*, which can affect what action the method takes.

For example, in the table that follows, you can see two methods that take a string as an argument; both of these will write the string into the page. (A *string* is a sequence of characters that may include letters, numbers, spaces and punctuation.)

Method Name	Purpose
write(string)	Allows you to add text or elements into a document
writeln(string)	The same as write() but adds a new line at the end of the output (as if you had pressed the Enter key after you had finished what you were writing)

You have already seen the write() method of the document object in ch14_eg01.html, which showed how it can be used to write content into a document:

```
document.write('This is a document')
```

The write() method can take a string as a parameter. In this case the string is the words This is a document.

You can also put something called an *expression* as a parameter of the write() method. For example, the following will write the text string Page last modified on followed by the last modified date of the document.

```
document.write('Page last modified on ' + document.lastModified);
```

You will see more about expressions later in the chapter, but in this case the expression *evaluates* into (or results in) a string. For example, you might see something like Page last modified on 12th December 2001.

Now that you've seen the properties and methods of the document object, it helps to look at the properties and methods of some of the other objects, too.

The Forms Collection

The forms collection holds references corresponding to each of the <form> elements in the page. This might sound a little complicated, but you can probably imagine a Web page that has more than one form—a login form, a registration form for new users, and a search box. In this case you need to be able to distinguish between the different forms on the page.

So, if the login form is the first form in the document and you want to access the action property of the login form you might use the following index number to select the appropriate form and access its properties and methods (remember that index numbers start at 0 for the first form, 1 for the second form, 2 for the third, and so on):

```
document.forms[0].action
```

Alternatively, you can directly access that form object using its name:

```
document.frmLogin.action
```

The form that you select has its own object with properties (mainly corresponding to the attributes of the <form> element) and methods. Once you have seen the properties and methods of the forms you will then see the objects, properties, and methods that correspond to the different types of form control.

Properties of the Form Objects

The following table lists the properties of the form objects.

Property	Purpose	Read/Write
action	The action attribute of the <form> element	Read/write
length	Gives the number of form controls in the form	Read only
method	The method attribute of the <form> element	Read/write
name	The name attribute of the <form> element	Read only
target	The target attribute of the <form> element	Read/write

Methods of the Form Objects

The following table lists the methods of the form objects.

Method	Purpose
reset()	Resets all form elements to their default values
submit()	Submits the form.

You learn about events and event handlers later in the chapter, but you should note that if you use the submit() method of a form object, any onsubmit event handler that is on the <form> element is ignored.

Form Elements

When you access a form you usually want to access one or more of its elements. Each form element has an elements[] collection object as a property. This works in a similar way to the forms[] collection; it allows you to access the elements you want by index (an index being a number corresponding to their order in the document beginning with 0). Alternatively, you can use their name.

Here are some of the things you might want to do with the elements in a form:

❑ **Text fields:** Read data a user has entered or write new text to these elements.

❑ **Checkboxes and radio buttons:** Test if they are checked and check or uncheck them.

❑ **Buttons:** Disable them until a user has selected an option.

❑ **Select boxes:** As with checkboxes and radio buttons some of the properties and methods of individual form element objects.

Properties of Form Elements

The following table lists the properties of form elements.

Property	Applies to	Purpose	Read/Write
checked	Checkboxes and radio buttons	Returns true when checked or false when not	Read/write
disabled	All except hidden	Returns true when disabled and user cannot interact with it (supported in IE 4 and Netscape 6 and later versions only)	Read/write

Continues

Property	Applies to	Purpose	Read/Write
form	All elements	Returns a reference to the form it is part of	Read only
length	Select boxes	Number of options in the `<select>` element	Read only
name	All elements	Accesses the name attribute of the element	Read only
selectedIndex	Select boxes	Returns the index number of the currently selected item	Read/write
type	All	Returns type of form control	Read only
value	All	Accesses the value attribute of the element or content of a text input	Read/write

If you want one of the form controls to be disabled until someone has performed an action—for example if you want to disable the Submit button until the user has agreed to the terms and conditions—you should disable the form control in the script as the page loads, rather than disabling it in the form control itself using XHTML; you will see more about this topic in Chapter 15.

Methods of Form Elements

The following table lists the methods of form elements.

Method	Applies to	Purpose
blur()	All except hidden	Takes focus away from currently active element to next in tabbing order
click()	All except text	Simulates the user clicking the mouse over the element
focus()	All except hidden	Gives focus to the element
select()	Text elements except hidden	Selects the text in the element

Try It Out   **Collecting Form Data**

In this example you are going to retrieve the value of a text box and write it into something known as a JavaScript alert box. The main purpose of the example is to show you how the value of the form can be retrieved, although it will also introduce you to an event and the JavaScript alert box.

The simple form will contain just one text input and a submit button. When you enter something into the text box and click the submit button the value you have entered in the text box will appear in the alert box. You probably have seen alert boxes on a Web site before. You can see the page once the user has clicked the submit button in Figure 14-4.

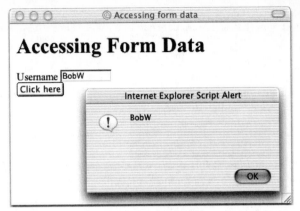

Figure 14-4

When you click the OK button the alert disappears.

1. Create a skeleton document for a Transitional XHTML page:

```
<?xml version="1.0" encoding="UTF-8"?>
<!DOCTYPE html PUBLIC "-//W3C//DTD XHTML 1.0 Transitional//EN"
    "http://www.w3.org/TR/xhtml1/DTD/xhtml1-transitional.dtd">
<html xmlns="http://www.w3.org/1999/xhtml" lang="en">
<head>
  <title>Accessing form data</title>
</head>
<body>

</body>
</html>
```

2. Add a `<form>` element to the body of the document. The form should contain a text input for a username and a submit button, like so:

```
<body>
<form name="frmLogin">
  Username <input type="text" name="txtUsername" size="12" /> <br />
  <input type="submit" value="Click here" />
</form>
</body>
```

3. Add the `onsubmit` attribute to the `<form>` element, and give it the following value:

```
<form name="frmLogin" onsubmit="alert(document.frmLogin.txtUsername.value)">
  Username <input type="text" name="txtUsername" size="12" /> <br />
  <input type="submit" value="Click here" />
</form>
```

Save the file as ch14_eg3.html, and open it in your browser. When you enter something into the text input and click Submit, you should see an alert box like that in Figure 14-4, which displays the value you entered into the text box.

How It Works

The line that creates the alert box and makes sure it displays what you entered into the text box is the value of the onsubmit event handler attribute:

```
<form name="frmLogin" onsubmit="alert(document.frmLogin.txtUsername.value)">
```

When the onsubmit even fires (which happens when the user clicks the Submit button, this simple line of script is run. In this case the alert() method is called:

```
alert(document.frmLogin.txtUsername.value
```

The alert(*string*) method allows you to write a string into the text box. Like the write() method of the document object, which you saw earlier, the string does not need to be the actual text you want to display. In the case of this example, rather than writing the same string to the alert box every time the script is run, whatever the user has entered into the text box will be written to the alert box.

You can see that inside the alert() the text input has been selected along with its value property. So, the value of the text input is written to the alert box.

So, when the user clicks the Submit button the onsubmit event fires, which creates the alert box that contains the value of the text input.

Images Collection

The images collection provides references to an image object that represents each image in a document. These can again be referenced by name or by their index number in the collection. So the src attribute of the first image could be found using the following:

```
document.images[0].src
```

Or, the image object corresponding to an image can be accessed directly using its name. For example, if the image had a name attribute whose value was imgHome, you could access it using the following:

```
document.imgHome.src
```

The main property you are likely to want to change is the src property, especially when creating rollover images.

There are no methods for the image objects, although there are several properties. These properties are supported only in Netscape 3+ and IE 4+.

Properties of the Image Object

The following table lists the properties of the image object.

Property	Purpose	Read/write
border	The border attribute of the `<img>` element	Read/write
complete	Indicates whether an image has loaded successfully	Read only
height	The height attribute of the `<img>` element	Read/write
hspace	The hspace attribute of the `<img>` element	Read/write
lowsrc	The lowsrc attribute of the `<img>` element (indicating a lower resolution version of the image)	Read/write
name	The name attribute of the `<img>` element	Read/write
src	The src attribute of the `<img>` element	Read/write
vspace	The vspace attribute of the `<img>` element	Read/write
width	The width attribute of the `<img>` element	Read/write

Try It Out   A Simple Image Rollover

In this example, you are going to see how to replace one image with another one when the user rolls over the image with her mouse. These kinds of images are commonly used in navigation items to indicate that a user can click on them.

While they require that two images be loaded rather than just one in order for the rollover to work, they can be quite effective, and if you are careful with your choice of images (making sure that the image files are not too large), then the extra overhead of loading another image for each rollover will not be a problem.

In this example you are going to see two simple images, both saying "click here." When the page loads the image will be in green with white writing, but as soon as the user hovers over the image with his mouse it will turn red with white writing.

1. Create the skeleton of a Transitional XHTML document:

```
<?xml version="1.0" encoding="UTF-8"?>
<!DOCTYPE html PUBLIC "-//W3C//DTD XHTML 1.0 Transitional//EN"
    "http://www.w3.org/TR/xhtml1/DTD/xhtml1-transitional.dtd">
<html xmlns="http://www.w3.org/1999/xhtml" lang="en">

<head>
  <title>Image Rollover</title>
</head>

<body>

</body>
</html>
```

2. Add the following link and image to the body of your document:

```
<p>Hover over the image with your mouse to see the simple rollover effect.
<br/>
<a href=""
  <img src="images/click_green.gif" width="100" height="50" border="0"
 alt="Example button" name="button" />
</a>
</p>
```

3. Now add the following onmouseover and onmouseout event handler attributes with the specified values:

```
<a href=""
  onmouseover="document.images.button.src='images/click_red.gif';"
  onmouseout="document.images.button.src='images/click_green.gif'">
```

4. Save this example as ch14_eg4.html and open it in your browser. Then roll your mouse over the image (without clicking it). You should see something like Figure 14-5 with the mouse over the image.

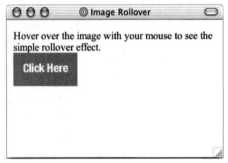

Figure 14-5

How It Works

When the user rolls over the image the onmouseover event fires, and when the user moves off it again the onmouseout event fires. This is why there are two attributes that correspond to these events. And when the events fire, the script held as a value for these attributes is executed.

The script in the onmouseover and onmouseout event handler attributes tells the browser to change the src attribute of the image, and therefore a different image is displayed to the user.

The first (onmouseover) indicates what should happen when the mouse is placed over the image; the second (onmouseout) indicates what should be done when the mouse is moved off the image.

You can see in the code for ch14_eg04.html that when the user puts his or her mouse over the image the src property of the image inside the link—named using the notation document.images.link—is changed.

```
<a href=""
   onmouseover="document.images.button.src='click_red.gif';"
   onmouseout="document.images.button.src='click_green.gif'">
   <img src="click_green.gif" width="100" height="50" border="0" name="button">
</a>
```

The <img> element must have a name attribute so that the image can be referenced in this way in the link (otherwise you would have to use its index in the images collection). It is generally best to use the name in situations like this because if you were to add another image into the document before this one the whole script would need changing.

Note that if no event indicated what should happen when the user takes the mouse off the image it would remain red rather than turning back to green. An image rollover script is a good example of not only retrieving a property from a document, but also changing that property as well.

You learn about a more complex version of the image rollover in Chapter 15, which shows you how to create a function that can change several images within the same document; this is particularly helpful if you are using rollovers in a navigation bar.

Different Types of Objects

You will come across several types of objects in JavaScript, each of which is responsible for a related set of functionality. For example, the document object has methods and properties that relate to the document; the forms collection, which is part of the document object, deals with information regarding forms, and so on. As you are about to see there can be lots of different objects, each of which deals with a different set of functionality and properties.

So, here are some of the types of objects you are likely to come across:

❑ **W3C DOM objects:** Like those covered already in this chapter, although in more recent browsers there are several more objects that are made available that allow you more control over a document. There are also additional objects in each of the different levels of the DOM released by the W3C.

❑ **Built-in objects:** Several objects are part of the JavaScript language itself. These include objects such as the date object, which deals with dates and times, and the math object, which provides mathematical functions. You will be learning more about these built-in objects later in the chapter.

❑ **Custom objects:** If you start to write advanced JavaScript you might even start creating your own JavaScript objects that contain related functionality; for example, you might have a validation object that you have written just to use to validate your forms.

While it is not possible to cover the creation of custom objects in this chapter, you learn about the built-in objects later in this chapter.

Starting to Program with JavaScript

Having learned about the DOM, you can see how it allows you to access a document in a Web browser. However, it is JavaScript that introduces real programming concepts. You know that the DOM allows you to retrieve and set properties and that methods can be used to evoke actions such as writing new content to a page. Now it is time to look at how you use these values and properties in scripts to create more powerful documents.

As I mentioned earlier, a programming language mainly performs calculations. So, here are the key concepts you need to learn about in order to perform different types of calculation:

❑ A *variable* is used to store some information; it's like a little bit of memory where you can store numbers, strings, or references to objects. You can then perform calculations to alter the data held in variables within your code.

❑ *Operators* allow you to do things to strings (remember strings are just a set of one or more characters). There are different types of operators. For example:

    ❑ Arithmetic operators allow you to do things such as add variables together, or subtract one from another (providing they are numbers). For example, there are the + and – operators.

    ❑ Comparison operators allow you to compare two strings and see if one is the same as the other, or different (for example whether x is equal to y).

❑ *Functions* are related bits of code containing rules that you create to perform a function. For example, you could have a function that calculates loan repayments when you pass it variables indicating an amount of money to be borrowed, the number of years the loan would last for, and the interest rate the loan should be paid back at. (Functions are just like methods, except methods belong to objects, whereas functions are written by the programmer.)

❑ *Conditional statements* allow you to specify a condition using variables and operators. For example, a condition might be whether a variable called varTimeNow (which contains the current time) has a value greater than 12. If the condition is met and the current time has a value greater than 12 then something can happen based upon this condition—perhaps the document says "Good afternoon." Otherwise, if it is less than 12 the document might say "Good morning."

❑ *Loops* can be set up so that a block of code runs a specified number of times or until a condition is met. For example, you can get a document to write your name 100 times.

❑ There are also several built in JavaScript objects that have methods that are of practical use. For example, in the same way that the document object of the DOM had methods that allowed you to write to the document, the date object can tell you the date, time, or day of the week.

The following section looks at these key concepts in more detail.

Variables

Variables are used to store data. To store information in a variable you can give the variable a name and put an equal sign between it and the value you want it to have. For example, here is a variable that contains a username:

```
userName = "Bob Stewart"
```

The variable is called userName and the value is Bob Stewart. If no value is given then its value is *undefined*.

When you first use a variable you are creating it. The process of creating a variable is referred to as *declaring* the variable. You can declare a variable with the `var` statement, like so:

```
var userName = "Bob Stewart"
```

I should note here that you need to use the `var` keyword only if you are creating a variable inside a function that has the same name as a global variable—although to understand this point you need to understand functions and global and local variables, which are covered later.

A variable's value can be changed in the script, and when you want to see a variable or change its value, you use its name.

There are a few rules you must remember about variables in JavaScript:

❑ Variable names are case-sensitive.

❑ They must begin with a letter or the underscore character.

❑ Avoid giving two variables the same name within the same document as one might override the value of the other, creating an error.

❑ Try to use descriptive names for your variables. This makes your code easier to understand (and will help you debug your code if there is a problem with it).

Assigning a Value to a Variable

When you want to give a value to a variable you put the variable name first, then an equal sign, and then the value you want to assign to the variable on the right. You have already seen values being assigned to these variables when they were declared a moment ago. So, here is an example of a variable being assigned a value and then the value being changed:

```
var userName = "Bob Stewart"
userName = "Robert Stewart"
```

`userName` is now the equivalent of "Robert Stewart".

Lifetime of a Variable

When you declare a variable in a function it can be accessed only in that function. (As promised you will learn about functions shortly.) After the function has run you cannot call the variable again. Variables in functions are called *local variables*.

Because a local variable works only within a function, you can have different functions that contain variables of the same name (each is recognized by that function only).

If you declare a variable outside of a function all the functions on your page can access it. The lifetime of these variables starts when they are declared and ends when the page is closed.

Local variables take up less memory and resources than page-level variables because they require only the memory during the time that the function runs, rather than having to be created and remembered for the life of the whole page.

Operators

The operator itself is a keyword or symbol that does something to a value when used in an *expression*. For example, the arithmetic operator + adds two values together.

The symbol is used in an expression with either one or two values and performs a calculation on the values to generate a result. For example, here is an expression that uses the x operator:

```
area = (width x height)
```

An expression is just like a mathematical expression. The values are known as *operands*. Operators that require only one operand (or value) are sometimes referred to as *unary operators*, while those that require two values are sometimes known as *binary operators*.

The different types of operators you will see in this section are:

❑ Arithmetic operators

❑ Assignment operators

❑ Comparison operators

❑ Logical operators

❑ String operators

You will see lots of examples of the operators in action both later in this chapter and in the next chapter (indeed you already saw an example in ch14_eg02.html). First, however, it's time to learn about each type of operator.

Arithmetic Operators

Arithmetic operators perform arithmetic operations upon operands. (Note that in the examples in the following table x = 10.)

Symbol	Description	Example (x = 10)	Result
+	Addition	x+5	15
–	Subtraction	x-2	8
*	Multiplication	x*3	30
/	Division	x/2	15
%	Modulus (division remainder)	x%3	1
++	Increment (increments the variable by 1—this technique is often used in counters)	x++	11
--	Decrement (decreases the variable by 1)	x--	9

Assignment Operators

The basic assignment operator is the equal sign, but do not confuse this to mean that it checks whether two values are equal. Rather, it's used to assign a value to the variable on the left of the equal sign, as you have seen in the previous section that introduced variables.

The assignment operator can be combined with several other operators to allow you to assign a value to a variable *and* perform an operation in one step. For example, with the arithmetic operators the assignment operators can be used to create shorthand versions of operators. For example, take a look at the following statement:

```
total = total - profit
```

This can be reduced to the following statement:

```
total -= profit
```

While it might not look like much, this kind of shorthand can save a lot of code if you have a lot of calculations such as this to perform.

Symbol	Example Using Shorthand	Equivalent Without Shorthand
+=	x+=y	x=x+y
-=	x-=y	x=x-y
*=	x*=y	x=x*y
/=	x/=y	x=x/y
%=	x%=y	x=x%y

Comparison Operators

As you can see in the table that follows, comparison operators compare two operands and then return either `true` or `false` based on whether the comparison is true or not.

Note that the comparison for checking whether two operands are equal is two equal signs (a single equal sign would be an assignment operator).

Operator	Description	Example
==	is equal to	1==2 returns `false` 3==3 returns `true`
!=	is not equal to	1!=2 returns `true` 3!=3 returns `false`

Continues

Operator	Description	Example
>	is greater than	1>2 returns `false` 3>3 returns `false` 3>2 returns `true`
>=	is greater than or equal to	1>=2 returns `false` 3>=2 returns `true` 3>=3 returns `true`
<=	is less than or equal to	1<=2 returns `true` 3<=3 returns `true` 3<=4 returns `false`

Logical or Boolean Operators

Logical or Boolean operators return one of two values: `true` or `false`. They are particularly helpful because they allow you to evaluate more than one expression at a time. (Note that in the examples in the following table x=1 and y=2.)

Operator	Name	Description	Example (where x=1 and y=2)
&&	And	Allows you to check if both of two conditions are met	(x < 2 && y > 1) Returns `true` (because both conditions are met)
||	Or	Allows you to check if one of two conditions are met	(x < 2 || y < 2) Returns `true` (because the first condition is met)
!	Not	Allows you to check if something is not the case	! (x > y) Returns `true` (because x is not more than y)

The two operands in a logical or Boolean operator evaluate to either `true` or `false`. For example, if x=1 and y=2 then x<2 is `true` and y>1 is `true`. So, the following expression:

```
(x<2 && y>1)
```

returns `true` because both of the operands evaluate to true.

String Operator

You can also add text to strings using the + operator. For example, here the + operator is being used to add two variables that are strings together:

```
firstName = "Bob"
lastName = "Stewart"
name = firstName + lastName
```

The value of the name variable would now be Bob Stewart. The process of adding two strings together is known as *concatenation*.

You can also compare strings using the comparison operators you just met. For example, you could check whether a user has entered a specific value into a text box. (You will see more about this topic when you look at conditional statements shortly.)

Functions

At last we come to the function, which has been mentioned several times already. A function is some code that is executed when an event fires or a call to that function is made, and typically a function contains several lines of code. Functions are written in the <head> element and can be reused in several places within the page. Indeed, if the function is stored in an external file it could be used in several documents.

A function is just like a method, except a method belongs to an object, and a function lives on its own at the top of a document—but both perform actions.

How to Define a Function

There are three parts to creating or defining a function:

❑   Define a name for it.

❑   Indicate any values that might be required as arguments.

❑   Add statements.

For example, if you want to create a function to calculate the area of a rectangle, you might name the function calculateArea() (remembering a function name should be followed by parentheses). Then in order to calculate the area you need to know the rectangle's width and height, so these would be passed in as *arguments* (arguments are the information the function needs to do its job). Inside the function between the curly braces are the *statements*, which indicate that area is equal to the width multiplied by the height (both of which have been passed into the function). The area is then returned.

```
function calculateArea(width, height) {
   area = width * height
   return area
}
```

If a function has no arguments it should still have parentheses after its name; for example logOut().

How to Call a Function

The calculateArea() function does nothing sitting on its own in the head of a document; it has to be called. In this example, you can call the function from a simple form using the onclick event so that when the user clicks the Submit button the area will be calculated.

Here you can see that the form contains two text inputs for the width and height, and these are passed as arguments to the function like so:

```
<form name="frmArea" action="">
Enter the width and height of your rectangle to calculate the size:<br />
Width: <input type="text" name="txtWidth" size="5" /><br />
Height: <input type="text" name="txtHeight" size="5" /><br />
```

```
<input type="button" value="Calculate area"
  onclick="alert(calculateArea(document.frmArea.txtWidth.value,
  document.frmArea.txtHeight.value))" />
```

```
</form>
```

Take a closer look at what is happening when the onclick event fires. First a JavaScript alert is being called, and then the calculateArea() function is being called inside the alert so that the area is the value that is written to the alert box. Inside the parentheses of the calculateArea() function, the two parameters being passed are the values of the width text box and the height text box using the notation you learned early in the section on the DOM.

Note that if your function has no arguments you still need to use the parentheses at the end of the function name when you call it; for example you might have a function that will run without any extra information passed as an argument:

```
<input type="submit" onClick="exampleFunction()"
```

The Return Statement

Functions that return a result must use the return statement. This statement specifies the value that will be returned to where the function was called. The calculateArea() function, for example, returned the area of the rectangle:

```
function calculateArea(width, height) {
  area = width * height
  return area
}
```

Some functions simply return true or false values. When you look at events later in the chapter you will see how a function that returns false can stop an action occurring. For example, if the function associated with an onsubmit event on a form returns false the form is not submitted to the server.

Conditional Statements

Conditional statements allow you to take different actions depending upon different statements. There are three types of conditional statement you will learn about here:

❑　if statements, which are used when you want the script to execute if a condition is true

❑　if...else statements, which are used when you want to execute one set of code if a condition is true and another if it is false

❑　switch statements, which are used when you want to select one block of code from many depending on a situation

if Statements

`if` statements allow code to be executed when the condition specified is true. Here is the syntax for an `if` statement:

```
if (condition)
{
   code to be executed if condition is true
}
```

For example, you might want to start your home page with the text "Good Morning" if the time is in the morning. You could achieve this using the following script (`ch14_eg06.html`):

```
<script type="text/JavaScript">
   date = new Date();
   time = date.getHours();

   if (time < 12)
   document.write('Good Morning');
</script>
```

This example first creates a date object (which you learn about later in the chapter) and then calls the `getHours()` method of the date object to find the time in hours (using the 24 hour clock). If the time in hours is less than 12, then the script writes Good Morning to the page.

if...else Statements

When you have two possible situations and you want to react differently for each, you can use an `if...else` statement; this means, if the conditions specified are met, run the first block of code, otherwise run the second block. The syntax is as follows:

```
if (condition)
{
   code to be executed if condition is true
}
else
{
   code to be executed if condition is false
}
```

Returning to the previous example again, you could write Good Morning if the time is before noon, and Good Afternoon if it is after noon (`ch14_eg07.html`).

```
<script type="text/JavaScript">
   date = new Date();
   time = date.getHours();

   if (time < 12)
   document.write('Good Morning');
   else
   document.write('Good Afternoon');
</script>
```

As you can imagine there are a lot of possibilities for using conditional statements. Indeed you will see examples in Chapter 15 that include several such statements to create some very powerful and complex examples.

A switch Statement

A `switch` statement allows you to deal with several results of a condition. First you have a single expression, which is usually a variable. This is evaluated immediately. The value of the expression is then compared with the values for each case in the structure. If there is a match the block of code will execute.

Here is the syntax for a `switch` statement:

```
switch (expression)
{
case option1:
   code to be executed if expression is what is written in option1
   break
case option2:
   code to be executed if expression is what is written in option2
   break
case option3:
   code to be executed if expression is what is written in option3
   break
default:
   code to be executed if expression is different from option1, option2,
and option3
}
```

You use the `break` to prevent code from running into the next case automatically. For example, you might be checking what type of animal a user has entered into a text box, and you want to write out different things to the screen depending upon what kind of animal is in the text input. Here is a form that appears on the page. When the user has entered an animal and clicks the button, the `checkAnimal()` function contained in the head of the document is called (`ch14_eg08.html`).

```
<p>Enter the name of your favorite type of animal that stars in a cartoon:</p>
<form name="frmAnimal">
   <input type="text" name="txtAnimal" /><br />
   <input type="button" value="Check animal" onclick="checkAnimal()" />
</form>
```

Here is the function that contains the `switch` statement:

```
function checkAnimal() {
   switch (document.frmAnimal.txtAnimal.value){
     case "rabbit":
       alert("Watch out, it's Elmer Fudd!")
       break;
     case "coyote":
       alert("No match for the road runner - meep meep!")
       break;
```

```
     case "mouse":
       alert("Watch out Jerry, here comes Tom!")
       break;
     default : alert("Are you sure you picked an animal from a cartoon?");
   }
 }
```

The final option—the default—is shown if none of the cases are met. You can see what this would look like when the user has entered **rabbit** into the text box in Figure 14-6.

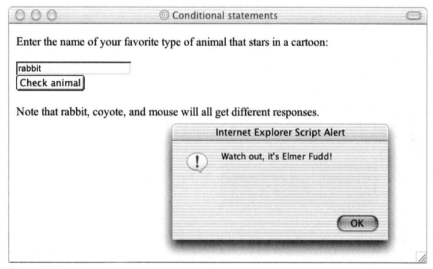

Figure 14-6

Note that, should the user enter text in a different case, it will not match the options in the `switch` statement. Because JavaScript is case-sensitive, if the letter's case does not match the value of the case in the `switch` statement it will not be a match. You could solve this by making the text all lowercase in the first place before checking it using the `toLowerCase()` method of the built-in JavaScript string object, which you will meet later in the chapter.

Conditional (or Ternary) Operator

A conditional operator (also known as the ternary operator) assigns a value to a variable based upon a condition:

```
variablename=(condition)?value1:value2
```

For example, say you have a variable called `instruction` and a variable called `color`. If the value of `color` is `red` then you want the variable instruction to be `STOP`; otherwise you want it to be `CONTINUE`.

```
instruction=(color=="red")?"STOP":"CONTINUE"
```

If the variable `color` is equal to `red` then the string `STOP` is added to the variable; if not then the string `CONTINUE` is used.

Looping

Looping statements are used to execute the same block of code a specified number of times:

❑   A while loop runs the same block of code while or until a condition is true.

❑   A do while loop runs once before the condition is checked. If the condition is true, it will continue to run until the condition is false.

❑   A for loop runs the same block of code a specified number of times.

while

In a while loop, a code block is executed if a condition is true and for as long as that condition remains true. The syntax is as follows:

```
while (condition)
{
   code to be executed
}
```

In the following example you can see a while loop that shows the multiplication table for the number 3. This works based on a counter called i; every time the while script loops the counter increments by one (this uses the ++ arithmetic operator, as you can see from the line that says i++). So, the first time the script runs the counter is 1, and the loop writes out the line 1 × 3 = 3, the next time it loops around the counter is 2, so the loop writes out 2 × 3 = 6. This continues until the condition—that i is no longer less than 11—is true (ch14_eg09.html):

```
<script type="text/JavaScript">
i = 1
while (i < 11) {
  document.write(i + " x 3 = " + (i * 3) + "<br />" );
   i ++
}
</script>
```

You can see the result of this example in Figure 14-7.

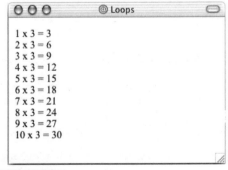

Figure 14-7

do...while

A do...while loop executes a block of code once and then checks a condition. For as long as the condition is true it continues to loop. So, whatever the condition, the loop runs at least once (as you can see the condition is after the instructions). Here is the syntax:

```
do
{
   code to be executed
}
while (condition)
```

For example, here is the example with the 3 multiplication table again—the counter is set with an initial value of 12, which is higher than required in the condition, so you will see the sum 12 × 3 = 36 once, but nothing after that (because when it comes to the condition, it has been met):

```
<script type="text/JavaScript">
i = 12
do {
  document.write(i + " x 3 = " + (i * 3) + "<br />" );
   i ++
}
while (i < 11)
</script>
```

Now, if you changed the value of the initial counter to 1 you would see that the script loops through the multiplication table as it did in the last example until it gets to 11.

for

The for statement executes a block of code a specified number of times like the loops you have just seen, but it takes a different approach in that you specify the conditions for the loop first. These are evaluated before the code executes. First, here is the syntax:

```
for (a; b; c)
{
   code to be executed
}
```

Now you need to look at what a, b, and c represent:

❑   a evaluates before the loop is run, and is only evaluated once. It is ideal for assigning a value to a variable; for example you might use it to set a counter to 0 using i=0.

❑   b should be a condition that indicates whether the loop should be run again; if it returns true the loop runs again. For example, you might use this to check whether the counter is less than 11.

❑   c is evaluated after the loop has run and can contain multiple expressions separated by a comma (for example i++, j++;). For example, you might use it to increment the counter.

So, if you come back to the 3 multiplication table example again, it would be written something like this:

```
for (i=0; i<11; i++) {
  document.write(i + " x 3 = " + (i * 3) + "<br />" );
  }
```

The a is where the counter is assigned to have a value of 0, b is where the condition is saying that the loop should run if the value of the counter is less than 11, and c is where the counter is incremented by 1 every time the loop runs. The assignment of the counter variable, the condition, and the incrementing of the counter all appear in the parentheses after the keyword for.

You can also assign several variables at once in the part corresponding to the letter a if you separate them with a comma; for example i = 0, j = 5;.

Infinite Loops and the break Statement

Note that, if you have an expression that always evaluates to true in any loop, you end up with something known as an *infinite loop*. These can tie up system resources or crash the computer, although IE tries to detect infinite loops and will usually stop the loop.

You can, however, add a break statement to stop an infinite loop; here it is set to 100 (ch14_eg12.html):

```
for (i=0; /* no condition here */ ; i++) {
  document.write(i + " x 3 = " + (i * 3) + "<br />" );

  if (i == 100) {
   break;
   }
  }
```

When the script gets to a break statement it simply stops running. This effectively prevents a loop from running too many times.

Events

You have already seen event handlers used as attributes on XHTML elements—such as the onclick and onsubmit event handlers. An event occurs when something happens. There are two types of event that can be used to trigger scripts:

❑ Window events, which occur when:

  ❑ A page loads or unloads (is replaced by another page or closed)

  ❑ Focus is being moved to or away from a window or frame

  ❑ Setting actions occur after a period of time has elapsed

❑ User events, which occur when the user interacts with elements in the page using a mouse (or other pointing device) or a keyboard.

Intrinsic events are those associated with an element or set of elements, and all browsers are expected to support them. They are used on the element just like an attribute and the value of attribute is the script that should be executed when the event occurs on that element (this could call a function in the <head> of the document).

For example, the onmouseover and onmouseout events could be used to change an image's source attribute and create a simple image rollover as you saw earlier in the chapter:

```
<a href=""
   onmouseover="document.images.link.src='images/click_red.gif';"
   onmouseout="document.images.link.src='images/click_green.gif'">
   <img src="images/click_green.gif" width="100" height="50" border="0"
   name="link">
</a>
```

The table that follows provides a recap of the most common events you are likely to come across.

Event	Purpose	Applies To
onload	Document has finished loading (if used in a frameset, all frames have finished loading).	<body> <frameset>
onunload	Document is unloaded, or removed, from a window or frameset.	<body> <frameset>
onclick	Button on mouse (or other pointing device) has been clicked over the element.	Most elements
ondblclick	Button on mouse (or other pointing device) has been double-clicked over the element.	Most elements
onmousedown	Button on mouse (or other pointing device) has been depressed (but not released) over the element.	Most elements
onmouseup	Button on mouse (or other pointing device) has been released over the element.	Most elements
onmouseover	Button on mouse (or other pointing device) has been moved onto the element.	Most elements
onmousemove	Button on mouse (or other pointing device) has been moved while over the element.	Most elements
onmouseout	Button on mouse (or other pointing device) has been moved off the element.	Most elements
onkeypress	A key is pressed and released over the element.	Most elements
onkeydown	A key is held down over an element.	Most elements
onkeyup	A key is released over an element.	Most elements

Continues

531

Event	Purpose	Applies To
onfocus	Element receives focus either by mouse (or other pointing device) clicking it, tabbing order giving focus to that element, or code giving focus to the element.	`<a> <area> <button>` `<input> <label>` `<select>` `<textarea>`
onblur	Element loses focus.	`<a> <area> <button>` `<input> <label>` `<select>` `<textarea>`
onsubmit	A form is submitted.	`<form>`
onreset	A form is reset.	`<form>`
onselect	User selects some text in a text field.	`<input> <textarea>`
onchange	A control loses input focus and its value has been changed since gaining focus.	`<input> <select>` `<textarea>`

You will see examples of these events used throughout this and the next chapter. You can also check which elements support which methods in Chapters 2 to 7 as those elements are discussed; almost every element can be associated with an event.

Built-in Objects

You learned about the document object at the beginning of the chapter and now it is time to see some of the objects that are built-in JavaScript objects. You will see the methods that allow you to perform actions upon data and properties that tell you something about the data.

> All of the properties and methods in this section are supported in Netscape 2 and IE 3 unless otherwise stated.

String

The string object allows you to deal with strings of text. Before you can use a built-in object you need to create an instance of that object. You create an instance of the string object by assigning it to a variable like so:

```
myString = new String('Here is some big text')
```

The string object now contains the words "Here is some big text." Once you have this object in a variable you can write the string to the document or perform actions upon it. For example, the following method writes the string as if it were in a `<big>` element:

```
document.write(myString.big())
```

Note that if you viewed the source of this element it would not actually have the `<big>` element in it; rather you would see the JavaScript so a user that did not have JavaScript enabled would not see these words at all.

You could check the length of this property like so:

```
alert(myString.length)
```

So, before you can use the string object remember you first have to create it and then give it a value.

Properties

The following table lists the properties and their purposes.

Property	Purpose
length	Returns the number of characters in a string.

Methods

The following table lists the methods and their purposes.

Method	Purpose
anchor(name)	Creates an anchor element (an `<a>` element with a name or id attribute rather than an href attribute).
big()	Displays text as if in a `<big>` element.
bold()	Displays text as if in a `<bold>` element.
charAt(index)	Returns the character at a specified position (for example, if you have a string that says "banana" and your method reads charAt(2) then you will end up with the letter n—remember that indexes start at 0).
fixed()	Displays text as if in a `<tt>` element.
fontcolor(color)	Displays text as if in a `<font>` element with a color attribute.
fontsize(fontsize)	Displays text as if in a `<font>` element with a size attribute.

Continues

533

Method	Purpose
indexOf(*searchValue*, [*fromindex*])	Returns the position of the first occurrence of the specified string *searchValue* inside another string. For example, if you have the word "banana" as your string, and you want to find the first occurrence of the letter n, you use indexOf(n). If the fromIndex argument is used, the search will begin at that index. For example you might want to start after the fourth character. The method returns -1 if the string being searched for never occurs.
italics()	Displays text as if in an <i> element.
lastIndexOf(*searchValue*, [*fromIndex*])	Same as indexOf() method, but runs from right to left.
link(*targetURL*)	Creates a link in the document.
small()	Displays text as if in a <small> element.
strike()	Displays text as if in a <strike> element.
sub()	Displays text as if in a <sub> element.
substr(*start*, [*length*])	Returns the specified characters. 14,7 returns 7 characters, from the 14th character (starts at 0). Note that this works only in IE 4 and Netscape 4 and later versions.
substring(*startPosition*, *endPosition*)	Returns the specified characters between the start and end index points. 7,14 returns all characters from the 7th up to but not including the 14th (starts at 0).
sup()	Displays text as if in a <sup> element.
toLowerCase()	Converts a string to lowercase.
toUpperCase()	Converts a string to uppercase.

Try It Out · Using the String Object

In this example you see a subsection of a string collected and turned into all uppercase letters. From the text "Learning about Build-in Objects is easy," this example will just collect the words "Built-in objects" and turn them into uppercase characters.

1. Create a skeleton XHTML document, like so:

```
<?xml version="1.0" ?>
<!DOCTYPE html PUBLIC "-//W3C//DTD XHTML 1.0 Transitional//EN"
    "http://www.w3.org/TR/xhtml1/DTD/xhtml1-transitional.dtd">
```

```
<html xmlns="http://www.w3.org/1999/xhtml" lang="en" xml:land="en">
<head>
  <title>String Object</title>
</head>

<body>

</body>
</html>
```

2. Because the code in this example is going to be run in only one place, the script can be added inside the body of the document, so add the `<script>` element and inside it write the following code:

```
<script type="text/JavaScript">
  myString = new String('Learning about Built-in Objects is easy')
  myString = myString.substring(15, 31)
  myString = myString.toUpperCase()
  document.write(myString)
</script>
```

3. Save this file as `ch14_eg14.html` and when you open it in the browser, you should see the text shown in Figure 14-8.

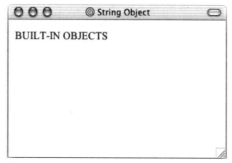

Figure 14-8

How It Works

The script for this example can sit in the body of the document because it is to be used for this example only (it need not be a function because it will not be called several times in the page and the script will not be used by other pages).

The interesting part is what is going on inside the `<script>` element. First you have to create an instance of the string object, which is assigned to the variable `myString`:

```
myString = new String('Learning about Built-in Objects is easy')
```

As it has been created, the string object has been made to hold the words `Learning about Built-in Objects is easy`. But, the idea of this exercise was just to select the words "Built-in Objects" so you use the substring() method. The syntax is as follows:

```
substring(startPosition, endPosition)
```

So, you select the string object (which is in the variable myString) and make its value the new substring you want (this is reassigning the value with the substring):

```
myString = myString.substring(15, 32)
```

This selects the string from the 16th character to the 33rd character—because it starts at position 0.

Next you must convert the string to uppercase using the toUpperCase() method:

```
myString = myString.toUpperCase()
```

And finally you can write it to the document like so:

```
document.write(myString)
```

The result looks quite simple, but when you consider the original string was Learning about Built-in Objects is easy it now looks substantially different.

Date

The date object helps you work with dates and times. You create a new date object using the date constructor like so:

```
new Date()
```

You can create a date object set to a specific date or time, in which case you need to pass it one of four parameters:

❏   **milliseconds:** This value should be the number of milliseconds since 01/01/1970.

❏   **dateString:** Can be any date in a format recognized by the parse() method.

❏   **yr_num, mo_num, day_num:** Represents year, month, and day.

❏   **yr_num, mo_num, day_num, hr_num, min_num, seconds_num:** Represents the hours, days, minutes, seconds, and milliseconds.

Here are some examples; the first uses milliseconds and will read Thu Nov 27 05:33:20 UTC 1975:

```
var birthDate = new Date(8298400000)
document.write(birthDate)
```

The second uses a dateString, and will read Wed Apr 16 00:00:00 UTC+0100 1975:

```
var birthDate = new Date("April 16, 1975")
document.write(birthDate)
```

The third uses yr_num, mo_num, and day_num, and will read Mon May 12 00:00:00 UTC+0100 1975:

```
var birthDate = new Date(1975, 4, 28)
document.write(birthDate)
```

There are a few things to watch out for:

- ❏ The first confusing thing you might notice here is that the number 4 corresponds to the month of May! That makes January 0. Similarly, when working with days Sunday is treated as 0.

- ❏ You might find that you get different time zones than I do. I am based in London, so I run on Greenwich Mean Time (GMT) or Coordinated Universal Time (UTC). All of the date objects workings are performed using UTC, even though your computer may display a time that is consistent with your time zone.

- ❏ While you can add or subtract dates, your result will end up in milliseconds. For example, if I wanted to find out the number of days until the end of the year, I might use something like this:

```
var today = new Date()
var newYear = new Date(2004,11,31)
var daysRemaining = (newYear - today)
document.write(daysRemaining)
```

The problem with this is that you end up with a result that is very long (either plus if you read this in 2004 or minus if you read it after 2004). With 86,400,000 milliseconds in each day, you are likely to see a very large figure.

So, you need to divide the daysRemaining by 86400000 to find the number of days:

```
var today = new Date()
var newYear = new Date(2004,11,31)
var daysRemaining = (newYear - today)
daysRemaining = daysRemaining/86400000
document.write(daysRemaining)
```

Bearing in mind that a user's computer clock may well be inaccurate and the fact that different users will be in different time zones, using the date object can quickly become very complicated. Calculating the number of days before an event could result in an inaccurate answer if the time you provide and the time zone of the user's computer are different.

If you're able to, it is better to use a server-side scripting language to provide things like time (you will see more about this in Chapter 16). But, for the record, the table that follows shows the methods you can use with the date object.

Method	Purpose
date()	Returns a Date object.
getDate()	Returns the date of a Date object (from 1 to 31).
getDay()	Returns the day of a Date object (from 0 to 6; 0=Sunday, 1=Monday, and so on).
getMonth()	Returns the month of a Date object (from 0 to 11; 0=January, 1=February, and so on).

Continues

Method	Purpose
`getFullYear()`	Returns the year of a `Date` object (four digits) only in Netscape 4 and IE 4 and later versions.
`getYear()`	Returns the year of a `Date` object using only two digits (from 0 to 99). You should use `getFullYear()` instead because it provides the four-digit year.
`getHours()`	Returns the hour of a `Date` object (from 0 to 23).
`getMinutes()`	Returns the minute of a `Date` object (from 0 to 59).
`getSeconds()`	Returns the second of a `Date` object (from 0 to 59).
`getTime()`	Returns the number of milliseconds since midnight 1/1–1970.
`getTimezoneOffset()`	Returns the time difference between the user's computer and GMT.
`parse()`	Returns a string date value that holds the number of milliseconds since January 01 1970 00:00:00.
`setDate()`	Sets the date of the month in the `Date` object (from 1 to 31).
`setFullYear()`	Sets the year in the `Date` object (four digits). Works in Netscape 4 and IE 4 and later versions only.
`setHours()`	Sets the hour in the `Date` object (from 0 to 23).
`setMinutes()`	Set the minute in the `Date` object (from 0 to 59).
`setMonth()`	Sets the month in the `Date` object (from 0 to 11. 0=January, 1=February).
`setSeconds()`	Sets the second in the `Date` object (from 0 to 59).
`setTime()`	Sets the milliseconds after 1/1–1970.
`setYear()`	Sets the year in the `Date` object (00 to 99).
`toGMTString()`	Converts the `Date` object to a string, set to GMT time zone.
`toLocaleString()`	Converts the `Date` object to a string, set to the current time zone.
`toString()`	Converts the `Date` object to a string. Works in Netscape 2 and IE 4 and later versions.

Many of the methods in the table that follows were then added again in version 4 browsers offering support for the universal (UTC) time, which takes the format `Day Month Date, hh,mm,ss UTC Year`.

Method	Properties
getUTCDate()	Returns the date of a Date object in universal (UTC) time
getUTCDay()	Returns the day of a Date object in universal time
getUTCMonth()	Returns the month of a Date object in universal time
getUTCFullYear()	Returns the four-digit year of a Date object in universal time
getUTCHours()	Returns the hour of a Date object in universal time
getUTCMinutes()	Returns the minutes of a Date object in universal time
getUTCSeconds()	Returns the seconds of a Date object in universal time
getUTCMilliseconds()	Returns the milliseconds of a Date object in universal time
setUTCDate()	Sets the date in the Date object in universal time (from 1 to 31)
setUTCDay()	Sets the day in the Date object in universal time (from 0 to 6. Sunday=0, Monday=1, and so on)
setUTCMonth()	Sets the month in the Date object in universal time (from 0 to 11. 0=January, 1=February)
setUTCFullYear()	Sets the year in the Date object in universal time (four digits)
setUTCHour()	Sets the hour in the Date object in universal time (from 0 to 23)
setUTCMinutes()	Sets the minutes in the Date object in universal time (from 0 to 59)
setUTCSeconds()	Sets the seconds in the Date object in universal time (from 0 to 59)
setUTCMilliseconds()	Sets the milliseconds in the Date object in universal time (from 0 to 999)

Math

The math object helps in working with numbers; it does not require a constructor. It has properties for mathematical constants such as pi and the natural logarithm of 10 (approximately 2.3026) and methods representing mathematical functions such as the Tangent or Sine functions.

For example, the following sets a variable called numberPI to hold the constant of pi and then write it to the screen:

```
numberPI = Math.PI
document.write (numberPI)
```

While the following example rounds pi to the nearest whole number (integer) and writes it to the screen:

```
numberPI = Math.PI
numberPI = Math.round(numberPI)
document.write (numberPI)
```

Properties

Property	Purpose
E	Returns the base of a natural logarithm
LN2	Returns the natural logarithm of 2
LN10	Returns the natural logarithm of 10
LOG2E	Returns the base-2 logarithm of E
LOG10E	Returns the base-10 logarithm of E
PI	Returns pi
SQRT1_2	Returns 1 divided by the square root of 2
SQRT2	Returns the square root of 2

Methods

Method	Purpose
abs(x)	Returns the absolute value of x
acos(x)	Returns the arccosine of x
asin(x)	Returns the arcsine of x
atan(x)	Returns the arctangent of x
atan2(y,x)	Returns the angle from the x-axis to a point
ceil(x)	Returns the nearest integer greater than or equal to x
cos(x)	Returns the cosine of x
exp(x)	Returns the value of E raised to the power of x
floor(x)	Returns the nearest integer less than or equal to x
log(x)	Returns the natural log of x
max(x,y)	Returns the number with the highest value of x and y
min(x,y)	Returns the number with the lowest value of x and y
pow(x,y)	Returns the value of the number x raised to the power of y

Method	Purpose
random()	Returns a random number between 0 and 1
round(x)	Rounds x to the nearest integer
sin(x)	Returns the sine of x
sqrt(x)	Returns the square root of x
tan(x)	Returns the tangent of x

Array

An *array* is like special variable. It's special because it can hold more than one value and these values can be accessed individually. Arrays are particularly helpful when you want to store a group of values in the same variable rather than having separate variables for each value. This might just be for the convenience of having several values in the same variable rather than in differently named variables, or it might be because you do not know how many items of information are going to be stored. For example, you often see arrays used in conjunction with loops, where the loop is used to add information into an array or read it from the array.

You need to use a constructor with an Array object, so you can create an array by specifying either the name of the array and how many values it will hold or by adding the elements straight into the array. For example, here is an array that holds the names of musical instruments:

```
instruments = new Array("guitar", "drums", "piano")
```

The elements of the array are indexed using their ordinal number, starting at 0, so you can refer to the guitar as instruments[0], the drums as instruments[1], and so on.

If you do not want to provide all of the values when you create the array, you can just indicate how many elements you want to be able to hold (note that this value does not start at 0 so it will create only three elements):

```
instruments = new Array(3)
```

Now the number is stored in the length property of the Array object and the elements are not actually assigned yet. If you want to increase the size of an array you can just assign it a new value to an element higher than the current length.

Here is an example that creates an array with five items and then checks how many items are in the array using the length property:

```
fruit = new Array("apple", "banana", "orange", "mango", "lemon")
document.write(fruit.length)
```

Here is an example of the toString() method, which converts the array to a string.

```
document.write('These are ' + fruit.toString())
```

Keeping the related information in the one variable tends to be easier than having five variables, such as `fruit1`, `fruit2`, `fruit3`, `fruit4`, and `fruit5`. Using one array like this also takes up less memory than storing five separate variables, and in situations when you might have varying numbers of fruit it allows the variable to grow and shrink in accordance with your requirements (rather than creating ten variables, half of which might be empty).

Methods

Methods	Purpose
`concat()`	Joins two or more arrays to create one new one; supported in Netscape 4 and IE 4 and later versions
`join(separator)`	Joins all of the elements of an array together separated by the character specified as a separator (the default is a comma); supported in Netscape3 and IE 4 and later versions
`reverse()`	Returns the array reversed; supported in Netscape 3 and IE 4 and later versions
`slice()`	Returns a specified part of the array; supported in Netscape 4 and IE 4 and later versions
`sort()`	Returns a sorted array; supported in Netscape 3 and IE 4 and later versions

Window

Every browser window and frame has a corresponding `Window` object that is created with every instance of a `<body>` or `<frameset>` element.

For example, you can change the text that appears in the browser's status bar using the `status` property. To do this, first you need to add a function in the head that is going to be triggered when the page loads, which will indicate what should appear in the status bar:

```
<script type="text/javascript">
  function statusBarText()
  {
    window.status = "Did you see me down here?"
  }
</script>
```

You then call this method from the body element's `onload` event, like so:

```
<body onload="statusBarText()">
```

Here's an example of how to open a new window known as a pop-up; you will see a more advanced function for performing this task that goes in the head of the document in Chapter 15, but as you can see, this example provides an inline script within the event handler:

```
<input type=button value="Open Window"
onclick="window.open('http://www.wrox.com')">
```

Properties

Property	Purpose
closed	A Boolean determining if a window has been closed. If it has, the value returned is true.
defaultStatus	Defines the default message displayed in a browser window's status bar (usually at the bottom of the page on the left).
document	The document object contained in that window.
frames	An array containing references to all named child frames in the current window.
history	A history object that contains details and URLs visited from that window (mainly for use in creating back and forward buttons like those in the browser).
location	The location object; the URL of the current window.
name	The window's name.
status	Can be set at any time to define a temporary message displayed in the status bar; for example, you could change the message in the status bar when a user hovers over a link by using it with an onmouseover event on that link.
statusbar	Whether the status bar is visible or not, has its own property visible whose value is a Boolean true or false for example window.statusbar[.visible=false](Netscape 4+ IE 3+).
toolbar	Whether the scrollbar is visible or not, has its own property visible whose value is a Boolean true or false for example window.toolbar[.visible=false]. This can be set only when you create the new window (Netscape 4 and IE 3 and later versions).
top	A reference for the topmost browser window if several windows are open on the desktop.
window	The current window or frame.

Methods

Method	Purpose
alert()	Displays an alert box containing a message and an OK button.
back()	Same effect as the browser's Back button.

Continues

Method	Purpose
`blur()`	Removes focus from the current window.
`close()`	Closes the current window or another window if a reference to another window is supplied.
`confirm()`	Brings up a dialog box asking the user to confirm that they want to perform an action with either OK or Cancel as the options. They return `true` and `false` respectively.
`focus()`	Gives focus to the specified window and brings it to the top of others.
`forward()`	Equivalent to clicking the browser's Forward button.
`home()`	Takes users to their home page.
`moveBy(horizonatalPixels, verticalPixels)`	Moves the window by the specified number of pixels in relation to current coordinates.
`moveTo(Xpostion, Yposition)`	Moves the top left of the window to the specified x-y coordinates.
`open(URL, name [, features])`	Opens a new browser window (this method is covered in more detail in the next chapter).
`print()`	Prints the content of the current window.
`prompt()`	Creates a dialog box for the user to enter an input.
`stop()`	Same effect as clicking the Stop button in the browser.

Writing JavaScript

You need to be aware of a few points when you start writing JavaScript:

❑ JavaScript is case-sensitive, so a variable called `myVariable` is different than a variable called `MYVARIABLE` and both are different than a variable called `myvariable`.

❑ When you come across symbols such as (, {, [, ", and ' they must have a closing symbol to match (', ",], }, and)).

❑ Like XHTML, JavaScript ignores extra spaces, so you can add whitespace to your script to make it more readable. The following two lines are equivalent, even though there are more spaces in the second line:

```
myVariable="some value"
myVariable = "some value"
```

❑ You can break up a code line within a text string with a backslash, as you can see here, which is very helpful if you have long strings:

```
document.write("My first \
  JavaScript example")
```

But you must not break anything other than strings, so this would be wrong:

```
document.write \
  ("My first JavaScript example")
```

❑ You can insert special characters such as ", ', ;, and &, which are otherwise reserved, by using a backslash before them like so:

```
document.write("I want to use a \"quote\" mark \& an ampersand.")
```

This writes out the following line to the browser:

```
I want to use a "quote" mark & an ampersand.
```

❑ If you have ever used a full programming language such as C++ or Java, you know they require a semicolon at the end of each line. Generally speaking this is optional in JavaScript unless you want to put more than one statement on a line.

A Word About Data Types

By now you should be getting the idea that you can do different things with different types of data. For example, you can add numbers together but you cannot mathematically add the letter A to the letter B. Some forms of data require that you are able to deal with numbers that have decimal places (floating point numbers); currency is a common example. Other types of data have inherent limitations; for example, if I am dealing with dates and time I want to be able to add hours to certain types of data without ending up with 25:30 as a time (even though I often wish I could add more hours to a day).

Different types of data (letters, whole numbers, decimal numbers, dates) are known to have different *data types*; these allow programs to manage the different types of data in different ways. For example, if you use the + operator with a string it concatenates two strings, whereas if it is used with numbers it adds the two numbers together. Some programming languages require that you specifically indicate what type a variable is and require you to be able to convert between types. While JavaScript supports different data types, as you are about to see, it handles conversion between types itself, so you never need to worry about telling JavaScript that a certain type of data is a date or a *string* (a string is a set of characters that may include letters and numbers).

There are three simple data types in JavaScript:

❑ **Number:** Used to perform arithmetic operations (addition, subtraction, multiplication and division). Any whole number or decimal number that does not appear between quotation marks is considered a number.

❏ **String:** Used to handle text. It is a set of characters enclosed by quotation marks.

❏ **Boolean:** A Boolean value has only two possible values: `true` and `false`. This data allows you to perform logical operations and check whether something is true or false.

There are two other data types that you are likely to use only rarely:

❏ **Null:** Indicates that a value does not exist and is written using the keyword `null`. This is an important value because it explicitly states that no value has been given. This can mean a very different thing to a string that just contains a space or a zero.

❏ **Undefined:** Indicates a situation where the value has not been defined previously in code and uses the JavaScript keyword `undefined`. You might remember that if you declare a variable but do not give it a value the variable is said to be undefined.

Keywords

You may have noticed that there are several keywords in JavaScript that perform functions, such as `break`, `for`, `if`, and `while`, all of which have special meaning; therefore these words should not be used in variable, function, method, or object names. Here is a list of the keywords, some of which are just reserved for future use, that you should avoid using:

```
abstract, boolean, break, byte, case, catch, char, class, const, continue,
default, do, double, else, extends, false, final, finally, float, for,
function, goto, if, implements, import, in, instanceof, int, interface, long,
native, new, null, package, private, protected, public, return, short, static,
super, switch, synchronized, this, throw, throws, transient, true, try, var,
void, while, with.
```

In order to indicate the default scripting language, a `<meta>` element should be used in the `<head>` of the document.

Summary

This chapter has introduced you to a lot of new concepts: objects, methods, properties, events, arrays, functions, object models, data types, and keywords. While it's a lot to take in all at once, by the time you have looked at some of the examples in the next chapter it should be a lot clearer. After reading that chapter you can read through this chapter again and you should be able to understand more examples of what can be achieved with JavaScript.

You started off by looking at how you can access information from a document using the document object model. This chapter focused on the Level 0 DOM, which is not a W3C recommendation like the other three levels of DOM that have since been released. Rather, it is based upon features that are common to both Netscape 2 and IE 3 and later versions that support these features.

The W3C is moving toward a standardized way of accessing all XML documents, including XHTML ones, although so many scripts have already been written using DOM level 0 code that it's still the best to get you started learning JavaScript and writing code that will be available in most browsers.

Once you have figured out how to get information from a document you can use JavaScript to perform calculations upon the data in the document. JavaScript mainly performs calculations using features such as the following:

❑ Variables (which store information in memory)

❑ Operators (such as arithmetic and comparison operators)

❑ Functions (which live in the `<head>` of a document and contain code that is called by an event)

❑ Conditional statements (to handle choices of actions based on different circumstances)

❑ Loops (to repeat statements until a condition has been met)

As you will see in Chapter 15, these simple concepts can be brought together to create quite powerful results. In particular, when you see some of the validation scripts that will check some of the form data users enter, you will see some quite advanced JavaScript, and you will have a good idea of how basic building blocks can create complex structures.

Finally, you looked at a number of other objects made available through JavaScript; you met the String, Date, Math, Array, and Window objects. Each object contains related functionality; they have properties that tell you about the object (such as the date, the time, the size of window, or length of string), while methods allow you to do things with this data about the object.

I hope you are starting to get a grasp of how JavaScript can help you add interactivity to your pages, but you will really get to see how it does this in the next chapter when you delve into my JavaScript library and look at examples that will really help you make use of JavaScript.

Exercises

1. Create a script to write out the multiplication table for the number 5 from 1 to 20 using a `while` loop.

2. Modify `ch14_eg06.html` so that it can say one of three things:

❑ "Good Morning" to visitors coming to the page before 12 a.m. (using an `if` statement).

❑ "Good Afternoon" to visitors coming to the page between 12 and 6 p.m. (again using an `if` statement. (Hint: You might need to use a logical operator.)

❑ "Good Evening" to visitors coming to the page after 6 p.m. up until midnight (again using an `if` statement).

Creating a JavaScript Library

You've learned the key concepts of JavaScript in Chapter 14; in this chapter you see how they come together. By examining lots of examples, you will learn how to make use of JavaScript in your own Web pages, and through these examples you will learn some new coding practices for writing JavaScripts.

The chapter covers the following major topics, each relating to different JavaScript techniques or parts of documents:

- ❏ **Validation of forms:** Checking that a user has filled in the appropriate form elements and has put a value that matches what you expect.
- ❏ **Other forms techniques:** Giving focus to elements when the page loads, auto tabbing between fields, disabling controls, and converting text case.
- ❏ **Navigation:** Image rollovers and highlighting navigation items.
- ❏ **Windows:** Creating pop-ups and changing text in the status bar.

By the end of the chapter, not only will you have learned a lot about using JavaScipt in your pages, but you will also have a library of helpful functions you can use in your own pages.

Practical Tips for Writing Scripts

Just before you start looking at the examples, there are a few practical hints on developing JavaScripts that should save you time.

Has Someone Already Written This Script?

Thousands of free JavaScripts are already out there on the Web, and before you start writing a script to do anything you are best off looking on some of these sites to see if someone has already done all of the hard work for you. Of course, some tasks will require that you create your own scripts, but if there is a script already written that you can use then there is no point reinventing the wheel; you should consider just using that script.

Here are a couple of sites that will help you get going (and don't forget you can search using a search engine such as Google, too):

- ❑   `http://www.HotScripts.com`

- ❑   `http://www.JavaScriptKit.com`

- ❑   `http://www.JavaScriptSource.com`

Even if you do not copy the script exactly, you can learn a lot by looking at how someone else has approached the same task.

Reusable Functions

Along with reusing other people's scripts and folders you should also write code that you can reuse yourself. For example, if you are going to write a function for a mortgage calculator, pass the values into the function when you call it rather than writing a function to retrieve them from the form. Consider the following function:

```
calculateLoan(loanAmount, repaymentPeriod, interestRate)
```

This function takes three parameters that have to be passed to it when it is called.

Now imagine the form that calls this function in your document. The `<form>` element will have an `onsubmit` event handler so that when the user clicks the button to calculate the loan repayments the function gets called. Because the function requires the three parameters to be passed the call to the event might look like this:

```
<form name="frmLoanCalc"
      onsubmit="calculateLoan(document.frmLoanCalc.txtAmount.value,
                              document.frmLoanCalc.txtRepayment.value,
                              document.frmLoanCalc.txtInterest.value)">
```

You might think that it would be better to collect the values from the form in the function itself; then you could just call the function in one line like so:

```
<form name="frmLoanCalc" onsubmit="calculateLoan()"
```

This second approach certainly looks easier to write, but it is a false economy. It is better to pass these values to the function than write a function to collect these values from the form itself because your function would have to start off collecting the values and might end up looking like this:

```
function calculateLoan() {
loanAmount = document.frmLoanCalc.txtAmount.value
loanValue = document.frmLoanCalc.txtRepayment.value
interestRate = document.frmLoanCalc.txtInterest.value
```

Why is this a problem if you otherwise have to write the same amount of code when you call the function? The answer is that if your function collects the information from the form, it is going to be of use only with that one page and that one form. By passing the values into the function as with the first approach the loan calculation could be used with lots of different forms.

You might think that you would not need a mortgage calculator on many sites, but then you might need some other form of loan calculator on a different site. For example, you might write a site for a car dealer who wants to allow users to work out how much they would have to pay for each installment if they got a loan to pay for the car—in which case you could use your loan calculator again. By making functions generic, they can be reused and you will soon be saving yourself time by reusing your own code.

So, you should aim to make your functions as reusable as possible rather than tying each script into the one page.

Using External JavaScript Files

Whenever you are going to use a script in more than one page it is a good idea to place it in an external JavaScript file (as you saw at the beginning of Chapter 14). For example, in the "Image Rollovers" section later in the chapter you will see an example of a script that creates image rollovers for a navigation bar. Because your navigation will appear on each page, rather than including the image rollover function in each page, you can just include the one script into every page. This has two advantages:

- ❑ If you need to change something about the navigation, you need to change only the one function, not every page.
- ❑ You do not have to copy and paste the same code into several files.

Place Scripts in a Scripts Folder

When you use external scripts you should create a special `scripts` folder—just like you would an `images` folder. This helps improve the organization of your site and your directory structure. Whenever you need to look at or change a script you know exactly where it will be.

You should also use intuitive names for your script files so that you can find them quickly and easily.

Form Validation

Form validation is one of the most common tasks performed using JavaScript. You have likely come across forms on the Web that have prompted you when you have not entered a value or when you have entered the wrong kind of value; this is because the form has been validated. That is, it's been checked to see whether the text you have entered or choices you have made match some rules that the programmer has written into the page. These rules may include things such as an e-mail address being required to contain an @ symbol or a username must be at least five characters long. These kinds of rules help ensure that the data provided by users meets the requirements before it's submitted.

When to Validate

Validation can happen in two places, either in the browser using JavaScript or on the server. In fact, most applications that collect important information using a form (such as e-commerce orders), will be validated both in the browser *and* on the server. The reason for the validation on the browser is that it helps the user enter the correct data required for the job without the form being sent to the server, being processed, and then being sent back again if there are any errors—it's much quicker to force the user to fix errors before ever submitting the form to the server. The server then double checks before passing the form data onto another part of the application—this second level of validation is performed because a simple wrong value in a database could prevent the application from running properly, and if the user does not have JavaScript enabled then the form can submit without the JavaScript validation occurring on the client.

How to Validate

When it comes to validating a form you cannot always check whether users have given you the correct information, but you can check whether they have given you some information in the correct format. For example, you cannot ensure that the user has entered his or her correct phone number; the user could be entering anyone's phone number, but you can check that it's a number rather than other characters, and you can check that the number contains a minimum number of digits. As another example, you can't ensure someone has entered their real e-mail address rather than a false address, but you can check that whatever was entered followed the general structure of an e-mail address (that it includes at least an @ sign and a period). So, form validation is a case of minimizing the possibility of user errors by validating form controls.

Forms are usually validated using the onsubmit event handler, which triggers a validation function stored in the head of the document, so the values are checked when the user presses the Submit button. The function must then return true in order for the form to be sent. If an error is encountered, the function returns false and the user's form will not be sent—at which point the form should indicate to the user what the problem with their code is.

The onsubmit function will often call a function with a name along the lines of validate(form) or validateForm(form). Because many forms contain several controls that require validation, you do not usually pass the values of each item you are checking into a validation function. The function is usually written explicitly for that form—although you can reuse the techniques you have learned in different forms.

> *If you use a validation function that is called by the onsubmit event handler, if the user's browser does not support JavaScript then the form should still be submitted but the validation checks do not take place.*

The first task in a validation function is to set a variable for the return value of the function to be true. Then the values entered are checked, and at any point the function finds an error with what the user has entered, this value can be turned to false.

Checking Text Fields

You have probably seen forms on Web sites that first ask you to enter a password, and then to re-enter it to make sure you did not mistype something. It might look something like Figure 15-1.

In such a form you might want to check a few things:

- ❑ That the username is of a minimum length
- ❑ That the password is of a minimum length
- ❑ That the two passwords match

Figure 15-1

As with all functions, the `validate()` function you are about to learn about will be live between the following `<script>` tags in the head of the document:

```
<script type="text/JavaScript">
</script>
```

To start, the `validation()` function assigns a variable called `returnValue` to `true`; if no errors are found this will be the return value and the form will be sent. Then the form collects the values of the form controls into variables, like so:

```
function validate(form) {

    var returnValue = true;

    var username = frmRegister.txtUserName.value;
    var password1 = frmRegister.txtPassword.value;
    var password2 = frmRegister.txtPassword2.value;
```

The first thing you want to do is check whether the username is at least six characters long:

```
if(username.length < 6) {
    returnValue = false;
    alert("Your username must be at least\n6 characters long.\nPlease
    try again.");
    frmRegister.txtUserName.focus();
}
```

The `length` property of the `username` variable is used to check whether the length of the username entered is longer than six characters. If it is not, the return value of the function will be `false`, the form will not be submitted, and the user will see the specified alert box with its error message. Note how the focus is passed back to the form control that has a problem using the `focus()` method on this control, saving the user from looking through the form to find that entry again. You can also see from this example how the line break is used in the `alert()` box to indicate breaks in the message presented to the user `\n`.

Next you want to check the value of the first password—this uses the same approach but also sets the values of the password boxes to blank again if the password is not long enough and gives focus to the first password box:

```
if (password1.length < 6) {
  returnValue = false;
  alert("Your password must be at least\n6 characters long.\nPlease
  try again.");
  frmRegister.txtPassword.value = "";
  frmRegister.txtPassword2.value = "";
  frmRegister.txtPassword.focus();
}
```

If the code has gotten this far, the username and first password are both long enough. Now, you just have to check whether the value of the first password box is the same as the second one, as shown here. Remember that the != operator used in this condition means "not equal":

```
if (password1.value != password2.value) {
  returnValue = false;
  alter("Your password entries did not match.\nPlease try again.");
  frmRegister.txtPassword.value = "";
  frmRegister.txtPassword2.value = "";
  frm Register.txtPassword.focus();
}
```

You can see here that when the user has entered passwords that do not match, the values are cleared and the focus is passed back to the first password box. This is done because the user will not be able to see the values they have entered into the password box (because it will show dots or asterisks rather than the characters); therefore they will have to enter both values again anyway.

The only thing left to do is return the value of the returnValue variable—which will be true if all the conditions are met or false if not.

```
return  returnValue;
}
```

Here is the form that is used with this example:

```
<form name="frmRegister" method="post" action="register.asp"
    onsubmit="return validate(this);">

  <table>
    <tr>
      <td>Username:</td>
      <td><input type="text" name="txtUserName" size="12" /></td>
    </tr>
    <tr>
      <td>Password: </td>
      <td><input type="password" name="txtPassword" size="12" /></td>
    </tr>
    <tr>
      <td>Please confirm your password:</td>
      <td><input type="password" name="txtPassword2"
```

```
      size="12" /></td>
    </tr>
    <tr>
      <td> </td>
      <td><input type="submit" value="Log in" /></td>
    </tr>
  </table>
</form>
```

In Figure 15-2 you can see the result if the user's password is not long enough.

Figure 15-2

Required Text Fields

Often you will want to ensure that a user has entered some value into a text field. You can do this for an individual element using the technique you saw in the last example for the username. As you saw then, if the user entered a value that was less than six characters long they were alerted.

An alternative technique is to use a loop to go through all of the required elements using a for loop, and if any of them are empty, return an error. When you use this technique you need to have a class attribute that has a value of required on each form element that is required so the loop can tell if the text input must have a value, and you must have a name attribute whose value matches the label for the element (because this will be used in any error message). Here is an example of what a text input should look like with the name and class attributes:

```
<input type="text" name="Username" size="5" class="required" />
```

This time the validate() function can loop through the elements of a form checking whether each has a class attribute whose value is required, and if it does, then it checks whether the value is empty. This function will be triggered using the onsubmit event again. The function is passed the form object as a parameter and starts by setting a return value to true:

```
function validate(form) {
  var returnValue = true;
```

Then the function loops through the elements on the form to find those that are required. You can see that the `for` loop has the three arguments: the first initializes a variable called `i` as a counter with a value of 0, the second is a condition to see if the counter is less than the number of elements in the form, and then the third increments the counter by 1 each time the loop is run:

```
var formElements = form.elements;
for (var i=0; i<formElements.length; i++)
 {
```

Then inside the loop the value of the current element is retrieved:

```
currentElement = formElements[i];
```

Now you get to see whether the `class` attribute has a value of `required`, and if it does you can check whether the value is blank. If both of these conditions are met, then the variable for the return value is set to `false`, and the alert tells the user where she has gone wrong. There is also a `break` here to stop the loop as soon as a required field that is blank has been found.

```
        if (currentElement.value=="" && currentElement.className=="required") {
        alert("The required field \""+currentElement.name +"\" is empty. Please
        provide a value for it.");
        currentElement.focus();
        returnValue = false;
      break;
        }
    return returnValue;
    }
 }
```

Note how the `alert()` method uses the value of the `name` attribute for the element to tell the user which element she has left off with `currentElement.name`.

You can see this function working with a form that is very similar to the one in the last example, although the values for the name attributes have to be descriptive for the user and match the labels for those forms:

```
<form name="frmEnquiry" method="post" action="register.asp"
     onsubmit="return validate(this);">

  <table>
    <tr>
      <td>Name:</td>
      <td><input type="text" class="required" name="Name" size="12" /></td>
    </tr>
    <tr>
      <td>E-mail: </td>
      <td><input type="text" class="required" name="Email" size="12" /></td>
    </tr>
    <tr>
      <td valign="top">Please enter your query here:</td>
      <td><textarea rows="8" class="required" cols="30" name="Query">
          </textarea></td>
```

```
      </tr>
      <tr>
        <td> </td>
        <td><input type="submit" value="Submit your query" /></td>
      </tr>
    </table>
  </form>
```

Figure 15-3 shows the error message generated when the user has not entered a value for the e-mail address. The word e-mail in quotes has been retrieved from the name attribute of that text input.

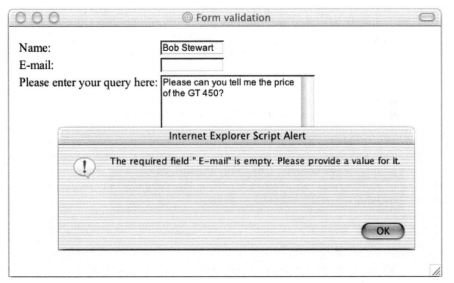

Figure 15-3

Finding Characters Using replace()

A feature that often comes in handy with text inputs is the ability to replace certain characters. JavaScript has the helpful replace() method that you can use to replace specified characters with an alternative set of characters.

The replace() method allows you to specify a character or set of characters that you want to replace using either a string or a regular expression; this is the first argument of the method. The second argument is the character(s) you want to replace the string with. This second argument may just be a replacement string, or it can be a function that determines what the replacement string should be—if it's a function the return value would be used as the replacement string. The replace() method can therefore use any of the following syntaxes:

```
string replace( oldSubString, newSubString);
string.replace( regEx, newSubString);
string.replace( regEx, function());
```

Here's a simple example that uses the `replace()` method with a text area and looks for the string url within the text box. When it finds the string url it will replace it with the string abc (ch15_eg03.html). First, here is the form:

```
<form name="myForm">
  <textarea name="myTextArea" cols="40"
            rows="10">I am interested in Curl, here is a url for it.</textarea>
  <input type="button" value="Replace characters url"
         onclick="document.myForm.myTextArea.value =
                  document.myForm.myTextArea.value.replace(/url/gi, 'abc');" />
</form>
```

Note, however, that this would also change the word Curl into Cabc, so it is a good idea to add a \b on either side of the string url to indicate a word boundary—indicating that you just want to look for whole words—so the string will be replaced only if the string url is a word on its own (you cannot just check for the presence of a space on either side of the letters url because there might be punctuation next to one of the letters):

```
onclick="document.myForm.myTextArea.value=
         document.myForm.myTextArea.value.replace(/\burl\b/gi, 'abc');"
```

The forward slashes around the string url indicate that it is looking for a match for that string. The g after the second slash (known as a *flag*) indicates that the document is looking for a global match across the whole of the text area (without the g flag, only the first match in the string is replaced), and the i flag indicates that it should be a case-insensitive match (so the string URL should also be replaced, or indeed any mix of these characters in upper- and lowercase).

You can match more than one string using the pipestem character; the following example looks for a match with link, url, or homepage:

```
/link| url| homepage/
```

Note that if you want to search for any of the following characters they must be escaped because they have special meanings in regular expressions:

```
\ | () [ { ^$ * + ? .
```

If you want to escape these characters, they must be preceded by a backslash (for example /\ \ / matches a backslash and /\$/ matches a dollar sign).

The table that follows lists some other interesting characters.

Expression	Meaning
\n	Linefeed
\r	Carriage return
\t	Tab
\v	Vertical tab

Expression	Meaning
\f	Form-feed
\d	A digit (same as [0-9], which means any digit 0 through 9)
\D	A non-digit (same as [^0-9] where ^ means not)
\w	A word (alphanumeric) character (same as [a-zA-Z_0-9])
\W	A non-word character (same as [^a-zA-Z_0-9])
\s	A whitespace character (same as [\t\v\n\r\f])
\S	A non-whitespace character (same as [^\t\v\n\r\f])

So, if you wanted to replace all carriage returns or linefeeds with an HTML <br /> tag, you could use the following:

```
onclick="document.myForm.myTextArea.value=
         document.myForm.myTextArea.value.replace(/\r\n| \r| \n/g),'<br />');"
```

In this case the replace() method is looking for either linefeeds using \n or carriage returns using \r. Then the replacement string is <br />. Figure 15-4 shows you what this example could look like replacing the carriage returns and line feeds for <br /> tags. (In reality you are more likely to use this function when the form is submitted by the user, rather than giving the user a button to perform the operation).

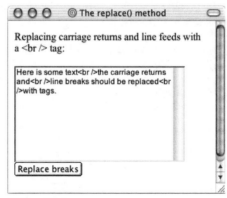

Figure 15-4

Netscape and IE have supported the replace() method with strings since version 3, and both introduced support for regular expressions in version 4. If you need to work with earlier browsers, you'll have to use indexOf() instead.

Testing Characters Using Test and Regular Expressions

Regular expressions can also be used to test patterns of strings entered by users. For example, they can be used to test whether there are any spaces in a string, whether the string follows the format of an e-mail address, whether it's an amount of currency, and so on. This uses the test() method like so: first you set variables to hold the return value of `true`, the value entered by a user, and a value to hold the regular expression:

```
function validate(form) {

var returnValue = true;
var amountEntered = document.frmCurrency.txtAmount.value;
var currencyFormat = /^ \d+(\.\d{1,2})?$/;
```

Then you test whether the value follows the correct format—if it does not you alert the user, give focus back to the correct form element, and set the `returnValue` variable to `false`:

```
if (currencyFormat != test(amountEntered))
{
alert("You did not enter an amount of money");
document.frmCurrency.txtAmount.focus();
returnValue = false;
}
```

If the user entered an amount she is reminded how much the amount was and the return value will still be at `true`, so the form will be submitted:

```
alert("You entered "+ amountEntered);
return returnValue;
}
```

Here is the simple form to test this example:

```
<form name="myForm" onsubmit="return validate(this);"
        action="money.asp" method="get">

Enter an amount of money here $ <input type="text" name="txtAmount" size="7" />

<input type="submit" value="Check format" />

</form>
```

Figure 15-5 shows this form in action.

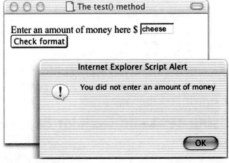

Figure 15-5

Regular expressions are not the easiest thing to learn to write, and you should pick up a book that covers how to write them if you want to start writing your own regular expressions. However, the table that follows lists some helpful ones that you can use to get you started.

Test for	Description	Regular Expression
Whitespace	No whitespace characters.	`/\S/;`
Alphabetic characters	No characters of the alphabet nor the hyphen, period, or comma may appear in the string.	`/[^a-z\-\.\,']/gi;`
Alphanumeric characters	No letters or number may appear in the string.	`/[^a-z0-9]/gi;`
Credit card details	A 16-digit credit card number following the pattern XXXX XXXX XXXX XXXX.	`/^\d{4}([ -]?\d{4}){3}$/;`
Decimal number	A number with a decimal place.	`/^\d+(\.\d+)?$/;`
Currency	A group of one or more digits followed by an optional group consisting of a decimal point plus one or two digits.	`/^\d+(\.\d{1,2})?$/;`
E-mail address	An e-mail address	`/^\w(\.?[\w-])*@\w(\.?[\w-])*\.[a-z]{2,6}(\.[a-z]{2})?$/i;`

Select Box Options

If you want to check whether a user has selected one of the items from a select box you need to use the `selectedIndex` property of the `select` object that represents the select box. If the user selects the first option then the `selectedIndex` property will be given a value of 0; if the user selects the second option the `selectedIndex` property will be given a value of 1; the third will be given a value of 2, and so on.

By default, if the user does not change the value that the control has when the page loads, the value will be 0 for a standard select box and 1 for a multiple select box. The value 1 indicates that none of the options are selected, whereas in a standard select box the first option is automatically selected when the form loads.

Look at the following simple select box, which asks the user to select a suit of cards:

```
<form name="frmCards" action="cards.asp" method="get"
      onsubmit="return validate(this)" >
  <select name="selCards">
    <option>Select a suit of cards</option>
```

```
      <option value="hearts">Hearts</option>
      <option value="diamonds">Diamonds</option>
      <option value="spades">Spades</option>
      <option value="clubs">Clubs</option>
  </select>
  <input type="submit" value="Send selection" />
</form>
```

Now, to check that one of the suits of cards has been selected you have the `validate()` function, which will have been passed the `form` object as a parameter. In the case of this example, if the value is 0, then you have to alert the user that he has not selected one of the suits of cards and ask him to do so.

```
function validate(form) {
   var returnValue = true;
   var selectedOption = form.selCards.selectedIndex;

   if (selectedOption==0)
   {
      returnValue = false
      alert("Please select a suit of cards.");
   }

   return returnValue;
}
```

In Figure 15-6 you can see the warning if the user has not selected a suit of cards.

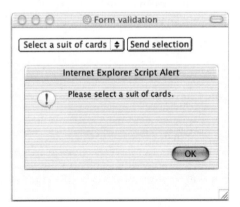

Figure 15-6

Note that if you wanted to collect the value of the selected option from the drop-down box you would use the following syntax:

```
form.selCards.options[selected].value
```

This is because you need to look at which of the option elements was selected to get its value rather than just the index number of the selected element.

Radio Buttons

A group of radio buttons is different than other form controls in that they share a value for the name attribute and only one of the radio buttons can be selected at a time.

If you want to ensure that a radio button has been selected you can either preselect one of the radio button values or you can loop through the RadioButton object's checked properties to see if one has been selected.

For example, here is a form with three radio buttons:

```
<form name="frmCards" action="cards.asp" method="post"
    onsubmit="return validateForm(this)" >
  <p>Please select a suit of cards.</p>
  <p><input type="radio" name="radSuit" value="hearts" /> Hearts </p>
  <p><input type="radio" name="radSuit" value="diamonds" /> Diamonds </p>
  <p><input type="radio" name="radSuit" value="spades" /> Spades </p>
  <p><input type="radio" name="radSuit" value="clubs" /> Clubs </p>
  <p><input type="submit" value="Submit choice" /></p>
</form>
```

As with the example for select boxes you need to loop through each of the radio buttons in the collection that share the same name and see if one has a checked property. This function actually uses a variable called radioChosen to indicate whether one of the radio buttons has been chosen; if a button has been chosen its value is set to true. Then there is a test after each of the radio buttons has been looped through to check this value:

```
function validate(form) {
   var radioButtons = form.radSuit;
   var radioChosen = false;

   for (var i=0; i<radioButtons.length; i++) {
    if (radioButtons[i].checked)
      {
         radioChosen=true;
         returnValue=true;
      }
   }

   if (radioChosen == false) {
     returnValue = false;
     alert("You did not select a suit of cards");
   }

   return returnValue;
}
```

Note that, while the order of attributes on an element should not matter in XHTML, Netscape 6 and Mozilla will show a checked property of the radio button only if the type attribute is the first attribute given on the <input /> element.

You can see the result in Figure 15-7.

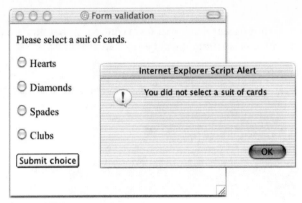

Figure 15-7

Checkboxes

Checkboxes allow a user to select zero, one, or more items from a set of choices. While a group of checkboxes can share the same name, they are not mutually exclusive like radio buttons are although they are made available in JavaScript as an array, just like the radio buttons.

Here is a slight change to the last example using checkboxes instead of radio buttons (and the user can select more than one suit of cards):

```
<form name="frmCards" action="cards.asp" method="post">
  <p>Please select one or more suits of cards.</p>
  <p><input type="checkbox" name="chkSuit" value="hearts" /> Hearts </p>
  <p><input type="checkbox" name="chkSuit" value="diamonds" /> Diamonds </p>
  <p><input type="checkbox" name="chkSuit" value="spades" /> Spades </p>
  <p><input type="checkbox" name="chkSuit" value="clubs" /> Clubs </p>
  <p><input type="button" value="Count checkboxes"
      onclick="countCheckboxes(frmCards.chkSuit)" /></p>
</form>
```

Here is the function that counts how many checkboxes have been selected and displays that number to the user. As with the last example, if no checkboxes have been selected you could alert the user that she must enter a value.

```
function countCheckboxes(field) {
  var intCount = 0
  for (var i = 0; i < field.length; i++) {
    if (field[i].checked)
        intCount++; }
  alert("You selected " + intCount + " checkbox(es)");
}
```

You can see the form in Figure 15-8 where the user has selected two checkboxes.

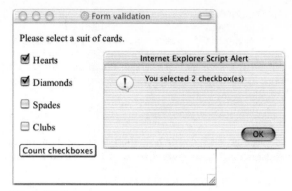

Figure 15-8

Disabling a Submit Button Until a Checkbox Has Been Selected

If you want to ensure that a checkbox has been selected—for example, if you want a user to agree to certain terms and conditions—you can do so by adding a function to the onsubmit event handler similar to those you have seen already. The function checks whether the checkbox has been checked, and if the function returns true the form will be submitted; if it returns false the user would be prompted to check the box. The function might look like this:

```
function checkCheckBox(myForm){
   if (myForm.agree.checked == false )
   {
      alert('You must agree to terms and conditions if you want to download
            this ' + 'product.');
      return false;
   } else
      return true;
}
```

However, you could use a script to simply disable the Submit button until users have clicked the box to say that they agree with the terms and conditions.

If you use a script to re-enable a disabled form control then you should disable the control in the script when the page loads rather than using the disable attribute on the element itself. This is important for those who do not have JavaScript enabled in their browsers. If you use the disabled attribute on a <form> element and users do not have JavaScript enabled they will never be able to use that form control. However, if you have used a script to disable it when the page loads, then you know that the script will be able to re-enable the form control when the user clicks the appropriate box. This is a great reminder that JavaScript should be used to enhance usability of pages and should not be required in order to use a page.

The following is a very simple page with a form. When the page loads, the Submit button is disabled in the onload event. If the user clicks the chkAgree checkbox then the Submit button will be re-enabled:

```
<body onload="document.frmAgree.btnSubmit.disabled=true">

<form name="frmAgree" action="test.asp" method="post">
```

```
I understand that this software has no liability:
<input type="checkbox" value="0" name="chkAgree"
        onclick="document.frmAgree.btnSubmit.disabled=false" />
<input type="submit" name="btnSubmit" value="Go to download" /><br />
<p>You will not be able to submit this form unless you agree to the
    <a href="terms.html">terms and conditions</a> and check the terms and
    conditions box.</p>
</form>
</body>
```

You can see this example in Figure 15-9; note how there is an explanation of why the Submit button might be disabled. This helps users understand why they might not be able to click the Submit button.

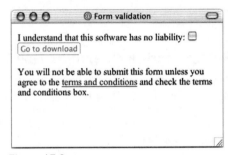

Figure 15-9

This technique can also be used with other form controls—you will see an example that enables a text input later in the chapter.

Form Enhancements

The examples you are going to meet in this section do not actually help you validate a form; rather, they are just used to enhance the usability of a form.

Focus on First Form Item

If your form starts with a text box, you can give focus to that text box so that users do not have to move their mouse, click the text input, and then move their hands back to the keyboard before they enter any text.

To give focus to the first text input on a form, simply add an `onload` event handler to the `<body>` element of the document. This handler selects the form control that you want to highlight and uses the `focus()` method of that control to give it focus like so (ch15_eg09.html):

```
<body onload="document.myForm.myTextBox.focus();">
```

When the page loads the cursor should be flashing in the form control that you have selected, ready for the user to enter some text.

Note that the `onload` event fires when the complete page has loaded (not as soon as it is come across in the order of the page).

Auto-Tabbing Between Fields

The `focus()` method can also be used to pass the focus of one control to another control. For example, if one of the controls on a form is to provide a date of birth in MM/DD/YYYY format then you can move focus between the three boxes as soon as the user enters a month and then again once the user has entered a day (`ch15_eg10.html`):

```
<form name="frmDOB">
  Enter your date of birth:<br />
  <input name="txtMonth" size="3" maxlength="2"
      onkeyup="if(this.value.length>=2)
      this.form.txtDay.focus();"/>
  <input name="txtDay" size="3" maxlength="2"
      onkeyup="if(this.value.length>=2)
      this.form.txtYear.focus();" />
  <input name="txtYear" size="5" maxlength="4"
      onkeyup="if(this.value.length>=4)
      this.form.submit.focus();" />

  <input type="submit" name="submit" value="Send" />

</form>
```

This example uses the `onkeyup` event handler to check that the length of the text the user has entered is equal to or greater than the number of characters specified in the `maxlength` attribute. If the user has entered the required number of characters the focus is moved to the next box.

Note how the length of the text input is discovered using `this.value.length`; `this` is a keyword that indicates the current form control, while the `value` property indicates the value entered for the control and then the `length` property returns the length of the value entered for the control. This is a quicker way of determining the length of the value in the current form control than the full path, which would be:

```
document.fromDOB.txtMonth.value.length
```

The other advantage of using the `this` keyword rather than the full path is that the code would work if you copied and pasted these controls into a different form, as you have not hard-coded the name of the form in.

You can see this example in Figure 15-10; the user has entered an appropriate number of digits in one field so the focus is moved onto to the next.

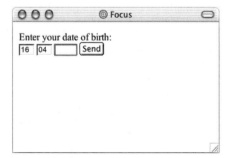

Figure 15-10

You might have noticed that the value of the size attribute is also one digit larger than the maximum length of the field to ensure that there is enough space for all of the characters (usually the width of the control will be slightly too small to see all of the characters at once).

I have seen this technique used to allow users to enter their credit card details using four blocks of four codes. While 16 digits is the most common length for a credit card number, and they are often printed in blocks of four digits, some Visa cards for example contain 13 digits and some American Express cards use 15 digits.

Disabling a Text Input

Sometimes you will want to disable a text input until a certain condition has been met—just like the Submit button was disabled until the user clicked the checkbox to agree to terms and conditions in Figure 15-9.

This example features a form that asks users how they heard about the site; radio buttons are used for several options such as Friend, TV ad, magazine ad, and then an option of Other. If the user selects the Other option, the text input next to that option allows the user to indicate how they heard about the site. You can see the form in Figure 15-11.

Figure 15-11

In this example, it's not just a case of enabling the text box when the user selects the other radio button, you really need to check the value of each radio button as it is selected—after all, if the user selects Other as her first choice, but then changes her mind and selects TV or one of the other options, you will want to disable the text input and change its value again. Therefore, each time the user selects a radio button, a function in the head of the document will be called that will be responsible for enabling and disabling the control and setting values.

First, here is the form that gives users the options (ch15_eg11.html). Note how the text input is disabled using the onload event handler of the <body> element and that the text input does not use the disabled attribute (this is the same as the earlier example with the Submit button).

```
<body onload="document.frmReferrer.txtOther.disabled=true;
              document.frmReferrer.txtOther.value='not applicable' ">
<h2>How did you hear about us?</h2>

<form name="frmReferrer">
```

```
        <input type="radio" name="radHear" value="1"
              onclick="handleOther(this.value);" />From a friend<br />
        <input type="radio" name="radHear" value="2"
              onclick="handleOther(this.value);" />TV Ad<br />
        <input type="radio" name="radHear" value="3"
              onclick="handleOther(this.value);" />Magazine Ad<br />
        <input type="radio" name="radHear" value="4"
              onclick="handleOther(this.value);" />Newspaper Ad<br />
        <input type="radio" name="radHear" value="5"
              onclick="handleOther(this.value);" />Internet<br />
        <input type="radio" name="radHear" value="other"
              onclick="handleOther(this.value);" />Other... Please specify:
        <input type="text" name="txtOther" />
    </form>
```

As you can see from this form, every time the user selects one of the options on this form, the onclick event calls a function called handleOther(). This function is passed the value of the form control as a parameter.

Looking at the function, you can see that it checks whether the value of the form control is equal to the text other (remember that checking whether one value is equal to another value uses two equal signs because the single equal sign is used to set a variable).

```
function handleOther(strRadio) {

    if (strRadio == "other") {
      document.frmReferrer.txtOther.disabled = false;
      document.frmReferrer.txtOther.value = ';
    }
    else {
      document.frmReferrer.txtOther.disabled = true;
      document.frmReferrer.txtOther.value = 'not applicable';
    }
}
```

Here you can see a simple if...else statement that looks at the value of the radio button, which has been passed in as an argument. If the value is other, the control is enabled, and the value set to nothing—otherwise it is disabled. If the value is other then the text input is enabled and its value is cleared. Otherwise txtOther is disabled and the value is not applicable.

Case Conversion

There are times when it is helpful to change the case of text a user has entered to make it all uppercase or all lowercase—in particular because JavaScript is case-sensitive. To change the case of text there are two built-in methods of JavaScript's string object:

❑   toLowerCase()
❑   toUpperCase()

To demonstrate, here is an example of a text input that changes case as focus moves away from the text input (ch15_eg12.html):

```
<form>
   <input type="text" name="case" size="20"
          onblur="this.value=this.value.toLowerCase();" />
</form>
```

If your form data is being sent to a server, it is generally considered better practice to make these changes on the server because they are less distracting for users—a form that changes letter case as you use it can appear a little odd to users.

Trimming Spaces from Beginning and End of Fields

You might want to remove spaces (whitespace) from the beginning or end of a form field for many reasons, even simply because the user did not intend to enter it there.

The technique I will demonstrate here uses the substring() method of the string object, whose syntax is:

```
substring(startPosition, endPosition)
```

This method returns the string from the given points—if no end position is given, then the default is the end of the string. The start and end positions are zero-based, so the first character is 0. For example, if you have a string that says Welcome, then the method substring(0, 1) returns the letter W.

Looking first at removing leading whitespace from the start of a string, the substring() method will be called upon twice.

First you can use the substring() method to retrieve the value the user has entered into a text control and just return the first character. You check if this first character returned is a space:

```
this.value.substring(0,1) == ' '
```

If this characters is a space, you call the substring() method a second time to remove the space. This time it selects the value of the control from the second character to the end of the string (ignoring the first character). This is set to be the new value for the form control; so you have removed the first character, which was a space.

```
this.value = this.value.substring(1, this.value.length);
```

This whole process of checking if the first character is a blank and then removing it if it is will be called using the onblur event handler; so when focus moves away from the form control the process starts. You can see here that the process uses a while loop to indicate that for as long as the first character is a blank then it should be removed using the second call to the substring() method. This loop makes sure that the first character is removed if it is a blank until the substring no longer returns a blank as the first character (ch15_eg13.html).

```
<form>
   <input type="text" name="txtName" size="100"
          value=" Enter text leaving whitespace at start. Then change focus."
          onblur="while (this.value.substring(0,1) == ' ')
```

```
            this.value = this.value.substring(1, this.value.length);" /><br />

</form>
```

To trim any trailing spaces the process is similar but reversed. The first `substring()` method collects the last character of the string, and if it is blank removes it:

```
<form>
<input type="text" name="txtName" size="100"
       value="Enter text leaving whitespace at end. Then change focus. "
       onblur="while (this.value.substring
           (this.value.length-1,this.value.length) == ' ')
             this.value = this.value.substring(0, this.value.length-1);" /><br />
</form>
```

Netscape 4 and IE 4 both introduced something called *regular expressions* that allow you to perform a wide variety of operations on strings. You could therefore use a regular expression to trim the spaces like so:

```
<form>
   <input type="text" name="removeLeadingAndTrailingSpace" size="100"
     value=" Enter text with white space, then change focus. "
     onblur = "this.value = this.value.replace(/^ \s+/, ").replace(/\s+$/, ");"
   /><br />
</form>
```

This removes both trailing and leading spaces.

Regular expressions are quite a large topic in themselves. If you want to learn more about them then you can refer to *Beginning JavaScript 2E* by Paul Wilton (Wrox, 2000).

Selecting All of the Content of a Text Area

If you want to allow users to select the entire contents of a text area (so they don't have to manually select all the text with the mouse), you can use the `focus()` and `select()` methods.

In this example the `selectAll()` function takes one parameter, the form control that you want to select the content of (ch15_eg14.html):

```
<html>
<head><title>Select whole text area</title>
<script language="JavaScript">
  function selectAll(strControl) {
    strControl.focus();
    strControl.select();
  }
</script>
</head>
```

```
<body>
  <form name="myForm">
    <textarea name="myTextArea" rows="5" cols="20">This is some text</textarea>
    <input type="button" name="btnSelectAll" value="Select all"
           onclick="selectAll(document.myForm.myTextArea);" />
  </form>
</body>
</head>
</html>
```

The button that allows the user to select all has an onclick event handler to call the selectAll() function and tell it which control whose contents should be selected.

The selectAll() function first gives that form control focus using the focus() method and then selects its content using the select() method. The form control must gain focus before it can have its content selected. The same method would also work on a single line text input and a password field.

Check and Uncheck All Checkboxes

If there are several checkboxes in a group of checkboxes, it can be helpful to allow users to select or deselect a whole group of checkboxes at once. Here are two functions that allow precisely this:

```
function check(field) {
  for (var i = 0; i < field.length; i++) {
    field[i].checked = true;}
}

function uncheck(field) {
  for (var i = 0; i < field.length; i++) {
    field[i].checked = false; }
}
```

In order for these functions to work, more than one checkbox must be in the group. You then add two buttons that call the check or uncheck functions, passing in the array of checkbox elements that share the same name like so (ch15_eg15.html):

```
<form name="frmSnacks" action="">

    Your basket order<br />
    <input type="checkbox" name="basketItem" value="1" />Chocolate
    cookies<br />
    <input type="checkbox" name="basketItem" value="2" />Potato chips<br />
    <input type="checkbox" name="basketItem" value="3" />Cola<br />
    <input type="checkbox" name="basketItem" value="4" />Cheese<br />
    <input type="checkbox" name="basketItem" value="5" />Candy bar<br /><br />

    <input type="button" value="Select All"
           onclick="check(document.frmSnacks.basketItem);" />
```

```
            <input type="button" value="Deselect All"
                    onclick="uncheck(document.frmSnacks.basketItem);" />
    </form>
```

You can see how this form appears in Figure 15-12.

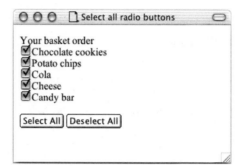

Figure 15-12

Try It Out   An E-mail Form

In this exercise you are going to create an e-mail form that has a few interesting features. It will use a regular expression to check the structure of an e-mail address and will also check that all fields have an entry of some kind. The form will include a quick address book that contains addresses of potential recipients of the e-mail. Figure 15-13 shows you what the form is going to look like; it also shows the message that appears when the user tries to submit the e-mail without entering a message.

1. First create a skeleton XHTML document with <head>, <title>, and <body> elements.

2. In the body of the document add the <form> element and a table to hold the form. The first row of the table will contain another table to hold the To, Cc, and Subject fields in one cell and then the quick address book in the second cell. So, add the first row of this table along with the part of the nested table that holds the three text inputs:

```
<form name="frmEmail" onsubmit="return validate(this)" action="sendMail.asp"
      method ="post">

  <table><tr><td>

  <table><tr valign="top">
     <td>Send to:</td><td><input type="text" size="70" name="textTo" /></td>
     </tr><tr>
     <td>CC: </td><td><input type="text" size="70" name="textCC" /></td>
     </tr><tr>
     <td>Subject:</td><td><input type="text" size="70" name="txtSubjct" />
     </td>
  </tr></table>

  </td>
  <td><!-- quick address book will go here --></td>
  </tr></table>
```

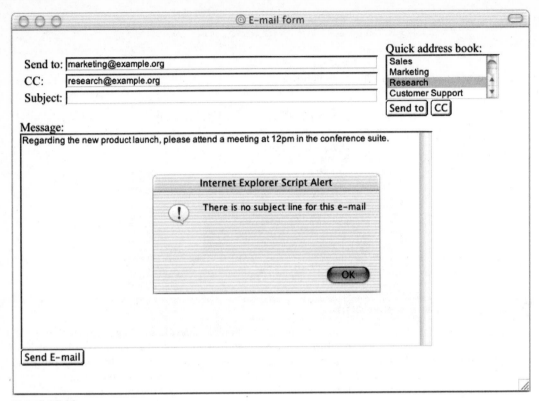

Figure 15-13

3. Next you need to add the quick address book into the second cell of the nested table. The address book uses a multiple select box. Underneath it are two buttons: one to add addresses to the `to` field and one to add addresses to the `cc` field. Both of these buttons call the `add()` function when clicked:

```
Quick address book:<br />
<select size="4" name="selectList1" style="width:150px">
   <option value="sales@example.org">Sales</option>
   <option value="marketing@example.org">Marketing</option>
   <option value="research@example.org">Research</option>
   <option value="support@example.org">Customer Support</option>
   <option value="it@example.org">IT</option>
</select><br />

<input type="button" onclick="add(textTo, document.frmEmail.selectList1);"
       value="Send to" />
<input type="button" onclick="add(textCC, document.frmEmail.selectList1);"
       value="CC" />
```

4. Add the message `<textarea>` element and a `Send E-mail` button:

```
Message:<br />
<textarea name="message" rows="20" cols="115"></textarea><br />
<input type="submit" value="Send E-mail" />
```

5. Now you need to add the validation function and the `add()` function. First, here is the `add()` function that adds e-mail addresses from the address book to the To or Cc fields:

```
function add(objInput, objList){

var strGroup = objList.options[objList.selectedIndex].value;

  if (objInput.value == "")
  {
     objInput.value = strGroup
  }
  else
  {
     objInput.value += ('; ' + strGroup)
  }
}
```

6. Here is the `validate()` function, which you can see is quite long:

```
function validate(form) {

  var returnValue = true;
  var sendTo = form.txtTo.value;
  var cc = form.txtCC.value;
  var subject = form.txtSubject.value;
  var message = form.txtMessage.value;

  if (sendTo == "")
  {
    returnValue = false;
    alert("There are no email addresses in the To field");
    form.txtTo.focus();
  }

  if (subject == "")
  {
    returnValue = false;
    alert("There is no subject line for this e-mail");
    form.txtSubject.focus();
  }

  if (message=="")
  {
    returnValue = false;
    alert("There is no message to this e-mail");
    form.txtMessage.focus();
  }
```

```
    var arrTo = sendTo.split("; ");
    var rxEmail=/^\w(\.?[\w-])*@\w(\.?[\w-])*\.[a-z]{2,6}(\.[a-z]{2})?$/i;

    for (var i=0; i<(arrTo.length); i++) {
      if (!rxEmail.test(arrTo[i]))
      {
        returnValue = false;
        alert("The e-mail address "+ arrTo[i] +" does not appear to be valid");
      }
    }

    var arrCC = cc.split("; ");
    for (var i=0; i<(arrCC.length); i++) {
      if (!rxEmail.test(arrCC[i]))
      {
        returnValue = false;
        alert("The e-mail address "+ arrCC[i] +" does not appear to be valid");
      }
    }

  return returnValue;
}
```

7.   Save the file as ch15_eg16.html, and when you open it up in the browser window it should look like the example you saw in Figure 15-13.

How It Works

The form in this example contains two functions. The first is the add() function, which passes the e-mail addresses from the select box to the To or CC fields. The add() function is very simple and takes two parameters:

❑   **objInput:** The field that the selected address is being sent to

❑   **objList:** The select list that contains the e-mail addresses

This function starts by collecting the value of the selected item using the selectedIndex property of the select list and placing it in a variable called strGroup. Next it checks whether the form field the address is being added to is empty; if it is the e-mail address stored in the strGroup attribute is added to the field. If the To or CC field is not empty, a semicolon and a space will be added before the e-mail address because this is the usual delimiter for multiple e-mail addresses:

```
function add(objInput, objList){

var strGroup = objList.options[objList.selectedIndex].value;

  if (objInput.value == "")
  {
    objInput.value = strGroup
  }
```

```
      else
      {
        objInput.value += ('; ' + strGroup)
      }
    }
```

The `validate()` function is slightly more complex, starting off by setting a `returnValue` variable to `true` and collecting the form's values into variables.

```
function validate(form) {

   var returnValue = true;
   var sendTo = form.txtTo.value;
   var cc = form.txtCC.value;
   var subject = form.txtSubject.value;
   var message = form.txtMessage.value;
```

The checks to see if the To, Subject line, and Message body fields take the same format as the examples you saw earlier in the chapter when checking to see if a field is empty or not:

```
if (sendTo == "")
{
   returnValue = false;
   alert("There are no e-mail addresses in the To field");
   form.txtTo.focus();
}
```

The `validate` function gets more interesting when it comes to checking that valid e-mail addresses have been entered into the form. The first thing that needs to be done is that the regular expression that's used to check the e-mail addresses needs to be stored in a variable—this time called `rxEmail`:

```
var rxEmail=/^\w(\.?[\w-])*@\w(\.?[\w-])*\.[a-z]{2,6}(\.[a-z]{2})?$/i;
```

Next the To field gets split into an array using the `split()` method of the string object. This function will take a string and split it into separate values whenever it comes across a specified character or set of characters. In this case, the method looks for any instances of a semicolon followed by a space, and wherever it finds these it creates a new item in the array.

```
var arrTo = sendTo.split("; ");
```

Imagine having the following e-mail addresses (note that this is just to illustrate the `split()` method; it is not part of the code):

```
sales@example.com; accounts@example.com; marketing@example.com
```

These would be split into the following array (again this is not part of the code from the example):

```
arrTo[0] = "sales@example.com"
arrTo[1] = "accounts@example.com"
arrTo[2] = "marketing@example.com"
```

So now there has to be a `for` loop in the code that will go through each e-mail address in the array and check that it follows the pattern described in the regular expression. The `for` loop has three parameters; the first sets a counter called `i` to be 0, checks that the counter is less than the number of items in the array, and finally increments the counter. Inside the loop is an `if` statement that checks whether the e-mail address matches the regular expression using the `test()` method; if it does not it will set the return value to `false` and alert the user that the value does not seem to be a valid e-mail address:

```
for (var i=0; i<(arrTo.length); i++) {
  if (!rxEmail.test(arrTo[i]))
  {
    returnValue = false;
    alert("The email address "+ arrTo[i] +" does not appear to be valid");
  }
}
```

After this you can see a similar setup for the CC field.

```
var arrCC = cc.split("; ");
for (var i=0; i<(arrCC.length); i++) {
  if (!rxEmail.test(arrCC[i]))
  {
    returnValue = false;
    alert("The e-mail address "+ arrCC[i] +" does not appear to be valid");
  }
}

return returnValue;
}
```

Now you have an example of a form that has more than one function. It uses JavaScript to create a quick address book and validates the entries to stop the user from trying to send an e-mail address that is not valid.

Breadcrumb Trails

If you have a good directory structure you can create a breadcrumb trail to help users know which section of your site they are in. This is really necessary only in a large site, where your site contains several sections.

Note that the approach described here requires that each of the sections lives in its own folder, and that folder contains clear names such as Products, Services, Music, or Film that reflect their content.

For this example to work well you also need to have descriptive filenames, and the file extensions for each page need to be the same length (for example file extensions must all be `html` or `htm` rather than a mix of both.

Sometimes you will see that people save HTML files with the extension .htm rather than .html. This is a throwback from when there were small limits on the length of filenames. As a result many authoring packages, and authors, wrote pages with the .htm extension rather than .html. In practice, both are treated exactly the same.

Figure 15-14 shows you an example of the breadcrumb trail this script will create:

Figure 15-14

This script works by collecting the URL of the page from the document object. The `split()` method of the string object is then used to split the URL into sections. The `split()` method takes a character as an argument, and each time that character is met in the string the section up to that is put into a new array.

The splitting character could be a space, period, comma, or (as in this case) a forward slash character. For example, consider the following URL:

```
http://www.wrox.com/books/xhtml/Beginning_Web_Development.html
```

Using the / character as a separator you will end up with an array that looks something like this:

```
array[0] = "http:"
array[1] =
array[2] = "www.wrox.com"
array[3] = "books"
array[4] = 'xhtml'
array[5] = "Beginning_Web_Development.html"
```

For the breadcrumb trail, you want to ignore the first two items of the array because you do not want the entries until after the second forward slash character. But then each item will form part of your breadcrumb trail. The resulting trail should look like this:

```
www.wrox.com > books > xhtml > Beginning Web Development
```

Here is the full script that creates the breadcrumb trail; it lives in a file called `breadcrumb.js` that should be included in the `<body>` of a document:

```
<script type="text/JavaScript">
var address = document.location.href;
var breadcrumb = "You are here ";
var arrAddress = address.split("/");

// you want to start after the second instance of the separator character
```

579

```
for (var i=2; i<(arrAddress.length-1); i++) {
  breadcrumb +="<a href=\""+address.substring(0,address.indexof("/"+
  arrAddress[i])+arrAddress[i].length+1)+"/\">"+arrAddress[i]+"</a> &gt; ";
}

i=arrAddress.length-1;
//remove the file extension html from the end of the name of the last item
endPos = (arrAddress[i].length -5)
name = arrAddress[i].substring(0,endPos)
breadcrumb +="<a
href=\""+address.substring(0,address.indexof(arrAddress[i])+arrAddress[i].le
ngth) +"\">"+name+"</a>";

document.writeln(breadcrumb);

</script>
```

Let's look at how this works a little more closely. The first variable called `address` collects the URL. The `breadcrumb` attribute is going to contain the final trail that will be written to the page, so this starts with the text "You are here." The third variable is now going to hold the array with the URL split into sections; this is going to be called `arrAddress`:

```
var address = document.location.href;
var breadcrumb = "You are here ";
var arrAddress = address.split("/");
```

To write out the breadcrumb trail the last item has to be treated separately from the rest of them. So this next section of code will take the parts of the URL between the two forward slashes and the final file name.

```
for (var i=2; i<(arrAddress.length-1); i++) {
```

You can see the three properties in the `for` loop:

❑ The first is a counter that will count the number of forward slashes that have been in the URL.

❑ The second is the condition for the loop to keep running. In this case it indicates that if the number of forward slashes (the value of the counter) is less than the number of elements in the `arrAddress` array minus one, the loop should run. It looks at the number of elements in the array minus one because the last item (the filename) will be dealt with separately in a moment.

❑ The third increments the counter by one every time the loop runs.

Each time the loop runs a new link will be added to the variable `breadcrumb`.

The first time the condition is met and the loop is run, the counter is at 2 so the first item to be added into the breadcrumb will be the third item in the array `arrAddress`.

First look at how the URL to the relevant subsection of the site is generated. Remember that the `substring(startPos, endPos)` method of the string object will return the part of the string between the start and end points provided as arguments. The `indexof()` method of the string object tests if a string contains a specified character and returns the position of that character.

```
address.substring(0,address.indexof("/"+arrAddress[i])+arrAddress[i].length+1)
```

So this line takes the address variable that contained the complete URL to the page and selects the substring of that URL up to the relevant part for this bit of the breadcrumb—which will obviously begin at position 0. The tricky thing is finding the end position. So, the end position is calculated using this part of the script:

```
indexOf("/"+arrAddress[i])+arrAddress[i].length+1
```

The `indexof()` method is looking for the forward slash character followed by the text that is in the current item of the array (the next time the loop runs it will look for a forward slash character followed by the next item in the array). For example, the first time it runs it will be looking for the first occurrence of the string `/www.wrox.com`. On its own this would indicate the start of the string, but you need to get the end of this string so you add the length of this element from the array, plus another character to count for the forward slash.

In between the `<a>` elements you can see that the current element from the array is written to the page as the part that is displayed to the user:

```
for (var i=2; i<(arrAddress.length-1); i++) {
  breadcrumb +="<a
    href=\""+address.substring(0,address.indexof("/"+arrAddress[i])+
    arrAddress[i].length+1)+"/\">"+arrAddress[i]+"</a> &gt; ";
}
```

This loop handles all of the items in the breadcrumb trail except for the filename. So you still need to add the filename, and for presentation purposes, the file extension will be removed.

You might have noticed that the loop adds an angle bracket after each iteration of the loop to separate links using `&gt;`, this must not appear on the last item and is why the last item in the array is treated separately.

To work with the final item of the breadcrumb trail, the filename, you need to set the counter to be the number of elements in the array minus one:

```
i=arrAddress.length-1;
```

Next you need to remove the file extension so that you can present it to the user. If your file extension is going to be `.html` then you have five characters to remove from the end of the last element in the array. You use the `length` property of this last element in the array and remove five characters from it to find the end position for a `substring()` method you will use next. The `substring()` method then takes that item from the array and selects the substring from the start to the specified end position:

```
endPos = (arrAddress[i].length -5)
name = arrAddress[i].substring(0,endPos)
```

The opening `<a>` tag is added to the breadcrumb variable as in the previous section, but the value displayed to the user is the one prepared in the name attribute:

```
breadcrumb +="<a
href=\""+address.substring(0,address.indexOf(arrAddress[i])+arrAddress[i].le
ngth) +"\">"+name+"</a>";
```

The breadcrumb trail is then written to the page using the `write()` method of the document object:

```
document.writeln(breadcrumb);
```

This script can now be included on any page of any site you create.

Image Rollovers

You met a simple example of an image rollover in the last chapter, but in this chapter you will meet a function that allows you to change several images on the same page. This function can then be used with all pages rather than repeating the same script in several pages.

To create a rollover image you need two different versions of an image:

❑ The normal image that the user sees when their mouse is not hovering over the image

❑ The other image that appears when the user rolls their mouse over the image.

In the last chapter you saw a very simple image rollover script that was added to an `<a>` element that contained the image. When the user rolls the mouse over the link (containing the image) an `onmouseover` event fires and the `src` property of the image object is changed to the mouseover image. When the mouse moves off the image the `onmouseout` event changes the image's `src` property back to the original image. (If only one of these events were monitored the image would simply change, not go back to its initial state, so it is important to monitor both.)

You can see that this image's name attribute has a value of `button`, which is used to identify the image in the event handler:

```
<a href=""
   onmouseover="document.images.button.src='click_red.gif';"
   onmouseout="document.images.button.src='click_green.gif'">
   <img src="click_green.gif" width="100" height="50" border="0" name="button">
</a>
```

Remember that each image in the document has its own corresponding object in the DOM, and one of the properties of the `image` object is the `src` property. The `src` property is the location for the image, which corresponds to the value specified in the `src` attribute on the `<img>` element in the document.

When creating rollover images that contain text, you should generally use the same size and weight of text on both images. Text that suddenly appears larger or bold can be hard to read. Changing the background color tends to be a better option.

Creating an image rollover function is the logical next step when you want to use the same rollover images on several pages—for example if you are creating a navigation bar that changes color as users move their mouse over each item. Figure 15-15 shows you a navigation bar that does just that.

Each image in this navigation bar is contained in a link and each image must have a different name. As with the last example, it is the `<a>` element that carries the event handlers. When the user places the mouse over and off the link, an `onmouseover` event calls the `changeImages()` function.

The `changeImages()` function has two arguments—the first is the name of the image, the second is the name of a variable that holds the URL of the image that will replace the current one. Note how the value

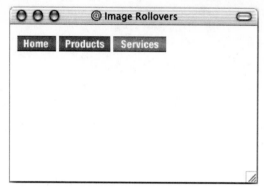

Figure 15-15

of the image's name attribute corresponds with the parameters being passed when the `onmouseover` and `onmouseout` events fire:

```
<a href="index.html"
    onmouseover="changeImages('image1', 'image1on')"
    onmouseout="changeImages('image1', 'image1off')">
    <img name="image1" src="images/home.gif" width="99" height="20"
        border="0" alt="home">
</a>
```

This script that does the real work lives in the `scripts` folder and is in a file called `rollover.js`. This script can be included in any page that is going to include a rollover.

Remember that there are two images for each rollover—when the mouse is over the image it is "on," and when the mouse is off the image it is "off."

Each image is assigned a variable, one for when the mouse is over it and one for when it is off it. The variable holds an image object whose `src` property is the URL for the image. First you see the images used when there are rollovers and then the images used in the normal state:

```
if (document.images) {
  image1on = new Image();
  image1on.src = "images/nav_home_on.gif";

  image2on = new Image();
  image2on.src = "images/nav_products_on.gif";

  image3on = new Image();
  image3on.src = "images/nav_services_on.gif";
```

Next come the variables holding the image objects that have the `src` property set for when the image is "off."

```
image1off = new Image();
image1off.src = "images/nav_home.gif";
```

```
   image2off = new Image();
   image2off.src = "images/nav_products.gif";

   image3off = new Image();
   image3off.src = "images/nav_services.gif";


}
```

Now, here's the function; it loops through the images and takes the arguments passed into the function:

```
function changeImages() {
  if (document.images) {
    for (var i=0; i<changeImages.arguments.length; i+=2) {
     document[changeImages.arguments[i]].src =
       eval(changeImages.arguments[i+1] + ".src");
      }
    }
   }
```

The lines that are doing the real work here are the ones in the middle. If the user has moved his mouse over the first image, the function will be called like this:

```
onsubmit="changeImages(image1, image1on)"
```

The first value being passed in is the value of the name property on the image. So the following line in the function tells the browser to take the first argument of the changeImages() function (which is image1) and change the src property of this element:

```
document[changeImages.arguments[i]].src =
```

The last thing on this line is the equal (=) sign. This property still has to be set and the code on the next line is the code that actually provides the value. This next line is saying the property should be given the value of the second argument in the function:

```
eval(changeImages.arguments[i+1] + ".src");
```

You may remember from the last chapter that the for loop takes three arguments:

❑ The first argument runs only once and in this case sets the value of the counter to be 0 (i-0).

❑ The second argument indicates whether the loop should run again. In this case, if the counter is less than the number of arguments passed to the changeImages() function it should run again.

❑ The third argument increments the counter by two.

This means that the changeImages() function can be used to change more than one image at a time. You can call the function with several sets of parameters.

Random Script Generator

The following script can be used to add random content to a page. You might like to use it to add random quotes or tips, or you could use it to rotate advertisements or images. The script contains a function called randomContent() that includes the content that will be selected at random.

The content is added to an array called arrContent and the array contains the data you want to appear randomly:

```
<script language="JavaScript">

function randomContent(){

var arrContent=new Array()
arrContent[0]='This is the first message.'
arrContent[1]='This is the second message.'
arrContent[2]='This is the third message.'
arrContent[3]='This is the fourth message.'
arrContent[4]='This is the fifth message.'
```

A variable called i is then set to a random value between 0 and the number of items in the array. In order to generate this random number you need to call two methods of the Math object. The random() method generates a random number between 0 and 1 and this is multiplied by the number of elements in the array. The number is then rounded to the nearest integer (whole number) equal to or less than the number generated using the floor() method.

The floor() method is used rather than the round() method because you could end up with a number higher than the number of items in the array.

```
var i=Math.floor(Math.random()*arrContent.length)
   document.write(arrContent[i])
}
</script>
```

Wherever you want to include the random content you just call that function:

```
<script type="text/JavaScript">
   randomContent();
</script>
```

You can see the result here in Figure 15-16.

If you wanted the random content to appear on several pages then you could simply place the function in an external file.

Pop-Up Windows

Pop-up windows have a bad name. People associate them with pop-up ads that appear when pages of a site load and they often feature advertisements or unwanted information. There are, however, some very legitimate uses for pop-up windows; for example, you might just want to keep users on the current page

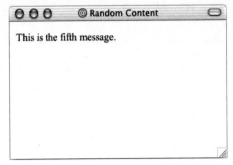

Figure 15-16

while allowing them to provide some other information in a pop-up, or you might want to open something from your site (such as an image) in a new window without the user losing his place.

Of course, you can create a normal link and make the page open in a new window by adding the `target="_new"` attribute, but when you create a popup in JavaScript you can control the dimensions of the window, indicate whether it can be resized or not, and whether it has scrollbars:

```
<a
  href="http://google.com/"
  onclick="window.open(this.href, 'search',
  'width=400,height=300,scrollbars,resizable');
  return false;"

>
Click here for the link to open in a popup window.
</a>
```

You can see the `open()` method of the `window` object can take several parameters; the syntax is as follows:

```
open(url, 'windowname', 'features')
```

You can list several features after the window name, and the following table shows you those available. As you can see, they allow you to control several properties of the window including size and position and whether the screen has scrollbars or not—but remember that users with different resolution might require scrollbars even if you do not.

Feature	Value	Sets
width	Number	The width of the new window in pixels
height	Number	The height of the new window in pixels
left	Number	The location where the left side of the window should appear
top	Number	The location where the top of the window should appear

Feature	Value	Sets
location	yes/no	Controls whether the browser should display the browser location toolbar
menubar	yes/no	Controls whether the browser should display the menu bar
resizable	yes/no	Allows the user to resize the browser window
scrollbars	yes/no	Controls whether horizontal or vertical scrollbars are shown
status	yes/no	Controls the display of the status bar (the area at the bottom of the browser)
toolbar	yes/no	Controls whether the browser should display the buttons toolbar

You should be aware that some pop-up blocking software might prevent functions like this from working. Netscape 6 and some versions of IE 6 contain pop-up blocking software that will prevent these links from working. You should also avoid using words like "pop-up" (or "popup") in your filenames even when creating pop-up windows because some pop-up window blockers look for words like these in your filenames and will not open files containing them.

You can create pop-up windows in JavaScript in several ways, but I strongly recommend that you use this approach if you choose to create them with JavaScript because many other methods prevent a user from right-clicking the link and opening it in a new window themselves. More experienced Web browsers often enable you to open a link in a new window with the right mouse button, and some methods of creating pop-ups mean that users who take this approach (choosing to open the link in a new window themselves) will just get a blank window. This approach solves the problem.

When *Not* to Use JavaScript

You've seen some great examples of when you should be using JavaScript, but I should warn you about some uses of it that are best avoided.

Drop-Down Navigation Menus

Some clients I've worked with have asked about creating effects that require JavaScript for navigation purposes. One of the more common requests is for drop-down navigation menus where subpages drop down from the main items on the menu. These rely on JavaScript and I discourage clients from using these for three reasons:

❑ The technique simply will not work for those who have JavaScript turned off on their browser. While this is quite a small percentage, it does mean that those users simply cannot access those pages.

❑ They tend to perform slightly differently on different browsers, and it is hard to get a script to work on all browsers.

❑ Users can find it difficult to click the appropriate part of a menu that moves.

Hiding Your E-mail Address

I have seen several articles on the Web that suggest you can use JavaScript to write your e-mail address to the pages (using the `write()` method of the document object to write out the e-mail address, rather than a normal <a> link and XHTML). The goal is to avoid getting so much spam. One of the sources for spam are little programs (that often go under the name of bots, spiders, or crawlers) that crawl through Web sites looking for e-mail addresses. These e-mail addresses are then used as a target for spam. The problem with this idea is that anyone without JavaScript turned on in their browser will not be able to see your e-mail address. A better alternative is to provide an e-mail form that sends inquiries to you—then once you have received an inquiry you can be fairly sure the user will not be doing this just to get an e-mail address and that you are safe giving your e-mail address to them.

Quick Jump Select Boxes

Some sites offer select boxes in forms (just like the select boxes you saw in Chapter 6) as a navigation menu—often referred to as a *quick jump menu* that takes you directly to different pages or sections of the site when you select that item from the drop-down list box. Some of these use scripts to automatically take the user to the selected page without the user actually pressing a GO or Submit button; rather, the script is set up to detect a change in the select box and then take the user to that page. This is bad practice for two reasons:

❑   You can use the up and down arrow keys to select items from a select box, and any user that tried to do this would automatically get taken to the first selection as soon as she pressed the down arrow the first time. Users would never be able to get further than this option using keys. While a savvy user might pick this up quickly, those with disabilities who are using keys rather than a mouse to navigate the site might be a lot more frustrated.

❑   And again, if the user has JavaScript disabled it simply won't work.

Anything the User Requires from Your Site

The bottom line in the decision when to use JavaScript or not is whether it will simply enhance the user experience or whether it is required for the user to perform an action or see some vital information. You should never design anything that requires JavaScript to function—remember the lesson from the "Disabling a Submit Button Until a Checkbox Has Been Selected" section.

Summary

In this chapter you have seen many uses for JavaScript and you should now have a better understanding of how to apply this language that you started to learn in the last chapter. With the help of these scripts you should now be able to use these and other scripts in your page. You should also have an idea of how you can tailor or even write your own scripts.

You have seen how you can help a user fill in a form correctly by providing validation, whether you are checking that required fields have something in them or that an e-mail address follows the expected pattern. This saves users time by telling them what they have to do before a page gets sent to a server, processed, and then returned with errors. The validation examples highlight the access the DOM gives to document content so that you can perform operations on the values users provide. This is a great example of interactivity—the document not only provides the form, but also helps in filling it out. And, of course, forms are a vital part of any Web site that wants to gather information from its visitors.

You also saw how the DOM can help make a form generally more usable by putting the focus in appropriate parts of the form and manipulating the text users have entered—by removing or replacing certain characters.

In the second half of the chapter you saw several other JavaScript techniques such as creating breadcrumb trails, image rollovers, random content, and pop-up windows. These examples will all help you understand what you can do with JavaScript and how to integrate scripts into your pages.

One of the key things to remember, however, is that you should use JavaScript to enhance a page, rather than relying on it to display content or offer some functionality.

Exercises

There is only one exercise for this chapter because it is quite a long one. The answers to all of the exercises are in Appendix A.

1. Your task is to create a validation function for the competition form in Figure 15-17.

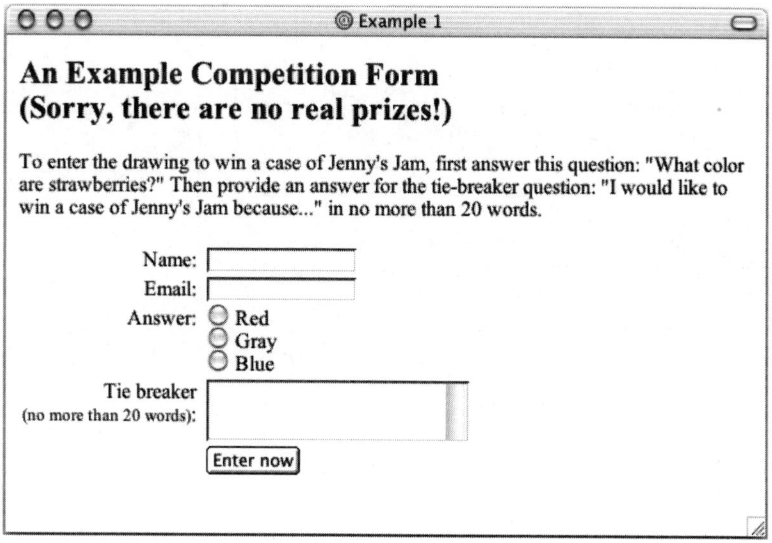

An Example Competition Form (Sorry, there are no real prizes!)

To enter the drawing to win a case of Jenny's Jam, first answer this question: "What color are strawberries?" Then provide an answer for the tie-breaker question: "I would like to win a case of Jenny's Jam because..." in no more than 20 words.

Name:
Email:
Answer: ○ Red ○ Gray ○ Blue
Tie breaker (no more than 20 words):
[Enter now]

Figure 15-17

The function should check that the user has done the following things:

❑ Entered his or her name

❑ Provided a valid e-mail address

❑ Selected one of the radio buttons as an answer to the question

❑ Given an answer for the tiebreaker question and that it is no more than 20 words

These should be in the order that the controls appear on the form.

Here is the code for the form:

```
<form name="frmCompetition" action="competition.asp" method="post"
onsubmit="return validate(this);">
<h2>An Example Competition Form <br />(Sorry, there are no real prizes!)</h2>
<p> To enter the drawing to win a case of Jenny's Jam, first answer
this question: "What color are strawberries?" Then provide an answer for
the tie-breaker question: "I would like to win a case of Jenny's Jam
because..." in no more than 20 words.</p>
<table>
  <tr>
    <td class="formTitle">Name: </td>
    <td><input type="text" name="txtName" size="18" /></td>
  </tr>
  <tr>
    <td class="formTitle">Email: </td>
    <td><input type="text" name="txtEmail" size="18" /></td>
  </tr>
  <tr>
    <td class="formTitle">Answer: </td>
    <td><input type="radio" name="radAnswer" value="Red" /> Red<br />
        <input type="radio" name="radAnswer" value="Gray" /> Gray<br />
        <input type="radio" name="radAnswer" value="Blue" /> Blue
    </td>
  </tr>
  <tr>
    <td class="formTitle">Tie breaker <br/ ><small>(no more than 20 words)
    </small>: </td>
    <td><textarea name="txtTieBreaker" cols="30" rows="3" /></textarea></td>
  </tr>
  <tr>
    <td class="formTitle"></td>
    <td><input type="submit" value="Enter now" /></td>
  </tr>
</table>

</form>
```

Taking Your Site Live

Once you have created your Web site you will want to get it out on the Web for everyone to see. As you might remember from Chapter 1, Web sites live on special computers called Web servers that are constantly connected to the Internet. Rather than buying and running your own Web server, it is generally far more economical to rent space on a Web server owned by a *hosting company*, and in order to help you choose the right hosting company and indeed the right package from the hosting company you need to learn some of the key terminology that they use. In this chapter you will find out what things like shared and dedicated hosting are, how to decide how much space or bandwidth you need, and so on.

But before you put your site on a Web server, you should perform some checks and tests, from validating your documents and checking links to making sure the site works in different screen resolutions and that the text is readable. Putting a site on the Web only to have customers tell you that the link to the products page does not work or that they cannot see the site on their computer will not do your reputation any good. So, you must learn how to test your site before it goes live. And then once you have put your site on a Web server you can perform other kinds of checks and tests—after all, while a site can seem to work fine on your computer, there may be issues with the way it is set up on your new server when you move it there.

Once your site is ready for the public to see, you will then want to make sure they know about it! You will want to make sure it gets indexed by the major search engines, such as Google, Yahoo, AltaVista, the dmoz Open Directory, and MSN; this can be quite a complex process with lots of trial and error to get your site as near to the top of the rankings as possible. You might also consider a number of other strategies to let people know you are out there. After putting all the hard work into creating a site, you want it to be a success.

In addition, an element that you haven't learned about yet provides information about documents and their content—the <meta> element.

In this chapter you learn how to do following:

- ❑ Use the <meta> element
- ❑ Perform tests to make sure your site will work as you intended
- ❑ Check that your site is accessible

- ❑ Find a *host* to make your site available to everyone on the Web
- ❑ Move your site from your computer to your host's Web server using FTP
- ❑ Submit your site to search engines
- ❑ Increase visitor numbers
- ❑ Control different versions of your site so that you can make changes without making mistakes

Meta Tags

Before you start looking at how to test your site, you need to learn about one last tag: the `<meta>` tag. Meta tags live in the `<head>` of a document and contain information about a document—rather than living in the `<body>` of the document and being part of actual content. The information can be used for a number of purposes including helping search engines index your site, specifying the author of a document, and, if the document is time-sensitive, specifying when it should expire.

The `<meta>` element is an empty element and so does not have a closing tag; rather, `<meta>` elements carry information within attributes, so you need a forward slash character at the end of the element. For example, here is a `<meta>` element that provides a description of a computer book shop Web site:

```
<meta name="description" content="Buy computer books online, and get them
delivered to your door the next day" />
```

The `<meta>` element can take eight attributes, four of which are universal attributes—dir, lang, xml:lang, and title. The other four, however, are specific to the `<meta>` element:

- ❑ schema
- ❑ name
- ❑ content
- ❑ http-equiv

The name and content attributes tend to be used together as do the http-equiv and content attributes. These pairings will be addressed next.

name and content Attributes

The name and content attributes specify properties of the document; the value of the name attribute is the property you are setting and the content attribute is its value. In the example you just saw a moment ago, the `<meta>` element was setting a description property for the content of the document or site. As you can see, the name attribute had a value of description, and its value is a description of what the site is about:

```
<meta content="Wrox Press Books, Articles and Online Resources"
name="description">
```

The value of the `name` attribute can be anything; no restrictions are published in any standards. It is therefore a very helpful way to add in your own information about a document. There are, however, some predefined values you will regularly see used this way. These are:

❑ **description:** Sets a description of the page or site

❑ **keywords:** Contains a list of comma-separated keywords that a user might search on to find the page

❑ **robots:** Indicates how search engines should index the page

The `description` and `keywords` properties can be used by programs called crawlers, bots, or spiders, which most search engines use to help index Web sites. These programs go through documents adding information to the databases used by the search engines, following links as they come across them, indexing those pages, and so on—this is how search engines manage to index so many sites.

Sometimes search engines will display the description property when your site is returned in response to a user's search.

A description should be a maximum of 200 characters long, although some search engines, such as Google, display only the first 100 characters.

The `keywords` property supplies a list of keywords that a search engine can use to index the site. If someone types in one of the words or a combination of the words you use as your keywords then a search engine has a better chance of returning your site.

Some people think that the keywords property is useless in determining rank in a search engine. As you will see later in the chapter, search engines have become a lot more sophisticated in the way they index sites, but my personal opinion is to use every technique available—that the combination of approaches is likely to result in the best possible ranking.

An online computer bookstore might use keywords like this:

```
<meta name="keywords" content="computer, programming, books, web, asp,
asp.net, vb, visual basic, c++, Java, Linux, XML, professional, developer,
html, html, css, xslt, access, sql, php, mysql" />
```

You could also use the `lang` attribute to indicate the language and offer keywords in different languages; for example, for U.S. English:

```
<meta name="keywords" content="computer, programming, books" lang = "en-us" />
```

In French:

```
<meta name="keywords" content="livres, ordinatteur, programmation"
lang = "fr" />
```

In German:

```
<meta name="keywords" content="" lang="programmierenbucher, computers" />
```

The more words you supply the better the chance your page will show up; however you should not use words that do not directly relate to the content of the site.

Most search engines create their own limit for the number of keywords they will index, and this number varies between search engines, but you should generally keep your keywords down to less than 1,000 characters.

You can also get a higher search page ranking if the keywords you supply also appear in the body of the document.

Using name with a Value of robots

As I mentioned earlier, many search engines use little programs to index Web pages on their behalf. You can use the name attribute with a value of robots to prevent one of these programs from indexing a page or links from the page (because many of these programs follow the links they find on your site and index those, too). For example, you probably would not want a search engine to index any administration pages for the site—because you do not want people to just happen across them.

Here you can see that the <meta> element tells search engines not to index this page or to follow any of the links on it to index those.

```
<meta name="robots" content="noindex, nofollow" />
```

The content attribute can have the values shown in the table that follows.

Value	Meaning
all	Index all pages.
none	Index no pages.
index	Index this page.
noindex	Do not index this page.
follow	Follow links from this page.
nofollow	Do not follow links from this page.

By default the values would be all, index, and follow, allowing Web crawlers to follow any link and index all pages.

You should use this technique in conjunction with a file called robots.txt, which is discussed in the "robots.txt" section later in this chapter if you want to prevent pages from being indexed.

http-equiv and content

The http-equiv and content attributes are paired together to set HTTP header values. Every time a Web browser requests a page, HTTP headers are sent with the request and each time the server responds sending a page back to the client it adds HTTP headers back to the client:

❑ The headers sent with a request for a page when made by a browser contain information such as the formats the browser will accept, the type of browser, the date, and other information about the user's configuration.

❑ The headers returned from a server with a Web page contain information such as the server type, the date and time the page was sent, and the date and time the page was last modified.

Of course, the headers *can* contain much more information, and using the `<meta>` tags is one way of adding new headers to be sent with the document. For example, you might want to refresh a page after a period of time, or add a header to indicate when the page should expire (no longer be valid)—which is especially helpful if the document contains things such as prices.

Expiring Pages

It can be important to expire pages because browsers have something known as a *cache*, a space on the hard drive where they store pages of Web sites you have visited. If you go back to a site you have already visited again, the browser can load some or all of the page from the cache rather than having to retrieve the whole page again.

Here you can see a `<meta>` tag that will cause the page to expire on Friday April 16, 2004 at 11:59 (and 59 seconds) p.m. Note that the date must follow the format shown.

```
<meta http-equiv="expires" content="Fri, 16 April 2004 23:59:59 GMT" />
```

If this were included in a document and the user tried to load the page after the expiry date, then the browser would not use the cached version; rather it would find a fresh copy from the server. This helps ensure that users get the latest copies of documents and thereby prevents people from using out-of-date information.

Preventing a Browser from Caching a Page

You can prevent some browsers from caching a page altogether using the value `pragma` for the `http-equiv` attribute and a value of `no-cache` for the `content` attribute like so:

```
<meta http-equiv="pragma" content="no-cache" />
```

Unfortunately, IE 4 and later versions ignore this rule and cache the page anyway.

Refreshing Pages

You can set a page to refresh after a certain number of seconds using the following `<meta>` tag, which gives the `http-equiv` attribute a value of `refresh`:

```
<meta http-equiv="refresh" content="10;URL=http://www.wrox.com/latest.asp" />
```

This will cause the page to refresh itself after 10 seconds. You can see the number of seconds given as the first part of the value for the `content` attribute. This is followed by a semicolon, the keyword `URL`, an equal sign, and the address of the page to be refreshed.

You can even refresh to a different page. For example, if your site moves from one domain to another, you can leave a page up for visitors who go to the old domain saying that you have moved and that the user will be redirected automatically in five seconds.

You should avoid refreshing a page too often as it will distract users, especially if they are trying to read a document. You should also be aware that regularly refreshing a document also places extra load on your Web server.

Refreshing and Redirecting Pages

You might have figured out that, because you can refresh pages to load up a different URL, you can use the same technique to redirect a user to a different page altogether. For example, look at the following `<meta>` tag:

```
<meta http-equiv="refresh" content="0;URL=http://www.myNewSite.com" />
```

This tells the browser to immediately ask for a new URL because the wait is 0 seconds.

Specifying Ratings

You can specify ratings regarding the content of your page. Without a rating it would be possible for some browsers (or programs designed to control what can be viewed) to prevent access to your site. As with all of the `<meta>` tags, the user will not see the rating, but the browser can process it. If you do provide a rating, the browser is more likely to show it to those who have agreed to view that sort of content.

Initially Internet ratings were introduced to help parents and schools block certain content from children, although the main technology in this area, PICS (the Platform for Internet Content Selection), has developed to allow lots of other uses.

In order to specify a rating value for a page, the value of the `http-equiv` attribute needs to be `pics-label`. The part that actually indicates what the content is known as a *rating label*, and the label must be created according to the Internet Content Ratings Association (ICRA).

The rating label is made up of four parts:

- ❑ An ICRA identifier
- ❑ The ICRA label
- ❑ The RSACi identifier (the old name for the ICRA)
- ❑ The RSACi ratings

As you will see the label can look quite complicated, but a form on the ICRA Web site `http://www.icra.org/` helps you create a label for your site. The RSACi rating is also generated on the same site as part of the process.

Once you have your label, the `<meta>` tag should look something like this one, which was created for the `http://www.wrox.com/` site:

```
<meta http-equiv="pics-label" content='(pics-1.1 "http://www.icra.org/
ratingsv02.html"
comment "ICRAonline EN v2.0" l gen true for
"http://www.wrox.com/" r (nz 1 vz 1 lz 1 oz 1 cz 1)
"http://www.rsac.org/ratingsv01.html" l gen true for "http://www.wrox.com/"
r (n 0 s 0 v 0 l 0))' />
```

While this might look complicated, the form on the ICRA site makes generation of a rating simple, and it shouldn't take longer than a couple of minutes.

Setting Cookies

Cookies are small text files that the browser can store on your computer. You can create them in a scripting language that runs in the browser such as JavaScript or using technologies on the server such as ASP, PHP, or JSP.

You are not likely to use cookies until you start working in depth with JavaScript or a server-side language, but they are mentioned here for future reference.

You can use the `<meta>` element to set cookies by giving the `http-equiv` attribute a value of `set-cookie` and then using the `content` attribute to specify a cookie name, value, and expiry date, like so:

```
<meta http-equiv="Set-Cookie" content="cookie_name=myCookie; expires=Fri
16 April 2004 23:59:59 GMT" />
```

If you do not provide an expiry date then the cookie will expire when the user shuts his or her browser window.

Specifying the Author Name

You can set the name of the author of the document using a value of `author` for the `http-equiv` attribute and then using the author's name as the value of the content attribute, like so:

```
<meta http-equiv="author" content="Jon Duckett" />
```

Setting the Character Encoding

Character encodings indicate the character encoding that was used to store the characters within a file. You can specify the encoding used in a document with a `<meta>` tag whose `http-equiv` attribute has a value of `Content-Type`. The value of the `content` attribute should then be the character encoding used to save the document; for example:

```
<meta http-equiv="Content-Type" content="ISO-8859-1" />
```

Here you can see that the document was written using the ISO-8859-1 encoding. You will see more about character encodings in Appendix E.

Setting a Default Style Sheet Language

You can specify the type of style sheet language you will be using in a document by setting the `http-equiv` attribute to have a value of `content-style-type`, and specifying the MIME type of style sheet language in the `content` attribute.

```
<meta http-equiv="content-style-type" content="text/css" />
```

When style sheet rules are inside a `<style>` element, the `type` attribute indicates the style sheet language used inside that element; but when you have inline style sheet rules using the style attribute on an element, there is no explicit indication of the language used. Therefore, setting the default to CSS removes any doubt. While CSS is the most popular language for styling HTML and XHTML documents, some applications support other languages such as XSLT and DSSSL.

Setting a Default Scripting Language

If you are going to use scripts throughout your page you can use the `<meta>` element to indicate the language your scripts are in. While you should still be using the `type` attribute on any `<script>` element, you can often use scripts in event handlers, and setting this `<meta>` tag indicates the language used in those attributes.

```
<meta http-equiv="content-script-type" content="text.JavaScript" />
```

scheme

The `scheme` attribute can be used to specify a scheme or format for a property value. For example, if you are working with dates, you can write them in several ways. In the U.S., the date format is written mm-dd-yyyy while in Europe it is written dd-mm-yyyy. So, you might use the `scheme` attribute to indicate a date format. In the U.S. you could use the following:

```
<meta scheme="usa" name="date" content="04-16-1975" />
```

In Europe you might use the following:

```
<meta scheme="Europe" name="date" content="16-04-75" />
```

The use of the `scheme` attribute does assume that the processing application understands the value of the `scheme` attribute and `name` attribute—and given that the mainstream browsers would not understand this, it would fall upon either a script or a customer application to interpret the use of this element.

Testing Your Site

Before you set your site loose for everyone to look at, you should perform some tests. Even if your site seems to work fine on your computer, it is not so easy to ensure that it will work as well on other people's computers. After all, different people have different makes and versions of browsers, different Internet connections, and different screen sizes and resolution, and what worked on your computer might not work when you take the site out onto the Web.

So, the two stages of testing are:

❑ **Pre-publishing tests:** These are performed on your computer before asking anyone else to look at the site.

❑ **Pre-release tests:** Performed on the site exactly as it will be published on the Web (on a Web server).

In this section you will learn about several tests that can help make sure your site is available to as many people as possible.

The Importance of Directory Structure and Relative URLs

In this section you will learn a valuable point about the importance of a good directory structure and the use of relative URLs. Say you have already built a site and you want to create a new version of it. You might want to test the new site on the Web server, but it will have to be in a separate folder, and therefore it will have a different URL than your current site if that is to remain live. For example, you might test the new site in a folder called `newsite` so the home page might have the following URL:

```
http://www.example.com/newsite/index.html
```

But when you are ready to make the switch to the new site you are going to want it to appear here:

```
http://www.example.com/index.html
```

If you are using relative URLs to link to all of your other pages, images, script files and so on, then moving a site to a new folder or even a new URL will not be a problem. However, if you hard code your links using items such as your logo onto your front page using an `<img>` tag like this:

```
<img src="http://www.example.com/newsite/images/our_logo.gif" alt="Our Logo" />
```

this image would not be loaded when you move the site to a new domain or a different folder. It is better to use something like this:

```
<img src="images/our_logo.gif" alt="our_logo" />
```

Now, as long as the `images` folder is within the folder for this page, the image will be loaded, no matter where the site is put.

Validating HTML, XHTML, and CSS

One of your best guards for making your site work on the majority of browsers is to validate your code and make sure that you have stuck to the rules of the language. A *validator* will check things such as whether you have closed all tags correctly, that the attributes you have used are actually allowed on that element, and so on. All it takes is for you to miss something as simple as one closing `</td>` tag and, while the page may look fine on your browser, it will not necessarily work on someone else's computer.

> *It is helpful to validate a design after you have built the first page, as it is quite tempting to copy and paste parts of your code from one file to the other and use your first page as a template. If you have an error in the page you use as a template and you use it to create all the other sites before you test it, you might have to rewrite every page.*

As you might remember from Chapter 1, each version of HTML and XHTML has at least one document containing the rules for that version of the language, known as a DTD or schema. Any Web page can be validated against this document to make sure it follows the rules. Therefore, by validating your pages you will know if you have left out a tag or other important part of the markup. The DOCTYPE declaration at the start of your page will tell a validation tool which DTD or schema your page should match the rules of.

Many authoring tools, such as Dreamweaver, contain tools that allow you to validate your site. But if you are not using such a tool, or if you want to check your site with more than one validation tool, you can use the W3Cs free Web page validator at http://validator.w3.org/.

You can see the W3Cs markup validator in Figure 16-1; it allows you to enter a URL for a site or upload a page from your computer.

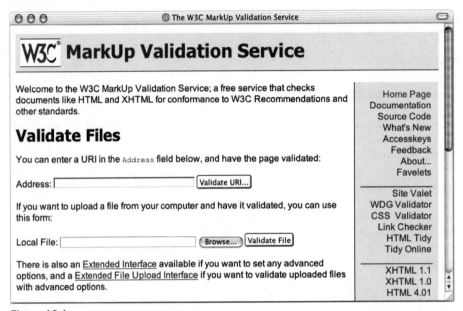

Figure 16-1

It will then tell you if errors are in your document. In Figure 16-2 you can see errors for a page.

While the W3C validation tool is very helpful—and free—having to validate each page individually can be a bit of a nuisance. Deamweaver MX (which certainly appears to be by far the most popular Web authoring tool among Web professionals) introduced excellent validation features for XHTML pages (far better than validation offered by earlier versions of Dreamweaver). Validating a page is as simple as saving it and then pressing Shift+F6; you should see errors appear in the results panel, as in Figure 16-3.

Note that for this to work properly you must have the correct settings in Dreamweaver. To get the settings you can right-click in the results panel and choose the setting dialog box (or Option+click on a Mac). You will then see a whole range of document standards appear in the new Preferences dialog box. You want to make sure that each option is unchecked except the version you want to check against. So, if you are trying to validate Transitional XHTML 1.0 you must have only that box checked, as shown in Figure 16-4.

Now revalidate the page.

Link Checking

It is important to check your links both before your site goes live and after you have published it on the Web. There are some tools that will help you check links. If you search for link checking tools you will

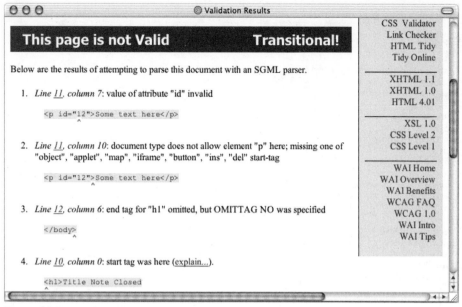

Figure 16-2

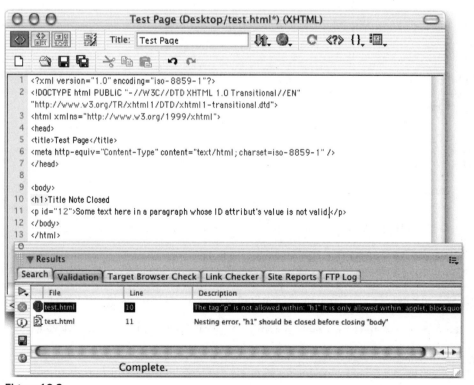

Figure 16-3

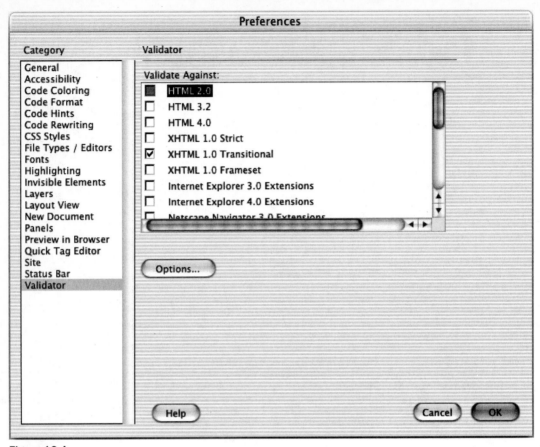

Figure 16-4

find several sites that charge for the service. However, there are some free link-checking services such as:

❏ The W3C's validation at `http://validator.w3.org/checklink/`

❏ HTMLHELP's Link Valet at `http://www.htmlhelp.com/tools/valet/`

You can also use the Link Valet tool to check whether any site you link to has been changed since a specified date. This can be very helpful because an external site might restructure its pages, and the old URL will no longer be valid, or it might start publishing content you no longer wish to link to.

In Figure 16-5 you can see the results of a single page validated with the W3Cs link validator.

The way in which these services output their results might appear quite verbose, but you should be able to tell which links are bad by looking for some kind of highlighting—which tends to be in red for broken or questionable links.

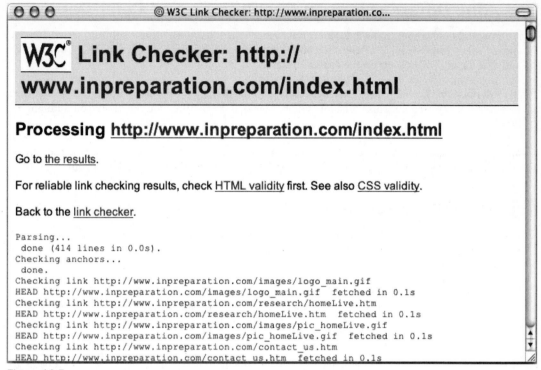

Figure 16-5

Macromedia's Dreamweaver also contains its own link-checking tool. You can access this from the results menu or by pressing Control+Shift+F9.

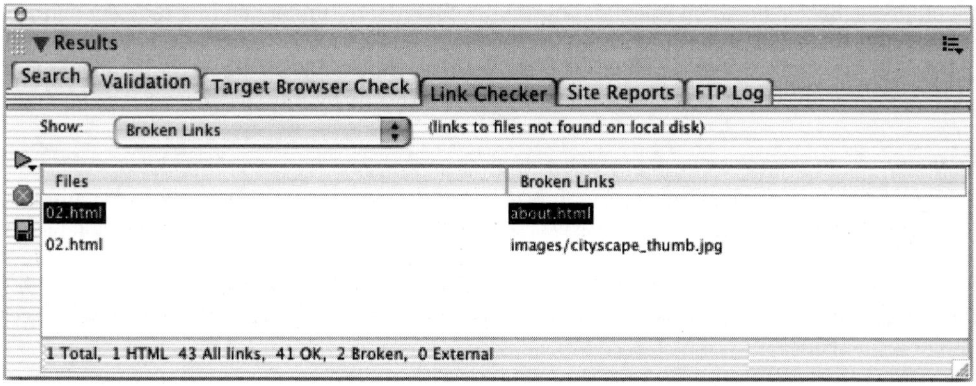

Figure 16-6

There are options to check a page, a folder, or a whole site.

Once Dreamweaver has found your broken links you can fix them in either the Results window or the Properties window.

603

Checking Different Screen Resolutions and Color Depths

As you might remember from Chapter 10, not everyone will have the same resolution screen as you; you should check your site with different screen resolutions to make sure that all of the text is still readable and that the information fits on the page adequately.

In most operating systems there are ways (usually in the display properties dialog boxes) to change the resolution of your screen. This will allow you to see what the picture would look like on different monitors.

You can also change the colors from millions of colors to 256 colors and make sure that the text can be read (even if the images don't look as good as you hoped). This is a good way to check that your text is readable.

Accessibility Checkers

It is becoming ever more important to create accessible Web sites; often people think of this as making your site available to visitors with visual or physical disabilities, although it really simply means making the site accessible to as many people as possible.

You have learned about lots of accessibility issues throughout the book, such as providing alternative text for all images, providing a link for users to skip navigation that is repeated, and more. You have learned that it's important to make sure that the colors you choose have enough contrast to be able to read any text, that tables should linearize well, and that you should not use color alone to convey information.

A lot of tools are available to help you check some of the main points of accessibility, but probably the most popular two are:

❑ Bobby from CAST (The Center for Applied Special Technology) at `http://www.cast.org`

❑ LIFT from UsableNet at `http://www.usablenet.com`

All of these tools are based on rules, and none is a substitute for understanding the issues surrounding accessibility. While a tool can check whether you have used `alt` attributes on each image, it cannot check that the alternative text used will make sense to someone who cannot see the image within the context of the page. A very good reference is *Constructing Accessible Web Sites* by Jim Thatcher, et al. (Glasshauss, 2002).

Bobby

Bobby was the first accessibility checker. It was released in September 1996 and was free until late 2001. Then a version called Bobby Worldwide was released, and now it costs US$99 for a single user license.

There is, however, a Web-based trial version of Bobby that you can use free of charge, although you can check only one page at a time. It applies the U.S. Section 508 Accessibility rules or the Web Accessibility Initiative guidelines (priorities 1, 2, and 3).

When you submit a page, the Web site generates a report. The report will start by telling you the page you checked and whether it passed. If no problems are discovered it will display the image to indicate the page has passed the text.

If there are errors, you are shown a version of your page with icons displayed where it finds potential problems. These icons are links to descriptions of the errors at the bottom of the page. A helmet indicates that a specific issue has been identified, while a question mark indicates a point where a problem may occur. Icons are shown for all of the W3C's WCAG (Web Content Accessibility Guidelines) priority 1 issues (not 2 or 3, otherwise the screen may be too busy) and all issues in the U.S. Web-based accessibility standards, taken from Section 508.

The full licensed version of Bobby is more customizable, can run on local files (rather than ones on Web sites), and can be tailored more than the free Web version, but you get a good idea of what the software will do for you if you try out the free version.

LIFT

A free Web-based trial version is on the home page, but it uses only a subset of the rules available in a paid version and tests only five pages at a time. LIFT was first released in April 2000 as a testing tool for usability, but later developed to cover accessibility guidelines.

LIFT is available in several different versions including:

❑ **LIFT for Macromedia Dreamweaver:** Aimed at users developing sites in Dreamweaver for Mac and Windows

❑ **LIFT Online tool:** An online tool allowing unlimited URLs to be checked.

❑ **LIFT Machine:** An enterprise server-side application allowing an organization to test and monitor its Web site

To use the trial version you enter a URL and an e-mail address where a link to the analysis report for your site can be sent.

The report you get back (using the online trial) looks like Figure 16-7.

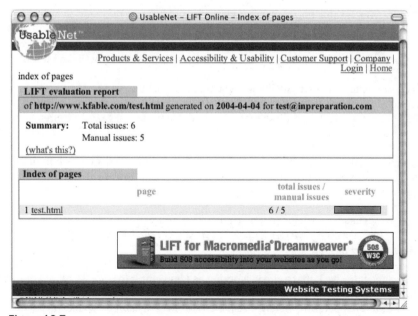

Figure 16-7

You can then look at each page in detail and see the issues it has detected along with links to documentation about them.

Development Server or Live Server

Once you have performed the checks mentioned so far, you will be ready to move it somewhere where other people can test your site. You will be looking at Web hosting shortly, but you probably want to put your site in a place where the public will not start looking at it until you have performed the second phase of tests. If you have a version of your site already live and you are working on an update then you will need to have a different place for the new site to be tested—this could be as simple as a different folder on your computer or it could be a separate server altogether.

If you are making changes to an existing site, you should always work on a separate copy of the site rather than the version the public will be looking at. It is also good practice to have a backup copy of each version of the site.

Once you have finished the following tests you can then make the site live, ready for the public.

Checking in Different Versions of Browsers

Even if you write your pages to the letter as far as the recommendations go and your pages validate perfectly, different versions of browsers on different operating systems behave differently. The page that looked perfect on your monitor just doesn't look the same on a friend's or colleague's monitor. So, you should always try to test your Web page on as many different browsers and platforms as possible. You should at the very least have the latest versions of Internet Explorer and Netscape on your computer.

Unfortunately, you are able to install only one version of Internet Explorer on a single computer (unless you have a partition running a second version of Windows or run a Windows emulator) and you are likely to want the latest version for day to day use. So, if you have an old PC lying around, you can keep older versions of browsers on that and use it to test your pages once you have built them.

Even if you can install an older version of IE on a spare machine, you have to find a version first because Microsoft does not distribute versions of IE other than the most recent version; one of the best places to check is on older cover CDs and disks that came with computer magazines from a few years back to find older versions of browsers.

You are in much better luck when it comes to Netscape because you can install multiple versions on a single machine and you can find older versions at `http://wp.netscape.com/download/archive.html`.

Some Web sites and services offer to take screenshots of each page of your Web site on many different versions of several makes of browser for you, so that you can check how the pages appear on different browsers; however this can be quite expensive.

Another great way to check that a site is working as you want it to is to ask all of your friends to check it before it goes live. The hope is that among them you will find at least one or two users who have older browsers or different operating systems. Ask them to check what it looks like and send you a screenshot of a couple of pages in their browser. If you want to you can even offer a small prize in return. A colleague of mine recently asked all of a client's staff to ask their friends to test the new Web site, and one lucky person who responded to the related questionnaire won an iPod.

Pilot Testing

If you are able to, get people that have not been involved in the project to test your site before it is released to the public. This is important because what might seem perfectly obvious to you is not always so clear to someone who is coming to the site for the first time. By the time you have built the site you will be so close to the designs and workings that it will be very difficult to look at it with the same objectivity as someone who has never seen it.

Ideally the people performing this kind of test on your site would be your target audience.

The first thing you can do is ask your participant to sit down in front of the site and then just watch what they do. You must resist all temptation to intervene at any point, whether you want to ask what someone is trying to do or if you want to tell them how to get to something you think they are trying to find. As soon as you start talking to them, you will affect what is their normal behavior—and you will not learn as much.

Watching where people go first, how long they spend on each page, and how they navigate can teach you a lot about your site.

You can also sit people in front of the site and give them a set of imaginary scenarios; for example, you might have a site that sells bikes and you could ask the user to:

❑   Find a bike they think would be suitable for their son or daughter

❑   Work out how much a certain model of bike is

❑   Find out how to visit the store and when they are open

❑   Check whether a helmet meets a certain safety standard

Any more than five tasks and the user will be getting used to the layout and operation of the site. Some people prefer to watch silently while participants perform these tasks. Others prefer to ask participants to talk their way through what they are doing. In this second scenario (sometimes known as talking aloud protocol) you need to make sure that users talk their way through every thought process that goes through their head. You often get broken sentences, but it can help to give the idea of what you expect of them by performing the task first yourself on a different site. Here is an example of a transcript you might end up with:

1.   "I'm supposed to look for a bike for Julia."

2.   "Looking at menu . . . home, store . . ."

3.   "Clicking on store . . ."

4.   "List of brands appears on the left, not heard of many of these."

5.   "Pictures on right saying men's bikes, women's bikes, boys' bikes, girls' bikes . . ."

6.   "Click on picture for girls' bikes . . ."

7. "Shows ages, so click on 'first bikes' . . ."

8. "Looking at pictures . . ."

9. "This one looks good; click on that picture . . ."

10. "Doesn't do anything . . . thought it would show more information about it . . ."

11. "Click on 'Raleigh Butterfly'."

12. "There, that one looks fine."

You are best off recording the voice if you can, as long as it doesn't put the user off too much. Again you must resist the temptation to interrupt if the user is doing something that is not what you think they should be doing in order to achieve the task—after all, in this example you learned that the user thought they would be able to click on the image of the bike to see more details, but they couldn't.

Proofreading

If you are working on a commercial site it can often help to hire a proofreader to check all of your text. Silly typos can affect people's impression of your site and make both you and the client you are developing the site for look less professional.

If a client you are working on a site for finds errors throughout the site they will think that you have not been paying close attention to what you are doing—even if they supplied the error-ridden copy for the site.

Proofreaders need not be expensive, and as far as your reputation goes, they can certainly be worth their fee (in saving you face—and helping you win continuing contracts).

Taking the Leap to Live

Now your site should be ready for the public to view it. So it is time to look at how you get your site on the Web. In order to do this you will need to get a domain name, some hosting space, and transfer the site to the new server using an FTP program. You will learn about each of these in the following section. In particular you will be learning what to look for when deciding with whom to host your site.

Getting a Domain Name

If you are creating a personal site you do not necessarily need your own domain name, but it is always a good idea if you are creating a site for a business. The *domain name* is the part of the name you commonly see after the www in a site address; for example Wrox Press uses the domain name wrox.com whereas Amazon use the domain name amazon.com in the U.S., amazon.co.uk in the U.K., amazon.de in Germany, and so on (although, as you might have noticed, some sites do not use the www in their name).

You can register your domain name with a domain registration company, of which there are hundreds; just search on your favorite search engine and you will find plenty. Most companies go for the suffix .com, but several other suffixes are available. For example, there are country-specific domain suffixes (also known as *top-level domains*) such as .co.uk for the UK, .de for Germany, .com.au for Australia, and .ru for Russia. You should choose a country-specific domain only if you are based in that country. Indeed, some domain names (such as .com.au domains) can be bought only by people with registered companies or companies with products by that name being sold in that country. Then there are also suffixes such as .me.uk, which is for personal sites; .info, which is for information-based sites; and .org, which is for registered organizations.

> *You do not need all available suffixes for your domain name, although you should make sure that your site is not very similar in name to someone you would not want to be associated with, just in case the user mistypes. For example, you would not want a children's site to have a very similar URL to an adult content site.*

Before you register your name you need to see if it is available; all domain name registration companies should have a form that allows you to search to see if your domain name is available. You might find this a frustrating process, as an incredibly high proportion of .com domain names you might conceive have been taken already—as well as most popular words, many numbers have also been taken.

You can order a domain name without actually having a site ready; this is sometimes known as *domain parking*. You order the name as soon as you know you are going to create the site (after all you will probably want to use the URL in the site design, and will therefore need to order it before you start designing the site), but you do not put anything up there until you have built the site.

Several domain name registration companies also offer hosting, but there is no need to order your domain name from the same people that host your site with; you can get the domain name registration company to point the domain to your hosting company's servers (usually there is a simple control panel on the site you registered the name with where you control where your domain name actually points to).

Your domain name should be easy to remember, and should not be so long that users will find it hard to remember or too long to type in. For example, if you were called the Sydney Slate Roofing Services Limited, you might choose a domain such as www.SydneySlate.com rather than www.SydneySlate RoofingServicesLimited.com.

When you register the domain name you will also likely be able to use this for your e-mail addresses. For example, if you choose the domain www.example.com then no one else will be able to use the e-mail address bob@example.com without your permission (although it is possible for spammers to make e-mails *appear* as if they come from your domain, simply by changing the from address in their e-mail program).

Hosting

You already know that in order to view a Web page a browser requests a page from a Web server. The Web server is a special computer that is constantly connected to the Internet.

When you access a page using a domain name, such as http://wwww.example.com/, something called a name server changes the name into a number. The number (known as an IP address) uniquely identifies a machine on the Web and this machine holds your Web site.

So, when you are ready to put your site out on the Web you are going to need some space on a Web server. Hundreds of companies will allow you to put your Web site on their server and they will, of course, charge you for the service. The service is known as *Web hosting* because the company hosts your site for you.

Many ISPs will give you a small amount of Web space free when you choose them to access the Internet. There are also other sites that offer free hosting (these are often paid for by the use of pop-up advertisements that appear when your pages load). For a personal site you may need only a small amount of Web space and you might be prepared to put up with any pop-up ads that come with the free service. For commercial sites, however, it is better to choose some paid hosting—which can still be very cheap but will not serve advertisements.

Key Considerations for Choosing a Host

As I said, literally hundreds of companies offer Web hosting, and it can seem like a minefield deciding which to go with. Following is a discussion of the key points you need to understand and consider when choosing a site:

❑   **Backups:** You should check whether your host performs backups on your sites and, if so, how often. A backup is simply a copy of the site taken in case there is a problem with the computer it is on. While the types of sites you are creating when you start working on Web sites probably will not require regular backups, it is good to know whether the hosting company keeps a copy of the site in case something should go wrong with their servers. When you start developing sites that change frequently and can be updated by several people you will need to look at the issue of backups more closely.

❑   **Bandwidth:** This is the amount of data you are allowed to send from your site. It can be given as a rate per day, month, or year. If the average size of one of your Web pages is 75KB including images, then if you get 100 visitors to your site per month and each visitor looks at 10 pages, you will need at least 75000kb (or 75MB) of bandwidth per month. In reality, you will find that hosts often allow a lot more than this, but it helps you get an idea of how to calculate bandwidth.

> *The tricky part of judging how much bandwidth you will need is judging how successful your site will be. You can never predict how popular your site will be, and if it is mentioned in a popular newspaper or magazine it can suddenly get a lot more traffic. One way around the problem of how much bandwidth you need is simply to choose a hosting service that will just charge you extra if you exceed the bandwidth you are allowed on your account. You should check regularly whether you have exceeded your level because you do not want to end up with a large surprise bill at the end of the month, and ensure you have enough money to pay for it if you go over the limit, or you may get cut off.*

❑   **Country:** You might like to consider which country your site is hosted in. It is best to host the site in the same country that you expect the majority of your customers to be in because the data has less distance to travel, which should therefore make your site appear to those users more quickly. If you are setting up a site for an Australian market, for example, it can be more quickly loaded by users there than if you hosted it in Europe. In practice, however, you are rarely likely to see much of a performance difference.

❑   **Data centers:** You will see a lot of companies say that they have multimillion dollar data centers. This is because most hosting companies hire space in a large data center and they put their services in these facilities.

❑   **Disk space:** You will usually see a figure given in MB (megabytes) of the amount of space you get on the computer that serves your site. The disk space governs how large your site can be and needs to be larger than the total of all of the XHTML, CSS, script files, and images that make up your site. You can check how large your Web site is by simply looking at the size of the folder that it is in (as long as you do not have any other files in that folder).

❏ **E-mail accounts:** Hosting companies generally provide e-mail services with Web hosting. You need to consider two factors here: the size of mailbox you are allowed, and the number of mailboxes you are given. Some hosts give you unlimited mailboxes but set a maximum amount of storage space across all of them, so if you have 5 mailboxes and only 10 megabytes of space to share between them, each account can hold only 2MB at capacity. Some hosting companies allow you only a few mailboxes, but will allow a fixed amount for each mailbox (say 10MB each). Finally, some hosting companies allow you to take up the amount of space you have allocated for your domain with mail, so the only limit is your storage limit.

❏ **Shared versus dedicated hosting:** The cheaper Web hosting is nearly always provided on what is known as a *shared host*. This means that your Web site is on the same physical computer as many other sites. Because the smaller sites do not have as many visitors, the computer can easily cope with hosting several sites. However, larger sites that have many thousands of visitors a month or that serve large files (such as music downloads or a lot of heavy graphics) require extra bandwidth and take up more resources on that server. This is when your site starts to exceed the bandwidth limit set and your charges start increasing. Therefore, if your site becomes extremely popular you might find it cheaper to get your own server (or indeed your host might insist you get your own server), which is known as a *dedicated server* because it is dedicated to your use.

Some of the very popular sites on the Web are actually hosted across several servers—the site may be so busy that one computer alone cannot handle the traffic, or one machine may require maintenance so there are others to take the strain. Banks, large online stores, and multinational corporations are examples of sites that would use this kind of setup—known as a *load-balanced server*.

> *Don't be put off by this talk about dedicated or load-balanced servers. Generally, if your site is that popular that you require your own dedicated server, you should be making enough money from it to warrant the extra cost.*

❏ **Statistics packages:** Every time a user requests a file from your site the Web server can log certain details about the user—for example, their IP address, browser version, language of the operating system, and so on. This information comes in the HTTP headers from the browser. Statistics packages can look at the log files that contain this information and interpret some very useful information from them. For example, you can see how many pages you have served to visitors, what users typed into search engines to find you, and what the most common page people leave your site from is. All this information helps you understand what users are doing on your site and can help you improve the site and the number of visitors it receives. You will see more about statistics packages later in the chapter.

❏ **Uptime:** *Uptime* refers to the percentage of time your Web server is working and available for people to look at your site. You will generally see figures such as 99 percent uptime, which means that on average 99 out of every 100 minutes your site will be available. But then that also means that your site might be down for 1 percent of the time, which could be 87.6 hours per year, or *four days*. If your site is your main source of income, you should find an alternative with more uptime.

Unless you are a running a *very* large company, it is rarely worth the investment of running your own servers because you are likely to need someone capable of administering the machines and taking care of them on a regular basis. If you decide that you do need your own dedicated servers, several hosting companies will manage a server on your behalf, updating it with new patches for the operating system to fix security holes when needed. While this is still very expensive, you will generally find it cheaper than hiring someone yourself to manage your servers.

Putting Your Site on a Server Using FTP

Once you have paid for some space on a Web server, you need to be able to get the files that make up your Web site onto this computer—which can be on the other side of the world. The most efficient way to do this is using *FTP*.

FTP stands for File Transfer Protocol. The Internet uses a number of different protocols for sending different types of information. For example, HTTP (Hypertext Transfer Protocol) is used for transmitting hypertext files, which are better known as Web pages. FTP is a protocol used to transfer binary files across the Internet and is much quicker at sending whole Web sites to a server than HTTP.

Most hosting providers actually require that you use FTP to transfer your pages onto their servers, which means that you need an FTP program (sometimes referred to as an FTP client) to put your files on a server.

Most FTP programs have two windows, each with a file explorer. One represents the files and folders on your computer; the other represents the folders on the Web server. In Figure 16-8 you can see the folders on my computer, and on the right you can see those on a Web server.

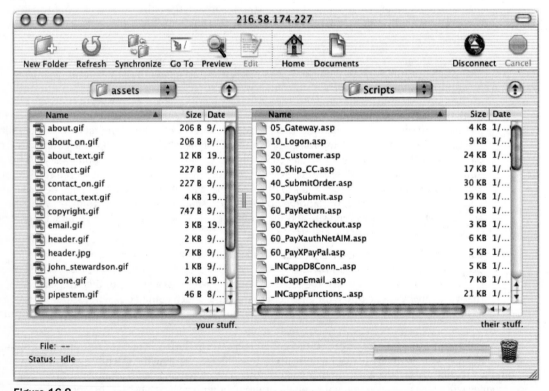

Figure 16-8

The table that follows shows some of the most popular FTP programs.

Product Name	URL	OS
Cute FTP	`http://www.cuteftp.com/`	Windows and Mac OS X
FTPX	`http://www.ftpx.com/`	Windows
BulletProofFTP	`http://www.bpftp.com/`	Windows
Fetch	`http://www.fetchsoftworks.com/`	Mac
Transmit	`http://www.panic.com/transmit/`	Mac

Each of the programs is slightly different, but they all follow similar principles.

When you register with a host they will send you details of how to FTP your site to their servers. This will include:

❑   An FTP address (such as `ftp.example.com`)

❑   An FTP username (usually the same as your username for the domain)

❑   An FTP password (usually the same as your password for the domain)

Figure 16-9 shows you how these are entered into the FTP program called Transmit on a Mac.

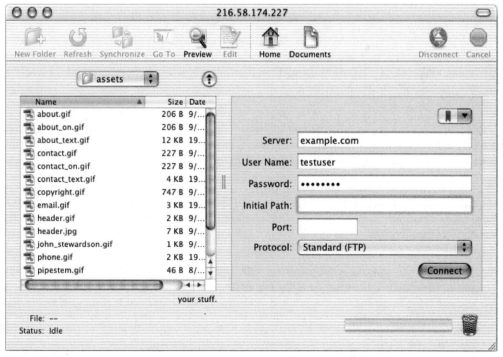

Figure 16-9

While you can download trial versions of several of these programs before you buy them to find out which one you are most comfortable using, most of these programs have graphical user interfaces that are very similar.

Search Engine Strategies

Now that you have your site on the server you want people to come and visit it. One of the best ways to get visitors to your site is by making sure that users can find your site in a search engine when they enter words that are relevant to the content of your site. Preferably they find you in the top ten values returned.

Beyond <meta> Tags

You have already seen how search engines can use the <meta> tag's description and keywords properties to help search a site, but search engines are becoming much more complex in the way in which they address the task of indexing all of the sites on the Web. You, too, therefore need to continue to work on your search engine strategies a lot more than just adding in <meta> tags.

> Staying on top of your search engine rankings is an ongoing exercise and should form part of your standard marketing practice. It is good to review your search engine ranking at least once a quarter—or once a month if possible.

You should never just rely upon the search engine sites to find your site and index it. For example, sites such as Yahoo, Lycos, and dmoz, are Internet directory sites based upon categories, and you have to navigate through the categories to find the site you want. This manual categorization of sites requires that you submit the URL of your site to them; it can then take anywhere between a couple of weeks and a few months for your site to appear on theirs.

Some sites even charge for the privilege of being listed on their site. You should carefully consider whether it is worth the money paying for this service. While it may be worthwhile on larger sites such as Yahoo or MSN, many other companies will try to take money off you without providing as many referrals as the larger sites. This is discussed more in the next section.

Once you have manually notified a search engine you should wait for at least a month before submitting the URL again. If you over-list a site it is considered spamming, and you might not get listed at all. If you have made significant changes to your site, it is always worth re-submitting it (not too frequently) so that the changes get identified.

Personally, I ignore programs that promise to submit my site to thousands of Internet directories and would rather do the work myself. Spending just an hour a day for a couple of weeks, first submitting the site with major search engines manually and then looking for other relevant Web sites and asking them to list the new site I have been working on. I do this because some of the programs used generate so many submissions to Web search engines that they are considered spam (and as a result are ignored). Remember that if the offer of results sounds too good (guaranteeing you top ten placements on thousands of search engines), the offer may well be too good to be true!

Designing Your Page to Maximize Rankings

Search engines that use programs to automatically index sites are using increasingly sophisticated rules of how they determine who gets the highest raking (top) results in a Web page. Following are some points to consider when designing your pages to help ensure that your site gets the highest ranking it can:

❑ The titles of your pages are the most important words in your site and are one of the most important things indexed. So, avoid using titles that just contain words such as "Home Page" and instead go for descriptive titles such as "Wrox Press—Computer Programming Book Publishers." Then, on specific pages the title could change to something like "XHTML Programming Books." If the words the user types into the search engine are found in your title, the engine will consider your site more relevant. But don't make the title longer than one sentence or the program will realize you are trying to fool it and count this against you.

❑ Most sites search the text content of a page and will index that, too. The first words tend to be considered the most relevant. So you should try to strategically place the keywords for your site in the text near the start of the page as well as in the title. You can also expand on that list of keywords here.

❑ If the keywords a user searches on appear in the page with more frequency than other words, then they are considered to be more relevant. However, do not make them too high—if the frequency with which the word appears is too high, again the search engine will count this against you.

❑ If your site uses images instead of text, you will have only your `alt` text that the site can index, not real text words.

❑ If you try to add words to your pages using the same color writing as the background in order to fool the search engine into thinking that you have words written even though the user cannot see them, some search engines will count this against you.

❑ Using keywords that are not related to the subject matter or content of the site can count against you.

❑ The more sites that link to yours the better. Some search engines will give you higher priority if you are linked to by lots of other sites.

❑ Finally, the more users that click on links to your site when it comes up in the search engine, the better your rating should be. If things such as the title, keywords in the text, `<meta>` tags, and the number of links to you give you a great ranking but nobody clicks the links to visit your site, your ranking will fall.

It can take a long time to build up your search engine rankings, but constant attention will help you get better and better. In the "Other Web Marketing Possibilities" section a bit later in this chapter you will also see some other marketing tips that will help you build traffic on your site. But first I'll show you what to do if you do *not* want your pages indexed.

robots.txt

On some Web sites there will be pages that you do not want to be indexed—for example administration pages, banner advertisements, and scripts. To prevent pages from being indexed by a search engine you can include a simple text file on your site called `robots.txt` (which you write in a simple text editor such as Notepad on Windows or SimpleText or TextEdit on a Mac).

The `robots.txt` file can contain simple commands that prevent parts of the site being indexed by the Web crawlers (the little programs that index sites), which are often programmed to read these files.

You should have only one `robots.txt` file for your site, and it should be placed in a folder called `htdocs` in the root folder of your Web server. Some Web hosting companies create the `htdocs` folder for you, other hosts require you do this yourself if you need one.

The first line of this simple text file should be:

```
USER_AGENT:  web_crawler_name
```

Given that you are likely to want all crawlers to obey the rules you can simply use an asterisk instead of the names of any Web crawlers—a wildcard character indicating that all crawlers should obey the rules.

Next you can specify which folders you want to disallow the crawler from indexing (another reason why a well-organized site is important) by using the `DISALLOW` command next. This command may be repeated for each folder you do not want indexed:

```
USER-AGENT: *
DISALLOW: /admin/
DISALLOW: /scripts/
```

This simply indicates that no crawler should attempt to index the `admin` or `scripts` folders (or any of their child folders).

While there is no requirement for the crawlers to obey the rules in this file, it is in their interest not to index pages people don't want displayed (usually because they will not allow the user to do something) so the main search engines will obey the rules.

Other Web Marketing Possibilities

Even with all the effort you put into getting a good search engine ranking, you can attract visitors to your site—and they do not all take advantage of the Web. Marketing your site both on and off the Internet are important tactics in getting a lot of visits to your site and maintain regular traffic.

Here are just some of the tactics you can use to attract visitors to your site:

❑ Search for other Web sites that are related to your industry. Some of these sites will have links to sites of interest and you can ask to be added to the page featuring those links.

❑ A lot of industries also have sites that act as directories for that industry and some of those charge you to advertise on their sites—whether you do this or not you will have to judge based on cost and the amount of traffic you think you will get in return.

❑ Many sites offer reciprocal links; that is, they will link to you in return for you linking to them—it is a way for everyone to boost traffic. But make sure that you are not putting someone on the front page of your site when they are going to put a link to you tucked away on a page that few people will come across—the term is *reciprocal linking* after all.

❑ Use a few search engines to search for related companies and find out who is linking to them—the sites that link to related sites may well link to you, too, if you ask. You may find sites that you had never heard of before but that are very relevant.

- ❑ You can provide buttons or banners on your site so that people can integrate them into their site. This is more likely to happen with community sites than with commercial sites, but hobbyists will often link to special interest sites and it is a lot easier for them to do this if you have already provided links for them. If the links look great, too, they are more likely to want to add them.

- ❑ Google has a system called AdWords, for which you specify keywords, and when a user searches using those words, the ads appear on the right side of the page. These ads can also appear on other special interest sites. The way AdWords works is very clever. You pay for an advertisement only when the user clicks it. The ranking of which ads appear first is based upon the amount you are prepared to pay each time someone clicks the ad *and* the number of people who actually click the AdWords link. If users do not click the ad, it slips down in position, no matter how much you pay (after all, Google stands to make more money if 10 people click a cheaper link than if one person clicks a slightly more expensive link, and more users are getting value from their service). Generally speaking this is a very cost effective way to generate traffic to your site.

- ❑ There are many other forms of paid advertising you can take out on the Web. Lots of sites take out banner advertising, and lots of sites allow you to pay to be listed. You will have to judge each of these on whether you think you will get enough traffic to justify the money. Remember that a lot of Web users are immune to advertising and just scan pages to find what they really want—so if you are going to create a banner, make it visually attractive to make it worth the money.

- ❑ If there are any newsgroups, bulletin boards, or forums for your particular industry, answer questions on them and add your Web site address as a signature beneath your name when you sign the posts. But be careful to do this only when you can be helpful to someone—do not start posting to newsgroups unless it is relevant; you are likely to annoy people rather than attract any visitors if you do so.

- ❑ If you have regularly changing content, consider adding a newsletter feature to your site so that people can sign up to receive regular updates. This is discussed more later in the chapter, but it is a great way to keep people up-to-date with your site and let them know about new content.

- ❑ Of course, you should not just use the Web to market your site; a good site should generate traffic by word of mouth. You can also use printed leaflets, place ads in related magazines, put your site address on your letterhead or the side of your car. You could even find a conference or event that relates to the area you cover and use that as a way to make people in your industry more aware of what you do.

Statistical Analysis

If your hosting provider has a statistics or analysis package on their servers, once your site is live you can find out lots of helpful information about your visitors. These packages analyze the log files of your Web server; log files contain information about files they send out and who they send them to.

The terms used in site analysis can be confusing. You may have heard people say that a site gets 10,000 hits, but this can be quite confusing. The term "hits" tends to refer to the number of files that have been downloaded from the site—and an image is a file as well as the XHTML pages, so a single Web page with eight images and a script file will receive ten hits (and some graphics intensive pages can have over thirty images) for each page that is served.

You may also come across the term "visits." You should be aware, however, that different statistics packages calculate visits in different ways. Some count everyone with the same IP address as the same visitor—so if there are ten people, all of whom use the same ISP, looking at the same site at once, then that might look like only one user instead of ten. Different packages also tend to count visits as different lengths of times; some packages only count an IP address once a day as a visit, while others will count the IP address as a new visit if it has just been inactive for 15 minutes.

I have found page views to be one of the most reliable figures to use, and it gives you an idea of how many pages of your site users have been to.

You should look deeper into these statistics packages, however, as many have much more useful information than just the number of visits. For example, it is quite common for these packages to tell you how people arrived at your site—what pages and sites people came from and how many came from each. This helps you learn how people are finding out about and coming to your site. This therefore helps you determine good places to market your site.

Statistics packages also frequently tell you what terms people were searching on in order to find you site—so you can tell what keywords have been entered into search engines for users to find you, and then work on enhancing the frequency of these words in pages and enhancing your search engine position. Figure 16-10 shows you some of the terms used to find a site about printing equipment and services.

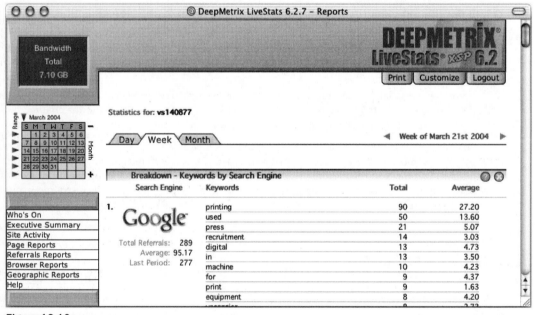

Figure 16-10

Some other information you might be able to find out includes:

- ❑ Which page users arrived at and which they left from. This is very helpful because you can get an idea what people are coming to the site for and where they leave. If there is one page that makes a lot of people leave you can do something about improving the design of that page.

- ❑ Where users are from.

- ❑ What browser they were using.

- ❑ The language their operating system is set to, and therefore which language they are likely to speak.

- ❑ How long they spent on the site.

Be aware that all of these figures are approximate and there can be anomalies between figures given by different reporting packages, but they are nevertheless very helpful tools in analyzing how people found out about you and what people are doing on your site.

If your host does not implement site analysis you can also find services on the Web that will do the job for you (such as `http://www.theCounter.com` or `http://www.WebTrends.com`). These sites use small scripts or images, which reside on their server, that you have to insert in your page. So each time a page on your site loads, the user has to request a page from the statistics company's server as well, giving them most of the same information you have. Some of the more expensive services are far more powerful than the packages used with hosting companies and are worth looking into if your site is doing well.

Version Control

In time, you are likely to want to make changes to your site. As mentioned already you should not make changes on your live server. Rather, you should have another copy of the site you can use for testing both on your local machine and the Web server before you make the changes active.

When you are working on any kind of file it is easy just to work on one version of a document and save changes as you go. However, this opens you up to problems:

- ❑ First, you might save over the file when you did not mean to, or make an error and want to go back to the original.

- ❑ You might open a file, make some changes, and save it, and while you are editing your version a colleague might come along and open the same file, make their changes, and then save their version after yours—saving over all of your changes.

- ❑ You might be working on a site for a client and decide that you want to go back to an earlier version of a design or some earlier content.

- ❑ You might need a copy of something your site contained at an earlier date—but if you do not have these files, you will not be able to.

Therefore, when more than one person is working on the same files or if you are updating your own files it can be a good idea to come up with a naming convention to save all older files before saving new documents with the same name. For example, you could simply add a date and time to any file before saving over it. If you wanted to change your home page `index.html` you can save a copy with the date you change it; this has the advantage that you also know when it was last changed.

This does take up more space on your hard drive, but if you regularly make an archive copy of your sites and remove older files that were never used, you can clear up the space they take regularly and maintain a manageable set of files.

You can also use your own `<meta>` tags to indicate a version as well as the name of the last person to update the file. You might remember from the beginning of the chapter that I said you can use anything you like as the value of the name attribute of the <meta> tag; this is a good example of doing exactly that. For example, here are <meta> tags to indicate the last modified date and who made the last changes:

```
<meta type="last-modified" content="16-04-04:12:34:00 GMT" />

<meta type="last-changes-by" content="Jon Duckett" />
```

Remember that you also have the <ins> and <del> elements, although these are not likely to be as much use when simply making updates to a site—they are more useful for tracking versions of documents.

It is also good practice to add comments into code when you change something that other people have done. For example, if you are working on a site and want to add in a new script, you might do something like the following:

```
<!-- start of new section added 12/12/03 by Bob Stewart -->
<b><a href="specials.html">Click here for special offers on end of stock
items.</a>
<!-- end of new section added 12/12/03 by Bob Stewart -->
```

You are not likely to do this for large changes to sites, but for small changes (especially ones in script or programming languages), the comment will help someone coming back to the site later see what and where changes have been made.

You can buy software to handle version control for you. This software allows you to book out files, as if they were library books—preventing two people from working on the same file at the same time. Some of these applications can be quite expensive, although free tools are available such as CVS (Concurrent Versions System) at http://www.cvshome.org/.

If you use Macromedia Dreamweaver there is also a function that allows you to indicate whether files should be allowed to be used by only one person at a time when you create a site—this is handy for preventing someone from opening a file while you are working on the same page and then saving over changes you have made and saved since they opened the file.

What Next?

You've learned all about XHTML and CSS, made a good start at learning JavaScript, and learned how to put your site live on the Web. You might wonder why there is a section entitled "What Next?" This section covers two topics:

❑ Tools you can use to add powerful features to your site using knowledge you already have

❑ What technologies might be appropriate to learn next

So, the first part of this final section will look at services provided on the Web that you can use to enhance your site. You will be learning about things such as blogs, how to add discussion groups or forums to your sites, and how to add search features to your site. While these might all sound complicated—and they certainly are advanced features—they can be remarkably easy to implement and you will see how they can be powerful and impressive features on any site.

In a similar way to how Hotmail offers e-mail over the Web, most of these services are implemented using other companies' servers and code—all you have to do is customize them to make them appear like part of your site.

Blogs

The word "blog" is short for *weblog*. Blogs were initially devised as a way to add online journals or diaries to a personal Web site. The idea behind blogs was to allow users to easily add new entries or *posts* to their Web site without having to manually re-code the page (often called *one-click publishing*). The user goes to the Web site of the company who made the blog, writes a post into a form, and the entry then appears on the Web site.

The posts are then added to the site in a chronological order, and while they are often used for online diaries or journals, they have been used for a wide variety of other purposes, such as a way for people to add news, posts about a topic of shared interest, links, and so on.

Indeed, while blogs started off their life as a way for anyone to share their thoughts with the rest of the Web, they soon started to appear on company intranets (as a way of sharing information), and on public Web sites as a news feature (rather than just being used as a diary).

Several different companies and Web sites give you the tools to add a blog to your Web site. Just two of the more popular ones are:

❑　`http://www.blogger.com/`

❑　`http://www.movabletype.org/`

Both of these sites give you the tools to add posts to your blog without having to manually update your page each time you want to write something new. Nor do you have to install software or scripts on your server (although both have applications where you *can* do so). Furthermore, they can look like they are on part of your site under your domain name (rather than the company you use for your blog).

You provide a template for how your posts should appear or choose one of the templates already designed that you can choose from when you sign up for the blog; then, when you want to add a new post to your blog, you simply go to the Web site of the company you signed up with (for example, `http://www.blogger.com/`) and add your post.

Templates can be heavily customized as they rely mainly on CSS for styling and positioning.

Discussion Boards or Forums

Discussion boards are a great way of adding a community feeling to your site and to attract visitors back to your site again and again—providing new content without you having to add it yourself. A discussion group is most commonly found on special interest Web sites and allows users to post questions or comments and then have other users reply to those questions.

For example, if you were running a site about a particular type of car, you might have one discussion group for technical questions that people could ask and answer regarding fixing problems with that model of car, and you might have another forum that allows users to indicate when they are buying or selling parts for that car.

One of the great things about discussion boards is that, if your site gets known for answering questions, people will come to that site whenever they have a problem. You may well have to start the community off by answering all questions yourself, but with luck, other members will start adding their thoughts.

As with blogs, there are companies that create software and offer it on their servers so that functionality-wise it looks as though your site has a discussion group (even though it runs on their servers). One of the best is http://www.ezboard.com/. And, as with blogs, you can usually customize the look of the discussion board using CSS.

You should note, however, that you might be held legally responsible for what people write on your discussion board. If someone takes offense to something written on a board or forum on your site, you can be held accountable as the publisher of the content on the Web—even if you do not share the opinion of the person who wrote the item.

Some discussion boards get around this by allowing the owner to moderate each post (read it before allowing it to go on the site); others simply regularly check the site for offensive material and remove any posts they consider offensive as soon as possible.

Adding a Search Utility

As mentioned in Chapter 12, you might want to add a search utility to your site. In Chapter 12 you saw that you can add a Google search utility to your site by going to http://www.google.com/services/free.html and adding a free search. Another site that offer a free customizable search service on sites of up to 500 pages is the Atomz Express service at http://www.Atomz.com/ (you may need to follow the links for the trial service).

The addition of a search facility to your site can mean the difference between users finding what they hoped to find or simply giving up and leaving. Not all users will hang around long enough to search through lots of pages if the information they wanted is not easily accessible.

With both the Google and Atomz services, you are given the code for a form that will allow users to send queries to the respective company's Web site. Their servers will then return a page to your users with the results of the search. Both services allow you to create custom headers for the page so that it contains your branding, although the results are generated by their servers.

Introducing Other Technologies

This section provides an introduction to some other technologies, what they can do, and how you can make use of them on Web sites. I hope this helps you decide what technology you might want to start learning next when you have gained experience with everything you have learned in this book.

Server-Side Web Programming: ASP, JSP, and PHP

You have already seen the very basics of what a programming language such as JavaScript can do in a browser, but when a programming language is used on a Web server, it becomes even more powerful.

Any time you want to collect information from a visitor to your site and return a page that is customized for them, you will want to look at server-side programming. Here are some examples of applications where different users will need different pages:

❑ **Searching for content on a site.** The user enters a term that he or she wants to search for into a form, which is sent to the application on the server. The application then creates a page that contains results the user enquired about.

❑ **Checking train times.** The user enters the point she is traveling from and the destination she is going to, along with preferred travel times, and the application creates a page that contains the requested journey times.

❑ **Shopping online.** Users browse through a catalog of products and select which ones they want. Their choices are often reflected in a shopping basket displayed in each page. After they have chosen what they want they provide their payment details and contact/delivery details. At the same time, the people running the store are likely to have a browser-based interface that allows them to add new products to the site (rather than having to create each new page and link to it individually).

❑ **Discussion boards and forums.** The examples you have already seen mentioned in this chapter of discussion boards and forums rely on another company's server-side programming and code to handle all of the posts.

When you see the term "server-side application," it can be something as simple as one page that contains a script that is executed on the server. However, it can be much more complex; it could be made up of hundreds of pages of code that use databases, things called components, even other programs running on the server. The complexity of the application usually depends upon the features it has.

Indeed, most sites that have content that changes regularly will use a server-side programming language because the content of the site will be in a database. You will learn more about this in the "Content Management" section shortly.

Choosing a Server-Side Language

You can work in several different server-side languages and environments, such as ASP or ASP.NET, PHP, and JSP. Each offers very similar capabilities—the first choice is usually whether you are going to be using Microsoft Web servers or a version of UNIX to host your site on. Generally speaking:

❑ ASP and ASP.NET run on Microsoft IIS and Windows 2000+ servers

❑ PHP and JSP run on UNIX servers

There are exceptions to this; you can find some UNIX servers running something called Chili!ASP (which is a version of ASP for UNIX servers), and you can find a Microsoft server running PHP. But these are less common.

It used to be the case that Web hosting companies charged more for running ASP and ASP.NET because they required the company to buy licenses for their servers from Microsoft, whereas PHP and JSP can be run on free software such as Linux. However, the price comparisons between the two are now very similar if you shop around, and you need to worry about the extra cost only if you are running several of your own servers (which is unlikely).

The first applications created using a script on a server were known as CGI scripts. You may still see CGI or CGI-bin in the URL of some applications. However, the languages discussed here are in far higher demand and are more powerful.

You can develop all three on your desktop computer with the right installations. Windows 2000 and later supports ASP by default (earlier versions need to install a program called Personal Web Server that can be hard to obtain these days), Mac OS X comes with a version of Apache installed (which is a UNIX Web server), and Linux or any other flavor of UNIX can also run Apache and other UNIX-based Web servers.

I have noticed a couple of real differences after working on the ASP/ASP.NET compared with PHP and JSP technologies:

❑ Microsoft makes a lot of server software itself, and it tends to work well with other Microsoft products. This means a Microsoft database will integrate easily with a Microsoft Web server and Microsoft E-mail components.

❑ By contrast, several different vendors make PHP and JSP tools that should operate in harmony but can be harder to get talking to each other.

❑ Often more free software is written for PHP, which you can use on your sites; whereas there are more commercial companies developing applications for ASP and ASP.NET that you are charged to use. So, if you want lots of programs you can start using for free, such as gallery scripts and shopping carts for eCommerce stores, then you are more likely to find more free PHP programs than ASP programs.

Different developers will have different opinions about which language to choose. But most people learn one environment and stick to it (although to a certain degree it is much simpler to learn a second language and environment when you understand one in the first place and know what can be done with server-side scripting languages).

If you are learning any technology in order to get a job then it is a good idea to keep an eye on job advertisements. You will be able to track the technologies required and also (if you look regularly) you will be able to see the emerging technologies early on—first there will be only one or two mentions of these technologies, and then they will start becoming ore regular. Job ads can therefore be quite a good barometer for technologies you should consider learning. (And if your boss catches you looking at job ads, you've got a great excuse—you're just researching which technologies are going to be more popular in the near future.)

Content Management

One of the key aspects of many sites is a *content management system*. This is actually a fancy name for something that will allow you to easily update the content of your Web site without actually having to create a new page for each new article, posting, product for sale, and so on, that you make.

Content management systems tend to be based around a relational database. Relational databases contain one or more tables, each of which is like a spreadsheet. Figure 16-11 shows you a database used in a site that runs classified ads.

You can see that there are several rows in this table, each containing the details of a different advertisement. The columns each contain different information about the ad in that row:

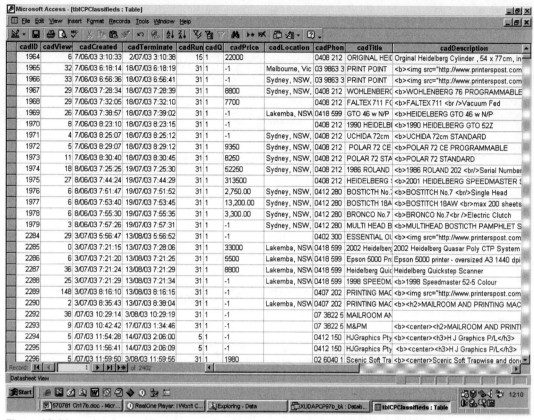

Figure 16-11

❑   cadRun is the number of days the ad should run.

❑   cadQ is the quantity available of the item for sale.

❑   cadPrice is the price of the item for sale.

❑   cadLocation is the location of the item for sale.

❑   cadPhone is the phone number of the vendor.

❑   cadTitle is the title of the item for sale.

❑   cadDescription is a description of the item that is for sale—as you can see this contains XHTML itself.

This table actually contains a lot more fields that are out of view and several more tables. But this gives you an idea of how the information is stored. When users come to the site that uses this database they will navigate through categories to find the items they are interested in. Rather than having a page containing the details of each item, the site contains only one page that displays all ads, called viewItem.asp. This is like a template for all of the ads, and the title, description, and sellers' details are added into the page at the one specific point. You can see an example of an advertisement in Figure 16-12.

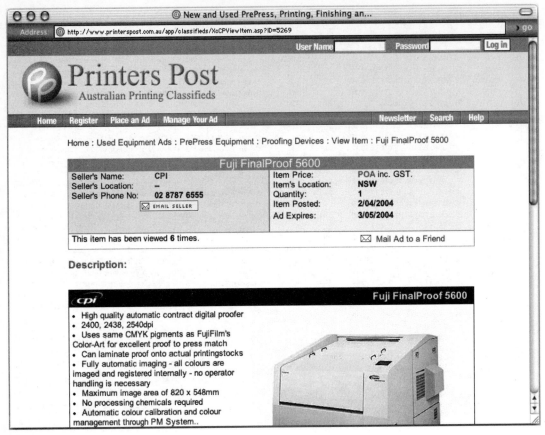

Figure 16-12

Look at the structure of the URL for this ad; it is the key to how this template-based system works:

```
http://www.printerspost.com.au/app/classifieds/viewItem.asp?ID=5269
```

The `viewItem.asp` page is requested, and when it is requested, the ID `5269` is also requested. This corresponds with the number in the first column of the table in Figure 16-11. All the details of this ad are then placed into the template. So, where the text says "Fuji Final Proof 5600," this is the title, and whatever is written in the `cadTitle` field of the database table for this ad will appear in that position on the page.

This approach is also what makes it possible for users to submit their own ads to the site. You cannot expect each user of a Web site to be able to create his or her own pages in the style of the site, and if someone working for the site had to manually create each page it would not be financially viable. However, a set of pages can be created that allow users to upload their own ads to the server. You can see in Figure 16-13 one of the pages that allows users to enter the details of the item they are selling.

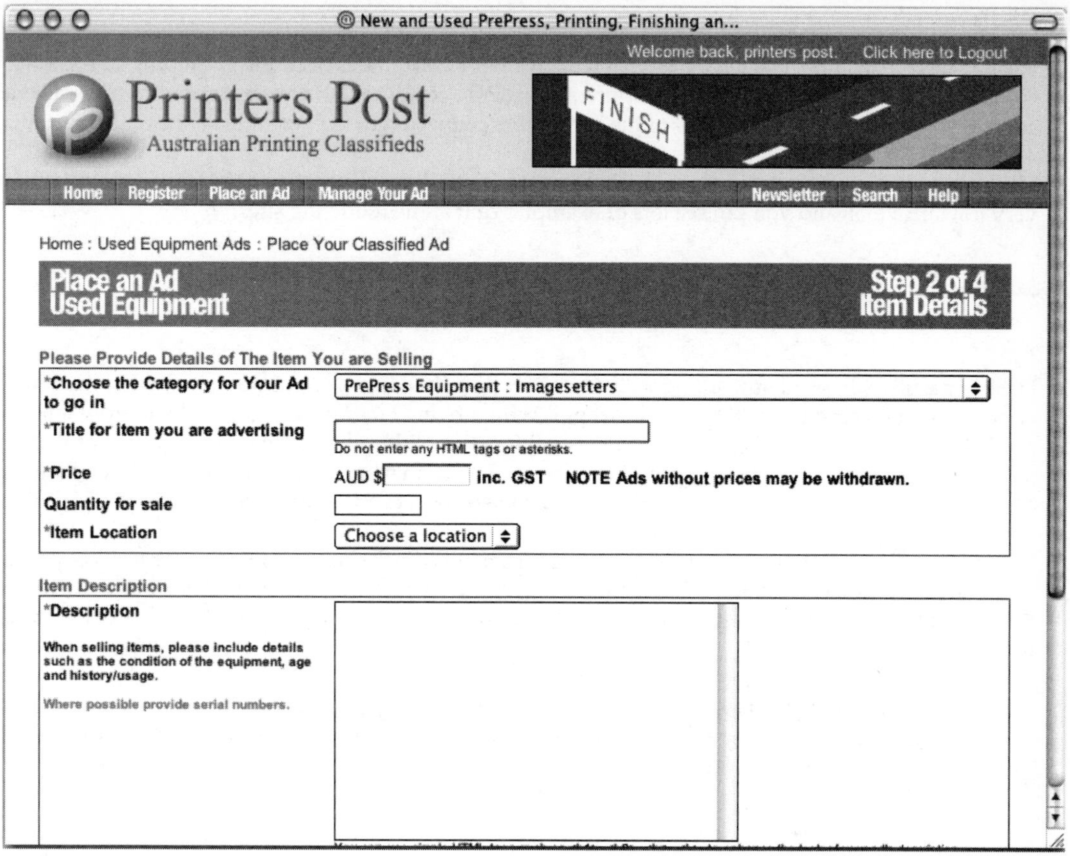

Figure 16-13

This application also allows the following:

- ❑ Users to upload images of their products to the server, and the company running the site can remove the images from the server if necessary

- ❑ Visitors to contact vendors via e-mail, so it can generate e-mails without users having to open e-mails

- ❑ The owner of the site to view each ad before allowing it to go live

- ❑ People to pay for the advertisement online (through a third-party payment company)

This approach of storing content in a database is employed in many different types of sites. For example, many news sites are run from databases with each article being stored in a row within one of the tables, just like the ads were in the example you saw. Likewise, e-commerce stores tend to store product details in a database, with each product stored in a row of one of the tables. When these sites use a row of a table for each article or product, new articles or products can be added using XHTML forms (rather than having to hand-code pages), and contents pages can list all of the articles or products without having to be modified each time a new one is added.

Flash

Flash is written in a tool created by Macromedia (called Flash). Users need the Flash plug-in—known as the Flash Player—installed on their computers in order to see the Flash files, but statistics from several sources suggest that over 90 percent of the computers connected to the Web already have this installed.

Flash started off as a way to create animations on the Web—from cartoons to animated logos or text. It is a very powerful tool, and you can see lots of examples of it at the following sites:

❑   http://www.macromedia.com/software/flash/

❑   http://www.flashkit.com/gallery/

Flash is particularly good at working with vector art (line drawings). It was not designed to work with photos, and to a certain extent it can still struggle with moving bitmaps (images made up from lots of tiny pixels like GIFs and JPEGs). Bitmaps tend to scroll less smoothly, whereas the line drawings of vector art move easily and with much more grace. You also get much smaller file sizes if you use vector drawings and text rather than importing images. You can also use Flash to add video and audio to your Web site.

Very few sites need to be designed completely in Flash; it is much more common to see parts of pages created in Flash (such as banner ads and animations). This is partly because it is much quicker to develop a site in XHTML and partly because fewer people have the skills to integrate Flash well with databases than they do with XHTML.

The Flash movie creation software does cost money, but the plug-in is, of course, free. If you are not sure whether Flash is the right thing for you to learn next, you can download a free trial version from http://www.macromedia.com/software/flash/.

Learning Graphics Packages

Learning how to deal with text, illustrations, photos, and images correctly is very important if you are going to be involved with designing pages as well as coding them. The difference between an okay-looking site and a visually great site is often its use of graphics.

There are two key types of graphics package you might want to learn:

❑   A photo editing and manipulation package such as Adobe Photoshop or the lite version Photoshop Elements. These work with bitmapped graphics.

❑   A vector art package such as Adobe Illustrator or Macromedia Freehand. These work with vector graphics—(line drawings created using coordinates) that are then filled in with colors.

You learned a bit about the difference between bitmapped graphics and vector graphics in Chapter 4.

Adobe Photoshop is by far the most popular graphics program used for developing Web graphics. You need only look at job ads for Web designers and you will see that it is often a prerequisite. Photoshop not only allows you to work with photos, but it can also be used for creating text and logos (although an experienced designer would usually favor a vector program when it comes to creating logos and diagrams from scratch).

Photoshop is a valuable tool to know because it not only allows you to edit photos, but also allows you to create all kinds of images, such as navigation images and logos. It will then take these images and create optimized versions of them ready for the Web with smaller file sizes for quicker downloads.

When working in Photoshop you can create an image built up from many layers—each layer is like a piece of clear film over the first image you start with, allowing you to make changes on top of the image.

When you have experience with a photo package you might like to go on to learn a vector image package—especially if you are going to be creating lots of logos or diagrams. Vector packages are of little use if you are working with photos, but they are great for doing line-based work. By their nature vector graphics scale very well, and logos are often created in a vector format because they allow you to scale an image to a large size for a poster or shrink it down for a small Web graphic. By contrast if you blow up a bitmapped image to a very large size it will look grainy—you will be able to see all of the pixels that make up the image.

Of course, there are many other technologies you could learn, but the ones you have learned about in this section offer you the next logical steps in your Web development career. If you want to work more with graphics I advise you to start with Photoshop or Flash, whereas if you want to work more on programming, start learning a server-side programming language.

Summary

In this chapter you have seen how to prepare your Web site for a waiting world. You started off learning about the <meta> tags that you can use to add content *about* your documents (such as the author, expiry date, or default scripting language)—hence the name <meta> tags; they contain information about the document rather than being part of the document themselves.

You then went on to learn about different sorts of tests that you should perform on your pages before you put them on a server, and once they are on the server but before you are ready for the world to see them. These tests included validating your pages (to make sure that your markup is written according to the relevant recommendation and that you are following the rules you should), checking links to make sure that all of them work and are not pointing to the wrong place, and checking that your site meets accessibility guidelines.

Next you looked at the potential minefield of choosing a host whose Web servers you can put your Web site on. This ever-changing market is hard to keep up-to-date with, but it can be well worth checking up on a few hosts before going with the first one you find. New deals with more storage, greater bandwidth, larger mailboxes, and newer features are coming out all the time, so it pays to shop around.

Once your site is live you will want people to come and look at it. One of the major ways of attracting new visitors is through a combination of techniques such as carefully chosen titles, keywords, content on your pages, and manual submission to sites. This is an ongoing process that requires regular attention. Of course, online is not the only way to market your site, and there are plenty of other ways you can attract visitors.

You can also gain valuable information about your visitors by using statistics packages that analyze your log files, working out how people came across your site, how many pages they looked at, what terms they searched on in search engines to arrive at your site, and so on.

This chapter also covered version control so that when you come to make updates to your site you do not end up losing important files, or having someone else save over your work. The keywords here are to play safe, and keep a copy of everything you change, at least until you have finished the job, and then you can archive that version of the site and delete older files.

The final part of the chapter looked at where you could go next with your site. You saw how there are services such as blogs, discussion boards, and search features that have already been developed by companies that allow you to integrate these services into your site. You also saw some other technologies and programs you might want to learn more about when you are comfortable with the topics you have learned in this book. If you are interested in programming, you should consider learning a server-side language such as ASP.NET, PHP, or JSP. Alternatively, if you are more interested about the visual appearance and design of sites you should consider learning a graphics program such as Adobe Photoshop, and possibly some animation software such as Macromedia Flash.

This book covered a lot, and the best way to make sure you have understood it properly is to get out there and build some sites. Perhaps you can create a site about a hobby or interest of yours, or maybe you can create a site for friends who run their own small business.

Remember that if you like the way someone has done something on a site (perhaps you like the layout, or the size and type of font they use) you can simply go to the View menu on your browser and select the option to display the source for the page. While you should never copy someone else's design or layout, you can learn a lot from looking about how other people have built their sites. But remember that they might not be using XHTML; a lot of pages are out there that were built using earlier versions of HTML. HTML is not strict about how you write your pages, and there are a lot of coders out there who are not as aware of things such as which elements require closing brackets, when to use quotes for attributes, or how to use CSS well.

While older, more relaxed ways of coding may seem easier, by being strict with how you use markup, separating as much of your markup from styling as possible, and using JavaScript only to enhance pages, you end up with pages that will be available to more browsers and more people for a longer period of time.

So, thank you for choosing this book, and congratulations on making it to the end. I wish you all the best in creating your first Web site and hope that it is the first of many!

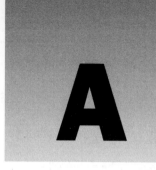

Answers to Exercises

Chapter 1

1. Look at the following HTML document and turn it into a Transitional XHTML document. There are some optional changes, as well as some required changes to make this document an XHTML document.

```
<html>
  <head>
    <TITLE>London</TITLE>
  </head>
  <body>
    <h1>Where I Live: London</h1>
    <p>London is the capital of England with a population of over seven
       million.
    <p>The Romans were the first to develop London as a port on the River
       Thames and as the main hub of their road network,
       although the banks of the Thames had previously been inhabited
       by the Celts.
  </body>
```

A. In order to make the HTML document a Transitional XHTML document, you had to make the following changes:

1. The document could have started with an optional XML declaration and the DOCTYPE declaration for Transitional XHTML.

```
<?xml version="1.0" ?>
<!DOCTYPE html PUBLIC "-//W3C//DTD/ XHTML 1.0 Transitional//EN"
  "http://www.w3.org/TR/xhtml-transitional.dtd">
```

2. The `<TITLE>` element should be in lowercase letters, as all element and attribute names in XHTML should be in lowercase.

```
<html>
  <head>
    <title>London</title>
  </head>
  <body>
    <h1>Where I Live: London</h1>
```

3. The `<p>` elements that make up the paragraphs of your document must have closing `</p>` tags. Whereas HTML was forgiving about the inclusion of some closing tags, all elements in XHTML must be closed (or be marked as empty elements).

```
<p>London is the capital of England with a population of over seven
    million.</p>
<p>The Romans were the first to develop London as a port on the River
    Thames and as the main hub of their road network, although the banks
    of the Thames had previously been inhabited by the Celts.</p>
  </body>
```

4. Finally, the document was missing a closing `</html>` tag.

```
</html>
```

2. Write the XHTML for the page shown in Figure 1-8.

A. The XHTML required to create the page shown in Figure 1-8 should look like this:

```
<?xml version="1.0" ?>
<!DOCTYPE html PUBLIC "-//W3C//DTD/ XHTML 1.0 Transitional//EN"
  "http://www.w3.org/TR/xhtml-transitional.dtd">
<html>
  <head>
    <title>ACME Product Recall</title>
  </head>
  <body>
    <h1>ACME Product Recall - Dehydrated Boulders</h1>
    <p><b>The ACME Toy Company</b> is asking all customers to return any
        <i>Dehydrated Boulders</i> purchased in the month of March 2004.</p>
    <p>Because of a fault at our manufacturing plant, the boulders would
        not form when the user adds water as per instructions. Therefore
        these items carry great risk of flattening the user.</p>
  </body>
</html>
```

Chapter 2

1. Mark up the following sentence with the relevant presentational elements.

The 1st time the **bold** man wrote in *italics*, he underlined several key words.

A.   The sentence used superscript, bold, italic, and underlined presentational elements.

```
<p>The 1<sup>st</sup> time the <b>bold</b> man wrote in <i>italics</i>, he
<u>underlined</u> several key words.</p>
```

2.   Mark up the following list, with inserted and deleted content:

Ricotta pancake ingredients:

❑   1 1/2 3/4 cups ricotta

❑   3/4 cup milk

❑   4 eggs

❑   1 cup plain white flour

❑   1 teaspoon baking powder

❑   75g 50g butter

❑   pinch of salt

A.   Here is the bulleted list with the editing elements added:

```
<h2>Ricotta pancake ingredients:</h2>
<ul>
  <li>1 <del>1/2</del><ins>3/4</ins> cups ricotta</li>
  <li>3/4 cup milk</li>
  <li>4 eggs</li>
  <li>1 cup plain <ins>white</ins> flour</li>
  <li>1 teaspoon baking powder</li>
  <li><del>75g</del> <ins>50g</ins> butter</li>
  <li>pinch of salt</li>
</ul>
```

Chapter 3

1.   Look back at the Try It Out example where you created a menu, and create a new page that has links, like those at the top of the menu page, to each of the courses in the menu example. Then add a link to the main Wrox Press Web site (www.wrox.com). The page should look something like Figure 3-8.

A.   Your code should look something like this:

```
<?xml version="1.0" encoding="UTF-8"?>
<!DOCTYPE html PUBLIC "-//W3C//DTD XHTML 1.0 Strict//EN"
    "http://www.w3.org/TR/xhtml1/DTD/xhtml1-strict.dtd">
<html xmlns="http://www.w3.org/1999/xhtml" lang="en">

<head>
  <title>Links to menu</title>
</head>
<body>
<h1>Links to the Wrox Cafe Menu</h1>
```

```
<div id="links">
  <a href="menu.html#starters">Starters</a> |
  <a href="menu.html#mains">Main courses</a> |
  <a href="menu.html#deserts">Deserts</a>
</div>
<p>Wrox Cafe is a fictional cafè brought to you from <a
href="http://www.wrox.com">Wrox Press</a></p>
</body>
</head>
```

In order for it to be a Strict XHTML 1.0 document, the links that form the menu have been placed inside a `<div>` element, and each link uses the pound or hash sign (#) after the filename followed by the value of the `id` attribute to indicate the part of the page the link should go to.

The link to the Wrox Web site, meanwhile, uses the full URL you would type into a browser window as the value of the `href` attribute.

2. Take the following sentence and place `<a>` elements around the parts that should have the link.

```
<p>To find out why advertising on our site works, visit the testimonials
page.</p>
```

A. The link is well placed around the word "testimonials." Remember that when a link is in the middle of text, the actual content of the link should be short and to the point so that users can scan the page for key items they are interested in.

```
<p>To find out why advertising on our site works, visit the
<a>testimonials</a> page.</p>
```

3. What is wrong with the positioning of the `<a>` element here?

```
<p>You can read the full article <a>here</a>.</p>
```

A. This link is not very descriptive for someone who is scanning the page. The word `here` will stick out when you probably want to draw people's attention to the words `full article`.

```
<p>Click on the link to read the <a>full article</a>.</p>
```

Chapter 4

1. Add the images that describe a shade, a tint, and a tone to the following example. All of the images are provided in the `images` folder in the download code for Chapter 4.

```
<h1>Color Definitions and Examples</h1>
<p>A <b>hue</b> is a pure color; it contains no black or white. It is the key
part of a color that allows it to be identified as red, green or blue.</p>
<img src="images/hue.gif" alt="Color sample for hues" />
<p>A <b>shade</b> is a hue with black added</p>
   Add shade1.gif here
```

```
<br />
<p>A <b>tint</b> is a hue with white added</p>
  Add tint1.gif here
<p>A <b>tone</b> is a hue with gray added</p>
  Add tone1.gif here
```

Your finished page should look like Figure 4-14.

A. Here you can see the body of the page that contains the new images; the lines with the images have been highlighted:

```
<?xml version="1.0" ?>
<!DOCTYPE html PUBLIC "-//W3C//DTD XHTML 1.0 Strict//EN"
    "http://www.w3.org/TR/xhtml1/DTD/xhtml1-strict.dtd">
<html xmlns="http://www.w3.org/1999/xhtml" lang="en" xml:lang="en">

<head>
  <title>Color Definitions and Examples</title>
</head>

<body>
  <h1>Color Definitions and Examples</h1>
    <p>A <b>hue</b> is a pure color; it contains no black or while. It is the
       key part of a color that allows it to be identified as red, green or
       blue.</p>
    <img src="images/hue.gif" alt="Color sample for hues" />
    <p>A <b>shade</b> is a hue with black added</p>
    <img src="images/shade1.gif" alt="Color sample for shades" width="317"
         height="78" /><br />
    <p>A <b>tint</b> is a hue with white added</p>
    <img src="images/tint1.gif" alt="Color sample for tints" width="317"
         height="78" />
    <p>A <b>tone</b> is a hue with gray added</p>
    <img src="images/tone1.gif" alt="Color sample for tones" width="317"
         height="78" /><br />

</body>

</html>
```

2. Look at the four images shown in Figure 4-15 and decide whether you are more likely to get smaller file sizes if you save them as JPEGs or GIFs.

A. You should probably save the images in the following formats:

- ❑ Image 1: JPEG
- ❑ Image 2: GIF
- ❑ Image 3: GIF
- ❑ Image 4: JPEG

As discussed in Chapter 4, images with large flat areas of color, such as images 2 and 3, compress better as GIFs than JPEGs, while JPEGs are better for saving photographic images. You could also have suggested PNGs instead of GIFs, as PNGs are a replacement for GIFs.

Chapter 5

1. Where should the `<caption>` element for a table be placed in the document, and by default where is it displayed?

A. The `<caption>` element should appear after the opening `<table>` element but before the first `<tr>` element.

2. In what order would the cells in Figure 5-12 be read out by a screen reader?

A. The names would be read in the following order: Emily, Jack, Frank, Mary, Dominic, Amy, Thomas, Angela, and David.

3. Create a table to hold the data shown in Figure 5-13. To give you a couple of clues, the document must be Transitional XHTML 1.0 because the `width` attribute is used on the cells of the first row of the table. You should also have seen examples of how the border is generated in this chapter, using another deprecated attribute, but this time on the `<table>` element rather than the cells.

A. Here is the example for the cinema timetable (`cinema.html`).

```
<?xml version="1.0" encoding="UTF-8"?>
<!DOCTYPE html PUBLIC "-//W3C//DTD XHTML 1.0 Strict//EN"
    "http://www.w3.org/TR/xhtml1/DTD/xhtml1-strict.dtd">
<html xmlns="http://www.w3.org/1999/xhtml" lang="en">

<head>
  <title>Classic Movies Times</title>
</head>

<body>
<table border="1" width="500">
<caption>Classic Movie Day</caption>
  <tr>
    <th></th>
    <th width="200">5 pm</th>
    <th width="200">7 pm</th>
    <th width="200">9 pm</th>
    <th width="200">11 pm</th>
  </tr>
  <tr>
    <th>Screen one</th>
    <td>Star Wars</td>
    <td>Empire Strikes Back</td>
    <td>Return of the Jedi</td>
    <td>The Exorcist</td>
  </tr>
  <tr>
    <th>Screen two</th>
    <td colspan="2">Dances with Wolves</td>
    <td colspan="2">Gone With the Wind</td>
  </tr>
  <tr>
    <th>Screen three</th>
    <td colspan="2">2001: A Space Odyssey</td>
```

```
      <td>The Conversation</td>
      <td>5 Easy Pieces</td>
    </tr>
  </table>

  </body>
  </html>
```

Chapter 6

1. Create an e-mail feedback form that looks like the one shown in Figure 6-25.

Note that the first text box is a `readonly` text box so that the user cannot alter the name of the person the mail is being sent to.

A. Here is the code for the e-mail feedback form:

```
<?xml version="1.0" ?>
<!DOCTYPE html PUBLIC "-//W3C//DTD XHTML 1.0 Transitional//EN"
    "http://www.w3.org/TR/xhtml1/DTD/xhtml1-transitional.dtd">
<html xmlns="http://www.w3.org/1999/xhtml" lang="en">

<head>
  <title>Reply to ad</title>
</head>

<body>
<h2>Reply to ad</h2>
<p>Use the following form to respond to the ad:</p>

<form action="http://www.example.com/ads/respond.asp" method="post"
      name="frmRespondToAd">
<table>
  <tr>
    <td><label for="emailTo">To</label></td>
    <td><input type="text" name="txtTo" readonly="readonly" id="emailTo"
        size="20" value="Star Seller" /></td>
  </tr>
  <tr>
    <td><label for="emailFrom">To</label></td>
    <td><input type="text" name="txtFrom" id="emailFrom" size="20" /></td>
  </tr>
  <tr>
    <td><label for="emailSubject">Subject</label></td>
    <td><input type="text" name="txtSubject" id="emailSubject" size="50" /></td>
  </tr>
  <tr>
    <td><label for="emailBody">Body</label></td>
    <td><textarea name="txtBody" id="emailBody" cols="50" rows="10">
        </textarea></td>
  </tr>
</table>
```

```
    <input type="submit" value="Send email" />

  </form>

</body>
</html>
```

2. Create a voting or ranking form that looks like the one shown in Figure 6-26.

    Note that the following <style> element was added to the <head> of the document to make each column of the table the same fixed width, with text aligned in the center (you see more about this in Chapter 8).

```
<head>
  <title>Voting</title>
  <style type="text/css">td {width:100; text-align:center;}</style>
</head>
```

A. Here is the code for the voting form. Note how the checked attribute is used on the middle value for this form so that it loads with an average score (in case the form is submitted without a value selected):

```
<?xml version="1.0" ?>
<!DOCTYPE html PUBLIC "-//W3C//DTD XHTML 1.0 Transitional//EN"
      "http://www.w3.org/TR/xhtml1/DTD/xhtml1-transitional.dtd">
<html xmlns="http://www.w3.org/1999/xhtml" lang="en">

<head>
  <title>Voting</title>
  <style type="text/css">td {width:100; text-align:center;}</style>
</head>

<body>
<h2>Register your opinion</h2>
<p>How well do you rate the information on this site (where 1 is very poor and
5 is very good)?</p>

<form action="http://www.example.com/ads/respond.asp" method="get"
      name="frmRespondToAd">

<table>
  <tr>
    <td><input type="radio" name="radVote" value="1" id="vpoor" /></td>
    <td><input type="radio" name="radVote" value="2" id="poor" /></td>
    <td><input type="radio" name="radVote" value="3" id="average"
        checked="checked" /></td>
    <td><input type="radio" name="radVote" value="4" id="good" /></td>
    <td><input type="radio" name="radVote" value="5" id="vgood" /></td>
  </tr>
  <tr>
    <td><label for="vpoor">1 <br />Very Poor</label></td>
    <td><label for="poor">2 <br />Poor</label></td>
    <td><label for="average">3 <br />Average</label></td>
```

```
    <td><label for="good">4 <br />Good</label></td>
    <td><label for="vgood">5 <br />Very Good</label></td>
  </tr>
</table>
<input type="submit" value="Vote now" />
</form>

</body>
</html>
</body>
</html>
```

Chapter 7

1. Re-create the frameset document shown in Figure 7-10, where clicking a fruit loads a new page in the main window. When the page loads it will carry the details for the appropriate fruit.

A. The first example required five files:

❏   A frameset document

❏   A navigation document

❏   The apple page

❏   The orange page

❏   The banana page

Here is the frameset document (example1.html):

```
<?xml version="1.0" encoding="iso-8859-1"?>
<!DOCTYPE html PUBLIC "-//W3C//DTD XHTML 1.0 Frameset//EN"
  "http://www.w3.org/TR/xhtml1/DTD/xhtml1-frameset.dtd">
<html>
<head>
  <title>Fruit example</title>
</head>

<frameset cols="200, 450, *">
  <frame src="frames/fruitNav.html" />
  <frame name="main_frame" src="frames/apple.html" />

  <noframes><body>This site makes uses of a technology called frames.
  Unfortunately the browser you are using does not support this technology.
  We recommend that you update your browser. We apologize for any inconvenience
  this causes.
  </body></noframes>

</frameset>

</html>
```

This is a frameset document type that contains two columns that are a fixed size, and then the remainder of the window is left blank (hence there are only <frame> elements for the first two columns). Note how the second <frame> element carries the name attribute so that the links in the navigation frame can load in that part of the page.

Here is the navigation pane (fruitNav.html):

```
<?xml version="1.0" encoding="iso-8859-1"?>
<!DOCTYPE html PUBLIC "-//W3C//DTD XHTML 1.0 Transitional//EN"
"http://www.w3.org/TR/xhtml1/DTD/xhtml1-transitional.dtd">
<html xmlns="http://www.w3.org/1999/xhtml">
<head>
  <title>Navigation</title>
  <style type="text/css">img {border-style:none; border-width:0px;}</style>
</head>
<body>

<h1> Navigation </h1>
<p>Click on the fruit to find out more about it.</p>
<a href="../frames/apple.html" target="main_frame"><img src="../images/
   apple.jpg" alt="apple" /></a>
<a href="../frames/orange.html" target="main_frame"><img src="../images/
   orange.jpg" alt="orange" /></a>
<a href="../frames/banana.html" target="main_frame"><img src="../images/
   banana.jpg" alt="banana" /></a>
</body>
</html>
```

This is a normal XHTML document; the only things of note in this document are the target attributes on the links to indicate that the link should open in the other frame, and the <style> element in the <head> (which you learn about in Chapter 8).

The pages about the fruit (apple.html, orange.html, and banana.html) are all the same except for their text content. Here is apple.html:

```
<?xml version="1.0" encoding="iso-8859-1"?>
<!DOCTYPE html PUBLIC "-//W3C//DTD XHTML 1.0 Transitional//EN"
"http://www.w3.org/TR/xhtml1/DTD/xhtml1-transitional.dtd">
<html xmlns="http://www.w3.org/1999/xhtml">
<head>
  <title>Apple</title>
</head>

<body>
<h1>Apples</h1>

<p>Apples come in different colors, and there are over 7500 varieties of
apples.</p>

<p>An apple contains about 5g of fiber (1/5 recommended daily average).</p>

</body>
</html>
```

2.   Re-create the <iframe> element shown in Figure 7-11.

Here is the new exercise code; the only change is to the text:

```
<?xml version="1.0" encoding="iso-8859-1"?>
<!DOCTYPE html PUBLIC "-//W3C//DTD XHTML 1.0 Transitional//EN"
"http://www.w3.org/TR/xhtml1/DTD/xhtml1-transitional.dtd">

<html xmlns="http://www.w3.org/1999/xhtml">
<head>
  <title>Football focus</title>
</head>

<body>
  <h1>Quarter Final - Wintertons Cup</h1>
  <h3>
    <a href="frames/teamA.html" target="iframe">Manchester Rangers</a>
      vs
    <a href="frames/teamB.html" target="iframe">Birmingham United</a>
  </h3>

  <p><iframe name="iframe" width="300" height="150" src="frames/clickForTeams
.html" align="left"></iframe>
      Today's big soccer game ise between Manchester Rangers and Birmingham
      United.
<br />The match will be played at Highgate Fields stadium, and
      is sure to be the big game of the week. <br /> All eyes on the underdogs
      Birmingham United who did not expect to get this far in the competition.
  </p>
</body>
</html>
```

A. The inline frame example requires four files:

- ❏ example2.html contains the page that you load.

- ❏ teamA.html contains the names of players in Team A.

- ❏ teamB.html contains the names of players in Team B.

- ❏ clickForTeam.html is what loads in the iframe before the user clicks either team.

First up is example2.html, which contains the <iframe> element. It is a normal XHTML document, with two links that carry the target attribute so that they can indicate which frame the document should go into.

```
<?xml version="1.0" encoding="iso-8859-1"?>
<!DOCTYPE html PUBLIC "-//W3C//DTD XHTML 1.0 Transitional//EN"
"http://www.w3.org/TR/xhtml1/DTD/xhtml1-transitional.dtd">
<html xmlns="http://www.w3.org/1999/xhtml">
<head>
  <title>Football focus</title>
</head>
<body>
<h1>Quarter Final - Wintertons Cup</h1>
<h3>
  <a href="frames/teamA.html" target="iframe">Manchester Rangers</a>
  vs
```

```
  <a href="frames/teamB.html" target="iframe">Birmingham United</a>
</h3>
  <p>
   <iframe name="iframe" width="300" height="150" src="frames/clickForTeams
.html" align="left" />

   Today's big soccer game with Manchester Rangers playing Birmingham
   United. The match will be played at Highgate Fields stadium, and is sure
   to be the big game of the week, with all eyes on the underdogs Birmingham
   United who did not expect to get this far in the competition, although the
   gate receipts will be a welcome relief for the team who have been
   facing financial difficulties.
  </p>
</body>
</html>
```

As you can see from the `<iframe>` element, it carries an `src` attribute that indicates that a page called `clickForTeams.html` should load into the iframe when the page loads. This is just a plain XHTML page:

```
<?xml version="1.0" encoding="iso-8859-1"?>
<!DOCTYPE html PUBLIC "-//W3C//DTD XHTML 1.0 Transitional//EN"
"http://www.w3.org/TR/xhtml1/DTD/xhtml1-transitional.dtd">
<html xmlns="http://www.w3.org/1999/xhtml">
<head>
  <title>Teams</title>
</head>
<body>
<h3>Click on a team name to load their players here</h3>
</body>
</html>
```

Now here is the page `teamB.html`, which contains a table for the players in the starting lineup of the team. The page `teamB.html` is exactly the same, just with different players.

```
<?xml version="1.0" encoding="iso-8859-1"?>
<!DOCTYPE html PUBLIC "-//W3C//DTD XHTML 1.0 Transitional//EN"
"http://www.w3.org/TR/xhtml1/DTD/xhtml1-transitional.dtd">
<html xmlns="http://www.w3.org/1999/xhtml">
<head>
  <title>Team B</title>
</head>
<body>
<h3>Birmingham United</h3>
  <p>The players of Birmingham United are</p>:
  <table>
    <tr><th>Number</th><th>Name</th></tr>
    <tr><td>1</td><td>Chris Warner</td></tr>
    <tr><td>2</td><td>Felix Thomlinson</td></tr>
    <tr><td>3</td><td>Barry Carr</td></tr>
    <tr><td>4</td><td>Mike Patterson</td></tr>
    <tr><td>5</td><td>Richard Neilson</td></tr>
```

```
      <tr><td>6</td><td>Brian Childer</td></tr>
      <tr><td>7</td><td>Micky Stephens</td></tr>
      <tr><td>8</td><td>Richard Brooks</td></tr>
      <tr><td>9</td><td>Nick Evans</td></tr>
      <tr><td>10</td><td>Joseph Barton</td></tr>
      <tr><td>11</td><td>Rob Bishop</td></tr>
    </table>
  </body>
</html>
```

Chapter 8

1. The following is an old HTML page that contains a fictional listing of files a user might be able to download. Your task is to re-create it using XHTML.

```
<html>
  <head>
    <title>Example of the value Attribute</title>
  </head>
  <body>
  <h1>Code Download</h1>
  The code download folder contains the following files and folders:

    <dir>
      <li>index.html</li>
      <li>sampleCode</li>
      <li>images</li>
    </dir>

  </body>
</html>
```

A. The main change you should have made to this example was to replace the old `<dir>` element with the `<ul>` element. Both elements create bulleted lists. You should also have put the paragraph (or line) of text describing what the list is inside either a `<p>` or `<div>` element:

```
<?xml version="1.0" encoding="UTF-8"?>
<!DOCTYPE html PUBLIC "-//W3C//DTD XHTML 1.0 Transitional//EN"
    "http://www.w3.org/TR/xhtml1/DTD/xhtml1-transitional.dtd">
<html xmlns="http://www.w3.org/1999/xhtml" lang="en">

  <head>
    <title>Example of the value Attribute</title>
  </head>

  <body>
  <h1>Code Download</h1>
  <p>The code download folder contains the following files and folders:</p>

    <ul>
      <li>index.html</li>
```

```
      <li>sampleCode</li>
      <li>images</li>
   </ul>

 </body>
</html>
```

2. Take the following code sample and turn it into XHTML. It contains only a few lines of code, but there are a few things you need to watch out for.

```
<HTML>
  <HEAD>
    <TITLE>Exercise 2</TITLE>
  </HEAD>
  <BODY>
    <H1>The &lt;title&gt; Element</H1>
    The following line shows the title of a document:
    <XMP><title>Exercise 2</title></XMP>
  </BODY>
</HTML>
```

A. Here you can see the XHTML version of the file with the example of the `<title>` element.

Not only did you have to change the `<xmp>` element to either the `<code>` or `<pre>` elements, but you also had to make a lot of changes to capitalization. All of the tags in the old version of the file were written in uppercase—whereas in XHTML all elements and attributes should be in lowercase.

You also had to escape the < and > characters in the `<code>` or `<pre>` elements because, while the `<xmp>` allowed you to put markup inside the element and it would display it, all occurrences of angle brackets that the user should see in XHTML must be escaped using the escape characters covered in Appendix F.

In addition, you could have added the XML declaration, the DOCTYPE declaration, and the namespace identifier in the root element (all shown up to and including the first `<head>` element). And you should have put the line of text before the code into a `<p>` or `<div>` element.

Eventually, you should have ended up with something like this:

```
<?xml version="1.0" encoding="UTF-8"?>
<!DOCTYPE html PUBLIC "-//W3C//DTD XHTML 1.0 Transitional//EN"
    "http://www.w3.org/TR/xhtml1/DTD/xhtml1-transitional.dtd">
<html xmlns="http://www.w3.org/1999/xhtml" lang="en">
  <head>
    <title>Exercise 2</title>
  </head>
  <body>
    <h1>The &lt;title&gt; Element</h1>
    <p>The following line shows the title of a document:</p>
    <code>&lt;title&gt;Exercise 2&lt;/title&gt;</code>
  </body>
</html>
```

Chapter 9

1. Go back to the first Try It Out example in this chapter and add styles to show what bold and italic versions of each font would look like. You should end up with something looking like Figure 9-31.

You are allowed to use only <span> and <br /> elements in the source document and class selectors in the style sheet. You also need to add a top margin to the content of the <div> elements to separate them from each other.

A. First, looking at the XHTML, here is the new structure of the document. I have used the <span> elements to repeat the line about the quick brown fox. Each <span> element has a class attribute whose value is either bold or italic. After each line of text there is a line break element. The <link /> element's href attribute also points to the new style sheet.

Here is the new font-test2.html file:

```
<?xml version="1.0" encoding="iso-8859-1"?>
<!DOCTYPE html PUBLIC "-//W3C//DTD XHTML 1.0 Transitional//EN"
    "http://www.w3.org/TR/xhtml1/DTD/xhtml1-transitional.dtd">
<html xmlns="http://www.w3.org/1999/xhtml" lang="en">

<head>
  <title>Font test</title>
  <link rel="stylesheet" type="text/css" href="font-test2.css" />
</head>

<body>

<div class="arial">
  Arial The quick brown fox jumped over the lazy dog.<br />
  <span class="bold">Arial The quick brown fox jumped over the lazy dog.</span>
  <br />
  <span class="italic">Arial The quick brown fox jumped over the lazy
  dog.</span><br />
</div>

<div class="helvetica">
  Helvetica The quick brown fox jumped over the lazy dog.<br />
  <span class="bold">Helvetica The quick brown fox jumped over the lazy
  dog.</span><br />
  <span class="italic">Helvetica The quick brown fox jumped over the lazy
  dog.</span><br />
</div>

<div class="TimesNewRoman">
  Times New Roman The quick brown fox jumped over the lazy dog.<br />
  <span class="bold">Times New Roman The quick brown fox jumped over the lazy
  dog.</span><br />
  <span class="italic">Times New Roman The quick brown fox jumped over the lazy
  dog.</span><br />
</div>
```

```
<div class="MrsEaves">
  Mrs Eaves The quick brown fox jumped over the lazy dog.<br />
  <span class="bold">Mrs Eaves Bold The quick brown fox jumped over the lazy
    dog.</span><br />
  <span class="italic">Mrs Eaves Italic The quick brown fox jumped over the lazy
    dog.</span><br />
</div>
</body>
</html>
```

Now it's time to look at the `font-test2.css` style sheet. The first new property is the `margin-top` property, which divides up the examples for each font. Then there are new class selectors for the bold style, which uses the `font-weight` property, and the italic style, which uses the `font-style` property.

```
/* CSS Style sheet for font-test.html */

body {background-color:#ffffff;}

div {line-height:28px;
margin-top:20px;}

div.arial {font-family:arial, courier;}
div.helvetica {font-family:Helvetica, courier;}
div.TimesNewRoman {font-family:"Times New Roman", courier;}
div.MrsEaves {font-family:"Mrs Eaves", courier;}

.bold {font-weight:bold;}
.italic {font-style:italic;}
```

2. Take a look at the following XHTML page:

```
<?xml version="1.0" encoding="iso-8859-1"?>
<!DOCTYPE html PUBLIC "-//W3C//DTD XHTML 1.0 Transitional//EN"
    "http://www.w3.org/TR/xhtml1/DTD/xhtml1-transitional.dtd">
<html xmlns="http://www.w3.org/1999/xhtml" lang="en">

<head>
  <title>Font test</title>
  <link rel="stylesheet" type="text/css" href="tableStyles.css" />
</head>

<body>
<table>
  <tr>
    <th>Quantity</th>
    <th>Ingredient</th>
  </tr>
  <tr class="odd">
    <td>3</td>
    <td>Eggs</td>
```

```
        </tr>
        <tr>
          <td>100ml</td>
          <td>Milk</td>
        </tr>
        <tr class="odd">
          <td>200g</td>
          <td>Spinach</td>
        </tr>
        <tr>
          <td>1 pinch</td>
          <td>Cinnamon</td>
        </tr>
      </table>
  </body>
</html>
```

Now create the `tableStyles.css` style sheet that makes this example look like it does in Figure 9-32.

Don't worry about getting the sizes exactly the same as the screenshot, but do make sure you have padding in the cells and a border around the outside. Just to let you know, the white border is created by default in IE and you find out how to remove this in Chapter 10.

A. You can create this style sheet in several ways. Here is one way:

```
/* CSS Style sheet for tableStyles.html */

body {
  background-color:#ffffff;
  font-family:arial, verdana, sans-serif;
  font-size:14px;}

table {
  border-style:solid;
  border-width:1px;
  border-color:#666666;}

th {
  color:#ffffff;
  background-color:#999999;
  font-weight:bold;
  border:none;
  padding:4px;}

tr {background-color:#cccccc;}

tr.odd {background-color:#efefef;}

td {
  color:#000000;
  padding:2px;}
```

Chapter 10

1. In this exercise you will create a linked table of contents that will sit at the top of a long document in an ordered list and link to the headings in the main part of the document.

    The XHTML file, example1.html, is provided with the download code for this book ready for you to create the style sheet. Your style sheet should do the following:

    ❏   Set the styles of all links including active and visited links

    ❏   Make the contents of the list bold

    ❏   Make the background of the list light gray and use padding to ensure the bullet points show

    ❏   Make the width of the links box 250 pixels wide

    ❏   Change the styles of heading bullet points to empty circles

    ❏   Change the style of link bullet points to squares

A. Here is the style sheet for the linked table of contents:

```
body {
  background-color:#ffffff;
  font-family:arial, verdana, sans-serif;
  font-size:12px;}
```

The selector for the first `<ul>` element should have rules for the `list-style` property to be a circle and the `font-weight` property to be bold.

```
ul {
  list-style:circle;
  font-weight:bold;
```

It is also on this first `<ul>` selector that you place the rules for the background of the links, so you should have rules like these in the same declaration. Note how the `padding-left` property ensures that the bullets remain visible.

```
background-color:#efefef;
padding-left:30px;
width:250px;}
```

A second selector should then indicate that a `<ul>` element inside another `<ul>` element should have a `list-style` property with a value of `square` so that the nested linking elements are preceded by squares.

```
ul ul {list-style:square;}
```

Finally, the rest of the rules indicate how the links should appear:

```
a:link {
  color:#0033ff;;
  text-decoration:none;}
```

```
a:visited {
  color:#0066ff;
  text-decoration:none;}

a:active {
  text-decoration:underline;}

a:link:hover {
  color:#003399;
  background-color:#e9e9e9;
  text-decoration:underline;}
```

2. In this exercise you will test your CSS positioning skills. You should create a page that represents the links to the different sections of the chapter in a very different way. Each of the sections will be shown in a different block, and each block will be absolutely positioned in a diagonal top left to bottom right direction. The middle box should appear on top as is shown in Figure 10-35.

You can find the source XHTML file (exercise2.html) with the download code for this chapter.

A. First you needed to set up some background properties for the <body> element:

```
body {
  background-color:#ffffff;
  font-family:arial, verdana, sans-serif;
  font-size:12px;}
```

In order to give each <div> element a border, fixed width, and padding, the rules should be placed on a selector for all <div> elements. These should also have a background-color property (in this case with a value setting it to white) to prevent the text from becoming a mess (because otherwise boxes are transparent):

```
div {
  background-color:#ffffff;
  padding:10px;
  border-style:groove; border-width:4px; border-color:#999999;
  width:300px;}
```

Each <div> element then individually needs different positioning properties to make sure they appear in diagonal positions. The z-index property must also be set to present the chosen boxes in the correct order.

```
div.page1 {
  position:absolute;
  top:70px;
  z-index:2;
  background-color:#f2f2f2;}

div.page2 {
  position:absolute;
  top:170px; left:100px;
  z-index:3;}
```

```
div.page3 {
   position:absolute;
   top:270px; left:200px;
   z-index:1;
   background-color:#efefef;}
```

Chapter 11

1. Take a look at the page shown in Figure 11-25. List all of the different elements on the page that would have been listed in the design stage, and put them together in their relevant grouping or categories.

For example, for the search box you might list the following:

```
Search Box
   Text input
   Search button
```

A. Exactly how you write down your list of elements for a page is up to you, but when coming up with this design, these were the elements I decided to fit on the page:

```
Search Box
   Text input
   Search button
Logo and branding
Navigation
   Home
   Products
   Stockists
   About Us
   Contact Us
Main Page Content
   Heading
   Text
   Image
Testimonials (x2)
Copyright notice
```

2. Look again at Figure 11-25 and use tables to create a layout similar to this one. In order to help you, try working out where the grid of the table might be. Hint: One table contains the whole page, and the search bar, logo and branding, navigation, main page, and footer each live in their own rows. Two tables (one inside the other) are nested in the main page.

A. This page is built entirely in one fixed-width table. The search bar, logo, navigation bar, main body of the page, and footer all live in separate rows of the table.

In the main body of the table is a nested table, which contains a column for the main text and picture, and a second column to the right for the testimonials about the company. After the paragraph of text there is another table with two cells—one containing the picture and the other containing the text to be displayed next to the picture.

```
<?xml version="1.0" encoding="UTF-8"?>
<!DOCTYPE html PUBLIC "-//W3C//DTD XHTML 1.0 Transitionalt//EN"
    "http://www.w3.org/TR/xhtml1/DTD/xhtml1-transitional.dtd">
<html xmlns="http://www.w3.org/1999/xhtml" lang="en">
<head>
  <title>Wheely Good Bins</title>
  <link rel="stylesheet" type="text/css" href="ch11_exercise.css" />
</head>
<body>
<table width="700" border="0" cellpadding="0" cellspacing="0" align="center"
class="page">

  <tr class="searchBar">
    <td align="right">
      <form action="search.asp" method="post" name="frmSearch">
        <input type="text" size="18" name="txtSearch" /> 
        <input type="submit" value="Search" />
      </form>
   </td>
  </tr>

  <tr>
    <td>
    <img src="images/masthead.gif" width="700" height="80" alt="LearnLatin
        Logo" />
   </td>
  </tr>

  <tr>
    <td class="nav">Home | <a href="">Products</a> | <a href="">Stockists
</a> | <a href="">About Us</a> | <a href="">Contact Us</a>
   </td>
  </tr>

  <tr>
    <td>
      <table width="700" border="0" cellpadding="0" cellspacing="0">
        <tr>
          <td valign="top" width="550" class="main">
            <h2>World Class Wheely Bins</h2>
            <p>Lorem ipsum dolor sit amet... </p>
            <table width="550" cellpadding="0" cellspacing="0" border="0">
              <tr>
                <td valign="top">
                  <img src="images/bin.jpg" width="200" alt="Picture of bin"
                      class="image" />
                </td>
                <td valign="top">
                  <p>Mauris quis urna. Donec sodales, risus...</p>
                </td>
              </tr>
            </table>
          </td>
```

651

```
                    <td valign="top" width="100" class="quotes">
                        Our first order from Wheely Good Bins was for over 4000 bins,
                        these were supplied in record time and have lasted very well.
                        <br /> <span class="credit">Tom Winters - CEO BoxTree Hotels
                        </span><br /> We take out wheely bins to all kinds of functions -
                        their smart appearance and easy clean design makes them ideal for
                        the most formal of functions.<br />
                        <span class="credit">Bob Crank - Event Catering</span>
                    </td>
                </tr>
            </table>
        </td>
    </tr>

    <tr class="footer">
        <td>&copy; 2004 Example.org</td>
    </tr>

</table>
</body>
</html>
```

Chapter 12

1. In this exercise you should add a second page to the Try It Out form at the end of the chapter (`registration.html`). The table that follows shows the new items you must add to the form.

Information	Form Control	Required
Address 1	Text input	Yes
Address 2	Text input	No
Town/Suburb	Text input	No
City/State	Text input	Yes
ZIP Code	Text input	Yes

You should also add the following:

❑   An indication at the top of the page as to how much of the form the user has completed

❑   A Back button and a Proceed button at the bottom (instead of the Submit button)

When you have finished the page should look something like Figure 12-31 (`registration2.html`).

A. Here is the code for the `registration2.html` file. It starts off like many of the other examples that use an external CSS style sheet:

```
<html>
  <head>
    <title>Try it out</title>
    <link rel="stylesheet" type="text/css" href="registration.css" />
  </head>
  <body>
```

Next is a table that indicates there are three pages to the form. These use different styles to indicate whether the user is currently on that step (indicated with the class stepOn):

```
<table class="steps">
  <tr>
    <td class="stepOff">Login details</td>
    <td class="stepOn">Contact details</td>
    <td class="stepOff">Confirm details</td>
  </tr>
</table>
```

Next comes the actual form itself. The form is laid out inside a table so that the labels and form elements align neatly. Each of the form elements has a <label> element whose for attribute has a value that corresponds with the id of the form control:

```
<form name="frmExample" action="" method="post">
  <fieldset>
  <legend>Contact details:</legend>

  <table>
    <tr>
      <td class="label"><label for="address1">Address 1:</label></td>
      <td class="form">
        <input type="text" name="txtAddress1" id="address1" size="30" />
      </td>
    </tr>
    <tr>
      <td class="label"><label for="address2">Address 2:</label></td>
      <td class="form">
        <input type="text" name="txtAddress2" id="address2" size="30" />
      </td>
    </tr>
    <tr>
      <td class="label"><label for="town">Town/Suburb:</label></td>
      <td class="form">
        <input type="text" name="txtTown" id="town" size="12" />
      </td>
    </tr>
    <tr>
      <td class="label"><label for="city">City/State:</label></td>
      <td class="form">
        <input type="text" name="txtState" id="city" size="12" />
      </td>
    </tr>
    <tr>
      <td class="label"><label for="postcode">Postal/Zip Code:</label></td>
      <td class="form">
```

```
            <input type="text" name="txtPostCode" id="postcode" size="12" />
      </td>
    </tr>
  </table><br />
```

Finally, a Back button is on the left side of the page and a Proceed button is on the right side. These are again positioned using a table. A key shows that the asterisk indicates a form field must be filled in:

```
<table class="steps">
  <tr>
    <td class="back"><input type="submit" value="Back" /></td>
    <td class="proceed"><input type="submit" value="Proceed" /></td>
  </tr>
</table>
</fieldset>
<br /><span class="required">*</span> = required
</form>

</body>
</html>
```

Chapter 13

1. Take a look at the XHTML page for a cookery site shown in Figure 13-8.

The following is the code for this page. Create a cut-down version that shows only the name and ingredients in XHTML MP that a shopper can see on his or her phone in the supermarket. You might want to leave on the preparation time and cooking time, and as a hint, all of the element names are still available in XHTML MP.

```
<?xml version="1.0" encoding="UTF-8"?>
<!DOCTYPE html PUBLIC "-//W3C//DTD XHTML 1.0 Transitional//EN"
    "http://www.w3.org/TR/xhtml1/DTD/xhtml1-transitional.dtd">
<html xmlns="http://www.w3.org/1999/xhtml" lang="en">

<head>
  <title>Roving Recipes - Summer Chicken</title>
  <link rel="stylesheet" type="text/css" href="exercise1.css" />
</head>

<body>

<h1>Summer Chicken</h1>
  <p>This recipe is for a light summer meal with strips of fried chicken
    breast on a base of saffron cous cous with steamed vegetables and pine
    nuts.</p>

  <div>
    <span class="leftColumn">Preparation time</span>
    <span class ="rightColumn">10 minutes</span>
  </div>
```

```
<div>
  <span class ="leftColumn">Cooking time</span>
  <span class ="rightColumn">15 minutes</span>
</div>
<div>
  <span class ="leftColumn">Serves</span>
  <span class ="rightColumn">2</span>
</div>

<div class="page">
  <div class="ingredients">

    <h2>Ingredients</h2>
      <ul>
        <li>200g chicken breast</li>
        <li>200g cous cous</li>
        <li>2 stems saffron</li>
        <li>50g raisins</li>
        <li>50g pine nuts</li>
        <li>50g sweet corn</li>
        <li>1 zucchini</li>
        <li>1 green pepper</li>
        <li>1 lemon</li>
        <li>2 teaspoons olive oil</li>
        <li>Fresh coriander</li>
      </ul>

  </div>
  <div class="cooking">

    <h2>Cooking</h2>
      <ol>
        <li>Prepare the dressing</li>
            <li><ol>
              <li>Juice the lemon</li>
              <li>Add in the olive oil</li>
              <li>Add in finely chopped coriander</li>
            </ol></li>
        <li>Add raisins to the cous cous and place in a heatproof bowl that
            you have a lid for</li>
        <li>Boil 300ml of water and add to the bowl of cous cous and cover;
            then <b>let it stand for 15 minutes</b></li>
        <li>Steam pepper and zucchini</li>
        <li>Add chicken to frying pan or wok on high heat for 5 minutes,
            turning regularly so all sides are brown</li>
        <li>Put pine nuts and sweet corn in the pan with the chicken, turn
            down heat, and leave for a further 2 minutes, stirring
            occasionally</li>
        <li>Remove chicken from pan and place to one side</li>
        <li>Add zucchini and pepper to the pan</li>
        <li>Loosen the cous cous with a fork and add to pan and stir for
            1 minute</li>
        <li>Serve cous cous on plate, place chicken on top, and pour over
            dressing</li>
```

```
        </ol>
      </div>
    </div>

</body>
</html>
```

A. The main point to note about this exercise in which you change the XHTML page into an XHTML MP page is that you need to use the XHTML MP DTD. You should remove the cooking instructions.

The elements and attributes for XHTML MP were not covered in great detail in this chapter, because you already knew them from earlier on in the book; they are the same as their HTML counterparts.

```
<?xml version="1.0" charset="iso-8859-1"?>
<!DOCTYPE html PUBLIC "-//WAPFORUM//DTD XHTML Mobile 1.0//EN"
  "http://www.wapforum.org/DTD/xhtml-mobile10.dtd">
<html xmlns="http://www.w3.org/1999/xhtml">
<head>
  <title>Summer Chicken</title>
  <link rel="stylesheet" type="text/css" href="article.css" />
</head>
<body>
<h1>Summer Chicken</h1>
  <div>
    <span class="leftColumn">Prepare:</span>
    <span class ="rightColumn">10min</span>
  </div>
  <div>
    <span class ="leftColumn">Cook:</span>
    <span class ="rightColumn">15min</span>
  </div>
  <div>
    <span class ="leftColumn">Serves</span>
    <span class ="rightColumn">2</span>
  </div>

      <h2>Ingredients</h2>
        <ul>
          <li>200g chicken breast</li>
          <li>200g cous cous</li>
          <li>2 stems saffron</li>
          <li>50g raisins</li>
          <li>50g pine nuts</li>
          <li>50g sweetcorn</li>
          <li>1 courgette</li>
          <li>1 green pepper</li>
          <li>1 lemon</li>
          <li>2 teaspoons olive oil</li>
          <li>fresh corriander</li>
        </ul>
```

```
<ul>

</body>
</html>
```

This should look something like Figure A-1 when you have finished.

Figure A-1

Chapter 14

1. Create a script to write out the multiplication table for the number 5 from 1 to 20 using a `while` loop.

A. This exercise uses code very similar to `ch14_eg09.html`; in fact, you need only to change the appropriate numbers from the example—otherwise it is identical. The file `ch14_eg09.html` calculated the 3 multiplication table up to 10. This example calculates the 5 multiplication table up to 20.

The example is based around a counter (to work out where you are in your tables); each time the code is run the counter increments by 1. So, you need to make sure the counter can go up to 20, rather than 10. This goes in the condition of the `while` loop:

```
while (i < 21) {
```

Then you need to change the multiplier, which is both written out and used in the calculation, as you can see where there are the number 5s in this line:

```
document.write(i + " x 5 = " + (i * 5) + "<br />" );
```

The final code should look like this:

```
<script type="text/JavaScript">
i = 1
while (i < 21) {
 document.write(i + " x 5 = " + (i * 5) + "<br />" );
  i ++
}
</script>
```

As you can see, this code is no longer than the loop in ch14_eg09.html, but it writes out twice the numbers, which really shows you the power of using loops in your code.

2. Modify ch14_eg06.html so that it can say one of three things:

- ❑ "Good Morning" to visitors coming to the page before 12 a.m. (using an if statement).

- ❑ "Good Afternoon" to visitors coming to the page between 12 and 6 p.m. (again using an if statement. (Hint: You might need to use a logical operator.)

- ❑ "Good Evening" to visitors coming to the page after 6 p.m. up until midnight (again using an if statement).

A. The following simple script modified from ch14_eg16.html will greet the user with the words "Good Morning" in the morning, "Good Afternoon" in the afternoon, and "Good Evening" in the evening.

It uses the getHours() method of the date object to determine the time and then uses if statements to check the appropriate time for each statement presented to the user.

Note how the afternoon uses a logical operator to check that it is after 12 but before 6 p.m.

```
<script type="text/JavaScript">
  date = new Date();
  time = date.getHours();

  if (time < 12)
  document.write('Good Morning');

  if (time > 12 && time < 18)
  document.write('Good Afternoon')

  if (time > 18)
  document.write('Good Evening');
</script>
```

Chapter 15

1. Your task is to create a validation function for the competition form in Figure 15-17.

The function should check that the user has done the following things:

- ❑ Entered his or her name

- ❑ Provided a valid e-mail address

    ❏   Selected one of the radio buttons as an answer to the question

    ❏   Given an answer for the tiebreaker question and that it is no more than 20 words

These should be in the order that the controls appear on the form.

Here is the code for the form:

```
<form name="frmCompetition" action="competition.asp" method="post" onsubmit=
"return validate(this);">
<h2>An Example Competition Form <br />(Sorry, there are no real prizes!)</h2>
<p> To enter the drawing to win a case of Jenny's Jam, first answer
this question: "What color are strawberries?" Then provide an answer for
the tie-breaker question: "I would like to win a case of Jenny's Jam
because..." in no more than 20 words.</p>
<table>
  <tr>
    <td class="formTitle">Name: </td>
    <td><input type="text" name="txtName" size="18" /></td>
  </tr>
  <tr>
    <td class="formTitle">Email: </td>
    <td><input type="text" name="txtEmail" size="18" /></td>
  </tr>
  <tr>
    <td class="formTitle">Answer: </td>
    <td><input type="radio" name="radAnswer" value="Red" /> Red<br />
        <input type="radio" name="radAnswer" value="Gray" /> Gray<br />
        <input type="radio" name="radAnswer" value="Blue" /> Blue
    </td>
  </tr>
  <tr>
    <td class="formTitle">Tie breaker <br/ ><small>(no more than 20 words)
    </small>:
</td>
    <td><textarea name="txtTieBreaker" cols="30" rows="3" /></textarea></td>
  </tr>
  <tr>
    <td class="formTitle"></td>
    <td><input type="submit" value="Enter now" /></td>
  </tr>
</table>

</form>
```

A.   The `validate()` function for this example uses techniques you learned about in Chapter 15. It starts off by setting a variable called `returnValue` that will either be `true` or `false` when the function finishes running—it starts off with a value of `true`, which is switched to `false` if any of the form fields fail to meet the requirements.

```
<script type="text/JavaScript">

  function validate(form) {
    var returnValue = true
```

First you have to check whether the value of the txtName field has a value in it:

```
var name=form.txtName.value
if (name=="")
  {
     returnValue = false;
     alert("You must enter a name")
     document.frmCompetition.txtName.focus();
  }
```

Next you have to check whether the e-mail address follows the format it is supposed to. If the address is empty it will not match the regular expression; therefore you do not need to check if the control is empty first:

```
var email=form.txtEmail.value
var rxEmail = /^\ w(\.?[\w-])*@\w(\.?[\w-])*\.[a-z]{2,6}(\.[a-z]{2})?$/i;

if (!rxEmail.test(email))
  {
     returnValue = false;
     alert("You must enter a valid email address")
     document.frmCompetition.txtEmail.focus()
  }
```

Next you must loop through the radio buttons to see if an answer was provided. This involves looping through the buttons and testing whether each button has the checked property. If a radio button has been checked then a variable (in this case called radioChosen) is changed to have a value of true. Once all of the radio buttons have been looped through there is a conditional if statement checking whether the value of this attribute is true or false.

```
var radioChosen = false;
var radioButtons = form.radAnswer;
for (var i=0; i<radioButtons.length; i++) {
if (radioButtons[i].checked)
  {
  radioChosen=true;
  }
}

if (radioChosen == false) {
  returnValue = false;
  alert("You did not answer the question");
}
```

Finally you come to the <textarea> element and the tiebreaker. This one needs to have a value but must not be longer than 20 words. To start then, it is checked to see if it has any value at all:

```
var tieBreaker=form.txtTieBreaker.value
if (tieBreaker=="")
  {
     returnValue = false;
```

```
    alert("You must enter an answer for the tie breaker")
    document.frmCompetition.txtTieBreaker.focus();
}
```

Then the value entered is split into separate words using the split() function of the string object and a regular expression. Because the split() function splits the string after spaces, you can check how many words were entered simply by finding out the length of the array created by the split() function. Because the array is zero-based, you need to find out whether the number of items in the array is less than or equal to 20. If there are too many words, the user is warned and told how many words she entered in order to help her make the response shorter.

```
var tieBreakerWords = tieBreaker.split(/\s+/g);
wordCount = tieBreakerWords.length;

if (wordCount > 20) {
  returnValue = false;
  alert("Your tie breaker answer must be no more than 20 words. You entered "+
        wordCount+ "words.");
  document.frmCompetition.txtTieBreaker.focus();
}
```

That is the final test and the returnValue (either true or false) indicates whether the form will be submitted or not.

```
    return returnValue
}

</script>
```

XHTML Element Reference

This appendix is a quick reference to the elements that are in the HTML and XHTML recommendations. They are listed with the attributes each element can carry and a brief description of their purpose.

You will see deprecated elements marked with the word "deprecated" next to them. You should avoid using these elements where possible. It is also recommended that stylistic markup and elements should also be replaced with CSS rules.

The first version of Internet Explorer (IE) and Netscape (N) that supported the element are given next to the element's name, starting with IE 3 and N3. Where you see the word "all," it is supported in all browsers from IE 3 and N3 and later. Note, however, that not all of the attributes will work with the same versions of the browsers—some attributes were introduced in later versions.

Following are a few notes on syntax:

❑   All element names should be given in lowercase.

❑   Any attribute listed without a value should have the name of the attribute repeated as its value in order to be XHTML-compliant; for example:

```
disabled = "disabled"
```

❑   All attribute values should also be given inside double quotation marks.

Core Attributes

Unless otherwise stated, the core attributes can be used with all of the elements in this appendix.

class = name	Specifies a class for the element to associate it with rules in a style sheet
dir = ltr | rtl	Specifies the direction for rendering text (left to right or right to left)

Continues

id = name	Defines a unique identification value for that element within the document
lang = language	Specifies the (human) language for the content of the element
onclick = script	Specifies a script to be called when the user clicks the mouse over this element
ondblclick = script	Specifies a script to be called when the user double-clicks the mouse over this element
onkeydown = script	Specifies a script to be called when the user presses down on a key while this element has focus
onkeypress = script	Specifies a script to be called when the user presses and releases a key while this element has focus
onkeyup = script	Specifies a script to be called when the user releases a key while this element has focus
onmousedown = script	Specifies a script to be called when the user presses down on the mouse button while the cursor is over this element's content
onmousemove = script	Specifies a script to be called when the user moves the mouse cursor while over this element's content
onmouseout = script	Specifies a script to be called when the mouse is moved off this element's content
onmouseover = script	Specifies a script to be called when the mouse is moved over this element's content
onmouseup = script	Specifies a script to be called when the user releases a mouse button while the cursor is over this element's content
style = style	Specifies an inline CSS style rule for the element
title = string	Specifies a title for the element
xml:lang	Specifies the (human) language for the content of the element

<a> (all)

Defines a link. The href or name attribute must be specified.

accesskey = key_character	Defines a hotkey/keyboard shortcut for this anchor
charset = encoding	Specifies a character set used to encode the target document
coords = x_y coordinates	Specifies a list of coordinates
href = url	Specifies the URL of the hyperlink target

hreflang = *language_code*	Specifies the language encoding for the target of the link
rel = *relationship* (same | next | parent | previous | string)	Indicates the relationship of the document to the target document
rev = *relationship*	Indicates the reverse relationship of the target document to this one
shape = circ | circle | poly | polygon | rect | rectangle	Defines the shape of a region
tabindex = *number*	Defines this element's position in the tabbing order
target = *<window_name>* | _parent | _blank | _top | _self	Defines the name of the frame or window that should load the linked document
type = *MIME_type*	Defines the MIME type of the target

<abbr> (IE 4+, N6+)

Indicates that the content of the element is an abbreviation.

<acronym> (IE 4+ N6+)

Indicates that the content of the element is an acronym.

<address> (all)

Indicates that the content of the element is an address.

<applet> Deprecated (all)

Used to place a Java applet or executable code in the page.

Takes only the attributes listed in the table that follows.

align = top | middle | bottom | left | right | absmiddle | baseline | absbottom | texttop	Aligns the applet within the containing element
alt = *text*	Specifies alternative text to replace the <applet> for browsers that support the element, but are unable to execute it

Continues

665

archive = *url*	Specifies a class archive that must be downloaded to the browser and searched for
class = *name*	Specifies a class for the element to associate it with rules in a style sheet
code = *classname*	Specifies the class name of the code (required)
codebase = *url*	Specifies a URL from which the code can be downloaded
height = *number*	Specifies the height of the <applet> in pixels
hspace = *number*	Specifies the width to allow to the left and right of the <applet> in pixels
id = *name*	Specifies a unique ID for the element
name = *name*	Specifies the name of this instance of the applet
object = *data*	Specifies the filename of the compiled code to run
vspace = *number*	Specifies the height to allow to the top and bottom of the <applet> in pixels
width = *number*	Specifies the width of the <applet> in pixels

<param> (all)

name = *name*	Specifies the name of the parameter
type = *MIME_type*	Defines the MIME type of the parameter
value = *string*	Defines the value of the parameter

<area> (all)

Used to specify coordinates for a clickable area or hotspot in an image map.

accesskey = *key_character*	Defines a hotkey/keyboard shortcut for this area
alt = *text*	Specifies alternative text for the area if the image cannot be loaded
coords = *string*	Specifies a list of coordinates for the area
href = *url*	Specifies the URL of the hyperlink target
name = *string*	Specifies a name for the element that can be used to identify it
nohref	Specifies that there is not a document associated with the area

notab	Specifies that this element does not take part in the tabbing order for the document
shape = circ | circle | poly | polygon | rect | rectangle	Defines the shape of a region
tabindex = number	Defines this element's position in the tabbing order
target = <window_name> | _parent | _blank | _top | _self	Defines the name of the frame or window that should load the linked document.

<b> (all)

The content of the element should be displayed in a bold font.

<base>

Specifies a base URL for the links in a document.

Supports only the attributes listed in the table that follows.

href = url	Specifies the URL of the base for the links in this document
id = id	Specifies a unique identifier for the element
target = <window_name> | _parent | _blank | _top | _self	Defines the name of the frame or window that should load the linked document

<basefont> Deprecated (all)

Specifies a base font to be the default font when rendering a document.

Supports only the attributes listed in the table that follows.

color = color	Specifies the color of text in this element
face = font_family_name	Specifies the font family in this element
size = value	Specifies the size of the font (required)

<bdo> (IE 5+, N6+)

Turns off the bidirectional rendering algorithm for selected fragments of text.

dir = ltr | rtl	Specifies the font family in this element

<bgsound> (IE only—IE 3+)

Specifies a background sound or audio file to be played when the page is loaded.

loop = number	Specifies the number of times the audio file should be played (can be an integer or the keyword infinite)
src = url	Specifies the URL of the audio file to be played.

<big> (IE 4+, N4+)

Renders text in a font size larger than its containing element.

<blink> (Netscape only—N3+)

The content of the element blinks on and off. Netscape only.

<blockquote> (all)

The content of the element is a quotation. Usually used for a paragraph quote or longer (otherwise use the <q> element).

cite = url	Specifies a URL for the source of the quote

<body> (all)

Specifies the start and end of the body section of a page.

accesskey = key_character	Defines a hotkey/keyboard shortcut for the
alink = color	Specifies the color of active links
background = url	Specifies the URL for a background image to be used as wallpaper for the background of the whole document
bgcolor = color	Specifies a background color for the document
bgproperties = fixed	Image does not scroll with document content
leftmargin = number	Specifies a margin in pixels for the left of the document
link = color	Specifies the color of unvisited links
onload = script event handler	Specifies a script to run when the page loads

onunload = *script event handler*	Specifies a script to run when the page is unloaded
text = *color*	Specifies a color for the text in the document
topmargin = *number*	Specifies a margin in pixels for the top of the document
vlink = *color*	Specifies the color of visited links

 (all)

Inserts a line break.

Supports only the attributes listed in the table that follows.

class = *name*	Specifies a class for the element to associate it with rules in a style sheet
clear = left | right | none | all	Breaks the flow of the page and moves the break down until the specified margin is clear.
id = *id*	Specifies a unique identifier for this element
style = *style*	Specifies inline CSS style rules for this element
title = *string*	Specifies a title for this element

<button> (IE 4+, N3+)

Creates an HTML button. Any enclosed markup is used as the button's caption.

accesskey = *key_character*	Defines a hotkey/keyboard shortcut for this
disabled = disabled	Disables the button, preventing user intervention
name = *name*	Specifies a name for the form control passed to the form's processing application as part of the name/value pair (required)
onblur = *script*	Specifies a script to run when the mouse moves off the button
onfocus = *script*	Specifies a script to run when the element gains focus
tabindex = *number*	Defines this element's position in the tabbing order
type = button | submit | reset	Specifies the type of button
value = *string*	Specifies the value of the parameter sent to the processing application as part of the name/value pair (required)

<caption> (all)

The content of this element specifies a caption to be placed next to a table.

`align = top|bottom|right|left`	For IE this specifies the horizontal alignment of the caption; in Netscape it sets vertical position
`valign = bottom|top`	Specifies the vertical position of the caption

<center> Deprecated (all)

The content of this element (and child elements) should be centered on the page.

<cite> (all)

The content of the element is a citation and tends to be rendered in italics.

<code> (all)

The content of the element is code and should be rendered in a fixed width font.

<col> (IE 3+, N4+)

Specifies column-based defaults for a table.

`align = center	left	right	justify	char`	Specifies the alignment of the column
`bgcolor = color`	Specifies a background color for the column
`char = string`	Specifies the alignment character for text within the cells
`charoff = string`	Specifies the offset character that the alignment character is set to
`span = number`	Number of columns affected by the <col> tag
`valign = bottom	top`	Specifies the vertical alignment of content within the element
`width = number`	Specifies the width of the column in pixels

<colgroup> (IE 3+, N4+)

Used to contain a group of columns.

align = center	left	right | justify | char	Specifies the horizontal alignment of content within the column
bgcolor = color	Specifies the background color for the group of columns
char = string	Specifies the alignment character for text within the cells
charoff = string	Specifies the offset character that the alignment character is set to
valign = bottom | top	Specifies the vertical alignment of content within the element
width = number	Specifies the width of the column group in pixels

<comment> (IE 4+ only)

The content is a comment that will not be displayed (IE 4+ only—not part of HTML or XHTML)

Supports only the attributes shown in the table that follows.

id = string	Specifies a unique identifier for the element
Lang = language_type	Specifies the language of the comment
xml:lang = language_type	Specifies the language of the comment

<dd> (all)

The definition of an item in a definition list. This is usually indented from other text.

<del> (IE 4+, N6+)

The content of the element has been deleted from an earlier version of the document.

cite = url	Specifies a URL for justification of deletion
datetime = date	Specifies the date and time it was deleted

<dfn> (all)

Defines an instance of a term.

<dir> Deprecated (all)

The content of the element is rendered in a directory-style file list.

type = bullet	Specifies the type of bullet used to display the list

<li> (all)

type = *format*	Specifies the type of bullet used to display the list item
value = *number*	Specifies the number of the list item

<div> (all)

A containing element to hold other elements, defining a section of a page. This is a block level container.

align = center | left | right	Specifies the alignment of text within the <div> element
nowrap = nowrap	Prevents word-wrapping within this <div> element

<dl> (all)

Denotes a definition list.

compact = compact	Makes the list more vertically compact

<dt> (all)

Denotes a definition term within a definition list.

<em> (all)

The element content is emphasized text, and is usually rendered in an italic font.

<embed> (all)

Embeds documents in a page that require another supporting application.

align = absbottom | absmiddle | baseline | bottom | left | middle | right | texttop | top	Specifies the alignment within the containing element
border = *number*	Specifies the width of the border around the embedded object in pixels

height = *number*	Specifies the height of the embedded object in pixels
hidden = hidden	Specifies that the embedded object should be hidden
hspace = *number*	Specifies the amount of additional space to be added to the left and right of the embedded object
name = *name*	Specifies a name for the embedded object
palette=foreground|background	Sets foreground and background colors of the embedded object
pluginspage = *url*	Specifies the URL of the page where the plug-in associated with the object can be downloaded
src = *url*	Specifies the URL of the data to be used by the object
type = *MIME_type*	Specifies the MIME type of the data used by the object
units = en|ems|pixels	Sets units for height and width attributes
vpsace = *number*	Specifies the amount of additional space to be added above and below the embedded object
width = *number*	Specifies the width of the embedded object in pixels

<fieldset> (IE 4+, N6+)

Creates a box around the contained elements indicating that they are related items in a form.

| align = center\|left\|right | Specifies the alignment of the group of elements |
| tabindex = *number* | Defines this <fieldset>'s position in the tabbing order |

<font> Deprecated (all)

Specifies the typeface, size, and color of the font to be used for text within the element.

color = *color*	Specifies the color of text in this element.
face = *font_family_list*	Specifies the family of font to be used for the text in this element
size = *value*	Specifies the size of the text used in this element

<form> (all)

Containing element for form controls and elements.

accept-charset = *list*	Specifies a list of accepted character sets the processing application can handle
action = *url*	Specifies the URL of the processing application that will handle the form
enctype = *encoding*	Specifies the encoding method for form values
method = get | post	Specifies how the data gets sent from the browser to the processing application
onreset = *script*	Specifies a script that is run when the form values are reset
onsubmit = *script*	Specifies a script that is run before the form is submitted
target = *<window_name>* | _parent | _blank | _top | _self	Defines the name of the frame or window that should load the results of the form.

<frame> (all)

Specifies a frame within a frameset.

Supports only the attributes listed in the table that follows.

[event_name] = *script*	The intrinsic events supported by most elements
bordercolor = *color*	Specifies the color of the border of the frame
class = *name*	Specifies a class name to associate styles with the element
frameborder = no | yes | 0 | 1	Specifies the presence or absence of a frame border
Id = *string*	Specifies a unique value for the element
lang = *language_type*	Specifies the language used for the content of the frame
longdesc = *url*	Specifies a URL for a description of the content of the frame
marginheight = *number*	Specifies the height of the margin for the frame in pixels
marginwidth = *number*	Specifies the width of the margin for the image in pixels
noresize = *noresize*	Specifies that the frame cannot be resized
scrolling = auto | yes | no	Specifies whether the frame can have scrollbars if the content does not fit in the space in the browser
style = *style*	Specifies inline CSS style rules
src = *url*	Specifies a URL for the location of the content for that frame
title = *title*	Specifies a title for the frame

<noframes> (all)

The content of this element should be displayed if the browser does not support frames.

<frameset> (all)

Specifies a frameset containing multiple frames (and possibly other nested framesets). This element replaces the `<body>` element in a document.

`border = number`	Specifies the width of the borders for each frame in the frameset
`bordercolor = color`	Specifies the color of the borders for frames in the frameset
`cols = list`	Specifies the number of columns in the frameset allowing you to control layout of the frameset
`frameborder = no | yes | 0 | 1`	Specifies whether borders will be present for the frames in this frameset
`framespacing = number`	Specifies the space between each frame in pixels
`onblur = script`	Specifies a script to run when the mouse moves off the frameset
`onload = script`	Specifies a script to run when the frameset loads
`onunload = script`	Specifies a script to run when the frameset is unloaded
`rows = number`	Specifies the number of rows in a frameset allowing you to control the layout of the frameset

<head> (all)

Container element for heading information *about* the document; its content will not be displayed in the browser.

Supports only the attributes listed in the table that follows.

`class = classname`	Specifies a class to associate style rules with this element
`dir = ltr | rtl`	Specifies the direction of text within this element
`Id = string`	Specifies a unique identifier for this element
`lang = language_type`	Specifies the language used in this element
`profile = url`	Specifies a URL for a profile of the document
`xml:lang = language_type`	Specifies the language used in this element

\<h*n*> (all)

Headings from \<h1> (largest) through to \<h6> (smallest).

align = left | center | right	Specifies the horizontal alignment of the header within its containing element

\<hr /> (all)

Creates a horizontal rule across the page (or containing element).

Supports only the attributes listed in the table that follows.

[event_name] = *script*	The intrinsic events supported by most elements
align = center | left | right	Specifies the horizontal alignment of the rule
class = *classname*	Specifies a class for the element to associate it with rules in a style sheet
color = *color*	Specifies the color of the horizontal rule
dir = ltr | rtl	Specifies the direction of the text
id = *string*	Specifies a unique identifier for this element
noshade = *noshade*	Specifies that there should not be a 3D shading on the rule
style = *string*	Specifies inline CSS style rules for the element
title = *string*	Specifies a title for the element
width = *number*	Specifies the width of the rule in pixels or as a percentage of the containing element

\<html> (all)

Containing element for an HTML or XHTML page.

class = *classname*	Specifies a class for the element to associate it with rules in a style sheet
dir = ltr | rtl	Specifies the direction of the text within the element
id = *string*	Specifies a unique identifier for this element
lang = *language_type*	Specifies the language used in this element
version = *url*	Specifies the version of HTML used in the document—replaced by the DOCTYPE declaration in XHTML

xmlns = *uri*	Specifies namespaces used in XHTML documents
xml:lang = *language_type*	Specifies the language used in this element

<i> (all)

The content of this element should be rendered in an italic font.

<iframe> (IE 3+, N6+)

Creates an inline floating frame within a page.

align = absbottom | absmiddle | baseline | bottom | top | left | middle | right | texttop | top	Specifies the alignment of the frame in relation to surrounding content or margins
frameborder = no | yes | 0 | 1	Specifies the presence of a border: 1 enables borders, 0 disables them
height = *number*	Specifies the height of the frame in pixels
longdesc = *url*	Specifies a URL for a description of the content of the frame
Marginheight = *number*	Specifies the space above and below the frame and surrounding content in pixels
marginwidth = *number*	Specifies the space to the left and right of the frame and surrounding content in pixels
scrolling = auto | yes | no	Specifies whether scrollbars should be allowed to appear if the content is too large for the frame
src = *url*	Specifies the URL of the file to be displayed in the frame
width = *number*	Specifies the width of the frame in pixels

<img> (all)

Embeds an image within a document.

align = absbottom | absmiddle | baseline | bottom | top | left | middle | right | texttop | top	Specifies the alignment of the image in relation to the content that surrounds it
alt = *text*	Specifies alternative text if the application is unable to load the image (required); also used in accessibility devices

Continues

border = *number*	Specifies the width of the border of the image in pixels—you must use this property if the image is a link to prevent borders from appearing
controls	Displays playback controls for video clips (IE 3 only)
dynsrc = *url*	Specifies the URL of a video clip to be played
height = number	Specifies the height of the image in pixels
hspace = *number*	Specifies the amount of additional space to be added to the left and right of the image
ismap = *ismap*	Specifies whether the image is a server-side image map
longdesc = *url*	Specifies a URL for a description of the content of the image
loop = *number*	Specifies the number of times the video should be played; can take a value of infinite
lowsrc = *url*	Specifies a URL for a low-resolution version of the image that can be displayed while the full image is loading
name = *name*	Specifies a name for the element
onabort = *script*	Specifies a script to run if loading of the image is aborted
onerror = *script*	Specifies a script to run if there is an error loading the image
onload = *script*	Specifies a script to run when the image has loaded
src = *url*	Specifies the URL of the image
start=fileopen| mouseover | number	Specifies when to play a video clip
usemap = *url*	Specifies the map containing coordinates and links that define the links for the image (server-side image map)
vspace = *number*	Specifies the amount of additional space to be added above and below the image
width = *name*	Specifies the width of the image

<input type="button"> (all)

Creates a form input control that is a button a user can click.

accesskey = *key_character*	Defines a hotkey/keyboard shortcut for this
disabled = disabled	Disables the button, preventing user intervention
name = *name*	Specifies a name for the form control passed to the form's processing application as part of the name/value pair (required)

notab = notab	Specifies that this element does not take part in the tabbing order for the document
tabindex = number	Defines this element's position in the tabbing order
taborder = number	Specifies the element's position in the tabbing order
value = string	Specifies the value of the parameter sent to the processing application as part of the name/value pair

\<input type="checkbox"\> (all)

Creates a form input control that is a checkbox a user can check.

accesskey = key_character	Defines a hotkey/keyboard shortcut for this
checked = checked	Specifies that the checkbox is checked (can be used to make the checkbox selected by default)
disabled = disabled	Disables the checkbox, preventing user intervention
name = name	Specifies a name for the form control passed to the form's processing application as part of the name/value pair (required)
notab = notab	Specifies that this element does not take part in the tabbing order for the document
readonly = readonly	Prevents user from modifying content
tabindex = number	Defines this element's position in the tabbing order
taborder = number	Specifies the element's position in the tabbing order
value = string	Specifies the value of the control sent to the processing application as part of the name/value pair

\<input type="file"\> (all)

Creates a form input control that allows a user to select a file.

accesskey = key_character	Defines a hotkey/keyboard shortcut for this
disabled = disabled	Disables the file upload control, preventing user intervention
maxlength = number	Maximum number of characters the user may enter
name = name	Specifies a name for the form control passed to the form's processing application as part of the name/value pair (required)

Continues

notab = notab	Specifies that this element does not take part in the tabbing order for the document
onblur = *script*	Specifies a script to run when the mouse leaves the control
onchange = *script*	Specifies a script to run when the value of the element changes
onfocus = *script*	Specifies a script to run when the element gains focus
readonly = readonly	Prevents user from modifying content
size = *number*	Specifies the number of characters to display for the element
tabindex = *number*	Defines this element's position in the tabbing order
taborder = *number*	Specifies the element's position in the tabbing order
value = *string*	Specifies the value of the control sent to the processing application as part of the name/value pair

<input type="hidden"> (all)

Creates a form input control, similar to a text input, but is hidden from the user's view (although the value can still be seen if the user views the source for the page).

name = *name*	Specifies a name for the form control passed to the form's processing application as part of the name/value pair (required)
value = *string*	Specifies the value of the control sent to the processing application as part of the name/value pair

<input type="image"> (all)

Creates a form input control that is like a button or submit control, but uses an image instead of a button.

accesskey = *key_character*	Defines a hotkey/keyboard shortcut for this
align = center | left | right	Specifies the alignment of the image
alt = *string*	Provides alternative text for the image
border = *number*	Specifies the width of the border in pixels
Disabled = disabled	Disables the image button, preventing user intervention
name = *name*	Specifies a name for the form control passed to the form's processing application as part of the name/value pair (required)

notab = notab	Specifies that this element does not take part in the tabbing order for the document
src = *url*	Specifies the source of the image
Readonly = *readonly*	Prevents user from modifying content
tabindex = *number*	Defines this element's position in the tabbing order
taborder = *number*	Specifies the element's position in the tabbing order
value = *string*	Specifies the value of the control sent to the processing application as part of the name/value pair

\<input type="password"> (all)

Creates a form input control that is like a single-line text input control but shows asterisks or bullet marks rather than the characters to prevent an onlooker from seeing the values a user has entered. This should be used for sensitive information—although you should note that the values get passed to the servers as plain text. (If you have sensitive information you should still consider making submissions safe using a technique such as SSL.)

accesskey = *key_character*	Defines a hotkey/keyboard shortcut for this
disabled = disabled	Disables the text input, preventing user intervention
maxlength = *number*	Maximum number of characters the user can enter
name = *name*	Specifies a name for the form control passed to the form's processing application as part of the name/value pair (required)
notab = notab	Specifies that this element does not take part in the tabbing order for the document
onblur = *script*	Specifies a script to run when the mouse moves off the element
onchange = *script*	Specifies a script to run when the value of the element changes
onfocus = *script*	Specifies a script to run when the element gains focus
onselect = *script*	Specifies a script to run when the user selects this element
readonly = *readonly*	Prevents user from modifying content
size = *number*	Specifies the width of the input in numbers of characters
tabindex = *number*	Defines this element's position in the tabbing order
taborder = *number*	Specifies the element's position in the tabbing order
value = *string*	Specifies the value of the control sent to the processing application as part of the name/value pair

<input type="radio"> (all)

Creates a form input control that is a radio button. These appear in groups that share the same name attribute value and create mutually exclusive groups of values (only one of the radio buttons in the group can be selected).

accesskey = key_character	Defines a hotkey/keyboard shortcut for this
checked = checked	Specifies that the default condition for this radio button is checked
disabled = disabled	Disables the radio button, preventing user intervention
name = name	Specifies a name for the form control passed to the form's processing application as part of the name/value pair (required)
notab = notab	Specifies that this element does not take part in the tabbing order for the document
readonly = readonly	Prevents user from modifying content
tabindex = number	Defines this element's position in the tabbing order
taborder = number	Specifies the element's position in the tabbing order
value = string	Specifies the value of the control sent to the processing application as part of the name/value pair

<input type="reset"> (all)

Creates a form input control that is a button to reset the values of the form to the same values present when the page loaded.

accesskey = key_character	Defines a hotkey/keyboard shortcut for this
disabled = disabled	Disables the button, preventing user intervention
notab = notab	Specifies that this element does not take part in the tabbing order for the document
tabindex = number	Defines this element's position in the tabbing order
taborder = number	Specifies the element's position in the tabbing order
value = string	Specifies the value of the control sent to the processing application as part of the name/value pair

<input type="submit"> (all)

Creates a form input control that is a submit button to send the form values to the server.

accesskey = *key_character*	Defines a hotkey/keyboard shortcut for this
disabled = disabled	Disables the button, preventing user intervention
name = *name*	Specifies a name for the form control passed to the form's processing application as part of the name/value pair
notab = notab	Specifies that this element does not take part in the tabbing order for the document
tabindex = *number*	Defines this element's position in the tabbing order
taborder = *number*	Specifies the element's position in the tabbing order
value = *string*	Specifies the value of the control sent to the processing application as part of the name/value pair

<input type="text"> (all)

Creates a form input control that is a single-line text input.

accesskey = *key_character*	Defines a hotkey/keyboard shortcut for this
disabled = disabled	Disables the text input, preventing user intervention
maxlength = *number*	Maximum number of characters the user can enter
name = *name*	Specifies a name for the form control passed to the form's processing application as part of the name/value pair (required)
notab = notab	Specifies that this element does not take part in the tabbing order for the document
onblur = *script*	Specifies a script to run when the mouse moves off the element
onchange = *script*	Specifies a script to run when the value of the element changes
onfocus = *script*	Specifies a script to run when the element gains focus
onselect = *script*	Specifies a script to run when the element is selected
readonly = readonly	Prevents user from modifying content
size = *number*	Specifies the width of the control in characters
tabindex = *number*	Defines this element's position in the tabbing order
taborder = *number*	Specifies the element's position in the tabbing order
value = *string*	Specifies the value of the control sent to the processing application as part of the name/value pair

<ins> (IE 4+, N6+)

The content of the element has been added since an earlier version of the document.

cite = *url*	Specifies a URL indicating why the content was added
datetime = *date*	Specifies a date and time for the addition of content

<isindex> Deprecated (all)

Identifies a searchable index.

Only the attributes listed in the table that follows are supported.

accesskey = *key_character*	Defines a hotkey/keyboard shortcut for this
action = *url*	IE only specifies the URL of the search application
class = *clasname*	Specifies a class for the element to associate it with rules in a style sheet
dir = ltr | rtl	Specifies the direction of the text within the element
id = *string*	Specifies a unique identifier for this element
lang = *language_type*	Specifies the language used in this element
prompt = *string*	Specifies an alternative prompt for the field input
style = *string*	Specifies inline CSS style rules for the element
tabindex = *number*	Defines this element's position in the tabbing order
title = *string*	Specifies a title for the element
xml:lang = *language_type*	Specifies the language used in this element

<kbd> (all)

The content of the element is something that should be entered on a keyboard, and is rendered in a fixed-width font.

<keygen> (Netscape only, N3+)

Used to generate key material in the page—key material referring to encryption keys for security.

Takes only the attributes listed in the table that follows.

challenge = *string*	Provides a challenge string to be packaged with the key
class = *classname*	Specifies a class for the element to associate it with rules in a style sheet
id = *string*	Specifies a unique identifier for this element
name = *string*	Specifies a name for the element

<label> (IE 4+, N6+)

The content of the element is used as a label for a form element.

accesskey = *key_character*	Defines a hotkey/keyboard shortcut for this
for = *name*	Specifies the value of the id attribute for the element it is a label for
onblur = *script*	Specifies a script to run when the mouse moves off the label
onfocus = *string*	Specifies a script to run when the label gains focus

<layer> (Netscape only, N4+)

Defines an area of a page that can hold a different page. Netscape-specific; not covered in this book.

above = *name*	Positions this layer above the named layer
background = *url*	Specifies the URL for a background image for the layer
below = *name*	Positions this layer below the named layer
bgcolor = *color*	Sets the background color for the layer
clip = *number* [, *number, number, number*]	Specifies the layer's clipping region
left = *number*	Specifies the position of the layer's left edge from the containing document or layer
Name = *name*	Specifies the name for the layer
src = *url*	Specifies another document as the content of the layer
top = *number*	Specifies the position of the layer from the top of the containing document or layer

Continues

visibility=show | hide | inherit	Specifies whether the layer should be visible
width = *number*	Specifies the width of the layer in pixels
z-index = *number*	Specifies the stacking order of the layer

\<legend\> (IE 4+, N6+)

The content of this element is the title text to place in a \<fieldset\>.

accesskey = *key_character*	Defines a hotkey/keyboard shortcut for this
align = top | left | bottom | right	Specifies the position of the legend in relation to the fieldset

\<li\> (all)

The content of this element is an item in a list. The element is referred to as a line item. For appropriate attributes see the parent element for that kind of list (\<ul\>, \<ol\>, \<menu\>).

type = *bullet_type*	Specifies the type of bullet used to display the list items
value = *number*	Specifies the number the list will start with

\<link\> (all)

Defines a link between the document and another resource. Often used to include style sheets in documents.

Takes only the attributes listed in the table that follows.

charset = *character_set*	Specifies a character set used to encode the linked file
href = *url*	Specifies the URL of the linked document
hreflang = *language_type*	Specifies the language encoding for the target of the link
media = *list*	Types of media the document is intended for
rel = same | next | parent | previous | string	Indicates the relationship of the document to the target document
rev = *relation*	Indicates the reverse relationship of the target document to this one
type = *type*	Specifies the MIME type of the document being linked to

<listing> Deprecated (IE 3+)

The content of this element is rendered in a fixed-width font.

<map> (all)

Creates a client-side image map and specifies a collection of clickable areas or hotspots.

name = *string*	Name of the map (required)

<marquee> (IE only, IE 3+)

Creates a scrolling text marquee (IE 3+ only).

accesskey = *key_character*	Defines a hotkey/keyboard shortcut for this
align = top | middle | bottom	Positions the marquee in relation to its surrounding content
behavior = alternate | scroll | side	Specifies the action or behavior of the marquee
bgcolor = *color*	Specifies the background color of the marquee
direction = down | left | up | right	Specifies the direction in which the text scrolls
height = *number*	Specifies the height of the marquee in pixels
hspace = *number*	Specifies the amount of additional space to be added to the left and right of the marquee
id = *string*	Specifies a unique identifier for this element
loop = *number*	Specifies the number of times the marquee loops or can have the keyword infinite
scrollamount = *number*	Specifies the number of pixels moved each time the text scrolls
scrolldelay = *number*	Specifies the delay in milliseconds between each movements of the scroll
tabindex = *number*	Defines this element's position in the tabbing order
vspace = *number*	Specifies the amount of additional space to be added above and below the marquee
width = *number*	Specifies the width of the marquee in pixels

\<menu\> Deprecated (all)

Renders the child elements as individual items. Replaced by lists (\<ol\> and \<ul\>). Deprecated in HTML 4.01.

type = *bullet_type*	Specifies the type of bullet used to display the list items

\<li\> (all)

type = *bullet_type*	Specifies the type of bullet used to display the list items

\<meta\> (all)

Allows for information about the document or instructions for the browser; these are not displayed to the user.

Takes only the attributes listed in the table that follows.

charset = *character_set*	Specifies a character set used to encode the document
content= *meta_content*	Specifies the value for the meta-information
dir = ltr | rtl	Specifies the direction of the text within the element
http-equiv = *string*	Specifies the HTTP equivalent name for the meta-information; causes the server to include the name and content in the HTTP header
lang = *language_type*	Specifies the language used in this element
name = *string*	Specifies the name of the meta-information
scheme = *scheme*	Specifies the profile scheme used to interpret the property
xml:lang = *language_type*	Specifies the language used in this element

\<multicol\> (N3, N4 only)

Used to define multiple-column formatting. (Netscape 3 and 4 only—not part of XHTML.)

cols = *number of columns*	Specifies the number of columns
gutter = *number*	Specifies the size of the gutter (space between columns) in pixels
width = *number*	Specifies the width of the columns in pixels

<nextid> (not supported in browsers)

Used to define values for text editing software when parts in or creating a document (was part of the HTML 2.0 specification only, not implemented by browsers)

Takes only the attribute listed in the table that follows.

n = *string*	Sets the nextid number

<nobr> (all)

Means "no break," and prevents the content of the element from wrapping onto a new line.

<noembed> (N2, N3, N4)

The content of the element is displayed for browsers that do not support <embed> elements or the required viewing application.

<noframes> (all)

The content of the element is displayed for browsers that do not support frames.

<nolayer> (N4+ only)

The content of the element is displayed for browsers that do not support layers.

<noscript> (all)

The content of the element is displayed for browsers that do not support the script. Most browsers will also display this content if scripting is disabled.

<object> (IE 3+, N6+)

Adds an object or non-HTML control to the page. Will be the standard way of including images in the future.

align = absbottom | absmiddle | baseline | bottom | left | middle | right | texttop | top	Specifies the position of object in relation to surrounding text
archive = *url*	Specifies a list of URLs for archives or resources used by the object

Continues

border = *number*	Specifies the width of the border in pixels
classid = *url*	Specifies the URL of the object
codebase = *url*	Specifies the URL of the code required to run the object
codetype = *MIME-type*	Specifies the MIME type of the code base
data = *url*	Specifies the data for the object
declare	Declares an object without instantiating it
height = *number*	Specifies the height of the object in pixels
hspace = *number*	Specifies the amount of additional space to be added to the left and right of the embedded object
name = *name*	Specifies a name for the object
notab = notab	Specifies that this element does not take part in the tabbing order for the document
shapes = shapes	Specifies that the object has shaped hyperlinks
standby = *string*	Defines a message to display while the object is loading
tabindex = *number*	Defines this element's position in the tabbing order
type = *MIME type*	Specifies the MIME type for the object's data
usemap = *url*	Defines an image map for use with the object
vspace = *number*	Specifies the amount of additional space to be added above and below the embedded object
width = *number*	Specifies the object's width in pixels

\<param> (IE 3+, N6+)

Used as a child of \<object> to set properties of the object.

id = *id*	Specifies a unique ID for this parameter
name = *name*	Specifies a name for the parameter
type = *MIME type*	Specifies the MIME type for the parameter
value = *string*	Specifies a value for the parameter
valuetype = *type*	Specifies the type of value attribute

\<ol> (all)

Creates an ordered or numbered list.

compact = compact	Attempts to make the list more vertically compact
start = number	Specifies the number with which the list should start
type = bullet_type	Specifies the type of bullet used to display the list items

<li> (all)

type = bullet_type	Specifies the type of bullet used to display the list items
value = number	Specifies the number of the list item

<optgroup> (IE 6+, N6+)

Used to group <option> elements in a select box.

disabled = disabled	Disables the group, preventing user intervention
label = string	Specifies a label for the option group

<option> (all)

Contains one choice in a drop-down list or select box.

disabled = disabled	Disables the option, preventing user intervention
label = string	Specifies a label for the option
selected = selected	Indicates that the option should be selected by default when the page loads
value = string	Specifies the value of this option in the form control sent to the processing application as part of the name/value pair

<p> (all)

The content of this element is a paragraph.

align = center | left | right	Specifies the alignment of the text within the paragraph

<param>

Used as a child of an <object> or <applet> element to set properties of the object. See under the <object> or <applet> element for details.

\<plaintext\> Deprecated (IE 3+, N2, N3, N4)

Renders the content of the element without formatting (deprecated in HTML 3.2).

\<pre\> (all)

The content of this element is rendered in a fixed-width type that retains the formatting (such as spaces and line breaks) in the code.

width = number	Specifies the width of the preformatted area in pixels

\<q\> (IE 4+, N6+)

The content of the element is a short quotation.

cite = url	Specifies the URL for the content of the quote in question

\<s\> Deprecated (all)

The content of the element should be rendered with strikethrough.

\<samp\> (all)

The content of the element is a sample code listing. Usually rendered in a smaller fixed-width font.

\<script\> (all)

The content of the element is a script code that the browser should execute.

charset = encoding	Specifies a character set used to encode the script
Defer = defer	Defers execution of the script
language = name	Specifies the language used in this element
src = url	URL for the location of the script file
type = encoding	Specifies the MIME type of the script

\<select\> (all)

Creates a select or drop-down list box.

`disabled = disabled`	Disables the select box, preventing user intervention
`Multiple = multiple`	Permits selection of multiple items from the list
`name = name`	Specifies a name for the form control passed to the form's processing application as part of the name/value pair (required)
`onblur = script`	Specifies a script to run when the mouse moves off the control
`onchange = script`	Specifies a script to run when the value of the element changes
`onfocus = script`	Specifies a script to run when the element gains focus
`size = number`	Specifies the number of items that may appear at once
`tabindex = number`	Defines this element's position in the tabbing order

`<small>` (all)

The content of this element should be displayed in a smaller font than its containing element.

`<span>` (all)

Used as a grouping element for inline elements (as opposed to block level elements); also allows for the definition of non-standard attributes for text on a page.

`<strike>` Deprecated (all)

The content of this element should be rendered in strikethrough text.

`<strong>` (all)

The content of this element has strong emphasis and should be rendered in a bold typeface.

`<style>` (IE 3+, N4+)

Contains CSS style rules that apply to that page

`<sub>` (all)

The content of this element is displayed as subscript.

`<sup>` (all)

The content of this element is rendered as superscript.

<table> (all)

Creates a table.

align = center | left | right	Specifies the alignment of the table within its content
background = *url*	Specifies a URL for a background image
bgcolor = *color*	Specifies a background color for the table
border = *number*	Specifies the width of the border in pixels
bordercolor = *color*	Specifies the color of the border
bordercolordark = *color*	Specifies the darker border color
bordercolorlight = *color*	Specifies the lighter border color
cellpadding = *number*	Specifies the distance between the border and its content in pixels
cellspacing = *number*	Specifies the distance between the cells in pixels
cols = *number*	Specifies the number of columns in the table
frame = above | below | border | box | hsides | lhs | rhs | void | vsides	Defines where the borders are displayed
height = *number*	Specifies the height of the table in pixels
hspace = *number*	Specifies the amount of additional space to be added to the left and right of the table
nowrap = nowrap	Prevents the content of the table from wrapping
rules = all | cols | groups | none | rows	Specifies where the inner dividers are drawn
summary = *string*	Offers a summary description of the table
valign = bottom | top	Specifies the alignment of content in the table
vspace = *number*	Specifies the amount of additional space to be added above and below the table
width = *number*	Specifies the width of the table in pixels

<tbody> (IE 3+, N6+)

Denotes the body section of a table.

align = center | left | right	Specifies the alignment of the content of the body of the table

char = *string*	Specifies an offset character for alignment
charoff = *string*	Specifies the offset within the cells of the alignment position
valign = bottom	top	Specifies the vertical alignment of content in the body of the table
width = *number*	Specifies the width of the table body in pixels

<td> (all)

Creates a cell of a table.

abbr = *string*	Specifies an abbreviation for the cell's content
align = center	left	right	Specifies the alignment of the content of the cell
axis = *string*	Specifies a name for a related group of cells
background = *url*	Specifies a URL for a background image for the cell
bgcolor = *color*	Specifies the background color of the cell
border = *number*	Specifies the border width of the cell in pixels
bordercolor = *color*	Specifies the border color of the cell
bordercolordark= *color*	Specifies the dark border color of the cell
bordercolorlight= *color*	Specifies the light border color of the cell
char = *string*	Specifies the cell alignment character
charoff = string	Specifies the offset from the cell alignment character
colspan = *number*	Specifies the number of columns this cell spans
headers = *string*	Specifies the names of header cells associated with this cell
height = *number*	Specifies the height of the cell in pixels
nowrap = nowrap	Prevents the content of the cell from wrapping
rowspan = *number*	Specifies the number of rows the cell spans
scope = row	col	rowgroup	colgroup	Specifies the scope of a header cell
valign = bottom	top	Specifies vertical alignment of the content of the cell
width = *number*	Specifies the width of the cell in pixels

<textarea> (all)

Creates a multiple-line text input control in a form.

accesskey= *key_character*	Defines a hotkey/keyboard shortcut for this
cols = *number*	Specifies the number of columns of characters the text area should be (the width in characters)
disabled = disabled	Disables the text area, preventing user intervention
name = *string*	Specifies a name for the form control passed to the form's processing application as part of the name/value pair (required)
onblur = *script*	Specifies a script to run when the mouse moves off the text area
onchange = *script*	Specifies a script to run when the value of the element changes
onfocus = *script*	Specifies a script to run when the element gains focus
onselect = *script*	Specifies a script to run when the text area is selected
readonly = readonly	Prevents the user from modifying content
rows = *number*	Specifies the number of rows of text that should appear in the text area without the scrollbar appearing
tabindex = *number*	Defines this element's position in the tabbing order
wrap = physical | vertical | off	Specifies whether the text in a text area should wrap or continue on the same line when width of text area is reached

\<tfoot\> (IE 3+, N6+)

Denotes row or rows of a table to be used as a footer for the table.

align = center | left | right	Specifies the alignment of the content of the footer of the table
char = *string*	Specifies an offset character for alignment
charoff = *string*	Specifies the offset within the cells of the alignment position
valign = bottom | top	Specifies the vertical alignment of content in the foot of the table
width = *number*	Specifies the width of the table body in pixels

\<thead\> (IE 3+, N6+)

Denotes row or rows of a table to be used as a header for the table.

align = center | left | right	Specifies the alignment of the content of the head of the table
char = *string*	Specifies an offset character for alignment

charoff = string	Specifies the offset within the cells of the alignment position
valign = bottom | top	Specifies the vertical alignment of content in the head of the table
width = number	Specifies the width of the table body in pixels

\<th\> (all)

Denotes a header cell of a table. By default content is often shown in bold font.

abbr = string	Specifies an abbreviation for the cell's content
align = center | left | right	Specifies the alignment of the content of the cell
axis = string	Specifies a name for a related group of cells
background = url	Specifies a URL for a background image for the cell
bgcolor = color	Specifies the background color of the cell
border = number	Specifies the border width of the cell in pixels
bordercolor = color	Specifies the border color of the cell
bordercolordark= color	Specifies the dark border color of the cell
bordercolorlight= color	Specifies the light border color of the cell
char = string	Specifies the cell alignment character
charoff = string	Specifies the offset from the cell alignment character
colspan = number	Specifies the number of columns this cell spans
headers = string	Specifies the names of header cells associated with this cell
height = number	Specifies the height of the cell in pixels
nowrap	Prevents the content of the cell from wrapping
rowspan = number	Specifies the number of rows the cell spans
scope = row | col | rowgroup | colgroup	Specifies the scope of a header cell
valign = bottom | top	Specifies vertical alignment of the content of the cell
width = number	Specifies the width of the cell in pixels

\<title\> (all)

The content of this element is the title of the document and will usually be rendered in the top title bar of the browser.

Supports only the attributes listed in the table that follows.

dir = ltr | rtl	Specifies the direction of the text within the element
id = *string*	Specifies a unique identifier for this element
lang = *language_type*	Specifies the language used in this element
xml:lang = *language_type*	Specifies the language used in this element

\<tr> (all)

Denotes a row of a table.

align = center | left | right	Specifies the alignment of the content of the row
background = *url*	Specifies a URL for a background image for the row
bgcolor = *color*	Specifies the background color of the row
border = *number*	Specifies the border width of the row in pixels
bordercolor = *color*	Specifies the border color of the row
bordercolordark= *color*	Specifies the dark border color of the row
bordercolorlight= *color*	Specifies the light border color of the row
char = *string*	Specifies the row alignment character
charoff = *string*	Specifies the offset from the row alignment character
nowrap = nowrap	Prevents the content of the cell from wrapping
valign = bottom | top	Specifies vertical alignment of the content of the cell

\<tt> (all)

The content of this element is rendered in a fixed-width font, as if on a teletype device.

\<u> (all)

The content of this element is rendered with underlined text (deprecated in HTML 4.01).

\<ul> (all)

Creates an unordered list.

compact = compact	Attempts to make the list more compact vertically
type = *bullet_type*	Specifies the type of bullet used to display the list items

<li> (all)

type = *bullet_type*	Specifies the type of bullet used to display the list items
value = *number*	Specifies the number of the list item

<var> (IE 3+, N6+)

The content of this element is a programming variable, and is usually rendered in a small fixed-width font.

<wbr> (IE 3, N2, N3, N4)

Creates a soft line break within a <nobr> element.

<xmp> Deprecated (all)

The content of this element is rendered in a fixed-width typeface for example or sample code. Replaced by <pre> and <samp> elements.

CSS Properties

This appendix is a reference of the main CSS properties that you will be using to control the appearance of your documents.

For each property covered you will first see a very brief description of the property and then an example of its usage. Then the tables on the left show the possible values the property can take, along with the first versions of IE and Netscape to support these properties. The table on the right indicates whether the property can be inherited, what the default value for the property is, and which elements it applies to.

At the end of the appendix are units of measurement.

While Netscape supports the `inherit` value of many properties, if it is unable to set the property to some other value in the first place, then this value is of little use.

> *Note that the tables indicating which browser version supported a value are based on browsers on the Windows platform. Internet Explorer 5 on a Mac has notably better support for many of the properties than its Windows counterparts.*

Font Properties

The font properties allow you to change the appearance of a typeface.

font

Allows you to set several font properties at the same time, separated by spaces. You can specify `font-size`, `line-height`, `font-family`, `font-style`, `font-variant`, and `font-weight` in this one property.

```
font {color:#ff0000; arial, verdana, sans-serif; 12pt;}
```

Value	IE	Netscape
[font-family]	3	4
[font-size]	3	4
[font-style]	3	4
[font-variant]	4	6
[font-weight]	3	4
[line-height]	3	4
inherit	-	6

Inherited	Yes
Default	n/a
Applies to	All elements

font-family

Allows you to specify the typefaces you want to use. Can take multiple values separated by commas, starting with your first preference, then your second choice, and ending with a generic font-family (serif, sans-serif, cursive, fantasy or monospace).

```
p {font-family:arial, verdana, sans-serif;}
```

Value	IE	Netscape
[generic family]	3	4
[specific family]	3	4
inherit	-	6

Inherited	Yes
Default	Set by browser
Applies to	All elements

font-size

Allows you to specify a size of font. The font-size property has its own specific values:

- ❑ **Absolutes sizes:** xx-small, x-small, small, medium, large, x-large, xx-large
- ❑ **Relative sizes:** larger, smaller
- ❑ **Percentage:** Percentage of the parent font
- ❑ **Length:** A unit of measurement (as described at end of the appendix)

Value	IE	Netscape
[absolute size]	3	4
[relative size]	4	4
[percent]	3	4
[length]	3	4
inherit	-	6

Inherited	Yes
Default	medium
Applies to	All elements

font-size-adjust

Allows you to adjust the aspect value of a font, which is the ratio between the height of a lowercase letter x in the font, and the height of the font.

```
p {font-size-adjust:0.5;}
```

Value	IE	Netscape
[number]	-	-
none	-	-
inherit	-	6

Inherited	Yes
Default	Specific to font
Applies to	All elements

font-stretch

Allows you to specify the width of the letters in a font (not the size between them).

- ❑ **Relative values:** normal, wider, narrower
- ❑ **Fixed values:** ultra-condensed, extra-condensed, condensed, semi-condensed, semi-expanded, expanded, extra-expanded, ultra-expanded

```
p {font-family:courier; font-stretch:semi-condensed;}
```

Value	IE	Netscape
[relative]	-	-
[fixed]	-	-
inherit	-	6

Inherited	Yes
Default	Specific to font
Applies to	All elements

font-style

Applies styling to a font. If the specified version of the font is available it will be used; otherwise the browser will render it.

```
p {font-style:italic;}
```

Value	IE	Netscape
normal	3	4
italic	3	4
oblique	4	6
inherit	-	6

Inherited	Yes
Default	normal
Applies to	All elements

font-variant

Creates capital letters that are the same size of normal lowercase letters.

```
p {font-variant:small-caps;}
```

Value	IE	Netscape
normal	4	6
small-caps	4	6
inherit	-	6

Inherited	Yes
Default	normal
Applies to	All elements

font-weight

Specifies the thickness of the text—its "boldness."

- ❑ **Absolute values:** normal, bold
- ❑ **Relative values:** bolder, lighter
- ❑ **Numeric value:** Between 0 and 100

```
p {font-weight:bold;}
```

Value	IE	Netscape
[absolute]	3	4
[relative]	4	6
[number 1–100]	4	6
inherit	-	6

Inherited	Yes
Default	normal
Applies to	All elements

Text Properties

Text properties change the appearance and layout of text in general (as opposed to the font).

letter-spacing

Specifies the distance between letters as a unit of length.

```
p {letter-spacing:1em;}
```

Value	IE	Netscape
[length]	4	6
normal	4	6
inherit	-	6

Inherited	Yes
Default	normal
Applies to	All elements

text-align

Specifies whether text is aligned left, right, center, or justified.

```
p {text-align:center}
```

Value	IE	Netscape
left	3	4
right	3	4
center	3	4
justify	4	4
inherit	-	6

Inherited	Yes
Default	Depends on user agent and element (usually left except for <th> elements, which are center)
Applies to	All elements

text-decoration

Specifies whether text should have an `underline`, `overline`, `line-through`, or `blink` appearance.

```
p {text-decoration:underline;}
```

Value	IE	Netscape
none	3	4
underline	3	4
overline	4	6
line-through	3	4
blink	-	4
inherit	-	6

Inherited	No
Default	none
Applies to	All elements

text-indent

Specifies the indentation in length or as a percentage of the parent element's width.

```
p {text-indent:3em;}
```

Value	IE	Netscape
[length]	4	4
[percentage]	4	4
inherit	-	6

Inherited	Yes
Default	zero
Applies to	Block elements

text-shadow

Creates a drop shadow for the text. It should take three lengths; the first two specify X and Y coordinates for the offset of the drop shadow, while the third specifies a blur effect. This is then followed by a color, which can be a name or a hex value.

```
.dropShadow {text-shadow: 0.3em 0.3em 0.5em black}
```

Value	IE	Netscape
[shadow effects]	-	-
none	-	-
inherit	-	6

Inherited	No
Default	none
Applies to	All elements

text-transform

Specifies capitalization of text in an element

- ❑ **none:** Removes inherited settings
- ❑ **uppercase:** All characters are uppercase
- ❑ **lowercase:** All characters are lowercase
- ❑ **capitalize:** First letter of each word is capitalized

```
p {text-transform:uppercase;}
```

Value	IE	Netscape
none	4	4
uppercase	4	4
lowercase	4	4
capitalize	4	4
inherit	-	6

Inherited	Yes
Default	none
Applies to	All elements

white-space

Indicates how whitespace should be dealt with:

- ❑ **normal:** Whitespace should be collapsed
- ❑ **pre:** Whitespace should be preserved
- ❑ **nowrap:** Text should not be broken to a new line except with <br /> element

```
p {white-space:pre;}
```

Value	IE	Netscape
normal	5.5	4
pre	5.5	4
nowrap	5.5	6
inherit	-	6

Inherited	Yes
Default	normal
Applies to	Block elements

word-spacing

Specifies the gap between words:

```
p {word-spacing:2em;}
```

Value	IE	Netscape
normal	6	6
[length]	6	6
inherit	-	6

Inherited	Yes
Default	normal
Applies to	All elements

Color and Background Properties

The following properties allow you to change the colors and backgrounds of both the page and other boxes.

background

Shorthand for specifying background properties for color, url, repeat, scroll, and position; separated by a space. By default the background is transparent.

```
body {background: #efefef url(images/background.gif) }
```

Value	IE	Netscape
[background-attachment]	4	6
[background-color]	3	4
[background-image]	3	4
[background-position]	4	6
[background-repeat]	3	4
inherit	-	6

Inherited	No
Default	Not defined (by default background is transparent)
Applies to	All elements

background-attachment

Specifies whether a background image should be fixed in one position or scroll along the page:

```
body {background-attachment:fixed; background-image: url(images
/background.gif);}
```

Value	IE	Netscape
fixed	4	6
scroll	4	6
inherit	4	6

Inherited	No
Default	scroll
Applies to	All elements

background-color

Sets the color of the background. This can be a single color or two colors blended together. Colors can be specified as a color name, hex value, or RGB value. By default the box will be transparent.

```
body {background-color:#efefef;}
```

Value	IE	Netscape
[color]	4	4
transparent	4	4
inherit	-	6

Inherited	No
Default	transparent
Applies to	All elements

709

background-image

Specifies an image to be used as a background, which by default will be tiled. Value is a URL for the image.

```
body {background-image: url(images/background.gif);}
```

Value	IE	Netscape
[url]	4	4
none	4	4
inherit	-	6

Inherited	No
Default	none
Applies to	All elements

background-position

Specifies where a background image should be placed in the page, from the top-left corner. Values can be an absolute distance, percentage, or one of the keywords. If only one value is given, it is taken to be horizontal.

❑ Keywords available are: top, bottom, left, right, center

```
body {background-position:center; background-image: url(images
/background.gif);}
```

Value	IE	Netscape
[length – x y]	4	6
[percentage – x% y%]	4	6
top	4	6
left	4	6
bottom	4	6
right	4	6
center	4	6
inherit	-	6

Inherited	No
Default	top, left
Applies to	Block level elements

background-positionX

Position of a background image to run horizontally across page. Values are the same as for background-position (default: top).

background-positionY

Position of a background image to run vertically down page. Values are same as for `background-position` (default: `left`).

Border properties

The border properties allow you to control the appearance and size of a border around any box.

border (border-bottom, border-left, border-top, border-right)

Shorthand for specifying `border-style`, `border-width`, and `border-color` properties

Value	IE	Netscape
`<border-style>`	4	6
`<border-width>`	4	6
`<border-color>`	4	6
`inherit`	-	6

Inherited	No
Default	none, medium, none
Applies to	All elements

border-style (border-bottom-style, border-left-style, border-top-style, border-right-style)

Specifies the style of line that should surround a block box.

```
div.page {border-style:solid;}
```

Note that Netscape did not support properties for individual sides until version 6.

Value	IE	Netscape
`none`	4	4
`dotted`	5.5	6
`dashed`	5.5	6
`solid`	4	4
`double`	4	4
`groove`	4	4
`ridge`	4	4

Inherited	No
Default	none
Applies to	All elements

Continued

711

Value	IE	Netscape
inset	4	4
outset	4	4
hidden	-	-
inherit	-	6

border-width (border-bottom-width, border-left-width, border-top-width, border-right-width)

Specifies the width of a border line; can be a width or a keyword.

```
div.page {border-width:2px;}
```

Value	IE	Netscape
[length]	4	4
thin	4	4
medium	4	4
thick	4	4
inherit	-	6

Inherited	No
Default	medium
Applies to	All elements

border-color (border-bottom-color, border-left-color, border-top-color, border-right-color)

Specifies the color of a border; values can be a color name, hex code, or RGB value.

```
table {border-color:#000000;}
```

Value	IE	Netscape
[color value]	4	4
inherit	-	6

Inherited	No
Default	none
Applies to	All elements

Dimensions

The dimensions properties allow you to specify the size that boxes should be.

height

Specifies the vertical height of a block elements; can scale the element.

```
table {height:400px;}
```

Value	IE	Netscape
auto	4	6
[length]	4	6
[percentage]	4	-
inherit	-	6

Inherited	No
Default	auto
Applies to	Block level elements

width

Specifies the horizontal width of an element; can scale the element.

```
td {width:150px;}
```

Value	IE	Netscape
auto	4	4
[length]	4	4
[percentage]	4	4
inherit	-	6

Inherited	No
Default	auto
Applies to	Block level elements

line-height

Specifies the height of a line of text, and therefore the leading (space between multiple lines of text).

```
p {line-height:18px;}
```

Value	IE	Netscape
normal	3	4
[number]	4	4
[length]	3	4
[percentage]	3	4
inherit	-	6

Inherited	Yes
Default	Depends on browser
Applies to	All elements

max-height

Specifies the maximum height of a block level element (same values as for height).

```
td {max-height:200px;}
```

Value	IE	Netscape
auto	-	-
[length]	-	-
[percentage]	-	-
inherit	-	6

Inherited	No
Default	auto
Applies to	Block level elements

max-width

Specifies the maximum width of a block level element (same values as for width).

```
td {max-width:400px;}
```

Value	IE	Netscape
auto	-	-
[length]	-	-
[percentage]	-	-
inherit	-	6

Inherited	No
Default	auto
Applies to	Block elements

min-height

Specifies the maximum height of a block level element (same values as for `height`).

```
td {min-height:100px;}
```

Value	IE	Netscape		Inherited	No
auto	-	-		Default	auto
[length]	-	-		Applies to	Block level elements
[percentage]	-	-			
inherit	-	6			

min-width

Specifies the minimum width of a block level element (same values as for `width`).

```
td {min-width:200px;}
```

Value	IE	Netscape		Inherited	No
auto	-	-		Default	auto
[length]	-	-		Applies to	Block elements
[percentage]	-	-			
inherit	-	6			

Margin Properties

Margin properties allow you to specify a margin around a box and therefore create a gap between elements' borders.

margin (margin-bottom, margin-left, margin-top, margin-right)

Specifies the width of a margin around a box.

```
p {margin:15px;}
```

Value	IE	Netscape		
			Inherited	No
auto	3	4	Default	zero
[length]	3	4	Applies to	All elements
[percentage – relative to parent element]	3	4		
inherit	-	6		

Padding Properties

Padding properties set the distance between the border of an element and its content. They are important for adding whitespace to documents (in particular table cells).

padding (padding-bottom, padding-left, padding-right, padding-top)

Specifies the distance between an element's border and its content.

```
td {padding:20px;}
```

Value	IE	Netscape		
			Inherited	No
auto	4	4	Default	zero
[length]	4	4	Applies to	All elements
[percentage – relative to parent element]	4	4		
inherit	-	6		

List Properties

List properties affect the presentation of bulleted, numbered, and definition lists.

list-style

Shorthand allowing you to specify list-style-position and list-style-type.

```
ul {list-style: inside disc}
```

Value	IE	Netscape		Inherited	Yes
`<position>`	4	6		Default	Depends on browser
`<type>`	4	4		Applies to	List elements
`<image>`	4	6			
`inherit`	-	6			

list-style-position

Specifies whether the marker should be placed with each item of a list or to the left of them.

```
ul {list-style-position:inside;}
```

Value	IE	Netscape		Inherited	Yes
`inside`	4	6		Default	`outside`
`outside`	4	6		Applies to	List elements
`inherit`	-	6			

list-style-type

Indicates the type of bullet or numbering that a bullet should use.

```
ul {list-style-type:circle;}
```

Value	IE	Netscape		Inherited	Yes
`None`	4	4		Default	`disc`
`disc (default)`	4	4		Applies to	List elements
`Circle`	4	4			
`square`	4	4			
`decimal`	4	4			
`decimal-leading-zero`	-	-			
`lower-alpha`	4	4			
`upper-alpha`	4	4			
`lower-roman`	4	4			
`upper-roman`	4	4			

Additional numbered list styles are available in CSS, but unfortunately they are not supported in IE 6 or Netscape 7.

hebrew	Traditional Hebrew numbering
georgian	Traditional Georgian numbering (an, ban, gan, . . . , he, tan, in, in-an, . . .)
armenian	Traditional Armenian numbering
cjk-ideographic	Plain ideographic numbers
hiragana	(a, i, u, e, o, ka, ki, . . .)
katakana	(A, I, U, E, O, KA, KI, . . .)
hiragana-iroha	(i, ro, ha, ni, ho, he, to, . . .)
katakana-iroha	(I, RO, HA, NI, HO, HE, TO, . . .)

marker-offset

Specifies the space between a list item and its marker.

```
ol {marker-offset:2em; }
```

Value	IE	Netscape		Inherited	No
[length]	-	-		Default	auto
auto	-	-		Applies to	Marker elements
inherit	-	6			

Positioning Properties

Positioning properties allow you to use CSS for positioning boxes on the page.

position

Specifies the positioning schema that should be used for an element. When an element is positioned you also need to use the box-offset properties covered next (top, left, bottom and right). Note that you should not use top and bottom or left and right together (if you do top and left take priority).

❑   absolute can be fixed on the canvas in a specific position from its containing element (which is another absolutely positioned element); it will also move when the user scrolls the page.

- ❏ static will fix it on the page in the same place and keep it there even when the user scrolls.
- ❏ relative will be placed offset in relation to its normal position.
- ❏ fixed will fix it on the background of the page and not move when the user scrolls.

```
p.article{position:absolute; top:10px; left:20px;
```

Value	IE	Netscape
absolute	4	4
relative	4	4
static	4	4
fixed	-	6
inherit	-	6

Inherited	No
Default	static
Applies to	All elements

Top

Sets the vertical position of an element from the top of the window or containing element.

Value	IE	Netscape
auto	4	-
[length]	4	6
[percentage – relative to parent's height]	4	-
inherit	-	6

Inherited	No
Default	auto
Applies to	Positioned elements

Left

Sets the horizontal position of an element from the left of the window or containing element.

Value	IE	Netscape
auto	4	-
[length]	4	6
[percentage – relative to parent's width]	4	-
inherit	-	6

Inherited	No
Default	auto
Applies to	Positioned elements

bottom

Sets the vertical position of an element from the bottom of the window or containing element.

Value	IE	Netscape
auto	5	-
[length]	5	-
[percentage – relative to parent's height]	5	-
inherit	-	6

Inherited	No
Default	auto
Applies to	Positioned elements

right

Sets the horizontal position of an element from the window or containing element.

Value	IE	Netscape
auto	5	-
[length]	5	-
[percentage – relative to parent's width]	5	-
inherit	-	6

Inherited	No
Default	auto
Applies to	Positioned elements

vertical-align

Sets the vertical positioning of an inline element:

- ❏ baseline aligns element with base of parent
- ❏ middle aligns midpoint of element with half the height of parent
- ❏ sub makes element subscript
- ❏ super makes element superscript
- ❏ text-top aligns element with top of parent element's font
- ❏ text-bottom aligns element with the bottom of parent element's font
- ❏ top aligns top of element with top of tallest element on current line
- ❏ bottom aligns element with bottom of lowest element on the current line

```
span.superscript {vertical-align:superscript;}
```

Value	IE	Netscape
baseline	4	4
middle	4	4
sub	4	6
super	4	6
text-top	4	4
text-bottom	4	4
top	4	4
bottom	4	4
[percentage relative to line height]	-	6
[length]	-	-
inherit	4	6

Inherited	No
Default	baseline
Applies to	Inline elements

z-index

Controls which overlapping element appears to be on top; works for absolutely positioned elements only. Positive and negative numbers are permitted.

```
p {position:absolute; top:10px; left:20px; z-index:3;}
```

Value	IE	Netscape
auto	4	-
[number]	4	4
inherit	-	6

Inherited	No
Default	Depends on position of element in XHTML source document
Applies to	Positioned elements

clip

Controls which part of an element is visible. Parts outside the clip are not visible. If value is rect(), takes following form:

❑   rect([*top*] [*right*] [*bottom*] [*left*])

```
rect(25 100 100 25)
```

Value	IE	Netscape
auto	4	-
rect	4	6
inherit	-	6

Inherited		No
Default		auto
Applies to		Block elements

overflow

Specifies how a container element will display content that is too large for its containing element.

```
p {width:200px; height:200px; overflow:scroll;}
```

Value	IE	Netscape
auto	4	-
hidden	4	-
visible	4	-
scroll	4	-
inherit	-	6

Inherited		No
Default		visible
Applies to		Block elements

overflow-x

Same as overflow, but only for the horizontal x-axis. First supported in IE 5.

overflow-y

Same as overflow, but only for the vertical y-axis. First supported in IE 5.

Outline Properties

Outlines act like borders, but do not take up any space—they sit on top of the canvas.

Outline (outline-color, outline-style, outline-width)

Shortcut for the outline-color, outline-style, and outline-width properties:

```
outline {solid #ff0000 2px}
```

Note that `outline-color`, `outline-style`, and `outline-width` take the same values as `border-color`, `border-style`, and `border-width`. They are not covered individually because they are not supported yet.

Value	IE	Netscape
<outline-color>	-	-
<outline-style>	-	-
<outline-width>	-	-

Inherited	No
Default	none
Applies to	All elements

Table Properties

Table properties allow you to affect the style of tables, rows, and cells.

border-collapse

Specifies the border model that the table should use (whether adjacent borders should be collapsed into one value or kept separate).

```
table {border-collapse:separate;}
```

Value	IE	Netscape
collapse	5	-
separate	5	-
inherit	-	6

Inherited	Yes
Default	collapse
Applies to	Table and inline elements

border-spacing

Specifies the distance between adjacent cells borders.

```
table {border-spacing:2px;}
```

Value	IE	Netscape
[length]	-	-
inherit	-	6

Inherited	Yes
Default	0
Applies to	Table and inline elements

caption-side

Indicates which side of a table a caption should be placed on.

```
caption {caption-side:bottom;}
```

Value	IE	Netscape
top	-	-
left	-	-
bottom	-	6
right	-	-
inherit	-	6

Inherited	Yes
Default	top
Applies to	<caption> elements in <table> elements

empty-cells

Specifies whether borders should be displayed if a cell is empty.

```
td, th {empty-cells:hide;}
```

Value	IE	Netscape
show	5	6
hide	5	6
inherit	-	6

Inherited	Yes
Default	show
Applies to	Table cell elements

table-layout

Specifies how the browser should calculate the layout of a table; can affect the speed of rendering a large or graphics-intensive table.

Value	IE	Netscape
auto	5	-
fixed	5	-
inherit	-	6

Inherited	No
Default	auto
Applies to	Table and inline elements

Classification Properties

Classification properties affect how the boxes in the box model are rendered.

clear

Forces elements, which would normally wrap around an aligned element, to be displayed below it. Value indicates which side may not touch an aligned element.

```
p {clear:left;}
```

Value	IE	Netscape
none	4	4
both	4	4
left	4	4
right	4	4
inherit	-	6

Inherited	No
Default	none
Applies to	All elements

display

Specifies if and how an element is rendered if at all. If set to none the element is not rendered and it does not take up any space. Can force an inline element to be displayed as a block or vice versa.

```
span.important {display:block;}
```

Value	IE	Netscape
none	4	4
inline	5	4
block	5	4
list-item	5	4
inherit	-	6

Inherited	Yes
Default	inline
Applies to	All elements

Other properties are either not supported or not required for XHTML.

While the default value of this property is inline, browsers tend to treat the element depending on its inherent display type. Block level elements, such as headings and paragraphs, get treated as if the default were block, while inline elements such as <i>, <b>, or <span> get treated as inline.

float

Subsequent elements should be wrapped to the left or right of the element, rather than below.

```
img.featuredeItem {float:left;}
```

Value	IE	Netscape
none	4	4
left	4	4
right	4	4
inherit	-	6

Inherited	No
Default	none
Applies to	All elements

visibility

Specifies whether an element should be displayed or hidden. Even if hidden, elements take up space on page, but are transparent.

Value	IE	Netscape
visible	4	-
show	-	4
hidden	4	-
hide	-	4
collapse	-	-
inherit	4	4

Inherited	No
Default	inherit
Applies to	All elements

Internationalization Properties

Internationalization properties affect how text is rendered in different languages.

direction

Specifies the direction of text from left to right or right to left. This should be used in association with the unicode-bidi property.

```
td.word{direction:rtl; unicode-bidi:bidi-override;}
```

Value	IE	Netscape
ltr	5	6
rtl	5	6
inherit	5	6

Inherited	Yes
Default	ltr
Applies to	All elements

unicode-bidi

The `unicode-bidi` property allows you to override Unicode's built-in directionality settings for languages.

```
td.word{unicode-bidi:bidi-override; direction:rtl; }
```

Value	IE	Netscape
normal	5	-
embed	5	-
bidi-override	5	-
inherit	-	6

Inherited	No
Default	normal
Applies to	All elements

Lengths

Following are the unit measurement for lengths that can be used in CSS.

Absolute Lengths

Unit	IE	Netscape
cm	3	4
in	3	4
mm	3	4
pc	3	4
pt	3	4

Relative Lengths

Unit	IE	Netscape
em	4	4
ex	4	4
px	3	4

Color Names and Values

The following table shows the 16 color names that were introduced in HTML 3.2 to support the 16 colors that 8-bit graphics cards offered:

Color Name	Hex Value
aqua	#00ffff
black	#000000
blue	#0000ff
fuchsia	#ff00ff
green	#008000
gray	#808080
lime	#00ff00
maroon	#800000
navy	#000080
olive	#808000
purple	#800080
red	#ff0000
silver	#c0c0c0
teal	#008080
white	#ffffff
yellow	#ffff00

All of the colors listed in the table that follows are available in IE, and most in Netscape, too. However, they are browser extensions, not part of the HTML or XHTML recommendations.

Color Name	Hex Value
aliceblue	#f0f8ff
antiquewhite	#faebd7
aqua	#00ffff
aquamarine	#7fffd4
azure	#f0ffff
beige	#f5f5dc
bisque	#ffe4c4
black	#000000
blanchedalmond	#ffebcd
blue	#0000ff
blueviolet	#8a2be2
brown	#a52a2a
burlywood	#deb887
cadetblue	#5f9ea0
chartreuse	#7fff00
chocolate	#d2691e
coral	#ff7f50
cornflowerblue	#6495ed
cornsilk	#fff8dc
crimson	#dc143c
cyan	#00ffff
darkblue	#00008b
darkcyan	#008b8b
darkgoldenrod	#b8860b
darkgray	#a9a9a9
darkgreen	#006400
darkkhaki	#bdb76b
darkmagenta	#8b008b
darkolivegreen	#556b2f

Color Name	Hex Value
darkorange	#ff8c00
darkorchid	#9932cc
darkred	#8b0000
darksalmon	#e9967a
darkseagreen	#8fbc8f
darkslateblue	#483d8b
darkslategray	#2f4f4f
darkturquoise	#00ced1
darkviolet	#9400d3
deeppink	#ff1493
deepskyblue	#00bfff
dimgray	#696969
dodgerblue	#1e90ff
firebrick	#b22222
floralwhite	#fffaf0
forestgreen	#228b22
fuchsia	#ff00ff
gainsboro	#dcdcdc
ghostwhite	#f8f8ff
gold	#ffd700
goldenrod	#daa520
gray	#808080
green	#008000
greenyellow	#adff2f
honeydew	#f0fff0
hotpink	#ff69b4
indianred	#cd5c5c
indigo	#4b0082

Continues

Color Name	Hex Value
ivory	#fffff0
khaki	#f0e68c
lavender	#e6e6fa
lavenderblush	#fff0f5
lawngreen	#7cfc00
lemonchiffon	#fffacd
lightblue	#add8e6
lightcoral	#f08080
lightcyan	#e0ffff
lightgoldenrodyellow	#fafad2
lightgreen	#90ee90
lightgrey	#d3d3d3
lightpink	#ffb6c1
lightsalmon	#ffa07a
lightseagreen	#20b2aa
lightskyblue	#87cefa
lightslategray	#778899
lightsteelblue	#b0c4de
lightyellow	#ffffe0
lime	#00ff00
limegreen	#32cd32
linen	#faf0e6
magenta	#ff00ff
maroon	#800000
mediumaquamarine	#66cdaa
mediumblue	#0000cd
mediumorchid	#ba55d3
mediumpurple	#9370db
mediumseagreen	#3cb371

Color Name	Hex Value
mediumslateblue	#7b68ee
mediumspringgreen	#00fa9a
mediumturquoise	#48d1cc
mediumvioletred	#c71585
midnightblue	#191970
mintcream	#f5fffa
mistyrose	#ffe4e1
moccasin	#ffe4b5
navajowhite	#ffdead
navy	#000080
oldlace	#fdf5e6
olive	#808000
olivedrab	#6b8e23
orange	#ffa500
orangered	#ff4500
orchid	#da70d6
palegoldenrod	#eee8aa
palegreen	#98fb98
paleturquoise	#afeeee
palevioletred	#db7093
papayawhip	#ffefd5
peachpuff	#ffdab9
peru	#cd853f
pink	#ffc0cb
plum	#dda0dd
powderblue	#b0e0e6
purple	#800080
red	#ff0000

Continues

Color Name	Hex Value
rosybrown	#bc8f8f
royalblue	#4169e1
saddlebrown	#8b4513
salmon	#fa8072
sandybrown	#f4a460
seagreen	#2e8b57
seashell	#fff5ee
sienna	#a0522d
silver	#c0c0c0
skyblue	#87ceeb
slateblue	#6a5acd
slategray	#708090
snow	#fffafa
springgreen	#00ff7f
steelblue	#4682b4
tan	#d2b48c
teal	#008080
thistle	#d8bfd8
tomato	#ff6347
turquoise	#40e0d0
violet	#ee82ee
wheat	#f5deb3
white	#ffffff
whitesmoke	#f5f5f5
yellow	#ffff00
yellowgreen	#9acd32

Character Encodings

When I discussed colors in Chapter 4, you saw a little bit about how computers store information and how a character-encoding scheme is a table that translates between characters and how they are stored in the computer.

The most common character set (or character encoding) in use on computers is ASCII (The American Standard Code for Information Interchange), and this is probably the most widely used character set for encoding text electronically. You can expect all computers browsing the Web to understand ASCII.

Character Set	Description
ASCII	American Standard Code for Information Interchange, which is used on most computers

The problem with ASCII is that it supports only the upper- and lowercase Latin alphabet, the numbers 0–9, and some extra characters: a total of 128 characters in all. Here are the printable characters of ASCII (the other characters are things such as line feeds and carriage return characters).

	!	"	#	$	%	&	'	(	)	*	+	,	-	.	/
0	1	2	3	4	5	6	7	8	9	:	;	<	=	>	?
@	A	B	C	D	E	F	G	H	I	J	K	L	M	N	O
P	Q	R	S	T	U	V	W	X	Y	Z	[	\	]	^	_
`	a	b	c	d	e	f	g	h	i	j	k	l	m	n	o
p	q	r	s	t	u	v	w	x	y	z	{			}	~	

However, many languages use either accented Latin characters or completely different alphabets. ASCII does not address these characters; therefore you need to learn about character encodings if you want to use any non-ASCII characters.

Character encodings are also particularly important if you want to use symbols, as these cannot be guaranteed to transfer properly between different encodings (from some dashes to some quotation mark characters). If you do not indicate the character encoding the document is written in, some of the special characters might not display.

The International Standards Organization created a range of character sets to deal with different national characters. ISO-8859-1 is commonly used in Western versions of authoring tools such as Macromedia Dreamweaver, as well as applications such as Windows Notepad.

Character Set	Description
ISO-8859-1	Latin alphabet part 1 Covering North America, Western Europe, Latin America, the Caribbean, Canada, Africa
ISO-8859-2	Latin alphabet part 2 Covering Eastern Europe
ISO-8859-3	Latin alphabet part 3 Covering SE Europe, Esperanto, miscellaneous others
ISO-8859-4	Latin alphabet part 4 Covering Scandinavia/Baltics (and others not in ISO-8859-1)
ISO-8859-5	Latin/Cyrillic alphabet part 5
ISO-8859-6	Latin/Arabic alphabet part 6
ISO-8859-7	Latin/Greek alphabet part 7
ISO-8859-8	Latin/Hebrew alphabet part 8
ISO-8859-9	Latin 5 alphabet part 9 (same as ISO-8859-1 except Turkish characters replace Icelandic ones)
ISO-8859-10	Latin 6 Latin 6 Lappish, Nordic, and Eskimo
ISO-8859-15	The same as ISO-8859-1 but with more characters added
ISO-2022-JP	Latin/Japanese alphabet part 1
ISO-2022-JP-2	Latin/Japanese alphabet part 2
ISO-2022-KR	Latin/Korean alphabet part 1

It is helpful to note that the first 128 characters of ISO-8859-1 match those of ASCII, so you can safely use those characters as you would in ASCII.

The *Unicode* Consortium was then set up to devise a way to show *all* characters of different languages, rather than have these different incompatible character codes for different languages.

Therefore, if you want to create documents that use characters from multiple character sets, you will be able to do so using the single Unicode character encodings. Furthermore, users should be able to view documents written in different character sets, providing their processor (and fonts) support the Unicode standards, no matter what platform they are on or which country they are in. By having the single character encoding, software development costs can also be reduced because the programs do not need to be designed to support multiple character encodings.

One problem with Unicode is that a lot of older programs were written to support only 8-bit character sets (limiting them to 256 characters), which is nowhere near the number required for all languages.

Unicode therefore specifies encodings that can deal with a string in special ways so as to make enough space for the huge character set it encompasses. These are known as UTF-8, UTF-16, and UTF-32.

Character Set	Description
UTF-8	A Unicode Translation Format that comes in 8-bit units. That is, it comes in *bytes*. A character in UTF8 can be from 1 to 4 bytes long, making UTF8 variable width.
UTF-16	A Unicode Translation Format that comes in 16-bit units. That is, it comes in *shorts*. It can be 1 or 2 shorts long, making UTF16 variable width.
UTF-32	A Unicode Translation Format that comes in 32-bit units. That is, it comes in *longs*. It is a fixed-width format and is always 1 "long" in length.

The first 256 characters of Unicode character sets correspond to the 256 characters of ISO-8859-1.

By default, HTML 4 processors should support UTF-8, and XML processors are supposed to support UTF-8 and UTF-16; therefore all XHTML-compliant processors should also support UTF-16 (as XHTML is an application of XML).

For more information on internationalization and different character sets and encodings see `http://www.i18nguy.com/`.

Special Characters

Some characters are reserved in XHTML; for example, you cannot use the greater than and less than signs or angle brackets within your text because the browser could mistake them for markup. XHTML processors must support the five special characters listed in the table that follows.

Symbol	Description	Entity Name	Number Code
&	Ampersand	&	&
<	Less than	<	<
>	Greater than	>	>
"	Double quote	"	"
	Non-breaking space		

To write an element and attribute into your page so that the code is shown to the user rather than being processed by the browser (for example as `<div id="character">`) you would write:

```
&lt;div id=&quot;character&quot;&gt;
```

There is also a long list of special characters that HTML 4.0–aware processors should support. In order for these to appear in your document, you can use either the numerical code or the entity name. For example, to insert a copyright symbol you could use either of the following:

```
&copy; 2004
&#169;
```

The special characters have been split into the following sections:

- ❑   Character Entity References for ISO 8859-1 Characters
- ❑   Character Entity References for Symbols, Mathematical Symbols, and Greek Letters
- ❑   Character Entity References for Markup-Significant and Internationalization Characters

Appendix F

They are taken from the W3C Web site at `http://www.w3.org/TR/REC-html40/sgml/entities.html`.

Entity Name	Symbol	Number Code	Description
Character Entity References for ISO 8859-1 Characters			
			No-break space = non-breaking space
&iexcl;	¡	&#161;	Inverted exclamation mark
&cent;	¢	&#162;	Cent sign
&pound;	£	&#163;	Pound sign
&curren;	¤	&#164;	Currency sign
&yen;	¥	&#165;	Yen sign = yuan sign
&brvbar;	¦	&#166;	Broken bar = broken vertical bar
&sect;	§	&#167;	Section sign
&uml;	¨	&#168;	Diaeresis = spacing diaeresis
&copy;	©	&#169;	Copyright sign
&ordf;	ª	&#170;	Feminine ordinal indicator
&laquo;	«	&#171;	Left-pointing double angle quotation mark = left-pointing guillemot
&not;	¬	&#172;	Not sign
&shy;		&#173;	Soft hyphen = discretionary hyphen
&reg;	®	&#174;	Registered sign = registered trademark sign
&macr;	¯	&#175;	Macron = spacing macron = overline = APL overbar
&deg;	°	&#176;	Degree sign
&plusmn;	±	&#177;	Plus-minus sign = plus-or-minus sign
&sup2;	²	&#178;	Superscript two = superscript digit two = squared
&sup3;	³	&#179;	Superscript three = superscript digit three = cubed
&acute;	´	&#180;	Acute accent = spacing acute
&micro;	µ	&#181;	Micro sign
&para;	¶	&#182;	Pilcrow sign = paragraph sign
&middot;	·	&#183;	Middle dot = Georgian comma = Greek middle dot
&cedil;	¸	&#184;	Cedilla = spacing cedilla

Entity Name	Symbol	Number Code	Description
Character Entity References for ISO 8859-1 Characters			
&sup1;	¹	&#185;	Superscript one = superscript digit one
&ordm;	º	&#186;	Masculine ordinal indicator
&raquo;	»	&#187;	Right-pointing double angle quotation mark = right pointing guillemet
&frac14;	¼	&#188;	Vulgar fraction one-quarter = fraction one-quarter
&frac12;	½	&#189;	Vulgar fraction one-half = fraction one-half
&frac34;	¾	&#190;	Vulgar fraction three-quarters = fraction three-quarters
&iquest;	¿	&#191;	Inverted question mark = turned question mark
&Agrave;	À	&#192;	Latin capital letter A with grave = Latin capital letter A grave
&Aacute;	Á	&#193;	Latin capital letter A with acute
&Acirc;	Â	&#194;	Latin capital letter A with circumflex
&Atilde;	Ã	&#195;	Latin capital letter A with tilde
&Auml;	Ä	&#196;	Latin capital letter A with diaeresis
&Aring;	Å	&#197;	Latin capital letter A with ring above = Latin capital letter A ring
&AElig;	Æ	&#198;	Latin capital letter AE = Latin capital ligature AE
&Ccedil;	Ç	&#199;	Latin capital letter C with cedilla
&Egrave;	È	&#200;	Latin capital letter E with grave
&Eacute;	É	&#201;	Latin capital letter E with acute
&Ecirc;	Ê	&#202;	Latin capital letter E with circumflex
&Euml;	Ë	&#203;	Latin capital letter E with diaeresis
&Igrave;	Ì	&#204;	Latin capital letter I with grave
&Iacute;	Í	&#205;	Latin capital letter I with acute
&Icirc;	Î	&#206;	Latin capital letter I with circumflex
&Iuml;	Ï	&#207;	Latin capital letter I with diaeresis
&ETH;	Ð	&#208;	Latin capital letter ETH

Continues

Entity Name	Symbol	Number Code	Description
Character Entity References for ISO 8859-1 Characters			
&Ntilde;	Ñ	&#209;	Latin capital letter N with tilde
&Ograve;	Ò	&#210;	Latin capital letter O with grave
&Oacute;	Ó	&#211;	Latin capital letter O with acute
&Ocirc;	Ô	&#212;	Latin capital letter O with circumflex
&Otilde;	Õ	&#213;	Latin capital letter O with tilde
&Ouml;	Ö	&#214;	Latin capital letter O with diaeresis
&times;	×	&#215;	Multiplication sign
&Oslash;	Ø	&#216;	Latin capital letter O with stroke = Latin capital letter O slash
&Ugrave;	Ù	&#217;	Latin capital letter U with grave
&Uacute;	Ú	&#218;	Latin capital letter U with acute
&Ucirc;	Û	&#219;	Latin capital letter U with circumflex
&Uuml;	Ü	&#220;	Latin capital letter U with diaeresis
&Yacute;	Ý	&#221;	Latin capital letter Y with acute
&THORN;	Þ	&#222;	Latin capital letter THORN
&szlig;	ß	&#223;	Latin small letter sharp s = ess-zed
&agrave;	à	&#224;	Latin small letter a with grave = Latin small letter a grave
&aacute;	á	&#225;	Latin small letter a with acute
&acirc;	â	&#226;	Latin small letter a with circumflex
&atilde;	ã	&#227;	Latin small letter a with tilde
&auml;	ä	&#228;	Latin small letter a with diaeresis
&aring;	å	&#229;	Latin small letter a with ring above = Latin small letter a ring
&aelig;	æ	&#230;	Latin small letter ae = Latin small ligature ae
&ccedil;	ç	&#231;	Latin small letter c with cedilla
&egrave;	è	&#232;	Latin small letter e with grave
&eacute;	é	&#233;	Latin small letter e with acute

Entity Name	Symbol	Number Code	Description
Character Entity References for ISO 8859-1 Characters			
&ecirc;	ê	&#234;	Latin small letter *e* with circumflex
&euml;	ë	&#235;	Latin small letter *e* with diaeresis
&igrave;	ì	&#236;	Latin small letter *i* with grave
&iacute;	í	&#237;	Latin small letter *i* with acute
&icirc;	î	&#238;	Latin small letter *i* with circumflex
&iuml;	ï	&#239;	Latin small letter *i* with diaeresis
&eth;	ð	&#240;	Latin small letter *eth*
&ntilde;	ñ	&#241;	Latin small letter *n* with tilde
&ograve;	ò	&#242;	Latin small letter *o* with grave
&oacute;	ó	&#243;	Latin small letter *o* with acute
&ocirc;	ô	&#244;	Latin small letter *o* with circumflex
&otilde;	õ	&#245;	Latin small letter *o* with tilde
&ouml;	ö	&#246;	Latin small letter *o* with diaeresis
&divide;	÷	&#247;	Division sign
&oslash;	ø	&#248;	Latin small letter *o* with stroke, = Latin small letter *o* slash
&ugrave;	ù	&#249;	Latin small letter *u* with grave
&uacute;	ú	&#250;	Latin small letter *u* with acute
&ucirc;	û	&#251;	Latin small letter *u* with circumflex
&uuml;	ü	&#252;	Latin small letter *u* with diaeresis
&yacute;	ý	&#253;	Latin small letter *y* with acute
&thorn;	þ	&#254;	Latin small letter *thorn*
&yuml;	ÿ	&#255;	Latin small letter *y* with diaeresis
Character Entity References for Symbols, Mathematical Symbols, and Greek Letters			
Latin Extended-B			
&fnof;	*f*	&#402;	Latin small *f* with hook = function = florin

Continues

Greek

Α	A	Α	Greek capital letter alpha
Β	B	Β	Greek capital letter beta
Γ	Γ	Γ	Greek capital letter gamma
Δ	Δ	Δ	Greek capital letter delta
Ε	E	Ε	Greek capital letter epsilon
Ζ	Z	Ζ	Greek capital letter zeta
Η	H	Η	Greek capital letter eta
Θ	Θ	Θ	Greek capital letter theta
Ι	I	Ι	Greek capital letter iota
Κ	K	Κ	Greek capital letter kappa
Λ	Λ	Λ	Greek capital letter lambda
Μ	M	Μ	Greek capital letter mu
Ν	N	Ν	Greek capital letter nu
Ξ	Ξ	Ξ	Greek capital letter xi
Ο	O	Ο	Greek capital letter omicron
Π	Π	Π	Greek capital letter pi
Ρ	P	Ρ	Greek capital letter rho
Σ	Σ	Σ	Greek capital letter sigma
Τ	T	Τ	Greek capital letter tau
Υ	Y	Υ	Greek capital letter upsilon
Φ	φ	Φ	Greek capital letter phi
Χ	X	Χ	Greek capital letter chi
Ψ	ψ	Ψ	Greek capital letter psi
Ω	Ω	Ω	Greek capital letter omega
α	α	α	Greek small letter alpha
β	β	β	Greek small letter beta
γ	γ	γ	Greek small letter gamma
δ	δ	δ	Greek small letter delta
ε	ε	ε	Greek small letter epsilon

Greek

&zeta;	ζ	&#950;	Greek small letter zeta
&eta;	η	&#951;	Greek small letter eta
&theta;	θ	&#952;	Greek small letter theta
&iota;	ι	&#953;	Greek small letter iota
&kappa;	κ	&#954;	Greek small letter kappa
&lambda;	λ	&#955;	Greek small letter lambda
&mu;	μ	&#956;	Greek small letter mu
&nu;	ν	&#957;	Greek small letter nu
&xi;	ξ	&#958;	Greek small letter xi
&omicron;	ο	&#959;	Greek small letter omicron
&pi;	π	&#960;	Greek small letter pi
&rho;	ρ	&#961;	Greek small letter rho
&sigmaf;	ς	&#962;	Greek small letter final sigma
&sigma;	σ	&#963;	greek small Greek sigma
&tau;	τ	&#964;	Greek small letter tau
&upsilon;	υ	&#965;	Greek small letter upsilon
&phi;	φ	&#966;	Greek small letter phi
&chi;	χ	&#967;	Greek small letter chi
&psi;	ψ	&#968;	Greek small letter psi
&omega;	ω	&#969;	Greek small letter omega
&thetasym;	θ	&#977;	Greek small letter theta symbol
&upsih;	υ	&#978;	Greek upsilon with hook symbol
&piv;	π	&#982;	Greek pi symbol

General Punctuation

&bull;	•	&#8226;	Bullet = black small circle
&hellip;	…	&#8230;	Horizontal ellipsis = three dot leader
&prime;	′	&#8242;	Prime = minutes = feet

Continues

General Punctuation			
&Prime;	″	&#8243;	Double prime = seconds = inches
&oline;	‾	&#8254;	Overline = spacing overscore
&frasl;	/	&#8260;	Fraction slash

Letterlike Symbols			
&weierp;	℘	&#8472;	Script capital P = power set = Weierstrass p
&image;	ℑ	&#8465;	Blackletter capital I = imaginary part
&real;	ℜ	&#8476;	Blackletter capital R = real part symbol
&trade;	™	&#8482;	Trademark sign
&alefsym;	ℵ	&#8501;	Alef symbol = first transfinite cardinal

Arrows			
&larr;	←	&#8592;	Left arrow
&uarr;	↑	&#8593;	Up arrow
&rarr;	→	&#8594;	Right arrow
&darr;	↓	&#8595;	Down arrow
&harr;	↔	&#8596;	Left-right arrow
&crarr;	↵	&#8629;	Down arrow with corner leftward = carriage return
&lArr;	⇐	&#8656;	Left double arrow
&uArr;	⇑	&#8657;	Up double arrow
&rArr;	⇒	&#8658;	Right double arrow
&dArr;	⇓	&#8659;	Down double arrow
&hArr;	⇔	&#8660;	Left-right double arrow

Mathematical Operators			
&forall;	∀	&#8704;	For all
&part ;	∂	&#8706;	Partial differential
&exist;	∃	&#8707;	There exists

Mathematical Operators

∅	Ø	∅	Empty set = null set = diameter
∇	∇	∇	Nabla = backward difference
∈	∈	∈	Element of
∉	∉	∉	Not an element of
∋	∋	∋	Contains as member
∏	∏	∏	*n*-ary product = product sign
∑	∑	∑	*n*-ary summation
−	−	−	Minus sign
∗	∗	∗	Asterisk operator
√	√	√	Square root = radical sign
∝	∝	∝	Proportional to
∞	∞	∞	Infinity
∠	∠	∠	Angle
∧	∧	∧	Logical and = wedge
&or ;	∨	∨	Logical or = vee
∩	∩	∩	Intersection = cap
∪	∪	∪	Union = cup
∫	∫	∫	Integral
∴	∴	∴	Therefore
∼	∼	∼	Tilde operator = varies with = similar to
≅	≅	≅	Approximately equal to
≈	≈	≈	Almost equal to = asymptotic to
≠	≠	≠	Not equal to
≡	≡	≡	Identical to
≤	≤	≤	Less than or equal to
≥	≥	≥	Greater than or equal to
⊂	⊂	⊂	Subset of
⊃	⊃	⊃	Superset of

Continues

747

Mathematical Operators

&nsub;	⊄	&#8836;	Not a subset of
&sube;	⊆	&#8838;	Subset of or equal to
&supe;	⊇	&#8839;	Superset of or equal to
&oplus;	⊕	&#8853;	Circled plus = direct sum
&otimes;	⊗	&#8855;	Circled times = vector product
&perp;	⊥	&#8869;	Up tack = orthogonal to = perpendicular
&sdot;	·	&#8901;	Dot operator

Miscellaneous Technical

&lceil;	⌈	&#8968;	Left ceiling = apl upstile
&rceil;	⌉	&#8969;	Right ceiling
&lfloor;	⌊	&#8970;	Left floor = apl downstile
&rfloor;	⌋	&#8971;	Right floor
&lang;	⟨	&#9001;	Left-pointing angle bracket = bra
&rang;	⟩	&#9002;	Right-pointing angle bracket = ket

Geometric Shapes

&loz;	◊	&#9674;	Lozenge

Miscellaneous Symbols

&spades;	♠	&#9824;	Black spade suit
&clubs;	♣	&#9827;	Black club suit = shamrock
&hearts;	♥	&#9829;	Black heart suit = valentine
&diams;	♦	&#9830;	Black diamond suit

Character Entity References for Markup-Significant and Internationalization Characters

C0 Controls and Basic Latin

&quot;	"	&#34;	Quotation mark = APL quote
&amp;	&	&#38;	Ampersand

C0 Controls and Basic Latin

&lt;	<	&#60;	Less-than sign
&gt;	>	&#62;	Greater-than sign

Latin Extended-A

&OElig;	Œ	&#338;	Latin capital ligature OE
&oelig;	œ	&#339;	Latin small ligature oe
&Scaron;	Š	&#352;	Latin capital letter *S* with caron
&scaron;	š	&#353;	Latin small letter *s* with caron
&Yuml;	Ÿ	&#376;	Latin capital letter *Y* with diaeresis

Spacing Modifier Letters

&circ;	^	&#710;	Modifier letter circumflex accent
&tilde;	~	&#732;	Small tilde

General Punctuation

			En space
			Em space
			Thin space
&zwnj;		&#8204;	Zero width non-joiner
&zwj;		&#8205;	Zero width joiner
&lrm;		&#8206;	Left-to-right mark
&rlm;		&#8207;	Right-to-left mark
&ndash;	–	&#8211;	En dash
&mdash;	—	&#8212;	Em dash
&lsquo;	'	&#8216;	Left single quotation mark
&rsquo;	'	&#8217;	Right single quotation mark
&sbquo;	‚	&#8218;	Single low-9 quotation mark
&ldquo;	"	&#8220;	Left double quotation mark
&rdquo;	"	&#8221;	Right double quotation mark
&bdquo;	„	&#8222;	Double low-9 quotation mark

Continues

General Punctuation			
&dagger;	†	&#8224;	Dagger
&Dagger;	‡	&#8225;	Double dagger
&permil;	‰	&#8240;	Per mille sign
&lsaquo;	<	&#8249;	Single left-pointing angle quotation mark (proposed, but not yet standardized)
&rsaquo;	>	&#8250;	Single right-pointing angle quotation mark (proposed, but not yet standardized)
&euro;	€	&#8364;	Euro sign

Language Codes

The following table shows the two-letter ISO 639 language codes that are used to declare the language of a document in the `lang` and `xml:lang` attributes. It covers many of the world's major languages.

Country	ISO Code
Abkhazian	AB
Afan (Oromo)	OM
Afar	AA
Afrikaans	AF
Albanian	SQ
Amharic	AM
Arabic	AR
Armenian	HY
Assamese	AS
Aymara	AY
Azerbaijani	AZ
Bashkir	BA
Basque	EU
Bengali; Bangla	BN
Bhutani	DZ
Bihari	BH

Continues

Country	ISO Code
Bislama	BI
Breton	BR
Bulgarian	BG
Burmese	MY
Byelorussian	BE
Cambodian	KM
Catalan	CA
Chinese	ZH
Corsican	CO
Croatian	HR
Czech	CS
Danish	DA
Dutch	NL
English	EN
Esperanto	EO
Estonian	ET
Faroese	FO
Fiji	FJ
Finnish	FI
French	FR
Frisian	FY
Galician	GL
Georgian	KA
German	DE
Greek	EL
Greenlandic	KL
Guarani	GN
Gujarati	GU
Hausa	HA

Country	ISO Code
Hebrew	HE
Hindi	HI
Hungarian	HU
Icelandic	IS
Indonesian	ID
Interlingua	IA
Interlingue	IE
Inuktitut	IU
Inupiak	IK
Irish	GA
Italian	IT
Japanese	JA
Javanese	JV
Kannada	KN
Kashmiri	KS
Kazakh	KK
Kinyarwanda	RW
Kirghiz	KY
Kurundi	RN
Korean	KO
Kurdish	KU
Laothian	LO
Latin	LA
Latvian; Lettish	LV
Lingala	LN
Lithuanian	LT
Macedonian	MK
Malagasy	MG

Continues

Country	ISO Code
Malay	MS
Malayalam	ML
Maltese	MT
Maori	MI
Marathi	MR
Moldavian	MO
Mongolian	MN
Nauru	NA
Nepali	NE
Norwegian	NO
Occitan	OC
Oriya	OR
Pashto; Pushto	PS
PERSIAN (Farsi)	FA
Polish	PL
Portuguese	PT
Punjabi	PA
Quechua	QU
Rhaeto-Romance	RM
Romanian	RO
Russian	RU
Samoan	SM
Sangho	SG
Sanskrit	SA
Scots Gaelic	GD
Serbian	SR
Serbo-Croatian	SH
Sesotho	ST
Setswana	TN

Country	ISO Code
Shona	SN
Sindhi	SD
Singhalese	SI
Siswati	SS
Slovak	SK
Slovenian	SL
Somali	SO
Spanish	ES
Sudanese	SU
Swahili	SW
Swedish	SV
Tagalog	TL
Tajik	TG
Tamil	TA
Tatar	TT
Telugu	TE
Thai	TH
Tibetan	BO
Tigrinya	TI
Tonga	TO
Tsonga	TS
Turkish	TR
Turkmen	TK
Twi	TW
Uigur	UG
Ukrainian	UK
Urdu	UR
Uzbek	UZ

Continues

Country	ISO Code
Vietnamese	VI
Volapuk	VO
Welsh	CY
Wolof	WO
Xhosa	XH
Yiddish	YI
Yoruba	YO
Zhuang	ZA
Zulu	ZU

MIME Media Types

You have seen the `type` attribute used throughout the book on a number of elements, the value of which is a MIME media type.

MIME (Multipurpose Internet Mail Extension) media types were originally devised so that e-mails could include information other than plain text. MIME media types indicate the following things:

❑ How the parts of a message, such as text and attachments, are combined into the message

❑ The way in which each part of the message is specified

❑ The way the items are encoded for transmission so that even software that was designed to work only with ASCII text can process the message

As you have seen, however, MIME types are not just for use with e-mail; they were adopted by Web servers as a way to tell Web browsers what type of material was being sent to them so that they could cope with that kind of file correctly.

MIME content types consist of two parts:

❑ A main type

❑ A sub-type

The main type is separated from the subtype by a forward slash character—for example, `text/html` for HTML.

This appendix is organized by the main types:

❑ `text`

❑ `image`

❑ `multipart`

❑ `audio`

❑ `video`

- ❑ `message`
- ❑ `model`
- ❑ `application`

For example, the `text` main type contains types of plain text files, such as:

- ❑ `text/plain` for plain text files
- ❑ `text/html` for HTML files
- ❑ `text/rtf` for text files using rich text formatting

MIME types are officially supposed to be assigned and listed by the Internet Assigned Numbers Authority (IANA).

Many of the popular MIME types in this list (all those that begin with "x-") are not assigned by the IANA and do not have official status. (Having said that, I should mention that some of these are very popular and browsers support them, such as `audio/x-mp3`. You can see the list of official MIME types at `http://www.iana.org/assignments/media-types/`.)

Those preceded with `.vnd` are vendor-specific.

The most popular MIME types are listed in this appendix in a bold typeface to help you find them.

text

Note that, when specifying the MIME type of a content-type field (for example in a `<meta>` element) you can also indicate the character set for the text being used. For example:

```
content-type:text/plain; charset=iso-8859-1
```

If you do not specify a character set, the default is US-ASCII.

calendar	**sgml**	vnd.IPTC.NITF
css	t140	vnd.latex-z
directory	tab-separated-values	vnd.motorola.reflex
enriched	uri-list	vnd.ms-mediapackage
html	vnd.abc	vnd.net2phone.commcenter.command
parityfec	vnd.curl	vnd.sun.j2me.app-descriptor
plain	vnd.DMClientScript	vnd.wap.si
prs.fallenstein.rst	vnd.fly	vnd.wap.sl
prs.lines.tag	vnd.fmi.flexstor	vnd.wap.wml
rfc822-headers	vnd.in3d.3dml	vnd.wap.wmlscript
richtext	vnd.in3d.spot	**xml**
rtf	vnd.IPTC.NewsML	**xml-external-parsed-entity**

image

bmp	tiff-fx	vnd.mix
cgm	vnd.cns.inf2	vnd.ms-modi
g3fax	vnd.djvu	vnd.net-fpx
gif	vnd.dwg	vnd.sealed.png
ief	vnd.dxf	vnd.sealedmedia.softseal.gif
jpeg	vnd.fastbidsheet	vnd.sealedmedia.softseal.jpg
naplps	vnd.fpx	vnd.svf
png	vnd.fst	vnd.wap.wbmp
prs.btif	vnd.fujixerox.edmics-mmr	vnd.xiff
prs.pti	vnd.fujixerox.edmics-rlc	**x-portable-pixmap**
t38	vnd.globalgraphics.pgb	**x-xbitmap**
tiff	vnd.microsoft.icon	

multipart

alternative	**form-data**	related
appledouble	header-set	report
byteranges	mixed	signed
digest	parallel	voice-message
encrypted		

audio

32kadpcm	GSM-EFR	vnd.3gpp.iufp
AMR	L8	vnd.cisco.nse
AMR-WB	L16	vnd.cns.anp1
basic	L20	vnd.cns.inf1
CN	L24	vnd.digital-winds
DAT12	LPC	vnd.everad.plj
dsr-es201108	**MPA**	vnd.lucent.voice
DVI4	**MP4A-LATM**	vnd.nokia.mobile-xmf
EVRC	mpa-robust	vnd.nortel.vbk
EVRC0	**mpeg**	vnd.nuera.ecelp4800
EVRC-QCP	**mpeg4-generic**	vnd.nuera.ecelp7470
G722	parityfec	vnd.nuera.ecelp9600
G.722.1	PCMA	vnd.octel.sbc
G723	PCMU	vnd.qcelp—deprecated, use audio/qcelp
G726-16	prs.sid	vnd.rhetorex.32kadpcm
G726-24	QCELP	vnd.sealedmedia.softseal.mpeg
G726-32	RED	vnd.vmx.cvsd
G726-40	SMV	**x-aiff**
G728	SMV0	**x-midi**
G729	SMV-QCP	**x-mod**
G729D	telephone-event	**x-mp3**
G729E	tone	**x-wav**
GSM	VDVI	

video

BMPEG	MP4V-ES	vnd.mpegurl
BT656	MPV	vnd.nokia.interleaved-multimedia
CelB	**mpeg**	vnd.objectvideo
DV	mpeg4-generic	vnd.sealed.mpeg1
H261	nv	vnd.sealed.mpeg4
H263	parityfec	vnd.sealed.swf
H263-1998	pointer	vnd.sealedmedia.softseal.mov
H263-2000	**quicktime**	vnd.vivo
JPEG	SMPTE292M	**x-sgi-movie**
MP1S	vnd.fvt	**x-msvideo**
MP2P	vnd.motorola.video	
MP2T	vnd.motorola.videop	

message

CPIM	http	s-http
delivery-status	news	sip
disposition-notification	partial	sipfrag
external-body	rfc822	

model

iges	vnd.gdl	vnd.parasolid.transmit.binary
mesh	vnd.gs-gdl	vnd.parasolid.transmit.text
vnd.dwf	vnd.gtw	vnd.vtu
vnd.flatland.3dml	vnd.mts	**vrml**

application

activemessage	eshop
andrew-inset	font-tdpfr
applefile	http
atomicmail	hyperstudio
batch-SMTP	iges
beep+xml	index
cals-1840	index.cmd
cnrp+xml	index.obj
commonground	index.response
cpl+xml	index.vnd
cybercash	iotp
dca-rft	ipp
dec-dx	isup
dicom	mac-binhex40
dvcs	macwriteii
EDI-Consent	marc
EDIFACT	mathematica
EDI-X12	mpeg4-generic

msword
news-message-id
news-transmission
ocsp-request
ocsp-response
octet-stream
oda
ogg
parityfec
pdf
pgp-encrypted
pgp-keys
pgp-signature
pidf+xml
pkcs10
pkcs7-mime
pkcs7-signature
pkix-cert
pkixcmp
pkix-crl
pkix-pkipath
postscript
prs.alvestrand.titrax-sheet
prs.cww
prs.nprend
prs.plucker
qsig
reginfo+xml
remote-printing
riscos
rtf
sdp
set-payment
set-payment-initiation
set-registration
set-registration-initiation
sgml
sgml-open-catalog
sieve
slate
timestamp-query
timestamp-reply
tve-trigger
vemmi
vnd.3gpp.pic-bw-large
vnd.3gpp.pic-bw-small
vnd.3gpp.pic-bw-var
vnd.3gpp.sms
vnd.3M.Post-it-Notes
vnd.accpac.simply.aso

vnd.accpac.simply.imp
vnd.acucobol
vnd.acucorp
vnd.adobe.xfdf
vnd.aether.imp
vnd.amiga.ami
vnd.anser-web-certificate-issue-initiation
vnd.anser-web-funds-transfer-initiation
vnd.audiograph
vnd.blueice.multipass
vnd.bmi
vnd.businessobjects
vnd.canon-cpdl
vnd.canon-lips
vnd.cinderella
vnd.claymore
vnd.commerce-battelle
vnd.commonspace
vnd.cosmocaller
vnd.contact.cmsg
vnd.criticaltools.wbs+xml
vnd.ctc-posml
vnd.cups-postscript
vnd.cups-raster
vnd.cups-raw
vnd.curl
vnd.cybank
vnd.data-vision.rdz
vnd.dna
vnd.dpgraph
vnd.dreamfactory
vnd.dxr
vnd.ecdis-update
vnd.ecowin.chart
vnd.ecowin.filerequest
vnd.ecowin.fileupdate
vnd.ecowin.series
vnd.ecowin.seriesrequest
vnd.ecowin.seriesupdate
vnd.enliven
vnd.epson.esf
vnd.epson.msf
vnd.epson.quickanime
vnd.epson.salt
vnd.epson.ssf
vnd.ericsson.quickcall
vnd.eudora.data
vnd.fdf
vnd.ffsns
vnd.fints

vnd.FloGraphIt
vnd.framemaker
vnd.fsc.weblaunch
vnd.fujitsu.oasys
vnd.fujitsu.oasys2
vnd.fujitsu.oasys3
vnd.fujitsu.oasysgp
vnd.fujitsu.oasysprs
vnd.fujixerox.ddd
vnd.fujixerox.docuworks
vnd.fujixerox.docuworks.binder
vnd.fut-misnet
vnd.genomatix.tuxedo
vnd.grafeq
vnd.groove-account
vnd.groove-help
vnd.groove-identity-message
vnd.groove-injector
vnd.groove-tool-message
vnd.groove-tool-template
vnd.groove-vcard
vnd.hbci
vnd.hhe.lesson-player
vnd.hp-HPGL
vnd.hp-hpid
vnd.hp-hps
vnd.hp-PCL
vnd.hp-PCLXL
vnd.httphone
vnd.hzn-3d-crossword
vnd.ibm.afplinedata
vnd.ibm.electronic-media
vnd.ibm.MiniPay
vnd.ibm.modcap
vnd.ibm.rights-management
vnd.ibm.secure-container
vnd.informix-visionary
vnd.intercon.formnet
vnd.intertrust.digibox
vnd.intertrust.nncp
vnd.intu.qbo
vnd.intu.qfx
vnd.ipunplugged.rcprofile
vnd.irepository.package+xml
vnd.is-xpr
vnd.japannet-directory-service
vnd.japannet-jpnstore-wakeup
vnd.japannet-payment-wakeup
vnd.japannet-registration
vnd.japannet-registration-wakeup

vnd.japannet-setstore-wakeup
vnd.japannet-verification
vnd.japannet-verification-wakeup
vnd.jisp
vnd.kde.karbon
vnd.kde.kchart
vnd.kde.kformula
vnd.kde.kivio
vnd.kde.kontour
vnd.kde.kpresenter
vnd.kde.kspread
vnd.kde.kword
vnd.kenameaapp
vnd.kidspiration
vnd.koan
vnd.liberty-request+xml
vnd.llamagraphics.life-balance.desktop
vnd.llamagraphics.life-balance.exchange+xml
vnd.lotus-1-2-3
vnd.lotus-approach
vnd.lotus-freelance
vnd.lotus-notes
vnd.lotus-organizer
vnd.lotus-screencam
vnd.lotus-wordpro
vnd.mcd
vnd.mediastation.cdkey
vnd.meridian-slingshot
vnd.micrografx.flo
vnd.micrografx.igx
vnd.mif
vnd.minisoft-hp3000-save
vnd.mitsubishi.misty-guard.trustweb
vnd.Mobius.DAF
vnd.Mobius.DIS
vnd.Mobius.MBK
vnd.Mobius.MQY
vnd.Mobius.MSL
vnd.Mobius.PLC
vnd.Mobius.TXF
vnd.mophun.application
vnd.mophun.certificate
vnd.motorola.flexsuite
vnd.motorola.flexsuite.adsi
vnd.motorola.flexsuite.fis
vnd.motorola.flexsuite.gotap
vnd.motorola.flexsuite.kmr
vnd.motorola.flexsuite.ttc
vnd.motorola.flexsuite.wem
vnd.mozilla.xul+xml

vnd.ms-artgalry
vnd.ms-asf
vnd.mseq
vnd.ms-excel
vnd.msign
vnd.ms-lrm
vnd.ms-powerpoint
vnd.ms-project
vnd.ms-tnef
vnd.ms-works
vnd.ms-wpl
vnd.musician
vnd.music-niff
vnd.nervana
vnd.netfpx
vnd.noblenet-directory
vnd.noblenet-sealer
vnd.noblenet-web
vnd.novadigm.EDM
vnd.novadigm.EDX
vnd.novadigm.EXT
vnd.obn
vnd.osa.netdeploy
vnd.palm
vnd.paos.xml
vnd.pg.format
vnd.picsel
vnd.pg.osasli
vnd.powerbuilder6
vnd.powerbuilder6-s
vnd.powerbuilder7
vnd.powerbuilder75
vnd.powerbuilder75-s
vnd.powerbuilder7-s
vnd.previewsystems.box
vnd.publishare-delta-tree
vnd.pvi.ptid1
vnd.pwg-multiplexed [RFC3391]
vnd.pwg-xhtml-print+xml
vnd.Quark.QuarkXPress
vnd.rapid
vnd.s3sms
vnd.sealed.doc
vnd.sealed.eml
vnd.sealed.mht
vnd.sealed.net
vnd.sealed.ppt
vnd.sealed.xls
vnd.sealedmedia.softseal.html
vnd.sealedmedia.softseal.pdf

vnd.seemail
vnd.shana.informed.formdata
vnd.shana.informed.formtemplate
vnd.shana.informed.interchange
vnd.shana.informed.package
vnd.smaf
vnd.sss-cod
vnd.sss-dtf
vnd.sss-ntf
vnd.street-stream
vnd.svd
vnd.swiftview-ics
vnd.triscape.mxs
vnd.trueapp
vnd.truedoc
vnd.ufdl
vnd.uiq.theme
vnd.uplanet.alert
vnd.uplanet.alert-wbxml
vnd.uplanet.bearer-choice
vnd.uplanet.bearer-choice-wbxml
vnd.uplanet.cacheop
vnd.uplanet.cacheop-wbxml
vnd.uplanet.channel
vnd.uplanet.channel-wbxml
vnd.uplanet.list
vnd.uplanet.listcmd
vnd.uplanet.listcmd-wbxml
vnd.uplanet.list-wbxml
vnd.uplanet.signal
vnd.vcx
vnd.vectorworks
vnd.vidsoft.vidconference
vnd.visio
vnd.visionary
vnd.vividence.scriptfile
vnd.vsf
vnd.wap.sic
vnd.wap.slc
vnd.wap.wbxml
vnd.wap.wmlc
vnd.wap.wmlscriptc
vnd.webturbo
vnd.wqd
vnd.wrq-hp3000-labelled
vnd.wt.stf
vnd.wv.csp+xml
vnd.wv.csp+wbxml
vnd.wv.ssp+xml
vnd.xara

vnd.xfdl
vnd.yamaha.hv-dic
vnd.yamaha.hv-script
vnd.yamaha.hv-voice
vnd.yamaha.smaf-audio
vnd.yamaha.smaf-phrase
vnd.yellowriver-custom-menu
watcherinfo+xml
whoispp-query
whoispp-response
wita
wordperfect5.1
x400-bp
x-debian-package

x-java
x-javascript
x-gzip
x-msaccess
x-msexcel
x-mspowerpoint
x-rpm
x-zip
xhtml+xml
xml
xml-dtd
xml-external-parsed-entity
zip

Index